"In a decade's time, I envision the coaching profession will be as widely-respected as any other major industry. A relentless focus on ethics is paramount to getting there. The Ethical Coaches' Handbook is a vital step in that direction, featuring a vast compilation from many of the industry's most respected thought leaders. Our field is grateful for this contribution!"

Brian O. Underhill, Ph.D., PCC.
Founder and CEO,
CoachSource

"A superb read and a much needed addition to the evidence-based literature on coaching! It is exciting to be part of the growth of coaching worldwide, but in order to be taken seriously as practitioners, coaches need to reflect, deepen and expand their knowledge of the ethical aspects of this fast-growing helping profession. That's why we need this book! With a wide range of essays on ethics in coaching – technology, culture, team dynamics, feedback and more – this book is a must-read for any coach who is committed to working ethically in an increasingly complex world. Bravo!"

Jeffrey W. Hull, PhD, BCC,
Executive Director,
Institute of Coaching, a Harvard Medical School Affiliate

"An exciting book for coaches offering a rich diversity of chapters in four sections. Ethical maturity as an integral aspect of professional development for coaches is finally being given the attention it deserves in this bumper guidebook, that offers a wealth of topics and perspectives around ethical thinking in all its complexity as a key part of everyday coaching practice. Chapters on offer include topics on ethical foundations and frameworks, chapters on ethical practices and the psychological contract within coaching, a fascinating variety of topics on 'pushing the boundaries of conventional ethical thinking' and a set of useful case studies. I recommend this as a practical resource for coaches at all stages of training and experience who are keen to advance their professionalism and coaching maturity."

Dr Ceri M Sims
Centre for Positive Psychology
Associate Professor, Bucks New University
Director of Positive Minds Alliance Ltd

"Ethics feeling increasing confusing in the quagmire of cultural relativism and woke self-righteous imposing one way of thinking on everyone. When coaching others, the confusion is contagious to our clients. This collection of essays

help to clear the fog. It helps us do the right thing, for the right reason in the right way."

Richard E. Boyatzis, PhD
Distinguished University Professor, Case Western Reserve University
author of best selling *Primal Leadership* and *Helping People Change*

"Ethics is what defines coaching. Ethical practice is essential for a successful engagement between a coach and a client and other stakeholders. As it is more an art than a science. This guide is such a useful tool for coaches and clients alike and a fantastic addition to the coaching body of knowledge. With contributions from so many amazing coaches and scholars, this book is a "must read" for everyone engaged with coaching!"

Magdalena Nowicka Mook
CEO, International Coaching Federation
United States

"The editors have brought together a broad range of experts from across the coaching field and beyond to create an authoritative and timely resource. I can see this book having a significant positive impact on the professionalism and ethics of coaching for decades to come."

Prof. Christian van Nieuwerburgh
Professor of Coaching and Positive Psychology
Centre for Positive Psychology and Health
RCSI University of Medicine and Health Sciences
Dublin, Ireland

"With the rise in popularity of coaching as an intervention, especially after what the world has experienced in the last few years, it has become more important that coaching psychologists particularly get clearer about their ethics and values and boundaries. With many things getting more complex, it's more critical to get clarity for oneself. This books serves as an important guide for practitioners, containing voices and thoughts from some of the leading thinkers in the area of coaching and coaching psychology. Highly recommended."

Mongezi C Makhalima, PhD
Chartered Coach (ABCCCP)
South Africa

"Coaches and Supervisors committed to reflective practice and their continuing development will welcome this book.
The breadth of the inquiry both mirrors and supports the growing interest for a more considered approach to ethics as a profession and a more subtle ethical-intelligence as individual practitioners.

Against the backdrop of the individual and societal challenges we face, how do we move beyond the guardrails of ethical codes to find new ways of being in question together?"

Ant Mitchell
Chair, APECS (Association for Professional Executive
Coaching & Supervision)

The Ethical Coaches' Handbook

What does it mean to be ethical as a coach? Just how ethical are you? How does ethics influence your coaching and how do you know if you are engaging in ethical practice? This important and eye-opening volume provides critical insight from the thought leaders in coaching across a full range of ethical issues.

Presented in four parts, this new edition works to guide the reader towards ethical maturity to strengthen their practice, though examination of theory and thought-provoking practice examples. Part 1, *Foundations of Ethics in Coaching,* provides a detailed overview of the basic principles of ethical coaching. Part 2, *Ethics in Coaching Practice,* details specific examples of where you will need to think ethically and be guided by good ethics within your practice. Part 3, *Pushing the Boundaries of Ethical Thinking in Coaching*, dives deeper into topics such as race, managing mental health, the environment and marketing. Part 4, consists of 12 case studies which encourage you to think about putting the theory of the book into practice.

The Ethical Coaches' Handbook: *A Guide to Developing Ethical Maturity in Practice* will provide ideal support to students, practitioners and coach educators looking to deepen, broaden and enhance their ethical coaching practice.

Wendy-Ann Smith
Eclorev Coaching and Consulting, France
L'École de Psychologues Praticiens, France
Visiting Fellow, Centre for Positive Psychology, Buckinghamshire New University, UK

Wendy-Ann is a coach and psychologist. She enjoys leveraging her expertise in consulting projects. She is a co-founder of the Coaching Ethics Forum (CEF), where she led and coordinated an international team to produce the first international conference dedicated to ethics in coaching. She is the lead editor of *Positive Psychology Coaching in the Workplace*. Wendy-Ann regularly coaches a small number of one-to-one clients. She designs and delivers lectures, training and workshops internationally in a variety of settings including universities. Her interest is supporting the development of coaches through coaching psychology, positive psychology, and increasing ethical awareness in practice. She also enjoys exploring geography and culture through travel and photography.

Jonathan Passmore
CoachHub & Henley Business School, UK

Jonathan is a professor of coaching and behavioural change at Henley Business School, UK and Senior Vice-President at CoachHub, the digital coaching platform. He is a chartered psychologist, European Mentoring and Coaching Council (EMCC) Master Coach, International Coaching Federation (ICF) PCC, holds qualifications in team coaching, coaching supervision and five degrees including an MBA and doctorate in psychology. He has written and edited over 30 books and nearly 200 scientific papers and book chapters, making him one of the most widely published coaching researchers.

Eve Turner
Fellow, University of Southampton Business School, Professional Development Foundation, UK

Eve has had three careers, in music, broadcasting and coaching and supervision. She sees their links through her interest in communication, collaboration and interrelationships. As a classical guitarist and then a willing, if not very able, orchestral conductor, she learned how the whole can be so much more than the sum of the parts and how the quality of the communication and relationships affected the outcome. Eve was a journalist, senior leader and internal coach in the BBC (British Broadcasting Corporation) before setting up her own practice. She has won many awards for her research, writing, coaching and supervision, and volunteers, alongside a busy practice. This includes co-founding the Climate Coaching Alliance, founding and co-leading the Global Supervisors' Network, immediate past chair of the coaching and supervision professional body Association for Professional Executive Coaching and Supervision (APECS) and for the AC and EMCC. Her books include *Ecological and Climate-conscious Coaching: A Companion Guide to Evolving Coaching Practice* (2023) co-edited with the late Alison Whybrow, Josie McLean and Peter Hawkins, *Systemic Coaching* (2020) with Peter Hawkins, and *The Heart of Coaching Supervision – Working with Reflection and Self-care* (2019) co-edited with Stephen Palmer.

Yi-Ling Lai
Department of Organizational Psychology, Birkbeck, University of London, UK

Yi-Ling Lai (PhD, CPsychol) joined the Department of Organizational Psychology as a Lecturer in January of 2020. Prior to working at Birkbeck. Yi-Ling's research mainly concentrates on the psychological evidence in the coaching process. For instance, the application of coaching intervention to facilitate cancer patients' illness identity sponsored by The Fountain Centre NHS Royal Surrey Hospital and Health Education England (2019–22). Yi-Ling is also taking active roles in several sub-committees of the British Psychological Society (BPS), such as the Editor of the BPS's *International Coaching Psychology Review*. Recently, Yi-Ling extended her research focus by drawing social psychological theory such as social identity to organization studies (e.g., workplace well-being and resilience).

David Clutterbuck
Co-founder of the European Mentoring and Coaching Council (EMCC), UK

David Clutterbuck is one of the earliest pioneers of coaching and mentoring. David is a visiting professor at four business schools and co-founder of the European Mentoring and Coaching Council EMCC. He is the author of more than 70 books, over 100 papers and book chapters on ethics and coach behaviour. David was a lead coach on the Ethical Coach project and has trained hundreds of ethical mentors in the UK health service and elsewhere.

The Ethical Coaches' Handbook

A Guide to Developing Ethical Maturity
in Practice

Edited by
Wendy-Ann Smith, Jonathan Passmore,
Eve Turner, Yi-Ling Lai and David
Clutterbuck

Routledge
Taylor & Francis Group

LONDON AND NEW YORK

First published 2023
by Routledge
4 Park Square, Milton Park, Abingdon, Oxon OX14 4RN

and by Routledge
605 Third Avenue, New York, NY 10158

Routledge is an imprint of the Taylor & Francis Group, an informa business

British Library Cataloguing-in-Publication Data
A catalogue record for this book is available from the British Library

Library of Congress Cataloging-in-Publication Data
A catalog record has been requested for this book

ISBN: 978-1-032-23060-3 (hbk)
ISBN: 978-1-032-23463-2 (pbk)
ISBN: 978-1-003-27772-9 (ebk)

DOI: 10.4324/9781003277729

Typeset in Times New Roman
by Taylor & Francis Books

Contents

SECTION 3
Pushing the boundaries of conventional ethical thinking in coaching

Illustrations

Figures

Tables

Contributors

Julie Allan
Independent supervisor and coaching psychologist, UK

Julie Allan MSc C Psychol FRSA is an experienced supervisor, Associate Fellow of the International Society for Coaching Psychology and Master Executive Coach with APECS. She has served on the ethics committee of the British Psychological Society, of which she is an Associate Fellow. Human creativity and potential have remained constant threads through her work, from a prior career encompassing theatre, media and publishing, to chartership as a psychologist and doctoral research in metacognition. Julie applies 25+ years of varied public, private and not-for-profit experience, and expertise in adult development, to her work with leadership. Underpinned by gestalt and a sense of enquiry-based adventure, Julie supports those seeking to engage in the challenges of our times with finesse, focus and integrity. Julie has spoken at conferences and for webinars on ethics, supervision and the psychology of wisdom, and has written on ethics, supervision, gestalt, wisdom, metacognition and complexity, including for the international Wiley-Blackwell Handbook of the Psychology of Coaching and Mentoring, Supervision in Coaching: Supervision, Ethics and Continual Professional Development and 101 Coaching Supervision Techniques, Approaches, Enquiries and Experiments. She is also co-author of The Power of the Tale: using narratives for organisational success.

Carrie Arnold
Evidence Based Coaching Program Director, Fielding Graduate University
Principal Coach & Consultant, The Willow Group, US

Carrie Arnold is a Master Certified Coach with a Ph.D. in Human Development. She works in private practice, coaching and consulting in education, healthcare, and government. Dr. Arnold is also a coach educator and the program director for evidence-based coaching at Fielding Graduate University. She is an author with published research on silencing, voice, and leadership; she enjoys blending her academic pursuits with creativity and authenticity.

Mona Ashok
Henley Business School, UK

Mona Ashok is an Associate Professor of Digital Transformation, Diversity, Equity and Inclusion committee member at Henley Business School, UK, University (of Reading) Board for Research and Innovation member, Director of Academic Tutoring for post-experienced programmes. Mona has extensive senior management industry experience. Worked with customers in Asia, Australia, Europe, and Northern America. She is a Fellow of the UK Higher Education Academy (FHEA), a member of the Institute of Chartered Accountants of India, a Certified Software Quality Analyst, and a Six Sigma Master Black Belt. Mona has successfully secured research grants.

Marc Bürgi
DMB-Consulting, Switzerland

Marc Bürgi is an independent certified coach for leaders, teams, and talents. He works digitally and in person with international professionals from the Zurich area, Switzerland. As a trained solution-focused coach, systemic practitioner with a PhD from the University of St. Gallen, and as an adult educator with diploma, Marc is a trusted partner for leadership, people and organisational development. Among his multi-sector clients are international corporations, SMEs, NGOs, and governmental institutions.

Roger Bretherton
University of Lincoln, UK

Roger Bretherton is Associate Professor in the School of Psychology, at the University of Lincoln. He is an HCPC accredited Clinical Psychologist, an Associate Fellow of the British Psychological Society and a Senior Fellow of the Higher Education Academy. He is the director of Character Lab Lincoln, which conducts training, consultancy and research on the positive qualities of character related to psychological wellbeing and effective living. His research team is currently investigating the benefits of humility in leaders, the role of mindfulness in character development, a strengths-based approach to pro-environmental behaviours, the role of wisdom in business leadership, and character strengths in entrepreneurs. He has authored two books, and dozens of articles and book chapters, and is a reviewer for several leading academic journals in applied psychology. He delivers coaching, training and keynotes across a broad range of public and private sector organisations.

Francine Campone
F. Campone Coaching & Consulting, US

Francine Campone, Ed.D. MCC is Editor (Americas) for the International Coaching Psychology Review, a member of EMCC, ICF and the Global Supervisors' Network. Francine is the Lead Editor for the forthcoming *Coaching Supervision: Voices from the Americas* (in press) and co-edited *Innovations in Leadership Coaching Research and Practice*. Her research publications include a case study on the coaching/psychotherapy boundary; the impact of life events on coaches and their coaching; and book chapters on adult learning theories in coaching, reflective learning for coaches, coaching in the adult workplace and trends in coaching related research. As principal for F. Campone Coaching & Consulting, Francine offers coach supervision, mentoring and coach training.

Catherine Carr

Carr Kline & Associates, Renewal Associates, Resilience@Work, Global Team Coaching Institute, Canada

Catherine Carr is a Master Corporate Executive Coach, supervisor, psychotherapist and university instructor, with 25 years experience in the public and not for profit sector. Catherine's early doctorate research advanced the team coaching field. Publications include peer reviewed research articles along with the co-authored *High performance team coaching* and *50 tips for terrific teams*. Catherine is currently Head of the Systemic Team Coaching Practitioner Practicum for the Global Team Coaching Institute, leads Resilience at Work (North America) and co-leads the Systemic Team Coaching Supervision Training. Catherine is grateful to do work that supports people to be well, live well, and to meaningfully contribute around them and to our world. She lives in beautiful Victoria, British Columbia (traditional territories of the W̱SÁNEĆ and Ləkʷəŋən speaking peoples).

Michael Cavanagh

Deputy Director, Coaching psychology Unit, University of Sydney (Australia)

Michael Cavanagh is an internationally recognized academic, practitioner and consultant in the fields of leadership and coaching psychology. Michael's work focuses on preparing leaders, teams and coaches to work in complex settings. As an academic he is the Deputy Director of the Coaching Psychology Unit at the University of Sydney – where he and Tony Grant established the world's first master's degree in coaching psychology. He is also a visiting Professor at Middlesex University (UK). He has coached leaders and managers at all levels from a diverse range of industries. Along with numerous publications in the peer reviewed press, Michael is the principal author of the Standards Australia Handbook of Organisational Coaching. He is also the Australian editor of the International Coaching Psychology Review. Michael's passion is assisting leaders, organisations and individuals to understand and address complex challenges in ways that increase the sustainability of the organisation, its people and the planet.

Sarah Corrie
University of Suffolk, UK

Sarah Corrie is a Chartered Coaching Psychologist and founder and co-director of Inspiring Transformation Ltd which specialises in bespoke coaching interventions for individuals and organisations. She is a Founder Member and former Chair of the British Psychological Society's Special Group in Coaching Psychology and has a particular interest in how coaching might contribute to some of the most challenging issues of our time, including sustainable emotional well-being and positive mental health. She is the author of nine books including, *The Art of Inspired Living: Coach Yourself with Positive Psychology*. Amongst her other roles, Sarah is a Professor of Cognitive Behaviour Therapy and Counselling at the University of Suffolk and a Visiting Professor at Middlesex University. In 2016, she was the recipient of the British Psychological Society's Achievement Award for Distinguished Contributions to Coaching Psychology.

Jule Deges
CoachHub – the digital coaching platform, Germany

Jule Deges is an organizational psychologist with a MSc in Positive Psychology and Coaching Psychology. Jule has extensive experience working with organizations to design evidence-based employee experience solutions that help organizations grow happier and healthier workforces. As a Senior Behavioural Scientist at CoachHub, she works with organizations in democratizing coaching across all career levels worldwide.

Rosie Evans-Krimme
CoachHub, Germany

Rosie Evans-Krimme is a psychologist, coach, mindfulness practitioner, and researcher. Rosie holds an MSc in Mental Health Studies from King's College London and is Principal Behavioural Scientist for CoachHub. Her writing and speaking covers themes including coaching for mental health and wellbeing, leadership, culture transformation, and the coaching industry.

Pauline Fatien
Associate Professor in Management, Grenoble Ecole de Management, France

Pauline Fatien is a critical researcher and educator in Management with a focus on coaching studies. For the past 20 years, she has developed an expertise in power and ethics in coaching, motivated by documenting the complexities of this helping practice. She is the author of several books, edited books, book chapters and peer-reviewed articles. She is Associate Professor at Grenoble Ecole de Management, France. She graduated with a Ms in Management (HEC Paris), a Research Master in Sociology of Power (University of Paris) and a PhD in Management (HEC Paris). She has an international career in France, the USA and Colombia.

Bob Garvey
Leeds Business School, UK

Professor (Emeritus) Bob Garvey PhD, FRSA, is one of Europe's leading academic practitioners of mentoring and coaching. He is an experienced mentor/coach working with a range of people in a variety of contexts. Bob works internationally and he subscribes to the 'repertoire' approach to mentoring and coaching. He is in demand as a keynote conference speaker, webinar facilitator and workshop leader. He is an active researcher and very widely published. His latest book, with Paul Stokes, *Coaching and Mentoring: Theory and Practice* was published in 2022 as a 4th Edition.

Andrea Giraldez-Hayes
University of East London, UK

Andrea Giraldez-Hayes is a chartered psychologist, coach, supervisor and consultant specialising in the use of arts and creative approaches to positive psychology and coaching psychology. She is the Director of the MSc in Applied Positive Psychology and Coaching Psychology and the Wellbeing and Psychological Services Centre at the University of East London's School of Psychology. Andrea has served in different roles within the arts, education, and coaching psychology sectors, having worked for universities, education departments, and international organisations. She has authored more than forty books and book chapters as well as peer-reviewed papers.

Stephen Gresty
Consultant, Facilitator and Coach, UK

Stephen Gresty is a coach, facilitator, and consultant, over the years he's been fortunate to have travelled the globe, where he has worked in EMEA, BRIC, Asia as well as North and South America, delivering numerous management development and sales training programmes, very often working through simultaneous translation This was a result of being a certified trainer and programme developer for the L'Oréal Sale Academy (LSA) and more recently the Service & Retail Academy (SRA). Stephen is also a licensed distributor and trainer of Insights Discovery, and certified

NLP practitioner. Stephen studied "Efficient Business Management at CEDEP and is co-founder of Positive Organisations & People (POP). He also claims to be a budding poet, whose philosophy is "see in others, more than they see in themselves".

Peter Hawkins
Chairman Renewal associates and Honorary President AoEC and Emeritus Professor of Leadership Henley Business School, UK

Peter Hawkins, Chairman of Renewal Associates, co-founder of the Global Team Coaching Institute, Emeritus Professor of Leadership at Henley Business School, and Senior Visiting Fellow, Civil Service College (Singapore), is a leading consultant, coach, writer and researcher in organizational strategy, leadership, culture change, team and board development and coaching. He has worked with many leading organizations all over the world facilitating major change and organizational transformation projects. He has coached over 100 boards and senior executive teams, in a wide range of organizations and leads masterclasses in over 50 different countries. He is the author of many best-selling books including *Leadership team coaching*, Kogan Page; 2011 (4th edition, 2021); *Leadership team coaching in practice* (3rd edition 2022, *Systemic coaching* with Eve Turner (Routledge 2020); *Coaching, mentoring and organizational consultancy: supervision, skills, and development* with Nick Smith, McGraw-Hill/Open University Press, (2nd ed, 2013); *Creating a coaching culture*, McGraw Hill, 2012; and *The wise fool's guide to leadership*, O Books, 2005.

Rachel Hawley
Sheffield Hallam University, UK

Rachel Hawley is a leadership associate, coach, researcher, and author with teaching experience in healthcare leadership and management. She was awarded Doctor in Professional Studies by Sheffield Hallam University for a piece of research on 'Relational Leadership in the NHS: how healthcare leaders identify with public engagement (2021). Her passion for collaborative practice is reflected in the publication of the first complete guide to exploring values and ethics in coaching – Iordanou, I., Hawley R. and Iordanou, C. (2017) Values and Ethics in Coaching: Sage, London and Thousand Oaks, CA. Rachel and her co-authors received the Coaching Book of the Year 2017 from The Coaching Centre, Henley Business School. She is Senior Follow HEA (2015) in recognition for her contributions to teaching and learning featuring coaching and mentoring approaches.

Hellen Hettinga
Hellen Hettinga Executive Coaching • Change Leadership, France

Hellen Hettinga is an ICF PCC executive coach, supervisor and change leadership facilitator, who partners with individuals, teams and organisations navigating complex challenges in uncertain environments, bringing a systemic approach in our interconnected eco-systems. Her intention is to enable conversations that matter to learn collectively and inclusively for people and planet to thrive. An explorer by nature, she has lived through career changes, rough seas, global relocations, mergers, acquisitions and societal transformations.

Angela Hill
European Mentoring and Coaching Council Global, The OCM Group Ltd, UK

Angela Hill is a Fellow of the CIPD, and an accredited senior coach practitioner and supervisor, EMCC EIA and ESIA. As a volunteer she was EMCC Global Centre for Excellence – Ethics Lead to 2022 and part of the international workgroup leading on the EMCC Supervision Competence Framework 2019. Formerly Head of Supervision with The OCM Group and now Consultant Supervisor and Professional Coach. Angela held a senior corporate client relationship role for 16 years in outplacement, change management, leadership development, well-being and critical incident services. As a freelance she has experience of ensuring quality and respectful delivery of social coaching in deprived UK communities. Angela has written several articles for annual OCM Journals and Chapter 15 'Supervision in Practice', Coaching and Mentoring: Practical Techniques for Developing Learning and Performance, 3rd Edition (2017). She continues to contribute to the quality of professional delivery and ethical practice internationally for EMCC Global.

Christiana Iordanou
University of Kent, UK

Christiana Iordanou is a Lecturer in Developmental Psychology and Mental Health at the University of Kent, with research interests in the use of creative methods as memory aids and the effects of trauma on wellbeing. She is an HCPC registered Dramatherapist, with more than 15 years clinical experience as a practitioner psychologist and dramatherapist. She is the co-author of the award winning book *Values and Ethics in Coaching* (Sage, 2017) and author of several book chapters and peer reviewed journal articles which involve, amongst others, the use of creative methods in coaching and supervision as well as safeguarding mental wellbeing in children and in Higher Education.

Ioanna Iordanou
Oxford Brookes University, UK

Ioanna Iordanou is a Reader in Human Resource Management (Coaching and Mentoring) at Oxford Brookes Business School, where she is an active member of the International Centre for Coaching and Mentoring Studies. She is the co-author of the award winning book *Values and Ethics in Coaching* (Sage, 2017) and co-editor of *The Practitioner's Handbook of Team Coaching* (Routledge, 2019). She is also co-editor-in-chief of the peer reviewed journal *Coaching: An International Journal of Theory, Research and Practice*.

Aaron Jarden
University of Melbourne, Centre for Wellbeing Science, Australia

Aaron Jarden, Associate Professor, is Director of the Masters of Applied Positive Psychology (MAPP) program at the Melbourne Graduate School of Education, University of Melbourne. He is a wellbeing consultant, social entrepreneur, has multiple qualifications in philosophy, computing, education, and psychology, and is a prolific author and presenter. He has previously been a Senior Research Fellow at Flinders University, and Head of Research at the Wellbeing and Resilience Centre at the South Australian Health and Medical Research Institute (SAHMRI). He is past president of the New Zealand Association of Positive Psychology, also co-editor of the International Journal of Wellbeing, and lead investigator for the International Wellbeing Study amongst others.

Kristin Kelly
International Coaching Federation, US

Kristin Kelly has served the International Coaching Federation (ICF) since 2007 in numerous capacities (including marketing, membership, and leadership development) before her current position as the Director of Ethics, Compliance and Culture. The ICF is the world's largest membership organization, accreditation, and credentialing body for professionally trained coaches. In her role, she works closely with the Independent Review Board, the body that oversees the ICF Ethical Conduct Review Process, as well as leading ethics, compliance, policy, and trademark matters across the organization. She oversees ICF's New Employee Onboarding Process and has been a driver in the creation of ICF staff culture and values and is actively involved in the ICF Strategic Planning Core Team. She recently served as a member of the ICF Values Summit that was tasked with updating the organizational values of the organization.

David A Lane
Professional Development Foundation, United Kingdom

David A Lane – is Director and co-founder of the Professional Development Foundation, which has for forty years pioneered work-based professional development. As well as contributing to research and the professional development of coaching Professor Lane has coached in a wide range of organisations including major consultancies, multinationals, and public sector and government bodies. He also pioneered the international development of work based masters and doctorate degrees for experienced coaches in South Africa, New York and London. He has published widely on coaching. He has served on committees of the BPS, CIPD, WABC and EMCC, working to create accreditation systems as well as being a founder member of the Global Coaching Community. In 2009 the British Psychological Society honoured him for his Distinguished Contribution to Professional Psychology. and also was elected a Fellow of the Academy of Social Sciences. He holds the Lifetime Achievement Award for contribution to Applied Psychology from Surrey University and from Coaching at Work for lifetime contributions to coaching and supervision.

Lise Lewis
Bluesky International EMCC Global Special Ambassador, United Kingdom

Lise Lewis D. Prof MBA CFCIPD EMCC accredited coach mentor supervisor and master coach mentor. Bluesky International founder providing accredited coach|mentor|supervisor training. Practising Executive Coach and Supervisor for independent|in-house practitioners. Immediate Past President of EMCC Global and currently Special Ambassador. Honorary Member of APECS and AOCS. Lise's immersion in a doctoral study of human behaviour culminated in authoring Relational Feedback: Why Feedback Fails and How to Make it More Meaningful 2020. Global keynote speaker and webinar contributor: AI, Cultural Diversity, Ethics, EQ/SQ, Trends in Coaching and Supervision, Leadership Tomorrow, Relational Feedback. Contributor to Coaching Supervision Advancing Practice, Changing Landscapes. Volunteer with EMCC Global 20+ years initiating and contributing to professional standards in coaching, mentoring and supervision. Building on a human resources senior management career, Lise's private| public sector work focuses on Relational Leadership. Assignments help leaders and teams to sharpen existing people skills that sustain a high level of interpersonal intelligence. Team relationships improve and consequently team effectiveness is responsive to the rapid pace and changing world of work. Training focuses on creating organisational coaching facilities. 2019 Winner EMCC Global Supervisor Award, 2018 Highly Recommended: Coaching at Work Coaching Supervision Award and Highly Recommended: Coaching|Mentoring Champion Award.

Tim Lomas
Harvard University, United States

Tim Lomas is a Psychology Research Scientist at the Harvard T.H. Chan School of Public Health and the Human Flourishing Program at Harvard University. Before that he was a lecturer in positive psychology at the University of East London from 2013–2020. Tim's main research focus is exploring cross-cultural perspectives on wellbeing, such as his lexicography of 'untranslatable' words. Tim completed an MA and MSc at the University of Edinburgh, and spent six years working as a musician and psychiatric nursing assistant before undertaking his PhD at the University of Westminster from 2008 to 2012 (exploring the impact of meditation on men's mental health).

Pam McLean
ICF, Master Certified Coach; Fellow American Group Psychotherapy AssociationMember, ACTO (Association for Coach Training Organizations) Member, American Psychological Association Certified Coach Supervisor, United States

Pamela McLean, PhD, Co-Founder of The Hudson Institute of Coaching, brings more than three decades of experience as a clinical psychologist, master coach, coach supervisor, business leader, and contributor in the field of leadership coaching. McLean authored The Completely Revised Handbook of Coaching (2012) examining key theories and evidenced based research informing the field; examining the essential methodology, key steps in the coaching engagement; and focusing on the impact of coaching on the leader and the system. In 2016 she authored LifeForward, Charting the Journey Ahead focused on intentionally charting a course through the chapters and transitions in one's life. McLean's most recent book, Self as Coach, Self as Leader (2019), takes a close look at developmental coaching that focuses on deeper, lasting changes and examines the internal landscape of the coach and the leader and all that is required to be at our very best when working with others. Pam served the Board of The Association of Learning Providers; Harvard's JFK Women's Leadership Board, Editorial Board of IJCO and LikeMinded, and on the faculty of Saybrook University in San Francisco. Pam lives in Santa Barbara, California, where she and her late husband raised three sons.

Dumisani Magadlela
Development Bank of Southern Africa, South Africa

Dumi Magadlela is an executive and team coach working for the Development Bank of Southern Africa (DBSA). He is Senior Faculty at The Coaching Centre (TCC) where he has delivered a module on "Coaching in the African Context" (14 years). Dumi is part-time faculty at the University of Stellenbosch Business School's MPhil in Management Coaching, where he teaches "Ubuntu Team Coaching". He is part of the international faculty at Coaching.com's Global Team Coaching Institute (GTCI). He is accredited by the European

Mentoring and Coaching Council (EMCC) as a Senior Practitioner in Team Coaching. Dumi lives in Johannesburg, South Africa.

Terrence E. Maltbia
Teachers College, Columbia University, United States

Terrence E. Maltbia, Associate Professor of Practice in the Department of Organization and Leadership, at Teachers College, Columbia. Scholarly interest includes strategic learning; leadership and organizational development; diversity and cultural intelligence; executive and organizational coaching. Terry came to Columbia after over 20 years of diverse experience as an external and internal organizational effectiveness consultant, thought leader and educator—in positions ranging from field sales, sales management, sales training, to Vice President Organizational Effectiveness Center of Excellence for a major Fortune 200 Corporation—as well as two consulting firms. He is the recipient of The Academy of Human Resources Development's Malcolm Knowles Dissertation of the Year Award for his pioneering diversity practitioner research; was recognized as #1 In Coach Education in the World by Thinkers50 | Marshall Goldsmith's Top Global Coaches 2019, 2021; AIIR Consulting's 2020 Coaching Leadership Award Recipient; and Outstanding Contribution to Coaching Award – Henley Business School, University Reading, in 2021.

Eric Mellet
Mellet Consulting, France

Eric Mellet is a coach, consultant and trainer, he works as an enabler to help organisations initiate and implement positive organisational transformation, staff engagement and client centric strategy. He previously worked for 29 years for L'Oréal. In his last appointment as Professional Products Division Business Development General Manager, Eric initiated, and piloted worldwide projects based on Collective Intelligence to develop customer's centric approach and commercial excellence. Eric aims to combine economic performance, quest of meaning and individual and collective potential flourishing. Eric is the co-founder of Positive Organisations & People (POP), he is also President of SOL France Association (Society for Organizational Learning). Co-author of *La Boîte à Outils de la Psychologie Positive au Travail*, and co-author of Développer une université d'entreprise. Créer un levier de business development.

Alexandra Morgan
Abbey Communication Ltd. and De Montfort University, United Kingdom

Alexandra Morgan has been training coaches for over 15 years, has led a post-graduate level programme in Professional Coaching at a university in the United Kingdom. Her own coaching focuses on leadership and communication coaching, particularly in international teams. She is author of "Coaching International Teams" and is a coach supervisor.

Stephen Murphy
EMCC Global VP Thought Leadership & Development, Poland

Stephen Murphy is a professional Individual Coach/ Mentor and a Team Coach, accredited *in both* at Master Practitioner level by the EMCC. He is also an accredited Coach/Mentor Supervisor. He has a multi-cultural and multi-functional background. British, living in Poland with a 30+year corporate career spanning P&G, Reckitt Benckiser, Coca-Cola Bottlers and PZ Cussons; on-the-ground in UK, Greece, Morocco, Tunisia, Yemen, Russia & Poland; with assignments in Sales, Marketing & Country/ Regional General Management. He has personally led and been responsible for international start-up operations, in developed and hardship locations; significant organisational change projects; business turnaround assignments and re-shaping leadership teams into effective operating units. He currently coaches and mentors in Europe, North & Central America, Africa and Asia, with senior business leaders, individually and in teams, towards greater self-awareness and operational impact. Sectors include AI, Banking, Chemicals, Consulting, FMCG, Insurance, IIoT, Legal, Logistics, Media, Pharma, Retail, Software and Wines & Spirits.

Angela M. Passarelli
Department of Management and Marketing College of Charleston, Charleston, SC USA
Institute of Coaching McLean/Harvard Medical School, Belmont, MA USA

Angela Passarelli is an Associate Professor of Management at the College of Charleston, SC, and Director of Research at the Institute of Coaching, McLean/Harvard Medical School. She also serves as a research fellow with the Coaching Research Lab at the Weatherhead School of Management, Case Western Reserve University. Her research focuses on how developmental relationships support learning, particularly in the context of leader development. She draws on neuroscience and psychophysiology to explore the implicit dynamics of these relationships. Her work has been published in both academic and practitioner outlets such as the *Leadership Quarterly, Social Neuroscience, Organizational Research Methods,* and the *Consulting Psychology Journal: Practice and Research.*

Liz Pavese
CoachHub– the digital coaching platform, US

Liz Pavese, PhD, is a Director of Behavioral Science (N. America), where she marries her expertise in organizational psychology, employee experience, and organizational development to close the gap between coaching research and practice. Liz has over 15 years of experience working with world-class organizations across industries to design and implement scalable talent solutions ranging from development programs, to performance practices, career architecture, culture assessment and change initiatives to drive transformation in organizations. Over the years as a leader in HR Tech, she has built global advisory teams to deliver on customer employee experience programs and provided expertise in the design of new product features and solutions. Liz earned her Ph. D. in Industrial- Organizational Psychology from Seattle Pacific University and is an ICF Certified Professional Coach. Liz is a member of the Society of Industrial-Organizational Psychology, Society for Consulting Psychology, International Coaching Federation, and Portland Women in Tech.

David Matthew Prior
Columbia Coaching Certification Program (3CP), United States

David Matthew Prior, MCC, BCC, MBA, has served on the Core Facilitator Team for the Columbia Coaching Certification Program since 2008. Leveraging over two decades of coaching, finance, ethics training and theatre performance, he has the honor to guide and coach more than 1,000 senior leaders in more than 30 countries, train 5,000+ executive coaches and create results for more than 100 organizations. His work in executive and team development benefits a global client roster, applying his gift with language to the nuances that exist within various cultural landscapes. Before coaching, he worked as a Trust & Financial Planning Officer for Texas Commerce Bank (now Chase), followed by completing a two-year acting conservatory as a graduate of the American Academy of Dramatic Arts, New York. As one of the founders of the PPCA (Professional & Personal Coaches Association) in 1986 (which merged with ICF in 1998), David served as Co-Chair of the ICF Ethics & Standards Committee (2003–2006) and Executive Committee member (Vice President) of the ICF Global Board of Directors (2006–2007). As founder of Getacoach.com, David's approach is rooted in helping leaders and their teams perform with integrity.

Annalise Roache
University of Melbourne, Centre for Wellbeing Science, Australia

Annalise Roache is a Positive Psychology Practitioner, credentialed coach, mentor, educator and wellbeing researcher. She works with emerging leaders, managers, business owners, coaches, and individuals in personal and workplace settings. Favouring an evidence-based, solution-focused approach informed by the fields of Coaching Psychology and Positive Psychology, she develops psycho-educational short courses and online wellbeing content to promote knowledge sharing and active practice to support personal transformation. Annalise works closely with the Centre for Wellbeing Science at the University of Melbourne and is a Faculty member of the Institute of Positive Psychology Coaching (IPPC). She is an active board member of the New Zealand Association of Positive Psychology and author of The Ethical Guidelines for Positive Psychology Practice (2019; 2021; 2023).   In 2017 Annalise gained a Master of Science in Applied Positive Psychology and Coaching Psychology (MAPPCP) from the University of East London. In 2018, she commenced Doctoral studies at Auckland University of Technology upon receiving a Vice-Chancellors Doctoral scholarship. Her research focuses on lay conceptions of wellbeing and how these compare to academic theory and models to bridge the gap and ensure more effective policy, programme and intervention design and delivery.

Tayyab Rashid
University of Melbourne, Centre for Wellbeing Science, Australia

Tayyab Rashid is a licensed clinical psychologist and Senior Lecturer at the Centre for Wellbeing Science, Melbourne Graduate School of Education, University of Melbourne. Prior to this Tayyab was a faculty member at the University of Toronto Scarborough (UTSC). For more than 15 years, Dr. Rashid has worked with individuals experiencing complex mental health issues including severe depression, debilitating anxiety, borderline personality disorder and PTSD using a culturally contextualized strengths-based therapeutic approach. His work has been published in academic journals, included in textbooks of psychiatry and psychotherapy and been featured media. His book Positive Psychotherapy (2018), co-written with Martin Seligman, is considered one of the most comprehensive clinical resources in the field and has been translated into ten languages so far. Dr. Rashid won the Outstanding Practitioner Award (2017) from the International Positive Psychology Association (IPPA) and Chancellor Award (2018) from the University of Toronto.

Kevin M Rogers
Director, Solent Law School, Southampton, UK

Kevin M Rogers is Director of Solent Law School, Southampton and has held senior management positions with other institutions within the UK. He has a strong background in quality assurance, learning and teaching, partnership working, and university governance. His teaching/research background is within commercial law-related fields, with a particular interest and specialism in aspects of internet/e-commerce law and he has published widely in these areas. Kevin has a particular interest in data protection and over the last few years has applied this research by providing consultancy work to various law firms and multi-national companies. Kevin has worked with a range of external organisations. He was Director for the Central Application Board (Lawcabs) and sat on a National Working Group on Law Degree Apprenticeships. He was secretary of the British and Irish Law, Education and Technology Association (BILETA) (2011–2018) and was a member of the Law Society's Technology and Law Reference Group from 2006–2016. In 2018, Kevin was appointed to the Access Qualification Development Group, which is a committee of the QAA and is focused particularly on the development of the Access qualifications, and he is also a QAA Institutional Reviewer.

Philippe Rosinski
Rosinski & Company, Belgium Kenichi Ohmae Graduate School of Business, Japan

Philippe Rosinski, MCC, is the author of two seminal books, Coaching Across Cultures and Global Coaching. For 30 years and across continents, Philippe has helped people, teams, and organizations thrive and make a positive difference in the world. He is the first European to have been designated Master Certified Coach by the International Coach Federation. He has also developed an integrative coaching supervision approach. A Master of Science from Stanford University, Philippe has received numerous awards including the Thinkers50 Marshall Goldsmith Leading Global Coaches Award (2019) and he is listed among the Global Gurus Coaching Top 30 (#9 in 2022). Philippe is the principal of Rosinski & Company, a consultancy based in Belgium with partners around the globe, and a professor at the Kenichi Ohmae Graduate School of Business in Tokyo, Japan. He intervenes in several other academic institutions including HEC Paris, Henley Business School, and the University of Cambridge.

Katharine St John-Brooks
Working Solutions, UK

Katharine St John-Brooks trained as an executive coach in 2003 and had coached over 500 clients in the public, private and not-for-profit sectors by the time she hung up her coaching boots in 2020. Her book, *Internal Coaching: The Inside Story* (Karnac Books, 2014), was based on research with 123 internal coaches and she has contributed chapters on internal coaching to the *Complete Handbook of Coaching* (3rd and 4th editions) and *Coaching Supervision: Advancing Practice, Changing Landscapes* (2019). Katharine holds an MSc in Organisational Behaviour, an MA in Professional Development (Coaching), is a Fellow of the Institute of Consulting and now concentrates on delivering workshops to internal coaches – many of them focusing on dealing with ethical dilemmas – and providing consultancy support for the strategic use of internal coaches within organisations. She chairs the European Mentoring & Coaching Council UK's Third Sector Coaching and Mentoring Forum, is launching a podcast series about supervision for internal coaches and is President of a charity providing support to isolated and lonely older people living in Southwark. Katharine is writing a thriller – working title Blind Faith – exploring a coach's relationship with her crooked Government minister client and the questionable ethical choices that she makes.

Lisa Sansom
LVS Consulting, Canada

Lisa Sansom is the owner of LVS Consulting, a boutique consulting firm that helps to build positive and effective organizations. Lisa shares positive psychology tools and techniques with her clients through speaking, corporate training, consulting, and coaching. Lisa has been working in Organizational Development, Leadership Development and Change Management since 2000. She is a certified coach at the PCC level with the International Coaching Federation. Lisa obtained her MBA from the Rotman School of Management, she holds an HonoursBachelor of Arts from the University of Waterloo and a Bachelor of Education from Brock University. She completed her MAPP (Master of Applied Positive Psychology) from the University of Pennsylvania in 2010, one of the first five Canadians to do so. Lisa is currently enrolled in the DBA (Doctor of Business Administration) program at Royal Roads University researching the workplace impacts of positive feedback. Additional certifications include Prosci Change Management, ShiftPositive 360, Designing Your Life (Stanford), Gallup Strengths Certified Coach, Process Management (Excellence Canada) and Change Cycle™. She recently (2022) won an award with CASE as part of her ground-breaking inclusive facilitation cocreating new remote working environments for a previously traditional work unit.

Sarah Smith
University of Lincoln, UK

Sarah Smith is an experienced leadership coach, consultant and researcher. With over 20 years' experience in developing individuals and teams, Sarah works with a wide variety of organisations in a range of sectors. Prior to establishing her own consultancy business Sarah was Deputy Head of Professional Development at Cranfield University where she held responsibility for management and leadership development across the university. Sarah continues to work with Cranfield as a visiting lecturer. She has designed and led international executive education and corporate programmes, taught at post-graduate and under-graduate levels and presented at international conferences. Sarah has a MSc in Applied Positive Psychology from Buckinghamshire New University. Her research focuses on the psychology of wisdom and she is currently engaged in doctoral research into this area at The University of Lincoln. This informs her approach; she brings a philosophical and deeply relational way of understanding the challenges of being human into her work with her clients.

Silvina Spiegel
ICF Brazil/ ICF Latam, Brazil

Silvina Spiegel is a multi-cultural ontological and executive coach, supervisor-mentor coach, and coach trainer, with coaching experience in Spanish, Portuguese, Hebrew and English. She is also a Coaching Clinic® certified trainer, a Co-development® facilitator and a Symbolon Reflection Method® Coaching Expert. She is the current representative from Latin America for the Regional Coordination Team NALAC – ICF Professional Coaches –, working towards the integration and collaboration of the Region on matters such as DEIJB (diversity, equity, inclusion, justice and belonging) and volunteer engagement and succession. Brazilian representative since 2020 for the Latin America Forum, responsible for the inclusion of Portuguese translation in every event. She served as ICF Brazil Chapter Vice President. founder, director and former VP of the Rio de Janeiro Nucleus. Silvina is passionate about human development and works as an independent coach and facilitator for several world leading consulting companies, training and coaching executives from all over the world and supporting them in the attainment of their goals. She holds a Professional Certified Coach (PCC) credential issued by the International Coaching Federation since 2015, and is currently working towards her MCC.

Catherine Steele
University of Leicester, UK

Catherine Steele is a Coaching Psychologist and an Occupational Psychologist. She works as an Associate Professor of Psychology at the University of Leicester where she leads the delivery of postgraduate programs in psychology. Catherine is also qualified as a Functional Medicine Certified Health Coach and her work is now mostly in the area of Occupational Health and Corporate Wellness. Catherine is the Research Lead for the Division of Coaching Psychology and a member of the Accreditation and Standards Board for the UK Health Coaches Association.

Paul Stokes
Sheffield Business School Sheffield Hallam University, UK

Paul Stokes is Associate Professor of Coaching & Mentoring at Sheffield Business School, Sheffield Hallam University in the UK. He currently leads the Business & Enterprise agenda for the Department of Management within the University. Paul is an EMCC Master Practitioner accredited coach and works as a mentor, supervisor and consultant. He has published widely on coaching & mentoring theory and practice and has 25 years of experience in working in the leadership development space with a range of organisations from public, private and third sectors as well as NGOs. He is also an active researcher and evaluation expert within coaching & mentoring.

Ng Phek Yen
The Borneo Consulting Co., Ltd., China

Ng Phek Yen FCCA, FCPA is a trilingual (English, Chinese and Cantonese) leadership coach and facilitator with a strong business background of more than 19 years of working experience in Mainland China, Hong Kong, and Malaysia. She was the Finance Director cum Qualified Accountant for one of the largest Chinese listed companies in HKSE and NYSE. She was the first and only expatriate with more than 300,000 employees during that period. Her extensive leadership experience in Chinese State-Owned companies and MNCs has provided her with rich intercultural management experience in developing and leading teams of diverse cultures. She is the co-author of the chapter 'Keeping with Times – Coaching, Culture & Positive Psychology' in "Positive Psychology Coaching in the Workplace Phek co-facilitated with Prof. Philippe Rosinski on the world acclaimed Leading and Coaching Across Cultures – Cultural Orientations Framework Certification program. She specializes in global leadership development, intercultural management, DEI in Asia, team effectiveness, women's leadership, and well-being. Originally from Malaysia, Phek Yen is now based in Beijing. She received her EMBA from The Hong Kong Polytechnic University. She is the Master Certified Coach of Cultural Orientations Framework. She is also an Organizational Consultant and LEGO® Serious Play™ facilitator.

Ivan Yong Wei Kit
Corporate Disruptors Forum, Hong Kong

Ivan Yong is an organisational psychologist, angel investor, sales coach and mentor. He is a frequent speaker on startup culture, disruptive innovation for corporations and sales strategy for growth. Ivan engages startups, multinationals and academia in corporate innovation through the collaborative effort of open innovation. Ivan is passionate about social justice, having initiated various global social responsibility programs with the European Mentoring & Coaching Council (EMCC) as the Head of EMCC Global Social Responsibility Initiatives. He is also an official mentor at the Chinese University of Hong Kong for the past 10 years and a startup mentor for the Malaysian Government.

Acknowledgements

This title was preceded by the first conference dedicated to ethics in coaching, organised and co-founder of the Coaching Ethics Forum (CEF) by one of our team Wendy-Ann, which generated many of the ideas contained in this volume. Wendy-Ann would like to acknowledge David Clutterbuck for his support for co-founding CEF. She would also like to make special mention of the conference organising team in alphabetical order: Angela Hill, Bob Garvey, Carol Kauffman, Carrie Arnold, David Lane, Dumisani Magadlela, Kristin Kelly, Ioanna Iordanou, Ivan Young, Lise Lewis, Jeff Hull, Michael Cavanagh, Pam McLean, Paul Brown, Paul Stokes, Pauline Fatien, Peter Hawkins, Rachel Hawley, Robert Biswas-Diener, Terrance Maltbia and Victoria Leath.

We would also like to pay tribute to all of the contributors of this volume who have worked extraordinarily hard on a challenging but engaging and thought-provoking subject matter - ethics - to bring this invaluable and important volume to the coaching community, as well as to our colleagues at Routledge who have brought this title to publication.

Lastly, each of us as editors has been supported by others in this journey. Wendy-Ann by Mila, her attention-seeking cat whose loving attention was a mainstay during this and past projects, her editing colleagues and broader professional coaching network. Jonathan by his wife, Katharine. Eve by family, especially Peter, Dom and Dawn, and the remarkable coachees and supervisees who inspire her. Yi Ling by H. C. James and her first little one, Ellie, who was only four months old when the editing work was officially kicked off. And David, by the ghost of colleagues in the Coaching and Mentoring International network.

Foreword: Where does ethical coaching start?

This book is about ethics in coaching. The title of the handbook implies that it will provide a guide to resolving in a right way complex ethical issues that are abundant in the multiple situations that arise in our work – easier said than done! Although there are ethical codes in all professions, they are not precise for a good reason and do not offer ready-made answers every time we face a dilemma or ethical concern. Furthermore, what is 'right and wrong' or 'good and bad', even in principle, are notoriously among the most difficult questions in philosophy. This means that to hope for clear and simple answers in applied practices is more than optimistic.

Why are decisions about ethical action so difficult? Because what is morally right or wrong is rarely a question that can be answered simply by rational analysis or empirical investigation. Although both are often useful to some extent, they can bring us to logical dead ends in many situations. These questions are so difficult because human beings frequently hold to system of values that may vary not only from culture to culture but often also from one individual to another. Although as human animals we are similar to each other in having certain basic needs and desires, and there are some moral imperatives that seem to apply to all of us, these often turn out to be general principles that tend to crumble in concrete situations when subjected to factual, cultural and subjective interpretation. This is why there are conflicting moral theories and general ethical principles, but these serve only as general guidance. At the point of application, they too often stumble on the personal values of those who are having to make the ethical decision. Even such an 'obvious' ethical principle as 'do no harm', for example, does not help definitively because it depends on how the individual evaluates 'harm' relative to the context in which it arises – it is far from always being obvious.

As an example, we can look at a psychological puzzle that thoughtful coaches often recognise in their work, and which clearly has ethical significance. On the one side, it goes without saying that coaches should not be involved in supporting the clients' actions that might be unethical. This requires that we see clients as agents and recognise their autonomy. As such, we must hold them responsible for their action and be able to judge that action in ethical terms. On the other side, with deeper understanding of the clients and knowing their circumstances we feel compassion for them. We know that individuals and their behaviours are affected by multiple forces in the complex dynamic systems within which they act with multiple commitments to the varying parts of these systems - all of which inevitably impose restrictions on their agentive autonomy. Perhaps because of this, coaches work so hard to avoid being judgmental. So, should we judge or not? Most likely it is our personal values that would determine our attitude to the client and our course of actions. It is also quite likely that often we are not even aware that we hold these important values simultaneously (e.g., autonomy and responsibilities of a human agent vs complex realities of life and compassion), but they clash in some situations involving ethical decision making.

In addition to personal doubts, often we also need to come to an agreement with others about ethical action. In such cases, the difficulties continue because our values may be only superficially compatible on the level of principles. In the concrete situations they might even be irreconcilable from the 'spectator's point of view'. This might be inviting a relativist worldview, that is to say, proclaiming that each person can decide what their values are and only need to be consistent to these values. Another relativistic attitude may be that values are different in each culture and we should not judge them as wrong simply from our cultural perspective, e.g., one person's terrorist is another person's freedom fighter. This can be seen as an interesting dilemma in theory, but in coaching we are not in a spectator's position – we have to make decisions and act. It is not defensible being a relativist, respecting other people's values and rights to act on them, when we are in a position to prevent the avoidable harmful consequences of these actions. There is surely a distinction to be made between respecting differences and having moral obligations.

You have probably noticed that so far, I have been using the terms 'moral' and 'ethical' interchangeably as there seem to be no watertight distinction between them. They are both about right and wrong in human action. The only difference that I see in the context of this book is that morality is concerned with *universal prescriptions* about the ways of being a good person. Any sincere moral judgment implies a command (*a prescription*), to anyone in similar circumstances (*universally*) to act in accordance with that judgment. Although, being something of an 'idealist', I am sympathetic towards any ambition to identify and agree upon imperatives that are universal, I see this as a task of enormous magnitude. At the same time, I am intensely worried when certain groups advocate their chosen imperatives and rules with a stringency bordering on fanaticism. Such moral rules are often a manifestation of the need to control others by any cost. I also dislike psychological and behavioural consequences of moralism such as righteous anger, moralistic posturing and debilitating guilt.

Ethics, on the other hand, is generally expected to be a *reliable guide to life, as a practical philosophy* for an individual or a society (Marks, 2013). Although this also might sound like a universal intention, for it to be reliable and practical, ethical codes are usually developed with reference to a specific area of life and practice. I think this difference means that the enormity of realising moral ideals can be thought of as divided into sizable and manageable chunks in specific contexts. At the same time, in order for this to happen, important conditions should be in place. In this Foreword I want to explore these conditions for coaching practice and raise some questions that might have been skipped in our field in the haste of implementing the important task of ensuring that coaching is an ethical practice. If these questions are not addressed, we will continue to wobble when facing ethical dilemmas, puzzle over interpreting our codes of ethics, and struggle with making decisions in ethically difficult situations.

One of the important conditions for an ethical code to be viable for a particular group of people is that this group should share core values in relation to the area of life or work in question. However, this is only possible when that particular group has established that they have an agreed upon *common purpose*. With this purpose and these values, they are in a position to define common strategies – ethical codes of practice. This highlights the first major problem, as I see it, for ethical guidance in coaching. It is clearly connected to the uncertainty of what we hold as the purpose of coaching in organisations. We are not explicit about what coaching is for and we do not have a commonly held agreement about who we serve as coaches: individual clients or sponsoring organisations or other parties.

Let me demonstrate the difficulty caused by the absence of agreed purpose by one of the valuable Kantian moral imperatives: one should not treat others as the means to an end. I personally align myself with this intention (thus my lifetime crusade against manipulation) and I am sure it makes sense for any coach in spite of various philosophical issues (e.g., see Marks, 2013). This principle is based on the value of respect and preservation of human dignity. But let's see what emerges when we apply this imperative in the wider context of different stakeholders of coaching. If coaching is mainly a *performance-enhancing organisational intervention*, the organisation has a priority in terms of defining the goals of coaching, the need to monitor the process and often even specifies tools and interventions that the coach should use. Using this Kantian imperative, both the coach and the client in this case are used as means to the organisation's ends. However, if coaching takes individual *clients' priorities and interests* as its end, it is the organisation and its financial investment in coaching that become means for the clients' and coach's ends. Therefore, if we do not have an agreed purpose of coaching among all those involved, this moral principle appears impotent.

Where we are now and what we do in practice amounts to manoeuvring around this issue in order to make coaching work, and that seems to involve trying to sit on more than one chair. Of course, a more difficult but honest way is not to give up in terms of establishing a common purpose of organisational coaching. Being on the same side with organisations in this pursuit is a long-term ambition, but I think we owe it at least to ourselves in the coaching world to bite the bullet and decide what coaching is for. I believe it is possible, but this is a topic for a different conversation. Meanwhile, one might say, our codes of ethics are there partially to counteract some of the issues that are created by this lack of clarity about our purpose.

It must be admitted that even without the above problems, creating codes of ethics is a challenge. There are no unified moral theories to guide our codes of ethics. This is why ethical codes contain information that sounds a little vague. They are developed with the recognition that it is difficult to ground ethics in moral theories when all of these theories are important and valuable in their own right. These theories (e.g., deontology, consequentialism, virtue ethics, contract theory and so forth) are aiming for universal prescription based on rational argument. However, each of these theories, unsurprisingly, meets with well-justified objections in the philosophy of ethics, and in real situations they clash in the same way as our values also clash. In real situations we do not have the power to anticipate how they would unfold with a full score of who will benefit and who will be harmed. (Although some of us seem to be intent on playing God and offering specific '10 commandment'-type scenarios for coaches, I guess this can only be useful among those who already share the same purpose and moral theory). Therefore, codes are not precise things, but they should at least indicate a general intention towards negotiation between complex factors.

Let me show an example of what happens when we wish to demand more of our codes than core principles and general intention. Below are 2.4 and 2.8 from our Global Code of Ethics in coaching (GCoE:2021, p. 4).

2.4 "Members will use their professional knowledge and experience to understand their clients' and sponsors' expectations and reach agreement on how they plan to meet them. Members will also try to take into account the needs and expectations of other relevant parties."

2.8 "Members should be guided by their client's interests and at the same time raise awareness and responsibility to safeguard that these interests do not harm those of sponsors, stakeholders, wider society, or the natural environment."

Although I can clearly see the high value of the intention behind this new clause 2.8 in the Global Code of Ethics and recognise how much effort has been put to carefully construct it, I am not sure about the practicality of this formulation. If we look first at clause 2.4 about contracting, we can see that it is less categorical – 'try[ing] to take into account the needs and expectations of other relevant parties'. In comparison, the style of 2.8 involves the terms such as 'responsibility' and 'safeguard' which in themselves require clarification. For example, it is not clear 'whose responsibility', 'what is the nature of the safeguard', etc. Even more difficult is to identify what it means ('do not harm') in principle and particularly in situations with multiple stakeholders. A simple example could be coaching clients in the organisations and businesses the activities of which are considered detrimental e.g., for the natural environment. Because of such confusion I doubt that this formulation is of great help to the admirable intention that motivates this clause.

In addition to highlighting these types of problems, I would like to raise in the Foreword to the book some specific questions in relation to ethics in general and for coaching in particular. I will also attempt to answer them in short, knowing that the rest of this impressive volume will be addressing these and many other questions in useful detail.

Can moral and ethical principles be universal for the whole of humanity?
This may sound as a too abstract question, but I think it highlights many issues that we have, not only in coaching, but also in the world. We are hugely divided. Therefore, I don't think such universality is possible at this stage, unless we, as the whole world population, identify a unified purpose and work to overcome differences in values that are connected to this purpose. There are some signs that issues with the environment might be able to unite us at some stage, but at the moment the discrepancies in preferences, even in evaluating this situation, are quite strong.

Is there any moral theory that is most applicable to coaching at this stage of development?
The theory that might be most helpful, as I see it, is that of moral particularism which has a close connection with philosophy of pragmatism. This theory recognises how difficult it is to apply moral principles to each morally challenging situation. So, it requires from us to explore each situation in its context with consideration of as many potential consequences of an action as we can. Although this position is also not perfect, it is practical and in tune with the main ideals of coaching such as recognition of complexity and uncertainty and the value of reflective exploration. Supervision is an invaluable setting for applying this position in coaching practice. I believe that the book you are about to read is a manifestation of moral particularism and pluralistic attitude to difficult issues. It takes the reader right to the specific contexts and typical difficulties that coaches face and explores these situations with determination and rigour.

What else would be required from coaches in line with moral particularism?
This question is the most important as it gives us an opportunity not only to explore multiple situations of ethical significance, but also to develop a general capacity for processing such situations whenever it is needed. With this purpose I am offering four areas for development of coaches with importance for ethical coaching practice. All four of these overlap in many important respects and are only separated for the purpose of punctuating the argument:

- Dealing with otherness
- Developing the self as an instrument of ethical practice
- Developing ethical maturity
- Developing trustworthiness

Dealing with otherness

In applied disciplines such as coaching, ethics is about relationship; about dealing with otherness. It is not a prescription about how to deal with diversity and inclusion, which is a wider agenda of many fields including coaching. It is about aiming for completeness in gaining an understanding of our practice and all its aspects. Aiming for completeness in understanding, we need to value as many sides and positions as possible, even if marginal. Only with this intention can we eventually establish a common purpose of coaching which would help in refining ethical codes.

Fair dealing with otherness also implies that we act as guardians of human rights in principle, aware of others' and our own needs and limitations. It implies transparency in our interactions with clients with an intention to prevent manipulation, however well-meaning its intended outcome might be. This has to be pursued at all stages of our work, starting from the point of attracting clients. It would involve providing them with information about your qualifications and how your model of coaching works, as well as sharing your values and personal interests in the outcomes of your work with them.

Developing the self as an instrument of ethical practice

Within the context of moral particularism, the onus is on us as coaches as the main instrument of practice to explore each situation as thoroughly as possible, to examine our own values and what role they might have in the decision making in addition to guidance provided by the codes of ethics that are available to us. It is an ability to ask useful questions about 'what is a better action?', 'who is affected?', 'what are the consequences?' and so forth.

It is also important to continue to work towards a better understanding of oneself. Recognising your own complexity and the many potential clashes of values you might come up against, means that you need:

> "to figure out what you really want, that is, the hierarchy of your desires all things considered, and then figure out how to achieve or acquire it by means that are themselves consonant with the prioritised set of your considered desires."
>
> (Marks, 2013, p. 86)

Marks's description of the essence of ethics is related to the big question of 'how shall I live?'. But it is also really important how you see yourself as a practitioner and what your purpose is when you engage in this practice. It requires the same careful exploration of your model of practice and what you consider as ends and means in achieving your professional purpose. There are also two specific qualities that I would like to add with a view to making this section more practical in relation to ethics: ethical maturity and trustworthiness.

Developing ethical maturity

We have already discussed the complexity of ethical dilemmas in coaching, the limitations of codes and regulations and competing moral perspectives. These problems indicate a need for coaches of all genres and levels of experience to seek help with ethical issues in supervision and to continue developing their own ethical maturity. Ethical maturity implies an ability to explore complex situations closely and intently, but also without forming strong attachments to a particular outcome. It implies someone who is aware of the impossibility of 'the view from nowhere' and so welcomes ideas from all perspectives but also welcomes their critique. It implies growing out of defensiveness as an obstacle to understanding and growth.

Extending the idea of oneself as an instrument of practice, ethical maturity starts with oneself, with recognition of one's own conflicting nature. It requires awareness that our own personal interests can create a tendency to simplify those issues that have ethical implications. Our own tendencies for self-deception can hide from us the nuances that work against our personal interests (Bachkirova, 2015). At the same time, ethical maturity does not imply turning our back to our shadows. I cannot agree more with Mary Midgely, who said: "To deny one's shadow is to lose solidity, to become something of a phantom. Self-deception about it may increase our confidence, but it surely threatens our wholeness" (Midgley, 1984, p. 13). I believe that when the shadow is befriended, it provides another string to the bow of ethical maturity.

Developing trustworthiness

Coaches know that the quality of our work with clients is in direct correlation with the trust that we are able to create with them. Onara O'Neill (2013) argues that trust between people requires an intelligent judgement of trustworthiness. So, if we want others' trust there are two conditions. First, we have to be trustworthy, which requires competence, honesty and reliability. Second, we have to provide intelligible evidence that we are trustworthy, enabling others to judge intelligently where they should place or refuse their trust. I believe, that for our own moral guidance in the context of difficulties with universal moral norms, conflicting values, vague ethical codes, etc, O'Neill's suggestion offers something very special.

For the first condition, it is paramount to keep asking ourselves when we are trustworthy and when not. For example, are we trustworthy if we claim to be experts in our work without proper education / training and continued professional development (CPD)? Are we trustworthy if we promise sponsors and clients too much, e.g., transformation as the result of each assignment? Are we trustworthy if we are not willing to expose our work to scrutiny in supervision? Asking these and other questions provides us with an opportunity to develop trustworthiness.

For the second condition - providing intelligible evidence that we are trustworthy, this book is not only a guide for coaches on how to think about ethics and become more trustworthy. It also shows to those we work with how serious we are, how carefully we consider the nuances of many situations and contexts, recognise the issues in the midst of external or internal nuances, explore the difficulties of ethical judgement and how motivated we are to develop ourselves as ethical instruments of practice. I hope this book can be one of the types of evidence for them to judge our trustworthiness.

Tatiana Bachkirova
Oxford Brookes University, UK

References

Bachkirova, T. (2015). Self-deception in coaches: an issue in principle and a challenge for supervision, *Coaching: An International Journal of Theory, Research and Practice*, 8(1), 4–19.

Global Code of Ethics. (2021). www.globalcodeofethics.org.

Marks, J. (2013). *Ethics without Morals: In Defense of Amorality*. London: Routledge.

Midgley, M. (1984). *Wickedness*. London: Routledge.

O'Neill, O. (2013). How to trust intelligently. *TEDBlog*. https://blog.ted.com/how-to-trust-intelligently (accessed 16 May 2022).

Section 1

Foundations of ethics in coaching

Chapter 1

Ethical coaching and its relationships

Wendy-Ann Smith and Carrie Arnold

Introduction

> *"Ethics is not something we choose to have or not have. We have it – it's a given. But we do choose how we make ethical decisions and what we allow to influence us in making those decisions"*
> (Kees de Vries, 2019, pp. 135–136)

Integrity and ethics are the foundations to all helping professions. This chapter outlines the definitions and purpose of ethical practice and what it means to work in an ethical manner with fidelity to the duty of care for another. A brief history of the coaching profession and its emergence is discussed while introducing the ethics of coaching and the use of ethical coaching guidelines. Dual relationships and power are highlighted while exploring coaching as a profession and a practice by discussing the differences between those who consider themselves a coach from other helping professions. The conversation about these distinctions is essential given how rapidly coach training grows globally as more mid-career professionals enrol in educational programs. Just as the definitions, descriptions, or roles of coaching vary, ethical considerations in the coaching profession remain subjective, undefined and, at times, problematic. Other chapters in this volume are referenced for further exploration as these important topics are named. Furthermore, this volume is completed with a number of case studies in Part 3, Chapter 26, to illustrate a variety of ethical coaching dilemmas and encourage the identification of resources, reflection and discussion, which is much needed, given the rise of coaching.

The International Coaching Federation (ICF) 2020 survey found the percentage of individuals seeking to become coaches goes up 33% every four years. In 1998 there were 34 credentialed coaches. In 2020 there were over 30,000, with the ICF just one global credentialing body. Coaching education is also attractive to operational leaders, with a 50% increase among professionals who have undertaken coach education but have not become a coach. These percentages suggest that coaching is an attractive vocation. What is it about coaching that attracts so many?

DOI: 10.4324/9781003277729-1

Kees de Vries (2019, p. 135) states, "Ethics comes alive in relationships. Ethics is about how we treat and deal with one another." Coaching only exists within a relationship. Whether the relationship is with the self, one to one, one to many, cross-cultural, transnational (see Chapter 15 for an in-depth discussion on the topic), or with artificial intelligence (discussed in Chapter 23). Ethical coaching and its relationships are addressed in this chapter with two coaching scenario vignettes to consider. One scenario is set within the corporate domain; the other focuses on the challenges of a coaching relationship within a remote external assignment. The chapter, like all chapters in this volume, concludes with discussion points and recommended reading.

Coaching, the profession and practice

Consider this question: When did you first discover a role in the world known as a *professional coach*? At what point in someone's life or career does awareness of this occupation, profession, or, as many would suggest, vocation – emerge as a possibility for a human being to hire or become? When did knowledge surface that coaching, a verb used to describe how to do something, was different from a coach? The latter example is a title, a proper noun; it identifies a person or their role.

LinkedIn is the world's largest professional network; if one searches the word 'coach,' more than one million results surface. Are there really millions of trained professional coaches in the world? Are these people coaches, as in the noun? Or are these individuals coaching as part of their expertise, as in the verb? What makes this conversation and distinction even necessary? This chapter and the ones that follow will highlight how essential it is that those who are the nouns versus those who occasionally do the verb need to be clear on the service they are providing to other human beings trying to do good work in the world. Consider the following examples:

- How parents coach their teenagers to parallel park the old family car is far different from coaching a manager of a motor vehicle construction department facing worker shortages, hostile customers, and complicated regulatory requirements.

- An operational leader can coach a direct report on the best ways to deliver a PowerPoint presentation to a significant group of stakeholders and board members. This type of coaching is not the same as a coach working with an emerging leader who consistently struggles to communicate clearly and concisely without unnecessary context and narration.

- How an educational leader coaches a school teacher on the best instructional moves to ensure classroom management and learner engagement is different from coaching the principal of a school on how to lead during pandemic times requiring distancing, masking, testing, and other dynamics never before integrated into the life of a school leader, who is managing an urban school serving students from multiple socioeconomic environments.

These examples could go on and on, but here is one more to finalise the point between the verb and the noun.

Many professionals see 'coaching' as part of their essential function. They coach on how to do things in the most efficient manner, which might be considered advice. Others coach on the best approaches to do the work because they have done it themselves and know how to get the desired results – also called mentors. Managers coach their direct reports on behaviours they want to see more or less of, and we could call this management. Coaching is a word (again, a verb) that could run parallel to terms like showing, teaching, demonstrating, or explaining. Sentient humans as young as two years old can show, teach, demonstrate, or explain, and we will keep performing this function until we take our last breath. Like those other action words, coaching is part of the human experience. Yet, a professional coach is different. This vocation requires education and training that exceeds natural emerging knowledge as we age.

This role – coaching – lives outside the realm of sport, mentoring, consulting, therapy, management, training, or instruction. Despite being distinct from these disciplines, coaching emerged from those social science fields that have long represented how we make sense of human potential, lived experience and organisational development.

One could argue that a professional coach was birthed during the Socratic years of Western philosophy between 469–399 BC; in other parts of the globe, by Eastern philosopher Siddhartha Gautama (Buddha in 525 BC), or perhaps in ancient Egypt that cannot be accurately dated (see Passmore & Evans, 2021 for a discussion of coaching pre-1900). Roots and traces of philosophy have left heart and head prints in every area of the world, with indigenous people seeking to understand themselves, their world, and their way of being with others. An ancient African philosophy, Ubuntu, translates to "a person can only be a person through others" (Shutte, 2001). The Socratic method invites deeper critical thinking; it is about discovery through inquiry and answers through questions. It is about how we change minds, our own and possibly others (Paul & Elder, 2019).

These few, among many, give glimpses of how coaching extends far beyond the mid-1990s when the world saw an explosion of post-modern organisations and leaders seeking thought partners as their day-to-day work became more complicated and complex. The density created by emerging matrixed organisations, globalisation, advanced technology and the World Wide Web are just a few examples that have shifted the way people need to be in the world. The decades and centuries of hard labour, manufacturing, domestic responsibilities and gendered roles have faded as knowledge work, and new technologies have catapulted society into the twenty-first century. The last seventy years alone have manifested significant shifts in the balance of labour between men and women.

Statistics vary by continent and country, but a woman's role continues to evolve with her occupying more and more space in the labour force (Catalyst, 2021).

As the world shifts, our sense-making strategies shift, and new phenomena require us to delve more deeply into knowing and being. The branches of thought that pre-date our modern understanding of coaching have also shifted. Philosophy opened a path for psychology and from this rich field emerged human potential movements like positive and humanistic psychology. As the world began understanding the give and take of economics, new thinking arose: management and consulting. Athletics has been around for centuries and is deemed a root discipline that informs and influences all sectors (Brock, 2014). There has been a waterfall of leadership theories, models and styles arising to describe what it means to be an effective person leading others. These bodies of social science and philosophy are just a few giants that have created this rich soil for coaching to grow and become its own field.

Coaching was birthed because of multiple socioeconomic factors. This field became a vehicle for professional development in a world that no longer primarily promotes based on tenure, next in line, or name. To get ahead or have career success in this information age, people need to balance managing tasks and relationships. There needs to be a focus on interpersonal development, conflict management, savvy communication, listening and a whole host of other skills that have historically been considered 'soft' or as we suggest 'essential' but are primarily the competency models that many leadership theories build upon.

History is the mosaic backdrop that supports the work of a coach. One could argue that the most successful people in the coaching field will understand, appreciate and incorporate former ways of knowing. They will study the social science evidence and make connections to deepen their work with other human beings.

But what do coaches do?

Assuming, that coaching (as a verb) is an action available to everyone, what makes a person the coach? What makes this a proper noun?

There are more than a dozen definitions of the role of a coach. Most combine the definition with a set of things a coach may do. The process of doing so creates quite a bit of variation. As the field of coaching matures, these definitions and descriptors need to form a more cohesive global framework that unites the purpose of a coach and delineates it from other disciplines. Here is a sample of how scholars and thought leaders define the role of a coach.

- John Whitmore (1996) – Coaching unlocks a person's potential to maximize their performance, helping them to learn rather than teaching them.
- Laura Whitworth (2007) – Partnering with a client for discovery, awareness, and choice; it is about empowering people to find their own answers.
- Jenny Rogers (2016) – Coaching aims to close the gap between a person's potential and current state.

- Peter Hawkins and Eve Turner (2020) – Coaching the individual influences the systems they are embedded in and the broader systems they are connected to.
- Ofer Atad, Wendy-Ann Smith, and Suzy Green (2021) – Coaching facilitates a person's self-directed learning, development, and wellbeing.

Outside the key nouns like potential, choice, and process, various definitions also include action words like *collaborate, maximise, unlock, help, teach, empower, inspire, become, stimulate, reflect, develop, facilitate* and *question* (Passmore, 2020). These verbs and nouns might be used interchangeably by coaches assuming they all mean something similar. From the client's perspective, when they experience a phenomenon of feeling heard, seen and valued by their coach, they may describe a coaching session as therapy, mentoring, or consulting. This is often where the confusion arises. Clients can get away with those mixed descriptions; the coach cannot. The disciplines cannot be treated, nor should they be described the same (see Chapter 13 in this volume for ethics in mental health and suicide management in coaching).

Within our deeply complex and ruptured world of blame and judgment, when someone (the coaching practitioner) treats another as capable, resourceful and whole with unlimited potential to create their own future, most (coachees) walk away breathing a sigh of relief for what may feel and look akin to a remedy of sorts or a way forward. They may not tease out all the coach said or did; they just experience something that feels better. But how does being in service to another human within this context get appropriately described? How does this transaction between humans get legitimately quantified? Grant and Cavanagh (2004) and Kauffman (2005) argue only through a coherent body of knowledge grounded on evidenced base practice and ethical standards can the progression from being of service, in a service industry, to a legitimate profession be found.

Whether a shared definition of coaching is required, there is a coherency in how many view the work. Peeling back all the similarities and differences (the nouns and verbs), one thing is consistently true of all definitions. Coaching creates. It does not diagnose, teach, train, or perform. Coaching fosters many different things, such as:

- space to reflect and think;
- opportunity for someone to (further) develop self-awareness;
- new interactive conversations; and
- possibilities to be different and do things differently.

Remember the game *I Say You Say*? I say, Queen. You say Elizabeth. I say snow. You say angels. I say warm. You say cold. It can go on and on. Within the realm of unwinding coaching from other disciplines, perhaps this simple exercise can create some shared answers.

- I say athletics. You say sports.
- I say consulting. You say solutions.

- I say mentoring. You say experience.
- I say advisor. You say expertise.
- I say therapy. You say healing.
- I say coaching. You say *create*. Eventually, the answer will be *co-create*.

Healing, expertise and solutions may also surface within the coaching relationship, but the role of a coach is not to do any of those primary functions. Coaching being a future oriented practice, the coach's role is to partner with the coachee to create the relationship, to go on to co-create a psychologically safe space for reflection, which then invites enhanced self-awareness for, learning wellbeing and goal pursuit (Atad, Smith & Green, 2021; Smith, King & Lai, 2021).

People are unable to adjust or change what they cannot see. At the heart of coaching is the emergence of agency. When people are agents of their own life, work and decisions, they can be creators of a new projects, new learning and increase their wellbeing. The process of developing self through awareness is a lifelong pursuit never done in isolation. Referring again to Ubuntu, "a person can only be a person through others" (Shutte, 2001) is essential. This philosophy suggests we must coach others in their work, family and with the broader system they interact in mind. We are never separate from our environmental factors (see Chapter 22 in this volume), and development emerges through relationships. We guide you to Chapter 19 in this volume to explore cultural considerations to coaching presence and engagement. We refer you to Grant and Spence's engagement wellbeing framework (see Figure 1.1) a valuable tool for reflective practice.

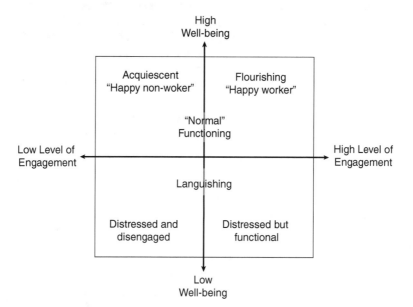

Figure 1.1 The Engagement and Wellbeing Framework (Grant and Spence, 2010)
Note: Permission kindly granted from Gordon Spence, who would like to acknowledge Anthony (Tony) Grant's pioneering work in the framing of Wellbeing and Engagement within the coaching space

Coaching and ethics: what's all the fuss?

The mere mention of 'ethics' in coaching circles elicits a range of reactions: *The rules do not cover all scenarios. I love ethics! I don't have ethical issues in my coaching.* or *Ethics – who needs them? Ethics are boring!*, and so forth. In early 2020 one of the authors (Wendy-Ann) of this chapter had the experience of an engaging discussion on power in coaching relationships. The topic itself was engaging, yet the mood was not, the longer the discussion the deeper the gloom and doom feeling of the conversation – it was depressive. This experience led the author to interrupt the conversation, address the mood and the need to, as she describes it, *make ethical conversations attractive to engage in.* Her motto became – *let's make ethics sexy!* That is to give ethics in coaching conversations an uplifting and inviting energy. Another example is the author's surprise when during group coaching supervision, and in the company of a number of very experienced coaches, the coaches were unsure of topics that were relevant for supervision, which to the author's mind these topics are often ethical in nature, and such topics being the very essence of supervision enquiry. If coaching is a creditable service for the betterment of all communities, there is an obligation to make ethics inviting, to be regularly engaging and building ethical awareness. We, the authors suggest engaging in ethical conversations is the foundation to good quality coaching engagement. It is about the practice of regularly reflecting, discussing, being open and curious and within the laws of the land, making well-thought-out decisions and actions. Perhaps consider the motto of 'Least-Harm – Most-Good' as you grow into the depths of ethical awareness and of 'being' an ethical coach, not just for yourself but also for your clients and the field of coaching more broadly.

Ethics, governance and frameworks

Ethics are often defined as morals, values, beliefs and principles to help guide and support decision-making and justify actions (we refer you to Chapter 2 of this volume for an in-depth discussion on What are ethics in coaching?). Ethical clauses are usually included in coaching engagement contracts. Ethics should also guide how coaches represent themselves as professionals in the community. However, a set of determined morals, values, or principles is limited and does not safeguard a coach from all possible scenarios or dilemmas. Rather, they, and coach supervision and a professionally defined ethical code, provide a grounding point of reference when deliberating, making decisions, or discerning and choosing possible courses of action.

Commencing with coach education and moving into a coaching practice, individuals face critical decisions and a need to take action at every stage. How are ethics taught? What is an institution's approach to ethical frameworks? Are there ethical discussions in the curriculum? These are questions educational programs need to address (see Chapter 17 in this volume for ethics in education).

Once coaches enter into practice, they must represent themselves professionally in conversations, on social media, or professional websites. They need to express who they are and what they promise ethically. We suggest reading Chapter 25 in this volume for further exploration of the ethical considerations or hazards of how coaches promote themselves as practitioners.

How coaches practice with individuals, groups or teams must be governed by an ethical mindset and presence. Ethical conversations need to be part of all third-party agreements, organizational interviews and the coaching community of practice groups. Hence, personally and professionally, ethics in all forms and guidelines help serve as a point of reference to ensure 'best practice,' protecting the coach, the coachee, other stakeholders and the coaching profession – before, during and after coaching engagements.

Debate about the governance and regulation of coaching is ongoing. Some argue global regulation and a common code of ethics are the only assurance of accountability, others prefer a tailored approach. The topics of governance and regulation for 'professional' status, as opposed to a field of practice like a facilitator or trainer of which anyone can partake without specific training and education - depending on the country they are working – and the pros and cons of professionalisation are too large for this chapter (see various chapters in this volume for discussion, for example Chapter 3, ethics and coach accrediting bodies). Suffice to say, the jury is still out and not likely to have a conclusion to satisfy all anytime soon, if ever.

We propose, more importantly than the legal regulation or universality of coaching ethical codes, that the coaching community as a whole move to strengthen its ethical fitness, akin to strengthening or building muscles by working out at the gym. Engaging in regular ethical conversations with ourselves and others, e.g., supervisor and colleagues (Biswas-Diener & Kauffman, 2022) with a continuous referral to a coaching code of ethics is your ethical gymnasium. Coaches should regularly challenge and stretch their ethical awareness and maturity, as this fosters and integrates a shared ethically aware mindset into the coaching community's professional identity. Bond (2015, p. 47) suggests a professional value-driven ethical guide and conduct is "an integral part of professional identity". We argue that integrating ethics into one's professional identity from the individual coach to coaching organisations, educational institutions and coaching bodies is the cornerstone of best-practice coaching and continually matures the field of practice. "Maturity is not a static or abstract state of being to which we can aspire as an ideal steady state that lifts us above the risks and uncertainties of professional life." Rather, "… [M]aturity suggests a quality of engagement in how we respond to the challenges of professional life" (Bond, 2013. p. 10).

From where do we draw on the guidance?

The British Psychological Society (BPS: 2018, p. 1) provides guidance to their communities on working with ethics in practice. A code of ethics and practice for coaching psychologists informs the practitioner that the code is a framework to guide decision making, that "the framework allows sufficient flexibility for a variety of approaches, contexts and methods and reflects the ethical standards that apply to all." The onus is on the coaching psychologist to know, refer to, understand and determine the best course of action for the specific scenario (BPS, 2018, p. 1). The same can be said for coaches whether they use a code of ethics from coach accrediting bodies such as the European Mentoring and Coaching Council (EMCC), ICF, or regulatory bodies such as American Psychology Association, The Psychology Board of Australia and others.

Much work is in place to identify ethical themes and define ethical frameworks across many professions such as medicine, law and psychology. Allard de Jong (2010, p. 208) produced a taxonomy of six primary issues: beneficence, non- maleficence (that is, doing no harm), fidelity, promoting autonomy, justice, respect and self-care (a dilemma often overlooked in coaching). Interestingly self-care is not explicitly listed in Law's (2011, p. 53) "six R's" of ethical practice (rights, respect, recognition, relationship, representation and responsibility). These categories were adapted as the Code of Ethics and Practice for the Society for Coaching Psychology within the BPS, prior to the regulation of coaching psychology (CP). The United Kingdom has since regulated CP as a specific division within the BPS, which provides recognition through the status of 'Chartered Coaching Psychologist', being applicable in the United Kingdom alone. Coaching psychology and positive psychology are expanding their reach in the coaching community. Both are grounded in psychology and help coaching practitioners understand the how and why of human thriving as opposed to disfunction. Positive ethical practice for 'least harm – most good' to support thriving is essential, we refer you to Chapter 16 in this volume for further exploration of positive ethics.

Fisher & Cathelt (in Carrol & Shaw, 2009, p. 113) provide a more nuanced set of ways of being that are required to be at play for one to be perceived as having integrity. They are: "self-knowledge, self-differentiation, courage, honesty, lack of duplicity, ability to be consistent and reliable, direct and willing to self-disclose, non-defensive, loving and compassionate, empathetic, independent, tolerant, inclusive, interested in growth and a search for meaning."

Brennan and Wildflower (2014) have identified five common themes among ethical codes across various disciplines such as counsellors, lawyers, human resources and psychologists, they are:

1. Do not harm or cause needless injury to others.
2. Act with a duty of care that promotes the welfare of other people.

3.   Know your limits and practice within your scope of competence.
4.   Respect the client's interests.
5.   Respect the law.

Each of these themes is as applicable to coaching as any other profession. However, in their commonality, they may not attend to the unique nuances of coaching specifically. They could be construed as too broad and not bringing awareness to the depth and complexity of ethical concerns. Others argue the codes and themes can be overly prescriptive and their variations from body to body are holding back the integrity of the field (Iordanou, Hawley, & Iordanou, 2017). On this last point, it could be argued the desire for the globalization of ethical codes for coaching does not take into account the variation of needs, similar to other professional domains such as psychology or medicine. Here you will find each nation's or intra nation's governing body has its code of ethics and common language use, that fit with the law and culture of the land and have been in use for centuries that are updated across time and are able to function with integrity.

How do we engage in ethical decision-making and action?

Ethical engagement requires contact with various sources of support and resources to ensure best practice and a continued cycle of ethical maturity. Carroll and Shaw (2013) suggest three categories of resources, skills and tools for ethical decision-making:

1.   *Resources* (ethical codes, principles, decision-making models, peers, and discussions)
2.   *Skills* (integrating the needs of self, community, society, and professions; emotions, intuition, openness to discussing challenging topics, noticing external pressures)
3.   *Self-Awareness* (access to feelings, intuition; awareness of own beliefs and ethics; knowing the self, vulnerabilities, and biases; understanding how you make decisions)

Passmore and Turner (2018) have detailed a comprehensive ethical decision-making process framework *APPEAR*: Awareness, Practice, Possibilities, Extending the Field, Action on Reflections and Reflecting on Learning. We refer you to Chapter 5 in this volume, which explores the model and decision-making frameworks in greater depth. A primary, but certainly not the only, source of guidance is a coaching code of ethics. The utility of a code is to help ensure accountability for best practice in the nuanced diverse circumstances that arise and to promote trust within the coaching and broader community who seek coaching services. See Chapter 4 in this volume, for further discussion of the utility of codes. A code of ethics alone is insufficient; a primary resource is colleagues, particularly coach supervision (see Chapter 9 in this volume for ethics in supervision). So, what is coaching – a noun, a verb, a profession, an industry, a field of practice, by whom and for who?

Coaching and its relationships

Effective relationships are not one-dimensional or one-sided. *'"Relational" in … [coaching] context means acknowledging the inherently mutual nature of all social processes, and therefore prioritizing the importance of the co-created, 'here and now' relationship [bound in ethics] as the central vehicle for development and transformation"* (Critchley, 2010. p. 1). An effective coaching alliance is contingent on establishing trust and credibility between both parties (Graßmann, Schölmerich, & Schermuly, 2020; Alvey & Barclay, 2007).

Unlike other relationships, a coach creates space for the other to explore their contexts, which is essential to deepening awareness, creating trust and safety, modelling a high-quality relationship (see Smith, King, and Lai, 2021) and fostering adult development (see Chapter 18 in this volume for further discussion on adult development and ethics). According to the ICF (2020), the age of a typical coaching client is between 35 and 54 years old (76%), suggesting most people who experience coaching are mid-career with at least ten years of work experience. They are already deeply immersed in multiple relationships e.g. teams and systems (see Chapter 10 in this volume for discussion and practice of ethics of team coaching). All will have various life experiences, with many having histories of broken trust, breakdowns, breakups, betrayal. They have worked in functional systems and systems that are disorganised, controversial and at times unjust. Few will have full awareness of themselves within these relationships or systems as they interact to sustain dynamics or disrupt them.

Coaches partner in ways many individuals may not experience in any other professional relationship both in person and increasingly online, see Chapter 23 of this volume for ethics and the digital environment. This partnership is not always intuitive or natural – it requires intentional skill, knowledge of theory and a well-developed sense of self.

Ethics in coaching relationships

The coaching relationship is a nuanced, complex psychological exchange where ethics is consciously or unconsciously embedded. Whether a one-to-one engagement or a contract with multiple stakeholders (see Chapter 14 of this volume for ethics in multiparty contracting), all coaching exists within broader personal and professional systems. It can also be argued that one-to-one coaching relationships are multilayered as humans rarely bring just one point of focus to coaching, but also that working on one focal point will have influence on other areas of their intrapersonal and interpersonal lives. Ethics require open and honest conversations, a dialogue with the self and with the other(s), all within the context of and fidelity to the primary relationship/s (De Vries, 2019).

Bachkirova (2020, p. 42) suggests the coach grows to understand they are "... [the] main instrument of coaching". We suggest a coach become aware of their thoughts, emotions, intuitions, behaviour and values in each moment of coaching and their professional relationships. Requiring constant curiosity about the implications of decisions and actions in personal and professional relationships (Bond, 2013) and understand each require monitoring and regulation, and that they have ethical implications on coaching practice. Ethical maturity is the cornerstone of best practice within coaching.

Ethical behaviour in a coaching relationship

In all coach-related relationships, including the coach's relationship with themselves, many ethical situations arise as a result of power imbalances, practice boundaries, a duty of care, confidentiality, contracting, ending, or extending. Consider these relationships:

- coach – coachee
- coach – coachee's stakeholders
- coach – sponsoring organisation
- internal coach – their organisation
- coach supervisor – coach
- coach – other coaches
- coach – coach accrediting or affiliated body

Coaches must remain aware of all relationships, including and especially the paying or sponsoring organisation. Clarity about the contracted engagement, individual expectations, practice boundaries and the various interconnections is imperative. A clear understanding of psychological contracting and the more tangible contracting is also required (see Chapter 8 of this volume for an exploration of psychological contracting).

While experience or knowledge of ethical considerations within these relationships may exist at one point, it does not mean coaches should assume ethical boundaries will remain static and not stray. Change naturally occurs over time, and personal or professional identities can shift as people experience and learn from life events and so relationships evolve. Every interaction or moment within the domain of coaching creates an opportunity for conscious ethical choice. Hence, all coaching relationships need monitoring and reflection.

Boszoremyi-Nagy's theory of relational ethics suggests trust, loyalty and empathy are crucial for effective relationships (2013). Relational accountability and self-awareness are required skills (Carroll & Shaw, 2013). As discussed earlier in this chapter, coaching is a relationship, and ethics is fundamental to the relationship.

Coaches need to be grounded in ethical practice rooted in coaching education, regular reflective practice and supervision. When coaches ignore the needed ethical balance, coaching can cause harm. Consider the following scenario set within a human resources department.

Vignette 1

Florence is a human resources (HR) director for a global apparel company of approximately 1,000 employees. She recently completed a coach training programme but has decided not to pursue a coaching credential. She envisions herself in a vice president role as a decision-maker at the senior leadership table. In her excitement to demonstrate her professional growth, she uses her coach training within the apparel company to help novice managers become better leaders. She invites four operational managers to be her clients offering 12 sessions over six months. She creates a coaching contract outlining roles and confidentiality within the coaching relationship and clarifies the client's coaching objectives. As she nears the end of her engagement with them, a hostile work environment complaint is lodged against one of her four coaching clients. Florence's role as the HR director requires her to oversee the investigation. The coachee shared several confidential and personal issues within the coaching context. One of the issues was the coachee's struggles with anger issues from a recent divorce.

Consider the following questions:

What are the implications for coaching and ethical practice are in this scenario? Can a human resources director maintain their role and be a coach inside the organization simultaneously?
Is it ethical to have a coach-client engagement with a power differential as outlined in this scenario?
When it comes to ethical maturity, is it appropriate to have a dual relationship with a coachee?
What is the ethical obligation when determining if you should hold the role of a coach versus employ coaching skills in your professional relationships?

As the above vignette highlights it is challenging to deconstruct any one ethical concern of prominence in a relationship. All chapters in this volume speak to a variety of domains a coach is in relationship with ethics, those that are not already mentioned in this chapter are:

- Ethics in the use of psychometrics – Chapter 12
- Ethics and having a coaching exit strategy – Chapter 21
- Ethics in transnational coaching assignments – Chapter 15
- Ethics in coaching feedback – Chapter 24 and
- Research in practice – Chapter 6

We have chosen two topics that are not explicitly covered in this volume to briefly explore here - power and dual relationships.

Power

Ethical decisions for relationships are situational and contextual with implications. Professional practice and relationship building foundational to coaching require "not exploiting power and status, avoiding conflicts of interest and keeping confidences" (Brennan and Wildflower, 2014, p. 432). We refer you to Chapter 7 of this volume for a more detailed discussion on the legal implications of ethics in decision making and confidentiality, and Chapter 11 for confidentiality in note taking and record keeping.

The onus is placed on the coach to create the relationship ethically. Stokes (in Iordanou et al., 2017, p. 52) speaks to the challenges during coaching with what he calls a "skilled coachee" and their ability to derail, block or stall progress and hinder the coaching of even the most experienced coach. We suggest the intentions of the coachee are not malicious; instead, they may not be ready to do their work as a client and so will be evasive or defensive. Stokes suggests the coachee's role in building and working on the relationship has implications for ethical coaching, in that perhaps the power is with the coachee, not the coach. We suggest ethical practice and awareness of the coach's power as a specialist remains the coach's responsibility regardless of how the coachee is showing up or what defensive demonstrations a coachee may exhibit in the relationship. Coaches must reflect on the coaching, their capacities, and whether to have a frank conversation with the coachee about what their experience, they perceive, think and question. This sharing by the coach is an important part of the process of coaching and when undertaken with care and compassion can be relationship building as well as providing the coachee more information for further reflection.

Co-creating, rules of engagement, regular contracting, re-contracting and understanding how the coach reacts to and uses power are fundamental to ethical practice and require prominent levels of awareness. Power dynamics can cause reactivity in everyone. Rescuing someone is an example of a use of power as it suggests there is a victim in need of a hero. Another example is the subservient posture to the opposite gender. This power dynamic could influence ethical decision-making when one gender has perceived or actual greater power, status, culture, race (see Chapter 20 for ethics and race) or any combination.

Dual relationships – Boundaries

Dual relationships mean one has more than one relationship with another. These may appear in multiple forms. Examples include:

- coach and coachee are friends or become friends
- coach holds a role of power within the coachee's organisation (such as the human resources leader)
- coach has a relationship with a coachee's family member
- coach and coachee are peers in a professional community of practice
- coachee is the coach's doctor, dentist, real estate agent

The Australian Psychological code of ethics speaks to dual relationships as non-professional or different professional relationships with the same client. Their definition also extends into relationships with an associated party or being the recipient of a service provided by the same client. Their code offers explicit instructions on personal relationships and the moratorium before a psychologist can be in an intimate relationship with a prior patient. An example of text from the Australian Code of Ethics, psychologists [should] refrain from engaging in multiple relationships that may:

a) impair their competence, effectiveness, objectivity, or ability to render a psychological service;
b) harm clients or other parties to a psychological service; or
c) lead to the exploitation of clients or other parties to a psychological service" (Australian Psychological Society, 2007, p. 28).

The ICF addresses sexual or romantic engagement with clients as follows:

"Do not participate in any sexual or romantic engagement with Client(s) or Sponsor(s). I will be ever mindful of the level of intimacy appropriate for the relationship. I take the appropriate action to address the issue or cancel the coaching engagement."

(ICF, 2021, p. 6)

Additionally, the ICF addresses internal coach responsibilities by addressing conflicts of interest with clients and sponsor(s). "Through coaching agreement (s) and ongoing dialogue. This should include addressing organizational roles, responsibilities, relationships, records, confidentiality, and other reporting requirements" (ICF, 2021, p. 5).

The EMCC provides additional guidance for various types of multiple relationships as follows:

"Members will strictly avoid pursuing and refrain from engaging in any romantic or sexual relationships with current clients or sponsors." and advised "To avoid any conflict of interest, members will clearly distinguish a professional relationship with a client from other forms of relationships"

(Global Code of Ethics: 2021, p. 6).

Dual relationships occur, sometimes without notice or perceived alternatives. Challenges arise when the nature of a coaching relationship changes. World events, lack of personal connection, constant volatility, uncertainty, complexity and ambiguity can quickly shift a professional relationship into a personal or dual relationship. Navigating dual or multiple relationships requires careful management, clearly defined roles, responsibilities and boundaries. Coaches must maintain a client-focused approach, engage in reflective practice and participate in coach supervision (Zur & Anderson, 2006) to prevent undue complications and ensure highest quality of coaching practice and no harm to either the coachee or the profession. While some codes of ethics are specific such as for coaching psychologists, or more explicit and broader than others in their dual/multiple relationship guidance, it is wise not to enter into a dual relationship, specifically a friendship or romantic relationship with a coachee. Consider the following vignette regarding the challenges of circumstance, location and the human need for connection.

Vignette 2

Cheryl has been coaching for 20 years, she regularly participates in coach supervision and is accredited by two coaching bodies internationally. She is married with three children and lives in a small remote town in central Australia. Cheryl regularly travels to the city to coach and via skype when working from home. Cheryl has been asked by a coaching organization to provide coaching services to several small business owners in towns and farmers in the local region.

Paul is the owner of an 8,000-sq-km generational cattle farm in the same region Cheryl resides. The nearest town with groceries and amenities is approximately100 km away. Paul is a recent divorcee and father of three boys. He throws himself into his work to combat the increasing loneliness.

While reviewing the assignment details, Cheryl notices the familiar name of a childhood friend. Her immediate reaction is that coaching Paul is acceptable: they have not had contact for years. However, she wants to know how he feels about the alternative of being coached remotely by someone else. Cheryl phones Paul to learn more about the conditions at home regarding internet coverage and Paul's preference for a coach.

Paul is happy to be coached by Cheryl and admits the internet at home is weak in strength and tends not to work well. Paul travels to the nearest town every two weeks to check emails.

Cheryl decides to coach Paul and travels to his homestead once a month. Paul looks forward to having Cheryl visit and arranges for lunch after each session. He offers Cheryl a meal and looks forward to her company. After four months, Cheryl is uncomfortable with Paul's efforts. She is unsure about his intentions and begins questioning whether she is the right person to coach him. Additionally, Cheryl experiences Paul as a stuck client who avoids certain topics. She questions her ability to partner with him on challenging issues.

Consider the following questions:

At what point are you concerned about the coach choice in this scenario?
Who are the stakeholders in this engagement?
How should Cheryl approach the ethical considerations of the coaching relationship?
What are the possible courses of action available to Cheryl?

Conclusion

For coaching to be a flourishing field of practice, ethical behaviour for all practitioners is essential. An ethical mindset and practice are the foundation for healthy professional relationships. Fundamentally, a coach is always in a process of becoming, increasing their ethical fitness and maturity and their coaching practice. Coaches have an obligation to act with integrity and be ethical – there is no separation. Therefore, coaches need to continuously work on their self and social awareness, recognise their practice limits, be humble in acting on that knowledge, understand how they interact with power and navigate or avoid dual relationships. As more coaches accept the invitation to engage in these critical conversations, the collective coaching community advances in service to the communities they serve.

Discussion points

1. Are you a professional coach, or do you use coaching in your profession? How might this distinction be essential when determining your ethical standards?
2. What are your values and morals? How have they influenced your coaching?
3. Power: what are your triggers? How do you navigate power of status and or gender in life and in particular your coaching life?
4. Dual relationships can sneak up on you. What value-driven and best practice boundaries work best for you? How do you ensure you work with your boundaries?

Recommended Reading

Carroll, M. & Shaw, E. (2013). *Ethical maturity in the helping professions: Making difficult life and work decisions.* Jessica Kingsley Publishers.

References

Alvey, S. & Barclay, K. (2007). The characteristics of dyadic trust in executive coaching. *Journal of Leadership Studies*, 1(1), 18–27.
Atad, O., Smith, W. A., & Green, S. (2021). Coaching as the Missing Ingredient in the Application and Training of Positive Psychological Science. In Smith, W. A.,

Boniwell, I., & Green, S. (Eds) *Positive Psychology Coaching in the Workplace.* Springer: Cham. https://doi.org/10.1007/978-3-030-79952-6_3.

Australian Psychological Society. (2007). Code of ethics. Melbourne, Vic. www.psychology.org.au/getmedia/d873e0db-7490-46de-bb57-c31bb1553025/18APS-Code-of-Ethics.pdf.

Bachkirova, T. (2020). Understanding yourself as a coach. In Passmore, J. (Ed.), *The Coaches' Handbook: The Complete Practitioner Guide for Professional Coaches.* Routledge, pp. 39–47.

Biswas-Diener, R. & Kauffman, C. (2022, February 24–25). Why are ethics so boring? [Conference fireside chat]. Exploring Ethics in Coaching Conference. Coaching Ethics Forum https://coachingethicsforum.com.

Bond, T., (2013), Foreword. In Carroll, M. & Shaw, E. *Ethical maturity in the helping professions: Making difficult life and work decisions.* Jessica Kingsley Publishers.

Bond, T. (2015). *Standards and Ethics for Counselling in Action*, 4th Ed. London: Sage.

Boszormenyi-Nagy, I. K. (2013). *Between give and take: A clinical guide to contextual therapy.* Routledge.

British Psychological Society. (2018). Code of ethics and conduct. www.bps.org.uk/news-and-policy/bps-code-ethics-and-conduct.

Brennan, D. & Wildflower, L. (2010) 369–380. Ethics in coaching. In Cox, E., Bachkirova, T., & Clutterbuck, D. A. (Eds). (2014). *The complete handbook of coaching.* Sage.

Brock, V. G. (2014). *Sourcebook of coaching history.*

Carroll, M. & Shaw, E. (2013). *Ethical maturity in the helping professions: Making difficult life and work decisions.* Jessica Kingsley Publishers.

Catalyst. Women in the Workforce: Global (Quick Take), February 11, 2021. Statistical Overview of Women in Global Workplaces: Catalyst Quick Take, accessed March 1, 2022.

Critchley, B. (2010). Relational coaching: Taking the coaching high road. *Journal of Management Development.*

De Vries, K. (2019). Moving from frozen code to live vibrant relationship – towards a philosophy of ethics of coaching supervision. In J. Birch & P. Welch (Eds), *Coaching Supervision – Advancing Practice, Changing Landscapes.* Abingdon: Routledge.

Global code of ethics. (2021). Retrieved from www.globalcodeofethics.org.

Grant, A. M. & Cavanagh, M. J. (2004). Toward a profession of coaching: sixty-five years of progress and challenges for the future. *International Journal of Evidence Based Coaching and Mentoring*, 2(1): 1–16.

Graßmann, C., Schölmerich, F., & Schermuly, C. C. (2020). The relationship between working alliance and client outcomes in coaching: A meta-analysis. *Human Relations*, 73(1), 35–58.

Hawkins, P. & Turner, E. (2020). *Systemic Coaching – delivering value beyond the individual.* Abingdon: Routledge.

International Coaching Federation. (2019). *Code of Ethics.* Lexington, KY. Retrieved from https://coachingfederation.org/ethics/code-of-ethics.

International Coaching Federation. (2020). Executive Summary 2020, ICF Global Coaching Study, accessed February 28, 2022. FINAL_ICF_GCS2020_ExecutiveSummary.pdf (coachfederation.org).

Law, H. (2011). Intellectual coaching approach for Asian family businesses. In M. Shams. and D. Lane (Eds), *Coaching in the Family Owned Business: A Path to Growth*. London: Karnac.

Kauffman, C. (2005) *De-mystifying research: an introduction for coaches*. In I. F. Stein, F. Campone, & I. J. Page (Eds), Proceedings of the Second ICF Coaching Research Symposium (pp. 161–168). Washington, DC: International Coach Federation.

Passmore, J. & Evans-Krimme, R. (2021). The future of coaching: a conceptual framework for the coaching sector from personal craft to scientific process and the implications for practice and research. *Frontiers in Psychology*, 12, 715228.

Passmore, J. & Sinclair, T. (2020). *Becoming a Coach: The Essential ICF Guide*. Berlin: Springer International Publishing.

Passmore, J. & Turner, E. (2018). Reflections on integrity – The APPEAR model. Coaching at Work. February 2018. Retrieved on February 18, 2022, from www.coaching-at-work.com/2018/02/23/reflections-on-integrity-the-appear-model.

Paul, R. & Elder, L. (2019). *The thinker's guide to Socratic questioning*. Rowman & Littlefield.

Rogers, J. (2016). *Coaching Skills: The definitive guide to being a coach*. Open University Press.

Shutte, A. (2001). *Ubuntu: An ethic for a new South Africa*.

Smith, W.A., King, S., & Lai, Y. L. (2021). Coaching with Emotions and Creating High Quality Connections in the Workplace. In Smith, W. A., Boniwell, I., & Green, S. (eds), *Positive Psychology Coaching in the Workplace*. Cham: Springer. doi:10.1007/978-3-030-79952-6_10.

Whitmore, J. (1996). *Coaching for performance*. N. Brealey Pub.

Whitworth, L. (2007). *Co-active coaching: New skills for coaching people toward success in work and life*. Davies-Black Publishing.

Zur, O. & Anderson, S. K. (2006). *Multiple-role relationships in coaching*. In P. Williams & S. K. Anderson (Eds), *Law and ethics in coaching: How to solve and avoid difficult problems in your practice* (pp. 126–129). Hoboken, NJ: John Wiley & Sons.

Chapter 2

What is ethics, and how does it apply to coaching?

Pauline Fatien and David Clutterbuck

Ethics as a rainbow

> There was an awful rainbow once in heaven: We know her woof, her texture; she is given in the dull catalogue of common things. Philosophy will clip an angel's wings
>
> John Keats

Keats' verses above capture why ethics in general, and in coaching in particular, is tricky. Like the rainbow, the more closely we examine ethics, the less meaning we can derive. A rainbow may be composed of atoms, but holds no wonder or meaning at the atomic level.

Therefore, perhaps it is useful to start by defining what ethics is *not*.

Ethics is *not moral reasoning*. While both ethics and moral reasoning are social constructs, they do not designate the same thing. Moral reasoning influences how we make ethical judgements in specific circumstances whereas ethics is a more general foundation, on which moral reasoning can occur. Victorian moral values in Europe and North America emphasised the notion of the 'deserving poor' – virtuous people whose ill-fortune or poverty was the result of circumstance – versus the undeserving poor, whose circumstances resulted from vices, such as alcohol addiction, loose living and so on. It was not only ethical but a moral imperative to apply different rules to the two categories. Ethics is to moral reasoning as literature is to poetry.

Ethics is *not a code of practice*, although a code may be written with moral and ethical principles in mind. Codes of practice change with the times. Moreover, the prescriptive approach lends itself to creative ways of observing the letter but not the spirit or content of the code. In the financial services sector, emphasising codes rather than morality or ethics may even have led to higher levels of deviant behaviour!

Ethicality *does not seek to provide one right answer*. Let's call this 'not one right answer' of 'zones of ethical acceptability' – a range of solutions within an ethical dilemma, where the acceptability of each choice depends on the weight given to the various conflicting values.

DOI: 10.4324/9781003277729-2

Then what is ethics?

Again, not easy! The Ancient Greeks, who gave us the term, would take a very different ethical stance compared to us today! This evolution shows that ethics can be considered a mirror of its times and contexts and evolves with societal changes. Then, in addressing ethics, in general, and ethics in coaching in particular, the issue is less one of definition and pinning things down with a risk of foreclosing ethics, than of asking the right questions, at the right time, from the right perspective (which is not that different from coaching!).

Thus, ethics can be considered a reflective practice that facilitates alignment of human behaviours with a sense of rightness or appropriateness. It is influenced by and influences, but is not the same as morality, as seen above. Ethics considers both the appropriateness of an action (is this a virtuous behaviour?) and the consequences (what good or ill will it create?).

Generic approaches to ethics typically assume that the heart of ethics is a dilemma, or a series of dilemmas, where we must make choices based on conscious or unconscious rules. From this perspective, ethical dilemmas occur when someone, or a group of people, is conflicted about the right choice to make, often when two or more values compete for priority. These values may be either personal, organisational, societal or any mixture of the three.

If, on the other hand, we approach ethics from the perspective of questions and a holistic understanding, we have a greater possibility of retaining its efficacy as an important construct, upon which to base our coaching. Ethics then addresses questions such as:

- Why do we do what we do and how we do it?
- With what intentions?
- In what ways does context (for example, national culture or our own life experience) influence what we regard as more or less ethical?

One way of looking at this is that coaching ethics lies in the centre of the three domains of general ethics, morality and codes of practice, as illustrated in Figure 2.1.

All of which leads us to suggest that ethics should be an open door inviting ongoing reflexivity. Hence, we constructed this chapter with a dialogical perspective in mind, engaging you in a dialogue with us and the coaching community on this major topic. We will be addressing two main questions: First, why talk about ethics in coaching – and we present three arguments. Second, what is the nature of ethics – and we offer two continua leading to a typology.

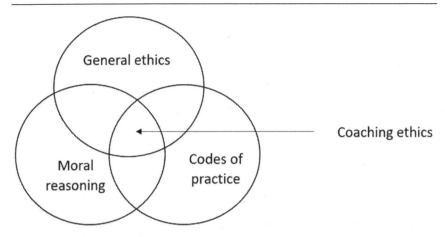

Figure 2.1 Situating coaching ethics

Why talk about ethics in coaching?

In this first section, we discuss the rationale for discussing ethics in coaching. We bring forth three main arguments (see Figure 2.2). First, the *instrumental* argument; talking about ethics in coaching is a necessary way to strengthen an emerging profession that needs structure and regulation. Second, the *socio-political*

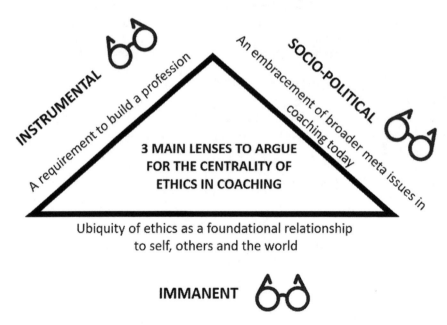

Figure 2.2 Why ethics in coaching? Three main lenses to argue for the centrality of ethics in coaching

argument; the ethical conversation is a requirement, given the broader societal, social, political and environmental issues that coaching is embracing. Third, the *immanent* argument; ethics is ubiquitous and surrounds us no matter what we do.

The instrumental argument

Let's start with the instrumental argument. A point that has long dominated the ethics conversations in coaching revolves around presenting ethics as an imperative to strengthening the burgeoning industry of coaching. Ethics would be a required condition to move coaching from an eclectic field of diversified practitioners to an established profession (Gray, 2011; Iordanou & Williams, 2017).

Indeed, early conversations in the domain of ethics in coaching concerned mainly raising awareness about the need for ethical practice (Allan et al., 2011), and defining its parameters through ethical frameworks and codes (Lowman, 2013; Townsend, 2011). In this effort though, a major challenge relates to the "great variety in approach and backgrounds of coaches" (Hannafey & Vitulano, 2012, p. 600) which makes it difficult defining what a good practice is. Portrayed a multifaceted cube (Segers et al., 2011), coaching remains a Wild West (Bennett et al., 2012), a contested terrain as a discipline (Bachkirova & Borrington, 2019; Boyatzis et al., 2022; Cox et al., 2014) where reaching an ethical consensus becomes challenging. And given the commercial interests involved, any attempt to impose a one best way or one unique view might be interpreted as an attempt to dominate the market and defend commercial interests. In brief, the relative newness of the market combined with its lack of structure constitute favourable grounds for greedy actors to make their ('ethical') voice louder.

This instrumental argument equating ethics to a normative imperative was confronted by a few researchers who argued that this normative tone in fact did not do justice to the complexity of the practice (Iordanou & Williams, 2017). They argued that "ethics cannot be applied by merely reading a book" (Gray, 2011, p. 16), since "instructions fail to equip coaches to deal with the twists and turns that they face in real practice" (Fatien, Diochon, & Nizet, 2015, p. 278). Rushing to find a clear-cut solution to ethics might just well be foreclosing it (Greenwood & Freeman, 2018).

The socio-political argument

While the instrumental view on ethics has paved the ground for the initial ethical conversation in coaching, it has recently been complemented by a socio-political imperative (Islam & Greenwood, 2021). This concern was made clear in several gatherings of coaching professionals and researchers. We can think for instance of a consortium where prominent coaching scholars and leaders gathered to discuss the future of coaching (Boyatzis et al., 2022). At a certain point, they were challenged to reflect about the "meta or hard to understand issues" beyond performance in coaching. Indeed, Jonathan Passmore asked (p. 4) echoing Zoe Cohen's (2019) concerns:

"what were coaches doing when the planet was burning? Maybe the answer is…actually, coaches were just simply helping their clients to make the fire glow hotter. We're focusing on amplifying individual and organizational performance, and those might be important issues, but what about the meta or hard to understand issues beyond those?"

In a similar vein, Micheal Cavanagh, in a fireside chat at the Exploring Ethics in Coaching conference (Smith, Cavanagh, & Magadlela, 2022), challenged coaches about the context in which they intervene. He mentioned:

"We have coaches coaching people in the military; (…) we have coaches coaching people in all of the companies that created the global financial crises; we have coaches in all of the companies that contributed to global warming; what's our ethical responsibility there? (…) Where do we draw those lines? Would you coach someone who works for a tobacco company for instance? Or for a casino, because there is something about these activities that does damage. What about an alcohol company? What about a soft drink manufacturer? Or a sugar company? Or what about McDonald's?"

These questions were already burgeoning a few years ago, with researchers questioning the political responsibility of coaches (Hawkins & Turner, 2020; Louis & Fatien Diochon, 2018; Shoukry, 2016). For instance, Fatien Diochon & Nizet (2012) documented coaches' concerns regarding their contributions to the institutions of Modernity as described by Giddens (1990), such as capitalism, industrialism, surveillance and military power. A current issue as we write is the relationship between the coaching profession generally and coaches in Russia, owing to the war between Russia and Ukraine. The international coaching community has taken various steps to support the isolation of the Russian state. But what about relationships with coaches in Russia, who oppose the Russia–Ukraine war, but face prison for making their views felt? If, as coaches, we hold strongly the value of caring for others, what is our responsibility towards these Russian coaches?

Therefore, we can say that this political concern that emerged a few years ago is getting increased momentum in the 2020s. In fact, coaching seems to embrace a "social turn" (Gannon, 2021) to include reflections on the social, societal, political impacts of their practice. The industry as a whole is encouraged to reflect on how they can "remedy the excesses of corporate behaviours, tackle social inequalities and disadvantage, address climate change and support empowerment in adverse political regimes" (Gannon, 2021, p. 5). With this socio-political turn in ethics, coaches are encouraged to act as citizens, which connects us to the original roots of working of self (Foucault, 1984). The care for the self should not be viewed as a selfish narcissist ambition but rather as a way to improve oneself, to be ready to serve others, and one's city, state or country.

In sum, with these 'bigger picture' issues raised, ethics in coaching moves from being only a way to strengthen a loosely defined and versatile profession, to a socio-political imperative given the global context in which coaches operate.

Next, we explore a third rationale for talking about ethics in coaching.

The immanent argument

Building on the above, another dialogue about ethics in coaching relates to the idea that ethics is in fact inherent to everything we do. In contrast to a perspective that will locate ethics to "moments of choices", i.e., specific and occasional moments when a doubt emerges (Iordanou & Williams, 2017), others think that ethics is ubiquitous, concerning our relationship to ourselves, others and the world (Greenwood & Freeman, 2018). It is present in everything we do, and informs our everyday actions, ways of thinking and behaving. In such a perspective, it is like a skin; present everywhere we go and informing our actions; for instance, in coaching, it can relate to our 'epistemic awareness' (Greenwood & Freeman, 2018), engaging our responsibility regarding the conceptual frameworks and models we use, and their embedded assumptions.

In a way, we could say that a restrictive perspective on ethics will locate it in specific difficult moments where one asks oneself about the do's and don'ts, while a holistic perspective will locate it in any activity that we are conducting, ethics concerning more about the being than the doing. This argument leads to the issue of the nature of ethical action. What do we consider to be ethical, or not? Interestingly, ethics coaching research conducted by Biquet (2022) reports that the number of ethical dilemmas experienced by coaches increases with years of experience; while 16.2% of experienced coaches (+10 years of experience) report having experienced more than 10 ethical dilemmas per year, only 4.7% report they did. The nature of dilemmas evolves too, with younger coaches more focused on managing their own weaknesses, and more experienced coaches dealing with conflicting interests between sponsor and coachees. This evidences that ethical sensitivity might increase with practice, meaning that the experience of ethical dilemmas might not be viewed as a sign of bad practice but rather as a signal of acute reflexivity of one's practice (Carroll & Shaw, 2012).

What is ethics? A typology to identify four types of coaching ethics

Another way to approach ethics is to ask where it is located, relating to the question of its nature. We will consider two questions: First, is ethics external and objective, or internal and subjective? Second, is ethics a stage or a contextual process? We will then offer a typology that crosses the two questions.

Ethics as external and objective, or internal and subjective?

Given the prevalence of the descriptive and normative tones in ethics overall (Painter-Morland, 2011; Schwartz, 2016) as well as in coaching (Fatien, Diochon, & Nizet, 2015), which tends to reduce coaching to the application of externally defined frameworks, coaching ethics can be viewed as an external objective knowledge that can obtained and therefore applied. Fatien Diochon and Nizet (2019, p. 463), referring to Weick (2001) use the metaphor of the Mastermind to explain this perspective in ethics: "ethical issues are comparable to a master code to be deciphered by removing the shield when the ethical individual—the code-breaker—has successfully guessed each piece of the concealed code. Consequently, "unethical behavior [can only be] attributed to flaws in reasoning" (Parmar, 2014, p. 1105). In such objectivist and rationalist approaches, issues are "out there" and their resolution requires the application of an individual judgement against externally given rules (Sonenshein, 2007). Some research conducted on ethics in coaching reveal that many coaches abide by this rational objective approach, while still struggling (Fatien Diochon & Nizet, 2015). For instance, and quite ironically, some coaches report how they ended up considering that they had been unethical by following what they described as externally imposed rules, such as codes, rather than follow their gut feelings. In the end, they experience misalignment and a lack of coherence with their decision based on an imposed reference.

Indeed, this external and objective view of ethics tends to override the emotional, intuitive, and sensorial dimensions of ethical decisions (Schwartz, 2016), while overestimating the rational capacity of actors (Palazzo et al., 2012). This allows us to introduce the other end of the continuum where ethics is experienced as fundamentally internal and subjective, highlighting its compassionate, embodied, sensorial, corporeal, and somatic dimensions (Pullen & Rhodes, 2013).

Coaches that embrace such a view tend to rely and trust their emotions, which play several roles. First, emotions can act as alerts to detect that something requires their attention and stop business-as-usual. For instance, feelings of betrayal, shame or guilt might be a signal of power dynamics in which coaches embark without full awareness. Then emotions can act also as compasses to guide decisions. Indeed, through our emotions, we can tell when it is a good moment to ask a powerful question or raise a challenging issue to a client. In fact, rather than providing a purely emotion-based emotional decision-making process in coaching, Fatien Diochon and Nizet (2018) suggest that emotions and rationality, under the form of reflexivity, are intertwined in the production of an ethical decision. These authors use the knitting metaphor to describe the interplay of emotions and reflexivity, which constitute for them two 'fibres' of the ethical process in coaching.

Ethics as a stage or a contextual process?

Another question to ask is whether ethics is as an individual characteristic, a stage one arrives at, or as a situated construction, a process, a never-ending quest.

The objective and rational perspective we above described in coaching ethics will tend to locate ethics in the individual, as part of who they are. Individuals, depending on their traits, skills and characters might reach a certain moral judgement stage (Rest, 1986), or development stages (Kohlberg, 1973). This presentation in terms of stages, steps, levels and intensities will lead to consider coaches as having more or less ethics, with training allowing them to become more ethically mature. This approach can be elitist, with a hierarchy of ethical maturity, with only very few or exceptional people reaching the top of the hierarchy in their lives. Current research into coach maturity generally suggests that experienced coaches may develop greater ethical awareness and more complex viewpoints about ethics – but this does not necessarily mean that they are 'more ethical'.

Other perspectives exist to capture the ethical decision-making process in coaching though, and they tend to be more socially constructed, processual and contextual. Here, ethics is not the property of an individual but more of a situation. Ethics there does not exist in a cultural vacuum, or independent of a context. Rather, ethics is an emerging process informed by the relational, social, political, ideological, etc. situation. For instance, using the metaphor of funambulism, Nizet and colleagues (2021) depict ethical decision-making in coaching as managing an equilibrium in a system of multiple commitments 'along the way'.

Ethical dilemmas are portrayed as a type of disequilibrium that emerges from a coach's conflicting commitments and the inability to maintain their compatibility. Their resolution revolves around the reestablishment of an equilibrium within the system of commitments; that is, compatibility between commitments. This emergent perspective portrays ethics as a practice that is dynamically constructed by a subject in interaction with others, with ethical meanings being mutable, unpredictable, and always transforming. In contrast to the property-based type of ethics described in the previous paragraph, here one might be tempted to say that a subject is never ethical outside of a context, or an action. This was a conclusion made by Fatien Diochon and Nizet (2018) who emphasised a performative dimension of ethics in coaching. If a subject makes an ethical decision, it is through this very decision that the subject becomes ethical. This performative perspective means that one is ethical as long as he is performing an action, but not before or after the action.

A typology

Building on the above, we propose a typology presenting four different ways to define ethics in coaching.

The intersection of the two above defined continuum allows us to propose a typology of four different ways of defining what ethics in coaching is.

A level: Coaching ethics as a level of maturity reached by an individual. Coaches understanding ethics as *a level* associate the views that ethics is a

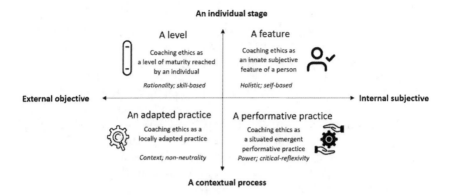

Figure 2.3 Nature of ethics and associated apprehensions coaching ethics

stage one arrives at, against externally defined references. It is likely a very rational process and might be typical of more compliant-based approaches to coaching ethics. One can anticipate that it is present in accreditation bodies or training programs that often use externally defined and objective references such as standards and codes delineating knowledge and skills to acquire. Such approaches will encourage coaches to abide by such standards and develop their practice to increase their ethicality, to arrive at predefined steps of coaching practice. Ethicality in coaching is defined by typical technical competencies; here, an ethical coach is able to do X, Y and Z.

A feature: Coaching ethics as an innate or subjective feature of a person. While this coaching ethics shares with the previous one above, that ethics is an individual property, it is not defined by external rules, but is rather more subjective. This approach will be more holistic (rational, emotional, corporeal, etc), when the former is mostly rational. Institutions (associations, schools, etc.) that favour such approaches might encourage the development of the self of the coach (Bachkirova, 2016), with attention paid to the self as an instrument of the practice. To develop their ethicality, coaches are encouraged to be self-reflexive (Fatien Diochon & Nizet, 2019) by paying attention to their own implication in the situation at stake. Through self-examination, coaches will question their own relationship with an issue at stake and identify any resonance between stories that might influence or interfere with his or her interpretations. This reflexive work is likely to enable them to create their own unique style of practice and to be authentic in their role as a coach (Bachkirova, 2016).

An adapted practice: Coaching ethics as a locally adapted practice. This approach might be well illustrated in coaching practices taking place outside of the Western world. As emphasised by Shoukry and Cox (2018), when they depict coaching as a social process, certain approaches to coaching might be unethical if not customised to the specific context of practice. For instance, "intercultural and oppressive contexts raise ethical questions around which values coaches seek to uphold: compassion or confrontation, acceptance or criticality, adaptability or resistance" (p. 414). Shoukry and Cox continue by raising the issue of neutrality. While certain learning approaches in coaching, such as behaviourism and cognitive constructivism (Hurlow, 2022), or world-views, such as value-neutral instrumentalism (Bachkirova, 2017), assume a neutral position of the coach, those are challenged by several authors emphasising the implicit Western white male bias inherent in coaching (Shoukry & Cox, 2018; Roche & Passmore, 2021; see Chapter 20 in this volume for further exploration of race in coaching ethically). Assuming neutrality in coaching might be another way to colonise minds under the argument of benevolence help. Hence being ethical here revolves around raising "epistemic awareness", consciousness about the conceptual and theoretical assumptions of the models we use and underpinning our practice, to avoid "epistemic violence", i.e., the imposition of one's views, and the silencing of others' (Greenwood & Freeman, 2018, p. 1).

A performative practice: Coaching ethics as a situated emergent performative practice. While here, coaching ethics shares with the previous conception that it is contextual, it does not mean the adaptation of externally defined practices as above, but rather a co-construction in context that involves not only self-reflexivity (like with above "feature" position) but also critical reflexivity. Critical reflexivity relates to questioning organisational practices, policies, social structures, and knowledge bases. For instance, a critically reflexive coach will examine discourses that sustain the use of coaching in organisations, ideologies and theoretical assumptions that inform coaching (Fatien Diochon & Nizet, 2019). Applied to intercultural contexts, coaches will demonstrate "integration and criticality" (Shoukry, 2017). This means that coaches are aware of the overall social context of their clients and recognise how the social context may drive many of the assumptions and behaviours that are discussed in coaching. Coaches are also aware of their own social context and how it influences them. Therefore:

> "coaches consciously try to create a balance between, on one hand, integrating the cultural aspects that may support their clients' needs and improve the effectiveness of coaching and, on the other, supporting their clients in critically reflecting on their social and cultural reality and empowering them to change that reality rather than to merely adapt to it."
>
> (Shoukry, 2017, p. 422)

In addition, the practice is performative insofar it the ethicality is attached to the situation rather than to the coach.

A reflexive framework

Throughout this chapter, we advocate for a dialogical approach to ethics, encouraging reflexive-based dialogue. Here we propose a six-step framework inspired from the practice of mentoring from the UK National Health Service. "Ethical mentors" are typically internal coaches or senior managers with coach training, who have a specific role helping clients work through real or potential ethical dilemmas. They work with a six-step ethical framework, aimed at helping the client identify the nature of the ethical dilemma and what they might do about it. The nature of the enquiry is not based in any particular moral perspective, code of conduct, or definition of ethics. The intent of the framework is to generate reflexivity on the part of the person involved, therefore to clarify, through the use of judicious questions, the *emergent ethical context*. The six steps to generate such reflexivity are:

1. *Articulate the issue.* Who does it affect, how and why? What is the nature of the conflict of interest? What specific personal, organisational and /or societal values are involved?
2. *What is the context?* Who is involved, directly and indirectly? Is this a new issue, or an old one in a new guise? What are your specific and general responsibilities? Who has been consulted? Who needs to be consulted? Is there a relevant code of conduct or guideline? What is the general ethical climate here?
3. *What are the implications?* What risks are involved? (Safety, financial, reputational, etc.) What precedents may be set by this decision? What would be the impact if this were done on a much larger scale? Would the implications be different if this were played out publicly v privately?
4. *What other opinions or perspectives might be relevant?* What might you be avoiding acknowledging? Who might provide a robust challenge to your thinking? How can you make other people feel more comfortable about speaking up? Have you genuinely sought and listened to dissenting views?
5. *Balance the arguments.* What would an impartial adviser see as fair? What priorities should we apply to conflicting objectives and values? What are the "zones of ethical acceptability" and what lies outside them?
6. *The final check.* What decision-making biases might you be applying without realising? How honest are you being with yourself? (How pure are your motives?) Do you truly feel this is the right thing to do? If you were to give this issue more time, would you come to a different conclusion?

Conclusion

If you ever for a passing moment thought that coaching ethics was a simple matter or right or wrong, hopefully this chapter and those that follow will inform you of the complexity. There are no easy answers, no neat solutions, no permanent fixes. Time and again in supervision, what looks like a straightforward difficult choice in working with a client turns out to have multiple ethical dimensions. When the dilemma involves multiple stakeholders, the ethical complexity becomes far greater still. The solution, we argue, is for coaches and supervisors to educate themselves systemically and eclectically, so they can approach ethical issues with both openness of mind and the ability to adopt different perspectives and approaches. Always bearing in mind that our perspective of appropriate ethical thinking may not be the same as that of the client! It may seem an unusual ending for a chapter, but we would be delighted if you disagree with our analysis. After all, multi-perspective dialogue is at the heart of effective ethical management!

Discussion points

1. How does ethics come into play in your own practice? When do you purposely question your practice?
2. How do you consider ethics in the context of your practice? As an obstacle? As a resource? As a framework?
3. How do you train/educate your ethical skills?
4. How does context come into play into your ethical decisions? What is your own zone of ethical acceptability?

Recommended reading

Louis, D. & Fatien Diochon, P. (2019). *Complex situations in coaching: a critical case-based approach*. Routledge.

References

Allan, J., Passmore, J., & Mortimer, L. (2011). Coaching ethics: Developing a model to enhance coaching practice. In J. Passmore (Ed.), *Supervision in coaching: Supervision, ethics and continuous professional development* (pp. 161–173). Kogan Page.

Bachkirova, T. (2016). The self of the coach: Conceptualization, issues, and opportunities for practitioner development. *Consulting Psychology Journal*, 68(2), 143–156. doi:10.1037/CPB0000055.

Bachkirova, T. (2017). Developing a knowledge base of coaching: Questions to explore. - PsycNET. In T. Bachkirova, G. Spence, & D. Drake (Eds), *The SAGE handbook of coaching* (pp. 23–41). Sage Publications. https://psycnet.apa.org/record/2017-07502-002.

Bachkirova, T. & Borrington, S. (2019). Old Wine in New Bottles: Exploring Pragmatism as a Philosophical Framework for the Discipline of Coaching. *Academy of Management Learning & Education*, 18(3), 337–360. doi:10.5465/amle.2017.0268.

Bennett, J. L., Campone, F., Fatien Diochon, P., & Page, L. (2012). Coaching Graduate Education: from Wild West to Established Territory. *Academy of Management Proceedings,* 2012(1), 11497. doi:10.5465/ambpp.2012.11497symposium.

Biquet, M. (2022). *Ethical dilemmas in coaching today*.

Boyatzis, R. E., Hullinger, A., Ehasz, S. F., Harvey, J., Tassarotti, S., Gallotti, A., & Penafort, F. (2022). *The Grand Challenge for Research on the Future of Coaching: Journal of Applied Behavioral Science*, 1–22. doi:10.1177/00218863221079937.

Carroll, M., & Shaw, E. (2012). *Ethical Maturity in the Helping Professions: Making Difficult Life and Work Decisions.* Jessica Kingsley Publishers.

Cohen, Z. (2019) *Where were all the Coaches when the planet warmed by 3 degrees?* LinkedIn post, published January 30, 2019.

Cox, E., Bachkirova, T., & Clutterbuck, D. (2014). Theoretical Traditions and Coaching Genres: Mapping the Territory. 16(2), 139–160. doi:10.1177/1523422313520194.

Fatien Diochon, P. & Nizet, J. (2012). Les coachs, ni muets ni inactifs face à la dimension critique de leur travail! *Management & Avenir,* 3(53), 162–182. doi:10.3917/mav.053.0162.

Fatien Diochon, P. & Nizet, J. (2015). Ethical Codes and Executive Coaches. *The Journal of Applied Behavioral Science,* 51(2), 277–301. doi:10.1177/0021886315576190.

Fatien Diochon, P. & Nizet, J. (2019). Ethics as a Fabric: An Emotional Reflexive Sensemaking Process. *Business Ethics Quarterly,* 29(4), 461–489. https://doi.org/10.1017/beq.2019.11.

Foucault, M. (1984). *Histoire de la sexualité III. Le souci de soi.* Gallimard.

Gannon, J. M. (2021). Applying the lens of social movements to coaching and mentoring. *An International Journal,* 6(1), 5–29. doi:10.22316/poc/06.1.02.

Giddens, A. (1990). *The consequences of modernity.* Polity Press.

Gray, D. E. (2011). Journeys towards the professionalisation of coaching: dilemmas, dialogues and decisions along the global pathway. *Coaching: An International Journal of Theory, Research and Practice,* 4(1), 4–19. doi:10.1080/17521882.2010.550896.

Greenwood, M. & Freeman, R. E. (2018). Deepening Ethical Analysis in Business Ethics. *Journal of Business Ethics,* 147, 1–4. doi:10.1007/s10551-017-3766-1.

Hannafey, F. T. & Vitulano, L. A. (2012). Ethics and Executive Coaching: An Agency Theory Approach. *Journal of Business Ethics, 115*(3), 599–603. doi:10.1007/S10551-012-1442-Z.

Hawkins, P. & Turner, E. (2020). *Systemic Delivering Value Beyond the Individual.* Routledge.

Hurlow, S. (2022). Revisiting the Relationship Between Coaching and Learning: The Problems and Possibilities. *Academy of Management Le,* 21(1), 121–138. doi:10.5465/AMLE.2019.0345.

Islam, G., Greenwood, M. (2021). Reconnecting to the Social in Business Ethics. Journal of Business Ethics, *170,* 1–4 (2021). doi:10.1007/s10551-021-04775-7.

Iordanou, I. & Williams, P. (2017). Developing Ethical Capabilities of Coaches. In T. Bachbirova, G. Spence, & D. Drake (Eds), *The SAGE handbook of coaching* (pp. 696–712). Sage Publications. www.researchgate.net/publication/310802183_Developing_Ethical_Capabilities_of_Coaches.

Louis, D. & Fatien Diochon, P. (2018). The coaching space: A production of power relationships in organizational settings. *Organization,* 25(6), 710–731. doi:10.1177/1350508418779653.

Lowman, R. (2013). Coaching ethics. In J. Passmore, D. Peterson, & T. Freire (Eds), *The Wiley-Blackwell handbook of the psychology of coaching and mentoring* (pp. 69–88). Wiley-Blackwell.

Nizet, J., Fatien Diochon, P., & Nair, L. B. (2021). When commitments conflict: Making ethical decisions like a funambulist. *M@n@gement,* 24(1), 44–58.

Painter-Morland, M. (2011). Moral decision-making. In M. Painter-Morland & R. ten Bos (Eds), *Business ethics and continental philosophy* (pp. 117–140). Cambridge University Press.

Palazzo, G., Krings, F., & Hoffrage, U. (2012). Ethical Blindness. *Journal of Business Ethics*, 109(3), 323–338. doi:10.1007/S10551-011-1130-4.

Pullen, A. & Rhodes, C. (2013). *Corporeal ethics and the politics of resistance in organizations, Organization*, 21(6), 782–796. doi:10.1177/1350508413484819.

Roche, C. & Passmore, J. (2021). *Racial Justice, Equity and Belonging in Coaching*. Henley Center for Coaching.

Schwartz, M. S. (2016). Ethical Decision-Making Theory: An Integrated Approach. *Journal of Business Ethics*, 139(4), 755–776. doi:10.1007/s10551-015-2886-8.

Segers, J., Vloeberghs, D., Henderickx, E., & Inceoglu, I. (2011). Structuring and Understanding the Coaching Industry: The Coaching Cube. *Academy of Management Learning & Education*, 10(2), 204–221. doi:10.2307/41318046.

Shoukry, H. (2016). Coaching for emancipation: A framework for coaching in oppressive environments. *International Journal of Evidence Based Coaching and Mentoring*, 14(2), 15–30. https://psycnet.apa.org/record/2016-45429-003.

Shoukry, H. (2017). Coaching for Social Change. In T. Bachkirova, G. Spence, & D. Drake (Eds), *The SAGE handbook of coaching* (pp. 176–194). Sage Publications.

Shoukry, H. & Cox, E. (2018). Coaching as a social process. *Management Learning*, 49(4), 413–428. doi:10.1177/1350507618762600.

Smith, W.-A., Cavanagh, M., & Magadlela, D. (2022, February 25). *Welcome Address.* [Conference welcome, fireside chat Wendy-Ann Smith and Micheal Cavanagh]. Exploring Ethics in Coaching Conference. Coaching Ethics Forum. https://coachingethicsforum.com.

Sonenshein, S. (2007). The Role of Construction, Intuition, and Justification in Responding to Ethical Issues at Work: The Sensemaking-Intuition Model. In *The Academy of Management Review* (Vol. 32, pp. 1022–1040). Academy of Management. doi:10.2307/20159354.

Townsend, C. (2011). Ethical frameworks in coaching. In J. Passmore (Ed.), *Supervision in coaching: Supervision, ethics and continuous professional development* (pp. 141–159). Kogan Page.

Chapter 3

Ethics and professional coaching bodies

Bob Garvey and Paul Stokes

Introduction

It has been argued (Shearing, 2001; Saul, 1997) that globalisation has brought societies around the world a new form of feudalism – neofeudalism. This concept brings with it the idea that power over the many is held globally by the few. More locally, this tendency has created a new style of leadership, driven by rules and an assumption of compliance and therefore control. Neofeudalism brings the modern workplace a plethora of surveillance processes, often driven through the Human Resources systems, for example, appraisal, professional development reviews, 360, performance management systems and perhaps, coaching itself (Nielsen & Nørreklit, 2009).

Lasch (1995) described these neofeudalistic barons in the global economy as having abdicated fundamental social or political responsibility within the societies they inhabit. They have dubious loyalties and temporarily commit to the highest bidder. These leaders hold the power and control the dominant discourse in their influence on governments and social and economic policy. They threaten to 'leave' the country if the government doesn't pander to them, and they call for deregulation and freedom at the same time as imposing greater regulation of those they control (Saul, 1997). Schwartz, (2000, p. 175) argues that this has created a paternal authority where the rights of individuals are side-lined *"under the guise of business ethics…"*.

Professional Bodies in coaching started to appear towards the end of the 1990s and early 2000s. Arguably at least, these were created to deal with what Morris & Tarpley (2000) referred to as *'The Wild West of Coaching'*. Later, in 2004, Stratford Sherman and Alyssa Freas published an article in the Harvard Business Review called *'The Wild West of Executive Coaching'* calling for controls on coaching activity and, following this, a wider range of Professional Bodies started to appear.

Professional bodies started to create a narrative that said that potential clients or sponsors needed reassurance and that quality control is maintained through membership and the policies to which members sign up to when

DOI: 10.4324/9781003277729-3

joining. The narrative extended to include slogans like '*it's what our members want*' and '*it's what the market demands*'.

In this chapter we critically review the policies and procedures of some of the main professional bodies and ask the question 'Are professional bodies behaving ethically or have they created neofeudalistic organisations with surveillance built into their policies and rules?'

Common ethical positions

First, we consider three common ethical positions:

- Utilitarianism/Consequentialism
- Kantian ethics
- Egoist

Utilitarianism/Consequentialism

Drawn from ethical ideas from the eighteenth, nineteenth and early twentieth century, the philosophy of utilitarianism claim that an ethical act is only 'right' if it maximises the 'good' and, only if that 'good' negates any 'bad' that may follow from the act. The utilitarian ethics position is concerned with the future benefit of an action. A broken promise, for example, is only bad if the effects of that broken promise negatively effects people in the future. The consequentialist position therefore is that the consequences matter more than the circumstances or the intrinsic nature of the act (see Bentham & Mills, 1987).

Kantian ethics

Kant was concerned with fundamental and universal moral principles (Wood, 2008). Most of the time, Kant thought that most things people do are not contingent on morality but, rather, contingent on our desires. So, if your desire is to get money, you ought to get a job. He called these 'hypothetical imperatives'. However, he believed in what he called 'categorical Imperatives', for example, it is wrong to lie under any circumstances even if it's a 'white lie' or a lie to help someone else. He believed strongly in the idea that people should be treated as 'ends in themselves' rather than 'means to an end'. Ethics, Kant believed, are based on reason and reason is a constant moral imperative. He also believed and respected human free-will. The 'categorical imperative' would put these two ideas together and conclude that each individual has their own autonomy, their own goals, ideas and to make their way in the world as they see fit, however, to lie, manipulate or deceive an individual is fundamentally wrong because that provides them with false information upon which to make their decisions (see Sullivan, 2008).

Egoist

Ethical egoism is a normative theory. Ethical egoism is based on self interest in that an individual is only interested in others if this contributes to their self-interest. While this position accepts that people may be able to act altruistically, ethical egoism thinks that people *should* act in their own self-interest. Therefore, an action that is 'good' is good for 'me'. It does not advocate that an individual just does whatever they feel but rather, acts need to be associated with personal objectives. (see Smith, 2006).

Is coaching a profession?

There is still conjecture as to whether or not coaching is a profession (Fillery-Travis & Collins, 2017; Gray et al., 2016; Lowman, 2013; Garvey, 2011). The basic tenet of a profession is that it is a norming process in which a trade or occupation sets rules, standards, qualifications and involves compliance measures and sanctions. A profession is often represented by a professional body with the purpose of controlling, vetting and objectifying the trade or occupation by differentiating itself as a body with integrity and competence. This may also mean establishing a code of ethics. However, a professional body also defines those who are amateurs, unqualified and of lower standing. Professionalisation could be seen positively, owing to the standards of membership and practice it creates or negatively as a narrow elitist group that excludes those of a 'lower standing'. Clearly, the question of inclusivity or exclusivity has ethical considerations and raises issues of diversity. This is discussed later.

The knowledge base of a profession should also be developed on the basis of research and continuous learning in order to progress the professional's understanding of the specialism to which they subscribe. Lowman (2013, p. 69) suggests that in the case of coaching, this is debatable, and that coaching is *"more akin to a proficiency than a speciality"*. He goes on to argue that in coaching it cannot be taken for granted that the coaching world is underpinned by *"mastery of scientific foundation for practice, science-based practice, socialization in the ethics of a profession"*. In 2005 Lowman stated that executive coaching has *"caught on more as an area of practice than as one of theory or research"* (p. 90).

As above, Garvey argues (2011) that the professionalisation agenda in coaching can be traced to the late 1990s and early 2000s. The argument was that the 'Wild West' of coaching needed to be tamed and it may have been the 'wild west' justification that led to the burgeoning numbers of the now, arguably, the 'wild west' of professional bodies; all with different conditions, standards and ethical codes (see below on perfect competition). Coaching activity has become a commercial activity and perhaps the entrepreneurial spirit found within the commercial world has driven these variations as different groups of people with different views have literally created their own professional bodies.

In considering the above arguments, a problem for ethics within a professional context is that there will be a tendency to develop a normative (Lowman, 2013) approach. This most commonly manifests as a code of conduct of a set of rules. To justify our use of the word 'rules', in the case of the European Mentoring & Coaching Council's (EMCC) Global Code of Ethics (GCoE: 2021, p. 1) the introduction points out that the code is *"intended as guidance"*, however, it also suggests that *"The Charter is drafted in accordance with European law..."*, although they say it's not *"legally binding"*. This rather confusing position that blends legality with ethics is unhelpful. Legality is not the same as ethics, for example, it may be the law to send asylum seekers from the United Kingdom to Rwanda, but this does not make it ethical or perhaps, Apartheid was legal in South Africa, but it certainly was not ethical. In reading into the code itself, the word *'will'* is used 54 times in the ethical statements and this is used as a *'command'* not as a choice or guidance. In this sense, they become rules and not guidance.

The International Coaching Federation's (ICF) Code (2021) attempts to position ethics as dilemmas and states that it sets standards of conduct globally. These standards are written as pledges made by individual coaches through the use of the word 'I' throughout and they say that these are *"ethical obligations"* (p. 2). They state that all members are *"expected to showcase and propagate"* (p. 4). It is this language that makes these statements 'rules' or standards to be complied with. Ultimately, this can mean that coaches can either be right or wrong and any consideration of genuine ethical dilemmas may be ignored, for example, when is it acceptable to break confidentiality? Professional bodies also argue that these codes offer *'protection from harm'* but do not consider the potential benefits of actions that a code might deem as unethical. Ethical thinking (rather than codes) considers benefit versus harm on a case-by-case basis and ethics are often socially and culturally (see Chapter 19 for cultural influences on ethics) defined and they are created in a moment of time to satisfy the prevailing conditions in any given context. Therefore, a set of rules created by one group of people to guide another at another point in time in the future may not remain contextually relevant. Therefore, from a utilitarianist's perspective, this may be relevant if the consequences in the future are not about maximum good. However, the Kantian position would question how far these rules fit with the categorical imperatives or if these rules are simply hypothetical imperatives based on the professional bodies desire to influence or control. If these rules are hypothetical imperatives based on desires, they become part of the ethical egoist's argument. So, either way, these codes of ethics from different ethical standpoints, appear rather dubious and to claim, as some professional bodies do, that these are 'global' and therefore apply to all coaches in every part of the world raises neofeudalistic questions of Professional Bodies being the paternal authority where the rights of individuals are side-lined *"under the guise of business ethics..."* (Schwartz, 2000, p. 175)

The context of coaching

Coaching activity happens in a wide range of sections of society. However, as stated above, the professional bodies tend to support the commercial and executive sections of society. Globalisation has brought neofeudalism (Shearing, 2001; Saul, 1997). With this has come a new confident entrepreneurial capitalism (Arnaud, 2003) where coaching, with its sporting analogies (Whitmore, 2002) translates into flattering the egos of the senior executives (Arnaud, 2003) and giving a narcissistic boost (Arnaud, 2003) to coaches as they develop the *'celebrated self'* (Western, 2012) of the executive. This seems like elitism.

Hutton (1997) argues that capitalism has triumphed over socialism, but this has been at the cost of the moral and religious values that informed social democratic movements. However, the loss of these values has been at the expense of, potentially at least, our very civilisation as an unchecked market has an *"inherent tendency to produce unreasonable inequality, economic instability and immense concentrations of private, unaccountable power"* (p. 4). Without controls, he argued in 1997, almost prophetically, we run the risk of *"collapsing into licence masquerading as liberty, spivery dressed up as risk-taking and exploitation in the guise of efficiency and flexibility"* (p. 4).

Consider the following statement put out on social media by one of the professional bodies:

"We condemn the war and humanitarian disaster occurring in Ukraine and call on all related parties to come together in a search of peaceful resolution. We continue to support the accreditation and development of coaching, mentoring and supervision all over the world, including with those impacted directly or indirectly by conflict, in our quest for a peaceful future for all humanity."

(EMCC Global, LinkedIn post, 2022)

What is noticeable about this is first, it is a neutral statement. In this war, our view is there is only one aggressor. What could be the reason for remaining neutral?

One possible argument is that this plays into the discourse of the coach as a reflective, non-directive observer of practice. However, this seems to run contrary to a condemnation of unethical behaviour. Second, the humanitarian sentiment is clear and not one many would argue with, which raises the question of the intent of the writer(s) in including it. Thirdly, it is a reminder that this professional body has 'business as usual'. While the intent may have been to position the professional body in support of peace, it is also possible to read this as a marketing opportunity for the organisation. This leads it open to accusations of seeking to capitalise on the humanitarian crisis in the Ukraine (paralleled by some individual coaches on social media seeming to promote themselves on this basis.) This also begs the question as to why this is the only conflict or humanitarian conflict this body has chosen to make a statement about, without reference to other previous and ongoing conflicts in many parts of the world – Sudan, Syria, Yemen, Ethiopia, for example, In Hutton's (1997) terms, discussed above, could this be labelled as opportunistic entrepreneurial '*spivery*'? In raising these questions, it is not our intent to arbitrarily attack coaching bodies on the decisions they make. Instead, we argue that this example brings into relief the challenges that coaching professional bodies have in taking up ethical positions. Our view is that such positions and approaches should be reflected upon and such thinking rendered transparent to members of these bodies. In this case, the rationale for making such a statement and the ethical position that underpins it is somewhat opaque currently. We will now go and explore the role of coaching professional bodies within the context of capitalist market economy, within which they are located.

The free market and the role of professional bodies

The unregulated free market raises issues that are central to ethics generally (see Chapter 25 for exploration of the promotion of coaching) and to the ethics of coaching in particular. The philosopher, Bertrand Russell (1928, p. 174) was clearly aware of this when he wrote:

> "Advocates of capitalism are very apt to appeal to the sacred principles of liberty, which are embodied in one maxim: The fortunate must not be restrained in the exercise of tyranny over the unfortunate."

In other words, it can be easy to be uncritical about the ethical underpinnings of the capitalist market economy generally, with this also applying to the coaching market in particular. This critique points to the economic oppression of the many by the few who wield significant economic power. We will tackle this later in relation to coaching specifically.

To counter this ethical critique, the supporters of free-market economics, drawing on egoist ethics, argue, after Adam Smith (1759) that the invisible hand of free-market economics creates social benefits and general public good brought about by individuals acting in their own interests. Smith viewed this argument as being the hand of God at work. Modern proponents of free market economics argue that the market is allocatively efficient; in other words, the invisible hand ensures that resources are given to those who use them most efficiently, in the form of surplus profits. However, critics of the current system argue that capitalist economies are distributively inefficient; they fail to distribute wealth equitably to the labour that created it but instead wealth goes to the few who own the means of production. Returning to the question of whether this market system is ethical, or not, depends on which ethical framework you are committed to.

For instance, it can be argued that, with 4.3 million children living in poverty in the UK (Action for Children, 2021), over 1,300 food banks (a 33% increase since 2020/21) and 2.5 million food packages currently being delivered as part of a three-day emergency food supply (House of Commons Library, 2022), that this level of distributive market failure is unacceptable ethically. Proponents of neofeudalism (e.g. Shearing, 2001; Saul, 1997) also make this point.

However, proponents of the free market argue that market failures exist because of the rigidities imposed by government legislation and other barriers to entry and that it is only by pursuing free markets more aggressively that social efficient outcomes can be attained. This economic argument for 'perfect competition' is relevant here in the case of *professional bodies.* Here, the notion is that the coaching market is structured in such a way so that all producers and consumers have the same information and no transaction costs and that there are a large number of producers and consumers competing with one another in this kind of environment. Perfect competition is the theoretical opposite of a monopoly. A further idea within this framework is that, because there are sufficient buyers and sellers in the perfect market, the prices reflect supply and demand and providers earn enough to stay in business and if they earn more, new entrants will enter the market to drive profits down. It also means that there is little differentiation between the suppliers' offerings. However, the current state of market for coaching professional bodies and their accreditation processes suggests a state closer to an oligopoly, which describes a market where there are a few large providers of goods or services who, while retaining some measure of monopoly power, compete against each other on the basis of price and/or product differentiation. Differentiation is a key concern and in the case of some professional bodies of coaching, with similar offerings, finding the differentiation is challenging. The ICF, for example, has recently changed its competency framework which might be argued to be an attempt to differentiate itself from other professional body providers. Others, such as The Association of Professional Executive Coaching and Supervision (APECS) differentiate through accreditation by portfolio and the recognition of university qualifications.

Finally, as with arguments for the free markets, it can be claimed that a key discourse in the coaching literature of coaching is that of libertarian humanism (e.g. Cox et al., 2014; du Toit, 2014; Rogers, 2012; Connor & Pokora, 2012; Western, 2012; Parsloe & Leedham, 2009; Whitmore, 2009; Rosinski, 2004) where individual choice and agency is paramount. However, this is seldom tied into an examination of the broader social impact of such choices, within the context of a global economy. We will now explore the possible reasons for this individual focus.

The individual focus

Arguably at least, the dominant model of coaching ethics is individualistic. Coaching practice is dominated by therapeutic psychological practices (de Haan & Gannon, 2016). Arnaud in referencing Brunel, (2007, p. 417) says that *"humanist psychology considers that human behaviour in organizations derives, above all, from the ethical disposition of individuals"*. Psychology, or at least organisational psychology almost by definition focuses on individuals and, not surprisingly, the individualistic view of ethics finds its way into the professional bodies who have largely adopted the psychological approach to coaching (Hawkins and Turner, 2020; de Haan & Gannon, 2016; Western 2012). This means that the wider context of ethical behaviour is not considered. Further, an often-unacknowledged assumption of ethical codes is that individuals are *"rational purposive actors who act in accordance with their intentions and understand the implications of their actions"* (De Cremer et al., 2010, p. 2). This can result in blame or punishment being easily delivered and that ethical problems are the result of 'a few bad apples' rather than the context in which these things happen. As raised earlier, the responses to the war in Ukraine by the EMCC Global on social media discussed above and the number of coaches on social media offering their unsolicited help could be viewed as 'a few bad apples' trying to promote themselves on the back of a war or it could be viewed as a contextual problem driven by the entrepreneurial discourse situated within the free-market capitalist agenda. In general terms, the shifting attention from the wider system and placing this in the hands of the individual is what Arnaud (2007, p. 415) refers to as the *"regression from the political"* (wider system) to the personal, wrongdoing becomes the individual's fault!

We are not suggesting that the latter is deliberate. Tenbrunsel & Messick (2004, p. 224) suggest that *"individuals do not 'see' the moral components of an ethical decision, not because they are morally uneducated, but because psychological processes fade the 'ethics' from an ethical dilemma"*, and this may be a case of the human capacity to reframe and reinterpret, justify and post-hoc rationalise.

There is an alternative to this individualistic orientation and this is potentially more challenging and difficult for professional bodies because it would mean abandoning rules based codes and instead applying a more sophisticated approach that moves away from binary distinctions of 'right' or 'wrong'.

Carroll and Shaw (2013) attempted to offer a framework, paraphrased below by Corrie and Lane, (2015, p. 148) that helps with this by publishing a six-point ethical framework that considers:

1. *Ethical sensitivity* – awareness of self, of harm of consequences, of impact of behaviour of intention.
2. *Ethical discernment* – reflection, emotional awareness, problem-solving process, ethical decisions.

3. *Ethical implementation* – what blocks me/what supports me, how to implement decisions.
4. *Ethical conversation* – defending the decision, going public, connecting to principles.
5. *Ethical peace* – living with the decision, support networks, crisis of limits, learning from the process, letting go.
6. *Ethical growth and development of character* – utilizing learning to enrich moral self-knowledge, extending ethical understanding, becoming more ethically attuned and competent.

While this is principally still an individual focus, it offers individuals a reflexive framework through which professional bodies might enable a discussion which takes account of the contextual issues and broader societal issues which we have raised above. Gray, (2011, p. 14) argued that *"ethics cannot be applied by merely reading a book"*. He went on to say that more discussion is needed in a non-judgmental manner rather than establishing a set of rules to be complied with and the professional bodies need to encourage debate. We intend to continue that debate here by next considering the ethical issues raised above, in terms of power, oppression and privilege, for the coaching market.

A question of access

The implications of the espoused discourse of the humanistic found in the coaching literature are that coaching helps individuals and groups of people to develop their full potential and this should be available to all. However, as discussed above this may not be the case with professional bodies. For example, one professional body states that their awards:

> EMCC's Global Quality Award (EQA) offers the market place the much-needed framework to enable the quality of mentoring/coaching services to meet and be recognised for meeting high quality standards of the profession.'
>
> (EMCC Global, 2022a)

This appears to be in line with the libertarian humanism running through the coaching literature but on the other, this statement is positioning the organisation in a marketplace. It claims its services are *'much needed'*, *'recognised'* and *'high-quality'* but fails to say by whom are these things *'much needed'*, *'recognised'* and who says they are *'high-quality'* other than themselves! It could be argued that playing into the market discourse here is revealing the EMCC's organisational egoist ethical position, where the only criteria that it should be judged on is whether it is acting in the interests of its members.

In a similar vein, the ICF accepts on its website that ICF credential holders are *'elite'* thus reducing the impact of its own professed *'humanity'*, *'collaboration'* and '*equity*' values (International Coaching Federation, 2022). It is hard to comprehend how 'elite' equates with these other values. Indeed, the very concept of the creation of an elite, reflects an aspiration to create significant barriers to entry so as to restrict supply. To continue the use of economic theory, a restriction of supply, other things being equal, means that market price for that service can be raised. This creation of a professional 'elite' is often couched, in professional bodies, as being one of quality control, where those who fail to meet the required standards are denied entry. Hence, this also plays up the notion of professional bodies as guardians of moral authority, as argued above. One way in which professional bodies can assert ethical control over their membership is through supervision. In the next section we will debate how supervision is enacted and justified ethically by professional bodies.

The ethics of supervision in professional bodies

All professional bodies require their members to receive supervision. They all claim that this reassures potential clients and sponsors and that it ensures quality control and continuous professional development of coaches.

Hawkins and Shohet (2006) acknowledge that there are many discourses that influence the idea of supervision in coaching, for example, psychotherapy, counselling, education, social work and management. Professional bodies seem to have latched on to these discourses, probably owing to the influence of psychotherapy on coaching practice (de Haan & Gannon, 2016; Western, 2012).

EMCC Global (2022b) states that supervision:

- Facilitates development
- Provides support
- Promotes professional standards

Promoting a professional standard, is presumably, the EMCC's professional standard and this would suggest that supervision is at least one-third about compliance. This thought leads into the issue of surveillance.

Foucault (1977, p. 202) stated:

> "He who is subjected to a field of visibility, and who knows it, assumes responsibility for the constraints of power; he makes them play spontaneously upon himself; he inscribes in himself the power relation in which he simultaneously plays both roles; he becomes the principle of his own subjection."

In this way, supervision could be viewed as a 'soft system' of control or 'quality control' and in making supervision a mandatory activity, coaches are subjecting themselves to their own subjection.

Nielsen and Nørreklit (2009) suggest that this form of control is endemic within organisations and that much of the dialogic exchanges within organisations are *'asymmetrical'*. This means that the person who asks the question, raises an issue or creates a mandatory statement, who is in a position of power, (like the EMCC) *"possesses the right to control the conversation"* (p. 208).

This ethical position for coaching professional bodies can indeed be justified depending on which ethical framework is being adopted. In terms of utilitarianism, the consequences for the quality of coaching received by clients can be framed as justification for the requirement for supervision. The moral imperative for intervening in the quality control of coaches could also be justified but this would depend on the desires of those enacting this process as to whether their true purpose was to promote the professional body as the provider for such services, hence aligning this more with an egoist position.

The ICF's view on supervision does not focus so much on professional compliance but rather on a wider range of issues, for example:

- Exploring the coach's internal process through reflective practice
- Reviewing the coaching agreement and any other psychological or physical contacts, both implicit and explicit
- Uncovering blind spots
- Ethical issues
- Ensuring the coach is "fit for purpose" and perhaps offering accountability
- Looking at all aspects of the coach and client's environment for opportunities for growth in the system

While the penultimate point has a 'quality assurance' feel, it is less explicit than the EMCC's statement but elsewhere on their website they claim to be 'thought leaders' and providers of the 'gold standard' of coach training. It is now important to turn to the demand side of the coaching market in relation to access to coaching, which we do in the following section.

Cost of accessing the market

In the ICF and EMCC, costs at the time of writing for professional body accreditation is about $500 per level. The Association for Coaching charges from $250–$500 per level and the APECS about $390. These fees are on top of any university qualification or other courses needed in concert with the application process. These levels arguably constitute a significant barrier to entry to professional body accreditation and are likely to militate against entry into the coaching profession by people from less affluent backgrounds.

In economics, a key concept is called 'distributive efficiencies'. In essence, this is where goods and services are consumed by those who need them most. As we argued earlier, capitalist economies are often inefficient in this sense and, as we also suggested earlier, professional bodies may well be raising the price of coaching services by restricting the supply of coaches. In the case of professional bodies, can it be said that they are ensuring that the services of a coach are consumed by those that need them most? The ICF Global Coaching Study (2020) shows that the global average earnings for coaches is $47,100 per annum but with figures of $60,000 or more in North America. Are these fee levels barriers for individual clients? While it is difficult to tell from one survey (albeit global), it seems likely that, as these earnings (purely from coaching work) are higher than average wage levels in those countries, the offer of coaching is beyond the reach of those at the lowest income levels, who arguably might be most in need of it.

Set against that, we are aware of other organisations in the UK context such as Coaching York (2022) and Coaching Reading (2022) where coaching is brought to those who need it rather than those who can afford it. Furthermore, there is evidence of a wide range of prices charged by coaches. These depend on the type of coaching, the organisational contexts and levels of experience. In life coaching for example, a coach's earnings may be anything from $27,000 to $210,000 per year.

Nevertheless, it is not clear what ethical stance many professional bodies within coaching are taking in relation to their own practice and impact on the coaching profession. This then leads us into the concluding part of the chapter, where we bring together the various debates outlined above and draw some conclusions from the ensuing discussion.

Professional bodies as guardians or neofeudalists?

As we have said above, it is possible to conceive of professional bodies in two main ways in ethical terms. Should they be seen as moral guardians of professional standards, empowered to exercise quality control over coaches, for the benefit of the clients they serve? Alternatively, should they be seen as neofeudalists, manipulating and distorting the market to serve their own interests and that of their members? Hopefully, it is clear that both of these positions can be justified from an ethical perspective.

Seeing professional coaching bodies as guardians of standards has some merit. As we mentioned earlier in the chapter, coaches often have to evidence participation in a credible coaching programme (often University delivered) plus evidence of reflecting on their coaching experience from an ethical perspective (among other things) to gain and maintain membership. Furthermore, professional bodies have engaged in numerous activities to promote the continuous professional development of coaches including supervision itself. Taking up this role within coaching can be justified from a utilitarian/ consequentialist perspective, seeking to achieve the greatest good for the greatest number.

Alternatively, professional bodies can be perceived as self- interested neofeudalist actors, seeking to seduce stakeholders into believing their hyperbolic rhetoric, hence acting unethically as judged by a Kantian categorical imperative ethical standards, while in reality pursuing a self-promoting, self-interested agenda. However, from an egoist position, pursuing a self-interested, 'good for us' agenda can at the same time be seen as ethically legitimate.

Looking at what has been written and said about professional coaching bodies, it is difficult to draw a clear and unambiguous conclusion to which of these positions reflects the current reality. Both positions are plausible. What is clear is that all professional bodies have attempted to position themselves to provide clarity in relation to the so-called 'wild west' of coaching before professional bodies were formed and express this with confidence and strong assertion. This itself can be criticised; as Bertrand Russell (2009, p. 204), the philosopher, wrote, *"The stupid are cocksure and the intelligent are full of doubt"* and *"Everything is vague to a degree you do not realize till you have tried to make it precise"* (Russell, 1998, p. 38). It is also clear that the professional bodies do seem to have moved down the *'make it precise route'* and seem intolerant of the complexity found within coaching, particularly with reference to ethics. This can be seen as evidence of the neofeudalistic discourse in action. However, it can be seen as an attempt to provide some measure of quality assurance for coaching clients as they search for a good fit for them in the coaching marketplace.

Conclusion

Depending on one's ethical standpoint, it can be argued that the professional bodies are the moral guardians, charged with upholding the ethical standards of coaching suppliers and consumers within the market. Certainly, this is how they would like to be positioned. However, they could be viewed as self-interested actors who ensure the restriction of supply of coaching thus making it possible to raise the market price and therefore the value to the beneficiaries of the bodies. Additionally, professional bodies could be seen as the neofeudalists, dominating the market for their own commercial and ethical interests. Some professional bodies also position themselves as providing the professional development of coaches and most accredit coaches. This approach is potentially flooding the market with coaches without expanding the demand for it. This, with other things being equal, might serve to lower the market price for coaching and perhaps make it more accessible to more clients.

What is also clear to us is that the professional body rhetoric coming from all professional bodies that we have experienced is relatively unsophisticated in terms of ethical theory. Ethical theory and definitions of ethical stance, approach and impact are vague, broad and lacking support from empirical data. The professional bodies remain relatively mute on their own ethical stances and seem to prefer instead to articulate professional standards for their members. While understandable from a practical point of view, relying only on written ethical codes of practice, which are largely context-free, does not necessarily help members resolve their ethical dilemmas and therefore casts doubt on the bodies' ability to act as moral guardians of ethical coaching standards. Rather, it lends weight to the neufeudalist tag, particularly when coupled with attempts to differentiate one's own professional body from others. As we have argued above, buying into a framework, like that of Carroll & Shaw (2013), which enables individuals to engage with their own practice by drawing on the broader contextual factors helps to develop a more nuanced notion of ethical maturity. Furthermore, by engaging actively and transparently with ethical theory, coaching professional bodies are much more likely to be enacting the moral guardian role that they espouse by role modelling the practice in their written discourses.

Discussion points

1. What ethical stance should professional bodies take up in relation to their ethical statements?
2. What responsibility do professional bodies have to act as the guardian of ethical standards?
3. To what extent can it be ethical for professional bodies to act in their own self-interest and those of its members?
4. How might coaching professional bodies support people who wish to move towards ethical maturity in their coaching practice?

Recommended reading

Carroll, M. & Shaw, E. (2013). Organisations, context, ethics and maturity. In Carroll, M. and Shaw, E. *Ethical Maturity in the Helping Professions: Making Difficult Life and Work Decisions*. London: Jessica Kingsley, p. 297.

References

Action for Children. (2021). www.actionforchildren.org.uk/blog/where-is-child-poverty-increasing-in-the-uk/#:~:text=Even%20before%20the%20pandemic%2C%204.3,child%20poverty%20data%20in%202021, accessed April 11, 2022.
Arnaud G. (2003) A Coach or a Couch? A Lacanian Perspective on Executive Coaching and Consulting. *Human Relations*, 256(9): 1131–1154.
Arnaud, G. (2007) Poweract and Organizational work: Gerard Mendel's socio-psychoanalysis. *Organization Studies*, 28(3):409–428.
Bentham, J. & Mills, S., (Ed. A. Ryan) (1987) *Utilitarianism and Other Essays*. St Ives: Penguin Classics.
Carroll, M. & Shaw, E. (2013) *Ethical Maturity in the Helping Professions: Making Difficult Life and Work Decisions*. London: Jessica Kingsley.
Coaching York. (2022) https://coachingyork.co.uk, accessed April 11, 2022.
Connor, M. & Pokora, J. (2012) *Coaching and Mentoring at Work: Developing Effective Practice*. Maidenhead: McGraw-Hill.

Coaching Reading. (2022) https://coachingreading.org, accessed April 11, 2022.

Corrie, S. & Lane, D. (2015) *CBT Supervision*. London: Sage Publications.

Cox, E., Bachkirova, T., & Clutterbuck, D. (Eds) (2014) *The Complete Handbook of Coaching*, 2nd Edition. London: Sage Publications.

De Cremer, D., van Dick, R., Tenbrunsel, A., Pillutla, M., & Murnighan, J. K. (2010) Understanding Ethical Behaviour and Decision Making in Management: A Behavioural Business Ethics Approach. *British Journal of Management*, 22 (Special Issue).

De Haan, E. & Gannon, J., 2017. *The coaching relationship*. In: T. Bachkirova, G. Spence, & D. Drake (Eds), *The SAGE handbook of coaching*, pp. 195–217.

Du Toit, A. (2014) *Making Sense of Coaching*. London: Sage Publications.

EMCC Global. Code of Ethics. (2021) https://emccuk.org/Common/Uploaded%20files/Policies/Global_Code_of_Ethics_EN_v3.pdf.

EMCC Global. (2022a) www.emccglobal.org/accreditation/eia, accessed April 10, 2022.

EMCC Global. (2022b) www.emccglobal.org/leadership-development/competences accessed April 11, 2022.

Fillery-Travis and Collins. (2017) Discipline, Profession and Industry: How or choices Shape our Future. In *The SAGE Handbook of Coaching*, T. Bachkirova, G. Spence, & D. DrakeLondon: Sage Publications.

Foucault, M. (1977) Discipline and Punish: The Birth of the Prison. In Foucault, M. (2020) *Discipline and Punish: The Birth of the Prison*, translated by Alan Sheridan, London: Penguin Classics.

Garvey, B. (2011) *A Very Short, Slightly Interesting and Reasonably Cheap Book on Coaching and Mentoring*. London: Sage Publications.

Gray, D., (2011) Journeys towards the professionalisation of coaching: dilemmas, dialogues and decisions along the global pathway. *Coaching: An International Journal of Theory, Research and Practice* 4(1): 4–19.

Gray, D., Garvey, B., & Lane, D. (2016) *A critical introduction to coaching and mentoring: Debates, dialogues and discourses*. Sage Publications.

Hawkins, P. & Shohet, R. (2006) *Supervision in the Helping Professions*, 3rd Edition. Maidenhead: Open University Press.

Hawkins, P. & Turner, E., (2020) *Systemic Coaching: Delivering Value Beyond the Individual*. Abingdon: Routledge.

House of Commons Library. (2022) https://commonslibrary.parliament.uk/research-briefings/cbp-8585/#:~:text=Both%20the%20number%20of%20food,over%20900%20independent%20food%20banks, accessed April 11, 2022.

How Much. (2022) https://rtt.com/how-much-should-i-charge-for-coaching/#:~:text=-for%20coaching%E2%80%9D%20exactly%3F-,Hourly%2DBased%20vs%20Value%2DBased%20Pricing,but%20more%20on%20this%20later, accessed April 10, 2022.

Hutton, W. (1997) *The State to Come*. London: Vintage.

International Coaching Federation. ICF Code of Ethics. (2021) https://coachingfederation.org/app/uploads/2021/01/ICF-Code-of-Ethics-1.pdf.

International Coaching Federation. (2022) https://coachingfederation.org/about/our-values, accessed April 11, 2022.

Lasch, C. (1995) *The Revolt of the Elites and Betrayal of Democracy*. New York: Norton.

Lowman, R. L. (2005). Executive Coaching: The Road to Dodoville Needs Paving With More Than Good Assumptions. *Consulting Psychology Journal: Practice and Research*, 57(1): 90–96.

Lowman, R. L. (2013). Coaching ethics. In J. Passmore, D. B. Peterson, & T. Freire (Eds), *The Wiley-Blackwell handbook of the psychology of coaching and mentoring* . Wiley Blackwell, pp. 68–88.

Morris, B. & Tarpley, N. A., (2000) So You're a Player, Do You Need a Coach? *Fortune*, 141(4).

Nielsen, A. E. & Nørreklit, H. (2009) A discourse analysis of the disciplinary power of management coaching. *Society and Business Review*, 4(3): 202–214.

Parsloe, E. & Leedham, M. (2009) *Coaching and Mentoring: Practical Conversations to Improve Learning*. London: Kogan Page.

Rogers, J. (2012) *Coaching Skills: A Handbook*, 2nd Edition. Milton Keynes: Open University Press.

Rosinski, P. (2004) *Coaching across Cultures*. London: Nicholas Brealey.

Russell, B. (1928) *Sceptical Essays*. London: George Allen & Unwin.

Russell, B. (1998) *The Philosophy of Logical Atomism* (reprint). La Salle, IL: Open Court.

Russell, B. (2009) *Mortals and Others: American Essays 1931–1935* (reprint). Abingdon: Routledge.

Saul, J. R. (1997) *The Unconscious Civilization*. Ringwood: Penguin.

Schwartz, M. (2000) Why Ethical Codes Constitute an Unconscious Regression. *Journal of Business Ethics*, 23: 173–184.

Shearing, C. (2001) Punishment and the Changing Face of the Governance. *Punishment & Society*, 3(2): 203–220.

Sherman, S. and Freas, A. (2004) *The Wild West of executive coaching. Harvard Business Review*, 82(11): 82–90.

Smith, T. (2006) *Ayn Rand's Normative Ethics: The Virtuous Egoist*, Cambridge: Cambridge University Press.

Sullivan, R. J., (2008) *An Introduction to Kant's Ethics*. Cambridge: Cambridge University Press.

Tenbrunsel, A. E. & Messick, D.M. (2004) Ethical fading: the role of self-deception in unethical behavior. *Social Justice Research*, 17, pp. 223–236.

Western, S. (2012) *Coaching and Mentoring: A Critical Text*. London: Sage Publications.

Whitmore, J. (2002) *Coaching for Performance: GROWing People, Performance and Purpose*, 3rd edition. London: Nicholas Brealey.

Whitmore, J. (2009) *Coaching for Performance: Growing Human Potential and Purpose*, 4th Edition. London: Nicholas Brealey.

Wood, A. E. (2008) *Kantian Ethics*, Cambridge: Cambridge University Press.

Chapter 4

Exploring ethical codes

Paul Stokes, Angela Hill and Kristin Kelly

Introduction

Following the advent of coaching professional bodies, there has come with them a concern with defining what constitutes professional coaching practice (see Chapter 3 of this volume for a fuller discussion of the role professional bodies take up generally in relation to ethics). From this has come a desire to generate codes of ethics which are used by the professional bodies to a) provide guidance about what constitutes ethical behaviour within coaching practice; and b) to assist members and other stakeholders (e.g., clients, sponsoring organisations). Arguably, professional bodies seek to position themselves as significant players in determining who can enter the coaching profession. This is done to reduce the volume of unregulated activity and thereby increasing the quality of services to clients. They achieve this by seeking to accredit training courses and other qualifications against their own professional standards. They also do this by developing codes of ethics which articulate expected standards of behaviour and practice by coaches. It is therefore important to look critically at these ethical codes and to understand how they have come into being, what the intent was in establishing them and what their impact might be on coaches who try to use them. Following this, it is then possible to critically examine the role of ethical codes in relation to ethical practice within coaching.

Are ethical codes relevant?

Most professional bodies have some sort of ethical code of practice which they publish via their websites and which they expect members to engage with. This is no different with coaching professional bodies. However, in their text, focusing on value and ethics in coaching, Iordanou, Hawley and Iordanou (2017, p. 1) raise the very pertinent question of the utility of such codes:

> "Can a well-defined list of explicit guidelines cater for the diversity of people and, in consequence, ethical issues that coaches encounter in their daily coaching practice?"

DOI: 10.4324/9781003277729-4

In other words, it raises the question of how useful ethical codes are to coaches and to other stakeholders in the coaching process. Others have raised this question in the past. For example, Fatien Diochon and Nizet (2015) undertook some research to investigate how ethical codes are applied to ethical dilemmas that coaches face. They used a qualitative research methodology, based on a social construction approach (Berger & Luckman, 1966), and interviewed 27 certified French executive coaches about their use of ethical codes in relation to ethical dilemmas they faced. They conducted the interviews using a critical incident methodology (Flanagan, 1954) and analysed the results thematically. Essentially, what Fatien Diochon and Nizet (2015, p. 278) found was that their results "confirm that reading and applying the code is rarely enough to solve an ethical dilemma". These challenges with using ethical codes were grouped into three main categories:

1. The code was not relevant
2. The code has 'shortcomings' itself
3. The code was an 'obstacle' to the ethics of the coach.

They then go on to explore these challenges across four different levels: micro (both interpersonal and intrapersonal challenges), meso level (organisational) and macro (societal level). In terms of the three categories above, their interview data reveals that, for some ethical dilemmas (e.g., an organisation pushing their coaching client to perform to the point of exhaustion), the code does not cover such an issue (not relevant). Instead, the coaches tended to use supervision or other people as sounding boards for dealing with this. In other cases, the interviewed coaches found that ethical codes did not fully articulate the processes required in order to comply with their ethical obligations (e.g., consulting with other qualified people) or felt the code failed to give a practical course of action for the coach to take (code shortcomings). Finally, a number of the coaches pointed to examples of where the coach feels compelled to act in defence of their client or pay attention to their own values which directly contradicts the position of neutrality or confidentiality advised in the code. One example would be advising a client to protect themselves legally against the actions of their line manager, another would be working for a nuclear energy company where the coach holds strong environmental objections. In all these examples cited by Fatien Diochon and Nizet (2015), the coaches interviewed in this piece of research were raising questions about how they should be expected to use ethical codes and, arguably, what the intent of the coaching professional body was when raising these.

In summary, it is important to engage with ethical codes in a critically reflexive way, because, as some commentators and researchers have shown, it is not necessarily clear how ethical codes should be used and related to that, how professional bodies intended that they should be used. In order to explore that, we will begin by briefly summarising the historical development of two ethical codes of practice – the Global Code of Ethics (GCoE:2021), driven by the European Mentoring and Coaching Council (EMCC), and the International Coaching Federation (ICF: 2020) code of ethics. There are many other coaching professional bodies in existence, each of which have their own ethical codes of practice, for example:

- Association for Coaching
- Division of Coaching Psychology, British Psychological Society
- Association for Professional Executive Coaching and Supervision
- Association of Corporate Executive Coaches
- International Association of Coaching
- The International Authority for Professional Coaching and Mentoring
- Asia-Pacific Coaching Alliance
- Coaches and Mentors of South Africa

Whilst a systematic review of all these codes could have been undertaken, this is not the primary intent of the chapter. Rather, this chapter is to shed light on the way in which ethical codes might be used by coaches in their practice and so the authors have chosen to selectively focus on two ethical codes. It is anticipated that the two codes chosen to focus on are those that most readers of this text will have seen and have engaged with at some level because of the scope and scale of the professional bodies who developed them.

These accounts will offer insight into the origins, intent and development of these codes from those that developed them. Following the presentation of these histories, an integrated thematic analysis will be presented, which critically examines these codes.

The Global Code of Ethics – Angela Hill

Origins

In July 2008 a gathering took place in Dublin. It was a mid-point in a series of international dialogues on the future vision and development needs of the emerging coaching profession. At a time of acute global economic crisis, a community of engaged, inspired and diverse coaches from 16 countries (source Global Community of Coaches Dublin Declaration Including Appendices Version 1.3, August 22, 2008) found common ground to articulate a shared vision for future growth and self-regulation.

This was a unique collaboration of professional coaches, coaching bodies, coaching service providers, academics and thought leaders with experience in different cultures and social contexts. The Appreciative Inquiry structure of Discovery, Dream, Desire, Deliver was used to examine many aspects of coaching practice and envision developments including standards to take the profession forward.

The seeds for the Global Code of Ethics (GCoE) for coaching and its ongoing development took root from here. At Dublin there was consensus on the value of having 'a strong, universal code of ethics' with support and practical techniques to raise ethical awareness and savvy across all coaching activities. It was acknowledged that there could not be predetermined answers for all ethical challenges. Therefore, the code needs to be dynamic across diverse contexts, balancing what was said with what was left unsaid. It needed to create space for emergent issues, meaning, values and beliefs to be explored as a way of expanding ethical consciousness.

Intent

The GCoE was intended to serve the coaching practitioner, mentor or supervisor and their clients' needs. It is intended as a framework or guide to quality service and is renewed on a regular basis. The current version (GCoE, V3 June, 2021) is structured around working with clients: set up or contracting, integrity, clarity of purpose, confidentiality and managed endings. Ethical principles embedded in the code include:

- Integrity
- Autonomy
- Respect for difference
- Professional conduct
- Responsibility

The GCoE (2021) has been expanded for different contexts and client range: in-house and external coaching, mentoring and supervision as well as increased use of Artificial Intelligence (AI) and digitalisation in coaching. Refinement that is still 'work in progress' and part of sustaining the code's relevance to the opportunities and challenges practitioners and clients may have.

The GCoE, as many other codes, is built on a universal commonality of understanding what is 'good' in our dealings with others e.g. To do no harm; Honesty; Accountability. For clients, sponsors and practitioners, the code is a touchstone before, during and after service delivery. It is not a rule book or instruction manual based on 'shoulds'. Other activities are encouraged and used in support of good practice and ethical behaviour: critical reflection; supervision; evaluation and feedback; leadership; continuing professional development (CPD); accreditation and an independent complaints process.

The GCoE will not by design provide all the answers but can act as a moral compass to help coaches reorientate to what may be the best course of action. The decision taken after that, and any consequences remain with the individual.

Development

The forward vision for the growth and development of coaching in 2008 anticipated societal change and very different potential contexts for coaching and opportunities from increased use of technology, including AI. Intended at the beginning of a universal code of ethics in coaching were endings and renewal with practitioners, clients and academic research individually and collectively contributing to ongoing relevance and value.

Following on from Dublin an ethics workgroup (EMCC, Association for Coaching [AC] and ICF and other thought leaders) consulted with members, clients and others to construct a best practice framework as an ethical guide through the coaching process. In 2016 the Global Code of Ethics (GCoE) was launched and signed by EMCC and AC. At the time of writing the GCoE had ten code signatories, some have their own code of ethics, some are specialists in mentoring, executive and business coaching; supervision; academia, high-level public sector or start-ups. The GCoE is available in 17 different languages. Recent additions include references to confidentiality and ownership of data, safeguarding, unconscious bias, systemic injustice and climate change.

The International Coaching Federation Code of Ethics – Kristin Kelly

Origins

An ICF Ethics Pledge was first created in 1997, two years after the ICF (then International Coach Federation) was founded and contained the following categories: honour the coach-client agreement, respect my limits, conflicts of interest, confidentiality, be respectful and constructive, be coachable, be professional, maintain professional distance, and be a model (Brock, 2008, pp. 226–227).

In 1998 the International Coaching Federation (ICF) merged with the Professional and Personal Coaches Association (PPCA). The PPCA entered the merger with numerous ethics and standards materials that would pave the way for the ICF to help regulate the profession and establish ethics by the late 1990s (Brock, 2008, pp. 226–227).

The ICF Ethical Guidelines were approved in August 1998 and contained the categories of coaching relationship and contract, client protection, confidentiality, conflicts of interest, referrals and terminations, and ethical violations (Brock 2008, pp. 226–227).

From this, the ICF Ethics Code was first published in 2000. The original code was created to promote professional and ethical coaching practices, and to raise the awareness of the public about the integrity, commitment, and ethical conduct of ICF Members and ICF Credential-holders.

The ICF Code was revised multiple times in the early 2000s, with the first revision happening in 2002. The purpose behind these updates was further clarification of their philosophy and definition of coaching. ICF members pledge to uphold this philosophy and the standards outlined in the code of ethics. During a 2003 code review, it was decided to group the standards of the code into four major areas: *professional conduct at large, professional conduct with clients, confidentiality/privacy,* and *conflicts of interest* (Brock, 2008, pp. 226–227). An extensive code review took place in 2004 and involved reviewing other organisation's codes and adding 12 new standards to create a more comprehensive and specific code, offering ICF Coaches greater guidance in their professional conduct.

In addition, the early 2000s saw the creation of an Ethics Committee, and later the Independent Review Board (IRB) to review ethical conduct of ICF Coaches. ICF is committed to providing a forum where individuals can bring complaints about alleged breaches of the ICF code by ICF members and credential-holders. The IRB oversees ICF's Ethical Conduct Review process. ICF is committed to providing a forum where individuals can bring complaints about alleged breaches of the code of ethics by ICF Members and credential-holders. Over time, ICF adopted a policy and set of procedures that provide for review of, investigation of and response to alleged unethical practices or behaviour deviating from the Code of ethics.

Intent

It's important to note that over time, the ICF's philosophy of its code of ethics and its application has shifted significantly. Initially, the ICF ethics philosophy was punitive in nature and rules-focused, 'as an ICF Coach, you must…'. However, over the last twenty years, this philosophy has gradually evolved into more of an expectation of professional conduct and behaviour. What was once a set of strict rules has evolved into guidelines of behavior for ICF Professionals, truly a way of *being* for every ICF professional. The ICF Code of Ethics is based on the ICF core values of:

- Professionalism
- Collaboration
- Humanity
- Equity

They being the foundation of the ethical principles and ethical standards of behavior for all *ICF Professionals.* The standards are divided into four major areas: Responsibility to Clients, Responsibility to Practice and Performance, Responsibility to Professionalism, and Responsibility to Society. The Code concludes with a Pledge of Ethics. Demonstration of ethical practice is also the first of ICF Core Coaching Competencies, giving the code importance and significance.

The ICF Code of Ethics serves to uphold the integrity of ICF and the global coaching profession by:

- Setting standards of conduct consistent with ICF core values and ethical principles;
- Guiding ethical reflection, education, and decision-making;
- Adjudicating and preserving ICF standards through the ICF Ethical Conduct Review process;
- Providing the basis for ICF ethics training in ICF-accredited programmes;
- Serving as a guide for developing continuing education in ethics, necessary for renewal of ICF Credentials.

Development

An *ICF Code Review Team* comprised of ICF Professionals – specifically from a variety of backgrounds, geographic locations and covering as many languages as possible. For reference, the most recent ICF Code Review took place over an 18-month period between 2018 and 2019 and included ICF Professionals from 16 different countries, cultures and backgrounds.

Depending on the revisions needed, the code review may be minor (edits, language updates) or more extensive (involving a complete review of each standard and how it should be revised or updated). The code review ensures the ICF organisational values are reflected throughout the code standards, that today's issues in coaching ethics are touched upon, and the code is as clear and concise as possible. Likewise, ICF finds it imperative that the code review emphasises language and word choice throughout the code of ethics.

At the time of writing, the most recent version of the ICF Code of Ethics was approved by the ICF Global Board of Directors in late 2019 and went into effect on January 1, 2020.

Thematic analysis

Looking at the preceding accounts, there are four key themes that can be drawn from these. These themes will be explored in turn with a comparison and contrast of the GCoE (2021) and the ICF (2020).

Acting ethically at a macro-societal level

In Fatien Diochon and Nizet's (2015) terms, there are parts of both codes which seem to be aimed at a macro-societal level. The intent of the developers of both codes, as suggested by their accounts above, seems to have been to generate a 'touchstone' for a range of coaching stakeholders – coaches, mentors, coachees, sponsors and supervisors – to refer to when seeking to assess their own actions (and those of others) in ethical terms. For example, in the

ICF code of ethics (2021, p. 6), reference is made to the importance of the coach being aware of 'my and my clients' impact on society" and "adhering to the philosophy of "doing good" versus "avoiding bad.". Similarly, the GCoE (2021, p. 7) makes reference to the requirement that "members will abide by their respective bodies' statements and policies on inclusion, diversity, social responsibility and climate change".

There do seem to be some assumptions embedded in the generation of the codes that are worth challenging and exploring. For example, it almost seems to be an axiom to say that there are universal ethical values around honesty and 'doing good' and, indeed, on the face of these, there is little to argue with. However, when the issues of context and values are introduced, this becomes more complicated. Is it always possible to do good in a universal sense without impacting on someone else's interest particularly within an organisational context? It may make sense to ask, 'doing good for whom'? The following vignette raises this question.

Application

A coach seeking to act ethically would need to consider the impact of their own interventions on wider society. For example, during the recent Covid-19 pandemic, and resulting challenges to ways in which people view their life and work, a coach could conceive of 'doing good' in ICF's terms, as offering pro-bono coaching to groups of people who may otherwise be excluded. This also seems to fit with the GCoE (2021) in terms of diversity and inclusion. However, is this offer only available to coaches who can afford to offer their services for free and does it militate against other coaches who cannot afford to do so?

Consider the following questions:

How might doing good be measured in ethical terms?
What ethical responsibilities do coaches have in terms of making coaching more inclusive?
What should ethical codes contain in order to articulate the ethical reach of coaches?

Furthermore, it could be argued that, by bringing in societal constructs such as climate change and inclusion, both bodies are raising concerns that are beyond their direct sphere of influence (Covey, 1989) as professional bodies. Implicit in the inclusion of these things is a tacit theory of ethics and of ethical behaviour – this will be explored in a later theme in this chapter.

Resolving ethical dilemmas

A key issue to consider with ethical codes is how they help coaches recognise and deal with ethical dilemmas that come up in their practice. What is noticeable about both codes is that in neither case do they offer prescriptive, rule based specific advice on how to deal with such ethical dilemmas. Instead, they both seem to stipulate values that they expect members to adhere to. For example, in ICF (2020, p. 6), there is a clear stipulation that an ICF coach should 'not participate in any sexual or romantic engagement with Client(s) or Sponsor(s)', should be 'ever mindful of the level of intimacy appropriate for the relationship' and should 'take the appropriate action to address the issue or cancel the engagement'. Similarly, the GCoE (2021, p. 6) states that "Members will strictly avoid pursuing and refrain from engaging in any romantic or sexual relationships with current clients or sponsors". However, both codes refrain from offering help and advice as to how to take the appropriate action in ethical terms, other than to terminate the coaching relationship.

Furthermore, it is expected that other mechanisms - critical reflection; supervision; evaluation and feedback; leadership, CPD; accreditation and an independent complaints process – are used by individuals to enable them to address and resolve ethical dilemmas. These other mechanisms may go some way to mitigating Fatien Diochon and Nizet's (2015)'s critique around code shortcomings i.e., the code was never intended to provide such a practical guide. Nevertheless, both codes are susceptible to the critique of *how* they might be used in conjunction with the aforementioned other mechanisms. What happens if these different mechanisms yield different answers from each other, for example? It is not clear from each code how individuals might integrate and reconcile these different modes of ethical guidance.

Application

In coaching contracting, reference is often made to the importance of a 'chemistry meeting', intended to establish whether there are sufficient grounds for a fruitful relationship. Also, much emphasis is placed on the relationship as the key vehicle through which help and support is offered. However, a coach needs help in being sensitive as to when such relationships become too intense and run the risk of moving into romantic/sexual relationships.

Consider the following questions:

What might be the things to look for in terms of being aware of the risk of ethical breach?
What role does the professional body play in these considerations?

In other words, the above vignette suggests that coaches may need to develop their ethical sensitivity so that they are able to notice when they may be moving towards behaviour that, by some, may be deemed unethical. What is not clear is what role ethical codes should and do play in this. Fatien Diochon and Nizet's (2015) research suggests that the coaches they spoke to struggled to use ethical codes in this way.

Lack of overt ethical theory in codes

Despite both codes being referred to as ethical codes, there is not an overt theory/ theory of ethics that runs through either framework. Both codes refer to acting ethically but neither seem to acknowledge that the same behaviours may be deemed either ethical or unethical depending on what theory of ethics is used. For example, ICF (2021, p. 2) states: "ICF Professionals who accept the Code of Ethics strive to be **ethical**, even when doing so involves making difficult decisions or acting courageously" (emphasis added). The implication is that we all know ethical behaviour when we see it because we are using the same criteria to assess that behaviour. We contest that assumption, owing to the existence of ethical theories such as utilitarian, Kantian and Egoist theories (Ioardannu et al., 2017) which have different and competing criteria for saying what is ethical. Likewise, where the GCoE (2021, p. 7) discusses the management of data, it asserts that members are responsible for the "maintenance of confidentiality of all information in relation to clients and sponsors with careful and **ethical** management of confidential, personal, or other data" (emphasis added). Again, at this point in the code, what constitutes 'ethical' is not explicitly theorised.

Both codes seem to suggest that, by engaging in critical reflexivity e, g. through supervision, CPD, etc., the individual coach will arrive at the 'correct' ethical decision. However, it could be argued that there are several outcomes that might be deemed 'correct' depending on what theory is adopted; for example, it can be seen to be ethical if you act purely in your own self-interest if the egoist ethical position is taken up (Rothstein, 2022). As articulated above, ethical codes were designed to work as moral compasses for those wrestling with ethical dilemmas. However, if a clear ethical position is not embedded and articulated within it, plus, the intent is to make the code 'flexible and dynamic' (for understandable reasons), then there is a risk of adopting a moral relativist position. This is where any course of action might be justified based on an individual's moral code and personal values. Whilst, for instance, the GCoE (2021) does articulate some core principles, individual engagement with what this means for the individual seems to be expected and encouraged. This porosity is to be expected in a code which has several organisational signatories, and which is intended to be 'universal', because it enables a larger number of people to engage with it. At the same time, though, this approach runs the risk of lacking relevance (another issue identified by Fatien Diochon and Nizet, 2015) because of the removal of context from the code and, owing to the various signatory bodies developing their own code of ethics for their coaching practitioners. By definition, contextualisation narrows, excludes and focuses the code and locates it somewhere more specific, which clearly works in opposition to the idea of being inclusive and universal in intent.

Application

In most coach development programmes, coaches are expected to reflect on their own values and, by being clear about those, decide to whom and where they offer their coaching services. A coach who cannot see their own values embedded clearly within a code of ethics, or where they can see a set of values that run contrary to their own, is unlikely to see such codes as being practically useful to them, particularly.

Consider the following questions:

What should coach training providers do to encourage reflexive engagement with ethical codes?
How might coaches resolve any tensions between their own values and those they see presented in ethical codes?

In other words, the above vignette suggests that without an overt exploration of ethical theory underpinning ethical codes, it makes it difficult for individual coaches to be able to use them as the original developers had intended. Those who wrote the ethical codes may have been concerned with making sure that the codes were practical and applicable, as opposed to theoretical and abstract. However, to adapt a phrase attributed to the psychologist, Kurt Lewin (Greenwood & Levin, 1998), there is nothing as practical as a good theory. Therefore, if the ethical theory being used has sufficient explanatory power and can be usefully applied to communicating key ethical values, it is difficult to see the counter-argument for not embedding ethical theory in ethical codes in coaching. Extending this logic further, it can be argued that coach training providers need to spend more time helping learners interrogate ethical codes using ethical theory. As Biquet (2022) argues, using ethical cases as part of this training may help developing coaches to identify their own reflexive processes. We explore this concept of ethical maturity below.

Ethical development and maturity

As we argued throughout, there are several similarities between the two codes of ethics examined. In both cases, there is clearly a long history of engaging with ethical issues in the case of ICF (2021), this goes back almost 30 years. In both codes, there is a clear emphasis on micro concepts around coaching relationships and contracts, client protection, confidentiality, conflicts of interest, referrals and terminations, and ethical violations. Similar also is the emphasis on moving away from a rules-based system, based on sanctions when rules are breached – to one which focuses on a set of values and guidelines of behavior. What appears slightly different, however, is the ICF's (2020) commitment to providing guidance on how to engage in ethical reflection, education and decision-making. This inclusion seems to have the potential to offer a way forward in terms of the challenges to using ethical codes posed by Fatien Diochon and Nizet's (2015) respondents in their research cited above.

Application

A coach who wishes to move towards ethical maturity will need to engage with their own critical reflexivity processes in terms of the assumptions and choices they make about their coaching practice. This is particularly the case when coaching someone who may seem to have different values and beliefs to theirs. If a coach aspires to create authentic, honest and transparent relationships with their clients, it is first important for them to decide what those terms mean for them.

Consider the following questions:

What is the best process for engaging in ethical reflexivity as a coach?
How will the coach know if they have established authentic, honest and transparent relationships with their clients?

It is not completely clear how this ethically reflective process will be achieved. Mention is made of the credentialing/accreditation programme as well as customised learning plans when breach occurs but there is not a clearly stated process of proactive ethical education. Whilst the standards and ethically reflective statements (supported by toolkits for members such as Association for Coaching, 2022) do seem to offer a steer in terms of expected values and behaviours, they do not seem to offer a clear process for reflexively engaging with the coach's own ethical values and framework. Carroll and Shaw's, (2013) framework does offer an example of such a framework. For example, when looking at the ICF values underpinning this, signatories are expected to show humanity by creating authentic relationships that support honesty, transparency and clarity. Whilst on the face of it, there would be few people who would disagree with these values – it is difficult to imagine anyone working in coaching wanting to see inauthentic relationships which support dishonesty, a lack of transparency and lack of clarity – such statements do not in of themselves provide help as to what such things look like in practice when we see them. Stripped of this context, they do not currently provide guidance as to how such behaviours and values might be enacted. As we argued above, this is critical when coaches experience a disconnect between their own personal values and those seeming to be required of them by the system (organisational or otherwise) that they find themselves engaging with. That said, what is also interesting about the ICF process is that there is clearly an ongoing process to refine and challenge the ethical codes that have been agreed via a multi-agency group across several countries and languages for it to be a living document. Ethical codes may be able to help with the decision-making approach but need to have embedded within them a process for how to use and engage with them in an ongoing and reflexive way.

Conclusion

What seems to be common to both codes is that it is important that individuals themselves engage reflexively with ethics in coaching. Both articulations of the code here reject the idea of a prescriptive, rule based contingent set of guidance and instead appear to advocate for ethical codes and statements as being a touchstone for ethical practice and guidance. They both also seem to emphasise the importance of personal reflexivity in relation to the coach's ethical practices. Iordanou, Hawley and Iordanou (2017, p. 96) explore the idea of such reflexivity in their text on values and ethics in coaching. They argue that the defining features of such reflexivity are that it is:

- "a conscious and cognitive process
- a combination of knowledge, theory and questioning applied to ethical issues we encounter to generate new meaning
- a process that encourages us to question who we are in coaching relationship
- something that can help us challenge and let go of basic assumptions and to enable changes in attitude and behaviour"

What is noticeable about both sets of codes is their lack of engagement with theory, in particular ethical theory. Clearly, this may partly be to do with perceptions as to the receptiveness of the intended professional audience for the codes, who may be put off by theoretical constructs. However, if the aspiration is to enable those who engage with the codes to move towards ethical maturity, as Iordanou, Hawley and Iordanou (2017) call it, then it seems incumbent on the developers and writers of both codes to make the theory accessible and useful to those who need to engage with it. Importantly, this also has implications for coach education (explored further in Chapter 17 of this volume) in terms of what ethical education needs to take place on coaching courses to ensure that novice and developing coaches have the necessary knowledge, theory and questioning insight to enable their own ethical development. Of course, as we point out above there are existing mechanisms for this such as coach supervision. However, articulation of codes of conduct from professional bodies could, as both codes acknowledge, provide guidance and support as to how to proactively engage with these issues as opposed to only dealing with them when an ethical breach has occurred. We, the authors, argue that it is only by signposting the 'what' and the 'how' of this process, that participants in coaching relationships can properly orientate themselves towards ethical maturity.

Discussion points

1. What guidance needs to be in place to help coaching participants understand how they might engage with ethical practice?
2. What ethical theories need to be embedded into Codes of Ethics, if any?
3. What does ethical maturity look like and how might these be enabled, using codes?
4. How will we know if we are engaging reflexively with coaching ethics?

Recommended reading

Fatien Diochon, P. & Nizet, J. (2015) Ethical Codes and Executive Coaches: One Size Does Not Fit All. *The Journal of Applied Behavioural Science*, 51(2): 277–301.

References

Association for Coaching. (2022) Ethical Supervision Resources. www.associationfor coaching.com/page/ethicalsupervisionresources, accessed August 26, 2022.

Berger, P. & Luckmann, T. (1966) *The Social Construction of Reality: A Treatise in the sociology of Knowledge*. Garden City, NY: Anchor Books.

Biquet, M. (2022). Ethical Dilemmas in Coaching Today. https://the-goodcoach.com/tgcblog/2021/9/6/ethical-dilemmas-in-coaching-today-by-maria-biquet#:~:text= Coaches%20have%20dilemmas%20about%20their,with%20the%20support%20of% 20supervision, accessed August 26, 2022.

Brock, V. (2008) Grounded Theory of the Roots and Emergence of Coaching. Doctoral Thesis, International University of Professional Studies. https://libraryofprofes sionalcoaching.com/wp-app/wp-content/uploads/2011/10/dissertation.pdf.

Carroll, M. & Shaw, E. (2013) *Ethical Maturity in the Helping Professions: Making Difficult Life and Work Decisions*. London: Jessica Kingsley.

Covey, S. (1989) *The 7 Habits of Highly Effective People*. New York: Free Press.

Fatien Diochon, P. & Nizet, J. (2019) Ethics as a Fabric: An Emotional Reflexive Sensemaking Process. *Business Ethics Quarterly*, 29(4): 461–489.

Global Code of Ethics. (2021) Retrieved July 27, 2022 from www.globalcodeofethics.org.

ICF Code of Ethics. (2020). International Coaching Federation. Retrieved July 12, 2022, from https://coachingfederation.org/ethics/code-of-ethics.

Iordanou, I., Hawley, R., & Iordanou, C. (2017) *Values and Ethics in Coaching*. London: Sage Publications.

Fatien Diochon, P. & Nizet, J. (2015) Ethical Codes and Executive Coaches: One Size Does Not Fit All. *The Journal of Applied Behavioural Science*, 51(2): 277–301.

Flanagan, J. (1954) "The critical incident technique". *Psychology Bulletin*, 51(4): 1–33.

Greenwood, D. J. & Levin, M. (1998). *Introduction to action research: Social research for socialchange.* Thousand Oaks, CA: Sage Publications.

Nizet, J., Fatien Diochon, P., & Nair, L.B. (2021) *'When Commitments Conflict: Making Ethical Decisions Like a Funambulist, M@n@gement,* 24(1): 44–48. doi:10.37725/mgmt.v24i1.4497.

Rothstein, J. K. (2022) *'Egoism and the Limits of Ethics' Journal of Mental Health & Social Behaviour,* 4(1): 161. doi:10.33790/jmhsb1100161.

Mooney, P (2008) Final Edit Including Appendices *Versi*on 1.3, 22nd August 2008. Global Community of Coaches Dublin Declaration. https://researchportal.coachfederation.org/Document/Pdf/598.pdf, accessed August 26, 2022.

Chapter 5

Ethical decision-making frameworks

Jonathan Passmore and Jule Deges

Introduction

Reminding us of the much-celebrated movie *Love Actually*, in which nine intertwined storylines invite the viewer to contemplate the complexities of love, Hawkins and Turner note that much like in the movie, where 'love is all around', "ethics is all around – it is in every conversation, it is part of the fabric of our societies, of being human, of everyday choices" (Hawkins & Turner, 2020, p. 167). Ethics has been defined as the practice that determines what is good or bad, or right or wrong, in our interactions with others (de Jong, 2010). In the daily quest to determine and balance the good or bad, right and wrong in interactions with a wide range of stakeholders, ethical behaviour can be viewed as a demonstration of one's moral values in action (Hawkins & Turner, 2020; Turner & Passmore, 2018, 2019). This view of ethical behaviour takes the question of ethics away from mere situational decision-making and instead assumes that an ethical coach is someone who places their values and ethics at the forefront of their practice (Iordanou & Hawley, 2020). De Vries notes aptly that "ethics is not something we choose to have or not have. We have it- it's a given. But we do choose how we make ethical decisions and what we allow to influence us in making those decisions" (De Vries, 2019, p. 135). The question is, how are such decisions made in the complex realities of the coaching profession? How might coaches determine appropriate action for ethical challenges in a profession which repeatedly reveals that ethical decisions are seldom binary? How might practitioners develop and apply a moral compass (Iordanou et al., 2017) or moral map (Malik, 2014) to guide ethical decision-making in coaching practice?

The complexities of ethical decision-making in coaching practice

Hawkins and Turner (2020, p. 166) paraphrasing Solzhenitsyn (1973), note:

"If only there were unethical coaches who were abusing their privilege and power for self-interest, and we could divide them from the rest, the ethical

DOI: 10.4324/9781003277729-5

coaches. But the line between ethical and unethical practice cuts through every coach and every coaching situation".For coaches, it is thus essential to recognise, and secondly, to be able to act thoughtfully in 'moments of choice', a term originally coined by Allard de Jong (2010). Van Nieuwerburgh (2014) expands the idea of ethical moments of choice and suggests that it is helpful to reframe one's thinking away from the 'ethical dilemma' toward seeing what might be considered 'ethical thinking' as part of daily practice. The more coaches think about their own personal values and ethics, and how they influence their decision-making and coaching practice, the easier and more natural it will be to confidently notice and handle the many potential ethical moments of choice as they arise in practice. Passmore and Duffy (2010), in one of the first papers exploring ethical decision models in coaching, suggested ethical dilemmas are most likely to arise under four broad areas:

i   Issues with coachee & stakeholders: These may be emotional, personality or behavioural issues. Each of which may be a precursor to the client being a danger to themself, those around them and the organisation within which they work.

ii   Issues with the coach: These may be personal, emotional or behavioural situated within the coach, such as ending the coaching relationship or making a referral to another helping professional when this is in the best interests of the coachee.

iii Boundary issues: Boundaries may be crossed by anyone in the coaching relationship or by activities while conducting research. These boundaries may be written explicitly in the form of professional codes or may be presented as standards of practice implicit within coaching.

iv   Multiple-dyadic & dual relationships: These dilemmas present themselves as a result of the coach working for many individuals, organisations or bodies at the same time, from the client, the line manager and the organisation. Or as a professional coach, bound by the ICF Code of Ethics and a psychologist bound by the British Psychological Society or American Psychological Association Code of Ethics.

There is a range of responses to any of the above-noted ethical moments of choice. De Haan (2012, p. 105) names a few:

- "We may not recognise an ethical moment until after the event
- We may recognise it but be confused about how to proceed
- We can be clear about what to do - but not follow through by doing it
- We can be clear about what not to do - and still do it

- We may know the right thing to do, take that action, yet be unable to explain our decision-making process or to justify our thinking and behavior, including in relation to the code of ethics with which we aspire to comply."

Another way to conceptualise ethical decision-making is offered by De Vries, who notes that "ethics is not a problem to be solved: it is a relationship to be lived" (De Vries, 2019, p. 137), challenging the commonly held view of ethical decision-making in coaching as a mere process of problem identification and subsequent response and solution-finding. Instead, the author emphasizes that "ethics comes alive in relationships. Ethics is about how we treat and deal with one another (...)" (De Vries, 2019, p. 135). This chapter proposes that there is a truth to both the process-based perspective on ethical decision-making, as well as the notion that ethics is always there, always present, and comes alive in ethical dialogue, much like "a river, a stream of different opinions, thoughts, and ideas" (De Vries, 2019, p. 136). A framework for ethical decision-making can give coaches and supervisors specific guidance in particular moments of choice, all the while knowing that ethics doesn't just happen when a challenge arises but is present at all times in the daily life of a coach, and comes alive when we engage in meaningful ethical dialogue.

Foundations of ethical decision-making in coaching

Given the range of options for responding to any potential moment of choice in coaching practice, coaches must understand the beliefs, values and assumptions which guide their ethical decision-making and the biases which may skew their decision-making. Both the coaching profession and coaching psychology as an academic discipline, have been informed by western beliefs and philosophical underpinnings, particularly humanistic psychology in its many manifestations. As a result, when considering the various beliefs, values and assumptions which influence our ethical decision-making, it is helpful to also acknowledge these systemic, cultural and societal influences. This is equally true of the present chapter which naturally reflects the author's western philosophical roots. This view posits that the way coaches arrive at an ethical decision is based on their position on a continuum between what is called the consequential or deontological position.

The consequentialist view suggests that the consequences of a decision determine right or wrong. Associated with the paradigm of utilitarianism and its proponents Jeremy Bentham (1789), John Stuart Mill (1861) and Henry Sidgwick (1907), Consequentialism is about bringing about the best outcome for the greatest number of people. An example for coaching practitioners would be that telling a lie might be acceptable if it brings the greatest benefit to the client organisation and its employees. The deontological position is based on whether an act is based on a certain moral standard. From this position, certain types of behaviour are considered right or wrong, independent of their consequences.

Arguably the most well-known proponent of this position is the German philosopher Immanuel Kant (1900), whose categorical imperative is the unconditional duty to act as if one's act could be applied as a universal law without exception: "Act only according to that maxim whereby you can, at the same time, will that it should become a universal law" (AA IV, 421). In the previous example, this would mean that the act of lying is always wrong, regardless of the potential consequences for the client or client organisation. In reality, most coaches sit on the continuum between the two positions, and when faced with an ethical moment of choice, coaches need to balance the complexity and ambiguity of personal ethics and values, context and often numerous stakeholders. As Passmore (2009, p. 8) puts it:

> "Most coaches are, in most cases, ethical pluralists, who hold to a few solid principles, but for most of what they do they consider the circumstances of the situation and consider the motives and situations of the characters involved to help them reach a decision about the course of action to follow".

This ethical pluralism in the coaching profession was highlighted by Turner and Passmore's (2018) global research with supervisors, which pointed to striking inconsistencies in how coaches and supervisors manage ethical decision-making. One in five supervisors included in the study did not discuss the role of values in ethical decision-making with their coachees, and 24.75% saw ethical codes of conduct as one possible factor in ethical decision-making.

One particular area of inconsistency between answers was that of illegal conduct. While Codes of Ethics of professional bodies precisely state courses of action for misconduct, only 18% of supervisors stated that they would report any illegal activity, and 23% said they would not report their supervisees to the professional body. Similar low standards of ethical compliance were found in a large-scale survey of coaches, exploring their ethical practices in a number of scenarios (Passmore, Brown, & Csigas, 2017).

Turner and Passmore (2018) draw multiple implications for practice from these findings. For one, there is a clear need for more inclusion of ethical work in coach and supervisor training, including access to ethical decision-making models and opportunities to use them. Furthermore, practitioners must actively engage in continued personal development to grow a conscious ethical practice. Iordanou and Hawley suggest that "engaging in the development of an ethical coaching practice stimulates a kind of critical self-dialogue, which is necessary to understand our personal and professional values within our coaching context with greater awareness" (Iordanou & Hawley, 2020, p. 336).

Turner and Passmore (2018) also note the need for increased activity and involvement from professional coaching bodies in promoting ethical decision-making through processes. This might include an ethical assessment at the point of membership application as well as training and re-assessment at the point of renewal. Interestingly this need has, in part, been answered with several professional bodies responding to this call by increasing their activity in ethical practice since the publication of the original research. The Association for Professional Executive Coaching and Supervision (APECS), for example, requires of members an annual Continuous Personal and Professional Development (CPPD) plan, including a supervisor's statement and review of the CPPD plan, and the EMCC has also taken steps to increase engagement with ethical practice. However, while the role of professional bodies in developing and advocating codes for ethical coaching practice is crucial, particularly in an unregulated profession such as coaching, codes are in themselves insufficient when it comes to navigating the complexity of moments of choice that coaches face. Ethical decision-making frameworks offer a practical solution, providing a compass, and helping coaches make the best use of the map (codes of ethics) to decide on their direction of travel (Iordanou et al., 2017; Turner & Passmore, 2018).

The *APPEAR* framework of ethical decision-making

In a study using grounded theory to analyse semi-structured interview data, Passmore and Duffy (2010) identified the key elements used by coaches in ethical decision-making. These included ethical principles informed by professional codes, personal ethics and moral values, societal norms, standards of practice, the law, conversations with others, experience, the view of respected others, implicit and explicit contracting with clients, and situational factors. The resulting ACTION model has since been further developed to create the *APPEAR* model (Passmore & Turner, 2018), arguably the most commonly cited model for ethical decision-making in coaching today (Figure 5.1). The six-step decision-making framework is a non-linear and multi-iterative model, with coaches moving through six steps to enhance their insights. This iterative process allows practitioners to learn, change perspective and broaden their thinking as they apply the model in practice. Or, as De Vries describes the process of ethical decision-making "(…) build the bridge as you are crossing it" (De Vries, 2019, p. 136).

The *APPEAR* model aims to:

- Offer coach trainers a model to teach as a practical tool, alongside ethical codes to support coaches in the application of ethical thinking and practice.
- Help coach practitioners move from a written professional code to a step-by-step guide to navigate real-world dilemmas.

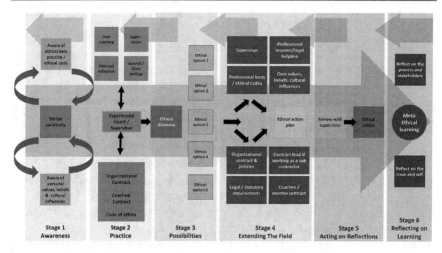

Figure 5.1 APPEAR decision-making model

Awareness

The starting point on any ethical journey is awareness. To notice when an ethical moment has arisen. This is not always easy, especially in the complex reality in which coaches and supervisors operate. In practical terms, awareness refers to the conscious state in coaching practice that enables one to notice such moments by being fully present, and simultaneously being prepared through prior reading and reflection.

The second dimension of awareness is self-awareness. Ethical coaches practice reflectively and reflexively, closely connected to their own beliefs, values and the broader context they are operating in Iordanou & Hawley (2020, p. 336). They aptly note:

> "So often we think we know our story well, yet as we explore our personal and professional values more closely, we tend to discover new insights, gaining greater awareness of how our values influence our coaching practice."

Iordanou et al. (2017) offer three questions for developing greater ethical awareness in coaching practice:

- *Who are you when you coach?*
- *Where are you when you coach?*
- *How do you coach?*

The first dimension of 'who' we are in the coaching relationship means understanding oneself and one's personal and professional values. Knowing oneself and how one's identity and rich background of lived experiences influence the coaching relationship is a critical element toward greater awareness. 'Where' we coach refers to understanding the context in which the coach practices and the complex nuances of ethical issues that arise when coaching across different professional, cultural, societal and organisational contexts. As a coach gains a greater understanding of who and where they are when they coach, they grow their competence and confidence in 'how' they coach and which combination of tools, theories and models might be applied as ethical practitioners. While many coaches and supervisors might not notice many ethical moments of choice, answering these questions and embracing ethical practice as a 'way of being' (Van Nieuwerburgh, 2014) will help the practitioner appropriately notice the nuances of ethical issues.

Carroll and Shaw believe that history "feels like a story of two extremes. While there is no other species that can equal humans for altruism, care and compassion, there is also no other species that matches us for harm, cruelty and sadism" (Carroll & Shaw, 2013, p. 44). As practitioners develop greater ethical awareness, the following strategies to make ethical choices proposed by Caroll and Shaw (2013, p. 60) might be a useful starting point and reflection for the development of ethical maturity and help one grow more confident in one's awareness of ethics in practice:

- do not think 'I', think 'we';
- consider issues of power, domination, and privilege and how they can move over easily into abuse and harm of others who are less privileged;
- ask yourself if you would recommend what you are about to do to someone else;
- try to look at the behavior, not the intention – what am I actually doing? Too often we use our intention (which is almost always good) to evaluate our behavior (which is often not that good);
- ask yourself how this might be perceived from the other's point of view – use empathy to view actions from the recipient's point of view, which helps us to realise that to experience it from that other viewpoint can create a radical change in what we do;
- look for the truth in the opposite position to the one you hold – this can expose the error in your point of view;
- ask yourself: what are my ways and habits of denial?
- identify your Achilles heel;
- beware of the extremity of your ideals (fundamentalism).

Practice

The second stage is the development and maintenance of ethical practice. Iordanou et al. (2017) note that coaches and supervisors can take specific steps toward enhancing their ethical practice, including education and training, continuing professional development and regular supervision. Given the wide range of educational and professional backgrounds that coaches typically come from, it is crucial to be aware and reflexive about personal training and development needs as coaches and supervisors (Iordanou & Hawley, 2020). This need goes hand in hand with the necessity of Continuing Professional Development (CPD). A crucial part of ethical practice is to regularly engage in a wide range of learning activities to grow one's professional knowledge and expertise. Regular journaling, personal reflection, peer coaching and externally engaging with organisational and individual clients might all play a role in regular CPD. The third, indispensable element of maintaining an ethical practice is regular supervision, Hawkins & Smith, (2006, p. 12) suggest:

> "the process by which a coach with the help of a supervisor can attend to understanding better both the client system and themselves as part of the client-coach system and, by so doing, transform their work and develop their craft."

While supervision is not universally mandatory in the coaching profession, unlike other helping professions such as psychotherapy, regular supervision is crucial for coaches to actively reflect, discuss and seek advice on their challenges and experiences with their clients and broader stakeholder systems. While the coaching profession still has a way to go towards universally requiring supervision, there is progress to be noted. The International Coaching Federation (ICF) has recently added supervision to its list of competencies for team coaches, noting that supervision is even more critical for team coaches, owing to the complexities of the role of a team coach, such as managing team dynamics (International Coaching Federation, 2020).

These three elements of education and training, continuing professional development and regular supervision are crucial in developing what many authors in the field refer to as 'ethical maturity', the "capacity to make ethical decisions" (Duffy & Passmore, 2010, p. 140).

Carroll and Shaw (2013, p. 137) offer a detailed definition:

> "Having a reflective, rational emotional and intuitive capacity to decide actions are right and wrong or good and better, having the resilience and courage to implement those decisions, being accountable for ethical decision made (publicly or privately), being able to live with the decisions made and integrating the learning into our moral character and future actions."

Noted as a core element in ethical decision-making (Duffy & Passmore, 2010), ethical maturity is a prerequisite for ethical coaching practice, and growing ethical maturity will help coaches as they move towards step three of the framework, 'Possibilities'.

Possibilities

While one should continuously develop ethical maturity and integrate ethical practice into one's 'way of being' as a coach and supervisor, serious ethical moments of choice do not arise every day. A coach might practice for several weeks or months without encountering a serious ethical issue. It is only when ethical moments of choice emerge that one turns to the third stage of the framework, 'Possibilities'. In this third stage, the coach considers multiple options for responding to the issue. The complexities of an ethical moment of choice often offer multiple solutions beyond the dichotomy of 'A' or 'B'. The supervisor might help the coach develop options for solving the issue at hand by helping the coach reconnect with their personal beliefs and values and review the relevant Codes of Conduct or their contract with the individual or organisation. Supervision also helps in considering the wider stakeholder group that is impacted by the issue at hand and learning about similar experiences and best practices that might help inform future action. Peer supervision and one-to-one conversations with colleagues also have a useful role to play as the coach reviews their options.

For experienced coaches, in particular, intuition might be another source for developing possibilities for approaching an ethical moment of choice (van Nieuwerburgh & Love, 2019). De Haan (2012, p. 108) notes:

> "There are convincing indications that many (if not most) decisions are made intuitively before our conscious mind notes, validates and justifies them using reason and language."

However, we urge caution. While many individuals may believe themselves to be highly intuitive, psychological research suggests that while intuition is useful for highly experienced practitioners, it can be a dangerous trap for those with little knowledge or experience in a particular sector or situation. As the coach grows their ethical maturity and coaching experience through reflective practice, they can gradually come to trust their intuition more.

When tapping into various resources to develop possibilities for solving an ethical moment of choice, coaches also need to expand their knowledge and thinking beyond what they know. This stage in the framework is known as 'Extending the field'.

Extending the field

In this fourth stage, the non-linear nature of the framework might be most obvious. As possibilities for action are developed, the coach needs to extend their knowledge and thinking, tapping into available resources. As the coach develops an ethical action plan in stage four by extending their thinking and considering a wider frame, they might continue to notice and develop possibilities for action. In the most practical terms, 'Extending the field' might involve a detailed review of the Codes of Conduct or seeking advice from an indemnity insurance provider's legal helpline, where available. This stage might also involve continued discussion with a supervisor and in-depth reflection of one's personal beliefs, values, background and resulting assumptions about the case at hand.

Other sources that can be pulled in to expand one's thinking might include a range of existing contracts and policies, such as the policies of the organisation which might have commissioned the coaching, the coach's or coaching provider's contract with the organisation, the coach's individual contract with the coach provider they are employed with, as well as the contract between the coach and coachee.

As the coach extends their thinking about a particular ethical moment of choice, they also have the opportunity and obligation to not only consider the effects of a potential decision on the coachee but also on their wider network, including how any decision will impact the coachee's relationships in their system. All coaching takes place within a system, and as such, considering not just the small number of directly impacted stakeholders but also the wider system is helpful. Brooks (2017) advocates for 'stakeholding', where all those with a stake should have a say about its outcomes. While this may be ideal, in reality, it is often hard to achieve in a multi-stakeholder environment.

Hawkins and Turner (2020, p. 178) suggest developing what they call "systemic ethical maturity" by developing "key capacities that counteract the human tendency to privilege the individual that is present". They propose four capacities:

1. *Cultural awareness.* Cultivating an awareness of our own biases and assumptions because of our cultural background.
2. *Listening not only to what is in the room but what is not in the room.* Growing the ability to not only hear what the coachee brings to the coaching session but see through the individual into their wider system and hear what the coachee might fail to notice.
3. *Wide-angled empathy.* Having empathy and compassion for everyone involved in the coachee's story, not only the individual coachee.
4. *Holding the future in mind.* Asking how a decision might impact the future, viewing a choice from the perspective of looking from 'future-back'.

Finally, as coaches and supervisors grow their ethical maturity, 'Extending the field' provides an opportunity to actively share and engage with the broader coaching community, to raise the collective awareness of ethical practice in the coaching profession. As coaches and supervisors, we have the responsibility to not only hold ourselves accountable for our own ethical choices and actions. We also have the responsibility to share our experiences with others, so that as a community, coaches and supervisors continuously engage in meaningful dialogue, because "ethics lives and breathes within individuals, couples, teams and organisations. Ethics is something between people, not above them or beneath them or even around them. It's a relational concept, like love" (de Vries, 2019, p. 140).

Acting on reflections

Once a decision is made based on the broad range of information collected through stages three and four of the model, the fifth stage, 'Acting on reflections', is about implementing the appropriate course of action. Before doing so, a coach might develop a concrete action plan on how to put the decision into action. In this process, a supervisor can help challenge and reflect on the practical elements of the plan. A supervisor might also be able to talk through the possible responses of different stakeholders who might be affected by the decision.

Using a framework such as constellations at this stage can be useful, helping to map each stakeholder in the system and consider how each might be impacted in turn (Finch, 2022).

Reflecting on learning

With every ethical moment of choice, coaches grow their ethical maturity and become more competent and confident in managing ethical issues. By reflecting on the learnings from an ethical decision-making process, practitioners strengthen their ethical practice muscle and their internal and external resources to draw from in future scenarios. This reflection should happen on two levels (Passmore & Turner, 2018):

1. Reflection of the process and the various stakeholders and what the coach has learnt from thinking through and implementing this ethical action.

Consider questions such as:

Which resources did I draw from to come to an appropriate decision?
How did supervision support the decision-making process?
What went well in the way that I implemented the decision? What might I have done differently in the way I implemented the decision?
How did the ethical issue change the coaching relationship/ the relationship with the organisation/ the relationship with other stakeholders?

2. Reflection on the issue and themselves.

Consider questions such as:

What have I learnt about myself in this process?
How has the issue and its resolution affected me through the various stages of the process?

How did I notice that I was facing an ethical moment of choice? Which role did my personal background and culture play?
How did my personal values and beliefs play into my decision-making?
How confident was I throughout the decision-making process? When did I have doubts? How did I approach these doubts?
What have I learnt about myself in this process?
How has this ethical decision-making process affected me personally?
How did I apply my strengths in the decision-making process?
What might I do differently in the future?

We would also advocate a continual reflective practice through journaling and the use of models such as the Henley8 as a framework to guide this reflection (Passmore & Sinclair, 2021), deepen self-awareness and enhance our capacities as reflective practitioners at all levels.

Case study

Eric is a senior coach working for a coach platform provider. He writes to his coach relations manager to advise he is really worried about a coachee whom he feels is on the edge of a breakdown as a result of long working hours, stress and demanding targets being imposed on him. He meets his supervisor, Jackie, who is aware of the *APPEAR* model.

Jackie's first step is to invite Eric to think about what alerted him to this issue and triggered his feeling that it was important to raise the topic in his supervision session. Jackie was particularly interested to explore with Eric what beliefs and values underpinned his thinking. Jackie invites Eric to look at his journal for the day of the session. In so doing, Jackie is encouraging Eric to be more consciously aware of the antenna that helped him highlight the issue as one that required deeper reflection and discussion. This also emphasizes to Eric the value of keeping a journal, as a space for reflecting and thinking. For some coaches writing a reflective journal is a challenge, as they often don't know where to start. The Henley8 model (Passmore & Sinclair, 2021) offers a framework to help with that experience (Table 5.1).

Table 5.1 Henley8 Questions

1. What do I observe?
2. What was my response?
3. What does this tell me about me?
4. What does this tell me about me as a coach?
5. What strengths does this offer?
6. What pitfalls should I be aware of?
7. What did I learn?
8. What will I do next time?

Secondly, in moving to explore 'Practice', Jackie invites Eric to think about the contract with the organisation, which is held by the platform provider, his professional code of practice and advice, guidance, or insights from reading similar issues or cases in the past. In this case, Eric was not a party to the contract with the client organisation. However, he had been briefed on the coaching project through a video recorded by the client and an organisation briefing by the provider. In addition, he had undertaken a multi-party contracting meeting with the client and their line manager. This provided useful insight into the relationship between the two, their shared expectations but also differences in how they framed their individual aspirations for the coaching assignment. Listening for such differences and seeking to address them at the start can be very useful in minimising subsequent misalignment. Further, understanding the tone, language and goals of the coach commissioner can also make a significant difference, ensuring the coach understands the commissioner's expectations and organisational priorities. In this case what stood out was the mismatch between the commissioner, seeking to protect the wellbeing of the workforce during a period of change and the language used by the line manager which focused on the delivery of targets, which was possibly playing into the stress being experienced by Eric.

The third step is 'Possibilities'. What options are available, first the obvious, and then the less obvious or more extreme options. Jackie can encourage fresh thinking by using different frameworks and tools during supervision. Fourthly she can help Eric to extend his field. If time allows, this may involve discussion with a legal advice line or with a peer to draw different perspectives. This is however not always possible, owing to time constraints. As a result, this stage may be more limited and simply involve thinking beyond the immediate and considering the wider stakeholders and system.

The fifth stage is to move to action and implement an agreed plan. In such situations, implementation almost always brings consequences for both the coach and the coachee. The coach thus needs to be prepared for negative and positive consequences and be prepared to see through their decision, even when resistance arises. Jackie's role as a supervisor is vital in supporting Eric to see through his decision and receive the ongoing support he needs to manage the emotional consequences. As Eric reflected on the options, these included a choice to continue with coaching, engage in a multi-party review meeting or suspend the coaching, while encouraging the employee to engage with others in the organisation such as Human Resources and the company's Employee Assistance Programme and secure counselling.

The final stage of *APPEAR* is a reflection on the process. This again is best done through the reflective journal and can be some weeks after the event. Such reflections allow insights to be captured and provide material to be reviewed at the end of each quarter or each year in search of themes or patterns.

Conclusion

In this chapter, we have reviewed in-depth the issue of ethical decision-making and offered a framework that coaches can use as a compass as they navigate the map of their personal and professional ethical code of practice. The *APPEAR* model is just one framework of many available, but by using such a model, the coach can draw on a range of perspectives and resources and develop both a deeper understanding of themselves and their situation, providing insight and learning and informing their course of action.

Discussion points

1. What key values inform your coaching practice?
2. How do you stay aware of ethical traps when coaching?
3. How do you currently navigate ethical decisions in your coaching practice?
4. How would you solve a past ethical moment of choice differently, after having read this chapter?

Recommended reading

Passmore, J. & Turner, E. (2018) Reflections on integrity – The APPEAR model. Coaching at Work. February 2018. Retrieved on February 18, 2022 from www. coaching-at-work.com/2018/02/23/reflections-on-integrity-the-appear-model.

References

Brooks, T. (2017). Leadership and Stakeholding. In J. Boaks & M. Levine (Eds), *Leadership & ethics*. London: Bloomsbury Academic.

Carroll, M. & Shaw, E. (2013). *Ethical maturity in the helping professions*. London: Jessica Kingsley Publishers.

de Haan, E. (2012). *Supervision in Action*. McGraw-Hill.

de Jong, A. (2010). Coaching ethics: integrity in the moment of choice. In J. Passmore (Ed.), *Excellence in coaching*. London: Kogan Page.

de Vries, K. (2019). Moving from frozen code to live vibrant relationship: Towards a philosophy of ethical coaching supervision. In J. Birch & P. Welch (Eds), *Coaching supervision: Advancing practice, changing landscapes*. London: Routledge.

Dryden, W. (1997). *Therapists' Dilemmas*. London: Sage Publications.

Duffy, M. & Passmore, J. (2010). Ethics in coaching: An ethical decision-making framework for coaching psychologists. *International Coaching Psychology Review*, 5(2): 140–151.

Finch, C. (2022). Constellations. In J. Passmore, C. Day, J. Flower, M. Grieve, J. J. Moon (Eds), *Coaching Tools: 101 Coaching tools and techniques for executive coaches, team coaches, mentors and supervisors*, Vol. 2. London: Libri Press, p. 169.

Hawkins, P. & Smith, N. (2006). *Coaching, mentoring, and organisational consultancy: Supervision and development*. London: Open University Press/McGraw Hill.

Hawkins, P. & Turner, E. (2020). *Systemic coaching: delivering value beyond the individual*. Abingdon: Routledge.

International Coaching Federation. (2020). ICF Team Coaching Competencies: Moving Beyond One-to-One Coaching. https://coachingfederation.org/app/uploads/2021/10/Team-Coaching-Competencies_10.4.21.pdf.

Iordanou, I. & Hawley, R. (2020). Ethics in coaching. In J. Passmore (Ed.), *The coaches' handbook: The complete practitioner guide for professional coaches*. Abingdon: Routledge, pp. 333–343.

Iordanou, I., Hawley, R., & Iordanou, C. (2017). *Values and ethics in coaching*. London: Sage Publications.

Kant, I. (1900). *Gesammelte Schriften*. Hrsg.: Bd. 1–22Preussische Akademie der Wissenschaften, Bd. 23 Deutsche Akademie der Wissenschaften zu Berlin, ab Bd. 24 Akademie der Wissenschaften zu Göttingen, Berlin 1900ff., AA IV, 421.

Malik, K. (2014). *The quest for a moral compass*. London: Atlantic Books.

Passmore, J. (2009). Coaching ethics: making ethical decisions- novices and experts. *The Coaching Psychologist*, 5(1): 6–10.

Passmore, J. & Sinclair, T. (2021). *Becoming a Coach: The Essential ICF Guide*. Shoreham on Sea: Pavilion.

Passmore, J. & Turner, E. (2018). Reflections on integrity – The APPEAR model. Coaching at Work. Retrieved on February 18, 2022 from www.coaching-at-work.com/2018/02/23/reflections-on-integrity-the-appear-model.

Passmore, J., Brown, H., Csigas, Z. et al. (2017) *The State of Play in Coaching & Mentoring: Executive Report*. Henley on Thames: Henley Business School-EMCC. Retrieved on November 1, 2021 from www.researchgate.net/publication/321361866_The_State_of_Play_in_European_Coaching_and_Mentoring.

Phillips, K. (2006). *Intuition in coaching*. Higher Poynton: Keri Phillips Associates.

Solzhenitsyn, A. (1973). *Gulag Archipelago 1918–1956*. New York: Harper & Row.

Turner, E. & Passmore, J. (2018). Ethical dilemmas and tricky decisions: A global perspective of coaching supervisors' practices in coach ethical decision-making. *International Journal of Evidence Based Coaching and Mentoring*, 16. doi:10.24384/000473.

Turner, E. & Passmore, J. (2019). Mastering Ethics. In J. Passmore, B. O. Underhill and M. Goldsmith (Eds), *Mastering Executive Coaching*. Abingdon: Routledge.

Van Nieuwerburgh, C. (2014). *An introduction to coaching skills: A practice guide*. London: Sage Publications.

van Nieuwerburgh, C. & Love, D. (2019). *Advanced Coaching Practice: Inspiring Change in Others*. London: Sage Publications.

Chapter 6

What might be an evidence base for coaching – ethical issues

David A. Lane and Sarah Corrie

Introduction

Professions have always held a duty of care to their clients but increasingly it is argued that they also need to include the wider society and the planet as part of that responsibility (Whybrow et al., 2022). Whether or not an intervention provided was evidence-based or consistent with best practice can form the basis of challenges to professionals in the form of client complaints over quality of care. Increasingly, professionals are required to be clear that their interventions are efficacious and go beyond doing no harm to being a source of sustainable value to the world. These evolving expectations raise important questions for us in coaching, concerning the types of evidence we use to inform practice and the extent to which that evidence encompasses higher values.

Acting in accordance with evidence is an ethical defence but understanding such judgements in a rapidly developing field is complex. In an established area such as health research, a randomised controlled trial may have empirically demonstrated that one procedure is superior to another. For example, a health and wellness coach may be working with a client who has been given a diagnosis leading to a prescribed treatment that is evidence-based. However, even in this apparently clear-cut situation of how to proceed two challenges arise. First, randomised controlled trials are based on a narrowly defined condition of a group and so if an individual fits the group definition but has several variant aspects to the way they present how should we proceed? Is the prescribed treatment still fit for purpose, or should adaptions be made? This use of group (generalisable) as opposed to individualised (idiographic) data is a longstanding dilemma for the professions (Miller & Frederickson, 2006), made more problematic as the world moves into the future of big data analytics (Hassad, 2022). Second, even though a person may be diagnosed as having a certain condition or may seemingly require a particular intervention based on psychometric or organisational feedback data (e.g. to learn how to delegate more) the meaning of that information to individuals may vary substantially. This is the question, well established in psychology, of the difference between a diagnosis and a case formulation (Corrie & Lane, 2010).

DOI: 10.4324/9781003277729-6

What is meant by evidence, the type of evidence that is useful and the extent or development of evidence for our practice in coaching is a major ethical issue for our emerging discipline.

This chapter considers some of the principal questions that arise in light of the dilemmas outlined above. It also examines the implications of these questions and dilemmas to try to understand how ethics is a central question if coaches are to practice professionally.

What is meant by evidence?

It has been argued (Cavanagh & Grant, 2006) that there is a fundamental distinction in the coaching industry between those who take the view that we need to develop and evaluate interventions based on a well-researched and continually developing body of knowledge and those who provide interventions from proprietary models built on ideas from both credible and spurious sources. In response to this dilemma, Cavanagh and Grant (2006) have argued for the value of coaching adopting the scientist-practitioner model. More recently, Passmore and Tee (2021) have acknowledged the challenge from coaches as to why research matters: if coaches and their clients are happy with the service delivered and coaches' own experience suggests that coaching works, why is research necessary at all? Similar to Cavanagh and Grant (2006), Passmore and Tee (2021) argue that research enables the development of a knowledge base from which practitioners can work. In the field of psychotherapy Singer (1980) raised the bar even higher. Replacing the term psychotherapy with coaching and intervention with treatment in the quote presents a cogent argument for how research has a central role in the ethics that are fundamental to practice (Singer 1980, p. 372):

> "The ethical practice of [coaching) must reflect the current status of knowledge.....The practitioner who has not examined recent developments in the research literature or who has not kept abreast of evaluation studies of various forms of [intervention] may well be violating a central ethic of the profession."

This sentiment is echoed by Kwaitowski (2013) who argues that, "...in undertaking any research ethical thinking is not optional." Consequently, this exploration starts by considering the different approaches to evidence and why the approach to evidence gathering is an ethical issue for coaching.

If the view is taken that judgements should be based on evidence that is well-founded then it follows that consideration should include what is meant by evidence. The concept of the scientist-practitioner arose early in the field of psychology and historically, is associated with the now famous conference in Boulder Colorado in 1949 where the role of psychologists as researchers and clinicians was debated (see Lane & Corrie, 2006, for a review). Later ideas included the role of the practitioner-scholar or researcher. As Lane and Corrie (2006) make clear professionals are both consumers and producers of research. As consumers of research, coaches use the ideas (theories, models, methods, etc.) of others and apply them to practice. As producers of research, coaches evaluate, ask questions about what works or explore theoretically driven or phenomenon-driven questions of relevance to the field of coaching and practice. In both cases coach practitioners are seeking to build practice from a knowledge base. However, coaches also need to innovate and create new ideas and practices where there may be either little or no evidence base. How, then, do coaches need to think about ethical practice in these situations?

When we ask, 'what do we mean by evidence?' any answer is underpinned by the question, 'evidence for what purpose?' If coaches can understand the purpose of their inquiry, they can then adopt an approach to evidence gathering that meets the need. That is, the purpose is established for which an explanation is required. Gibbons et al. (2010) argued that while traditional research was concerned with knowledge for its own sake and operated within specific disciplines – a form of knowledge termed Mode 1 knowledge – other approaches were transdisciplinary, and knowledge was produced in the context of application – a form of knowledge termed Mode 2 knowledge. While this distinction is not without its detractors for the purpose of this chapter, it raises the question of what ethical issues arise from undertaking different types of research. The coaching practitioner's duty of care to their research participants may be of a different order when operating from the position of Mode 2 as opposed to Mode 1 knowledge. In drawing upon different philosophical perspectives on research this becomes clear. For example, the coaching practitioner/researcher can ask:

What is the concept of evidence that guides your work?
How have your beliefs about evidence been influenced by your practice?
How has your practice been influenced by your beliefs about evidence?
What have been the key influences on your personal definition of evidence?
How is your approach to evidence influenced by the purpose of your enquiry?

Alternative discourses for coaching research

If the purpose in conducting research is to optimise effective practice through standardising a model of delivery, developing a knowledge base that is generalisable or justifying the effectiveness of a particular approach then the concept of evidence that guides a coaches practice is likely to be informed by an empiricist world view. The assumption is that knowledge becomes more robust to the extent it we can be enhance its findings through multiple observations can be generalised. Adopting an empiricist perspective would lead to questions such as:

What would be an appropriate justification for using a particular practice?
To what extent are ideas generated in one context transferable to a different application?
What techniques might be standardised into a protocol or practice manual?

The empiricist perspective, derived from the purpose outlined above raises ethical questions relating to the way research is conducted and the coaches' responsibilities for adopting ideas from one source and applying them to another when there is no empirical research base to support it.

In contrast, the purpose in conducting research might be to work with the best theories currently available rather than seeking universal generalisable findings. In this case the aim could be to ensure best practice by refining existing approaches and seeking to explore theories by creating conjectures that can be tested. The concept of evidence guiding work here, might be the falsification of a well-established theory and confirmation of newer speculative ones to gradually advance knowledge. This would lead to questions such as:

What are the relative merits of each competing theory in the context of my enquiry?
At what point and what evidence, would lead me to reject my existing theories?
What are the factors that would lead me to reject certain ideas in favour of others?

The notion of theory testing, derived from the purpose outlined above raises ethical questions about the willingness to use current evidence to change practice and the use of particular theoretical models which might not be underpinned by a sound evidence base.

If the purpose in conducting research is to move away from universal laws towards contextually situated data which attempt to make sense of phenomena in terms of the meanings people bring to them then coaching might be guided by a social constructionist view. This perspective argues that all knowledge is socially created, politically driven and historically located. Underpinning a social constructionist worldview is the premise that knowledge and evidence emerge within human relationships with different types of social exchange predisposing certain types of action over others. The language that coaching practitioners use determines their understanding of the world and as such, enables and constrains thinking, expression and perception. Adopting this purpose and perspective would lead to questions such as:

What discourses underpin my practice?
In what historical, social or political traditions are these discourses based?
What dominant discourses are enabling and constraining my approach to practice and the practice within my area of coaching more generally?

This approach to research and evidence raises ethical questions about the way coaches relate to others when conducting in-depth enquiries about them, their experiences and their senses of self, and the practitioner's willingness to confront personal foundational historical, social and political perspectives.

If the purpose in conducting research is to understand the relationship between structures and systems in the world that exist independently of ideas about them alongside those aspects of the world that are socially constructed, then it is possible to draw upon a critical realist perspective on evidence. Critical realism differentiates three levels of reality: the empirical (based on our observations, experiences and what we can measure); the actual (those situations and events that form the basis of our experience) and the real (causal factors, structures and the generative mechanisms that produce events). Engaging with this perspective gives rise to questions such as:

As agents of change how do we create desirable outcomes for our practice?
What are the external factors we need to take into account to maximise the chances of obtaining a preferred outcome?
What types of practice enable or constrain the agency of our clients?

This approach to research and evidence raises ethical questions about how coaches relate to wider factors influencing clients and the need to evaluate consistently the ways in which practices might enable and inadvertently constrain the clients' agency.

Finally, as the world of professional practice becomes increasingly complex and faces challenges to our notion of an ordered and objective reality the need is to develop increasingly sophisticated techniques for understanding the world and that of clients. Faced with the necessity to understand non-linear systems that cannot be predicted or controlled the task is to seek to facilitate ways to enhance self-organisation. The critical determiner in complexity theory is the idea that the world unfolds in the process of interacting with it. When faced with complexity, relationships and movement towards self-organisation enable response to elements that cannot be predicted, rather than trying to work to defined plans. This perspective leads to questions such as:

Given the future is uncertain, how do we develop services that establish new directions?
How do we avoid being trapped in methodological, theoretical or intellectual dead-ends?
What connections with others do we need to make to break down any barriers and overcome difficulties to enhance co-operation?

This approach to research and evidence raises ethical issues about the way professions can codify restricted notions of competent practice (which can quickly become outdated), ways of thinking about ethics in a changing world and the ways in which talking just to like-minded professionals can perpetuate intellectual traps to the detriment of clients. Addressing such issues means moving beyond ethical codes to developing a personal moral compass and collectively exploring what it means to act ethically within communities.

The above approaches reflect different philosophical stances concerning the nature of knowledge and reality. Although beyond the scope of the chapter to address this literature in any depth (the interested reader is referred to a series of papers by Stanford University, 2022) for current purposes the questions above offer an initial means of reflecting on how different interpretations of reality might inform the areas of concern identified and the evidence gathering procedures that follow. They also enable us to consider the status of the evidence that underpins coaching. This is considered next.

What does evidence look like in coaching?

There has been a rapid growth in the delivery of coaching alongside a proliferation of models, methods and techniques that underpin this delivery, but this expansion is relatively unsupported by research (Gray, Garvey, & Lane, 2016). This has to be to the detriment of the field and also raises the ethical issue of how to substantiate claims to effective practice. The situation is improving with many trainee coaches on post-graduate programmes producing useful research exploring specific approaches, features of the relationship, coaching outcomes and so on. Moreover, there are increasing numbers of published research studies in coaching (Cavanagh & O'Connor, 2019; de Hahn, 2021). Nonetheless, only a limited number adopt an empirical perspective and consequently the purpose served, and ethical issues involved are not well covered. Hence, justifications for particular practices and issues of generalisation and the standardisation of practices are ethically difficult to sustain.

There are broad themes that do emerge from existing research (Gray, Garvey, & Lane, 2016; de Hahn, 2021). These include:

On the positive side:

- The benefits of coaching are overwhelmingly positive although most positive results come from self-report with fewer using external data such as 360° reporting.
- Coaching is effective for a wide range of goals.
- The characteristics of effective coaches such as integrity, support for the coachee, communication skills and behaviours and credibility appear consistently.

- The coaching relationship including matching coach and client is well-established as important.
- Aspects of the coaching process such as goal setting, agreeing a long-term focus and evaluating progress are identified by many studies as important.
- The organisational context and the necessity of a supportive environment is well established.

On the negative side:

- While questions of coachability have arisen comparatively little emphasis has been placed on the characteristics of the coachee.
- A wide range of theoretical approaches to guide coaching have appeared but much less attention has been paid to comparisons between them or their distinctive contributions.

An intriguing finding:

- In a review by de Hahn (2021) it appears that the outcome of coaching is not dependent on the number of sessions. Somehow coach and coachee adapt themselves to achieving outcomes within the available sessions. He suggests that we can trust coaches to determine the amount of input that makes sense for their coachees.

Hence, ethical questions are raised when certain claims for practice are made which cannot be supported. While coaching is effective for a wide range of issues more sophistication is needed in responding to the question, 'does coaching work?' (Fillery-Travis & Lane, 2006; Linley, 2006) by asking supplemental questions such as, 'who is the coaching for? What should we be researching? Where is the research happening? When is it happening/over what timescales and why is it happening (i.e. its purpose)?' It is possible to claim that establishing an effective coaching alliance matters but other aspects of the process also impact. There is a reasonable amount of data about what makes coaches effective but less about the coachee. There are many techniques and theories but still relatively little is known about how they compare.

Towards an evidence-based profession

Research and practice are often seen as opposite ends of a dichotomy where the worlds of research and practice rarely coincide (Fillery-Travis & Corrie, 2019). This research-practice divide leaves coaching practice relatively uninformed (Grant & O'Connor, 2019; Swanson, 2001) and prone to fads and the promise of panaceas. This question applies across many professions (see Denvall & Skillmark, 2021, who provide useful ways to explore this in practice). Those who seek to fill the research-practice gap are often those who identify as scientist-practitioners or researcher-practitioners. They also include those who undertake post-graduate qualifications that include a research dissertation, academics who are themselves practitioners (common in the coaching field) and coaches who strive diligently to evaluate the process or outcome of their work. Including the latter group, makes the research-practice gap less wide.

There is a view that the research-practice gap is based on a fundamental philosophical divide where those who produce knowledge from research are concerned with generalising their results to a wider population whereas practitioners seek specific solutions to the concerns that confront them in their daily practice (Lane & Corrie, 2006). While some have argued that the gap should be bridged (Fincham & Clark, 2009), others maintain that researchers and practitioners inhabit separate social systems leading to differences in how problems are defined and addressed (Kieser & Leiner, 2009). An example is found in Starkey et al. (2009) who claim that the prioritising of rigor leads to research that is of interest only to narrow scholarly communities. This challenges researchers to pay more attention to the world of practice. Blumberg and Lane (2011) have set out a range of approaches suitable for coaching practitioner research including a sequential guide to conducting projects. There are interesting developments in the understanding of practice in fields such as practice theory which seeks to explore not the practitioner but the practices that they and their clients engage upon in their interactions (Nicolini, 2012). This could open up interesting lines of enquiry for the practitioner-researcher in a variety of areas. These include the nature of the encounter in coaching practice, coaching accomplishments, discourses on practice, bounded creativity in the field and representing the texture of practice in coaching (Gherardi, 2012; Nicolini, 2012). This would go some way towards advancing understanding of other forms of evidence beyond the empirical.

Moving towards becoming an evidence-based profession – what is involved?

While Mode 1 research discussed earlier in this chapter seeks to uncover cause and effect relationships that can yield generalisations cannot be discounted, most coaching practitioner led research is likely to come from Mode 2 approaches. This may well be generated in the context of multiple stakeholder teams transcending the boundaries of traditional disciplines and aiming at a transdisciplinary approach that works on the real-life concerns arising in organisational or other practice contexts. Frameworks are generated in the practices themselves and involve a continuous interchange between application and academic theory. The potential consumers of any new knowledge are those practitioners who are creating it. Hence, an evidence-based profession becomes one in which production and consumption are both central to our understanding. Ethically this means considering how to use research findings in practice and how evidence is defined when practitioners seek to use or create it. Coaches also have to consider the ethical implications of being a practitioner-researcher often working with known client groups or in organisational groupings of which we are members.

Coaches are often insiders to the evidence-gathering process rather than objective observers. (There is doubt philosophically that an outsider position is ever tenable given that coaches are always part of a wider community of practice.) There are several approaches appearing that seek to address these issues. For example, Anderson et al. (2001) proposed a typology balancing practical relevance with methodological rigor. This results in four quadrants of research in table 6.1.

According to Anderson et al. (2001) the aim in wishing to become an evidence-based profession is to focus on Quadrant 2.

Another useful approach is the Research Consultancy Framework developed by Napier University (Francis et al., 2009). Here, the partnering between academics and coaching practitioners generates actionable knowledge that can help navigate the research-practice divide. The emphasis is on co-operative enquiry and the co-creation of ideas in a similar way to Appreciative Inquiry, Open Space, World Café, or Participant Directed Feedback (see Gray, Garvey, & Lane, 2016, for a review of the application of these approaches in coaching). Adapting the Napier Framework to coaching, Gray, Garvey and Lane (2016) suggest the following possibilities:

By developing complex conversations, it is possible to capture the essence of coaching practices. Coaches can try to balance work that meets clients' needs, based on a clear sense of direction, while also helping unearth embedded assumptions or interpretations that may benefit from reflection or revision. To build an evidence-based profession coaches need to:

- Develop approaches to the evaluation of coaching.
- Develop longitudinal studies that seek to understand long-term impacts for the individual, team and across the system more broadly.
- Seek to compare different approaches used and in particular consider how varied purposes are best met through different perspectives and processes.
- Report all results with transparency including those with neutral or negative outcomes.
- Fully understand the practices happening within coaching so that the nature of the encounters can be better understood.

Table 6.1 Four quadrants of research

Quadrant 1:	"Popularist Science" with a high practical relevance but limited rigor. Many personal development books sit in this quadrant.
Quadrant 2:	"Pragmatic Science" being both methodically rigorous and practically relevant. Coaching is increasingly moving in this direction.
Quadrant 3:	"Pedantic Science" where the methodology is rigorous, but the results are of little practical relevance. Coaching is not currently overburdened with this type of research.
Quadrant 4:	"Puerile Science" that lacks both rigor and practical value. Coaching research that consists of personal opinions falls into this category.

Being a consumer and producer of research

Based on the points discussed above, if coaching is to move towards becoming an evidence-based profession, coaches have to consider themselves to be both consumers and producers of research. To be evidence-based requires us to go beyond narrow definitions of research in order to draw upon much wider sources to inform our work (Barkham & Mellor Clark, 2000; Barkman et.al., 2001; Milton & Corrie, 2002; Newnes, 2001). These wider sources, alongside a critically reflective approach to the coaches' own experience, draws them towards intuitive knowledge as well as creativity in their practice and the role of story-telling in coaching. As Miller Mair (1988) in another context states we can learn to define ourselves in terms of the stories we tell.

In coaching we also place a premium on the client's agency and hearing their story and hence have an interest in the nature of the encounter between the coach and coachee in which each brings their own understanding to create a dialogue. We are all storytellers (Corrie & Lane, 2010). This means seeking new forms of collaboration that respect different ways of knowing. Lane and Corrie (2006) have argued for different ways to incorporate a scientist-practitioner model in psychology and as consumers and producers of research in coaching a similar position is suggested. In doing so it is possible to articulate and justify reasons for using one version of science and practice over another in a particular context. The limitations of choices can be evaluated as well as being clear about the purposes they can fulfil. If asked, can coaches explain their thinking but also continuously ask themselves why they are making certain choices over others. It becomes an ethical responsibility to hold in mind explicit frameworks for differentiating ways of knowing and systematic approaches to professional decision making (Lane & Corrie, 2006; 2012).

Given an approach to evidence gathering as a socially embedded activity, it is recognised that any evidence obtained will be contextually bound. It matters where, how, why and by whom the work is done. As consumers of research coaches are part of the audience and need a systematic way to reflexively engage with it as part of practice. This becomes an ethical issue and enables knowing if an activity is consistent with the existing evidence, is innovative or is simply off track (Corrie, 2021). In seeking to become skilled consumers of research it is necessary to understand how to evaluate the research encountered. In effect, a knowledge management strategy is needed.

Grant (2016) has offered the 'Research Relevance to Coaching Model' as a way to make judgements concerning whether or how to incorporate particular findings into work as a coach (see also Grant & O'Connor, 2019). In this two axes model, one axis concerns the relevance of the research to coaching that is specific or related, the other concerns the strength of the data as either weak or strong. This is a useful aid for exploring if the evidence reviewed has relevance. However, the world is increasingly confronted with problems that are messy (Lane, 1991) or as Brown et al. (2010) describes it, "wicked." That is, the need is to be able to consider complex issues that are not amenable to complete definition and for which generating a solution is not easy since each answer generates further concerns. Approaches are needed that go beyond the linear to incorporate non-linear decision making (Lane & Corrie, 2012).

To incorporate this broader way of conceptualising research as consumers or producers requires a way to frame thinking. One approach has been offered by Corrie (2014; 2021; see Figure 6.1).

A comprehensive description of Figure 6.1 can be found in Corrie (2021). In essence, Corrie's (2014; 2021) lenses are presented as an organising framework that can help scholars and practitioners identify and navigate factors of influence on the way in which research evidence is designed, implemented and disseminated. Each of these carries varied ethical positions. Such influences are not always overtly declared but nonetheless shape the privileging of certain types of enquiry and methodology over others. The privileging of one perspective or approach over another carry's ethical implications.

In brief, the quadrants (or "lenses") that comprise the foreground of Figure 6.1 draw attention to different perspectives that can help us position ourselves within a broad and often complex landscape of knowledge. For example, examining a particular study or body of evidence (our own or the work of others) through the lens of Context takes us into an examination of some of the dominant priorities and needs at local, national and global levels (see Lane & Corrie, 2006, for a description of these levels of influence and Nutley, Walter, & Davies, 2007, for an in-depth analysis of diverse agendas that research can serve). Local, national and global priorities will privilege certain questions and forms of knowledge over

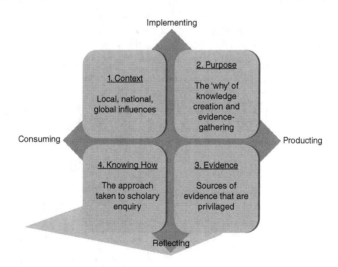

Figure 6.1 Lenses through which to understand Coaching Research

others. Therefore, when investigating context, Corrie (2014; 2021) suggests that questions (adapted for this chapter) worthy of exploration include:

Reflecting on your particular area of coaching, what are some of the current dominant areas of interest? Who determines which are the areas of interest? What ethical implications arise and are excluded by dominant interests?

Who is currently producing the evidence that influences your practice? Who is making use of this research and how? What is the ethical stance of those producing the evidence that you choose to inform your practice?

What are the contexts in which you are producing your own evidence? Who has a claim on that evidence? Who might use or misuse your evidence – with what ethical implications?

For whom is your research good or bad news? Who benefits and who loses as a result of your stance and how do you address the ethical sensitivities arising?

Examining any research endeavour or trend through the lens of Purpose encourages sharpening thinking around the "why" of any investigation but also what makes it worthwhile and ethical. Corrie (2014; 2021) proposes that questions arising from reviewing evidence through the lens of Purpose include:

What are the range of purposes (both declared and undeclared) of the research and evidence-gathering endeavours that are currently dominant in your field of coaching? What ethical assumptions underpin those dominant discourses?

What purposes do you want your own research to serve? What purposes do others want it to serve? What makes those purposes worthwhile and are there any contradictions which would give rise to ethical dilemmas?

What would 'success' look like? Who has the power to define success in relation to the research that you produce? What is the ethical basis of that power dynamic?

Who will benefit from your research and who might lose out in some way – and how? How will you ensure both the beneficiaries and victims of the research are treated ethically?

The third quadrant, Evidence, focuses attention on matters of an epistemological and ontological nature to position the findings of our enquiries within different interpretations of the nature of knowledge, of being and of reality itself. Questions arising from this perspective might include:

What are your beliefs about the nature of knowledge and how we acquire it? (See above, in the section "what do we mean by evidence?" to consider the specific ethical issues that arise from your stance.)

What types of evidence are personally persuasive for you and why? What do you gain and lose by favouring these sources of knowledge over others? How do you balance benefits to yourself with the benefit to others?

What would lie beyond the scope of knowledge that you would consider credible and why?

Who gets to define what is legitimate evidence in your specific context? Who are the dominant voices and how are they shaping your field of practice? Who are those shaping what is or is not considered an ethical basis for research?

Questions arising from the fourth quadrant, Knowing How, relate more to the design, development and implementation of any research enquiry. Questions arising might, therefore, include the following:

Given the vast range of studies and approaches to enquiry that now characterise coaching, what is your own, personal knowledge management strategy? What ethical assumptions underpin that strategy?

How do you synthesise externally produced evidence with the experience and knowledge acquired through your own practice? What will your response be if the available evidence and your own professional experience conflict? How will you resolve this and what ethical stance might inform your decisions?

What types of conversation, reflection and possibly further study would help you advance your knowledge at this point in your career? How might you enhance your understanding of ethical sensitivities?

What are some of the questions, and perhaps methods of enquiry, that you would like to see the coaching community champion more explicitly? What would they add to enhance the worthwhile and ethical contributions the community could make?

In contrast to the foreground quadrants of the model, Corrie (2014; 2021) uses the background in Figure 6.1 to represent how we can position ourselves as a consumer of the research of others or a producer of our own research (the horizontal axis). Equally, we can choose to position ourselves as reflecting on research that has been produced or actively implementing the evidence that we or others have gathered (the vertical axis). Depending on how we position ourselves within this terrain at any given point in time – which will likely vary as a function of the area of interest, question in hand and our working context – the following questions might assist us:

What issues, questions and ethical dilemmas are most pressing for you in your practice right now?

What methods of investigation with what ethical implications would help you answer those questions?

Does the evidence already exist for you to draw upon, or do you need to create what you need (that is, do you see yourself primarily as a consumer or producer of research, or both)?

If you have to produce the evidence you need, do you have the knowledge to apply those methods or do you need assistance?

If you choose to implement knowledge produced by others, what ethical issues arise and what areas might need particular reflection?

It is important to note that the different fields of Figure 6.1 are seen as interacting rather than mutually exclusive. The purpose in separating them is to provide a means of engaging in reflection and critique that promotes ethical awareness and use of different approaches to knowledge generation. If this way of approaching the complexities of ethical issues in relation to evidence gathering appeals try to experiment with this framework by selecting a piece of research that you have conducted or that has been conducted by someone else or identifying a trend in evidence gathering in your area of coaching and then working through the questions outlined above.

Ethical issues for the practitioner-researcher

There is a common problem for practitioner-researchers operating outside of university settings if they wish to have their findings published. Most journals require that the work has been through an ethics panel which poses a barrier for those who do not hold university positions. This dilemma would be addressed by professional bodies establishing practitioner ethics panels for members. However, there are common ethical issues that practitioners have to address when developing research proposals. These include:

1. *Your role as an insider researcher.* As a member of the community you are investigating, your insights will add value. However, this also means you are influenced by the prevailing ideologies, relationships and assumptions that are dominant within that community. It is important to articulate your own position so that you can be clear how it influences observations you make.
2. *Maintaining confidentiality for recognisable participants.* It is likely that those participating will know each other and consequently any views you analyse and report will be recognisable to others as well as the participants themselves. It is important to be open about this so that participants have choices in whether and how they wish to proceed.
3. *The right to withdraw.* While it is appropriate to offer the right to withdraw at any time with certain methods such as qualitative research, once you have coded participants' responses they are difficult to remove from the data so you need to be clear about the point at which withdrawal is no longer possible.

4. *Ethical codes.* The ethical codes that apply to you, those of a university, professional body and your employer (if relevant) all might need consideration but so too does your own moral compass. If you were a participant in one of your studies, ask yourself if you would be happy with the process involved.

5. *Relational ethics.* This centres on individual processes of engagement with what people do together. Thus, we have to be mindful of what our interactive processes are creating. We are not just observers but part of the act of creation.

6. *Choosing methodologies.* Research methods and methodologies are expanding which enable us to capture increasingly rich accounts of people, events and moments in time. It is therefore important to be clear about your purpose in asking others to participate and its value to them. Explore the range of perspectives that best serve that purpose then consider what research process best fits the questions you seek to answer and the needs of your participants.

7. *Duty of care when using more intrusive methodologies.* The more intimate or intrusive the process the greater our duty of care. We encourage in-depth exploration in some research approaches which increases the chance of uncovering distressing feelings or thoughts for participants. It is necessary, therefore, to think through how the process will be managed, what information is given to participants in advance of the study and what opportunities for subsequent debriefing or support might need to be offered.

8. *Protecting the vulnerable.* While it is standard to pay additional attention to the needs of vulnerable populations in any research, your close connections when conducting insider research can create vulnerabilities that may not be immediately obvious. You will learn about each other in ways not anticipated which has implications for your future relationships beyond the evidence gathering process. There is a potential power imbalance which needs to be considered.

9. *Publishing findings where anonymity is difficult to protect.* With qualitative research in particular the comments you draw upon may make the participants identifiable even without the names being used. Always share with participants any comments that they made which you wish to publish to ensure consent.

10. *Maintaining consent in an emergent research project.* Complex research endeavours appear more like a journey of discovery rather than a project with set goals and timeframes. The requirements and challenges will, therefore, vary over time. Consent given at the beginning may not cover what emerges so revisiting issues of consent as the journey progresses is important.

All of the issues above can be addressed but as a participant-researcher producing evidence and as a consumer of any findings it is worth reflecting on how the endeavour is conducted.

Vignette

Sarina is an experienced executive coach who has decided to undertake a piece of research into what learning happens during the coaching process. It has been her practice for many years to ask clients to keep a journal during coaching to reflect on their learning. She also keeps a journal relating to her experiences with a client to understand the context for any movement. This provides in her view an interesting database for a research project.

She discusses this in supervision and is challenged as to what she thinks this will reveal and therefore the purpose of the research and why it might be worthwhile. She takes the view that there is little known about the parallel journey of coach and client and consequently this adds to our understanding. She is asked in terms of the discourses for research (outlined above) where this sits as a perspective.

Vignette reflections

Stop and consider for a moment where within the alternative discourses this approach sits. This leads to further challenges on the ethical implications of taking this stance. Again consider for a moment what ethical implications are specific to the approach.

In terms of the points 1–10 above consider what further ethical issues arise.

The supervisor asks her to consider in particular points 1, 7 and 8 above. *Consider what these issues might be raised?*

Finally, Sarina is asked to consider point 10 above. Consent was given originally to use the journey notes for the purpose of coaching now a different purpose for the notes is envisaged.

What are the implications of this for consent, in particular, would the client have revealed matters in the sessions that they would not like to be the subject of research?

Conclusion

In coaching, currently, practice outstrips what can be claimed as an evidence-base. The situation is improving as is the quality of research work that is emerging. What is meant by evidence to inform coaching practice depends upon the type of questions asked and the purpose for which the answers are sought to seek an answer. Different research traditions offer an opportunity to address varied questions of interest to coaching practitioners/researchers, clients and the wider community. However, these traditions generate ethical issues that are not equivalent and require coaching practitioners to think carefully about how they operate in these encounters and the limitations to what they can do or claim for the field. There are those who take the view that the worlds of research and practice operate in such separate systems that there will always be a research-practice divide.

There are emerging research paradigms that come closer to practice which enable coaches to address multiple questions of interest. The ethics of such research is different and potentially far more challenging than traditional empirical evidence gathering. Concerns include sensitivities in managing power relationships, insider knowledge, confidentiality and the critical issue of how meaningful consent can be obtained in a research study that evolves into a different form of enquiry over time. Nevertheless, these challenges can be addressed and that the broadening scope of paradigms, methodologies and methods provide the opportunity to gather evidence that gradually closes the research-practice gap. Research that provides a meaningful way to conceptualise practice as coaches is increasingly within grasp.

In summary, coaching should strive towards becoming an evidence-based profession but that should never undermine the importance of innovation. This may take us beyond current understanding into worlds of ambiguity and complexity, but these are the very spaces in which coachees dwell. Coaches need to be able to hold the tension inherent in their encounters with clients and help them to navigate the challenges they face without a map or even a clear destination in mind. To do practice-based research ethically is the challenge.

Discussion points

1.   What role does the evidence base for coaching play in developing your own practice?
2.   To what extent do you regard keeping up-to-date with current knowledge essential to your work and an ethical imperative?
3.   In terms of the alternative discourses for coaching how have each or any of them influenced your practice?
4.   What issues do you find ethically most challenging and what knowledge base might you draw upon to help you address them?

Recommended reading

Gray, D. E. (2017). *Doing Research in the Real World*. London: Sage Publications.

References

Anderson, N., Herriot, P., & Hodgkinson, G. P. (2001) The practitioner-researcher divide in Industrial, Work and Organizational (IWO). Psychology: Where are we now and where do we go from here? *Journal of Occupational and Organizational Psychology*, 74(4): 391–411.

Athanasopoulou, A. & Dopson, S. (2018). A systematic review of executive coaching outcomes: Is it the journey or the destination that matters the most? *The Leadership Quarterly*, 29(1): 70–88.

Barkham, M., Margison, F., Leach, C., Lucock, M., Mellor-Clark, J., Evans, C., Benson, L., Connell, J., Audin, K., & McGrath, G. (2001). Service profiling and outcomes benchmarking using the CORE-OM: Toward practice-based evidence in the psychological therapies. *Journal of Consulting and Clinical Psychology*, 69(2): 184–196.

Barkham, M. & Mellor-Clark, J. (2000). Rigour and relevance: The role of practice based evidence in the psychological; therapies. In N. Rowland & S. Goss (Eds), *Evidence-based Counselling and Psychological Therapies: Research and Application*. London: Routledge, pp. 127–142.

Biswas-Diener, R. & van Nieuwerburgh, C. (2021). The Professionalization of Positive Psychology Coaching. In W.A. Smith, I Boniwell, & S. Green (Eds), *Positive Psychology Coaching in the Workplace*. Cham: Springer.

Blumberg, M. & Lane, D.A. (2011). Undertaking and reviewing coaching research as CPD. In J. Passmore (2011). *Supervision in Coaching Supervision, Ethics and Continuous Professional Development*. London: Kogan Page, pp. 237–262.

Brown, V. A., Harris, J. A., & Russel, J. Y. (2010). *Tackling Wicked Problems through the Transdisciplinary Imagination*. London: Earthscan.

Cavanagh, M. & Grant, A. M. (2006). Coaching psychology and the scientist-practitioner model. In D. A. Lane & S. Corrie (Eds), *The Modern Scientist Practitioner: A Guide to Practice in Psychology*. Hove: Routledge, pp. 146–157.

Corrie, S. (2014). Deconstructing the Concept of Evidence: Diverse Perspectives on the Quest for Legitimate Knowledge. Invited address as part of the Expert Seminar Series at the Institute for Work Based Learning, Middlesex University, London.

Corrie, S. (2021). Developing coaching through research. In M. Watts & I. Florance (Eds), *Emerging Conversations in Coaching Psychology*. London: Routledge, pp. 42–59.

Corrie, S. & Lane, D. A. (2010). *Constructing Stories Telling Tales: A Guide to Formulation in Applied Psychology*. London: Karnac.

de Hahn, E. (2021). *What Works in Executive Coaching Understanding Outcomes Through Quantitative Research and Practice-Based Evidence*. Hove: Routledge.

Denvall, V. & Skillmark, M. (2021). Bridge over troubled water: closing the research-practice gap in social work. *British Journal of Social Work*, 51: 2722–2739.

Fillery-Travis, A. & Lane, D. A. (2006). Does coaching work, or are we asking the wrong question? *International Coaching Psychology Review*, 1(1): 23–36.

Fillery-Travis, A. & Corrie, S. (2019). Research and the practitioner: Getting a perspective on evidence as a coaching psychologist. In S. Palmer & A. Whybrow (Eds). *The Handbook of Coaching Psychology*, 2nd Edition. Hove: Routledge, pp. 68–79.

Fincham, R. & Clark, T. (2009). Introduction: Can we bridge the rigour-relevance gap? *Journal of Management Studies*, 46(3): 510–515.

Gherardi, S. (2012). *How to Conduct a Practice-Based Study: Problems and Methods*. Cheltenham: Edward Elgar.

Gibbons, M., Limoges, C., Nowotny, H., Schwartzman, S., Scott, P., & Tow, M. (2010). *The New Production of Knowledge: The Dynamics of Science and Research in Contemporary Societies*. London: Sage Publications.

Grant, A. M. (2016). What constitutes evidence-based coaching? A two-by-two framework for distinguishing strong from weak evidence for coaching. *International Journal of Evidence Based Coaching & Mentoring*, 14(1): 74–85.

Grant, A. M. & O'Connor, S. (2019). A brief primer for those new to coaching research and evidence-based practice. *The Coaching Psychologist*, 15(1): 1–10.

Gray, D. E., Garvey, B. & Lane, D. A. (2016). *A Critical Introduction to Coaching and Mentoring*. London: Sage Publications.

Hassad, R. (2021), quoted in De Angelis, T. (2021). Can real-world data lead to better interventions?www.apa.org/monitor/2021/09/news-real-world-data, accessed July 22, 2022.

Kieser, A. & Leiner, L. (2009). Why the rigour-relevance gap in management research is unbridgeable. *Journal of Management Studies*, 46(3): 516–533.

Kwaitowski, R. (2013). 60 seconds with Dr Richard Kwiatkowski – Research Ethics. www.youtube.com/watch?v=njJ548j7WIo, accessed July 19, 2022.

Lane, D. A. (1990). Counselling psychology in organisations. *The Psychologist*, 12: 540–544.

Lane, D. A. (1993). Counselling psychology in organisations. *Revue Européenne de Psychologie Appliquée*, 43: 41–46.

Lane, D. A. & Corrie, S. (2006). *The Modern Scientist Practitioner A guide to Practice in Psychology*. Hove: Routledge.

Lane, D. A. & Corrie, S. (2012). *Making Successful Decisions in Counselling and Psychotherapy. A Practical Guide*. Maidenhead: Open University Press.

Miller, A. & Frederickson, N. (2006). Generalisable findings and idiographic problems: struggles and successes for educational psychologists as scientist-practitioners. In D. A. Lane & S. Corrie (Eds), *The Modern Scientist Practitioner A guide to practice in Psychology*. Hove: Routledge, pp. 146–157.

Miller, M. (1988). Psychology as story-telling. *International Journal of Personal Construct Psychology*, 1: 125–138.

Milton, M. & Corrie, S. (2002). Exploring the place of technical and implicit knowledge in therapy. *The Journal of Critical Psychology, Counselling and Psychotherapy*, 2(3): 188–195.

Newnes, C. (2001). On Evidence. *Clinical Psychology*, 1: 6–12.

Nicolini, D. (2012). *Practice Theory, Work & Organization*. Oxford: Oxford University Press.

Nutley, S. M., Walter, I., & Davies, H. T. O. (2007). *Using Evidence. How Research can Inform Public Services*. Bristol: Policy Press.

Passmore, J. & Tee, D. (2021). *Coaching Researched*. Hoboken, NJ: Wiley.

Singer, J. L. (1980). The scientific basis of psychotherapeutic practice: a question of values and ethics. *Psychotherapy, Theory, Research and Practice*, 17: 372–383.

Smith, W. A., Boniwell, I., & Green, S. (2021). *Positive Coaching Psychology in the Workplace*. Springer.

Stanford University. (2022) https://web.stanford.edu/class/symsys130/Philosophy%20of%20science.pdf, accessed July 27, 2022.

Starkey, K., Hatchuel, A., & Tempest, S. (2009). Management research and the new logics of discovery and engagement. *Journal of Management Studies*, 46: 547–558.

Whybrow, A., Turner, E., McLean, J., & Hawkins, P. (2022). *Ecological and Climate-Conscious Coaching: A Companion Guide to Evolving Coaching Practice*. Hove: Routledge.

Chapter 7

Legal considerations of ethical decision making in coaching

Kevin M. Rogers

Introduction

Coaches will be familiar with the ethical challenges of their profession. The requirement for confidentiality in coaching, ensuring that information acquired through the coaching engagement is not disclosed and ensuring that there are appropriate boundaries in places in the coach/coachee relationship are well-established and well-known. Coaches will also tend to focus more on the business processes, skills and accreditation to support the success of their work. What is perhaps less well known however are the ethical and legal implications of the work of a coach. While different business models may exist for a coach (perhaps self-employed, part of a firm or organisation or perhaps larger company), there are certain legal considerations that are universal in their application and essential that a coach operates within to maintain a legal and ethical approach to their practice. Arguably, chief among these legal considerations is the importance of the General Data Protection Regulation (GDPR). Following the United Kingdom's decision to leave the European Union, the GDPR was retained as part of domestic law (termed the 'UK GDPR') and, as such, is substantially the same legislation with minor amendments to reflect local law. Therefore, the GDPR effects coaches who work in the UK, European Union (EU) and even internationally as the reach of the GDPR purports to cover, under Article 3, all data controllers based in the EU who may not process data within the EU and individuals outside of the EU who process data within the EU. Whilst sanctions for breaching this legislation are significant, of parallel importance is the reputational harm that a data breach could cause to the coach. In light of this, this chapter will foreground some of the key requirements of this legislation and signpost methods to ensure best practice in terms of data protection and data security to support a coach in operating in a legal and ethical manner.

Context to the GDPR

After a long gestation period, the GDPR came into effect in May 2018. It replaced the European Union's Data Protection Directive (95/46/EC) which

DOI: 10.4324/9781003277729-7

dated back to 1995 where there were less than 40 million internet users worldwide, and less than 1% of the UK population had access to the web. Email marketing and social media platforms like Facebook, Instagram, TikTok and LinkedIn had not been developed, and were not harvesting personal data in pursuit of changing our views about products or how we intend to vote. The GDPR sought to make several enhancements to the data protection legislation landscape. It intended to harmonise data protection laws within the EU, while also being fit for purpose for the globalised and digital age. The GDPR placed a stronger focus on compliance and the rights of the data subject or individual the personal data relates to. The jurisdictional reach is almost globally universal and therefore this is of significance to coaches who may be based within the EU or UK, or perhaps will have clients based within the EU or UK or will be using technology to move within and outside of the EU and perhaps even the sharing of data across borders. All of which comes within the remit of the GDPR and as such needs to inform the professional practice of a coach.

Not only is the reach of the legislation all-encompassing, but the scope of the act was designed to ensure maximum impact. For example, key definitions were defined broadly. The definition of 'personal data' is an example of this. The GDPR is concerned with the protection of personal data. Under the pre-GDPR legislation (within the UK it was the Data Protection Act 1998), courts had got themselves tied in knots over the definition of personal data. *Durant v. Financial Services Authority*[1] is a good example of the complexity where it sought to define personal data as being biographical in a significant sense about the data subject and that the focus of the data should be on that individual. The consequence of this and some subsequent decisions was to narrow the scope of the legislation to the extent that it became opaque as to whether an individual could seek to rely on the provisions of the legislation where they felt their personal data had been misused.

These complexities were swept away with the introduction of the GDPR. Under Article 4(1) 'personal data' means *"any information relating to an identified or identifiable natural person ('data subject'); an identifiable natural person is one who can be identified, directly or indirectly, in particular by reference to an identifier such as a name, an identification number, location data, an online identifier or to one or more factors specific to the physical, physiological, genetic, mental, economic, cultural or social identity of that natural person."* The scope of the phrase 'personal data' has become much wider. This is more than simply an academic or theoretical point because by virtue of data being personal data, data subjects can then rely on the protections afforded by the legislation. The types of data held which could be classified as personal data would be anything which could identify the data subject and would include:

- contacts on a telephone or computer address book

---

1   [2003] EWCA Civ 1746.

- a person's email address (particularly a work email address which often identifies the name, place of work and usually location around the globe)
- a mailing list of clients
- holding details to facilitate invoicing (e.g., address, name of person to be invoiced)
- a record of coaching hours with client name
- recordings of coaching conversations for analysis

It is therefore more likely that the data coaches hold about their clients (who under the provisions of the legislation are known as 'data subjects') will be classified as personal data meaning a coach needs to be cognisant and engaged with the requirements of the legislation.

Another key term which is broader in its definition is that of processing. 'Processing' has a very wide definition and includes almost any action relating to data, specifically: "*'processing' means any operation or set of operations which is performed on personal data or on sets of personal data, whether or not by automated means, such as collection, recording, organisation, structuring, storage, adaptation or alteration, retrieval, consultation, use, disclosure by transmission, dissemination or otherwise making available, alignment or combination, restriction, erasure or destruction.*"[2] Again, when analysing the applicability of the legislation in any given circumstance, the data in question must be personal data and that personal data must be processed by the coach in question. It is clear that the approach of the GDPR by broadening the core definitions have ensured that a greater number of contexts fall within the remit of the legislation. Coaches will hold significant data on their clients. This ranges from digital and paper files about organisations as well as the individuals, such as contact details and meeting notes. They are also likely to hold files, or notebooks (electronic or otherwise) with personal details on coaching clients. This can relate to both general contact information, as well as personal issues raised during coaching conversations. Coaches have an obligation to ensure their handling of this data is within the parameters of the GDPR.

Requirements on a coach

Most coaches operate as sole practitioners, where coaching may be only part of their total income. As a result, few are aware of the requirements placed on them by the GDPR and may be unwittingly acting in a manner contrary to the legislation. If, as a coach is indeed operating as a sole practitioner, then the first thing to note is that they would be classified as the data controller. A data controller is "*the natural or legal person, public authority, agency or other body which, alone or jointly with others, determines the purposes and means of the processing of personal data; where the purposes and means of*

---

2   GDPR, Article 4(2).

such processing are determined by Union or Member State law, the controller or the specific criteria for its nomination may be provided for by Union or Member State law.[3] As data controller, this person is the main decision maker when it comes to how personal data is handled and crucially may be found to be liable for breaches of the GDPR. There is a severe regime of fines; up to 4% of worldwide turnover up to a maximum of £17m for serious breaches. This is significantly more than existed in the legislation prior to the GDPR (the Data Protection Act 1998), where the maximum penalty levied was a £5,000 fine (Smith & Chamberlain, 2015). Perhaps crucially for coaches, the liability for breaches of the GDPR extends beyond data controllers and companies onto individual data processors themselves. Meaning it is even more critical for the challenges in this area of law to be considered. It is important to note there the scope of the GDPR covers all engagement with personal data regardless of the size of business or type of organisation. The legislation applies as much to a sole trader processing personal data as it does a behemoth multi-national company.

Once identified as the data controller, the first responsibility for the coach is to notify their local supervisory authority that they are processing personal data. In the United Kingdom, the relevant authority is the Information Commissioner's Office (ICO)[4]. Under the Data Protection (Charges and Information) Regulations 2018, individuals and organisations that process personal data need to pay a data protection fee to the Information Commissioner's Office (ICO), unless they are exempt. The fee is tiered, and the amount depends on the size of the organisation. It is expected that a coach (or organisation they work for) has a privacy policy in place. This will cover the identity and contact details of the organisation, the data controller (who may or may not be the data protection officer), the purpose of processing personal data and ground for processing. The policy should also state what the data will be used for, whether the data will be shared with any third party, how long data will be retained for, the rights of the data subject (including access rights) and details of who the data subject should contact.[5] Furthermore, it would be helpful at the outset if the coach carries out an audit of data held along with the security measures currently in place. This will help a coach in the management of the personal data they hold. The Information

---

3　GDPR, Article 4(7).
4　Examples of equivalent authorities include the Bundesbeauftragter für den Datenschutz und die Informationsfreiheit (BfDI) (Germany), Commission nationale de l'informatique et des libertés (France), An Coimisinéir Cosanta Sonraí (DPC) (Republic of Ireland) and Agencia Española de Protección de Datos (Spain).
5　The Information Commissioner's Office contains a helpful checklist with details of what a privacy policy should contain: https://ico.org.uk/for-organisations/guide-to-data-protection/guide-to-the-general-data-protection-regulation-gdpr/the-right-to-be-informed/what-privacy-information-should-we-provide.

Commissioner's website has several audit tools that may be helpful for this purpose.[6] A coach also needs to be cognisant about third party platforms, particularly social networks (e.g. LinkedIn) where a coach may engage with clients. It is straightforward when a coach is holding information on their own platforms, although with contacts held and stored by a third party it is more complex. Not surprisingly, a coach may not target people on LinkedIn with unsolicited commercial communication advertising their services and the provisions of the Privacy and Electronic Communications are of relevance here explaining the difference between 'solicited' and 'unsolicited'. In terms of 'ownership' of the list of contacts, social networks will normally outline in their terms and conditions that ownership of the contacts resides with the account holder (so, the coach). Where a coach or individual is employed and leaves the employment it may be that the employer wants ownership of the contacts, although it will fall on the employer to demonstrate that the contacts are commercially confidential and it will be difficult for an employer to demonstrate that headline information about an individual or group of individuals is commercially confidential. There is very limited case law on this matter within England and Wales where the distinction between third party platforms (owned by the individual) and in-house platforms, such as an Outlook address list and owned by the employer, has been considered. The wisest approach in an employee/employer relationship is to clarify at the outset and have clear policies in place about who owns the data on third party platforms.

Within the GDPR there are several principles, which act as an umbrella over all the legislation. These principles set out how data should be handled and inform the entirety of the legislation. These principles are:

1. Lawfulness, fairness and transparency

The personal data should be used in a way which complies with the legislation and is in line with what has been told to the data subject. If a company or individual processes or uses personal data they need to have a reason (or lawful base) for doing so and they need to ensure that their use of the data does not extend beyond that purpose. There are six lawful bases for processing personal data. These are:

a) The data subject has given their clear consent for their personal data to be processed for a particular and specific purpose.
b) That the processing is necessary for a contract a data controller has with a data subject.
c) The processing is necessary in order to comply with a legal obligation.
d) The processing is in the vital interests of the data subject.

---

6   See for example: https://ico.org.uk/for-organisations.

e)   The processing is necessary to perform a task which is in the public interest.

f)   That the processing is necessary for the legitimate interests of the data subject or a third party.

It is suggested that the most likely lawful ground for a coach to process personal data will be consent. There are other grounds, however, if as a coach consent is the basis for processing data the coach will need to ensure that the consent provided is a freely given, specific, informed and unambiguous indication of the data subject's agreement and that this consent can be evidenced by the data controller.

The threshold for consent increases where a data controller is processing special category data. This is a data type which is more sensitive in nature, which reveals:

- racial or ethnic origin;
- political opinions;
- religious or philosophical beliefs;
- trade union membership;
- genetic data;
- biometric data (where used for identification purposes);
- health;
- a person's sex life; and
- a person's sexual orientation.

If a coach is processing the type of special category data and are using the legal basis for consent, the coach will need to ensure they have the *explicit* consent of the data subject.[7]

2. Purpose limitation

This principle is designed to prevent 'mission creep' or obtaining personal data for a purpose but then using the same data for wider purposes not originally outlined at the point of collection. In short, where personal data is collected by a coach it can only be used in a manner consistent with what is expected by the data subject and not for an extra or unrelated

---

7   Article 9 lists the other legal bases for processing special category data. Specifically, these are: Employment, social security and social protection (if authorised by law), vital interests of the data subject, carried out by not-for-profit bodies, where the data is made public by the data subject, legal claims or judicial acts, reasons of substantial public interest (with a basis in law), health or social care (with a basis in law), public health (with a basis in law) or archiving, research and statistics (with a basis in law). In reality, however, in the unlikely circumstance where a coach finds they are processing special category data explicit consent is likely to be the relevant legal base.

purpose.[8] This is important from a legal point of view, but also an ethical standpoint.

3. Data minimalisation

This principle is closely aligned to the principle of purpose limited and requires data controllers to limit the amount of personal data that they collect to the level of what is needed. In short, whilst the business focus between coaches will differ it is likely that in the majority of cases the personal data held will include contact details and notes of interactions with the client. In some cases, financial details may be held for payment purposes, but in a professional coaching context it is unlikely that wider information (for instance, medical records) will need to be held. Crucially, the data held needs to correspond to what a coach needs.

4. Accuracy

It is important both for the coach and the client that the personal data held should be accurate and kept up to date. There is a very practical purpose for this to ensure that a coach has the correct information to be able to contact the client and also ensure that notes of conversations are kept up to date to ensure relevance of future conversations. It is incumbent upon a coach to take reasonable steps to ensure that the data held is accurate. This could include the coach periodically checking details with the client to ensure accuracy.

5. Storage limitation

Under this principle, the coach has an obligation to ensure that they only keep personal data for as long as it is needed. When the data is no longer needed, it should be deleted and/or securely destroyed. The length of time that personal data is retained should be included as part of the privacy policy – this could be as part of a retention schedule. The length of time personal data is held for depends on the type of data held. So, for example, a coach would retain personal data of a client during the existence of their coach/client but would need to destroy this information after the relationship concludes. Twelve months is not an unreasonable period in this context (to cover situations where a client may get back in touch with a coach). A coach may wish to retain basic contact details for longer as part of a client database. When it comes to destroying data, a coach may need to consider

8   European Commission Article 29 Working Party Opinion 03/2013 on purpose limitation (2013). Available at: https://ec.europa.eu/justice/article-29/documenta-tion/opinion-recommendation/files/2013/wp203_en.pdf.

professional data services that can securely destroy data, clean computer hard drives and back-up devices and shred paper files and ensure their data retention schedule / policy details how long recordings of sessions will be retained for.

6. Integrity and confidentiality (security)

Although no principle is more important than any of the others, arguably this principle should inform a coach's entire practice with personal data. A coach needs to ensure that they keep the personal data they hold securely and this security should be maintained. A coach needs to ensure that their client list and records of conversations are kept security. The type and level of security will depend on the sensitivity of the data held, although passwords, encryption and secure databases are standard practices to ensure the security. As a basic rule of thumb, the more sensitive the personal data held a greater level of security is required. This principle was exemplified in the European case of *I v. Finland* where a data subject was able to show that a hospital holding sensitive data relating to medical records could be easily accessed by people within the hospital.[9] In this case, 'I' (who was a nurse who worked in the eye department of a Finnish hospital who also attended the same hospital's infectious diseases clinic) began to suspect that her fellow employees had become aware of her HIV diagnosis. 'I' requested to be informed of who had accessed her medical records and when, but the hospital advised that they only kept a record of the last five instances of patient records being accessed. In addition, there was nothing to stop colleagues in the eye department from accessing 'I's' records. The court held that there was sufficient evidence that the hospital had not taken sufficient steps to protect the security of the personal data and awarded 'I' compensation. Coaches may wish to share details of their client conversations with other coaches as part of a supervision group. It is recommended that coaches advise clients of this as part of their terms of engagement and where this takes place clients are suitably anonymised during the discussions.

Coaches also need to be mindful of the data breach notification rules within the GDPR, which place an obligation on a data controller to advise the supervisory body (for instance, the ICO in the UK) of a breach of security leading to the accidental or unlawful destruction, loss, alteration, unauthorised disclosure of, or access to, personal data. It could be that the personal data is accessed by a third party or where data is sent to the incorrect recipient. Where the loss could lead to serious harm to the data subject the data controller needs to advise the supervisory authority within 72 hours.[10]

---

9   Application no. 20511/03, European Court of Human Rights (2008).
10   Article 29 Data Protection Working Party *Guidelines on Personal data breach notification under Regulation 2016/679* (2018). Available at: https://ec.europa.eu/newsroom/article29/items/612052/en.

7. Accountability

The final principle underpins the other six principles and emphasises the importance of taking responsibility for the data and how it is managed. This prevents individuals from avoiding responsibility through ignorance, wilful or otherwise. As such, all coaches, whether self-employed or otherwise, have an obligation to ensure they are taking appropriate steps to adhere to the requirements of the data protection legislation.

Rights of the data subject

The GDPR does not only confer responsibilities on those that process personal data it also provides data subjects with several rights which a data controller needs to adhere to in situations where a data subject seeks to exercise these rights. A coach (or data controller) needs to ensure that they respond appropriately. The rights afforded to a data subject should be identified as part of the coach/client contract and are:

1. **The right to be informed** – meaning that a client has the right to be informed about the collection and use of their personal data, including privacy information such as the purpose and basis for processing.
2. **The right of access** – data subjects have the right of copies of the personal data held about them. This is commonly known as a data subject access request (SAR) and can be made verbally or in writing (including via social media). A data controller is unable to charge a fee to an individual making a SAR and should respond to the request within a month (where it would be complex to obtain the personal data this time period can be extended by two months).
3. **The right to rectification** – a data subject can request either verbally or in writing to correct inaccurate personal data held.
4. **The right to erasure** – this right contained within Article 17 was one of the main headlines of controversy when the GDPR was originally introduced and known as 'the right to be forgotten'. Where consent is the lawful basis for processing, data subjects can only rely on this right if the personal data is no longer needed for the purpose for which it was originally collected. Where legitimate interest is the lawful basis for processing the data needs to be erased if there is no overriding legitimate interest to continue the processing.[11] Initial concern about the right to be forgotten was that it would place onerous obligations on data controllers to remove personal data, although recent case law has tempered the perceived extremities of this data subject right.[12] The right to be forgotten has significant implications for

---

11 GDPR.eu, *Everything you need to know about the "Right to be forgotten"*. Available at: https://gdpr.eu/right-to-be-forgotten.
12 BBC News, *Google wins landmark right to be forgotten case* (24 September 2019). Available at: www.bbc.co.uk/news/technology-49808208.

some organisations like Google. But for small organisations, and individual coaches, this may simply require the ability to delete individuals and their records from the files. This might be easy for digital files, but does require some thought about back-ups, as well as for paper records, such as those contained in a notebook, supervision notes or personal journals.

5. **The right to restrict processing** – this is an alternative right to the right to erasure and it provides data subjects with the right to limit the way that an organisation uses their data. There are several occasions where this right can be used, with the main grounds being where the data subject is contesting the accuracy of the data or where the legal basis for processing the data is being challenged.

6. **The right to data portability** - this right allows data subjects to obtain and reuse their personal data for their own purposes across different services. The data needs to be transferred in a machine-readable manner (an example could be home meter readings).

7. **The right to object** – under this right, a data subject can object to the processing of their personal data. This would effectively stop the coach from processing their client's personal data. This is an absolute right where it concerns direct marketing (so, if a coaching business engaged in marketing to former clients, a recipient could request that this advertising stops with immediate effect).

8. **Rights in relation to automated decision making and profiling** – although very unlikely to apply to a coach in their business, this right provides the data subject the ability to stop automatic decision making where their personal data is used (for example, recruitment processes, which involve automatic aptitude tests).

In their operations, a coach needs to be mindful that not only do they have several responsibilities under the data protection legislation, but also a data subject has a number of rights, which they could seek to exercise during, or even after, their engagement with the coach. Alongside the legal imperative, it is also important for the coach that their business is conducted legally, ethically and properly so as to ensure there is no negative impact on the goodwill of the coach's practice.

Confidentiality

It would be remiss of any chapter on the legal and ethical considerations of coaching not to include a section on confidentiality. The Global Code of Ethics[13] states that *"…coaches maintain the strictest level of confidentiality*

---

13 Available at: https://emccuk.org/Common/Uploaded%20files/Policies/Global_ Code_of_Ethics_EN_v3.pdf (June 2021).

with all clients."[14] While confidentiality is a core component of all the international coaching governing bodies. Furthermore, there is a strong recommendation that at the outset of the coaching relationship the terms of engagement set out the boundaries of that confidentiality. That a client and coach have a confidential relationship will all greater openness, trust and greater insight to support the client in their practice, while a breach of this confidentiality could have serious implications on the coach, in no small way through reputational impact. Any information from the coaching relationship will belong to the client and should not be shared without the consent of the client. This is in the context of the protection afforded to a data subject in the data protection legislation. A coach ensuring the boundaries of confidentiality is important for their own practice as a coach's reputation and practice could be compromised where allegations of a breach of confidence are made by a client.

Confidentiality is important as it allows a client to speak freely, without fear of any of their comments or observations being fed back to the senior team of their organisation or business, or perhaps their customers, clients, or peers. That said, the parameters of this confidentiality are not absolute and there are limitations. For instance, it may be that there is an incidence of criminality or perhaps risk of serious harm to another (such as serious illegality, including insider dealing or fraud, threat to life or where there is a legal duty to disclose (such as certain safeguarding matters or matters relating to terrorism)). Rare situations may emerge where a coach is asked to give evidence in a court of law and may need to disclose some of the contents of their discussions with their client. A coach would be required under their code of ethics (which will speak about the importance of upholding the law in the country in which they are operating) to attend court and speak truthfully, which may, of course, lead to an impact on the coach/client confidentiality. Alternatively, there may be a risk of harm to either the client or another person. This is particularly pertinent in circumstances which involve children or adults at risk (or vulnerable adults). Where a coach breaches the client's confidence, a client can complain to either the coaching provider or the professional body and they may find themselves held responsible by their professional body should an allegation of breach of confidence be upheld.

In these circumstances, which are often tricky, the coach will need to come to a view about any reporting duties they may have, and it would be prudent for the coach to include their reporting duties as part of the coach/client contract. This is where it is important to ensure that a coach has an effective and anonymous supervision model in place. In this forum, a coach can explore with their supervisor the legal/ethical dilemma they are facing and explore together the more appropriate route to take. In doing so, it is likely a

---

14 Ibid, para 2.13.

coach will explore with their supervisor legal implications, the code of ethics and consider multiple perspectives before coming to a decision.

Contract of engagement

Key information around confidentiality and key privacy details should be set out in the contract of engagement established at the outset of the coaching relationship. This contract should fully outline the nature, terms and conditions of the coaching, mentoring, or supervision contract. This will also include the financial, logistical and confidentiality arrangements. It should set out the boundaries of confidentiality and should note that in instances of criminality or risk of serious harm that confidentiality could be broken. A coach should avoid saying that confidentiality would be absolute as there are grounds for this not being the case. In terms of data protection, the contract should set out the ground for processing data and if the ground is consent then the contract should expressly state this. Clear contact details should be provided to allow the client to be able to contact the coach should they wish to exercise any of their rights under the GDPR. It is important that this contract is clear, simple and easy to understand.

Conclusion

The legal and ethical ramifications of a coaching practice are extensive and the GDPR has a big impact on coaching, and particularly digital coaching. This chapter has focused on these data protection, confidentiality and privacy aspects. The important thing to stress to a coach is that most of these legal requirements can be adhered to through good practice in terms of a clear contract of engagement, good data handling practices and clear communication with the client around grounds and purposes of processing their personal data. Legal standards in this area can be maintained by ensuring that technical and organisational measures are put in place to safeguard the security of the data (for instance, ensuring that backups are available, that checks are there are regular checks in place to assure the accuracy of the data held and that any data held is kept secure through passwords and encryption. A data retention policy for a coach is good practice as it sets out the length of time that personal data is retained for. This should be identified as part of the contract of engagement with the client, which will also foreground the privacy policy which identifies to the client the purpose, grounds and basis for processing their personal data. Whilst penalties contained within the GDPR for a breach of the legislation are substantial and a sufficient stick to ensure adherence will the rules, the ethical standing of a coach, and the requirements of the professional bodies around the globe necessitate that a coach should seek to ensure best practice in this field to ensure the standing of their operation and that no negative impact is levelled against a coach's individual business, but also the broader coaching profession.

Discussion points

1. To what extent does your coaching practice adhere to the principles of the GDPR? Where do you think you could enhance your practice in this field?
2. Reflect on the occasions in your practice where you process (or handle) personal data and what steps do you need to take to ensure that you keep that data secure. For example, if you keep records of conversations with clients how do you ensure this information remains confidential? How do you ensure that your client database is kept secure? What could you do to enhance your practice around data security?
3. Where you engage with a client, does your contract set out the key parameters of your coaching relationship in matters relating to the lawful base for processing personal data, confidentiality and other ethical considerations outlined by the professional bodies?
4. Consider your approach to retention of personal data once a relationship with a client has concluded. Do you advise a client at the outset of your relationship of the length of time their data will be retained for? Do you have an operational data retention policy who sets out how long different types of data will be retained for?

Recommended reading

European Mentoring and Coaching Council. *GDPR Guidance for Members.* https://emccuk.org/Common/Uploaded%20files/Policies/GDPR-guidance-for-coaches.pdf.

References

Information Commissioner's Office. (2022) Guide for organisations. Retrieved on July 20, 2022 from https://ico.org.uk/for-organisations.

Smith, D. & Chamberlain, P. (2015) On the blacklist: how did the UK's top building firms get secret information on their workers? *The Guardian*, February 27. Retrieved on July 22, 2022 from www.theguardian.com/uk-news/2015/feb/27/on-the-blacklist-building-firms-secret-information-on-workers.

Ethics in coaching practice

Chapter 8

The psychological contract in coaching

Pam McLean

Introduction

Exploration of the concept of the psychological contract has been sparsely covered in the field of coaching and yet an ethical awareness of this dimension has profound implications for the work of the coach. The coach's developmental path on the road to ethical maturity warrants attention to multiple layers operating within the coach's internal landscape, in the client's sphere, and in the broader context and systems at play of the work of coaching. The psychological contract is one of those layers.

The term 'psychological contract' represents the implicit, unspoken, subconscious, and unconscious agreements that accompany any explicit and written contract. In the legal context, we are fully cognizant of the reality that inherent in every written contract are latent ambiguities open to multiple interpretations depending upon a variety of extrinsic facts.

Implicit contracts exist in most parts of our lives – our social contracts, employment contracts, families, and intimate relationships. We pay taxes based upon an implicit contract that governments will provide a certain level of services and do certain things that can remain largely ambiguous. We enter employment contracts and implicit in the contract might be any number of expectations on both parties including potential for advancement, opportunities to learn on the job, and more. The traditional marital contract can be fraught with implicit hopes, expectations, and trade-offs that are out of awareness until well into the marriage. One partner's hope might be that their partner will be fully supportive of their career wishes while the other partner might hope for quite a different arrangement.

The concept of a psychological contract has been studied most thoroughly within the organizational context and to a lesser extent in the field of psychology and psychotherapy. Yet, only recently has this dynamic been examined within the coaching relationship and the multiple systems at play in the work of coaching.

This chapter draws our attention to thoroughly understand the role of this key dynamic in our coaching work, interweaving our ethical responsibility for

DOI: 10.4324/9781003277729-8

becoming aware of *psychological contracting within our work*, in ourselves as coaches, within our clients, and within the broader systems in which we work.

The chapter begins with a brief summary of the literature on psychological contracting in related fields of study, then moves to an exploration of several useful conceptual frameworks from the fields of counseling and psychology that inform a coach's understanding of the nuances of the psychological contract – both conscious and unconscious – for the coach and coachee in a coaching engagement. Finally, this chapter will examine a linkage between coaching maturity and the psychological contract through vignettes and a series of simple tools for uncovering the unspoken contracts *will be offered.*

Distinctive ethical features

A coach's capacity to observe and consciously use this awareness in the engagement creates increased value and impact in the coaching work. An understanding of the psychological contract unfolds slowly as the coach matures. This understanding is an ethical practice for a coach that enhances the depth and value of the work for the coachee.

Taken a step further, if a coach is able to consider factors like transference and countertransference, generally embedded in the psychological contract, and make conscious choices about how to use the countertransference material on behalf of the coachee rather than in reaction to the coachee, this further deepens the meaning and impact of the coaching engagement.

Ethics spans the distance from the legalities of confidentiality to the alignment with a code of ethics, to the duty to report, to dual relationships, and all the way to the cultivation of one's capacities to be self-aware, observe, and explore what lies underneath the surface in the coaching work.

The context

This chapter examines research adjacent/peripheral to the field of coaching, focusing on several dimensions of psychological contracting that provide a helpful understanding of implicit contracts. With this backdrop as a first level foundation, the chapter will delve into the important role this concept and dynamic plays in a coaching engagement. Lastly, an examination of the value it can create in the coaching work when the practitioner has developed their ethical maturity sufficiently to become aware of the unconscious and implicit levels of agreements and hopes that can derail and limit what is possible in the coaching engagement.

The psychological contract inside the organization

The concept of the psychological contract has been most widely studied relative to the workplace employment contract. In organizational research, the concept of the 'psychological contract' refers to the implicit and undocumented needs, wants, and expectations of employers and employees in relation to each other (Argyris, 1960; Schein, 1980). Argyris is credited with developing this concept emphasizing the reality that even while this unspoken contract is not documented, it plays a powerful role in the behavior that shows up inside an organization. Schein further studied this concept and viewed it as is a set of undocumented expectations between the organization and its employees wherein when expectations between both parties' match, harmony prevails while when a mismatch exists, problems surface, such as distrust, disloyalty, and under-performance.

Rousseau (1995) extended the literature on this topic and underlined that while not explicitly included in the contract, the psychological contract is understood by both parties wherein the psychological meaning and interpretation doesn't come from the individual, but rather from a set of common beliefs exchanged between employee and employer for their mutual interests. Rousseau (2000) wrote of the psychological contract as "the individual's interpretation of an exchange of promises that is mutually agreed on and voluntarily made between two or more parties" (p. 284).

Hewson (1999) uses the image of an iceberg when describing the visible contract – that which is above water – and the unseen psychological contract that resides below the surface, noting the part that is below the waterline is much larger and potentially more powerful or destructive. In the organizational context, he suggests that transparency is particularly helpful in fostering healthy psychological contracts. He further advises that these contracts are fluid and changing based on what's unfolding for the employee and the employer and social forces at play at any particular time.

Rollinson (2008) defines this contract as the accumulation of unspoken expectations and commitments both parties have of each other. Dundon and Rollinson (2011) identify eight parameters that can influence the employee's psychological contract, including: safe working environment, satisfying work, job security, equal promotion opportunities, professional development opportunities, fair and equal pay, and having input into decisions that might affect them. Of these, probably the most easily understood dimension of the psychological contract has been job security (Shore and Tetrick, 1994), although that factor is rapidly becoming rarer in our world today. Guest (2014) goes a step further and examines the degree to which the psychological contract serves as a gateway into understanding employee turnover. His findings suggest that when employers fulfill their commitments and obligations to their employees, employees are less likely to voluntarily quit the organization. While all these parameters are likely fluid in our changing workplace, they provide a useful view into what role the psychological contract in the workplace might play.

These researchers and observers seem to agree that within an organization there may exist several written contracts based upon a variety of relationships; and, within each separate **contract,** a psychological contract exists that impacts the work agreement. Each written contract is open to two factors: a psychological-level contract unique to each employee/employer relationship, and the unique way in which each employee makes meaning (based on several external factors) and interprets the implicit realities of the contract. Michael Carroll (2005) offers a wide range of influences ranging from cultural norms and societal factors to the individual's specific needs and unresolved issues as depicted below (Figure 8.1).

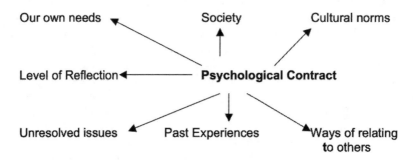

Figure 8.1 Influences on the Psychological Contract (Carroll, 2005)

The psychological contract in counseling frameworks

The psychological contract in the workplace provides a useful perspective on the implicit contract, an unwritten contract that is generally known to employee and employer even while unspoken; while the fields of counseling and psychology add more dimensions and complexities to this concept to incorporate the levels of a contract that are of a more individualized and personal nature; and which can either emerge out of awareness or remain at times fully unconscious.

In counseling and psychology, and by extension coaching, a successful engagement is dependent on the quality of the relationship between counselor and client (Bergin & Lambert, 1978; Hubble et al., 1999). Carroll applies more personal influences on the psychological contract in the field of counseling and suggests that one's present needs influence perception and expectations. He offers the quintessential example of the client who expects her counsellor might become her friend and brings gifts to each session. As suggested by the writing of Carroll, the field of psychology and psychodynamic therapy offers a view into the psychological contract that is more complex and potentially more relevant to the field of coaching than the employee-employer contract because it addresses the implicit and oft-times unconscious contracts of which we may not be aware that can easily impede the work of coaching if the coach isn't sufficiently skilled and aware of what lies beneath the surface.

Sills (1998) explores dimensions of psychological contract that are implicit, unspoken, and to various degrees, outside of awareness or are unconscious for the client. In Sills' study of the psychological contract as found in the field of counseling and psychology, she writes "the psychological contract is not usually even in awareness and the use of the word reminds us powerfully of the strength of such unspoken and unchosen pacts, what are at best empathic connections and at worst the enmeshment of an unrecognized transference and counter-transference symbiosis" (p. 21).

Berne (1966), father of transactional analysis, was one of the first to address the psychological contract in the field of psychology. He provides a model of three levels of contracts: the administrative, the professional, and the psychological. The administrative deals with logistics and practical arrangements along with confidentiality and its limits. The professional contract concentrates on goals of the work and the outcomes that are desired. The psychological contract consists of the unspoken and often unconscious and it contains two elements, the negative and the positive attributes.

Positive and negative psychological contracts

Berne (1966) and others in the field of psychology pay particular attention to this added analysis of the positive and negative psychological contract. According to Berne (1966) the positive dimension is established when the administrative and professional contracts are well articulated, and the practitioner and client feel confident they understand their agreements and have an early working alliance that is warm and respectful, creating conditions for the possibility of positive outcomes. Winnicott's (1958) concept of 'facilitative' transference and countertransference seem to be at play in the positive contract, creating an environment of warmth, respect, and safety – a holding environment that allows for meaningful work to unfold. The negative psychological contract represents the hidden agenda or the deeply held beliefs that are largely out of awareness and likely to thwart the goals of the counseling if left unexplored.

Sills (1997) suggests the negative psychological contract can adversely affect the course of an engagement in two ways. The first lies in what she describes as the hidden agenda: one's wishes, hopes and fantasies, as well as one's unspoken fears. The client may come to the counselor with a hope that her willingness to enter into psychotherapy will be sufficient to rescue her marriage; or the psychotherapist might be swayed to collude with his client in order to avoid fearful explorations or outcomes. The second, and largely inescapable, way the negative psychological contract can hinder the work is found in the unspoken expectations the client brings that will not be in his or her awareness and will be based on past experiences and relationships.

Berne (1966) takes this unspoken and unconscious expectation a step further and suggests that a client comes to psychotherapy in order to confirm or re-confirm their 'script' or past experiences and beliefs. The man who has always allowed others to dominate his decision making will expect the psychotherapist to take on that same role, thus confirming his script. The woman who never feels understood will expect the same dynamic to play out in the psychotherapy as her conversations moves from topic to topic in rambling and unconnected thoughts, leaving the therapist confused and resulting in the reconfirmation of her early script.

Cyclical dynamics

This second dimension of the negative psychological contract lies in the client's transference, and it opens the door for the psychotherapist's countertransference. Herein, lies the ethical landscape of the psychological contract. If the psychotherapist has not sufficiently cultivated their use of self, they may well accept the invitation to reconfirm the client's script. Wachtel (1977) describes this as 'cyclical dynamics' – instead of recognizing the invitation and pivoting to explore it together, the therapist may step into the 'dance' and reconfirm the client's old beliefs or script. A common example of accepting the invitation and creating Wachtel's 'cyclical dynamic' might be the psychotherapist who responds to the client's wish to be rescued by donning the cape and obliging by attempting (usually unsuccessfully!) to rescue the client by making suggestions, offering comfort. and digging for solutions that might serve the client. Once this cyclical dynamic is a part of the relational interaction, the psychotherapist is reaffirming a repeating cycle, or as Berne suggests, confirming a core script of the client.

Transference and countertransference embodies the psychological contract

Transference and countertransference happen regularly in psychotherapy because the relationship the client creates with the therapist naturally reflects the client's relationships in their everyday life. The ethical work of the therapist is a commitment to the cultivation of their own internal landscape such that they can observe and work with the dynamics rather than falling into a negative psychological contract.

Sills additionally notes that the practitioner will also regularly bring some transference into the psychotherapy room and the client will respond to this. The therapist that wants to provide answers may cull out acquiescence, denial, or rebellion depending upon the client's history. Again, the ethical work of the psychotherapist is to bring into awareness their own transference dynamics.

The psychological contract in the coaching engagement

As suggested by the writing of Carroll, the field of psychology and psychodynamic therapy offer a view into the psychological contract that is more complex and potentially more relevant to the field of coaching than the employee-employer contract because it addresses the implicit and often unconscious or *unknown* contracts that can easily impede the work of coaching if the coach isn't sufficiently skilled and aware of this dynamic in play.

In coaching, the positive psychological contract is fostered through a clear working contract, full presence, an empathic connection, and a strong working alliance. These dimensions are easier to teach, model, and convey in the coach's development than the negative form. The negative psychological contract asks much more of the coach and requires a willingness to explore one's inner landscape with diligence throughout one's journey from novice to maturity.

Literature in the field of coaching is just beginning to address this important concept that is present in every coaching engagement and in the work of coach supervision as well.

Hawkins and Turner (2020, p. 86) write extensively about contracting within multi-stakeholder systems and they allude to the psychological contract in their exploration of relational dynamics, noting:

> "Client's stories are often 'sticky' so that the coach may get caught within the story of their client…this can mean that [the coach] starts to see the world through the client's eyes and vicariously share their emotional reactions to situations and other people."

Beware of the 'Transference Cure'

Kets DeVries (2014) addresses the psychological contract, and the negative psychological contract, as the context for real change versus pseudo-change in the coaching engagement. He references the psychoanalytic term 'the transference cure', a dynamic whereby the cure represents a form of collusion between the coach and client with the client claiming victory or miraculous change to please their coach or therapist. He cautions that without adequate development, a coach can wind up colluding and believing a 'cure' has occurred! Emphasizing the role of supervision, he also raises the question about what kind of training is necessary to enable a coach to take a deeper look into the psychological contract.

'ABC' Approach allows the psychological contract to emerge

Hawkins and Turner (2020) underline the need for clear contracting at all levels to create support boundaries that equip the coach to resist the urge to get drawn into the client's story. In a recent discussion with Hawkins (private conversation) he shared that he often talks with coaches about the important ABC's of coaching – by which he means 'always be contracting'; a reminder that contracts at all levels are fluid, not static. 'Always be contracting' may additionally remind the coach to be alert for the overt, the implicit. and the unconscious.

Coach supervision gives voice to the psychological contract

In coaching the psychological contract is an evolving and emergent force that requires a coach to routinely engage in their own development in order that the coach might cultivate the capacity to become fully attuned to what is happening in one's head, heart, and gut. This entails noticing judgements and biases along with wishes and wants for the client. It includes paying close attention to reactions that arise in relation to the client including strong feelings like anger, disgust, pity, and confusion along with the more subtle sensations of boredom, feeling sleepy, wanting to pull back or withdraw, and more.

Hawkins and Shohet (2012) have written extensively of the role coach supervision plays in a coach's development and a coach's capacity to see multiple layers at play. They address the developmental function of coach supervision that is achieved through reflection and examination of all aspects of a coaching engagement and suggest through their experience that this helps the supervisee in the following ways (p. 62):

- To understand the client better;
- To become more aware of their own reactions and responses to the client;
- To understand the dynamics of the interactions between themselves and their clients;
- To look at how they intervened and the consequences of their interventions; and
- To explore other ways of working with this and other similar client situations.

Their articulation of what unfolds in supervision emphasizes the value of supervision in cultivating a capacity to uncover the complexities of the psychological contract viewed through the lenses of transference and countertransference.

Each coaching relationship has a unique 'dance', a distinctive tenor that holds some of the keys to changes the client wants to make. When the coach is unable to recognize this tenor, the dreaded 'transference cure', resulting in no real change, is the most likely outcome of the work. Consider the following vignette.

Vignette: Paul wants a promotion

Paul comes to coaching wanting to figure out what needs to change for him to be viewed as a candidate for a promotion in his department. He finds himself continually frustrated because he is passed over and, in his view, he is smarter than the candidates chosen. As the coach, you are aware that Paul is super-smart, and you want to help him figure out what he needs to alter to better position himself for a promotion. Paul is sincere and he is fully committed to coaching to solve this issue and finally get recognized. Even before stakeholder input is gained, you notice you find Paul tedious. He conveys situations and information to you in great detail, and you find yourself almost getting lost or distracted as he talks in a circuitous way and seems never to stop to even take a breath. Your third session with Paul is tomorrow and you find yourself dreading the meeting. You wish he could just stay focused, and you know it will be yet another session of Paul moving from one topic to another in his droning voice.

This coach may well be early in their development journey and instead of paying attention to the patterns of how Paul shows up and the reactions happening inside the coach, this coach finds himself in judgment – frustrated, distracted, bored, almost dreading the upcoming sessions. We might speculate that the psychological contract, or in Berne's terms, the script Paul seeks to have reconfirmed is "I keep trying to help people understand by my careful explanations, but nobody gets me!" The unaware coach may 'accept the invitation' to collude with Paul's psychological contract, and like everyone else, confirm for Paul that he is hard to understand, he's frustrating, and there is a wish to get away from him. Herein lies the 'the transference cure'! Nothing changes, nothing in 'the dance' is explored. Every coach has been in a situation similar to this, especially in the early days of their coaching journey. Some coaches may remain in this state if they don't view their own development as an essential, ethical practice.

Let's imagine this coach is further along on his developmental journey and he has built reflective practices along the way while regularly partaking in supervision. He may not yet discern all parts of the dynamics at play, but he is likely to bring this coaching engagement to supervision to explore. He notices what is triggered in him by Paul's meandering talking and he knows it is not a usual reaction for him as a coach. He hears in Paul's story that there is a pattern of not gaining a promotion that has occurred on several occasions. He is certain there is a dynamic to explore, but he's not quite sure precisely what it is and how to create an intervention that will serve Paul.

Finally, let's imagine this coach is even further along in his own development and maturation as a coach through reflective practices, some journaling and long-term supervision. He can notice what is uniquely triggered in himself and he also closely observes how his client is showing up. He is aware through Paul's story that there is a pattern that has occurred for Paul on several occasions. He engages in his own reflections and considers the possibility that Paul's psychological contract reinforces a script that 'no matter how much he tries (and how long he talks), nobody understands him'. The coach at this stage in their development also experiences the dance that happens when they come together. Paul talks ad nauseum; in the beginning the coach tries to understand, yet as the talking continues, the coach finds himself frustrated. Paul doesn't see the dynamic and if he can't see it, he can't change it. The coach's work is finding an intervention that surfaces this dynamic in a way that he and Paul can explore and find parallels of this dynamic that have an impact well beyond the coaching conversations. This coach will determine how to surface this pattern in a way that Paul will be open to considering and exploring it. The coach will be curious with Paul about where this might come from, how it shows up in everyday life, and allow Paul to begin to see what has previously been invisible.

Using the countertransference or unwittingly succumbing to it

According to Berne (1966), if we are unaware of our own countertransference reactions, we unwittingly accept the invitation to collude with our client's psychological contract or script. Our collusion renders the work ineffective; and without sufficient reflection and development, we may not even realize what has occurred.

If a coach is unable to manage boundaries, notice triggers, and ultimately discern the psychological contract the client is unconsciously attempting to reconfirm; the likelihood of the dreaded 'transference cure' is strong.

The psychological contract today

The field of coaching (Megginson & Clutterbuck, 2016; Hawkins & Shohet, 2016; McLean, 2022) has begun to study the developmental progression of the coach's maturity and a distillation of the coach's journey that supports the capacity to discern the complexities of the psychological contract can be viewed in Figure 8.2 below. This figure demonstrates a progression of developmental levels (McLean, 2022) that occurs over several years in supervision.

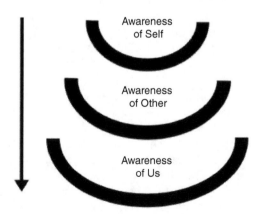

Figure 8.2 Levels of Awareness
(McLean, 2022)

These studies suggest that while development is not necessarily linear, there is a nested progression in the coach's levels of awareness that begins with a thorough awareness of self, including reactions, triggers, judgements, biases, wishes, wants, self-doubts, and self-critiques. This awareness takes time, reflection, practice, and optimally, regular supervision. This level of awareness needs to be in place before a coach is capable of being fully alert to how the client(s) is showing up without the contamination of the coach's own material.

Consider the following questions

What is the client saying?
What are the repeated phrases or well used words?
What patterns are discernable?
What somatic features are notable?

It is only when these two levels of awareness are fully developed that the coach is then able to pay close attention to the 'dance' that is 'the awareness of us' level, the unique interaction that occurs when this coach and this client come together.

The capacity to agilely move from awareness of self to full awareness of the client and then see and integrate the unique dance that unfolds in each session, while monitoring triggers and boundaries, requires a coach's dedication to their development. It does not come naturally to any of us, and it is most unlikely we can engage in this learning in isolation. Many in the field offer suggestions and practices to continually cultivate one's capacity. Kets DeVries (2014) recommends a leadership coach engage in a reflective practice like mindfulness to heighten their awareness of feelings and reactions that might be triggered in response to the client. Many in the field have documented the power of coach supervision in cultivating and deepening one's capacity to observe all levels of a coaching engagement, understand the psychological contract at work and devise ways to use the countertransference model instead of getting seduced by it.

Hawkins' (2012) 7-eyed model for coach supervision explicitly addresses the dynamics of the psychological contract through the exploration of what's occurring within the coach, within the client, and within the relationship. Hawkins writes that his impetus for building his model came from noticing the tendency of a coach supervisor and likely the coach as well to look at only some aspects of the coaching system at play. His model provides coach and coach supervisor with a process for exploring at all levels inside each system. Like the nested levels of development and the progression of coach maturity; the capacity to become aware at all levels sets the stage for discerning the psychological contract, the client's script, the coach's transference tendencies and the countertransference material that can be used to be of service to the client.

In multistakeholder contexts there are multiple psychological contracts

Meaningful coaching that delivers results does not exist in a vacuum. We reside inside nested systems, and we fool ourselves if we think our only client is the person in front of us. The HR partner or executive who recommended the coaching as well as the organization are key stakeholders. Each stakeholder has the potential for unspoken as well as out of awareness hopes and wishes. The mature coach understands the need to explore what might be unspoken in the contract by making a variety of inquiries, such as:

You've been working with this member of your team in several capacities over a period of time. What haven't you shared with me that is important for us to discuss?

In requesting me to provide this coaching, what hopes do you have that you may not have yet shared?

You've asked me to engage in coaching with this member of your team, what unspoken expectations and hopes might you have that we ought to surface for us to be fully aware of all that is at play?

What is the psychological contract or implicit agreements you have with your boss and your direct reports? How would your boss and direct reports define it?

Ethics and psychological contracts

It's easy to err on the side of viewing ethics in the simplistic terms of good decisions and bad ones; right and wrong, laws and common practices. Hawkins (2020) often writes of asking a group of coach supervisees what sorts of ethical issues they are confronting, and the prideful response is "oh, actually, we have had none come up in our work". Is this response a reflection on the work we need to do in the field of coaching to fully elucidate the complexities of ethics?!

Certainly, this topic of the psychological contract brings this to the forefront.

Consider the following questions

What is our ethical responsibility to discern the psychological contracts in our work?

What is our commitment to understanding our own transference tendencies that, if unchecked, will confuse and contaminate our work?

What is our ethical responsibility to use the countertransference on behalf of the client's growth rather than colluding with it?

What is our commitment to growing boundaries that are essential to best serve our clients?

What if we saw a significant portion of the ethics conversation as residing inside our own development as a coach?
What is our psychological contract with ourself?

Accepting that ethical issues will arise and being prepared for that is a key to forging strong psychological contracts as well as fielding critical questions about boundaries.

Conclusion

The ethical maturation of a coach is an evolving journey that requires cultivating one's capacity to observe more facets of oneself, one's client(s), and the unique interactional patterns of the dance. One aspect of this cultivation lies in the coach's capacity to discern the psychological contract present in coaching engagements, exploring the unspoken and examining old patterns at play with the client, while simultaneously managing any inclination to collude with an unexamined and largely unawares script. The coach's commitment to cultivating one's capacities ought to be one of our most important ethical commitments.

Discussion points

1. A good place to begin is to explore the concept of the implicit and psychological contracts deliberately and thoroughly, in your own life. Perhaps you are receiving coaching or engaged in supervision. What might be unspoken or out of your awareness that is at play in these contracted relationships. How might you explore these dimensions with your coach, coach supervisor or fellow colleagues?
2. In your work as a coach or coach supervisor, how might you give more attention to the psychological contract? In what ways might you create space for exploring this layer of the contract? What exploratory questions might you ask?
3. Think of a time when, like every coach, you were in danger of the 'transference cure'. What were the circumstances, what did you learn and what strategies might you use to stay alert to this dynamic?
4. How does coaching supervision intersect with ethics and impact psychological contracts? What questions about boundaries inform your thinking about ethics and psychological contracts?

Recommended reading

Kets DeVries, M. (2014) Mindful leadership coaching. London: Palgrave Macmillan.

References

Argyris, C. (1960) *Understanding organizational behavior*. London: Tavistock Publications.

Bergin, A. & Lambert, M. (1978). *The evaluation of therapeutic outcomes*. In S. Garfield and A. Bergin (Eds), *Handbook of psychotherapy and behavior change*. Hoboken, NJ: Wiley.

Berne, E. (1966) *Principles of group treatment*. New York: Grove Press (Reprinted, 1994, by Shea Press, Menlo Park).

Carroll, M. (2005). *Psychological contracts with and within organisations*. In R. Tribe & J. Morrissey. *Handbook of professional and ethical practice for psychologists, counsellors, and psychotherapist*. Hove: Brunner-Routledge.

Clinton, M. E. & Guest, D. E., 2014. Psychological contract breach and voluntary turnover: Testing a multiple mediation model. *Journal of occupational and organizational psychology*, 87(1): pp. 200–207.

Dundon, T., & Rollinson, D. (2011). *Understanding Employment Relations*, 2nd edition. London: McGraw-Hill.

Hawkins, P. and Shohet, R. (2012) *Supervision in the helping professions*, 4th edition. Maidenhead: Open University Press.

Hawkins, P. & Turner, E (2020) *Systemic Coaching: Delivering value beyond the individual*. London: Routledge Press.

Hewson, J. (1999) Training supervisors how to contract in supervision. In E. Holloway & M. Carroll (Eds) *Training counselling supervisors*. London: Sage Publications.

Hubble, M. et al. (1999) *The heart and soul of change: What works in therapy*. Washington, DC: American Psychological Association.

Kets DeVries, M. (2014) *Mindful leadership coaching*. London: Palgrave Macmillan.

McLean, P. (2011) *The completely revised handbook of coaching*. San Francisco, CA: Jossey-Bass.

Mcean, P. (2019) *Self as coach, self as leader: developing the best in you to develop the best in others*. Hoboken, NJ: Wiley.

McLean, P. (2022) Understanding the developmental journey of the coach supervisee. In , F. Campone, J. DiGirolamo, D. Goldvarg and L. Seto (Eds) *Coaching supervision: Voices from the Americas*. London: Routledge Press.

Rollinson, D. (2008) *Organizational behavior and analysis*. 4th Ed. London: Prentice Hall.

Rousseau, D. M. (1995) *Psychological contracts in organisations: Understanding written and unwritten agreements*. Thousand Oaks, CA: Sage Publications.

Rousseau, D. M. and Schalk, R. (Eds) (2000) *Psychological contracts in employment: Cross-national perspectives*. Thousand Oaks, CA: Sage Publications.

Schein, E. (1980). *Organizational psychology*. Englewood Cliffs, NJ: Prentice-Hall.

Shore, L. M. & Tetrick, L. E. (1994). The psychological contract as an explanatory framework in the employment relationship. In C. L. Cooper & D. M. Rousseau (Eds), *Trends in organizational behavior*, 1, pp. 91–109. Hoboken, NJ: Wiley.

Sills, C. (Ed) (1997). *Contracts in counselling*. London: Sage Publications.

Wachtel (1977). *Toward an integration*. New York: Basic Books.

Winnicott, D. (1958). *Collected papers*. London: Tavistock.

Chapter 9

Supervision ethics

Julie Allan and Lise Lewis

Introduction

> "Tell me to what you pay attention, and I will tell you who you are."
>> Jose Ortega y Gasset (1962) Man and Crisis (p. 94)

Supervision, initially imported from helping professions, has increasingly been adopted as a way to enable appropriate coaching practice. To consider ethics in supervision is to consider a purposeful relationship conducted within an evolving ecology of other relationships, attitudes and values, including the coaching landscape. We may seek stability and assurance for clients, through codes of ethics, however, with ethical guidance we inherit a long and partial history that does not provide unequivocal solutions in the face of arising dilemmas and human frailties.

Research focused on ethics related to supervision is building slowly and a short survey was created to sample views from supervisors and coaches concerning ethics in supervision at the time of writing (Lewis & Allan, 2022). Its title, 'What should excite us all about ethics in supervision?' reflected anecdotal concerns that the topic may remain unattractive - however important and relevant - which could hinder the acquisition of appropriate knowledge and skill. Would such a perception prove misplaced and/or might perspectives be offered to stimulate greater engagement? Readers are invited to reflect on extracts included here, and whether these impact on their own approach to ethics in supervisory practice.

This chapter explores ways in which an approach to supervision can understand and support three fundamental and inter-related lenses – *systemic/holistic, relational and developmental* - offering a vital space enabling coaches and supervisors to work with competence and integrity as ethically mature developers of others.

Ethics in supervision: some foundations

When seeking guidance, each relevant body has ethical codes for its members. Supervision is recognised as supporting the development of coaches,

DOI: 10.4324/9781003277729-9

alongside "education to improve the ability to read ethical dilemmas otherwise change towards ethical behaviours won't happen" (Dublin Declaration, 2008, p. 17, 2.3).

While supervision is included in the Global Code of Ethics (BCoE2016, 2021), the only direct reference to supervisors is to hold professional indemnity, where such insurance is available. Coaching and supervising are not regulated professions and neither has an agreed common ethics curriculum or mandated training. There are some resources including chapters in edited books, workshops and increasing opportunities to engage with scenario-based enquiries, however coaches still believe little support is available for ethics in supervision, and that very few coaches understand what ethics in coaching supervision is (Lewis & Allan, 2022).

Ethics concerns human actions and how people decide what to do. Ethics are built on values, the personal beliefs motivating and choices. Ethics in supervision therefore concerns choices of action in the room and outside it as supervised practitioners. Almost by definition, an ethical dilemma does not have an easy solution provided by a written code, and as people vary in what they judge most salient, this can produce different decisions based on the same circumstances. In supervision, exploring such differences helps inform a coaching practitioner's growing ethical maturity.

Supervision is defined as the " process by which a coach with the help of a supervisor, can attend to understanding both the client system and themselves as part of the client-coach system, and by so doing transform their work and develop their craft" (Hawkins, 2014, p. 393; Hawkins & Smith, 2006) and does this "by also attending to transforming the relationship between the supervisor and coach and to the wider contexts in which the work is happening" (Hawkins, 2011, p. 286).

These wider contexts include, for example, the fields of health, care, business and technology, each with its own codes, concerns and enquiries. And long overdue attention has turned to dynamics including intersectionality, exploitation, microaggression and AI-mediated relationships. Given each practitioner has unique viewpoints and vulnerabilities, influenced by personal histories, hopes and situations, ethical practice is likely to raise as many questions as it answers. Are coaching supervisors aware, when they supervise, of how they, the coach or their client include and exclude (Ryde et al, 2019)? What position do coaching supervisors take if the letter and spirit of the law have parted company? Can they find themselves wondering 'whose ethics?', as codes of ethics have tended to grow from Western roots – not necessarily the most appropriate option (Roche 2022; Chimakonam & Cordeiro-Rodrigues, 2022).

Curiously or shockingly, some supervisors report not having encountered ethical issues in practice (AC/AOCS working party, 2018). How could it be that ethical challenges never arise in supervision, between supervisor and supervisee or from the everyday economic, social, political and psychological challenges faced by coaching clients? Furthermore, Turner and Passmore (2018) report supervisors may not follow the course guided by codes they were subscribed to. Could this reflect that the codes seem insufficient, rather than disagreement or disinterest? It is suggested that ethics are not viewed as exciting by some coaches and supervisors, however this was a small number compared to those seeing ethics as a way to explore possibilities in practice (Lewis & Allan, 2022).

Ethics asks coaching practitioners and supervisors to understand where they are 'coming from' and what agreements are made; what they hold as true, and why; how clear and congruent they are in speech and actions; and how they approach doing "least harm – most good" (Smith & Arnold, 2023; Chapter 1, p. 53 in this volume). When seeking an ethical route, coaching practitioners and supervisors may quickly find a space of 'should' and 'ought' – even in discussions *about* ethics and creating guidance. They may experience power dynamics, misunderstandings, values clashes, fears of being judged and so on, which feel uncomfortable and can influence coaching and supervisory relationships. So, it is suggested to do as Rumi (Barks & Moyne, 1995, p.36) suggests, and move to the field "out beyond ideas of rightdoing and wrongdoing". Below are three important perspectives to guide discovery in supervision for supervisors and coaching practitioners to consider:

1. Taking a *systemic perspective*, practitioners may at first notice elements and permeable boundaries – from self to family, social group, colleague, to team, to organisation, to society, to planet and beyond. As products and producers of what is around them, they consider their cultures of origin and upbringing. Exploration of ecologies and how they relate with nature, whether they *are* nature. The practitioner (coach or coach supervisor) may appreciate that everything is intricately entwined, especially if working globally and with multi-cultural teams.

2. Taking a *relational perspective*, practitioners attend to what they might see as 'spaces between' themselves and others and/or between themselves and what is around them. They also consider their relationship with themselves or different aspects of themselves. Qualities of relationship and their abilities or capacity to be in and evolve their relationship with people, ideas and circumstances come to the fore.

3. Taking a *developmental perspective*, practitioners reflect on how they have grown and changed through ethical practice and the conversations on that journey. This is not just knowing 'about'; it concerns expanding their capabilities and capacity. They might notice how they can 'see' or make sense of things in different ways, which changes things around them in ways they wouldn't previously have thought.

The three above perspectives are interdependent. How might the responses of a coaching practitioner or supervisor to each of these perspectives illuminate their own values? Coaches regularly use their own values and moral compass as primary guides (Lewis & Allan, 2022) and in the absence of

structured input on ethical reasoning, few other choices may be available –
with personal intuitions and motivations prevailing (Haidt 2001; Batson
& Thompson 2001). This suggests that supervision is important in its
role to support the coaching practitioners develop a deepening awareness
of their values – how they have come by them and if they are, indeed,
their own.

Even if ethics education or indeed supervision are not mandated, this
chapter invites personal enquiry into supervision as a vital relational, systemic
and developmental space in which to generatively embrace ethics.

Avenues of ethical enquiry

The complexity of the field in relation to the potential simplicity of conduct
codes was highlighted by Raven (2000), reflecting on the gap being experienced between a routinised application of codes and the true seriousness of
ethical dilemmas facing psychologists in workplaces. Questions similarly arise
outside the scope of simple answers for ethical supervision:

*Where are the supervisory boundaries when a systemic-holistic frame is needed
to encompass the complexity of practice?*
*Who is the client? The supervisee, the sponsor of the supervision if different, the
wider stakeholders influenced by the supervision conversation?*
*How are agreements made in relation to revisiting multi-stakeholder contract-
ing given the emergent nature of supervision conversations?*
*Whose agendas come consciously to the room? How are spaces created to
allow/notice whose agendas have not (yet)?*
How might multi-organisational cultures influence a supervision session?
*How might you respond if/when areas of work become publicly contentious, or
personal values are challenged?*
What are the wider ethical implications of session recordings? (see Chapter 11 in
this volume for further exploration and Chapter 26 for examples)

> The Global Code of Ethics for Coaching, Mentoring and Supervision
> (2021) asks coaching practitioners to be conscious of the introduc-
> tion of Artificial Intelligence. *What might be the ethical issues of data
> security "accepting that transactional coaching may make coaches
> vulnerable and replaceable creates the question of who supervises the
> AI coaches?"*
>
> (Lewis & Clutterbuck, 2019, p. 215)

Of course, the lens doesn't have to be turned 'out there' into organisations.
Thinking systemically, relationally and developmentally: What might be
markers of ethical practice of supervision? Do they include considering if fees
are equitable, whether and how to travel for meetings, or which technology

platforms are used? If the supervisor is grieving, does this give pause for considering self-support and ability to work? If a supervisee or their coachees are also grieving, does this change anything? How would a supervisor discern and take action when a supervisee has grown beyond them in some way and needs some other provision?

Dilemmas associated with contracting is one area of note that frequently arrives at supervision (Turner & Passmore, 2018; Turner & Clutterbuck, 2019). This can cover a variety of topics including confidentiality, organisational behaviour, unspoken expectations and legality. Contracting for supervision requires a view that embraces the needs of stakeholders and has "at its centre a collaborative, co-created relationship" (Hawkins & Turner, 2020, p. 158). The top three good practices for effective contracting for supervisors are (Turner & Clutterbuck, 2019):

1. Shared understanding of supervision (67.7%)
2. Supervisor-supervisee relationship (63.6%)
3. Clarity of contracting (54.5%).

When asked, coaching practitioners reported having difficulties in contracting within the supervisory relationship, both as supervisor and coach. Some supervisors were concerned about the ethical alertness of those they supervise, and the interactive effect around suitable contracting, especially with organisations. Some coaches were not sure what they could do if they had a disagreement or concern about their supervisor (Lewis & Allan, 2022). Although contracting can be seen as agreements at the start of an engagement, things always emerge to change a landscape, requiring clarification or re-contracting. This includes 'things that are not said/written in the contract' – including the psychological contract (see Chapter 8 in this volume) that, when broken in organisational life, can lead people to exit (Rousseau 1989; 1995). If contracting for supervising can achieve ever-present attention to agreements about working – relationally, systemically and with developmental intent – we may more reliably provide what is needed, helpful and has integrity. In other words, we may improve our ethical navigation.

Given this complexity, the absence of consistency in practice noted by Turner and Passmore (2019), and differences in awareness and practice noted by Faire and colleagues (AC/AOCS working party, 2018), that touchstones and guidance for coaching supervision beyond written codes are needed.

How to frame ethical enquiry?

Frameworks help coaching practitioners bring reasons for action into the light and invite multiple lenses, triangulation and support. Table 9.1 compares three that offer coaching- and/or supervision-relevant perspectives: Steare's business-focused Ethicability, "how do we decide what's right and find the courage to do it?" (2006, p. 11), Carroll & Shaw's "six components [that] result in ethical maturity" (2013, p. 30), and Passmore and Turner's *APPEAR*

(2018), building on Duffy and Passmore's (2010) research to offer an aid to build ethical awareness and capability. Collaborative thinking helps to broaden and invite multiple perspectives that can enhance the ability to notice blind spots and make ethical navigations more transparent. Hawkins and Smith (2006, pp. 255–256) outline a guided group learning process (practicum) for supervisors in which co-reflection enables a shift from constraining or confining (ethics as following rules) to enabling (ethics as finding an expansive way through).

Table 9.1 Three ethical decision-making frameworks

	Steare (2006) Ethicability	*Carroll & Shaw (2013) Ethical maturity*	*Passmore & Turner (2018) APPEAR*
Form	Twenty questions in three stages: primarily linear sequence	Six components: inter-relating aspects that have a sequence as well as non-linear feedback loops	Six stages: overall step-by-step progression, however with a non-linear multi-iterative approach expected
Focus	Question sequence used to pragmatically ensure breadth of ethical consideration and RIGHT action in often non-reflective business settings	Navigating ethical dilemmas while constituting and helping develop ethical maturity for those in helping professions	For coaches and supervisors to navigate ethical dilemmas more actively and reflectively, drawing on research within the specific practitioner population
Components, with approximate equivalences. Note: exclusively linear use in practice NOT assumed	Stage 1: preparatory questions – eight areas of enquiry, including making time available and reflecting on dimensions including facts, feelings, characters and intentions	Sensitivity/ thoughtfulness – awareness of self, values, motivations etc and potential impact	Awareness – of good/best practice, codes and practitioners' own values, beliefs norms Practice – practitioner actions including supervision, reflection and engaging with work
		Discernment/ decision-making – expanding choice, taking responsibility, understanding the nature of the situation, being appropriate	Possibilities – going beyond 'do A or B' through reflection and conversation Extend the field – what else may be involved and how can it be brought in to give breadth and depth

Steare (2006) Ethicability	Carroll & Shaw (2013) Ethical maturity	Passmore & Turner (2018) APPEAR
Stage 2: RIGHT – exploring Rules, Integrity, Good, Harm and Truth, addressing different approaches to ethics including principled and social consciences and testing for accountability	Implementation/ competency – how to cross from knowing to doing, what helps and what hinders required/chosen action	Extend the field – see above Act on reflection – working with awareness and support through a plan of action, including considering possible responses from others
Stage 3: decision-testing questions – seven enquiries to make before, during and after acting, including others' perspectives, respect and learning	Conversations/going public – holding self-accountable and explaining choices and actions to others	Act on reflection – see above Reflect on learning – professional development/ learning from what was involved in the dilemma, and personal learning about self and how impacted
	Peace/living with decisions and actions – going forward from the experience, supported as needed and able to settle with and move on from the actions taken, including where circumstances or outcomes were difficult	Reflect on learning – see above
	Growth/moral character development – incorporate learning to increase ethical attunement and competence	Reflect on learning – see above, with emphasis on new insight and development

However, coaches choose to frame their thinking and explorations of ethical challenges, the importance of self-care and potentially time out of coaching or supervisory practice, is increasingly understood. Drawing through a gestaltist appreciation of the self being the instrument of the work (e.g. Nevis, 1987; Allan & Whybrow, 2020), there is recognition that 'the instrument' requires maintenance to function well – that is to be 'resourced' by participating in restorative actions(Hawkins & Smith, 2013) element of supervision. Coaching practitioners have reported awareness of the need to manage their wellbeing and that it is an ethical responsibility for best practice – able to name multiple support strategies within and external to supervision (Lewis & Allan, 2022). Supervisors have an opportunity to role model their own self-care practices.

As coaches move beyond *knowing about theories of ethics* towards ethical maturity, questions of purpose and who or what is being served through supervising arise. Here, again, ethical navigations are in prospect, related to differing views on, for example, what 'counts' as legitimate coaching (Einzig, 2017) and whether supervision is a space that can facilitate the coach to feel safe to be open, reflect, provoke or attempt to remain neutral when values-challenging topics arise.

Ethics through the researcher-practitioner lens

Friere (2000, p. 30) suggests, "Critical reflection on practice is a requirement of the relationship between theory and practice. Otherwise, theory becomes simply 'blah, blah, blah'", so this section is offered in the spirit of enquiry that arises through constructive conversation between theory and practice (see Chapter 6 in this volume for exploration of ethics of the researcher-practitioner).

The literature relating to each of the inter-twining systemic/holistic, relational and developmental aspects – that are advocated as important for ethical supervision – is extensive. These are:

• give touchstones to each of the three aspects and their relevance
• consider some personal challenges that follow from these, moving from declarative knowledge to embodied ethics in practice.

Systemic/holistic

Ethical enquiry: how well can coach supervisors and coaches notice, encompass and speak about what is happening?

Systemic and holistic stances have a long and broad history on which supervision can draw, including physicists (Bohm, 1985; Capra 1982, 1996, 2003), biologists (Maturana & Varela 1987), organisational systems theorists (Jackson 1982), those whose work crosses borders (G. Bateson 2000; N. Bateson 2016) and indeed moral psychologists (Rest, 1982). Gestaltists have holism as one of the underpinning principles (Clarkson, 1993; Allan & Whybrow, 2019), with Clarkson (2000) highlighting that ethical thinking is predicated on what can be noticed and spoken of. Supervision is a space in which to be alert to the complexity of experience, finding the perspectives and language that support embodied ethical decision making for today's contexts (Hawkins & Smith, 2013; Hawkins & Turner, 2020; Hawkins, Allan & Turner, 2021).

Relational

Ethical enquiry: are coach supervisors and coaches in danger of missing one another?

The important nature of the working alliance and other key relational contributors for therapeutic purposes (Clarkson, 1995; Lambert & Barley 2001) found parallels when adapted with a coaching focus (De Haan et al., 2013; 2016; Dryden, 2017). Overall, the relationship in coaching has been found to be an intricate and important one, explored from a wide variety of perspectives (O'Broin & Palmer, 2019). A strong working supervisory relationship that can encompass difficult explorations is likely to serve ethical practice well. Considering the overall relational field Lewin, (1951), suggests *how* coach supervisors and coaches consider ethical dilemmas is important because this will affect how a coach can behave in the situation of concern. Long's (2020) principles of regenerative healing highlight that there can be a sense of healing even if there is not an available cure. These relational elements are arguably crucial for situations in which outcomes may be imperfect and not fully resolvable.

Developmental

Ethical enquiry: are coach supervisors and coaches truly learning and growing?

People tend to take action that makes sense to them, that suits their perception of what's going on. Supervision offers a reflective opportunity to 'learn on purpose' and, with self-as-instrument in mind, address our psychological development – the who – alongside the what and the how of ethical practice. Adult developmental theories (for a summary see Jefkins & Allan 2019) address how different complexities of sense-making can impact our choices of action, with Hawkins (2011) offering a model for supervision based around one such theory. Coaching has received more attention than supervision (Laske, 1999, 2008; Berger, 2009) with Cox and Jackson (2014) critically examining the concept of development in relation to developmental coaching (see also Chapter 18 on wisdom, adult development and ethics). Bachkirova and Cox (2019) discuss relevant cognitive-developmental theories including how these might inform supervision: "… the role of educators, supervisors and coaches is to understand and nurture natural progression of individual capacities along the cognitive-developmental and ego-developmental dimensions…" (p. 559).

Given that developmental maturity is often held to enable increased capacity for uncertainty and complexity, supervisees might most benefit from a supervisor who is at least a match. As a supervisee may seek supervision for situations taxing their current developmental frames of reference, the supervisor's frame of reference would need to encompass and extend ways of considering the situation, to avoid collusion or over-simplification (Hawkins, 2011). During supervision how can a coach supervisor reflect on the learning space that is held and its different dimensions?

As many have said, it's hard to learn if you already know everything, so some humility in the coach supervisor's approach to learning and growing would seem an ethical requisite in supervision, reinforced by recognising the complexity of being human and how this can fuel interactions that 'interfere' with finding resolution to ethical issues. It is imperative coach supervisors and coaches extend their ways of seeing and being.

Living ethics

"We do not act rightly because we have virtue or excellence, but we rather have those because we have acted rightly. We are what we repeatedly do." (Durant, 2012, p. 98, on Aristotle's *Ethics*)

This section considers aspects of the self-emerging in different situational contexts that may be supportive or may instead lead the coaching practitioner into ethical dilemmas.

> "We spend much of life at ethical crossroads as life and work decisions confront us and demand answers. Sometimes we are aware when these crossroads confront us with moral issues and sometimes, we are not. Sometimes we don't realise there are crossroads."
>
> (Carroll & Shaw, 2013, p. 13)

How might values feature in ethical practice?

Taking an ethical stance means reflecting on the essence of who you are both personally and professionally – on your values and how these act as a conduit fuelling your beliefs, and how they may influence coaching and supervisory practice. Combined with social conditioning colouring people's worldviews it's clear that the value of self-awareness and continuous self-reflection is not to be underestimated. Becoming aware of each other's (i.e. the coach, coachee and supervisor) values helps to guide both the supervisor and the supervisee to recognise possible disconnects when seeking reasons for a faltering conversation. Self-reflection helps both supervisors and coaching practitioners to notice what they emphasise and what is missed, particularly when overly attached to personal values. The ability to recognise and be open to working with different values and opinions (De Haan, 2008) is a pre-requisite to ethical practice. Coaches and supervisors need to move beyond mere tolerance.

The word 'values' has several connotations: a monetary implication, the idea of relative worth – the usefulness or importance of a commodity – and what coaching practitioners and supervisors value as important – which relates intimately with their beliefs and personal ethics. The last of these can be a particularly strong driver influencing how they react and behave.

Vignette 1

Consider this scenario from a coach expressing feelings of discomfort with a client 'lacking' a religious tenet that the coach believes will 'solve their issue.':

The supervisor observes the coach's tone and language, when recalling a recent coaching conversation with their client, is judgemental, accusatory and without any sign of empathy in trying to understand the client's mindset, or readiness to work with what was presented. The supervisor's embodied reaction screams shock – "am I really hearing this?" – quickly followed by a realisation that this sensation is signalling 'attack alert' on personal values rather than their role as supervisor accepting that as humans we have 'different values and opinions'. The supervisor connects with their practice of 'responding not reacting' by remaining truly present, calming the supervisor. The session continues with the supervisor acknowledging the coach's deeply held religious beliefs. When the coach finished speaking without faltering in their resolve to be right, the supervisor reacted with honesty about feelings triggered with having a different perspective on religion. In silence both reflected on the exchange. The supervisor broke the silence with a question for the coach: "How did the coach feel about exploring their client's perspective'." The invitation was accepted to for the coach to try putting themself in the 'shoes of the client' and to notice what was observed.

Consider the following questions

Is exploring a clash of values between the supervisor and coach a similar scenario happening between the coach and their client?
How well does the supervisor calm the system?
Does the supervisor remain unconsciously disturbed by this clash of values and if so how does this manifest in the conversation?
What impact might 'being invited into the shoes of someone' perceived as a non-believer have on the coach?
Who are the stakeholders that could be impacted?

Coaches' and supervisors' unconscious selves inviting ethical boundaries

In addition to the very wide range of straightforward errors of processing that coaching practitioners may unconsciously make, they each travel with unexplored cultivated 'blind spots'. Banaji and Greenwald (2016, p. 20) use the term "mindbugs" that "slant how we see, remember, reason and judge, they reveal a particular disparity in us; between our intentions and ideals, on the one hand, and our behaviour and actions, on the other." Blind spots can lead to misconnections or mindbugs, they influence what/who they can see or hear with significant ethical implications to the coach supervision relationship.

The role of self-care as practitioner

How do coaching practitioners and supervisors know if they should pause coaching or coach supervising practice? How do they gauge if life events are impacting their practice negatively? Global disruptors, for example catastrophic influences of a pandemic, environmental damage or war, inevitably cause disturbances in the system that are absorbed both physically and mentally. Combined with the rapid growth of technological capability: expectations of constantly 'being on' and available when working in a global market becomes the norm; supervisors, coaching practitioners, their clients and their stakeholders become overwhelmed in a way that can deaden the senses and sanitise emotions. Supervisors and coaching practitioners can find they are left to work at the margins, processing the trauma or perhaps disassociating from what's happening.

Do they become so focused on their practice that they unconsciously cross ethical boundaries such as duty of care of self and client, competency of coaching practise, believing they act in service of the client to attend sessions when in effect they are incapacitated. The intention is well-meaning although they cease to role model what the field of practice aims to encourage in the–client - self-care with attention to diet, fitness, mental health and general wellbeing. "Look after yourself. Failure to do so means that sooner or later you will fail to look after your client or supervisee adequately" (Phillips, 2019, p. 101). Supervision can offer this decompression space where supervisors and coaches can draw on a range of practices that support wellbeing (Hawkins, Allan & Turner, 2021).

Vignette 2

How well do we as supervisors check in on the wellbeing of the supervisee?

A supervisor, practising for several years, with an accredited training and personal accreditation for practice, has a supervisee who doesn't have regularly timed sessions. They are usually arranged when a specific practice issue emerges for the supervisee. Today is no exception. The supervisor checks whether the contracting agreement needs reviewing before asking: "What brings you here today? What shall we discuss that will be of value to you and your client, and anyone who may be impacted by the topic?" As a fruitful session comes to a natural close, the supervisor decides to share the small asides punctuating the conversation that seem to imply 'something else needs to be heard'.

The supervisor reacts to the strength of this observation by slowing the pace of the conversation and curiously recalls what's been said about work pressures resulting from current world disruptions. These have influenced staffing levels, created difficulties for the organisations' business associates and cultural influences are stimulating challenges between team members holding strongly opposing alliances.

"How does coping with all this in addition to the responsibilities you have in your position make you feel right now?' asks the supervisor. The question opens a floodgate. An extended supervision conversation brings into consciousness acceptance of initiating and sustaining self-care activities at critical times when personal resilience can be depleted to the point of exhaustion. The supervisee recognised they were emotionally exhausted and realised this was 'time for self' to be resourced, to access medical help and to postpone coaching commitments until fully recovered.

Consider the following questions

What alerts you to explore when safeguarding wellbeing with the supervisee: 'what is not being said and that needs to be heard.'
How will you prevent yourself and your supervisees from unintentionally crossing boundaries into unethical practice?
How will you detect in your practice and in your supervisees' practice, a tendency beyond physical and psychological limits, to feel 'responsible for and care for others'?

Interpreting signals from the somatic self as a guide to ethical practice.

Attention to the somatic self is part of self-care. However, it is also an enabling discipline for supervision. The somatic self provides information about the physiology of the self that can be brought to open awareness within the supervision space. "The unconscious is the body ... Your body "knows" the whole of each of your situations, vastly more aspects of it than you can think. Here you find an intricate bodily knowledge and new steps that want to come, and will come, if you can wait here." These are the words of Eugene Gendlin introducing his Focusing (2003, pp. vii–viii). This approach encourages coaches and supervisors to notice what's happening inside them. It is a form of presence in the moment, without rushing to an answer, rather sit and listen to the information the bodily senses offer to the topic at hand.

Hawkins and Smith (2013), through the Seven-Eyed model, raise awareness of the need to be conscious of the energies coaches and supervisors absorb from and transmit into the field – what is happening in-between coaches and their clients and the wider system? What dynamics are at play that create or possibly displace energy within and between relationships? Such awareness can be a challenge for internal practitioners driven by a cognitive world of work.

What coaching practitioners and supervisors attempt, in service of ethical practice, is to broaden perception and perhaps decrease the unknown as well as maintain our overall functioning to support enquiry and action. The notion of somatics in relation to leadership and coaching has been explored (e.g. Brown & Brown, 2012; Palmer & Crawford, 2013; Strozzi-Heckler, 2014), however the discussion of such matters relevant to supervision has to date remained primarily within the therapeutic field. It is argued ethical practice requires the listening of the physical self as part of effective ethical practice and maturity.

The impact of today's world of work on ethical practice

The possibilities of boundaries becoming engulfed in a coaching supervisor's 'busyness' escalates when working with supervisees keeping pace with clients working in increasingly demanding environments. Parallel processing flourishes in this fertile soil of haste. How easily might supervision conversations be influenced by the same expediency for swift results that coaches may succumb to? Being drawn into the supervisee's narrative is a place where ethics can be easily missed. A reminder for the supervisor is that even when adopting a systemic lens only data available is presented in the session.

Consider the following questions

When does empathy become collusion?
How does a boundary become clear, in the face of other boundaries being blurred? And what are the consequences?
When can mutual understanding of different views be sufficient?
How are trust and transparency being challenged?
How does having only part of the story influence ethical engagement?
How might these moments give you the chance to explore possibilities led by supervision enquiry?

Power influencing ethical practice

The approach described above asks for alertness and mutuality of enquiry. However, it is of importance to also acknowledge that for the most part supervision starts asymmetrically (de Vries, 2019). Although some coach training and coaching practitioners hold that supervision relationships are learning partnerships, there is an 'asymmetric' attachment, with the word 'supervisor' traditionally implying a power position. In practice, the espoused balance of equality shifts when a supervisor finds reason to give a particular steer on a topic or piece of work, and again when a supervisee voices a different view or wants to change direction of the conversation. The supervisor may enjoy the power position bestowed by the supervisee; the supervisee may encourage 'being rescued' by a caring supervisor. Chemistry meetings may encourage the supervisor to exaggerate 'likeability' to engage the supervisee'.

Is this unethical or commercially sound practice if the business is won and the supervisee reports satisfaction with the service? (see Chapter 25 in this volume for the challenges of promoting coaching). The supervision space needs to be alert to the ethical impacts of vested interest and how compromise and boundaries are being navigated.

Carroll (2016) suggested that supervisors might prepare for supervising by standing in front of a mirror and asking a few questions of themselves. Such as: 'What am I pretending not to know?' and 'What feelings am I not expressing?' His premise was that the person most deceived in life is themselves. For ethical practice, attention to who and how you are, and not just alone but in company, is a perpetual requirement. Supervisors also need spaces and relationships that support their own ethical practice. When the world arrives at the door, everyone benefits from not opening it alone.

Conclusion

This chapter aimed to explore the waters at the confluence between ethics and supervision, informed by systemic/holistic, relational and developmental theories, as well as reflecting some of the ongoing work in coaching, coaching psychology, supervision and contemporary responses from supervisors and coaches from around the globe. Raven's (2000) expressed concern was that individualistic codes were not up to the task and something more systemic and collaborative is called for. Coaches have indicated preferences including simplifying and rationalising codes, case studies exploring different ethical perspectives and approaches, and virtual session dialogue to support greater understanding, engagement and enjoyment of ethics in coaching practice (Lewis & Allan, 2022). The quest to become ethically robust practitioners continues. Coaching practitioners and supervisors must recognise that ethics can be 'messy' and 'complex'. Humans are often involved in unanticipated issues, informed by personal values and beliefs that can make them more or less accepting of other views. There may not always be easy solutions to ethical issues, and supervision is vital for the continued development of compassion, for addressing difficult situations, and for encouraging practitioner engagement through courageous, creative and collaborative conversations.

Discussion points

1. Whose ethics are relevant in a supervision space? Could you make a 'map' of these in the supervisory space, to notice overlaps, gaps and opportunities?
2. How do your views and values around, for example, climate, sustainability and regenerative practice contribute to your supervision?
3. Given the word 'courage' understood for its root in the Latin 'cor' for 'heart', how would you 'show up' to courageously notice and work through ethical issues in the supervisory space?

4. How would you apply any of the available ethical decision-making frameworks or processes in supervision?

Recommended reading

Lane, D. & Cavanagh, M. (2021) Supervision for working ethically. In T. Bachkirova, P. Jackson, & D. Clutterbuck (Eds), *Coaching and Mentoring Supervision Theory and Practice*. London: McGraw Hill Open University Press.

References

AC/AOCS working party. (2018) Survey conducted by Faire, M. with Campion, H. & Allan, J. Ethical Supervision resources. www.associationofcoachingsupervisors.com/community/ethical-supervision-resources.

Allan, J., Passmore, J., & Mortimer, L. (2011) Coaching ethics – developing a model to enhance coaching practice. In J. Passmore (Ed.) *Supervision in Coaching: Supervision, ethics and continuous professional development*. London: Kogan Page, pp. 161–173.

Allan, J. & Whybrow, A. (2019). Gestalt Coaching. In S. Palmer & A. Whybrow (Eds) *Handbook of Coaching Psychology*, 2nd Edition. Abingdon: Routledge, pp. 180–194.

Allan, J. & Whybrow, A. (2020) A gestalt approach to coaching supervision. In M. Lucas (Ed.) *101 Coaching Supervision Techniques, Approaches, Enquiries and Experiments*. London: Routledge, pp. 144–170.

Bachkirova, T. & Cox, E. (2019) *A cognitive-developmental approach for coach development*. In S. Palmer & A. Whybrow (Eds) *Handbook of Coaching psychology*, 2nd Edition. London: Routledge, pp. 548–561.

Banaji, M. R. & Greenwald, A. G. (2016) *Blind Spot Hidden Biases of Good People*. New York: Bantam Books, an imprint of Random House, a division of Penguin Random House LLC, p. 20.

Batson, C. D. & Thompson, E. R. (2001) Why Don't Moral People Act Morally? Motivational Considerations. *Current Directions in Psychological Science*, 10(2): 54–57. www.jstor.org/stable/20182695.

Bateson, G. (2000) *Steps to an Ecology of Mind*. Chicago, IL: University of Chicago Press.

Bateson, N. (2016) *Small Arcs of Larger Circles: framing through other patterns*. Axminster: Triarchy Press.

Berger, J. G. & Atkins, P. (2009) Mapping complexity of mind: using the Subject-Object Interview in coaching. *Coaching: An International Journal of Theory, Research and Practice*. 2(1): 23–36.

Bohm, D. (1985) *Unfolding Meaning: a weekend of dialogue*. London. Routledge.

Brown, P. & Brown, V. (2012) *Neuropsychology for Coaches: understanding the basics*. Maidenhead: Open University Press.

Capra, F. (1982) *The Turning Point*. New York: Simon & Schuster.

Capra, F. (1996) *The Web of Life*. New York: Harper Collins; Hammersmith: Flamingo (1997) imprint.

Capra, F. (2003) *The Hidden Connections*. Hammersmith: Flamingo. First published 2002New York: Harper Collins.

Carroll, M. (2016) Keynote address for Supervision Conference UK: All Inclusive: Developing Dialogue in a Diverse World, October 15, Bristol. Retrieved on July 3, 2019 from www.severntalkingtherapy.co.uk/website/IGP797/files/Michael%20Carroll %20Keynote.pdf.

Carroll, M. & Shaw, E. (2013) *Ethical Maturity in the Helping Professions – Making Difficult Life and Work Decisions.* London: Jessica Kingsley.

Chimakonam, J. O. & Cordeiro-Rodrigues, L. (2022) *African Ethics: A Guide to Key ideas.* London: Bloomsbury.

Clarkson P. (1993) 2,500 years of gestalt: from Heraclitus to the Big Bang. *The British Gestalt Journal*, (2): 4–9.

Clarkson, P. (1995) *The Therapeutic Relationship.* London: Whurr.

Clarkson, P. (2000) Seven Domains of Discourse in Exploring Ethical and Moral Dilemmas. In P. Clarkson (Ed.), *Ethics: working with ethical and moral dilemmas in psychotherapy.* London: Whurr, pp. 191–198.

Commons, M. L. & Richards, F. A. (2002) Organizing components into combinations: How stage transition works. *Journal of Adult Development*, 9(3): 159–177.

Cook-Greuter, S. (2013) Nine Levels Of Increasing Embrace In Ego Development: A Full-Spectrum Theory Of Vertical Growth And Meaning Making. Updated and expanded from S. Cook-Greuter (1985). A detailed description of the successive stages of ego-development. www.researchgate.net/publication/356357233_Ego_Development_ A_Full-Spectrum_Theory_Of_Vertical_Growth_And_Meaning_Making, accessed April 2019.

Cox, E. & Jackson, P. (2014) Developmental Coaching. In E. Cox, T. Bachkirova, & D. Clutterbuck (Eds) *The Complete Handbook of Coaching*, 2nd Edition. London: Sage Publications, pp. 215–227.

De Haan, E., Grant, A., Burger, Y., & Eriksson, P.-O. (2016) A large-scale study of executive and workplace coaching. The relative contributions of relationship, personality and self-efficacy. *Consulting Psychology Journal: Practice and Research*, 68 (3): 189–207.

De Haan, E. (2008) *Relational Coaching Journeys Towards Mastering One-to-One Learning.* West Sussex: John Wiley & Sons.

De Haan, E., Culpin, V., & Curd, J. (2011) Executive coaching in practice: What determines helpfulness for clients of coaching?, *Personnel Review*, 40: 24–44.

De Haan, E., Duckworth, A., Birch, D. & Jones, C. (2013) Executive coaching outcome research: The contribution of common factors such as relationship, personality match, and self-efficacy. *Consulting Psychology Journal: Practice and Research*, 65: 40–57.

De Vries, K., (2019) Chapter 9. In *Moving from frozen code to live vibrant relationship: Towards a philosophy of ethical coaching supervision.* Abingdon: Routledge.

Dublin Declaration. (2008) Code of Ethics Appendix, 2. Dilemmas, queries and concerns 2.3 P.17. V1.4 GCC September 1, 2008.

Dryden, W. (2017) *The coaching alliance: theory and guidelines for practice.* Abingdon: Routledge.

Duff, M. & Passmore, J. (2010) Ethics in coaching: An ethical decision making framework for coaching psychologists. *International Coaching Psychology Review*, 5(2): 140–151. www.researchgate.net/publication/49290316_Ethics_in_ coaching_An_ethical_decision_making_framework_for_coaching_psychologists, accessed 2022.

Durant, W. (2012) *The Story of Philosophy: the Lives and Opinions of the Great Philosophers of the Western World*. New York: Simon & Schuster.

Einzig, H. (2017) *The Future of Coaching: Vision, Leadership and Responsibility in a Transforming World*. London: Routledge.

Erikson, E. H. (1997) *The Life Cycle Completed*. Extended Version with New Chapters on the Ninth Stage of Development by J. M. Erikson. New York: Norton.

Fischer, K. (1980) A theory of cognitive development: The control and construction of hierarchies of skills. *Psychological Review*, 87(6): 477–531.

Freire. P. (2000) *Pedagogy of Freedom: Ethics, Democracy, and Civic Courage*. Lanham, MD: Rowman & Littlefield.

Gendlin, E. (2003) *Focusing How to Gain Direct Access to Your Body's Knowledge*. Rider, an imprint of Ebury Publishing A Random House Group company, pp. vii–viii.

Gallagher, S. (2013) *How the body shapes the mind*. Oxford: Clarendon Press.

Global Code of Ethics. (2016, 2021). www.globalcodeofethics.org, accessed May 10, 2022.

Haidt, J. (2001) The emotional dog and its rational tail: A social intuitionist approach to moral judgment. *Psychological Review*, 108(4): 814–834. doi:10.1037/0033-295X.108.4.814.

Hawkins, P. (2011) Building emotional, ethical and cognitive capacity in coaches – a developmental model of supervision. In J. Passmore (Ed.), *Supervision in Coaching*. London: Kogan Page, pp. 285–305.

Hawkins, P. (2014) Coaching supervision. In E. Cox, T. Bachkirova, & D. A. Clutterbuck, (Eds.). (2014). *The complete handbook of coaching*. Sage Publications, pp. 381–393.

Hawkins, P. & Smith, N. (2006) *Coaching, Mentoring and Organizational Consultancy Supervision and Development*. Maidenhead and New York: Open University Press.

Hawkins, P. & Smith, N. (2013) *Coaching, Mentoring and Organizational Consultancy: Supervision and Development*, 2nd Edition. Maidenhead: Open University Press.

Hawkins, P. & Turner, E. (2020) Systemic Coaching Supervision; and Systemic Ethics. In *Systemic Coaching: Delivering value beyond the Individual*. London: Routledge.

Hawkins, P., Allan, J., & Turner, E. (2021) Supervision: Widening the Lens and Perspective—The Art of Reflective Practice. In: W. A. Smith, I. Boniwell, & S. Green (Eds), *Positive Psychology Coaching in the Workplace*. Cham: Springer. doi:10.1007/978-3-030-79952-6_8.

Jaques, E. & Cason, K. (1994) *Human Capability: A Study of Individual Potential and its Application*. Arlington, VA: Cason Hall.

Jefkins, C. & Allan J. (2019) Appendix: selected theorists and practitioners in adult development. In *Certain Uncertainties: measuring vertical development and its impact on leadership*. MDV Consulting. Downloaded May 2022. https://mdvconsulting.co/whitepaper/certain-uncertainties-measuring-vertical-development-and-its-impact-on-leadership.

Jackson, M. C. (1982) The nature of 'soft' systems thinking: the work of Churchman, Ackoff and Checkland. *Journal of Applied Systems Analysis*, 9: 17–29).

Kegan, R. (1980) Making meaning: The constructive developmental approach to persons and practice. *Journal of Counseling & Development*, 58(5): 373–380.

King, P. M. & Kitchener, K. S. (2002) The reflective judgment model: Twenty years of research on epistemic cognition. In B. K. Hofer and P. R. Pintrich (Eds), *Personal epistemology: The psychology of beliefs about knowledge and knowing*. Mahway, NJ: Lawrence Erlbaum, Publisher, pp. 37–61.

Lai, Y. & McDowall, A. (2014) A systematic review of coaching psychology: focusing on the attributes of effective coaching psychologists. *International Coaching Psychology Review*, 9(2): 118.

Lambert, M. J. & Barley, D. E. (2001) Research summary on the therapeutic relationship and psychotherapy outcome. *Psychotherapy: Theory, Research, Practice, Training*, 38(4): 357–361.

Laske, O. E. (1999) An integrated model of developmental coaching. *Consulting Psychology Journal: Practice and Research*, 51(3): 139.

Laske, O. (2008) On the unity of behavioural and developmental perspectives in coaching. *International Coaching Psychology Review*, 3(2): 125–147.

Lewin, K. (1951) *Field Theory in Social Science: Selected Theoretical Papers*. D. Cartwright (Ed.). New York: Harper & Row.

Lewis, L. & Allan, J. (2022) What would EXCITE us all about Ethics in Supervision? An enquiry into contemporary views from supervisors and coaches. www.researchga te.net/project/What-should-EXCITE-us-all-about-Ethics-in-Supervision?.

Lewis, L. & Clutterbuck, D. (2019) Co-Evolution: exploring synergies between Artificial Intelligence (AI) and the supervisor. In *Coaching Supervision. Advancing Practice, Changing Landscapes*. Abingdon: Routledge, p. 215.

Loevinger, J. & Hy, T. (1996) *Measuring ego development*, 2nd Edition. Mahweh, NJ: Lawrence Erlbaum Associates.

Long, K. (2020) Principles of Regenerative Healing. Workshop: Wisdom of Self-Healing Systems, March 18, 2022.

Maturana, H. R. & Varela, F. J. (1987) *The tree of knowledge: The biological roots of human understanding*. New Science Library/Shambhala Publications.

Nevis, E. (1987) *Organisational Consulting: a gestalt approach*. New York: Gardner Press for Gestalt Institute of Cleveland.

O'Brion, A. & Palmer, S (2019) The coaching relationship: a key role in coaching process and outcomes. In S. Palmer & A. Whybrow (Eds) *Handbook of Coaching Psychology*, 2nd Edition, pp 471–486.

O'Fallon, T. (2010) *StAGES: Growing Up is Waking Up. Interpenetrating quadrants, states and structures*. Seattle: Pacific Integral.

O'Fallon, T., Murray, T., Fitch, G., Barter, K., & Kesler, J. (2017) 8/31 A Response to Critiques of the STAGES Developmental Model. Integral Leadership Review August-November. Accessed April 2019. http://integralleadershipreview.com/15609-a-response-to-critiques-of-the-stages-developmental-model.

Ortega y Gassett, J. (1962) *Man and Crisis*. Trans. Adams, M. New York and London: W.W. Norton and Company, p. 94.

Page, N. & DeHaan E. (2014) *Does Executive Coaching Work … and if so. The Psychologist*, 27(8): 585. https://thepsychologist.bps.org.uk/volume-27/edition-8/does-ex ecutive-coaching-work.

Palmer, W. & Crawford, J. (2013) *Leadership Embodiment: How the way we sit and stand can change the way we think and speak*. St Rafael, CA: The Embodiment Foundation.

Passmore, J. (2009). West Midlands Local Government Annual Coaching Conference.

Passmore, J. & Turner, E. (2018) Reflections on Integrity – the APPEAR model. *Coaching at Work*, 13(2): 42–46.

Phillips, K., (2019). Working with Intense Emotions. In: *The Heart of Coaching Supervision*. Abingdon: Routledge.

Prinsloo, M. & Barrett, P. (2013b) Concept White Paper: Investigating the reliability and validity of the Cognitive Process Profile (CPP) Accessed June 2019. www.cogna dev.com/publications/Cognadev_concept_1_reliability_validity_and_the_CPP_June_%202013.pdf?cls=file.

Raven, J. (2000) Ethical Dilemmas. *The Psychologist*, 13: 404–407. Retrieved April 2022 from https://thepsychologist.bps.org.uk/volume-13/edition-8.

Rest, J. R. (1982) *A Psychologist Looks at the Teaching of Ethics. The Hastings Center Report*, 12(1): 29–36.

Roche, C. (2022) Decolonising reflective practice and supervision. *Philosophy of Coaching: An International Journal*, 7(1): 30–49. doi:10.22316/poc/07.1.03.

Rooke, D. & Torbert, W. (2005) Seven transformations of leadership. *Harvard Business Review*, 83(4): 66–76.

Rousseau, D. M. (1989) Psychological and implied contracts in organizations. *Employee Responsibilities and Rights Journal*, 2: 121–139.

Rousseau, D. M. (1995) *Psychological Contracts in Organizations: Understanding Written and Unwritten Agreements.* Thousand Oaks, CA: Sage Publications.

Rumi, J. (1995) Out beyond ideas of rightdoing and wrongdoing. In *The Essential Rumi* (trans. C. Barks with J. Moyne). San Francisco, CA: HarperCollins, p. 36.

Ryde, J., Seto, L., & Goldvarg, D. (2019) *Diversity and inclusion in supervision.* In E. Turner & S. Palmer (Eds), The heart of coaching supervision – working with reflection and self-care. Abingdon: Routledge.

Smith, W. A., King, S. & Lai, Y. L. (2021) Coaching with Emotions and Creating High Quality Connections in the Workplace. In: W. A. Smith, I. Boniwell, & S. Green (Eds), *Positive Psychology Coaching in the Workplace.* Springer, Cham. https://doi.org/10.1007/978-3-030-79952-6_10.

Steare, R. (2006) *Ethicability.* London: Roger Steare Consulting Limited.

Strozzi-Heckler, R. (2014) *The Art of Somatic Coaching: Embodying Skillful Action, Wisdom, and Compassion.* Berkeley, CA: North Atlantic Books.

Torbert, W. R. (1994) Cultivating post-formal adult development: Higher stages and contrasting interventions. In M. Miller & S. Cook-Greuter (Eds), *Transcendence and mature thought in adulthood: The further reaches of adult development.* Lanham, MD: Rowman & Littlefield, pp. 181–203.

Turner, E. & Clutterbuck, D. (2019) All in the small print. A brief study of contracting issues in coaching and supervision. Presentation to the 8th International Coaching Supervision Conference, Oxford, May 11.

Turner, E, & Hawkins, P. (2016) Multi-stakeholder contracting in executive/business coaching: An Analysis of practice and recommendations for gaining maximum value. *International Journal of Evidence Based Coaching and Mentoring.* 14(2): 48–65.

Turner, E. & Palmer, S. (Eds) (2019) *The Heart of Coaching Supervision: Working with Reflection and Self-Care.* Abingdon: Routledge, p. 101.

Turner, E. & Passmore, J. (2018) Ethical dilemmas and tricky decisions: A global perspective of coaching supervisors' practices in coach ethical decision-making. International Journal of Evidence Based Coaching and Mentoring, 16(1): 126–142. Retrieved August 3, 2022 from https://radar.brookes.ac.uk/radar/items/da4e8785-60aa-4867-8aa7-caebf259a94f/1.

Turner, E. & Passmore, J. (2019) Mastering Ethics. In J. Passmore, B. Underhill, & M. Goldsmith, *Mastering Executive Coaching.* Abingdon: Routledge.

Chapter 10

Ethics in team coaching

Peter Hawkins and Catherine Carr

The challenge

> Systemic team coaching is a process by which a team coach works with a
> whole team, both when they are together and when they are apart, in order
> to help them improve both their collective performance and how they work
> together, and also how they develop their collective leadership to more
> effectively engage with all their key stakeholder groups to jointly
> transform the wider business.
>
> (Hawkins, 2021)

It is hoped that both developing and experienced leadership and team coaches
will find that this chapter provides foundational and ongoing ethical anchoring
for themselves, and for the teamwork that is so needed in this world.

The reader may not be a team coach or supervisor of team coaches, however
even the coach who practice one to one coaching will need to understand the
complexities of the ethical dilemmas inherent in working with complex teams.
Why? Because one of the most common issues brought to individual coaching
is: 'How do I manage and develop my team?' So sooner or later the coach will
become involved in supervising the team coaching of their individual coachee.

With that in mind, consider: *What would a coach-practitioner do as the
systemic team coach in the following scenarios?*

Please assume that this hasn't been covered in the contract before this
situation occurred. It is impossible to circumvent all ethical dilemmas in
advance, thus the coach needs to be prepared for the unexpected and to think
through exceptions to the rule. These are only three of a myriad and multitude of possible quandaries team coaches will find themselves in.

Scenario 1: *What would you say to the team member who disclosed to you in
the 1–1 interview that they are hoping the team leader won't last in their position, and is collecting information to demonstrate incompetence?*

Scenario 2: *How would you supervise two co-coaches at loggerheads over
whether or not to share their individual session content with one another?* One

DOI: 10.4324/9781003277729-10

made a verbal contract with the CEO to share and the other created a contract with the COO stating they will not share.

Scenario 3: *What about the team leader who says?* 'Look, you are working with all of my team. I need you to help me figure out who should be on the short list for promotion and who you have concerns about. I need your honest opinion.'

What is the coach's ethical responsibility and what should they do in each of the above scenarios? We will return to these scenarios further along in the chapter.

Introduction to relational, systemic and eco-systemic ethical maturity

Helping professionals ranging from individual and team coaches, organisational consultants, psychologists, psychotherapists, social workers and trainers, have ethical codes with similar features. They focus on the behaviours and actions of the professional and try to define what the professional should and should not do. The language can often feel like a direct descendent from the Ten Commandments in the Old Testament of the Bible!

These statements of standards and ethics can provide useful guidance for the starting-out professional, but the danger is that they establish a framework whereby being ethical is just about the coaching practitioner sticking to the rules. In a complex engagement such as *systemic team coaching* in today's VUCA (volatile, uncertain, complex, ambiguous) world, many more different challenges emerge than can possibly be anticipated in a professional code. When training coaches and team coaches to address the wider stakeholder needs, including the 'more-than-human' world of the wider ecology (Whybrow et al., 2023), it is the authors experience that many coaches say they cannot be as encompassing as it contravenes their ethical code of coaching.

It is therefore proposed that for all coaching, and particularly *systemic team coaching* in the 21st century, there is a need for ethics that are less about pre-defining good and bad behaviour and more about guiding the developing professional toward greater ethical maturity, based on relational, systemic and eco-systemic principles. How is this better understood?

A relational perspective views what is happening as co-created between the coach and the coachee, whether the coachee is an individual or a team. It does not see coaching as being done by the coach, but as a partnership process done jointly by the coach and their individual or team coaching partner. Therefore, any ethical consideration needs to consider the nature of the partnership, how it was formed and contracted, cultural considerations, who the partnership is in service of, and who it is accountable to.

A systemic perspective. In any form of coaching in organisational settings, the coaching can never be solely in service of the coach and coachee, or team, but more importantly it is in service of all the team's stakeholders. Prior to the coaching process starting, neither the coach or coachee will know what the agenda is; rather, the agenda and the focus of the work will become co-discovered through a skilfully enabled inquiry process. This may involve generative dialogue, while also collecting feedback from important stakeholder groups. Many argue that to be both ethical and effective, *systemic team coaching* must be stakeholder-centric, bringing in the perspectives and voices of all the key stakeholder groups, now and in the future (Carr & Peters, 2021; Peters & Carr, 2013; Hawkins, 2021; 2022).

An eco-systemic perspective, in all forms of coaching, helps individuals and teams connect with all the nested systems they are part of, and which are also within them, and all that they are part of. This approach enables all members of the coaching eco-system to experience how their life is a constant flow between all the systemic levels. These levels include the many living elements within them and the many systems they are nested within, for example:

- family and teams they are part of;
- communities and organisations that these groupings are nested within;
- the stakeholder communities they serve;
- the wider cultures and one human family within which they are intricately interconnected; and
- the one Earth humanity shares with so many complex eco-systems and other living beings.

All are in a state of constant ever-changing flow and change. (These perspectives are addressed more fully in Whybrow et al., 2023; Hawkins, 2021; Hawkins & Turner, 2020).

12 key ethical principles of *systemic team coaching*

Grounded on the above foundational perspectives, these ethical principles serve to increase the coach's ethical maturity.

1. **Being ethical is more than avoiding unethical behaviour** – It is about increasing the orbit of both who the coach is both accountable to and responsible for.

   For example, in 2009, Peter asked a large group of coaches, 'What were you doing in 2008 while the banks were heading into a global financial crisis?' Thirteen years later and those ethical imperatives have multiplied. What did coaches do when the danger of coronavirus (COVID-19) was clearly predicted but not prepared for? And what are coaches doing now to help solve the climate crisis? Or the million species at risk of extinction in the biodiversity crisis? Or inequality around race, gender and socio-economic class? Or the doubling of refugees in the last decade? How does humanity ensure that they are not passive nor complicit in these global problems, and have significant positive impact?

Operationalizing these larger ethical concerns suggests that the team coach must be in service of at least two clients – the team and the orga-nisation. In order to balance the needs of both of these groups, it is necessary but not sufficient for *systemic team coaching* ethics; for both the individual and organisational client might invite the coach to collude in serving their particular interest at the cost of wider stakeholder needs.

2. **The coach is not there in service of individual coachees or team members or the team trying to suboptimise the system**.

   Many ethical codes for coaches focus on protecting the rights of the coachee, but this is just one level of systemic ethics. Five levels of sys-temic ethics with illustrations for each follow.

   - **Self-interest** over all other interests. For example:

     o Encouraging the team to invest in particular products and service lines v. what they really need, e.g.: 'I have this great assessment ... '

   - **Collusion** – Putting the team's collective self-interest over the purpose of the work.

     o Delaying the team offsite because team members state that they are too busy; and the coach concurs, because they are also very busy.

   - **Supporting tribalism and sub-optimisation of part of the organisation**

     o A team leader who runs a regional branch of a large financial organization asks the team coach to coach the team to be the best regional team, to stand-out as better than the other divisions.'

   - **Organisational exploitation** – This is where the coach is asked to support the organisation's interest over the interests of the wider stakeholders.

     o Coaching an international company that is tasked with expand-ing tobacco sales in developing countries where there are fewer government restrictions on sales and marketing.

   - **Human-centricity** – Here the coach may face situations where human interests are being privileged at the cost to the health of the wider 'more-than-human' ecology.

     o The coach is asked to work with an international environmental organisation that espouses a low carbon footprint however is routi-nely flying executive staff to meetings regardless of the length or type of meeting.

Coaches tend to focus on the immediate, short-term and local, and thus fail to bring in the longer-term implications, or the voices of the wider stakeholders including the 'more-than-human' world. It can be difficult to challenge the teams' stated agenda, but coaches need to be less interested in their agenda, and more interested in their purpose – and the agenda life is asking them to rise to. Systemic coaches remain steadfast and transparent in their alignment with the team's larger purpose, holding the question: 'what is in the best interests of the wider system?'

3. **Recognise subjective and socially constructed frames of reference, biases and assumptions.** No matter how objective coaches believe that they are, they are never as objective as they might believe. Knowing this allows the practitioner to 'unknow' and paradoxically to be able to see wider and deeper. Seeing once is not enough though. For instance, a single training session on unconscious bias seldom impact behaviour. Argyris and Schön (1974) showed how there is often a gap between our 'espoused theories' and our 'theories in action'. The team coach needs to keep the likelihood of unconscious bias on their radar, practice cultural humility and be cognisant that there are often underlying structural and organisational problems that will require sustained effort to change.

4. **Systemic thinking, doing and being** – The systemic challenge for coaches is to 'be the change' that will empower their clients, by practicing what they encourage in others.

   Who do the stakeholders need coaches to be for the team to become who they need to be? Coaches need focus on all levels of systemic thinking, doing, and being. Indeed, a coach don't get far with thinking and doing without anchoring those both in *systemic being*. Systemic being is a way of attuning to body signals via the nervous system, breath, and muscle tension, to intuition via listening inwardly, and to heartfulness via open presence, empathy, and compassion. How do coaches have wide-angled empathy so that they feel empathy and compassion for every individual, group, and system in the team narrative, not just empathy and compassion for the team? (Hawkins, 2019).

5. **Thinking future-back** – What will stakeholders require in the future? How can coaches leave a legacy for those who come after them, and be good ancestors responsible to future generations? This is about transgenerational ethics that move from short-termism to considering the long path (Wallach, 2017; Krynaric, 2020).

   This can present an ethical dilemma. How do coaches create rapport with their clients, by understanding their current concerns and aspirations, and also coach them to go beyond their current state? What does the world of tomorrow need them to see now? What are they open to seeing and how can coaches respectfully open that door further? North American indigenous teachings remind us that true leadership begins when people make decisions that incorporate the wisdom of the seven generations that come before them, and ethically consider the seven generations that come after, as well as all living beings with whom they share this moment in time. Connection to the sacred includes ancestors, the living world, and also the unborn.

Unfortunately, the majority of humans are selectively empathic. They engage in intergenerational discounting and are more concerned with their individual needs in the present, than that of future generations (Wade-Benzoni, 2008). This is borne out in scientific literature: humans have a difficult time relating to their own future self, let alone anyone else. MRI scans show people connect about as much to their future selves as they do to complete strangers (Hershfield and Bartels, 2018).

In this context, team coaches need to bring in the voice of the future, asking what they might regret in two years' time, having not addressed in the team coaching today; bringing in the imagined voice of the collective grandchildren and world at large; asking how the team's actions might now appear from their 'future-back' perspective. These practices can start to strengthen a felt sense of connection to the future. One practice is to query decisions asking, 'to what end?'.

6. **Co-working and collaborating with others** – Team coaching is a team sport. The systemic team coach comes alongside, not as a distant consultant but rather as an active partner.

   Using the sporting analogy, the coach can end up responsible for successfully moving the ball down the field. The other side of this trap is to not enter the game enough, and instead stay neutral on the sidelines, asking the team what they need to do to get the ball into motion. In contrast, systemic team coaches are very active; they are on the field with the team, encouraging them to pass the ball in new ways, creating new actions and sequence patterns. A systemic team coach enters from the position that neither the coach nor the team members have the answer to what the game is requiring – but rather can partner and discover this together.

7. **Practice ruthless compassion-** this brings together two seemingly opposite concepts: courageous steadfastness, even ruthlessness, on one hand, and loving kindness on the other. Aligned with the greater good, ethical practice is to speak the truth that needs to be spoken. It is essential to contract for this upfront. The coach must ask permission to challenge when needed with ruthless compassion. It may not be comfortable for a coach or the team, but comfortable doesn't create change. Challenge from the heart to the heart.

8. **Treat every ethical challenge as a learning opportunity-** never waste a good ethical crisis. Stretch the mind and heart to find a way through?

Team coaches need to watch that they don't line up on one side or the other of a team polarity, but rather help the team see that both can be true. If they are dealing with either/or opposites, it is important to strive for a balance between the polarities or find the third way. Marion Woodman (Mentor, 2018; Woodman, 1985), the Jungian psychotherapist, referred to the third way as synthesis – holding the tension of the opposites until synthesis and wholeness emerge.

9. **Bring the ethical issue into the room right here, right now.** It is easy to join the team in a state of wilful blindness – colluding, avoiding, and denying the truth; however, ethical coaches have a responsibility to help leaders and teams face issues squarely. They need to partner with the team to face the issue, right here, right now, to create a transformative shift in the room, not by talking about the ethical issue but rather by experiencing it.

10. **Strive to continually increase competency, capability, and capacity as a team coach** – lean into developmental learning edges, even if uncomfortable, to help teams do the same. The saying goes, when guiding others, they can only travel as far as one has ventured themselves. Always ask, 'What does one need to learn so that the team can learn?'

11. **Listen to not only what is in the room, but also what is not in the room** – Coaches are trained to listen deeply to the coachee's issues, feelings, and concerns. Systemic coaches need to be able to do this, while at the same time listen through the individuals and team to their world – both that which they bring into the coaching session and that which they fail to see, hear, or mention. This includes critical thinking about the pathways followed and what other ones would have been possible. Consider, where was there collusion with wilful blindness? (Heffernan, 2019).

12. **Work from source** – part of ethical practice is ensuring that coaches take care of themselves and care for the client. Working from source means 'letting the work come through us vs. coming from us.'

Teams can activate conditioned relationship patterns and be triggering. These triggers are teachers about what is unfinished, as well as giving important information about the team. Coaches can re-source themselves by clearing the team energy and dynamic they have picked up, monitoring their triggers, and by regularly replenishing their own wellbeing. Working from source also includes noticing and building upon what is going well and nurturing emergent team strength and resilience.

Systemic ethics

Systemic coaching ethics and differences in complexity between individual coaching and *systemic team coaching are abound*. The actions listed below (see table 10.1) for a team coaching response often build upon the individual response, albeit in a more complex fashion.

Table 10.1 Five examples of working systemically: individual and team coaching responses

Ethical challenges	Systemic individual coaching response	Systemic team coaching response
Confidentiality	Maintain confidentiality except for the usual limits. **Action**: Not sharing personal details. Keep in mind systemic (and all) coaching occurs at the interface of the individual and the organization and beyond. Encourage the client to bring forward concerns rather than be the conduit.	Offer anonymity, not confidentiality, as a team coach. **Action:** Be very clear upfront what is and isn't rolled up into themes from 1–1 interviews and sessions. Contract to feed back to the team non-attributable data that comes from multiple sources.
Avoiding being a go-between	Between coachee and their line manager, or coachee and HR. The systemic coach is in service of the greater agenda but is not directly *servicing*. **Action:** Encourage, and where helpful, facilitate direct communication between coachee and their manager. Example: Multi-stakeholder contracting sessions with coachee and key others (Hawkins and Turner, 2020).	The systemic coach is not there to represent the team and report out and report back. **Action:** Coach the connection between the team members and team leader, the team, and the levels above and below the team and between the team and their stakeholders.
Not taking sides when working with multiple clients (a subset of conflict of interest)	In this conflict of interest, the coach works with multiple clients in the same organization who have competing needs. **Action:** Encourage the client in conflict with other people and parts of the organization to take responsibility for the whole. 'I am only as whole as we are together.' Interrupt all blame. Turn blame into a request. Turn a problem into a challenge and locate it in the relationship, not in a person or part.	What happens when the coach meets with multiple teams across an organization? **Action:** Contract or recontract not to share material what belongs to a team but identify organizational issues if working with multiple teams. The systemic coach is not there on the side of one team leader or another, or the team against the team leader (e.g., a team that wants to get rid of the CEO). Rather, the coach is on the side of who the team serves. Be careful to not locate blame within the individual, unless there is a clear ethical breech (e.g., bullying, theft, breach of confidentiality).

Ethical challenges	Systemic individual coaching response	Systemic team coaching response
Coaching select clients	Here the coach is asked to only work with the super stars, those with performance issues, or the newer staff. **Action**: Think through the pattern regarding who the contract is with to coach. Are there implications for others who are not receiving coaching? For the organization? Do the coachees want coaching? What are the expectations regarding coaching results? What are the consequences if there are not results?	**Action:** When coaching the team leader, contract for them to share a higher level summary back to the team on what was talked about. The team is the client, too. Avoid becoming the keeper of secrets. If coaching team members, coach all of them. If only a few want coaching, this can create a biased perspective. The team has a right to know whom is being coached. Otherwise, this is modelling secret subgroups. **Action:** Consider possible ethical issues in advance and contract that the coach is there to serve the system as a whole.
Reflective/ pre-flective practice and supervision	Pre-empt, contain, and/or process personal reactivity. It is inevitable, and useful, in a team dynamic that the coach will pick up the process and polarities of a team. The coach is never just coaching one person or one team. Their family, team, organization, and systemic levels show up in the individual/team. Just like in a couple or family, the coach will start to engage in the dynamic if they are not mindful. Early patterning is primed to be reactivated. Parallel process occurs when the coach picks up the unconscious or unspoken dynamic in the room and is not aware of this themselves. They then embody and play out the dynamics of the team. **Action**: The work on 'self as instrument' is ongoing. Engage in a consistent reflective practice, much as one would tune an instrument before playing.	**Action:** Have a reflective practice such as reviewing work right after and before the next meeting. Engage in regular supervision, including the co-coach, if team coaching. The coach learns to observe their own triggers and parallel process, identify, contain, and then respond as helpful, rather than react. In co-coaching, how might the coach enact two sides of a team polarity? Recognize what is personal but also not personal. Process reactions together, in service of the co-coaching team and the larger system. If the co-coaches can't resolve the split, neither will the team.

Above are typical ethical challenges in systemic individual and team coaching. While the suggested actions are useful, they are not fixed, but fluid. Situations are nuanced and it is important to think them through carefully. As the coaching practitioner, it is typical to feel certain about one choice until presented with new information or considered in a different context – much like white paint looks like 'the only kind of white that exists' until another shade of white is painted right beside it. Through disciplined contemplation in working through issues, the coach expands their own and their clients' ethical discernment and maturity. Over time, the coach becomes more able to embrace wider systemic complexity, knowing that there is often not one right path, but many. Consider the next five scenarios that can occur at multiple levels of our systemic work.

Five examples for a coach to work ethically and systemically with any level: individuals, teams, complex and multifaceted teams and organisations

1. Partnering rather than supplier – customer relationship

It is not the coach doing the coaching. It is the coach, their team and the agenda that life is bringing.

Otherwise, the coach turns the team into a customer. Remember they are not paying. The organisation isn't even paying, as the money is derived from customers and investors. At whose expense does the coaching occur? Who benefits?

Thinking systemically, it is fundamentally unethical to only contract with the team. As Marc Kahn (2014) offers that the coach needs to coach the connection between the individual and all levels of the organisation. We would add other stakeholders such as the non-human world and future generations.

Action: The Systemic coach sets up a triangulated contract between themself and the team, the organisation and life's agenda.

Rather than asking 'What do you want from the coaching?' ask 'What's the work we need to do together in service of what your world is asking of you, now and in the future?

2. Disclosing conflict of interest

There are many traps here. Examples include, the coach is wanting great feedback from the client in order to open up other work or provide a reference.

Internal coaches may have an interest in how the coaching may promote or harm their own career advancement or loyalty to other parts of the organisation. External coaches may need successful cases for their professional accreditation.

Coaches are invited to write down their personal interests, reflect on what would be in the interest of the client and all their stakeholders rather than themselves, what interests they will set aside, and then share any remaining interests openly with their client/team.

3. Not overtaking or under doing

When the coach knows better or knows first, they become an expert-based consultant and even an alternative team leader, rather than a coach. Everyone even looks to them! Sometimes the reverse is true. It is hard to bring coaching presence and hold the space. *Systemic team coaching* is about partnering with full Authority, Presence, and Impact (API; Hawkins and Smith, 2013).

The coach's job is to bring the challenges that are in the wider system onto the table and make sure the individual coachee/team addresses them. The challenge is to be courageous about what is clear and necessary to address, and do so compassionately and without judgement or blame.

Partner through collaborative dialogical inquiry, discovering the way forward together.

Intentionally access a felt sense of API and act with courageous compassion.

4. Being a bystander

Failing to challenge unethical, illegal behaviour or behaviour contrary to the organisational values or stakeholder needs.

It is easy to watch something happen and not address it, particularly if it concerns or is in the presence of a supervisor.

Be courageous and compassionate. Hold the larger picture in mind. Speak the truth that needs to be spoken from a respectful, responsible and compassionate place.

5. Team coaches need to be clear about their level of competency and accreditation

Know when to pass on a new client and when to refer on.

A coaching practitioner may feel they are in over their head in coaching when delving into a realm they either didn't contract for or don't have the competency to address (e.g., serious and/or acute mental health issues or specialised business processes). In the team space, remember that it is common to feel overload as a team coach and this is quite likely what the team feels too.

Developing ethical maturity

Iordanou et al. (2017) argue strongly that the key to ethics is not solving problems but stimulating "the kinds of conversations and conditions that enable ethical issues to be surfaced" (2017, p. 3). As Bachkirova et al. (2011) point out, it is the coach (or other practitioner) not the application of particular methods or techniques that creates the difference in coaching. Maclean (2019) refers to this as 'self as instrument'. In order to achieve ethical maturity and coaching mastery, the coach needs to attend to their own growth and development as a disciplined practice.

Carroll and Shaw (2013, p. 137) define ethical maturity as:

> "Having the reflective, rational, emotional, and intuitive capacity to decide actions are right and wrong or good and better, having the resilience and courage to implement those decisions, being accountable for ethical decision making (publicly or privately), being able to live with the decisions made, and integrating the learning into our moral character and future actions."

Carroll and Shaw describe six components of ethical maturity, noting "components are not equal in terms of the tasks and time involved. Situations and stakeholders will demand more from some components than others on any given occasion" (2013, p. 135).

1. *Creating ethical sensitivity and mindfulness*: this is about creating an "antennae" for ethics, the coach using their self-awareness, moral compass, and beliefs to think through issues. Coaches need to also strive to deeply listen and practice "wide-angled compassion" for all stakeholders (Hawkins, 2019, p. 74).

2. *The process of ethical decision-making*: coaches want to expansively consider choices *and be accountable and responsible for them. They need to remember how powerfully the unconscious can influence their decision-making*: We, as a people are open to possibilities while considering what is appropriate in a particular context including the organization's rules and the law of the land.

3. *Implementing ethical decisions*: is about the intention to do what is right, and understanding and working with the space between "knowing and doing" (Carroll & Shaw, 2013, p. 223)

4. *Ethical accountability and moral defence*: when coaches try to make sense of what they have done they may face challenges from their own protective defensiveness, their ability to slightly alter facts, to rationalise, minimize and, to evade responsibility. Coaches tend to judge themselves by their intentions and others by their impact. This begs the question: what is 'truth' and whose truth is it?

5. *Ethical sustainability and peace*: coaches need to be able to live by their decisions. Carroll and Shaw argue that self-compassion and self-forgiveness are crucial, not to let ourselves off the hook but to accept our imperfection

and limitations. It is essential that coaches continue to reflect to facilitate their learning from the past, present and prepare for the future.

6. ***Learning from experience and integrating new learning into moral character*:** Carroll and Shaw warn that learning is not automatic. The coach needs to consider how they can revisit their ethical experiences, to move from "information to knowledge, and from wisdom to action" in a way that new knowledge becomes "embedded in who we are" (2013, p. 261).

Underpinning the coach's ethical maturity development is their ability to reflect, the use of supervision and own ability to self-supervise. John Heron (1982) points out how all human beings can easily and regularly fall into illusion, delusion and collusion. Similarly, Bachkirova (2011, p. 96) warns of "not noticing ethical dilemmas, forgetting the organisational client, colluding, particularly with powerful or famous clients," fear or attachment to one's personal image of self as coach, and external reasons such as a "lack of clear standards and accountability, no feedback mechanisms for clients to register concern; and high levels of competition for contracts" (Bachkirova, 2011, p. 97).

For a coaching practitioner to develop their systemic ethical maturity, they need to counteract the human tendency to privilege the individual that is present, the local, the tribal and be human-centric. Hawkins (2011) proposed a coach maturity model based on Torbert's developmental work (2004) that demonstrates how coaching practitioners mature as coaches. Shifting from an ego centric way of approaching issues to an eco-systemic way of not only helping the leader and team transform through the issue but rather, generating value for all stakeholders.

Let's return to the half-finished sentences at the beginning of this chapter. What changed from reading this chapter? What might the coaching practitioner add to what was done with each scenario and what levels of coach maturity was evident in the team coaches' approach?

Scenario 1: team member disclosure concerning team leader

What would you say to the team member who disclosed to you in the 1–1 interview that they are hoping the team leader won't last and is collecting information to demonstrate incompetence?

Main ethical traps: Confidentiality, potentially being a go-between, and not taking sides.

The team coach might offer an exploratory or more challenging reply:

Exploratory: 'I hear that you have significant concerns. What have you tried so far to address these issues directly with the team leader or if necessary asking HR.'

Challenging: 'What are you hoping for by telling me this? It concerns me that you are gathering information. Indeed, I think, without naming names, the Team Leader should know that her team is concerned at this level. Rather than me share that, how can I support you to have a direct conversation and address your concerns?'

Scenario 2: Co-coaching- what's private and what's not?

How would you supervise a team of two co-coaches at loggerheads over whether or not to share their individual session content with one another? One made a verbal contract with the CEO to share and the other created a contract with the COO stating they would not share.

Main ethical traps: Confidentiality, taking sides.
    Note: You might feel the increased pressure to give advice and come down on one side or other of their dilemma, rather than focus on using the dilemma to help grow the ethical capacity of the pair.'
    The team coach might offer an exploratory or more challenging reply:

Exploratory: 'It sounds like it might be helpful to reflect and consider what you both could agree to, that will also serve the team.'

Challenging: Supervisor might ask: 'How might you be replicating the dynamic of the team in your co-coaching relationship.' or 'If the board was in the room with us, what would they want from the two of you and from the CEO and COO?'

Scenario 3: Request to evaluation staff

What about the team leader who says 'Look, I've paid for you to work with all of my team. I need you to help me figure out who should be on the short list for promotion and who I should have concerns with. I don't need you to pick any one person, but I need your honest opinion.'

Ethical Traps: Confidentiality, potentially being a go-between.
    The team coach might offer an exploratory or more challenging reply:

Exploratory: 'I can understand your need to evaluate your staff and look at promotion and problems. The dilemma I have here is that if I give you my opinion, I help you but would damage my trust with the collective team. They would perceive me as evaluating them as individuals, rather than coaching them as a whole. What I can do is help you sort out your thinking around all of this and ask specific questions that will help you make these decisions.'

Challenging: 'Let's look at this from another angle to see if this is doable. How would it be if the board asked me to help them decide whether to keep you on or not and who your successor might be?' Do you see my dilemma here?'

Conclusion

It can be seen how the role of the team coach and supervisor is not to try to solve the ethical problem, but to use ethical challenges as an opportunity to explore the contending systemic needs that are involved in the situation. By doing this, coaching and coach supervision can help team coaches and teams develop their ethical sensitivity, ethical maturity, systemic thinking, doing and being. It is suggested one of the important core ethical values is that team coaching should be delivering value for many stakeholders, beyond the team being coached, and that bringing their voice and needs into the coaching room is essential for more ethically mature coaching.

Discussion points

1. What do you think of the statement, 'It can be difficult to challenge the teams' stated agenda, but we are less interested in their agenda, and more interested in their purpose – and the agenda life is asking them to rise to.'
2. Which of the three scenarios would you find most challenging and why? What would your response be?
3. Thinking systemically, what stakeholder gets forgotten in your work (or consider a particular assignment)?
4. Apply the six components of ethical maturity to an issue. Which components are most relevant?

Recommended reading

Hawkins, P. (2021) *Leadership team coaching: developing collective transformational leadership, 4th Edition*. London: Kogan Page.

References

Argyris, C. & Schön, D. (1974). *Theory in practice: increasing professional effectiveness*. San Francisco, CA: Jossey-Bass.

Bachkirova, T., Jackson, P., & Clutterbuck, D. (Eds) (2011). *Supervision in coaching and mentoring: theory and practice*. Maidenhead: Open University Press/McGraw-Hill.

Carr, C. & Peters, J. (2012). The experience and impact of team coaching: a dual case study. Doctoral dissertation, Middlesex University.

Carroll, M. & Shaw, E. (2013). *Ethical maturity in the helping professions: making difficult life and work decisions*. London: Jessica Kingsley Publishers.

Hawkins, P. (2011). Expanding emotional, ethical, and cognitive capacity in supervision. In J. Passmore (Ed.), Supervision in coaching. London: Kogan Page.

Hawkins, P. (2019). Resourcing – the neglected third leg of supervision. In E. Turner & S. Palmer (Eds), The heart of coaching supervision – working with reflection and self-care. Abingdon: Routledge.

Hawkins, P. (2020) We need to move beyond the high-performing teams. www.renewalassociates.co.uk/2020/07/we-need-to-move-beyond-high-performing-teams.

Hawkins, P. (2021). *Leadership team coaching: developing collective transformational leadership*, 4th Edition. London: Kogan Page.

Hawkins, P. (Ed.) (2022). *Leadership team coaching in practice*, 3rd Edition. London: Kogan Page.

Hawkins, P. & Smith, N. (2013) *Coaching, mentoring and organizational consultancy: supervision and development*, 2nd Edition. Maidenhead: Open University Press/ McGraw Hill.

Hawkins, P. & Turner, E. (2020). *Systemic coaching: delivering value beyond the individual.* London: Routledge.

Heffernan, M. (2011). *Wilful blindness: How we Ignore the obvious at our peril.* London: Simon & Schuster.

Heron, J. (1982). *Empirical validity in experiential research.* London: Sage Publications.

Hershfield, H. E. and Bartels, D. (2018). The future self. In Oettingen, G., Sevincer, A. T., & Gollwitzer, P. M. (Eds). *The psychology of thinking about the future.* The Guilford Press.

Iordanou, I.; Hawley, R., & Iordanou, C. (2017) *Values and ethics in coaching.* London: Sage Publications.

Kahn, M. S. (2014). *Coaching on the axis.* London: Karnac.

MacLean, P. (2019). *Self as coach: coach as self.* New York: Wiley.

Peters, J. & Carr, C. (2013). *High performance team coaching: a comprehensive system for leaders and coaches.* Victoria, BC: Friesen Press.

Torbert, B. (2004). *Action inquiry: the secret of timely and transforming leadership.* San Francisco, CA: Berrett-Koehler.

Wade-Benzoni, K. A. (2008). Maple trees and weeping willows: The role of time, uncertainty, and affinity in intergenerational decisions. *Negotiation and conflict management research*, *1*(3): 220–245. https://doi.org/10.1111/j.1750–4716.2008.00014.x.

Wallach, A. (2022). *Longpath: Becoming the great ancestors our future needs – an antidote for short-termism.* Harper Collins.

Whybrow, A., Turner, E., McLean, J., with Hawkins, P. (2023). *Ecological and climate-conscious coaching: a companion guide to evolving coaching practice.* Abingdon: Routledge.

Woodman, M. (1985). *The pregnant virgin: a process of psychological transformation.* Scarborough, ON: Inner City Books.

Chapter 11

Ethical issues in note taking and record keeping in coaching

Christiana Iordanou, Rachel Hawley and Ioanna Iordanou

Introduction

While writing and keeping effective records of coaching sessions has been deemed significant for an ethical coaching practice (Skoumpopoulou, 2017; European Mentoring and Coaching Council, 2018), research on the ethics of note taking and record keeping in coaching is overwhelmingly overlooked, apart from a few notable exceptions (see, for instance, Passmore & Sinclair, 2020, esp. pp. 189–194). Conversely, the ethical issues surrounding note taking and record keeping in relevant helping professions, such as psychology, counselling and psychotherapy, have been addressed both by scholars and practitioners in a variety of academic and practitioner publications (see, for instance, Mitchels & Bond, 2021, and bibliography therein). It is for this reason that substantial confusion still exists, not only on the practicalities of note taking and record keeping, but on the actual purpose, value and relational aspects of the practices. In this chapter, we synthesise the relevant literature on the ethics of note taking and record keeping in an initial effort to extract the transferable knowledge for the discipline and practice of coaching. While we have strived to consult any relevant sources in coaching, owing to their paucity or their lack of theoretical or empirical grounding, we have focused primarily on more robust literature stemming from psychology, counselling and medicine. Accordingly, we list some of the most pertinent practical considerations of ethical note taking and record keeping practices and discuss them against the backdrop of the relevant literature. Moreover, we provide, in the form of succinct vignettes, some reflections resulting from conversations with esteemed colleagues that have enabled us to forefront, aside from the practical aspects of ethical note taking and record keeping, the significance of the relational aspect of ethical note taking and record keeping. Our main argument is that conscious reflection on the purpose and value of our note taking and record keeping – aside from the practicalities of these practices – can help enhance the development of a respectful and trusting coaching relationship.

For the purposes of this chapter, note (or record) taking is defined as the "process of writing records", for the purpose of organising one's "thoughts

DOI: 10.4324/9781003277729-11

and feelings", in order to "reflect systematically on what has occurred and plan for future sessions" (Reeves & Bond, 2021, p. 236). This practice enables "accurate recall of client related information [...] in order to provide the best possible care to the clients" (Australian Psychological Society, 2007, p. 1). Record keeping, by extension, is the practice of creating and storing formal records. A definition of the word 'record' is more challenging. It would be easy to define records as, simply, "any notes" practitioners "keep about their work with their clients". From a legal perspective, however, the term "records" entails a lot more than mere notes (Mitchels & Bond, 2021, p. 12), including the diary of appointments, and jottings on scrap paper beyond what we deem more formal notes, the client's own notes or drawings during sessions, any assessment or psychological measurement records, reviews and reports, emails, audio or video recordings of sessions, and any other notes prepared for discussion, supervision, or training purposes (Ibid.).

The chapter starts by offering a brief introduction on the relevant literature on note taking and record keeping, as it emerges from relevant disciplines, such as psychology, counselling and psychotherapy. It moves on to consider an array of practical issues relating to note taking and record keeping. Interspersed with these issues, we provide three vignettes with the purposes of inciting further reflections on how note taking and record keeping may impact – positively or negatively – the development of a respectful and trusting coaching relationship. A case study with reflexive questions follows, before the chapter is closed with a summative conclusion and some pertinent discussion points.

Ethics in note taking and record keeping: the context

In helping professions such as psychology, counselling and psychotherapy and medicine, note taking and record keeping are an integral aspect of the work of professionals. In such settings, note taking and record keeping might not only enable the development of a trusting relationship between the client and the practitioner, but may also prevent the client from having to recount any painful information which, on occasion, may be traumatic (Australian Psychological Society, 2007). Record keeping is also important in cases a professional is subpoenaed by a court. In such cases, any kept notes and records can be used as evidence in court. Importantly, well-kept records can be used in support of a practitioner in case of a formal complaint against them and there seems to be discrepancy between the professional's and client's recollection of events (Ibid.).

Given that coaching also involves the collaboration of two or more individuals who work together respectfully and confidentially, note taking and record keeping may enhance the working relationship in several ways: firstly, keeping concise notes of what is shared in the coaching sessions may help both coach and coachee to remember the goals of the session, the actions that need to be taken, and any other key facts that are relevant to the coaching. (Skoumpopoulou, 2017). Passmore and Sinclair (2020) offer a simple framework – the PIPS framework – which can guide coaches on what to capture during sessions, that includes:

- Personal, non-sensitive issues, relating to the client;
- Ideas or passing remarks that might be worth exploring at a later time;
- Plans of action that we might encourage the client to summarise at the end of a session; and
- Suggestions from the client for the coach to implement.

From a practical perspective, this type of concise note taking and record keeping might enable the coach to plan the sessions, keeping track of what works and what can potentially be detrimental to the client's progress. Moreover, note taking and record keeping enable reflection on the coaching process and progress. If taken by the coach, brief notes might enable them to assess the effectiveness of the tools and methods used, in order to decide whether they work or whether alternative avenues need to be explored and adopted (Skoumpopoulou, 2017). If taken by the client, notes might empower them to take ownership of their progress, evaluating their skills, abilities and limitations. For all these reasons, coaches tend to take notes and keep records of their work with their clients, depending on their level of expertise. We would also like to emphasise the merits of encouraging clients to take notes for themselves, as part of the learning journey that they embark on during their coaching (Passmore & Sinclair, 2020).

As coaching is an unregulated profession, there are still no clear guidelines with respect to record keeping in line with the code of ethics of a licenced regulatory body (Afton, 2013). The International Association for Coaching Code of Ethics (n.d.) suggests that:

> "(a) Coaches create, maintain, disseminate, store, retain, and dispose of records and data relating to their practice, and other work in accordance with the law of the country in which they practice, and in a manner that permits compliance with the requirements of this Ethics Code.
>
> (b) Coaches are recommended to appropriately document their work in order to facilitate provision of services later by them or by other professionals, to ensure accountability, and to meet other legal requirements of their country."

This brings to the fore the issue of data protection and the lack of universal rules regarding data protection (Coron, 2021). In the European Union (EU), for instance, the use and management of personal data is dictated by the General Data Protection Regulation (GDPR: see Chapter 7 in this volume for further exploration). Accordingly, coaches are expected to have a strategy for the management, storage and destruction of clients' written and digital data, being aware that clients can request access to any personal data held by an organisation or an individual, such as a coach (Passmore & Rogers, 2018). It is important to emphasise that even if the coach is not based in the EU, coaching a client based in that region digitally is protected by GDPR (Passmore & Sinclair, 2020). Moreover, in the current climate, where the Covid-19 pandemic normalised digital ways of working across national boundaries, the variety of platforms that coaches use to work digitally might dictate coaches' legal responsibilities. Coaches, therefore, need to be aware of their contractual and legal obligations in the digital sphere, aside from national legal requirements that have traditionally protected face-to-face coaching practices. Accordingly, coaches are advised to understand how the law operates in their part of the world (Passmore & Turner, 2017), and their contractual responsibilities as dictated by the digital platforms they use for their coaching practice.

Even though these guidelines offer some direction as to how coaches should treat the notes and records they retain, they do not provide clear instructions with respect to the confidentiality and privacy of the client within an organisation (Afton, 2013). Thus, just like any other ethical issue in coaching, note taking and record keeping is dependent on each individual coach's professional values and ethical commitments (Afton, 2013; Iordanou, Hawley & Iordanou, 2017). It is for this reason that note taking and record keeping entail several challenges. Some of the pertinent issues pertaining to the ethics around them will be outlined in the following section.

Ethical issues in note taking and record keeping

There are several issues involving note taking and record keeping in coaching, with an emphasis on what should or should not be included in the coach's notes, the timing of writing such notes and their secure storage. These concerns have primarily been raised in neighbouring disciplines such as psychology, counselling and psychotherapy but are also relevant to coaching. Pope (2015) argues that the exponential increase in record keeping laws and professional guidelines and standards of ethics has resulted in great confusion for clinical professionals who work with clients. Pope (2015) clearly explicates a variety of challenges pertaining to note taking and record keeping, including confidentiality, informed consent and third parties. Although his work is situated in the discipline of psychology, some of his arguments and recommendations are relevant to coaching and will be outlined below.

The most obvious and prevalent issue with regard to note taking and record keeping is fairly straightforward: is there really an **obligation** on the part of the coach to take notes and keep records? As the profession is unregulated, the answer is not clear, with limited advice from professional bodies or thought leaders in the coaching sphere. In the neighbouring disciplines of psychology, counselling and psychotherapy in the UK, there is no consensus on the matter, although keeping records of a session is starting to become a requirement, even if the notes written are brief (Reeves & Bond, 2021). Nevertheless, effective note taking and record keeping are an integral part of the work of counsellors, psychotherapists and psychologists, because it allows them to recall information related to their clients (Australian Psychological Society, 2007).

According to the British Psychological Society's Code of Ethics (2006), all psychologists should keep records of their work, obtain their client's consent to disclose confidential information, when necessary, limit this disclosure to the purposes relevant to the request, and keep records in a way that does not put confidentiality at risk. Coaching marks a stark contrast to psychotherapy and other helping professions. One reason is that, as the emphasis is on the client taking responsibility for their learning and development, there is an argument for the client to be responsible for their own note taking. Whatever the approach, if coaches wish to keep their own records, they might consider either journaling as a reflexive practice after the session (Iordanou, Hawley, & Iordanou, 2017) or taking only brief notes during the session. The brevity of notes is essential for the coach to continue engaging in the conversation and, thus, not jeopardise the trust and intimacy that can result from the inevitable distraction of continuous note taking. Needless to mention that clients should be made aware, from the initial contracting, of coach's practice and purpose of note taking, of the possibility of confidentiality breaches and of their right to offer informed consent (British Psychological Society, 2008).

Vignette 1: Capturing the silences

In the literature on note taking and record keeping in coaching (and other helping professions) emphasis has primarily attended to the spoken word. Yet, the deeper we explore the nuances of the coaching process the more the issue of silence in the coaching conversation surfaces (Turner, 2021). This leads us to a fundamental question for all coaches who engage in note taking and record keeping: How do we capture the silences – their content, meaning, and quality? According to David,[1] a highly experienced coach and supervisor, silences are very important in coaching; it's where the coachee is engaging in real and deep thinking, engaging in the kind of reflection and reflexivity that leads to new understanding and, potentially, change. From a note taking perspective if all we are capturing as coaches is the words of the client, we could be missing out on an integral aspect of the coaching conversation. This is because, according to David, within the coaching conversation there is always a triad: firstly, the spoken conversation; secondly, the coach's silent

---

1   We would like to thank Professor David Clutterbuck, who allowed us to use the content of our discussion with him on the matter of ethical note taking and record keeping in order to produce the vignettes of this chapter.

conversation; and thirdly, the coachee's silent conversation. So, an ethical question to ask is: Are we actually doing our best by the client, if we are only capturing parts of the spoken conversation in our notes and records? Consequently, we would like to encourage coaches to reflect deeply on the purpose of their note taking practice and the ethical implications of what, how, when, and why they keep notes of coaching sessions.

Granted that notes and records are relevant, if not welcome, in coaching, the second issue coaches are encouraged to consider involves **confidentiality**, indeed, a concept that goes hand in hand with any written record of any therapeutic or developmental intervention (Pope, 2015; Mitchels & Bond, 2021). According to the Australian Psychological Society (2007), all entries involving clients should be accurate and factual and ascertain the client's confidentiality and integrity, especially when sensitive information is stored. The notes should be written in a format that shows respect towards the client, and in no way should the language used dishonour the client. It goes without saying that abusive language or prejudiced remarks should be avoided (Reevens & Bond, 2021), as should speculation and any types of labels or unauthorised diagnoses of client behaviour (Passmore & Sinclair, 2020). Coaches are also encouraged to bear in mind that tiredness, burnout and distractions, which are, at times, part of the job, may result in poor notes with counterfactual information and/or errors. Coaches, therefore, are encouraged to look after themselves, to minimise this risk. As already mentioned, coaches should bear in mind that clients may request access to any notes taken or records kept on them. For this reason, Passmore and Sinclair (2020) suggest that coaches make the assumption that clients will request to see their notes after the session. Doing so will encourage coaches to "focus on the essentials and avoid staying into areas of speculation" (Ibid., p. 191). It is further recommended that clients are informed from the initial session or contracting stage about the manner in which the records will be stored and the measures that will be taken to ensure their safety and, by extension, protect confidentiality (Coron, 2021). It is, thus, up to the professionalism of each coach to write notes in a respectful and factual manner which honours the client's right to privacy and informs the client about the steps taken to ensure the records' security. To be sure, there might be instances when confidentiality may have to be broken and the coach may be asked to disclose (parts of) their records. This is due to the moral obligation of the coach to protect the client and other members of the public from harm (Iordanou, Hawley, & Iordanou, 2017), as well as the more complex issue of the legal (or not) obligation of the coach to submit notes as evidence in court (Passmore & Sinclair, 2020), or to the police (Turner & Woods, 2015; Turner, Woods & Mountain, 2016).

This brings to the surface the perpetual question of who the client is, especially if the coach works for an organisation (Iordanou, Hawley, & Iordanou, 2017). Indeed, in coaching, the client may not be an individual, but rather a group of people or an organisation. A key ethical concern when more people or a whole organisation are involved is maintaining the confidentiality of each individual involved. If, for example, a coach's notes go missing, owing to loss or theft, the coachee's personal information could become exposed. With the exponential growth in the use of technology, especially as more and more coaches work in the digital sphere, mechanisms such as password protection or data storage in encrypted servers minimises some of these risks. However, as Fouracres (2022) has aptly shown, coaches' command of data security is still quite basic, if non-existent. Moreover, if a coach's notes must be presented as evidence for a court case, this means that information involving other parties of the group or the organisation might be disclosed, compromising, thus, confidentiality (Australian Psychological Society, 2007). To avoid confusion and act as professionally and ethically as possible, coaches are encouraged to consider informing everyone who might be affected about the possibility of disclosure of the records. This should be done from the initial contracting. It is in the interest of all parties involved that the coaching alliance is based on this knowledge from the outset.

What naturally stems from the above observation is the practical issue of **informed consent** to note taking and record keeping. Coachees have the right to be informed about who will have access to records kept on their coaching sessions, as well as the duration the records will be kept for and the manner in which they will be subsequently disposed of. But should consent be given verbally or in writing? In other helping professions there has been a lot of debate on the effectiveness of giving clients a form and asking them to read through dense legal jargon, in order to agree to its content (Pope, 2015). We hold the view that such an approach may sabotage the relationship between coach and client. Here, drawing from the related literature on psychotherapy is helpful. One study, for example, showed that patients perceived informed consent forms exist to protect therapists from patients (e.g. in cases of formal complaints) and not the other way around (Akkad et al., 2006). Seen through this lens, offering a written consent form and expecting a client to read through it and sign it may prove counterproductive for the development of a respectful and trusting working relationship. Coaches have the ability to communicate these issues simply and succinctly, building, rather than jeopardising, the trust between themselves and their clients (Passmore & Sinclair, 2020). This contrasts with the context of other helping professions. It is the coach's ethical responsibility to consider their client's rights and to initiate a dialogue which promotes and enables informed decisions for both (or all) parties. This type of open communication may prove extremely valuable in cases when informed consent involves people who come from different cultural backgrounds and are expected to work together (Wang, 2009; Pope, 2015).

Another key ethical issue in coaching, particularly in business environments, involves the **ownership of the records** and, by extension, reporting mechanisms on the progress of coaching. In the sphere of psychotherapy, the owner of the records is the company where the files were initially created unless the contract stipulates otherwise (Australian Psychological Society,

2007). It is expected that any records created on material provided by an employer or organisation or in the employer's premises for the benefit of the employer and/or organisation belong to said employer and/or organisation (Reeves & Bond, 2021). As a result, the employer may ask for access to these records. These practices are not common in coaching, where a carefully constructed contract can stipulate the reviewing and reporting tools for client progress. Passmore and Sinclair (2020) suggest that tripartite contracting, which is based on a pre- and a post-coaching assignment meeting, is an effective way to minimise the possibility of the sponsor asking for feedback reports or access to the coach's notes. This is because the priorities and the confidentiality of the coaching are mutually agreed upon. The client's progress can be discussed in the post assignment meeting or in a mid-assignment meeting, if deemed necessary. Throughout these interactions, the coach can act as the facilitator of the conversation without providing input (Ibid.). Overall, ethically minded coaches might anticipate ethical pitfalls and dilemmas by having clear guidelines on confidentiality and disclosure, which they can communicate to both the sponsor and the client from the contracting stage of a coaching programme (Iordanou, Hawley & Iordanou, 2017).

A note taking ethical challenge that has received more attention in the literature recently involves the **most appropriate time** to take notes. Put plainly, should notes be taken during the session or afterwards? Research with medical doctors who tend to create electronic records during the consultation using tablets, laptop or desktop computers makes for an uncomfortable read (Pope, 2015). Margalit et al. (2006) argued that typing on a keyboard during a medical appointment adversely affected doctors' and patients' therapeutic interaction. They further found that gazing at the screen disrupted the patient's emotional responsiveness and that screen contact rather than eye contact had a negative impact on the patient's ability to disclose information about their issue (Margalit et al., 2006). A systematic review by Kazmi (2013) showed that computer use with the purpose of note taking during the consultation negatively affected the physician-patient relationship, resulting in the reduction of eye contact and emotional support, as well as poor rapport building. These findings have significant implications for coaches. Considering the diversity the coaching discipline encompasses, such as the different cultural backgrounds of coaches and coachees, the plethora of approaches to coaching and the variety of issues that are brought in the coaching, one wonders when – if at all – is the right time for effective note taking during coaching?

Vignette 2: Balance between process and the developing coaching relationship

There is always a tension between the process – following the rules; a model; a framework – and the relationship that is evolving as a result of it.

According to David, coaching is about helping an individual to recognise patterns, for example, by opening new perspectives, and making new meaning. Within the context of note taking and record keeping, if too much of our attention, as coaches, is consumed by capturing words, we might lose sight of the patterns. From this situation, we can see that if we focus too much on the process of note taking, in order to maintain an effective coaching practice, paradoxically, we risk missing the point of ethical coaching, which is built on the development of a trusting and respectful relationship. It follows, therefore, that ethical note taking (and record keeping) involves a balancing act between adequate structure based on process and the unrestricted development of a respectful and trusting relationship, based on the coach's undivided attention. David, therefore, cautions coaches against an overreliance to process which could lead to low-quality coaching. Because, if we concentrate too much of our attention on recording what the client is saying, we might not listen to our own internal voice, upon which we depend in order to support the client, while losing sight of the whole. An important question to ask, then, is how do we rise above the process, to ensure some balance between taking notes and developing a respectful and trusting coaching relationship? Accordingly, when is the right time to take notes? Writing notes after the coaching session provides the coach with an invaluable tool for reflection, consolidation of information, and sense-making about what is going on for the coachee and the coach.

The limited coaching literature, which follows similar trends in psychology and psychotherapy, recommends that notes are taken as soon as possible after – and not during the session and to consider their **safe storage** (Australian Psychological Society, 2007; Passmore and Sinclair, 2020). While in psychology and psychotherapy the recommendation is that records are kept for seven to ten years after the end of the intervention (Australian Psychological Society, 2007; Reeves & Bond, 2021), some coaches suggest that two to three years after the completion of the coaching relationship are a good timeframe for deleting/destroying client notes (Passmore & Sinclair, 2020). Alas, more empirical research is needed in order to understand and reflect upon these practices by coaches. Nevertheless, coaches are advised to store their records safely and securely in line with the guidelines and/or recommendations of appropriate licensed bodies or legislation and their own integrity and professional standards. Moreover, as coaches increasingly work in digital environments, it is paramount that they familiarise themselves and keep up to date with technologically supported storage provisions and requirements, such as password protection (Coron, 2021). In fact, the British Psychological Society (2019) has published specific guidelines to help psychologists and coaching psychologists use, retain and manage electronic records, which coaches might find useful. Finally, the safe **disposal of the records** after the recommended storage period has elapsed should also be given careful consideration. Physical files can be shredded, while electronic files can be deleted both from their original folders and the computer's recycle bin. The disposal of computers and hard discs that contain sensitive records should also be considered in advance, to ensure clients' confidentiality (Passmore & Sinclair, 2020).

All these guidelines and recommendations are reflected in the Global Code of Ethics (2018), which suggests that:

> *"Members will keep, store and dispose of all data and records of their client work including digital files and communications, in a manner that ensures confidentiality, security, and privacy, and complies with all relevant laws and agreements that exist in their client's country regarding data protection and privacy."*

It goes without saying that each coach is expected to be familiar with and abide by recommended guidelines on ethical practice (Pope & Vasquez, 2011; Pope, 2015). These do not necessarily have to be a code of ethics by an established professional association, much as we fully recognise the value of such formal codes (Iordanou, Hawley, & Iordanou, 2017). As coaches are accountable for their decisions, they ought to be aware of the fact that formal codes are there to undergird their practice, not absolve them of difficult ethical decisions (Ibid.). Moreover, coaches are advised to be aware of the current legislation in their country of practice and ply their trade ethically and reflexively, welcoming and respecting equality and diversity. Indeed, as we live and work in societies enriched by individuals from diverse backgrounds, coaches can take advantage of this diversity to enhance their reflexivity on the aspect of ethical note taking and record keeping and, by extension, reflect on the variety of ethical issues pertaining to note taking and record keeping. As we, the authors hope to have shown here, these issues go beyond the clear-cut, straightforward practical ethical considerations involving process, such as confidentiality, informed consent, ownership, timing, storage and disposal. Importantly, what should be focusing on more – both as practitioners and scholars of coaching – is reflecting on the relational value of ethical note taking and record keeping, namely, how the purpose of these practices enriches and enhances, rather than stifles, the coaching relationship and the coaching practice, overall.

Vignette 3: What is the purpose of note taking and record keeping?

For the coach, the coaching conversation is a balancing act between looking inwards to themselves and looking outwards to the client. So, when considering the value of note taking and record keeping, David encourages coaches to ask themselves two questions: What value am I trying to create with my note taking for the client? What value am I trying to create with my note taking for myself as a coach? Coaches often take copious notes of sessions and, more often than not, share them with their clients. While, in principle, an ethical act could stop the coachee from doing their own thinking? Could this practice also, inadvertently, absolve the coachee from the more laborious act of deep reflection, as the coach is seemingly doing the work, while the client is doing the talking? So, according to David, when a coach shares their notes with a client, unless they invite them to reflect upon them and share their views, they could be imposing their views on the client. This could be unethical, as notes are subject to personal interpretations, time and space restrictions, amongst other issues. This brings us back to the issue of the real purpose of note taking and record keeping. Why do we take notes and keep records as coaches? Is it because it is a recommended process? Is it because it adds value to the client or the coach? Is it to protect ourselves in legal terms? In short, have we got more selfish or more altruistic motivations and how ethical are these motivations? These questions encourage reflection on what collaborative note taking might look like in practice, now and for the future.

Requests for notes lead to consider the purpose of record keeping for an ethical coaching practice. As stated at the outset of this chapter, there can be complex issues relating to the making, disclosure and retention of notes/records, and each situation needs to be assessed in context. However, some core principles emerge. The following case study shares the reflections of experienced coach Aisha, who explored the ethical threads of walking the tightrope.

Case study

Aisha, is an accomplished coach, experienced in working across a variety of professional contexts. As a seasoned coach, Aisha thought that she would be happy to disclose her coaching notes, if she thought that they could help a coachee but this is an issue she only spared a passing thought on, as she had never received such a request. With the advent of the Covid-19 pandemic in early 2020, which ushered in a more uncertain coaching landscape compared to the one she once felt at ease with, forced her to reflect deeply on the legal aspect of her note taking and record keeping. Indeed, as Aisha found herself engaging in more complex coaching relationships online, and although not coaching outside of her home country, she became aware of the need to protect herself and her clients through the notes she took and records she kept. More specifically, even though Aisha was open to sharing her notes, should a formal request be made, she began considering the potential implications of such requests, and how the content or format of her notes might impact on her practice. For this reason, she reached out to her insurer to explore the purpose of her note taking and record keeping for an ethical coaching practice.[2] Her ultimate goal was to be better prepared to

2 We would like the thank Jo Mountain, who allowed us to use the content of our discussion with her on the matter of navigating boundaries in order to produce this case study.

be able to respond to any request for her notes. Fundamentally, she recognised that a request for disclosure of a client's notes may come in different forms – it might be a simple informal request from a client; a letter from the client's solicitors; a Subject Access Request; a court order requiring disclosure; or even a request from the police without a court order. The nature of such requests varies according to the impending issue and, importantly, the regional legislation.

From the conversation with her insurer's legal team, Aisha became aware of the following valuable information: If the request for a coach's records has no legal authority, it might be helpful to explain to the client themselves (not their solicitor or the police) that the notes are written by the coach for their own use, covering a whole range of issues discussed; that they are not a verbatim account of what has been said in the sessions or a chronologically accurate account of any facts discussed; that, as the coach may only record things they feel are pertinent to the coaching work, that the notes may simply be reflections, or short memos to help them recall what issues they want to address; that, as such, that they could be taken out of context and misconstrued. Moreover, as it is likely that notes are being requested for a specific reason, it follows that the information needed and, in turn, the information which should be provided, should pertain to that issue at hand only; everything else should remain confidential. For this reason, the coach is encouraged to consider writing a statement on the actual issue based on their records, rather than offering their actual notes.

If the request for the coach's records has legal authority the coach must comply. Nevertheless, before they do so, coaches might have to seek legal advice, as they might not have to submit their actual notes but, possibly, a statement. Coaches are advised to familiarise themselves with the terms of their professional liability insurance, as legal advice will most probably be offered to them through that avenue, enabling them to understand whether they could get away with partial disclosure, should they wish to. Importantly, in all circumstances, coaches are advised to reflect on the purpose of their note taking and record keeping not only from a procedural perspective but from a relational, that is, how their note taking and record keeping practices affect the development of a respectful and trusting relationship with their clients.

Consider the following questions

What value do my notes and records create for my client?
What value do my notes and records create for myself as a coach?
How can I share the content of my notes and records in a way that ensures my client's safety and confidentiality?
What steps do I need to take now to become more consciously reflexive of the purpose of my note taking and record keeping?

Before this chapter is concluded, a final note is provided on the exponential increase of the use of digital technology and Artificial Intelligence (AI) in coaching (on AI in coaching, see Chapter 23 in this volume). This entails not only the use of technological means to support the delivery of coaching services, such as digital platforms that enable virtual coaching conversations (Coron, 2021); but also the use of tools, such as chatbots, that augment or even replace functions carried out by coaches (Ellis-Brush, 2021). Following the peak of the Covid-19 pandemic, such digital tools have enabled the rise of virtual exchanges, rendering coaching conversations ubiquitous despite differences in time zones. While, anecdotally, coaches are embracing this form of work, recent research has shown that they also find it challenging for several reasons, including testing their capacity to be fully present and to establish intimacy and trust (Schermuly et al., 2021; Coron, 2021). These challenges have an impact on note taking and record keeping. While empirical research on this issue is in its infancy, it is agreed with initial suggestions the encourage the coach to "pace the virtual coaching engagements to allow time for note taking and meta reflection on the session, as well as ensuring there is enough time between sessions for the coach to resource, refresh and refocus" (Coron, 2021, p. 375). While this chapter does not delve deeply into the opportunities the digital world offers to coaching, coaches are encouraged to reflect deeply on the nature, purpose and timing of their notes, as well as to become familiar with their contractual and legal responsibilities, as dictated by their chosen digital platform and the regions in which the coaching takes place.

Conclusion

There are several practical issues and legal challenges pertaining to ethical note taking and record keeping. A consciously ethical coach is reflexive and mindful of the purpose, value and practicalities of these practices and how they might impact on the development of a trusting coaching relationship. Mistakes might be made, at times, and unconscious biases might need to be reflected and worked on. This chapter has explored how ethical note taking and record keeping goes beyond the mere practicalities of process to embrace the coaching relationship as a whole. Indeed, aside from a practical issue, note taking and record keeping is a relational one, involving coaches' and clients' mutual learning, development and growth. Accordingly, it is encouraged for coaches to evaluate the practicalities and value of their note taking and record keeping against the backdrop of acknowledging (and capturing) the silences of the client – their content, meaning and quality; balancing the capture of what the client is saying with listening to their internal voice – process vs relationship; and, ultimately, consciously reflecting on the purpose of note taking and record keeping. Unavoidably, challenges and frustrations are part of the process. But if used and reflected upon productively, they can contribute to the personal and professional development of both the coach and the coachee.

Discussion points

1.   Ethical note taking and record keeping draws on many fields of knowledge. What are your views on the way different fields approach note taking and record keeping and how does this knowledge inform your own note taking and record keeping?
2.   What does ethical note taking involve for you in your practice?
3.   There could be a tension between having enough structure to keep people safe and to appreciate the richness of what is going on behind the process – the spoken and un-spoken words. This is the difference between linear and systemic thinking. In your practice, how do you ascertain you capture your client's verbal and nonverbal cues to offer a constructive coaching experience?
4.   How can you as a coach maintain a balance between process and relationship and place the latter at the heart of ethical note taking and record keeping?

Recommended reading

Mitchels, B. & Bond, T. (2021) Confidentiality and Record Keeping in Counselling and Psychotherapy, 3rd Edition. London: Sage Publications.

References

Akkad, A., Jackson, C., Kenyon, S., Dixon-Woods, M., Taub, N., & Habiba, M. (2006) Patients' perceptions of written consent: questionnaire study. *British Medical Journal*, 333(7567): 528.

Afton, M. (2013) The Ethics of Record Keeping in the Business Coaching Milieu. https://certifiedcoach.org/the-ethics-of-record-keeping-in-the-business-coaching-milieu, accessed April 1, 2022.

Australian Psychological Society. (2007) Ethical notetaking and record keeping guide. https://aapi.org.au/common/Uploaded%20files/Ethical%20Note%20Taking%20and%20Record%20Keeping%20Guide.pdf, accessed April 10, 2022.

British Psychological Society. (2006) Code of Ethics and Conduct. www.bps.org.uk.

British Psychological Society. (2008) Record keeping: Guidance on good practice. www.ucl.ac.uk/clinical-psychology-doctorate/sites/clinical-psychology-doctorate/files/SECTION_8_Appendix_7_BPS_Guidance_on_record_keeping_June_2013.pdf, accessed April 9, 2022.

British Psychological Society. (2019) Electronic records guidance. www.bps.org.uk/sites/www.bps.org.uk/files/Policy/Policy%20-%20Files/Guidelines%20on%20the%20Use%20of%20Electronic%20Health%20Records%20%28Updated%20March%202019%29.pdf, accessed April 9, 2022.

Coron, E. (2021) AI and Digital Technology in Coaching, in J. Passmore (ed.), *The Coaches' Handbook: The Complete Practitioner Guide for Professional Coaches*. Abingdon: Routledge.

Cox, E., Bachkirova, T., & Clutterbuck, D. (2018) *The Complete Handbook of Coaching*, 3rd Edition. London: Sage Publications.

Ellis-Brush, K. (2021) Augmenting Coaching Practice through Digital Methods. *International Journal of Evidence Based Coaching and Mentoring*, S15: 187–197.

European Mentoring and Coaching Council. (2018) *The Global Code of Ethics for Coaches, Mentors, and Supervisors*. https://emccuk.org/common/Uploaded%20files/Global-Code-of-Ethics-v2-2.pdf, accessed May 1, 2021.

Fouracres, A. J. S. (2022) *Cybersecurity for Coaches and Therapists: A Practical Guide for Protecting Client Data*. Abington: Routledge.

International Association for Coaching Ethical Principles and Code of Ethics. (n.d.) Code of Ethics. https://certifiedcoach.org/about/ethics, accessed April 1, 2022.

Iordanou, I. Hawley, R., & Iordanou, C. (2017) *Values and ethics in coaching*. London: Sage Publications.

Kazmi, Z. (2013) Effects of exam room EHR use on doctor–patient communication: a systematic literature review. *Informatics in Primary Care*, 21(1): 30–39.

Margalit, R. S., Roter, D., Dunevant, M. A., Larson, S., & Reis, S. (2006) Electronic medical record use and physician–patient communication: an observational study of Israeli primary care encounters. *Patient Education and Counseling*, 61(1): 134–141.

Mitchels, B. & Bond, T. (2021) *Confidentiality and Record Keeping in Counselling and Psychotherapy*, 3rd Edition. London: Sage Publications.

Passmore, J. & Sinclair, T. (2020) *Becoming a Coach: The Essential ICF Guide*. Cham: Springer.

Passmore J. & Rogers, K. (2018) Are you GDPR ready? *Coaching at Work*, 13(4): 30–33.

Pope, K. S. (2015) Record-keeping controversies: Ethical, Legal, and Clinical Challenges. *Canadian Psychology/Psychologie Canandienne*, 56(3): 348–356. http://dx.doi.org/10.1037/cap0000021.

Pope, K. S. & Vasquez, M. J. T. (2011) *Ethics in psychotherapy and Counselling: A practical guide*, 4th Edition. Hoboken, NJ: John Wiley.

Reeves, A. & Bond, T. (2021) *Standards and Ethics for Counselling in Action*. London: Sage Publications.

Schermuly, C. C., Graßmann, C., Ackermann, S., & Wegener, R. (2021) The Future of Workplace Coaching – An Explorative Delphi Study. *Coaching: An International Journal of Theory, Research and Practice*. doi:10.1080/17521882.2021.2014542.

Skoumpopoulou, D. (2017) Understanding Good Practice in Workplace Coaching, *Frontiers in Management Research*, 1(2): 37–45.

Turner, A. F. (2021) Silence in Coaching. In J. Passmore (ed.), *The Coaches' Handbook: The Complete Practitioner Guide for Professional Coaches*. Abingdon: Routledge.

Turner, E. & Passmore, J. (2017) The Trusting Kind, *Coaching at Work*, 12(6): 23–26.

Turner, E. & Woods, D. (2015) When the Police Come Knocking, *Coaching at Work*, 10(6): 28–34.

Turner, E., Woods, D., & Mountain, J. (2016) A Matter of Record, *Coaching at Work*, 11(3): 37–39.

Wang, C. (2009) Managing informed consent and confidentiality in multicultural contexts. Presentation at the annual meeting of the American Psychological Association, Toronto, Canada.

Chapter 12

Ethics in using psychometrics in coaching

Catherine Steele

Introduction

Psychometrics are designed to assess an individual's mental ability, personality or preferences, they are a specific type of assessment that has three specific properties; reliability, validity and norm groups. Increasingly this type of assessment is utilised in all areas of coaching (Passmore, 2008). This chapter will look at their use in a coaching setting by focusing on the key ethical considerations This includes the factors coaches need to consider when deciding whether or not to use these assessments with their clients and, once that decision is made, how to use them ethically.

McDowall and Kurz (2007) suggest that when used skilfully psychometrics can "add value to any coaching process" (p. 301). However, there are a number of factors that need to be thought through to ensure skilful use; ethics being a key one. For example, psychometric tests involve the collection of personal data which leads to issues around how that data is stored and accessed especially in light of GDPR legislation brought in in 2016 making this both an ethical and legal consideration. Another issue relates to the fact that the use and understanding of psychometric tests are often commercially available measures and the user needs to ensure they have the appropriate training in a particular measure (outside of their coaching skills) to be able to utilise the often sensitive data contained within their outputs responsibly.

Within the coaching relationship this chapter will suggest that psychometrics are best used as a tool to support the development of that relationship and understanding between the coach and coachee. For this to happen ethically the coach needs to have a good understanding of why they are using a measure, what it is assessing and how best to apply it within their coaching focus.

What are psychometrics?

People often refer to the term 'Psychometric tests' however in this chapter they will be referred to as assessments. The rationale for this is that in a

DOI: 10.4324/9781003277729-12

coaching context psychometrics are used as assessments rather than as a test, which might be more commonly associated with their use within a recruitment and selection context. There are three main types of psychometric assessments:

1. Assessments of ability
2. Assessments of personality
3. Assessments of motivation or preference.

A study from McDowell and Smewing (2009) found that personality measures were the most popular type of assessment used (followed by 360-degree feedback and learning styles and emotional intelligence. As stated in the introduction, psychometric assessments need to have three important features; reliability, validity and norm groups for comparison and benchmarking. Reliability refers to consistency of measurement, for example if you are measuring a space in which to put a washing machine with a tape measure you need the tape measure to give you consistent measurement, not 100 cm at one point and 120 cm the next time you measure it! The same is true for psychometric assessments, you need the assessment to measure whatever its focus is consistently.

Validity refers to whether or not the assessment is measuring what it is stating it measures. For example, if an assessment proposes that it measures mental ability, we need to be able to say that with some certainty. Therefore, there might be a need to compare it to an external measure of ability like exam results. There is a lot more to be said about these two statistical concepts that are outside the scope of this chapter and text, to learn more you would need to look at specific training in psychometric testing which is discussed in more detail below.

Finally, an assessment will ideally have norm groups that enable you to make sensible comparisons between like groups. For example, if you are assessing the verbal reasoning skills of a child aged eight and you compare it to a group of adults that won't give you a meaningful comparison, instead you need to compare to a group of similar aged children – a norm group. In addition to these it is important that assessments are fair and free from bias meaning that no group is either advantaged or disadvantaged by their use. For example, some assessments have cultural biases within them meaning that questions require a level of cultural knowledge to answer. A question might ask about something in United Kingdom politics which would require the person to understand that cultural context.

The Psychological Testing Centre part of the British Psychological Society offers testing qualifications in psychometrics for professionals working in Occupational, Forensic and Educational settings. In addition to this the publishers of tests also offer training in their own measures. The purpose of the training in psychometrics relates very much to ensuring their ethical use and how that is done will be discussed in more detail below. There are also a number of guidance documents on responsible and ethical usage of psychometric assessments. For example, the International Test Commission Guidance on Test Use and the Psychometric Testing Centre's Test Users Guide. The commercial nature of the psychometric testing industry is also worthy of note here with some measures being somewhat luxury in their pricing bracket and marketing being a factor in purchasing decisions. I'm sure most coaches will be aware that quality and cost of product are not always aligned. Therefore, to help you make ethical purchasing decisions publications such as the independent test reviews on the Psychological Testing Centre website can support a coach's choices.

Why would a coach use psychometrics?

There is a wealth of literature on psychometric assessments and increasingly there is a growing evidence base on coaching. However, the literature on psychometrics and coaching together is a little sparse! As stated above within coaching the types of psychometrics that are most often used are those that look at personality, motives or preferences. The literature we do have on the use of psychometrics in coaching suggests that they are supportive of both the coach and the coachee (Buckle, 2012). Coaches have also reported that psychometric assessments support their practice by enabling them to reflect on and examine their own style and strengths which in turns means they can adapt their style to the client in front of them (Krebs-Hirsch & Kise, 2000). In addition, measures such as the Hogan Development Survey can show a coach where they might have potential for derailment for example in times of pressure (Nelson & Hogan, 2009).

From the perspective of the coachee psychometrics assessments can help us to see how we are like and unlike others (Rogers, 2008). In that way they provide us with a metaphorical mirror showing us unique insights into who we are (Beddoes-Jones & Miller, 2007). Wallace, (2009) shows that they can also give us an indication of things like our preferred working style. Scoular and Campbell (2007) described that the experience of receiving feedback from a psychometric assessment can be a very powerful experience for a coachee and enable better self-insight and awareness relatively quickly that can then be used in the coaching sessions. These assessments provide a snapshot to both the coach and coachee of where the coachee is currently in their outlook, their preferences and perhaps their style of relating to others for example. They also offer a shared vocabulary between coach and coachee which can be used to enhance understanding and communication in coaching sessions (Harper, 2008).

However, whilst these all sound like very positive impacts and the kind of experiences all coaches want for their clients; (shared communication, self-insight, reflection and so on), these benefits can only be experienced when psychometric assessment is done appropriately and ethically. These key distinctive ethical features are the focus of the next section.

Distinctive ethical features

Psychometric assessments bring with them a number of distinctive ethical features that are outside of those perhaps normally associated with coaching. Firstly, as mentioned above, to be able to use an assessment the coach needs to ensure they are trained in the measure as a minimum and ideally more broadly in psychometric assessment. These training programmes will cover these ethical issues generally and then as a coach you will need to consider how these apply to your specific coaching practice, to your clients and their needs. Once the coach is trained and therefore able to access and use these assessments in their practice the next step is to consider *when, how and why* the assessments are introduce into your practice. This is a theme that is covered in detail in the following section as well as when and why it may not be appropriate to introduce them.

As outlined elsewhere in this book there are a number of codes of conduct that a coach can refer to that guide the ethical nature of their practice and for many of us that will depend on the affiliation with their professional body. However, there are similarities between them, and most will aim to guide a coaches ethical reasoning and support them in decision making. When it comes to ethics in psychometric assessment use the two main codes of conduct that we need to refer to are:

1. International Testing Commission Guidelines on Test Use (2013)
2. British Psychological Society Test User Guide (2017)

The key similarities in these documents relate to:

- being qualified and competent to use an assessment, which refers to the both the initial training and the maintenance of competence.
- issues around collection and storage of personal data. With these assessments that data comes in two main forms, raw data and then the interpreted, standardised data for example in the form of a feedback report. Any materials relating to assessments themselves must also be stored appropriately.
- consideration of when it is appropriate to use an assessment which will include consideration of fairness and bias.
- consideration of client welfare and consent in assessment use.

Often as assessments are now carried out online, a coach may have access only to the interpreted data in the form of either standardised scores or some form or interpretive/feedback report. So, the coach needs to consider how they will use this data as this is not just an ethical consideration but also a legal obligation. Best practice dictates that computer generated reports from psychometric assessments are not simply handed over to the client (even though it is their data). Instead, it is recommended that a feedback session is carried out where a trained user (the coach) of the assessment discusses the output from the measure with the coachee (in the context, which the assessment was undertaken). During that discussion there is an opportunity to consider the coaches previous experience with this type of assessment (more on that in the next section), how they felt completing the assessment and talk around the outcome using tentative language. This is expanded on in the next section with some examples of good, and room for development, practices!

Another issue to consider here is if the coach is working in an organisational context - what access will the organisation have to any data gathered through a process of assessment for example. This is something that must be boundaried and contracted for when any work is being agreed at its conception. For example, it is not unheard of to ask coaches to use existing psychometric assessments in their coaching or for a client to bring a previous report to a session and ask the coach to discuss it with them. These are things to be considered and to be sure of your own scope of practice and limitations in these scenarios. For example, if you are not trained in a measure then you can't really offer any insight.

We have now identified what psychometric assessments are, considered a little bit about how we might utilise them in our coaching practice and what the distinctive ethical features to be aware of are. What follows is a more detailed discussion of each of these features specifically in relation to coaching with examples of how these things might come up, the issues a coach may face and how to ensure you (the coach) can use psychometrics smoothly and ethically in coaching practice.

Being appropriately qualified to use psychometric tests

Hopefully as a qualified coach you understand the importance of being qualified to do what you do, to protect both yourself and your clients. When adding another thing to your coaching practice in the form of psychometric assessments you need to ensure you are appropriately qualified in their use – for the same reasons, to protect you and to protect your clients. However as touched on above as well as ethical issues there are also legal considerations in this area that we need to be aware of. Mainly this refers to the use of sensitive data. This is outside the scope of this text and chapter as we are centred here on ethics but if you train in psychometrics, it will be covered as part of that training either with a responsible test publisher or with an organisation like the Psychological Testing Centre.

A qualification in psychometrics will cover at the very least administering, interpreting and feeding back test results to the coachee (Steele, 2021). There will also be a requirement to have an understanding of the data, data analysis and statistics to understand how standardised scores are generated, what a norm group is and how to interpret scores and explain them appropriately without jargon to the client. The level of this will vary depending on the assessment being used. The training should also outline the contexts within which the assessment can be used, for example some are appropriate for use in coaching and developmental contexts whereas others are more suitable for us within a recruitment and selection context.

It can be thought of as adding to the coaches' toolkit, when it comes to the type of assessment a coach might use. It's likely that the training will be specific to one type of assessment. For example, a personality assessment like the MBTI which is a type of measure or perhaps a motives assessment like the MVPI which looks more generally at a coachees motivations and values. To use both of these a coach would need to attend training with both test publishers (two separate organisations) and there would be a significant undertaking of both time and finances to do so. Therefore, it is perhaps very important to think about the purpose of using the assessment and how that information will inform the coaching. That will guide the coach as to which assessment or which assessments qualify to be used and where time and money is invested. Passmore's (2012) text is an excellent resource for coaches looking to understand this area in more detail. The text covers a range of well-known measures and how these can be integrated into coaching practice.

How to decide when to use psychometrics in coaching practice

Once a coach has the appropriate training and has thought carefully about why they want to use psychometric assessment with their clients they will need to consider when they will be used. Will it be at the start of the relationship for example? In 2012 Buckle found that a coach's relationship building competencies were critical before the introduction of a psychometric within a coaching programme. She suggested that at least some level of rapport and trust has to be developed before the assessment is introduced. A study conducted by McDowell and Smewing in 2009, found that eighty eight percent of coaches they contacted were using assessments with the majority of their clients. Those coaches not using them felt that they either didn't add value to or that they didn't fit their coaching approach. In the same research McDowell and Smewing (2009) found that the main reason coaches report using assessment is to open up areas for discussion (96.3%). This might indicate that using them at the start of the coaching relationship is most important, once that initial rapport is there from a first conversation perhaps. 79.3% of coaches in that research stated that assessments provide a useful source of data to provide insight into the coachee and 73.2% said that the coachee found the outputs useful. There is also evidence to suggest that psychometric assessments can impact the speed at which important issues can be accessed and the level of depth of the work between the coach and coachee (Buckle, 2012).

There may be times when psychometrics assessment either is not necessary or is not the best approach and it would not be ethical to introduce an assessment when it was not appropriate. The coach would then be gathering sensitive personal data about the coachee without a clear rationale which may result in a lack of trust. The use of an assessment involves the individual being self-aware and able to answer questions about their preferences and tendencies honestly and authentically. Steele (2021) suggests that there may be occasions where the coachee's motivation is low, perhaps this might occur either in an organisational or a health coaching setting where the coachee has been sent for a session by a General Practitioner or a manager rather than self-selecting into the process. In this case it might be unlikely that the individual is going to build the necessary trust and rapport quickly enough so it may be best to focus on that rather than introducing an assessment. Similarly, if an individual has been on the receiving end of bad practice in psychometric assessment, for example they are sometimes used in redundancy decisions (even though that is bad practice and not advised) they may be very sceptical of them in a coaching process.

One of the risk areas here is once a coach has invested in training in a psychometric assessment, they then may expect to use it with every client. Each coaching relationship is unique, and the use of assessment needs to be tailored to the coachee's needs. If a coach has a very homogenous practice with clients coming in for similar issues, then it may be appropriate to have them as part of their standard coaching practice, but it would be more usual to make the decision on a client-by-client basis.

How to use psychometrics in coaching practice

As touched on in the section above it seems to make a lot of sense to use psychometrics at the beginning of coaching relationships and this certainly seems to be supported by researchers in this area (Kurz et al., 2008; Rogers, 2008; Carr et al., 2008; Nelson & Hogan, 2009). O'Riordan and Palmer (2012) discuss three ways in which psychometrics can be used, firstly ahead of a coaching assignment, secondly during an organisational/leadership programme that then subsequently feeds into one-to-one coaching or to support the development of a theme or issue that emerges as part of the ongoing coaching discussions and can also serve with appropriate permissions as data for future research. See the example in Vignette 1 for how a psychometric assessment can be used to support a health coaching relationship.

Vignette 1

In this example the coach is working in a health coaching capacity working with coaching clients who are trying to reverse a type 2 diabetes diagnosis. Following a referral from a GP the coach will look at the coachee's motivations for making lifestyle changes and work with the coachee to support and facilitate their implementation. Following their first session, where the coach spent the majority of the time gathering the background about the coachee and understanding what they wanted to achieve in their coaching session, the coach agreed with the coachee that they would undertake a strengths assessment. The coach outlined the purpose would be to learn more about the coachees strengths so that these could be discussed in their sessions and utilised to support the behaviour change process.

The coach emailed the links to complete the assessment to the client and received their report one week before the next session. This ensured that the coach had time to review the client report before their next session. They had agreed that the second session would be focused on providing feedback on the strengths measure, so the coach led the session and provided feedback on what the report showed and using best practice principles they also discussed this with the client to see how they felt about the report. Finally, the coach discussed how the data from the assessment would now be used to support their ongoing coaching relationship.

After the feedback session the coach sent some further information about the strengths assessment to the coachee to support their understanding of what their strengths are and how to use them in their day-to-day life. In following sessions these strengths provide an anchor for both the coach and coachee to fully understand the coachee's motivations and some of their preferences. Strengths were used to help the coachee implement some of the lifestyle changes they wanted to put in place to help manage and reverse their diabetes. For example, one of the coachees strengths was curiosity so they discussed how the client could use this to research diabetes and the impact of diet. Curiosity was also utilised in designing new diet plans and creating new family recipes.

Both the coachee and coach reported that the assessment really helped them to gain a shared understanding of how the coachee could use their preferences to move forward and felt that it really accelerated the coachee's understanding of herself.

As already considered here, trust is a key factor of the use of assessments in coaching. Buckle's (2012) research showed that this was crucial and one way this can be achieved is through the coach sharing their own psychometric profile with the coachee. The coaches in this research felt that was fundamental in helping the relationship to develop. Ethically any sharing of information of this nature needs to be done in a consensual relationship with appropriate boundaries of further sharing.

When introducing psychometrics into a coaching practice the coach needs to be able to articulate the purpose to the coachee so they understand why they are being asked to do something else. The coach also needs to ensure that the relationship is prioritised above anything else (Kauffman 2010; O'Broin & Palmer, 2010). As discussed earlier in this chapter choosing an appropriate assessment is important, this relates to understanding why the assessment is being used. Vignette 2 provides an example of when there is a mismatch between the assessment and the coaching focus.

Vignette 2

In this example the coach was working with a client who had approached them to support them through a career change. Before their first meeting the coach asked the client to complete a personality assessment based on the big 5 personality model. The link to complete the assessment was included in an initial email with a coaching contract but no detail of the purpose of the assessment or how it would be used in the coaching relationship.

The coach had recently qualified in the psychometric assessment and had taken a decision to use it with every coachee and to get a report from them before the first appointment. The coach hadn't yet had time to update their intake files to explain the background to the measure and how they intended to use it in their coaching. Upon reflection the coach realises they didn't think through the how and why of choosing the type of psychometric assessment, but after spending the money on the training they wanted to make sure their new skills were being used. The coachee completed the assessment as requested and the coach received a report outlining the results prior to their first session.

In the first session the coach started to discuss the results of the assessment and it emerged that the client had already completed a similar measure and been involved in some lengthy team workshops based around the big 5 personality model. As a result, the coachee had a thorough understanding of his personality type, how it impacted him and those around him. In fact, he stated that he was more interested in discussing how his personal values might impact his career choices going forward and wanted to discuss that. He was a little frustrated that the coach hadn't asked him if he had any knowledge of personality assessment and felt that he had wasted his own time and a large portion of the first coaching session on something he already knew.

As a result, the coachee started to question the professionalism of the coach and the value of the coaching he was signing up to. In the second session the coach and coachee did start to discuss how personal values may impact the coachee's next career steps which was a far more effective discussion. The discussion led to the coach considering getting trained in a broader range of assessments to ensure they were able to better match the assessment to the client needs in the future.

They did continue the coaching relationship, but it took longer than usual to develop trust and rapport after a difficult start. The coach also became aware that in this case both time and money had been wasted on the personality assessment and reviewed the decision to use it with every coachee.

Vignette 2 highlights how important it is to follow best practice and ethical guidelines when using psychometric assessments in your coaching practice.

You are asking for your coachee's time and for them to share personal information with you when you request that they complete a measure. As a coach you need to treat that sensitively. When this is done well it can enhance the relationship but when it is done superficially or at worst unethically it will damage the relationship and your reputation as a coach.

Conclusion

This chapter has considered two things in alignment; the role of psychometrics within a coaching context and the key ethical issues that relate to their use in our coaching practices. As outlined, there are many potential benefits to using psychometric assessments in coaching, for both ourselves and our coaching clients. However, to realise these benefits there are some key factors that need to be considered. The coach needs to be trained to use the assessment they intend to use, the coach also needs a clear idea of why they want to use it and how it will support their coaching work. Alongside the why the coach also needs to consider how, what will the process be for implementing the assessment? Finally given things like GDPR legislation a coach needs to make sure they are using any data gathered responsibly.

As long as you are adhering to sound ethical practices then psychometric assessments and skills in this can be a great addition to your coaching and also a new skill that you can utilise to develop a deeper understanding and awareness of both yourself and your clients.

Discussion points

1. What psychometric assessments that you are aware of would be best suited to coaching practice and what are the key ethical considerations in using a particular assessment?
2. What steps do you need to take to protect your client when using psychometrics in coaching?
3. What steps do you need to take to protect yourself when using psychometrics in your coaching practice?
4. What considerations do you need to make when organisations ask you to use existing psychometrics with coaching clients they are referring to you?

Recommended reading

Passmore, J. (2012) *Psychometrics in Coaching; Using Psychological and Psychometric Tools for Development*. London: Kogan Page.

References

Beddoes-Jones, F. & Miller, J. (2007). Short-term cognitive coaching interventions: Worth the effort or a waste of time? *The Coaching Psychologist*, 3(2): 60–69.

British Psychological Society. (2017) Psychological Testing; A Test Users Guide. https:// cms.bps.org.uk/sites/default/files/2022-07/ptc02_test_users_guide_2017_web.pdf.

Buckle, T. (2012). "It can be life changing" an IPA of the Coach and Coachee's experience of Psychometrics in Coaching. *International Journal of Evidence Based Coaching and Mentoring*, 6: 105–118.

Carr, S., Cooke, B., Harris, L., & Kendall, B. (2008). Coaching with MBTI. In J. Passmore (Ed.), *Psychometrics in Coaching*. London: Kogan Page, pp. 47–62.

Harper, J. (2008) Psychometric tests are now a multi-million-pound business: what lies behind a coach's decision to use them? *International Journal of Evidence Based Coaching and Mentoring*. Special Issue No. 2: 40–51.

International Testing Commission. (2013) ITC Guidelines on Test Use. www.intest com.org/files/guideline_test_use.pdf.

Kauffman, C. (2010) The last word: how to move from good to great coaching by drawing on the full range of what you know. *Coaching: An International Journal of Theory, Research and Practice*, 3(2): 87–98.

Krebs-Hirsch, S. & Kise, J. (2000) *Introduction to Type and Coaching. A dynamic guide for individual development*. Palo Alto, CA: Consulting Psychologists Press.

Kurz, R., Saville, P., & MacIver, R. (2008) Coaching using Saville Consulting Wave. In: J. Passmore, *Psychometrics in coaching*. London: Kogan Page, pp. 132–150.

McDowall, A. & Kurz, R. (2007) Making the most of psychometric profiles - effective integration into the coaching process. *International Coaching Psychology Review*, 2 (3): 299–309.

McDowall, A. & Smewing, C. (2009) What assessments do coaches use in their practice and why? *The Coaching Psychologist*, 5(2): 98–103.

Nelson, E. & Hogan, R. (2009) Coaching on the Dark Side. *International Coaching Psychology Review*, 4(1): 9–21.

O'Broin, A. & Palmer, S. (2010) Exploring key aspects in the formation of coaching relationships: initial indicators from the perspective of the coachee and the coach. *Coaching: An International Journal of Theory, Research and Practice*, 3(2): 124–143.

Passmore, J. (Ed.) (2012) *Psychometrics in coaching: Using psychological and psychometric tools for development*. London: Kogan Page.

Rogers, J. (2008) *Coaching Skills, a handbook*, 2nd Edition. Maidenhead: Open University Press.

Ruben, M. & Schmuckler, J. (2003) *Coaching for Results: An Overview of Effective Tools. The 2003 Annual: Volume 2, Consulting*. San Francisco, CA: Jossey-Bass/ Pfeiffer, pp. 1–19.

Scoular, A. and Linley, P. A. (2006) Coaching, goal-setting and personality type: What matters? *The Coaching Psychologist*, 2(1): 9–11.

Steele, C, (2021), *Assessment in Coaching Psychology, in: O'Riordan & S. Palmer Introduction to Coaching Psychology*. London, Routledge, pp. 66–79.

Wallace, E. (2009) Using Psychometrics and Psychological Tools in Business Performance Coaching. *Coaching Psychology International*, 2(1): 13–14.

Chapter 13

Ethics in mental health and suicide management in coaching

Rosie Evans-Krimme and Jonathan Passmore

Introduction

We all have mental health in the same way that we have physical health. The World Health Organization (2022) views mental health to be an integral component of our overall health and define it as 'a state of well-being in which an individual realises his or her own abilities, can cope with the normal stresses of life, can work productively and is able to make a contribution to his or her community'. This definition acknowledges there is more to mental health than the restoration of it. There are also benefits to the promotion and protection of mental health. This shift in perspective throughout the western world has echoed across the health sector, therapy and coaching. In this chapter we explore the three most common ethical principles reported across coaching, clinical psychology, psychotherapy, counselling and psychiatry professional bodies and demonstrate how coaches can apply them in decision-making around coaching for mental health and managing all be it rare but extreme risks such as suicidal clients.

Rationale for the importance of the topic area

The mental health pandemic

Mental illness continues to be stigmatising and disabling, with depression as one of the world's leading causes of disability (World Health Organization, 2021). An estimated 5% of adults suffer from depression worldwide; this is an estimated 280 million people with depression (Institute of Health Metrics and Evaluation, 2019). Within these statistics are disparities between genders, age, race and socio-economic variations. For example, women are more likely to be affected by depression than men; the greatest cause of death among 15–29-year-olds is suicide; and that evidence-based and affordable mental health care continues to be limited in low socio-economic countries. One example of the impact of a global event on individual mental health both now and in the future is the COVID-19 pandemic. COVID-19 has had a profound impact on

DOI: 10.4324/9781003277729-13

mental health and psychological distress (Cénat et al., 2021), with growing concerns about an increase in suicide (Gunnell et al., 2020). This increase results from measures such as quarantine, social distancing, and self-isolation which are associated with increased loneliness, social isolation and entrapment (Holmes et al., 2020). While it was estimated suicide would rise, preliminary data from 21 countries, has revealed there has not been an increase in suicide numbers during the pandemic (Pirkis et al., 2021). It is still too early to fully examine the long-term impact of COVID-19 of mental health (Pirkis et al., 2021; Appleby et al., 2022), and many researchers remain concerned about a looming global mental health pandemic (Antonova et al., 2021; Cuzco et al., 2021; Bak, Chin, & Chiu, 2022).

Another consequence of COVID-19 was disruptions to mental, neurological, and substance use services, with the prevention and promotion of mental health services and programmes most severely affected (World Health Organisation, 2020). The WHO (2020) reported that around three-quarters of school and workplace mental health services were either wholly or partially disrupted, which were already limited in availability. To counteract the disruption and adverse impact of COVID-19 on mental health services, many countries and organisations responded by adopting digital solutions, such as telephone or video conferencing, to replace the need for in-person services (World Health Organization, 2020). The combination of the global pandemic deteriorating people's mental health, reduced accessibility of mental health services, and an increased accessibility of coaching delivered through technical platforms (Passmore & Evans-Krimme, 2021) has led to a 'boom' in the interest of coaching for mental health and wellbeing. Coaching is said to offer greater variation in modes of delivery (Grant & Cavanagh, 2007; Bachkirova, Jackson, & Clutterbuck, 2021) with a growing evidence-based behind distance coaching (Berry et al., 2011) and coaching for wellbeing (Boniwell, Smith, & Green, 2021; Green, Jarden, & Leach, 2021; Green & Palmer, 2019). From this perspective, coaching can be considered an effective approach to prevent and manage mental health issues through the promotion of wellbeing and development of skills (Atad, Smith, & Green, 2021), mindsets and behaviours that help clients to deal with the long-term uncertainty and significant changes the COVID-19 pandemic has caused.

Whilst the growing number of applications of coaching is generally viewed as a positive development, there are concerns over the safety of people with mental illness engaging with coaching (Cavanagh, 2005; Bachkirova, 2007; Aboujaude, 2020). For example, encouraging clients with clinical depression to set goals beyond their capacity is detrimental to their recovery (Cavanagh, 2005). This is in part due to the huge variation in the level of mental health training among coaches so coaches may fail to recognise subtle signs of mental illness in their clients (Cavanagh, 2005; Bachkirova, 2007). As a result, Grief (2013) argues that coaching should explicitly exclude the treatment of mental health disorders. This recommendation is based on the current state of health coaching research (Todorova, 2022), despite a lack of research into the effectiveness of coaching for mental health. Although coaching is showing promising psychosocial outcomes in areas such as quality of life, self-efficacy, and other indicators of mental health (Totorova, 2022; Grover & Furnham, 2016; Theeboom, Beersma, & van Vianen, 2014), research remains limited on the impact of coaching on mental health (Bishop, 2018).

Ultimately, coaching is not a replacement for mental health treatments and coaching practitioners need to be clear on their professional boundaries and how to appropriately respond when a client presents with mental illness. At the same time, coaching can play an important role in the mental health pandemic as a proactive and preventative tool that enhances mental health and wellbeing in the general, 'non-clinical', population. This chapter offers ethical guidance on how coaches can maintain the boundaries of their coaching engagement and maintain the welfare of their clients should they present with mental illness during their coaching engagement.

Ethical principles of coaching practitioners for mental health

Fidelity and responsibility

Coaching practitioners depend on a relationship of trust with their clients and responsibility is a key element of the professional autonomy that coaching practitioners have. This requires an open communication and responsibility for appropriate action when client safety is compromised and when conflicts of interest arise during coaching. The coach has a responsibility to form a strong working alliance and maintain confidentiality, whilst also taking care to benefit the coach sponsor and other parties involved in the coaching agreement. The practitioner ensures that the coaching contract clearly outlines the circumstances in which a breach of confidentiality may occur, which is always the case when the client is at serious risk of harming themself or another person. Practitioners can gather informed consent from the client when referring them to therapy or counselling. This can be gathered prior to contracting as well as during the coaching when the client's mental health problems become apparent.

Integrity around establishing and maintaining boundaries between a coaching relationship and other helping professions is paramount. In addition to being aware of the limits to their competency and capability, practitioners must recognise that they are in a position of power and trust and must promote themselves accurately and honestly in the science, teaching, and practice of coaching. This includes the accurate representation of their professional competency, knowledge and limitations around mental health and wellbeing or ability to deal with emotional distress. Practitioners should apply evidence-based coaching approaches that are in line with the currently accepted scientific practice (Biswas-Diener & van Nieuwerburgh, 2021; see section 'Adopting an evidence-based approach to ethics for mental health in coaching').

Respect for people's rights and dignity

Coaching practitioners should recognise the rights of all clients as human beings and respect their individual value and dignity. They work in partnership with their client and involve them in the decision-making and response to mental illness, as appropriate. This is demonstrated with a commitment to kindness and compassion for all and includes the right to privacy, to be self-governing and autonomous; all key ingredients to a successful coaching process. This includes respecting a client's choice on how to approach or treat their mental health. Coaching practitioners are opposed to the manipulation of their clients' will, even if it is to the client's benefit. However, knowing when to appropriately act in response to indicators of serious mental illness is also part of coaching practitioners' responsibilities and demonstrates a deep respect for client welfare.

In addition to considering the client's welfare, the practitioner must also consider the impact of the client's mental health on the coach sponsor in their risk evaluation of breaching confidentiality and/or referral to counselling or psychotherapy. The boundaries around these processes must be clearly stated and agreed upon in the coaching contract by all parties involved. The coaching practitioner can play an important role in offering feedback on these processes and suggest pathways that best protect the client's welfare, rights and dignity.

Beneficence and non-maleficence

Coaching practitioners should be aware of their professional limits and know how to respond promptly when a client's mental health goes beyond their competency level and scope for coaching. The practitioner must evaluate the need to postpone, continue or terminate coaching. They are responsible for their client's welfare and strive to benefit the people they enter into a coaching agreement with and take care to do no harm. They are responsible for the safeguarding of their clients and are obligated to promptly address conflicts that may impact a client's mental health and wellbeing. This includes the fastest course of action when the practitioner has concerns of self-harm and suicide, while also considering how to protect their client's confidentiality around their mental health and treatment and reduce the stigma attached to mental illness. The pathways to mental health support should be clearly outlined in the coaching agreement. The welfare of the client, the coach sponsor and the public takes precedence over the coaching practitioner's self-interest.

Coaching practitioners should address their own biases towards mental health and refrain from allowing them to interfere with their professional judgement and partnership with their clients. They should continuously develop their self-awareness in relation to equality and diversity with continued professional development, on-going coaching supervision, and awareness of their own physical and mental health to practise competently.

Practitioners must consider the additional risks associated with disclosing their client's mental health status and consider how to reduce the potential stigma attached to mental illness in their client's individual context. Whilst mental illness does not discriminate, factors such as gender, age, race, disability, sexuality, religion, culture, immigration and socioeconomic status can increase the likelihood of clients experiencing some mental illnesses, which can exacerbate the client's experience of discrimination and injustice. Practitioners should commit to adopting a coaching mindset when exploring and understanding the needs of their clients and should reflect on the limits of their objectivity. They should be critical of just how equitable the coaching process is in order to aim for equality for all.

Theoretical discussion of ethical features in the coaching context

Navigating the "grey area" between coaching and therapy

When navigating the 'grey-area' between coaching and therapy, coaches can consider the differences in focus, purpose and population (Maxwell, 2009). Psychotherapy, therapy and counselling primarily adopts a medical model perspective of mental health, where the focus is on diagnosing psychopathological behaviour (American Psychological Association, 2013). Psychotherapy also tends to have a focus on psychosocial problems and the past in order to understand the present and mental illness symptomatology, whereas Auerach (2001) argues that coaching's focus tends toward visioning, success, the present, and moving into the future. The purpose of psychotherapy is on recovery from mental illness symptoms, which is often done by helping patients to develop skills for managing emotions or past issues. As a result, psychotherapists and therapists mainly work with patients from a clinical population, meaning that the patient has a diagnosed mental health disorder. Conversely, coaches work with clients who are psychologically robust that come from a non-clinical population. The purpose of coaching this population tends to be around performance improvement, learning, or development in some areas of life (Atad, Smith, & Green, 2021; Hullinger & DiGirolamo, 2018). In a revisit of the boundaries between coaching and counselling, Bachkirova & Baker (2019) reviewed the current state of literature and research and reported a need for clear guidelines around navigating the boundaries in a pragmatic way. The researchers identified two implications for practitioners: identifying mental health issues and extensive contracting that considers mutual responsibilities and potential obstacles to their collaboration.

The risk of causing harm to clients with mental health disorders

Mental health disorders include illnesses such as major depression, anxiety disorders, psychotic disorders, personality disorders, substance misuse disorders, self-harming behaviours and suicidal ideation. Mental illness can severely impair a person's overall functionality, characterised by a danger of harm to self or others, serious impairments to judgement, mood, relationships, or occupation (American Psychological Association, 2013; World Health Organization, 2019). When considering the coaching process, mental illness can reduce a person's capacity to make choices and be self-determining (Bora, et al., 2010) in addition to having low levels of intentional goal-striving (Grant, 2007). This can lead to a power imbalance in the coaching relationship that can negatively impact the strength of the working alliance (Bora et al., 2010). For example, in the United Kingdom, if a coach has the perception that their client has lost their capacity to participate in the coaching relationship and is perceived to be acutely unwell, there is the potential threat to the client of being detained under the Mental Health Act. Concerns such as these may be highly prevalent in clients who experience severe mental illness. Furthermore, failing to address a client's mental health problems in a timely manner could potentially escalate their mental health problems. There is also a risk of indirect harm caused to those around the client, such as their family and colleagues at work. Coaches must consider how to prevent these occurrences by remaining within their competency level and make continuous assessments throughout the coaching engagement about the client's suitability for coaching, making a referral to another helping profession where appropriate (see section 'How to refer coaching clients to other helping professionals'). Programmes such as the United Kingdom's 'Mental Health First Aid' training offer professionals the opportunity to develop their mental health literacy and may be a valuable tool for coaches (MHFA England, 2022).

Who is coaching most appropriate for?

Considering the concerns over the safety of people with mental illness engaging with coaching (Cavanagh, 2005; Bachkirova, 2007; Aboujaude, 2020) and lack of research into coaching for people with mental health disorders (Bishop, 2018), we argue that coaching is not appropriate for people with clinical mental health disorders. However, Grant (2007) highlights the crossover between counselling and coaching populations and that suggests some experienced and relevantly qualified coaching professionals may be able to work with clients who experience subclinical psychopathologies. In his 3D model (Figure 13.1), Passmore (2020) identifies three distinct groups along the distribution of mental health in the general population: Diagnosis, Damage and Desire. Diagnosis refers to the clinical population where a client needs to receive treatment for their mental health disorder by a mental healthcare professional and recover, which could take months to years. Damage is the poor mental health, also known as languishing, that the general non-clinical population will experience at some point in their lives and can recover from with little to no additional intervention from a helping professional. Clients in the desire phase tend to be experiencing some to high levels of mental health and wellbeing and this is where coaching is most appropriate.

Coaches with additional clinical, counselling and psychotherapeutic training, who are experienced in working with emotional topics as part of their coaching practice may wish to move to the section: '*Promotion of mental health rather than amelioration of symptoms*'. In this section we provide a more nuanced model on assessing clients for coaching suitability.

Identifying mental health issues

It is not the responsibility of the coach to diagnose a mental health disorder but coaches can benefit from enhancing their understanding and ability to recognise potential problems that may benefit from a referral to a healthcare professional. Table 13.1 is an adaptation of Grant's (2007) table of potential warning signs of mental illness and offers reflective questions that coaches can consider when assessing potential warning signs of mental illness (Grant, 2007). It is based on the clinically used mental state examination (Soltan & Girguis, 2017) and should also include an assessment of the level of the coachee's impairment to their daily functioning, amount of time issues are present and impact on progress in coaching. If uncertain, coaches can share and explore with their supervisor and refer to Hullinger & DiGirolama's (2018) detailed overview of signs for referral for the most common mental health issues, which are: anxiety, depression, eating disorders, post-traumatic stress disorder, substance abuse or addiction, suicidal ideation and thought disorders.

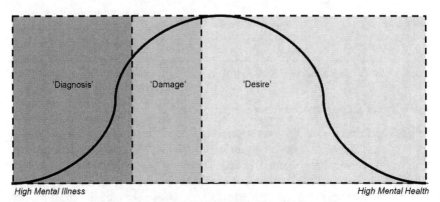

High Mental Illness   High Mental Health

Distribution of Mental Health in the General Population

Figure 13.1 Distribution of 3D model along the mental health continuum

Table 13.1 Potential warning signs of mental illness

Factor	Questions
Appearance	Is there anything unexpected with respect to dress? Is there anything unusual about the coachee's personal care? Are there clues in how the coachee moves? Is there any unusual body language?
Behaviour	Is there any behaviour that appears to be unusual? Is the coachee excessively agitated or lethargic? Can you observe any repetitive behaviours? How congruent is the body language with the coachee's expressions and what they are saying?
Mood	Does the coachee's mood fluctuate significantly with no apparent correlation with other information? Do you have the impression that the coachee is overly optimistic or pessimistic? Is the coachee possibly apathetic, and appears fixed emotionally?
Thoughts	Is the coachee 'stuck', preoccupied or fixated on a thought, idea, scenario or memory? How clearly is the coachee communicating their thoughts? Does the coachee appear rational or are there some signs of irrationality, such as possible delusions?
Perceptions	Are there any indications that the coachee's perception of the world is abnormal? Does the coachee appear to hear, see or feel phenomena that are not visible from your own perception?
Intellect	Has the coachee's intellect changed over time? Considering the information you have about the coachee, do they appear as intellectual as you expected? How present and active is the coachee in the session? Does the coachee appear to struggle with questions and exercises that require reflection or decision-making?
Insight & Judgement	How aware is the coachee of any unusual signs they present with? Can the coachee offer an explanation as to why they may present these unusual signs as reasonable?

Adapted from Cavanagh & Buckley, 2014, p. 410

Ethical contracting that considers mental health

Ethical contracting includes an assessment of a client's suitability for coaching. As 25–52% of people engaging with coaching present significantly high levels of psychological distress (Green et al., 2006; Spence & Grant, 2007; Kemp & Green, 2010), this initial 'screening' for mental health problems should become standard practice for all coaches. The coach must use this opportunity to assess whether the client's goal or topic, especially when around wellbeing, is within the scope of the coaching relationship or the coach's competency level.

Möller notes that clients find it easier to turn towards coaching than psychotherapy. The reasons for this include a comparatively lower threshold when compared to the long wait periods for therapy and the client potentially avoiding the stigma associated with psychotherapy or counselling (Möller, 2022). In a survey, Middendorf and Ritter (2022) found that stress-management, burn-out prevention and work-life balance were the fifth most commonly reported central topics of coaching. However, in his study on negative effects of coaching, Schermuly (2014) found that 26% of coach respondents had triggered deeper problems of the client and went beyond the scope of the coaching engagement. With evidence suggesting that all coaches, new and experienced, are willing to work beyond their capabilities (Bachkirova & Baker, 2019), there is a risk of coaching exacerbating their client's symptoms. This harm could be brought about by unskilled interventions that seek to explore deeper emotions (Baker, 2015) and potentially caused by a lack of awareness or understanding of the client's psychological and emotional distress (Bachkirova & Baker, 2019).

These findings highlight the likelihood of coaches working with clients on goals related to their wellbeing and the potential risk if the wellbeing goal is 'a wolf in sheep's clothing', especially considering the negative stigma associated with mental illness. Therefore, it is increasingly more important to include an assessment of the client's suitability for coaching during the contracting process. The following 'BE WELL' model of ethical contracting for mental health offers an overview of the core areas that coaches need to consider when contracting around mental health or wellbeing topics.

Be clear about professional qualifications
Explore the mental health or wellbeing goal/ topic
What is the impact of the topic on the client's daily life
Explain the difference between coaching and psychotherapy / therapy / counselling
Listen to the client's preferred route for mental health support
Look out for the potential risks of discrimination and conflict
The following vignette offers an example of how to apply to the BE WELL model in practice.

Vignette 1: Application of BE WELL model of ethical contracting for mental health

A client approaches a coach to work on their procrastination that is affecting their work performance. When introduced to each other, the coach explains the role of a coach and shares that they are certified and accredited with an international coaching governing body, in addition to having worked as a senior leader in the same industry as the client for 20 years (*Be clear about professional qualifications*).

The coach asks the client to expand on what they hope to achieve from coaching and the client expresses feeling 'stressed' because of their difficulties with procrastination, which is the cue for the coach to *Explore the mental health or wellbeing goal/ topic.* Here the coach can assess whether the topic is a 'wolf in sheep's clothing' and asks the client to share their understanding of what the terms they use mean, such as stress. In their answer, the client reports feeling like a failure because of their difficulties with procrastination and fears of losing their job.

The coach also wants to clarify *What the impact of the topic in the client's daily life,* and the client shares that they have had a final warning from their employer about needing to make a significant change or they may lose their job. At this point, the coach strongly suspects an underlying mental health problem and has confirmation that this problem has a significant impact on the client's life. The coach asks what outcome the client hopes to achieve from coaching and the client wants to 'feel less stressed'.

The coach decides to *Explain the difference between coaching and psychotherapy and counselling,* highlighting that psychotherapy and counselling focuses on treating difficult emotions that occur over a prolonged period of time and coaching on pursuing goals. The coach shares an observation that the client appears to be experiencing challenging emotions, which could potentially be a barrier to the client achieving their goals.

The client agrees and the coach *Listens to the client's preferred route for mental health support.*

The coach however, is *Looking out for the potential risks of discrimination and conflict,* they discuss whether sharing with their employer that they are seeking mental health support to resolve their issue with procrastination will be detrimental or helpful.

The benefits of adopting a systemic-biopsychosocial lens of mental health

Systemic coaching takes into account the greater system that surrounds the individual and how it affects the required coaching approach (Burchardt, 2015; Hawkins & Turner, 2020). By adopting a systemic approach, coaches are able to identify the complexity of their client's environment and leverage this contextual understanding to enable clients to formulate goals that are intrinsically satisfying (Burchardt, 2015). Adopting a systemic approach can enable a coach to better recognise and respond to clients' mental health problems. The addition of a biopsychosocial lens enables the practitioner to integrate an understanding of the biological, psychological and sociocultural factors of mental illness (Engel, 1997) and understand the interconnection and interdependence of these perspectives.

A biopsychosocial lens has been applied in research to create models that help practitioners understand the complex interplay between the various biological, psychological and social risk factors that contribute to the risk of mental health disorders, such as the diathesis-stress model of psychopathology (Broerman, 2017). This general framework explains the interaction between predispositional risk factors, an individual's experience of stressful events, and the development of mental health disorders. For example, someone who is highly vulnerable to a particular mental health disorder may develop the disorder as a result of seemingly minor stressors. Applications of this model to the understanding of mental health disorders include major depression (Colodro-Conde et al., 2018), schizophrenia (Jones & Fernyhough, 2007), and suicide (van Heeringen, 2012). Ultimately, taking a holistic view of a client's experience demonstrates a coach's respect for their client's rights and dignity. The benefits of such an approach include early identification of mental health disorders and decision-making for appropriate interventions.

Another benefit is that it can enable coaches to take into consideration the risks of discrimination and stigmatisation associated with disclosing information around their client's mental health. Coaches must consider where to draw the line at respecting their client's autonomy over their mental health and intervening when they are a risk to themselves or others. The risks to consider include understanding the potential discrimination the client may experience should the state of their mental illness be known to others and also the risk of not acting promptly. Table 13.2 is a tool that coaching practitioners can use alone and in supervision to generally assess these two risks and be used as an aid when considering how to best respond. To begin, the practitioner must gather the available demographic information and indicators of mental illness, which are highlighted in Figure 13.2. The addition of the demographic data is a step that encourages coaches to question how culturally relevant, appropriate and accessible the pathway to mental health treatment is for their client. For example, older people of colour are reported to experience the greatest mental healthcare disparities, owing to racism and discrimination (Jimenez, Park, Rosen et al., 2022). Coaches can play a vital role in working collaboratively with healthcare providers to increase equity in mental healthcare.

Table 13.2 Coaches risk assessment framework for mental health

Demographic data	Potential warning signs of mental illness
• Gender • Race • Age • Socioeconomic status • Disability • Culture • Employment status	• Appearance • Behaviour • Mood • Thoughts • Perceptions • Intellect • Insight Take note of the cluster of signs, their duration, frequency and intensity.

EMERGENCY RESPONSE:
• Risk of suicide: recurrent thoughts of death, suicidal ideation, suicidal plans, or reporting of suicidal attempts
• Risk of self-harm: recurrent thoughts of harming self, ideation of harming self, plans to self-harm, or reporting of recent self-harm

Recognising suicidal ideation and behaviours

One model that describes the biopsychosocial context of the common pathways to suicidal behaviour is the integrated motivational-volational (IMV) model of suicidal behaviour (O'Connor, 2011; O'Connor & Kirtley, 2018). It describes three phases (Figure 13.2) in which suicidal ideation and behaviour may emerge: the pre-motivational, motivational and volitional.

The pre-motivational phase is when suicidal ideation and behaviour may emerge and is when practitioners can identify individual and environmental vulnerability factors and potentially triggering negative events. Higher levels of perfectionism and socially prescribed perfectionism have been consistently associated with suicide risk and the likelihood of feeling defeated when faced with an interpersonal crisis. Combined with low socio-economic status and early life adversities this can further contribute towards an individual's risk of suicidal ideation and behaviour. However, negative life events are a potential risk factor at any stage in life. Table 13.3 gives an overview of the psychological risk and protective factors for suicidal ideation and behaviour that coaches can monitor as part of their risk of suicidal ideation and suicide assessment. In identifying pre-motivational factors of suicidal ideation and behaviour, coaches can assess which clients are more likely to be susceptible to the threat to self or motivational moderators outlined in the motivational phase and have planned pathways to mental health support if needed.

The motivational phase focuses on the relationship between the core constructs of defeat/ humiliation, entrapment, suicidal ideation and suicidal

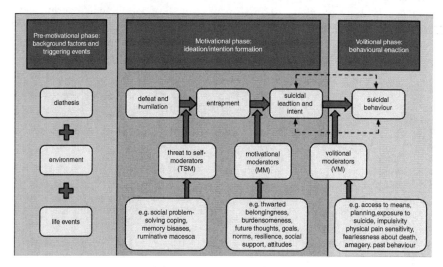

Figure 13.2 The IMV model of suicidal behaviour (Adapted from O'Connor & Kirtley, 2018, p. 2)

Table 13.3 Psychological risk and protective factors for suicidal ideation and behaviour

Personality and individual differences	*Cognitive factors*
Risk: Hopelessness, impulsivity, perfectionism, neuroticism and extroversion **Protective**: Optimism, resilience	**Risk**: Cognitive rigidity, rumination, thought suppression, autobiographical memory biases, lack of belonging, feeling like a burden, fearlessness about injury or death, insensitivity to pain, inability to problem solve and cope, agitated, implicit associations, attentional biases, defeat and entrapment **Protective**: Future thinking, goal adjustment, reasons for living, sense of belonging, ability to problem solve and cope
Social factors	**Life events**
Risk: social isolation, exposure to deaths by suicide of others, modelling, contagion, assortative homophily, social transmission **Protective**: social support	**Risk**: traumatic life events in childhood and/ or adulthood, physical illness, other interpersonal stressors, and psychophysiological stress response

Adapted from O'Connor & Nock, 2014, p. 77

behaviour. Clients who perceive that there is no escape from the defeat and/ or humiliation, such as social rejection or loss, are close predictors of suicidal ideation. However, the absence of threat to self or motivational moderators contribute towards the increase or decrease in entrapment translating into suicidal ideation. For example, unemployment has been shown to affect an individual's feelings of hopelessness or entrapment, which increases the risk of suicide, yet not everyone who is unemployed will feel suicidal. These predictors should be red flags to coaches, who can turn towards their supervisor for support on how to best respond to their client. When there is an urgent need to discuss a client's wellbeing, supervisors can contract with their supervisees the option to speak within hours rather than waiting for the next planned session. Coaches must honestly assess the need to terminate or delay coaching in the best interest of the client and refer to an appropriate helping professional.

The volitional phase outlines the transition from suicidal ideation to suicide attempts and suicide. The volitional moderators include: access to means, planning, exposure to suicide or suicidal behaviour, impulsivity, physical pain sensitivity/endurance, fearlessness about death, mental imagery of death/ dying, and past suicidal behaviour. Table 13.4 offers some questions practitioners can reflect on to assess if and how many of these factors are present. If the client shares any information that confirms one of these factors, then the coach must ask about suicide in a direct but sensitive manner. Asking individuals about suicide has been shown to be beneficial to those at high risk and does not increase the risk of suicidal ideation or self-harm (Dazzi et al., 2014).

Table 13.4 Volitional moderators within the IMV model and reflective questions for practitioners

Volitional moderator	*Question*
Access to means	*Does the coachee have ready access to likely means of suicide?*
Planning (If-then plans)	*Has the coachee formulated a plan for suicide?*
Exposure to suicide or suicidal behaviour	*Has a family member, friend or colleague engaged in suicidal behaviour?*
Impulsivity	*Does the coachee tend to act impulsively or on the spur of the moment?*
Physical pain sensitivity/ endurance	*Does the coachee have high or increased physical pain endurance?*
Fearlessness about death	*Is the coachee fearful about death? Has this changed?*
Mental imagery	*Does the coachee describe visualising dying or after death?*
Past suicidal behaviour	*Does the coachee have a history of suicide attempt or self-harm?*

Adapted from O'Connor & Kirtley, 2018, p. 5

The purpose of identifying these risk factors is to consider how they inter-act with one another in complex ways and potentially increase an individual's vulnerability to suicidal ideation and behaviour. In doing so, practitioners embody their ethical practice because they are taking responsibility for their client's welfare and can safeguard them more effectively. However, there are a number of dilemmas that coaching practitioners face when a client is at risk of self-harming or suicide. Lane & Boden (2014) outlined how therapists' own personal and ethical beliefs may conflict with their legal and professional responsibilities when responding to a client threatening suicide and offers some guidance that can be useful for coaching practitioners. As a result, coaches must become aware of how their biases may conflict with their ethical and legal responsibilities.

How to refer coaching clients to other helping professionals

It is imperative that coaches refer clients to other healthcare professionals as needed. As confidentiality is an essential ingredient in coaching, there are occasions when breaching confidentiality may be necessary and this poses a potential ethical dilemma that coaches may face. It must be noted that breaking confidentiality in order to protect the safety of the coachee or others is rare, however, coaches must be prepared to effectively manage these situations.

In the coaching agreement with the coachee and potential third parties, such as the sponsor, coaches can clearly state the circumstances in which they will break confidentiality. The non-negotiable circumstances include risk of serious illegal activities and harm to the coachee or others. Coaches can include circumstances such as the referral to a healthcare professional when mild to severe mental health problems arise, in the cases of physical illness, and when the topic is outside of the coaches' competencies.

Case study 1

Jack was referred by his parents for coaching, after dropping out of university and a period of time at home unable to find work. After meeting Jack, a more detailed and nuanced story emerged. Jack achieved reasonable grades and got access to his chosen course at university. He attended the first year, but owing to a combination of poor attendance and cannabis taking he failed. He shared the news of his course failure with his parents and explained the course was not the right fit for him and he wanted to change subjects. His parents agreed to fund a new course, and he was to live at home. Jack left the house each day as if to go to university. Jack told his parents over the following three years, he had attended, and passed. They agreed to fund a master's degree, and he continued to appear as if he was attending, dressing each day and leaving the house. After four years, he created a story of an internship he had secured, but that he needed money to support himself until a job offer came. For a year he left the house each day in a suit. This continued for a further year. Finally, five years later he shared the news, none of this was true, and the past five years had largely been spent in cafes, friends' houses and drug use had become a frequent habit.

What turned out to be a case on the surface of a careers coaching assignment was beneath the surface a significantly more complex case about habitual lying, drug use and a mental health disorder.

While the coach could have worked on Jack's curriculum vitae, or tried to spend time unpicking the issues, referral to a counsellor was the appropriate course of action to address the issue of drug use, what appeared to be habitable deception and depression.

While it can be tempting for coaches to get drawn into such cases, having worked with a client over two or three sessions as they share their story, few coaches have contracted or are trained to work with clinical issues. Coaches instead should have in the network, trained therapists who are happy to receive referrals and can work with cases of 'distress' or where a clinical 'diagnoses' is required and to instead focus on individuals who bring with them dreams and 'desires' about their future goals.

Promotion of mental health rather than amelioration of symptoms

Coaching has the potential to prevent the development of mental health disorders or help clients intervene at an earlier stage (Palmer & Gyllensten, 2008). However, coaches must maintain their fidelity by working with clients within the scope of their professional qualifications. Coaches qualified in areas such as coaching psychology, clinical psychology, psychotherapy and counselling will be able to better assist clients who experience subclinical mental health issues and are highly engaged in the coaching and goal striving process (Grant & Palmer, 2019). Grant and Spence (2010) developed their languishing-flourishing model of goal striving and mental health (Figure 13.3) to visually represent mental health as a continuum and highlight the overlapping areas between mental health and mental illness. Of note: Bachkirova and Baker (2019) argue even experienced coaches have been reported to exceed their competence and capabilities and may find the languishing-flourishing model useful when assessing the coachees' readiness and the coaches' competency.

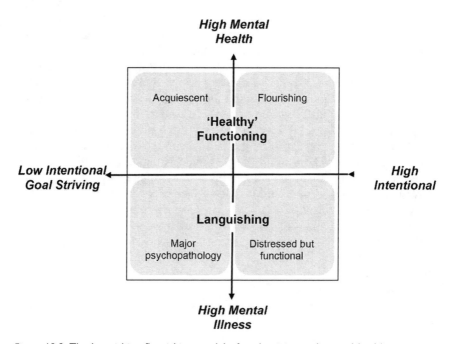

Figure 13.3 The languishing-flourishing model of goal-striving and mental health
Adapted from Grant & Spence 2010. Note: Permission kindly granted from Gordon Spence.

Adopting an evidence-based approach to mental health in coaching

What is the distinction between coaching for wellbeing and mental health? Arguably, coaching always aims to improve clients' wellbeing and there is some debate around whether coaching is an applied form of positive psychology (Atad, Smith & Green, 2021; Passmore & Evans-Krimme, 2021). If we draw on models of wellbeing, such as Seligman's PERMA model (2018), which states that the five pillars of wellbeing are performance, engagement, relationships, meaning, and accomplishment, then even traditional performance or goal-focused coaching will inevitably improve wellbeing. It has been repeatedly demonstrated (Theeboom, Beersma, & van Vianen, 2014) that measurable improvements of wellbeing are a common by-product of coaching; however, the goal or topic of coaching was rarely to directly improve wellbeing. This highlights the lack of research where coaching was intentionally offered to improve and strengthen mental health. However, one example of preliminary research is Atad and Grant's (2021) randomised controlled trial that compared the impact of health coaching on outcomes such as goal attainment, psychopathology, resilience, solution-focused thinking and self-insight within traditional tertiary education. Two groups of mature-age Israeli undergraduates who enrolled in a 13-week long health promotion course were compared: the traditional-education and health coaching conditions. Participants in the traditional-education condition completed lectures without the supplementation of health coaching and participants in the other condition had their lectures supplemented with health coaching delivered on Zoom video-conferencing. The findings highlighted that participants, in the coaching condition showed a significant improvement in their goal attainment and mental wellbeing whereas those in the traditional-education condition did not.

Despite advancements in positive psychology and coaching, and health coaching, many studies that assess the impact of coaching on mental health use assessments of mental illness to infer a lack of mental illness as an indicator of mental wellness (Theeboom, Beersma, & van Vianen, 2014; Grover & Furnham, 2016). For example, many pre-post measurements of wellbeing tend to include assessments of mental illness, such as depression and anxiety, rather than measuring the domains of wellbeing such as those outlined in the PERMA model of wellbeing. Green, Jarden, & Leach (2021) provides an overview of the latest research into coaching for wellbeing in the workplace with a focus on the PERMA model of wellbeing.

The advancement of coaching research into mental health and wellbeing will enable coaching practitioners to apply evidence-based coaching approaches or tools with greater precision. For example, if a client is in coaching due to experiencing burnout and the ultimate goal of coaching is to reduce their anxiety around setting boundaries at work, then the client wants the coaching to have a direct impact on their mental health. We recommend that the practitioner applies approaches or coaching tools with the strongest evidence based for direct impact on mental health. One example might be using a cognitive behavioural or MI approach. On the flip side, if a client is entering coaching with more performance-related goals, such as meeting the requirements to earn their promotion, but also reports wanting to improve their work-life balance, then the practitioner could apply approaches and tools that have an indirect impact on mental health, such as a solution-focused approach.

Conclusion

In this chapter we have explored the issue of mental health challenges in coaching, recognising that they are often more frequent than untrained and ill-informed coaches believe. Instead, mental health issues are widely scattered across the population and coaches need to be aware of these within the clients, the risks these might pose such as the risk of suicide for some clients, and how they can put in place actions, such as referrals, to support these clients. As a result, there is a greater need for coaches to develop their mental health literacy. By applying the ethical principles of coaching practitioners for mental health into their practice, coaching practitioners can enhance client welfare, navigate the boundaries between coaching, psychotherapy, therapy and counselling, and explore where they fall on the continuum of coaching for mental health and wellbeing. We emphasise the importance of a network around the practitioner, such as supervision, and have provided tools that can help both individual and collective reflection around clients' mental health and the appropriate course of action that includes a systemic-biopsychosocial perspective. We encourage the continued preliminary research into coaching for mental health and wellbeing and urge practitioners to adopt an evidence-based coaching approach.

Discussion points

1. What are the checkpoints for identifying mental health concerns with a client? What might the implications be of not recognising these indicators?
2. When and how should a coach be contracting for mental health support with their client? What are the implications for the coaching relationship and the welfare of the client?
3. Where should coaches be educated about mental health and suicidality in coaching? What are the resources available to a coach to support their decision making in such circumstances?
4. How should coaches consider suicidality and the management of such circumstances?

Recommended reading

Cavanagh, M. & Buckley, A. (2014) *Coaching and mental health. The complete handbook of coaching*, Vol. 2, pp. 405–417.

References

Aboujaoude E. (2020) Where Life Coaching Ends and Therapy Begins: Toward a Less Confusing Treatment Landscape. *Perspectives in Psychological Science*. 15(4): 973–977. doi:10.1177/1745691620904962.

American Psychiatric Association. (2013) *Diagnostic and statistical manual of mental disorders*, 5th Edition. doi:10.1176/appi.books.9780890425596.

Antonova, E., Schlosser, K., Pandey, R., & Kumari, V. (2021) Coping with COVID-19: Mindfulness-based approaches for mitigating mental health crisis. *Frontiers in psychiatry*, 12: 322.

Appleby, J. A., King, N., Saunders, K. E., Bast, A., Rivera, D., Byun, J., Cunningham, S., Khera, C., & Duffy, A. C. (2022) Impact of the COVID-19 pandemic on the experience and mental health of university students studying in Canada and the UK: a cross-sectional study. *BMJ open*, 12(1): 050187.

Atad, O., Smith, W. A., & Green, S. (2021) Coaching as the Missing Ingredient in the Application and Training of Positive Psychological Science. In Smith, W. A., Boniwell, I., & Green, S. (Eds), *Positive Psychology Coaching in the Workplace*. Cham: Springer. doi:10.1007/978-3-030-79952-6_3.

Bak, M., Chin, J. and Chiu, C. (2022) Mental Health Pandemic during the COVID-19 Outbreak: Calls for Help on Social Media. arXiv preprint arXiv:2203.00237.

Bachkirova, T. (2007) Role of coaching psychology in defining boundaries between counseling and coaching. In S. Palmer & A. Whybrow (Eds), *Handbook of Coaching Psychology*. Abingdon: Routledge, pp. 351–366.

Bachkirova, T. & Baker, S. (2019) Revisiting the issue of boundaries between coaching and counselling. *Handbook of Coaching Psychology: A Guide for Practitioners*, 2nd edition. Abingdon: Routledge.

Bachkirova, T., Jackson, P., & Clutterbuck, D. (2021) *Coaching & Mentoring Supervision Theory and Practice*. London: Open University Press.

Baker, S. (2015) *Practitioners' perceptions of the boundaries between coaching and counselling*. Unpublished PhD Thesis. University of Bedfordshire.

Berry, R. M., Ashby, J. S., Gnilka, P. B., & Matheny, K. B. (2011) A comparison of face-to-face and distance coaching practices: Coaches' perceptions of the role of the working alliance in problem resolution. *Consulting Psychology Journal: Practice and Research*, 63(4): 243.

Bishop, L. (2018) A scoping review of mental health coaching. *The Coaching Psychologist*, 14: 5–15.

Biswas-Diener, R., van Nieuwerburgh, C. (2021) The Professionalization of Positive Psychology Coaching. In Smith, W. A., Boniwell, I., & Green, S. (Eds), *Positive Psychology Coaching in the Workplace*. Cham: Springer. doi:10.1007/978-3-030-79952-6_2.

Boniwell, I., Smith, W. A., Green, S. (2021) PPC in the Workplace: The Business Case. In Smith, W. A., Boniwell, I., & Green, S. (Eds), *Positive Psychology Coaching in the Workplace*. Cham: Springer. doi:10.1007/978-3-030-79952-6_1.

Bora, R., Leaning, S., Moores, A., & Roberts, G. (2010) Life coaching for mental health recovery: the emerging practice of recovery coaching. *Advances in psychiatric treatment*, 16(6): 459–467.

Broerman, R. (2017) Diathesis-Stress Model. In V. Zeigler-Hill & T. K. Shackelford (Eds), *Encyclopaedia of Personality and Individual Differences*. Springer International Publishing, pp. 1–3. doi:10.1007/978-3-319-28099-8_891-1.

Burchardt, C. (2015) Business coaching and consulting–the systemic constellation approach in business. In *Modelling and management of engineering processes*. Berlin, Heidelberg: Springer. pp. 101–112.

Campone, F. (2014) At the border: Coaching a client with dissociative identity disorder. *International Journal of Evidence based Coaching and Mentoring*, 12(1): 1–13.

Cavanagh, M. (2005) Mental health issues and challenging clients in executive coaching. In M. Cavanagh, A. Grant, & T. Kemp (Eds) *Evidence-based coaching: in theory, research and practice from the behavioral sciences*, Vol. 1. Bowen Hills, Queensland: Australian Academic Press.

Cénat, J. M. et al. (2021) Prevalence of symptoms of depression, anxiety, insomnia, posttraumatic stress disorder, and psychological distress among populations affected by the COVID-19 pandemic: A systematic review and meta-analysis. *Psychiatry research*, 295: 113599.

Colodro-Conde et al. (2018) A direct test of the diathesis-stress model for depression. *Molecular Psychiatry*, 23(7): 1590–1596. doi:10.1038/mp.2017.130.

Cuzco, C., Carmona-Delgado, I., Canalias-Reverter, M., Martínez-Estalella, G., & Castro-Rebollo, P. (2021) Heading towards a Mental Health Pandemic. *Enfermeria intensiva*.

de Haan, E., Grant, A. M., Burger, Y., & Eriksson, P. O. (2016) A large-scale study of executive and workplace coaching: The relative contributions of relationship, personality match, and self-efficacy . *Consulting Psychology Journal: Practice and Research*, 68(3): 189–207. doi:10.1037/cpb0000058.

Engel, G. L. (1997) 'From Biomedical to Biopsychosocial: Being Scientific in the Human Domain'. *Psychosomatics* 38(6): 521–528. doi:10.1016/S0033-3182.

Gunnell, D. et al. & COVID-19 Suicide Prevention Research Collaboration. (2020) Suicide risk and prevention during the COVID-19 pandemic. *The Lancet Psychiatry*, 7(6): 468–471. doi:10.1016/S2215-0366(20)30171-1.

Grant, A. M. (2007) A languishing-flourishing model of goal striving and mental health for coaching populations. *International Coaching Psychology Review*, 2(3).

Grant, A. M. & Cavanagh, M. (2007) Evidence-based coaching: Flourishing or languishing? *Australian Psychologist*, 42(4): 239–254.

Grant, A. M. & Green, R. M. (2018) Developing clarity on the coaching-counselling conundrum: Implications for counsellors and psychotherapists. *Counselling and Psychotherapy Research*, 18(4): 347–355.

Grant, A. M. & Spence, G. B. (2010) Using coaching and positive psychology to promote a flourishing workforce: A model of goal-striving and mental health. In P. A. Linley, S. Harrington, & N. Garcea (Eds), *Oxford handbook of positive psychology and work*. Oxford University Press, pp. 175–188.

Green, S., Jarden, A., & Leach, C. (2021) Coaching for Workplace Wellbeing. In Smith, W. A., Boniwell, I., & Green, S. (Eds) *Positive Psychology Coaching in the Workplace*. Cham: Springer. doi:10.1007/978-3-030-79952-6_11.

Green, S. & Palmer, S. (2018) Positive psychology coaching: Science into practice. In S. Green & S. Palmer (Eds), *Positive psychology coaching in practice*. Abingdon: Routledge, pp. 1–15.

Green, S. & Palmer, S. (Eds). (2019) *Positive psychology coaching in practice*. Abingdon: Routledge.

Grover, S. & Furnham, A. (2016) Coaching as a developmental intervention in organisations: A systematic review of its effectiveness and the mechanisms underlying it. *PloS one*, 11(7): e0159137.

Holmes, E. A., O'Connor, R. C., Perry, V. H., Tracey, I., Wessely, S., Arseneault, L., et al. (2020) Multidisciplinary research priorities for the COVID-19 pandemic: a call for action for mental health science. *Lancet Psychiatry*, 7: 547–560.

Hullinger, A. M. & DiGirolamo, J. A. (2018) Referring a client to therapy: A set of guidelines. Retrieved from International Coaching Federation, www.coachingfederation.org/client-referral-whitepaper.

Jimenez, D. E., Park, M., Rosen, D., et al. (2022) Centering Culture in Mental Health: Differences in Diagnosis, Treatment, and Access to Care Among Older People of Color. *The American Journal of Geriatric Psychiatry*.

Jones, S. R. & Fernyhough, C. (2007) A new look at the neural diathesis–stress model of schizophrenia: The primacy of social-evaluative and uncontrollable situations. *Schizophrenia Bulletin*, 33(5): 1171–1177. doi:10.1093/schbul/sbl058.

Lane, P. & Boden, R. (2015). Self-harm and suicide risk: identifying some of the professional and ethical considerations. In Tribe, R. & Morrissey, J. (Eds). (2015). *Handbook of professional and ethical practice for psychologists, counsellors and psychotherapists*. Abingdon: Routledge.

MHFA England. (2022) Adult. Retrieved from https://mhfaengland.org/individuals/adult.

O'Connor, R.C. (2011) Towards an integrated motivational-volitional model of suicidal behaviour. In R. C. O'Connor, S. Platt, & J. Gordon (Eds), *International Handbook of Suicide Prevention: Research, Policy and Practice*. Wiley Blackwell.

O'Connor, R. C. & Kirtley, O. J. (2018) The integrated motivational–volitional model of suicidal behaviour. *Philosophical Transactions of the Royal Society B: Biological Sciences*, 373(1754): 20170268.

O'Connor, R. C. & Nock, M. K. (2014) The psychology of suicidal behaviour. *The Lancet Psychiatry*, 1(1): 73–85.

O'Riordan, S. & Palmer, S. (2012) Health and wellbeing coaching. In Neenan, M. & Palmer, S. (Eds) *Cognitive behavioural coaching in practice: an evidence-based approach*. Abingdon: Routledge.

Passmore, J. & Lai, Y. L. (2020) Coaching psychology: Exploring definitions and research contribution to practice. In J. Passmore & D. Tee (Eds) *Coaching Researched: A Coaching Psychology Reader*. London: Wiley, pp. 3–22.

Passmore, J. (2021) Digital Coaching. Definitions and boundaries. Internal document, CoachHub.

Passmore, J. & Evans-Krimme, R. (2021) The future of coaching: a conceptual framework for the coaching sector from personal craft to scientific process and the implications for practice and research. *Frontiers in Psychology*, 12. doi:10.3389/fpsyg.2021.715228.

Pirkis, J., John, A., Shin, S., Del Pozo-Banos, M., Arya, V., Analuisa-Aguilar, P., Appleby, L., Arensman, E., Bantjes, J., Baran, A., & Bertolote, J. M. (2021) Suicide trends in the early months of the COVID-19 pandemic: an interrupted time-series analysis of preliminary data from 21 countries. *The Lancet Psychiatry*, 8(7): 579–588.

Seligman, M. (2018) PERMA and the building blocks of well-being. *The Journal of Positive Psychology*, 13(4): 333–335.

Soltan, M. and Girguis, J. (2017) How to approach the mental state examination. *BMJ: British Medical Journal*, 357.

Theeboom, T., Beersma, B., & van Vianen, A. E. (2014) Does coaching work? A meta-analysis on the effects of coaching on individual level outcomes in an organizational context. *The Journal of Positive Psychology*, 9(1): 1–18.

Todorova, I., (2022) Health Coaching Research. In Grief, S., Möller, H., Scholl., W., Passmore, J., & Müller, F. (Eds), *International Handbook of Evidence-Based Coaching*. Cham: Springer, pp. 429–445.

van Heeringen, K. (2012). Stress–Diathesis Model of Suicidal Behavior. In Y. Dwivedi (Ed.), *The Neurobiological Basis of Suicide*. CRC Press/Taylor & Francis. www.ncbi.nlm.nih.gov/books/NBK107203/.

World Health Organization. (2019) ICD-11: International classification of diseases (11th revision). Retrieved from https://icd.who.int.

World Health Organization. (2020) The impact of COVID-19 on mental, neurological and substance use services. www.who.int/publications/i/item/9789240012455.

World Health Organization. (2021) Depression. Retrieved from www.who.int/newsroom/fact-sheets/detail/depression.

Chapter 14

Ethics of multi-party contracting in coaching

Yi-Ling Lai and Eve Turner

Introduction

Contracting in the coaching engagement has been identified as an important initial stage to establish expectations and alignments between the coach and clients (Lee, 2013). Whereas the conventional business or executive coaching contract has been based on business terms and conditions between the coach and organisation, research indicates (Louis & Fatien Diochon, 2014; Turner & Hawkins, 2016) multi-party contracting should be acknowledged, encouraged and entered into transparently. It would not achieve the ultimate and authentic purpose of coaching (e.g., to facilitate coachees' critical and creative thinking) if any of the coaching parties or stakeholders are not actively included in the contracting process. Louis and Fatien Diochon (2014) specified potential hidden agendas between different coaching parties and the ethical dilemmas that may arise when any of the party's interests are disregarded. De Haan and Nieß (2015) pointed out that coaches, coachees and organisational stakeholders in the same coaching process experienced significant emotional reactions concurrently because all collaborators share critical moments jointly. Therefore, the issues emerging in the coaching process should not be recognised as individual experiences but as group membership matters. Accordingly, contemporary coaching research has shifted its focus from positivism into critical approaches to explore in what way organisational factors, like power dynamics in coaching relationships and hierarchy affect the coaching relationship and contracting process. This chapter integrates existing literature to outline the best practice in a multi-party contracting and negotiation procedure. These practical suggestions can be used as a guideline for the coach's professional development (e.g., supervision).

Contracts in the coaching engagements

A contract is described as a written or spoken agreement, especially one concerning employment, sales or tenancy, that is intended to be enforceable by law (Passmore & Sinclair). In coaching scenarios, contracting has been

DOI: 10.4324/9781003277729-14

considered as one of the methods for establishing productive expectations among different stakeholders (coachee, organisation, human resources, coach etc.) involved in the coaching engagement (Lee, 2013; Turner & Hawkins, 2016). Contracts in the coaching context include formal and casual statements (or verbal accounts) that spell out intended outcomes, business arrangements, the methods the coach will be using, the coach's and coachee's responsibilities and duties or terms and conditions (e.g., confidentiality: Lai & Smith, 2021; Lee, 2013; Turner & Hawkins, 2016). A good contracting practice builds the foundation for evaluation processes and successful coaching outcomes for all parties (Ridler & Co, 2013). A transparent contracting process encourages communication flow and psychological exchanges among all collaborators that may enhance the coaching relationship (Lai & Smith, 2021). As Passmore and Sinclair (2021, p. 183) note it is also a safeguard for all the stakeholders. Clients here refers to the sponsors and other stakeholders such as team, human resources (HR), learning and development (L&D), as well as the individual client:

> *"A failure to use a written contract or an agreement leads to the potential risk of misunderstanding about the nature of coaching, how the coach will work and what the organization and the individual client can expect, and what the coach can expect. More importantly it also fails to provide a means for clients to hold their coach to account, what ethical standards can the client expect the coach to follow, and how can the client complain about their coach if they are unhappy."*

Contracting in the coaching process often can appear to consider only logistics or housekeeping contracting in the coaching process (Gettman, Edinger & Wouters, 2019). However, there are other forces at play such as the psychological contracting between all parties.

It is vital to distinguish contracts in coaching settings from other similar psychological interventions (e.g., counselling) and L&D activities (e.g., mentoring). The best way to start is to scrutinise their definitions and characterise similarities and differences. Overall, workplace mentoring is described as "involving a relationship between a less experienced individual (protégé) and a more experienced person (the mentor), where the purpose is the personal and professional growth of the protégé" (Eby et al., 2007, p. 16). Counselling is defined as a treatment which is entered into voluntarily, is responsive to the client's individual needs, and to bring about change in the domains of psychological and behavioural functioning (British Association for Counselling and Psychotherapy, 2021; McLeod, 2001).

Regardless of the variety of coaching definitions, contemporary coaching researchers place stress on the process of coaching, such as contracting, interpersonal interactions and working relationships rather than the formats and outcomes of coaching, (de Haan et al., 2013). Passmore and Fillery-

Travis (2011, p. 76) suggested coaching involves "a socratic based dialogue between a facilitator (coach) and a participant (client) where the majority of interventions used by the facilitator are open questions which are aimed at stimulating the self- awareness and personal responsibility of the participant." In general, the main focus of these three developmental activities is to improve a participant's professional growth through applying psychological, management, adult-learning or philosophical principles in the one-on-one interaction process. Hence, the working relationship appears to be the essential role to facilitate greater outcomes (Lai, 2015; McDowall & Mabey, 2008; Smith, King & Lai, 2021), highlighting the importance of the contracting between all parties.

Nevertheless, there are several distinctions to highlight the unique feature of coaching contracts. Slightly different to counselling, the sponsoring organisation of coaching may have a significant expectation of the desired outcomes. Contracts in the counselling relationship are usually two-way (i.e., between the counsellor and patient), and this may also be true in personal coaching. But most business and executive coaching contracts and relationships tend to include third parties, such as the coachee's line manager, HR/L&D or other senior stakeholders who are responsible for the coachee's workplace life (e.g., performance, career development and well-being: Lai, 2015). In comparison to the informality of mentoring contracts, coaching usually draws on a structured process, often involving specific tools and assessments, to provide both awareness in the client and the development of specific plans for improvement (Joo, 2005). Therefore, contracts in workplace coaching call for both explicit and informal spoken agreements (e.g., the mutual beliefs, perceptions and informal obligations between coaching parties) on expected outcomes, formats and roles and responsibilities. The contracting process often requires a multi-way negotiation between the coach, coachees and organisational stakeholders (e.g., line managers, HR professionals and senior executives (Turner & Hawkins, 2016), nevertheless it is less frequently undertaken in practice.

There are different types of contracts in the coaching engagement, such as commercial contracts, relational contracts, learning contracts and psychological contracts (Cardon, 2008; Fatien, 2012; Passmore & Sinclair, 2020; Salicru, 2009). The following section explains the main contracts in the workplace coaching process that involve various coaching parties.

Types of coaching contracts

Firstly, the coach needs to establish the so-called 'business' or 'commercial' contract with the sponsoring organisation. This is often conducted with certain HR professionals (especially those who are responsible for employees' L&D) to specify objectives and outcomes of this coaching engagement, roles and responsibilities, financial terms and outline a working plan for identified ethical issues. These ethical issues arising in information sharing and note taking (Fatien, 2012; Passmore & Sinclair, 2020 and see Chapters 7 and 11 in this volume for further exploration on the topics) that could impinge on confidentiality and in what circumstances it might be breached for example for legal or health and safety issues.

Secondly, the learning contract should be defined between the coach and coachee. This is usually discussed and agreed in the chemistry meeting or first session. The concept of a learning contract originated from self-directed learning to set out learning objectives, activities, evaluation methods, resources and strategies as well as roles and responsibilities (Knowles, 1986). A good learning contract promotes coachees' intrinsic motivation by encouraging them to take more learning responsibility (Lai & Smith, 2021).

Thirdly, the psychological contract is also required in the coaching engagement; it originally refers to the relationship between an employer and employee where there are unwritten mutual expectations for each side (Rousseau, 1995; see Chapter 8 in this volume for an exploration of psychological contracts in coaching). Given that advanced interpersonal interactions and collaborative relationships between the coaching dyad have been examined as essential factors to enhance affective and cognitive coaching outcomes (Graßmann, Schölmerich, & Schermuly, 2020), it is important to establish psychological connection and reciprocal obligations for the enhancement of coaching results.

The need for effective contracting applies to all types of coaching - whether one-to-one, group or team. While the growth of team coaching in particular can be seen in the burgeoning of both team coaching training programmes and accreditations, this has not yet been matched by research, clear when reading reviews of the team coaching literature (O'Connor & Cavanagh, 2017). Hawkins (2018), provides examples of team coaching practice, including some that refer to contracting processes. What stands out is the overriding need for clarity on the commission with "a clear purpose and defined success criteria by which the performance of the team will be assessed" (Hawkins, 2017, p. 48). The agreement with the sponsor will also cover areas such as methodology, processes, any assessments and establishing how the team will be in relationship - for example in a top-down culture, ensuring everyone's voice will be heard (for additional considerations in team coaching please see Chapter 10 in this volume).

Comprehensive contracts with various coaching parties align the coach's and coach's perceptions, create buy-in, reduce ambiguity for the coachee, clarify the role of third parties, and ease concerns regarding confidentiality that could obstruct the relationship (Lee, 2013; O'Broin & Palmer, 2010; Turner & Hawkins, 2016). Contracting has been found to be positively related to clients' beliefs about their coach's expertise and agreement on goals and methods for coaching (Gettman et al., 2019). Additionally, personal connection and trust are also requirements for effective contracting (Ibid.). For instance, strong contracting behaviours are one way of demonstrating knowledge and experience as a coach. Therefore, it would affect executive views of a coach's coaching ability and competency (Ibid.).

Quality contracting behaviours (e.g., discuss objectives, expectations around level of commitment, responsibilities) are more likely to reach a mutual understanding and agreement on the goals and methods for development through these discussions. In addition, the process of coming to mutual agreement on goals, roles and expectations engenders positive feelings of shared purpose, and clearly defined parameters should increase trust among all coaching parties.

Transparent contracting and negotiation process among all coaching parties promotes the creation of a shared identity or agreement, reduces psychological barriers and enhances the coaching relationship (Lai & Smith, 2021). Coaches frequently use writing contracts with organisations but oral agreements with other parties, this may cause some ethical dilemmas since oral agreements do not have the same legal force (Passmore et al., 2017). With the increased awareness of neoliberal values in coaching (a belief in sustained economic growth) and misuse of coaching as an instrumental tool and process of control for change (Shoukey & Cox, 2018), contextual factors relating to ethics in the coaching process (e.g., cultural differences and power dynamics in coaching relationships; see Chapter 1 in this volume for an introduction to relationships and power) have been brought to light. Coaching is understood to be a social process (reference please). Within multi-party contracting, there is an inherent tension as the result of socio-historical processes, organisational politics and power dynamics (Louis & Fatien Diochon, 2014; 2018; Shoukey & Cox, 2018).

Social influences on multi-party contracting process

Prior to the review of ethical issues in the coaching contracting process, it is important to understand in what way social influences in the organisation impact on various coaching parties' reasons for engaging in coaching. While the ultimate purpose of coaching is to "facilitate stimulating the self-awareness and personal responsibility of the coachee through interpersonal interactions" (Passmore & Fillery-Travis, 2011, p. 76), Despite the fact that coaching is often presented to employees as an opportunity for empowerment and growth, several authors have argued that workplace coaching may be acting as a control mechanism (e.g. Shoukry & Cox, 2018). For instance, organisational stakeholders may 'mistreat' coaching as an 'instrumental tool' or 'political action' to standardise coachees' behaviours. This may limit opportunity for coachees to develop creative thinking and behaviours (Fatien Diochon, 2012). With the increased use of digital platforms and AI coachbots for coaching sessions, the contracting should include the storage and usage of databases.

Shoukry and Cox (2018) argued that seeing coaching as a social process could allow the multi-party contracting to become an enabler for significant change. For example, it may help executives to take more holistic responsibility by means of a critically reflective approach to their actions (McLaughlin & Cox, 2016) and how their actions impact those around them. In addition, the critical approach encourages the linking of a social perspective with their organisational goals (Outhwaite & Bettridge, 2009; Hawkins & Turner, 2020). This social perspective of the coaching process raises two questions in the multi-party contracting procedure:

1. Is the purpose of coaching is for conformity or change?
2. In what way neoliberal values are embedded in the discourse of coaching (e.g., goal setting)?

These two questions are crucial as they may have consequential effects on the multiple party contracting process. When the coaching is established with authentic interest in helping coachees with the promise of development of their potentialities significant questions arise such as:

How can the coach ensure an alignment between the coachee's personal development and wellbeing goals?

How can these align with organisational objectives without breaching ethics, such as confidentiality? And

How can the coach ensure that in attending to the coachee's goals, they do not ignore, or sideline the legitimate outcomes agreed with the organisation, which is often paying for the intervention?

This point and above questions link to a long-debated question about who is the client? Scoular (2011) argues strongly that the organisation is the client. Huffington (2006) and Kahn (2014), among others, view both client and organisation as important. Bresser & Wilson (2006, p. 11) argue that the "effective coach needs to balance these competing priorities" linking to the need for transparency and clarity already discussed.

According to Diochon and Lovelace (2015, pp. 308–309), there are four types of power dynamics in workplace coaching contracting.

1. *Coaching as a tool of psychologicalisation*: organisations seek "control" by identifying the individual as the problem, not organisational systems, policies or practices.
2. *Coaching as a space for conformation*: organisations intend to use coaching to standardise individuals' behaviours and adapt to expected norms.

3. *Coaching as the externalisation of the management role*: coaches are portrayed as 'fulfilling activities and functions that other organisational members do not want to assume'.
4. *Coaching as a substitute for the collective*: coaching contributes to making people think they have to develop a personalised relationship to their work and organisation without any reference to the group.

Managing multiple agendas within the triangular coaching relationship

Louis and Fatien Diochon (2014) suggest there are multiple agendas in the triangular coaching relationship (coach, coachee and organisational stakeholders). These agendas are often hidden from different coaching parties as the result of the traditional coaching contracting process. In general, the business contract and part of the learning contract (expected outcomes, evaluation methods or available resources) are negotiated and agreed between the hired coach and organisational stakeholders or representatives (hereafter *organisation*). Some other parts of the learning contract (e.g., learning and development activities) are commonly taking place within the coaching pair or team. Potential hidden agendas that may breach coaching ethics during the contracting process are described in Table 14.1 below.

Table 14.1 Hidden Agendas Identified in the Coaching Literature

Hidden agendas	Initiator	References
The organisation excluded	Coachee	St John-Brooks (2010)
The individualisation	Organisation	Amado (2004), Tobias (1996)
The poisonous gift	Organisation	Fatien (2012)
The loudspeaker	Organisation	Fatien (2012)
The apparent compliance	Coachee	Bluckert (2006)

Louis & Fatien Diochon, 2014

This can be considered as important guidelines for coaches to identify issues emerging from contradictory agendas within multiple parties.

1. *The organisation excluded*: The coachee informs his/her coach in the one-on-one session that he/she would like to develop their personal career growth rather than work on the organisational objectives. Meanwhile, the coachee prefers the coach not to inform the sponsoring organisation (St John-Brooks, 2010).

2. *The individualisation*: The issues identified by the organisation should be related to the collective (e.g., organisational structure and policies), nevertheless the organisation considers this is a problem of individual motivation or behaviour. Therefore, the ethical issue here is about the coach's role, which isn't to fix anyone (Amado, 2004; Tobias, 1996).

3. *The poisonous gift*: The organisation has the intention of firing the coachee and uses coaching as a "last resort" or as an "excuse" to show that despite all their efforts, the executive still didn't meet the requirements of the role, and hence has to be laid off, making the coaching a "poisonous gift" (Fatien, 2012, p. 310).

4. *The loudspeaker*: The coach is used to deliver difficult messages to the coachee (e.g., bad performance) that the organisation tries to avoid doing directly. This is also called "externalisation of the manager's role" (Fatien, 2012, p. 310).

5. *The apparent compliance*: The coachee withholds his/her perspective and appears compliant. He/she could agree to being coached with the aim of modifying a specific behaviour, without intending to modify this behaviour in reality.

Coaches who regularly engage in supervision tend to learn to contract more effectively (Hawkins & Turner, 2020) and are less likely to experience misunderstandings, as a result of having a shared understanding of an assignment (Turner & Clutterbuck, 2019).

Vignettes

Please note – all vignettes are based on real situations, but names and details have been changed and cases merged, to ensure confidentiality.

Vignette I

An example of type 3 (see Table 14.1 for explanation) was when executive coach Omar came to supervision. He had agreed to a coaching assignment in a prestigious institution, brought in by the head of HR Jen, who was the first contact for all such engagements. His new coachee, Avyaan, was struggling in his relationship with his boss, Stephan, and felt that Stephan did not like him, was not interested in hearing his views, belittled him in front of others, and wanted to get rid of him. However, Omar was assured by the head of HR Jen that Stephan would take part in a multi-stakeholder meeting, and indeed a date and time was set.

Omar tried to talk to Stephan in advance of the meeting to briefly explain its purpose and what would happen and ensure that Stephan and Avyaan had discussed the coaching in advance and had agreed the potential outcomes. This did not happen. Omar first brought the case to supervision when Stephan failed to attend the first three-way meeting leaving him with Avyaan to set outcomes. He had sent these to Stephan for his thoughts and not got a reply. Omar was feeling unsure what to do next as he was worried coaching might be being used to get rid of Omar.

After supervision, Omar tried again to engage Stephan, and when that failed, he asked for Jen's (a staff member from HR) help in doing so. Instead, he was told by Jen that it seemed Avyaan was now under a formal performance management process which, if he failed, would lead to his dismissal. Jen offered to attend a three-way meeting and explain the process, and this appeared to be the only feasible three-way offer. Omar discussed this in supervision. He felt torn between ending the assignment, because of what he felt was the unethical behaviour of the company in deciding to go ahead with a formal process, without coaching being given an opportunity to work, and leaving Avyaan without any support during the process.

What would you do as the coach or the supervisor? In this case, given that Avyaan was being offered 6 coaching sessions, and he could use them with little organisational input – although of course he had his formal performance process objectives – Omar decided to keep working with Avyaan and they had the three-way meeting with Jen. Omar felt it would be wrong to withdraw from the assignment leaving Avyaan with very limited internal support. Ultimately while Avyaan did lose his job, he prepared for this outcome and found another role in a different institution that suited him better, and long-term he was much happier in the new role and organisation.

Vignette 2

Another common issue as in type 1 (see Table 14.1 above for explanation) is where the coachee tells the coach confidentially that they want to leave the organisation and asks for help in preparing to do so. In this instance such an outcome has not been agreed with the organisation; indeed, the coach knows the company is relying on the coachee's specific technical expertise to deliver a multi-million dollar contract in the next few months, and that no one else in the company, indeed the country, currently has the skills to roll this technology out. The coach is new to coaching, and to this organisation, and is worried about losing the possibility of any further work and feels torn. In supervision the coach is encouraged not to be drawn into binary thinking: either they give up the assignment or they discuss the coachee leaving, without telling the organisation. Instead, they concentrate on the relationship.

In the next session the coach explores with the coachee what lies behind their wanting to leave. The coach discusses with the coachee that they feel that they cannot provide active support (such as looking at CVs and covering letters), in preparation for them to leave as that goes beyond the scope of the outcomes they have agreed in the multi-stakeholder meeting, and would be done without the organisation's agreement or even knowledge. The coach discovers it all comes down to the coachee not seeing their young children between Sunday night and the following Saturday morning, not what the coach had expected! And through doing what the organisation wanted – helping the coachee delegate more so they were less under pressure - the coachee got home twice a week to bathe his children, and happily stayed to run the project and beyond!

Coaches' challenges while encountering multiple agendas and contracting processes

Coaches face a number of ethical challenges with multiple agendas and contracting processes. Some are explored below.

First, coaches often deal with issues related to confidentiality in a multi-party contracting process when communicating a certain amount of information to each of the different parties. For example, the organisation would expect to be updated on the progress of the coaching and its outcomes. However, the coach should be aware of not becoming "the ear of the powerful person in charge" and not to reveal any information given by the client during the sessions (Bluckert, 2006; Louis & Fatien Diochon, 2014, p. 34).

The coach might learn important information about the coachee from his/her organisation, such as performance issues, a takeover or a promotion opportunity. The coach needs to be careful with such sensitive and classified information and consider what can or cannot be shared between parties (St John-Brooks, 2010) within multi-stakeholder contracting, openly agreeing how feedback will be done and by whom is critical. Agreement of all parties is key (e.g. an agreed written review by the coach and coachee, interim three-ways etc.). In addition, the coach should make clear to all parties their stance on being given information that may not be passed on. The challenges this presents in not being able to 'un-know' information can lead to some coaches explicitly stating in the multi-stakeholder meetings that they did not want to be privy to such information (Clutterbuck & Turner, 2019).

Second, coaches may experience loyalty conflicts when multiple agendas create ethical issues, for instance, if the organisation has decided to terminate the employment of the coachee, regardless of coaching outcomes. The choices available to coaches include sharing their concerns with the coachee and/or the organisation (using the voice), ending the contract (exit) or staying involved by working on their values (loyalty). These choices are all ethical dilemmas requiring reflection, seeking the thoughts of colleagues and finding the best solution.

Third, coaches may also experience emotional stress when facing conflicts within multiple agenda situations. Last but not least, conflictual challenges sometimes occur between the coachee and organisation, owing to a pre-existing disagreement with coaches and the other parties falling prey to roles that can impede effective working relationships Karpman (1968) described the following roles as a 'drama triangle', where the coachee could be perceived as the 'victim,' the organisation as the 'persecutor,' and the coach as the 'rescuer'. This may result in the coach's excessive helping behaviours and failure to keep a non-biased position.

Vignette 3

An example of this was brought to supervision. James, the coach, really likes Anamika, his 'new' coachee. He has known her for some time, indeed she brought him into the organisation some years ago to work with her team. This introduction has been of great benefit to him financially. James has worked with several individuals and teams in what is a big organisation with many divisions. Now there is a new CEO, Sam. This CEO is not completely happy with Anamika's team's performance. Sam has heard good things about James from various teams and individuals and has asked James to work with Anamika. They start with a multi-stakeholder meeting and James admits he found it harder to be as detached as he normally is and found himself wanting to defend Anamika.

What is clear from supervision is that James has been 'sucked' into seeing the world from Anamika's position, and is seeing her as the victim, from a new persecutor boss. He found himself sympathising with her, and telling her how good he thought her, and her team's, work had been in the past – so becoming a potential rescuer. He realises that he is colluding with Anamika because of their past relationship and comes to supervision to step back and explore what is going on for him practically, emotionally, in the relationships with Anamika and Sam, and to consider what to do next.

Essential techniques for ethical issues in the multi-party contracting process

In order to offer evidence-based solutions for ethical dilemmas in the multi-party coaching contracting, based on the triangular coaching relationship and contracting research, Louis and Fatien Diochon (2014; 2018) suggested several essential skills and knowledge that would help coaches to deal with ethical dilemmas in the multi-party contracting process via supervision.

These skills and knowledge include:

1. Coaches' familiarity with tricky situations and capabilities to cope with emotional challenges.
2. Coaches' advanced interpersonal skills (e.g., good questioning and listening skills) to establish a trusting coaching relationship with all parties.
3. Coaches' strong self-awareness and reflective thinking to continuously enhance coaches' expertise. Furthermore,
4. Applying a systematic approach to strengthen all parties' working alliance. Meanwhile, their study also suggested coaches' experience of power and politics in the organisation should be included in the coach's

learning and development (e.g., supervision) to increase coaches' awareness of organisational factors in the multi-party contracting process.

Transparent multi-way contracting is a significant factor when engaging in an effective negotiation process. It is suggested involving the coachee and organisational stakeholders together in the contracting process and communicating with the coachee's supervisors for support, promotes a well-defined and mutually agreed contract (i.e., explicit objectives, accountabilities, resources and evaluation methods) providing a foundation of trust-building in the coaching process (Lai & Smith, 2021).

The most common practices facilitating multi-party coaching contracting meetings are when coaches saw their main roles in the contracting meeting as (Turner & Hawkins, 2016):

1. To clarify and ensure roles and responsibilities in this coaching engagement.
2. To make sure there is an agreed understanding about the coaching approach.
3. To be the facilitator of the dialogue.

Three key impact areas for coaches, clients and organisations are:

1. Aligning outcomes to organisational needs and strategic development.
2. Setting clear and specific goals.
3. Making the coaching more focussed on outcomes and action.

Numerous best practices in multi-party contracting can be reviewed in Turner and Hawkins (2016) work, the top five are listed and explained below (see Table 14.2).

Table 14.2 Top Five Best Practice Advice

Top themes	
Clarity	Be clear on expectations (of stakeholder, client and yourself), boundaries, confidentiality and what coaching is and isn't.
Honesty and transparency	Ensure honesty and transparency in communication. Do not fear to challenge the line manager and/or ask the important questions. Coach the line manager during the review meeting to ensure they provide meaningful feedback, by asking open questions and probing for evidence.
Leading and planning	Take the lead in contracting. Plan ahead, provide a clear, concise contract.
Setting outcomes and measures	Establish clear desired outcomes and measures of success.
Impartiality	Be impartial. Listen. Be curious.

Turner & Hawkins, 2016, pp. 60–61

Conclusion

To summarise recent research has stressed the multi and diverse agendas between different parties, such as coach, coachee and organisational stakeholders (e.g., coachee's line manager, senior executives and HR/LD professionals who are responsible for recruiting and evaluating coaches), that influence contracting in coaching. There are often hidden agendas emerging from multi-way contract negotiation processes, and these often affect working relationships with these parties. This chapter is a good starting point in developing new frameworks or schemes to evaluate the quality of multi-party coaching contracting.

Discussion points

1. As a coach or organisational stakeholder, have you experienced a multi-party contracting process? Are there any ethical issues you could think of?
2. As a coach, how did you solve the diverse agendas emerging from different parties?
3. What was the most difficult ethical dilemma you ever had in terms of the multi-party contracting process? What would you do the same or differently the second time?
4. How could coach education, development and supervision support coaches in understanding the complexities and ethical practices of multi-party contracting?

Recommended reading

Passmore, J. & Sinclair, T. (2020) *Becoming a Coach*. Springer International Publishing.

References

Amado, G. (2004) Le coaching ou le retour de narcisse? *Connexions*, 1(81): 43–51.
Athanasopoulou, A. & Dopson, S. E. (2018) A systematic review of executive coaching outcomes: Is it the journey or the destination that matters the most? *Leadership Quarterly*, 29(1): 70–88.
Bluckert, P. (2006) *Psychological dimensions of executive coaching*. Reading: Open University Press, McGraw-Hill.
Bresser & Wilson, (2006) What is coaching? In J. Passmore (Ed.) *Excellence in coaching*. London: Kogan Page/Association for Coaching.
British Association for Counselling and Psychotherapy. (2021) Introduction to counselling and psychotherapy. www.bacp.co.uk/about-therapy/what-is-counselling.
Cardon, A. (2008) *The triangular contract: Finding your way through collective contract complexity*. Retrieved from www.metasysteme.eu.
de Haan, E., Duckworth, A., Birch, D., & Jones, C. (2013) Executive coaching outcome research: the predictive value of common factors such as relationship,

personality match and self-efficacy. *Consulting Psychology Journal: Practice and Research*, 65(1): 40–57.

Eby, L. T., Rhodes, J. E., & Allen, T. D. (2007) Definition and evolution of mentoring. *The Blackwell handbook of mentoring: A multiple perspectives approach*, pp. 7–20.

Fatien Diochon, P. (2012) Ethical issues in coaching. In M. Esposito, M. Smith, & P. O'Sullivan (Eds), *Business ethics—a critical approach: Integrating ethics across the business world*. London, England: Routledge, pp. 302–316.

Fatien Diochon, P. & Lovelace, K. J. (2015) The coaching continuum: Power dynamics in the change process. *International Journal of Work Innovation*, 1(3): 305–322.

Fillery-Travis, A. & Cox, E. (2014) Researching coaching. *The complete handbook of coaching*, pp. 445–459.

Gettman, H. J., Edinger, S. K., & Wouters, K. (2019) Assessing contracting and the coaching relationship: Necessary infrastructure. *International Journal of Evidence Based Coaching & Mentoring*, 17(1): 46–62.

Graßmann, C., Schölmerich, F., & Schermuly, C. C. (2020) The relationship between working alliance and client outcomes in coaching: A meta-analysis. *Human relations*, 73(1): 35–58.

Gray, D., Garvey, D., & Lane, D. (2016) *A Critical Introduction to Coaching and Mentoring*. London: Sage Publications.

Hawkins, P. (2008) The coaching profession: Some of the key challenges. *Coaching: An International Journal of Theory, Research and Practice*, 1(1): 28–38.

Hawkins, P. (2017) *Leadership Team Coaching*, 3rd Edition. London: Kogan Page.

Hawkins, P. (2018) *Leadership Team Coaching In Practice*, 2nd Edition. London: Kogan Page.

Hawkins, P. & Turner, E. (2020) *Systemic Coaching – Delivering Value Beyond the Individual*. Abingdon: Routledge.

Huffington, C. (2006) A contextualized approach to coaching. In *Executive coaching – systems-psychodynamic perspective*. London: Karnac.

Joo, B. K. (2005) Executive coaching: A conceptual framework from an integrative review of practice and research. *Human resource development review*, 4(4), 462–488.

Kahn, M. S. (2014) *Coaching on the axis*. London: Karnac.

Karpman, S. (1968) Fairy tales and script drama analysis. *Transactional Analysis Bulletin*, 7(26): 39–43.

Knowles, M. S. & Knowles, M. S. (1986) *Using learning contracts: Practical approaches to individualizing and structuring learning*. San Francisco, CA: Jossey-Bass.

Korotov, K. (2017) Coaching for Leadership Development. In T. Bachkirova, G. Spence, & D. Drake (Eds), *The Sage Handbook of Coaching*. London: Sage Publications, pp. 139–158.

Lai, Y. (2015) Enhancing Evidence-based Coaching Through the Development of a Coaching Psychology Competency Framework: Focus on the Coaching Relationship (PhD Thesis), University of Surrey, Guildford.

Lai, Y. L. & Smith, H. (2021) An investigation of the three-way joint coaching alliance: A social identity theory perspective. *Applied Psychology*, 70(2): 489–517.

Lee, R. J. (2012) The Role of Contracting in Coaching: Balancing Individual Client and Organizational Issues. *The Wiley-Blackwell Handbook of the Psychology of Coaching and Mentoring*, pp. 40–57.

Louis, D. & Fatien Diochon, P. (2014) Educating coaches to power dynamics: Managing multiple agendas within the triangular relationship. *Journal of Psychological Issues in Organizational Culture*, 5(2): 31–47.

Louis, D., & Fatien Diochon, P. (2018) The coaching space: A production of power relationships in organizational settings. *Organization*, 25(6): 710–731.

McDowall, A. & Mabey, C. (2008) Developing a framework for assessing effective development activities. *Personnel Review*, 37(6): 629–646.

McLaughlin, M. & Cox, E. (2016) *Leadership coaching: Developing braver leaders*. Routledge.

McLeod, J. (2001) *Counselling in the Workplace: The Facts*. Rugby: British Association for Counselling and Psychotherapy.

Mulvie, A. (2015) *The Value of Executive Coaching*. Oxford, New York: Routledge.

Nielsen, A. E. & Nørreklit, H. (2009) A discourse analysis of the disciplinary power of management coaching. *Society and Business Review*, 4(3): 202–214.

O'Broin, A. & Palmer, S. (2010) Exploring key aspects in the formation of coaching relationships: Initial indicators from the perspective of the coachee and the coach. *Coaching: An International Journal of Theory, Research and Practice*, 3 (2): 124–143.

O'Connor, S. & Cavanagh, M. (2017). Group and Team Coaching. In T. Bachkirova, G. Spence, & D. Drake (Eds), *The SAGE handbook of coaching*. London: Sage Publications, pp. 486–504.

Outhwaite, A. & Bettridge, N. (2009). From the inside out: Coaching's role in transformation towards a sustainable society. *The Coaching Psychologist*, 5(2): 76–89.

Passmore, J., Brown, H., & Csigas, Z. (2017) *The state of play in European coaching & mentoring*. Henley Business School.

Passmore, J. & Fillery-Travis, A. (2011) A critical review of executive coaching research: a decade of progress and what's to come. *Coaching: An International Journal of Theory, Research and Practice*, 4(2): 70–88.

Passmore, J. & Sinclair, T. (2020) *Becoming a Coach*. Springer International Publishing.

Ridler & Co. (2013) Ridler report 2013: Trends in the use of executive coaching - in collaboration with EMCC UK. Retrieved June 5, 2022 from www.ridlerandco.com/ridler-report.

Rousseau, D. (1995) *Psychological Contracts in Organisations: Understanding the Written and Unwritten Agreements*. London: Sage Publications.

Salicru, S. (2009) *The impact of the psychological contract in executive coaching*. Paper presented at the Australian and New Zealand Academy of Management Conference, December, Melbourne, Australia.

Salman, S. (2014) Un Coach pour Battre la Mesure? La Rationalisation des Temporalités de Travail des Managers par la Discipline de Soi. *Revue d'Anthropologie des Connaissances*, 8(1): 97–122.

Scoular, A. (2011) *Business coaching*. Harlow: Pearson Education Ltd.

Shoukry, H. (2017) Coaching for social change. In T. Bachkirova, G. Spence, & D. Drake (Eds), *The SAGE handbook of coaching*. London: Sage Publications, pp. 176–194.

Shoukry, H. & Cox, E. (2018) Coaching as a social process. *Management Learning*, 49 (4): 413–428.

Smith, W. A., King, S., & Lai, Y. L. (2021) *Coaching with emotions and creating high quality connections in the workplace.* In *Positive Psychology Coaching in the Workplace.* Cham: Springer, pp. 173–198.

Tobias, L. L. (1996) Coaching executives. *Consulting Psychology Journal: Practice & Research,* 48(2): 87–95.

Turner, E. & Clutterbuck, D. (2019) *All in the small print.* A brief study of contracting issues in coaching and supervision. Presentation to the 8th international coaching supervision conference, May 11, Oxford.

Turner, E. & Hawkins, P. (2016) Multi-stakeholder contracting in executive/business coaching: An analysis of practice and recommendations for gaining maximum value. *International Journal of Evidence Based coaching and mentoring,* 14(2): 48–65.

Western, S. (2017) The key discourses of coaching. In T. Bachkirova, G. Spence, & D. Drake, (Eds) *The Sage Handbook of Coaching.* London: Sage Publications, pp. 42–61.

Whybrow, A., Turner, E., McLean, J. with Hawkins, P. (2023) *Ecological and Climate-Conscious Coaching: A Companion Guide to Evolving Coaching Practice.* Abingdon: Routledge.

Chapter 15

Ethics in transnational assignments in coaching

Philippe Rosinski and Liz Pavese

Introduction

Leading coaching associations have contributed significantly to the professionalization of coaching through codes of ethics that have increased in sophistication over the years. These ethical codes are essential for the coaching profession which is still predominantly unregulated. Ethical codes typically serve as guidelines leaving coaches to exercise their judgment to determine what they should and should not do in any given situation.

We all have opinions about what is right and wrong, and we may be quick to judge. Referring to coaching codes of ethics and exercising careful consideration, help us feel confident that it will be enough to make the right decisions.

However, we often don't go as far as exploring what philosophical ethics offers to go beyond the obvious. Moreover, we may not be aware of cultural biases that affect our judgment, nor do we go as far to use a cultural perspective as a basis of ethical decision making.

Coaches, at a minimum, need to be familiar with national cultural variations when they work on transnational assignments. However, it would be a mistake to confine cultural differences to national differences alone. This limited view of culture could inadvertently reinforce stereotypes while overlooking many other cultural factors that shape our behaviors, norms, values, and beliefs (generational, organizational, occupational, religious, etc.). Furthermore, this narrow view risks steering coaches away from a broader reflection about culture, which affects ethical judgment.

This chapter explores how different philosophical currents can enrich our conception of coaching ethics. We highlight links between philosophical ethics and cultural viewpoints, suggesting how this combination is essential for ethical coaching practice. These considerations are meant to equip coaches to act consciously whether they work on transnational assignments or not.

DOI: 10.4324/9781003277729-15

Context

Transnational coaching assignments are certainly becoming more of the norm in our ever-increasing globally and digitally connected world. Working with clients across time zones, in different languages, with various customs, norms, values, beliefs, experience, etc. introduces many exciting opportunities for coaching practitioners. It also introduces more complexity to the profession. To navigate the changing waters, coaches look to standards of professional practice. Prominent coaching associations (e.g., International Coaching Federation [ICF], European Mentoring and Coaching Council [EMCC], Association for Coaching[AC]) and university coaching programs (e.g., Henley Business School, University of Cambridge, HEC Paris, Columbia University) all outline with great similarity the codes of ethics to ensure the highest quality and integrity in coaching practice.

Codes of ethics consist in a mix of *rules*, which unambiguously spell out what can or cannot be done (e.g., "identify accurately... my ICF Credentials" (International Coaching Federation, 2022, Section III, 20), and *standards*, which state general principles that still give room to interpretation (e.g., "Commit to excellence"; International Coaching Federation, 2022, Section II, 16). While rules reduce the role of judgment and thus the noise in human decision making, standards allow us to adjust to the particulars of the situations (Kahneman, Sibony, & Sunstein, 2021, pp. 350–351, 360). With standards, the coaching codes are not as clear though in helping one to conclude a 'right' or better path. While it makes sense to grant some discretion to coaches so they can exercise ethical judgment to address complex situations (as opposed to mechanically applying a set of overly rigid rules), a difficulty is that coaches may lack the philosophical and cultural knowledge to do so most adequately. Moreover, most coaches do not see this gap as problematic and may therefore not make the intellectual effort to acquire it.

In a study conducted by Turner and Passmore (2018) of 101 participants (i.e., primarily coaching supervisors and coaches), only 9.5% of respondents mentioned cultural norms when asked: "What other factors are important for practitioners to consider within their ethical supervision/coaching practice in making good decisions?" So, while it is advantageous to have ethical codes urging to 'be sensitive to culture' (International Coaching Federation, 2022, Section III, 23; Global Code of Ethics, 2022, 2.18), there may not be enough emphasis on how to incorporate cultural sensitivity into one's practice and how to consider multiple cultural perspectives to deal with complex situations.

Despite the best intentions, codes of ethics reflect the biases of those who have created them. This presents another layered issue of ethics in the transnational coaching settings in which many coaches operate today. This is additionally problematic for coaching supervisors who inadvertently reinforce cultural norms they have been taught, even when they might be inadequate in a different cultural context. As such, it can be considered unethical to practice coaching supervision without proper intercultural training, which still appears to be the norm rather than the exception today. Vikki Brock notes that:

> "the 'coaching supervision' agenda appears to be predominantly driven by certain (some) coaching psychologists/psychotherapists. Coaching supervision first appeared in early 2000 in the UK during the same period that coaching psychology, a sub-discipline of psychology, was formed. This 'non-clinical' supervision stems from a therapeutic model."
>
> (Brock, 2015, pp. 11–12)

Coaching supervision cannot be the mere extension of supervision in psychotherapy but needs to draw from a wide range of disciplines. This is precisely what 'integrative coaching supervision' offers (Rosinski, 2016). Integrative coaching supervision builds upon 'Global Coaching' (Rosinski, 2010). It calls upon multiple perspectives ranging from the physical to the spiritual and including the cultural, which helps to consider a broader outlook when working with clients.

The following sections dive deeper into how coaching ethics can be informed by and augmented with philosophical ethics and interculturalism. We refer to the Cultural Orientations Framework (Rosinski, 2003; 2010), which is a roadmap to navigate the cultural terrain.

Distinctive ethical features

While it is beyond the scope of this chapter to explore diverse perspectives within philosophical ethics, a good place to start is the contrast between 'deontology' and 'teleology'.

Immanuel Kant is regarded as the central figure in deontological ethics (Stanford Encyclopedia of Philosophy, 2020). In this view, "no matter how morally good their consequences, some choices are morally forbidden". "Conformity with a moral norm" is what matters (Kant, 1785). Deontology is manifested when coaches adhere to a coaching association's code of ethics. It will hopefully be suitable across cultures but in practice it is hard to eliminate all cultural biases. This might make some norms inadequate in certain cultural contexts.

Deontology (from Greek δέον obligation and λόγος science, reason) includes three branches: the agent-centered (e.g., "Kant's locating the moral quality of acts in the principles or maxims on which the agent acts and not primarily in those act's effects on others"), the patient-centered (e.g., "Kant's injunction against using others as mere means to one's end"), and the contractualist (e.g., "Kant's insistence that the maxims on which one acts be capable of being willed as a universal law – willed by all rational agents) (Kant, 1785; Stanford Encyclopedia of Philosophy, 2020).

The first branch includes obligations and permissions for coaches. It constitutes the core of today's coaching ethics. The second branch is at the heart of coaching, which is about selflessly serving the coachees. The third branch implies regularly updating coaching codes of ethics considering multiple cultural perspectives in the spirit of achieving a universal synthesis. This is challenging given the diversity of cultures. Furthermore, it can only be work in progress as the world keeps changing.

Teleological theories (from Greek τέλος end, purpose, and λόγος science, reason) "first identify what is good in the state of affairs and then characterize right acts entirely in terms of that good" (Encyclopedia.com, 2022). Teleological theories vary in terms of what 'good' means, referring either to consequences (i.e., consequentialism) or to the intrinsic properties of actions (i.e., virtue ethics). For example, the former could be actions that effectively promote desirable ends such as happiness or sustainable development, while the latter could be acting with benevolence or compassion. By contrast, deontology focuses on rightness or wrongness of behaviors, regardless of the good that is produced. For example, acting with compassion (virtue ethics) does not make our action deontologically ethical if we have not first considered the morality of our choice.

The teleological/utilitarian notion of 'good' needs to be further defined and can vary widely. For Jeremy Bentham it is "the greatest happiness for the greatest number" (Bentham, 1789). Bentham insisted that "all forms of pleasure are of equal value" and was for "a fundamental human equality, with complete happiness being accessible to all, regardless of social class or ability". Bentham:

> "supported the idea of equal opportunity in education and his ideas contributed to the foundation of University College London in 1826, the first institution in England to admit students of any race, class or religion and the first to welcome women on equal terms with men"
>
> (University College London, 2022)

Two centuries ago, Bentham was already a proponent of "diversity and inclusion", a contemporary imperative coaches cannot ignore (Rosinski, 2022). Moreover, Bentham was concerned about sentient beings, not just humans: "The question is not, Can they reason? nor, Can they talk? but, Can they suffer?" (Bentham, 1789, p 144). Bentham devised a 'felicific calculus' to measure happiness. John Stuart Mill (1863) considered the quality of pleasures, not just the quantity, attributing more weight to higher, intellectual pleasures than to baser, physical ones. He was a proponent of liberty, believing that people should be free to do whatever makes them happy, even if it could harm them, but that they are not entitled to act in ways that could harm others. Even if they differed somewhat in their conception of 'good', for both Bentham and Mill the right ethical choice is the one resulting in "the greatest good for the greatest number".

Bentham and Mill's ideals are not so distant from the coaching aim of promoting joy (Rosinski, 2010) and positive psychology coaching which involves fostering happiness and flourishing (Seligman, 2002, 2011; Smith, Boniwell, & Green, 2021). However, it is difficult to imagine "doing the greatest good for the greatest number" in today's world without referring to planetary environmental, social, and economic imperatives, such as those captured in the United Nations 17 Sustainable Development Goals (United Nations, 2015). Coaches need to be mindful of cultural orientations that could lead to favoring certain goods while ignoring others, as important as they may be in other cultures and for our human society overall. From this perspective, it would be unethical for coaches to help corporations in their pursuit of profit, if their quest is unbridled, done at the expense of the environment and under undignified social conditions.

'Coaching across cultures' or 'intercultural coaching' (i.e., systematically integrating interculturalism into coaching; Rosinski, 2003) implies considering cultural variations within deontology while augmenting it with teleology. In other words, it implies adopting a more complete view of ethics. The Cultural Orientations Framework (COF) (see Table 15.1) is an integrative framework that can serve both to uncover limitations in traditional coaching ethics and to expand our cultural worldview for a more suitable and nuanced coaching ethics. The COF builds upon the findings of anthropologists, communication experts, and cross-cultural consultants, including Florence Kluckhohn and Fred Strodtbeck (1961), Edward Hall (1976), Geert Hofstede (2001), and Fons Trompenaars (1997), among others. A more detailed overview and analysis of the COF can be found in (Rosinski, 2003).

A 'cultural orientation' is an inclination to think, feel, or act in a way that is culturally determined, or at least influenced by culture. For example, Direct and Indirect are two polar-opposite cultural orientations, which make up the direct-indirect communication cultural dimension. The 'right' way of communicating depends on the cultural context. More generally, the COF points to possible variations in ethical choices, which extend beyond national cultural differences alone. For example, should we emphasize coherence (i.e., the same rule for everyone – Universalism) or flexibility (i.e., adjust to specific circumstances – Particularism), competitive stimulation (Competitive) or mutual support (Collaborative), etc.? Our responses are likely to reflect our cultural biases.

The COF provides a language to describe cultural preferences, regardless of their origins. As coaches, we need to be prepared to meet each coachee as a unique person, who is likely not going to fit the stereotype we may have of their national culture.

In some cases, the links between the COF and philosophical ethics are readily apparent. A utilitarian conception is more aligned with Collectivism than with Individualism. If we prefer individualism, the greatest sin would be to prevent self-actualization. However, if we prefer collectivism, it is worst to sacrifice the interests of the larger community for personal, selfish gain. Instead, it is desirable to promote "the greatest good for the greatest number". Even if Bentham and Mill are Western philosophers who have had considerable influence, it should not come as a surprise that their collectivistic philosophy is less present in coaching, particularly in individualist societies where coaching originated. Some coaching associations ethics have recently strived to address the imbalance (e.g.,

Table 15.1 Cultural Orientations Framework

Categories	Dimensions	Description
Sense of Power and Responsibility	Control/Harmony/Humility	**Control:** People have a determinant power and responsibility to forge the life they want. **Harmony:** Strive for balance and harmony with nature. **Humility:** Accept inevitable natural limitations.
Time Management Approaches	Scarce/Plentiful	**Scarce:** Time is a scarce resource. Manage time carefully! **Plentiful:** Time is abundant. Relax!
	Monochronic/Polychronic	**Monochronic:** Concentrate on one activity and/or relationship at a time. **Polychronic:** Concentrate simultaneously on multiple tasks and/or people.
	Past/Present/Future	**Past:** Learn from the past. The present is essentially a continuation or a repetition of past occurrences. **Present:** Focus on the "here and now" and short-term benefits. **Future:** Have a bias towards long-term benefits. Promote a far-reaching vision.
Definitions of Identity and Purpose	Being/Doing	**Being:** Stress living itself and the development of talents and relationships. **Doing:** Focus on accomplishments and visible achievements.
	Individualistic/Collectivistic	**Individualistic:** Emphasize individual attributes and projects. **Collectivistic:** Emphasize affiliation with a group.
Organizational Arrangements	Hierarchy/Equality	**Hierarchy:** Society and organizations must be socially stratified to function properly. **Equality:** People are equals who often happen to play different roles.
	Universalist/Particularist	**Universalist:** All cases should be treated in the same universal manner. Adopt common processes for consistency and economies of scale. **Particularist:** Emphasize particular circumstances. Favor decentralization and tailored solutions.
	Stability Change	**Stability:** Value a static and orderly environment. Encourage efficiency through systematic and disciplined work. Minimize change and ambiguity, perceived as disruptive. **Change:** Value a dynamic and flexible environment. Promote effectiveness through adaptability and innovation. Avoid routine, perceived as boring.
	Competitive/Collaborative	**Competitive:** Promote success and progress through competitive stimulation. **Collaborative:** Promote success and progress through mutual support, sharing of best practices and solidarity.

Categories	Dimensions	Description
Notions of Territory and Boundaries	Protective/Sharing	**Protective:** Protect oneself by keeping personal life and feelings private (mental boundaries), and by minimizing intrusions in one's physical space (physical boundaries). **Sharing:** Build closer relationships by sharing one's psychological and physical domains.
Communication Patterns	High-Context/Low-Context	**High-Context:** Rely on implicit communication. Appreciate the meaning of gestures, postures, voice and context. **Low-Context:** Rely on explicit communication. Favor clear and detailed instructions.
	Direct/Indirect	**Direct:** In a conflict or with a tough message to deliver, get your point across clearly at the risk of offending or hurting. **Indirect:** In a conflict or with a tough message to deliver, favor maintaining a cordial relationship at the risk of misunderstanding.
	Affective/Neutral	**Affective:** Display emotions and warmth when communicating. Establishing and maintaining personal and social connections is key. **Neutral:** Stress conciseness, precision and detachment when communicating.
	Formal/Informal	**Formal:** Observe strict protocols and rituals. **Informal:** Favor familiarity and spontaneity.
Modes of Thinking	Deductive/Inductive	**Deductive:** Emphasize concepts, theories and general principles. Then, through logical reasoning, derive practical applications and solutions. **Inductive:** Start with experiences, concrete situations and cases. Then, using intuition, formulate general models and theories.
	Analytical/Systemic	**Analytical:** Separate a whole into its constituent elements. Dissect a problem into smaller chunks. **Systemic:** Assemble the parts into a cohesive whole. Explore connections between elements and focus on the whole system.

Am aware of my and my clients' impact on society. I adhere to the philosophy of "doing good" versus "avoiding bad." (International Coaching Federation, 2022, p. 28); Acting responsibly (Global Code of Ethics, 2022, 3.3–3.8), but without describing more specifically what this would entail (for example by adhering to the UN 17 sustainable development goals).

Philosophical ethics are obviously not limited to Western philosophers (which is what we have described here). Lessons can be learned from philosophers and religious traditions across the world. For example, Confucianism stresses that individuals cannot reach their full potential outside of the group. Confucian ethics involves the sacrifice of individual aspirations to serve the community. Moreover, virtue does not imply exercising a personal choice. It is rather a matter of spontaneously adopting the right attitude thanks to one's education, which Westerners might equate to dressage (University of Geneva, 2022, 8.10 Ethique et Confucianisme). When working on a transnational assignment with China, we cannot ignore these variations in ethics (e.g., here a Collectivistic rather than Individualistic ethics). In fact, making the effort to learn about diverse world traditions is not only a good way to prepare for transnational coaching assignments. It is mostly a way to continuously enrich our worldview, to gain in wisdom and humility.

Combining philosophical ethics and intercultural coaching

The unique combination of philosophical ethics and intercultural coaching can best be explained by considering some concrete examples that may arise in coaching practice. We can expect transnational variations to address the following ethical dilemmas more adequately. However, once we become aware of our current cultural beliefs, we can learn to revisit these whenever they prove to be limiting. We can do so by learning from other cultures (national as well as other forms of cultures).

Case Study I

Which companies am I prepared to work for as a coach and under what conditions? More specifically, should I accept to work for an 'Oil and Gas' corporation?

This question was raised during a recent webinar. To preserve confidentiality, we use pseudonyms of those who shared their views. While one coach expressed a concern for serving a corporation that would not be committed to a sustainability agenda, another coach, 'George', argued that there is no right or wrong answer in this situation. In his view, the choice was a matter of personal values and consistency. Since he drives a combustion engine car and uses electricity at home that is still sourced from gas-powered stations, George is a consumer of Oil and Gas. It seems therefore ethical for him to work with a company in that sector. However, as a non-smoker, George would refuse to work for 'Big Tobacco'.

George's view seems to reveal different cultural orientations. One is Control, the notion of being in charge. Though, we may wonder about the level of Control in this situation. For example, despite the fact that bikes are more common around the world than cars (Poushter, 2015), the US specifically is more car dependent for a variety of reasons, including infrastructure being built around the automotive wave, fewer vehicle taxes, government funding for interstate and roadway systems, etc. (Buehler, 2014). While car ownership is still high, public transit and usage of bikes as a commuting option have higher rates in countries such as the Netherlands, Germany, and Finland and even when cycling is high, the use of bikes is generally still higher for non-work purposes (Goel, et al., 2022). When we compare how transportation services have advanced in other countries like in Western Europe, we potentially see differences in what is valued, practical and available. In the US, when there are few trains and other forms of clean energy public transportation and a system built around cars, what can you really do if you need to travel? Granted, electric vehicles are becoming more common; however, George may not necessarily be able to afford buying a new car, let alone an electric one that is still likely to be more expensive. Further, it is challenging to opt-out completely, as a significant portion of power in Westernized countries still comes from gas and carbon fuels. Being mindful of the other polarity, the Humility orientation, could have allowed George to appreciate that driving a car may not really be his personal choice.

His position also suggests an Individualistic orientation; that is, what is right for me does not have to be right for you, it is a matter of personal values. This view sounds tolerant and reasonable. Yet, it overlooks the fact that, as humans, we are also on the same boat (Collectivistic) facing the great dangers of pollution, destruction of ecosystems and climate change, which are exacerbated by unbridled oil consumption. This cultural dichotomy also relates to Analytical (i.e., addressing the issue in isolation) versus Systemic (i.e., examining the broader consequences), and Present (i.e., immediate impact) versus Future (i.e., the impact on future generations).

How might coaching supervision address this? The supervision conversation could be centered around respecting a coaching code of ethics (viewed as a universal code of conduct). George could be left with the sense that his choice is ethical in that he has abided by the various principles in the code (e.g., confidentiality, no conflict of interest). Yet, deeper questions informed by the COF and by philosophical ethics could allow George to make a more informed and more authentic choice.

- COF Being – Future orientations/Aristotle's virtue ethics (Aristotle, 335–322 BC): *What kind of person do I want to be? How can I increase my humanity in this situation?*

  - George could realize that increasing his humanity in the situation might not necessarily involve turning down the coaching engagement with Oil and Gas but could imply at least probing the leaders' intentions and vision. If their view is a cynical pursuit of profit with mere lip service to environmental protection, George could challenge their approach and accept the offer only if they reveal a genuine desire to change.

- COF Being – Humility orientations / Aristotle's virtue ethics: *What would be the prudent choice here?*

  o For Aristotle, prudence is the first cardinal virtue. It is the virtue that allows us to find the 'golden mean' (i.e., happy medium) between recklessness (a vice of excess, lack of temperance) and cowardice (a vice of defect, lack of courage). *What are George's financial needs in the situation? Is George in a situation where he needs a continuous stream of high income to support an affluent lifestyle? And in this case, how could George settle for a more modest way of life that would allow him to turn down unsavory projects?* This would involve some letting go and acceptance of limitations (COF Humility). *Or is George merely trying to make ends meet? And if so, how could George still embrace justice (i.e., attending to the rights of others (Stanford Encyclopedia of Philosophy, 2022), the fourth cardinal virtue?*

- COF Universalist orientation / Kant's categorical imperative: *How can I go beyond my inclination that could be harmful to others, and instead act in a way that could be universalized and makes us worthy of being called humans?*

  o *In other words, would it be okay if all coaches decided to help Oil and Gas companies without restriction?* If George's answer is "no", Kant's categorical imperative would lead him to decline the opportunity. Importantly, although Kant's name is associated with 'deontology', the choice here is not determined heteronomously (i.e., by something external such as a code of conduct) but is rather dictated freely by George's conscience.

- COF Collectivistic – Equality – Systemic orientations/ Bentham and Mill's utilitarianism: *How could I foster the greatest good for the greatest number?*

  o This question might lead George to potentially sacrifice a lucrative business opportunity by considering fellow humans around the world potentially affected by his decision as equal stakeholders, and by even considering the impact on other living species.

George could further attempt to reconcile various philosophical ethics and alternative cultural perspectives to make an optimal choice while helping potential clients navigate these complex dilemmas as well. Ranjaj Gulati argues for pursuing 'deep purpose', a form of practical idealism: to be purpose-driven, genuinely committed to solve social and environmental problems, while recognizing the necessity to generate wealth as well to build a lasting company. These leaders are ready to sacrifice one of these agendas in the short term when they must, in order to achieve long-term sustainable success, which requires purpose and profit (Gulati, 2022). In sum, these leaders have found a way to combine Kant's categorical imperative, Mill's pragmatic quest for great positive impact and Aristotle's prudence. They are able to leverage Control and Humility, acting with determination while accepting limitations, and Being and Doing, being exemplary in their human qualities while striving to achieve optimal meaningful results.

Even when we carefully consider our various options while facing ethical dilemmas, we still don't know what we don't know. Although we cannot hope to ever be fully informed, we can nevertheless become better aware of the unconscious psychological and cultural biases that may affect our judgments, so we don't fall prey to these biases. We can go beyond mere adherence to coaching codes of conduct and ad hoc reflection about coaching complicated situations, by making the intellectual effort to learn from various philosophical ethics, thereby giving ethics a new horizon in our coaching practices and in our lives.

Case Study 2

Let us consider another situation: is it appropriate to be friends with our coachees?

Julia Milner and colleagues (2013) examined several critical incidents in cross-cultural coaching. For example, some coaches have the impression that coachees from China and India want to be their friends, which they consider as a sign of 'transference'. In other words, in their views, coachees are not supposed to be friends!

A starting point is to clarify the nature of the relationship between the coach and the coachee. One can argue that, unlike what is typically the case among friends, there is an asymmetry between being a coach and being a coachee. Yet, if we consider culture and philosophical ethics, we could argue that it might be unethical to turn down the coachee's request right off the bat!

The idea that we should maintain hermetic boundaries between our personal and professional lives, that we should refuse a more personal connection with our coachee, exemplifies a Protective cultural orientation. This is not a universal panacea. In Sharing cultures, the boundaries are more permeable. From a personal example, one of us (Philippe) was working with a client in Morocco and was invited to his home. He also asked very personal questions. I obliged and enjoyed building a closer relationship. From my client's standpoint, how could we work together, if we don't get to know each other? Establishing intimacy allowed for trust-building, which is one of the cornerstones of a high-quality working alliance between coach and coachee, and with a strong working alliance, coaching engagements are likely to be more effective (Graßmann, Schölmerich, & Schermuly, 2020).

We could ask our coachees: what does friendship mean to you? What does it entail? This could lead to a rich conversation, which we could best approach in an open and learning mode. When examining from the philosophical ethical standpoint, here are some interpretations.

In Aristotle's virtue ethics (eudemonics), 'true friendship' is when two people are seeking to help each other become better people. It is not obvious to apply this notion to the coaching relationship. Some would say that the role of the coach is not to make the coachee a better person, but to help them achieve their objectives, whatever they are.

However, this neutral stance is neither possible (we all have cultural biases, whether we realize it or not), nor desirable (neutrality would be unethical considering both Kant's categorical imperative and Mill's utilitarianism). Coaching hopefully involves some form of human development, which typically goes together with a higher level of consciousness (Barrett, 2014). Virtue ethics has the merit of inspiring a noble coaching pursuit: yes, coaching can have the ambition of helping coachees become better people. What about us coaches? Aristotle emphasized the notion of model. As coaches, we want to be exemplary, to serve as models. Indeed, how can we help coachees to grow if we are not prepared to become better people ourselves? Aristotle had already highlighted how we are shaped and influenced by the people we interact with. We can model humility by being genuinely eager to learn from our coachees, to be challenged in our cultural assumptions, in a spirit of openness and curiosity. By letting our coachees allow us to become better people, we can become more powerful coaches in helping them become better people as well. In sum, far from being an obstacle, true friendship could be a coaching enabler.

Ethics of the gift (University of Geneva, 2022, 7. Les Ethiques du Don), with philosophers like Henri Bergson (1932), Emmanuel Levinas (2006) and Jacques Derrida (1999), go one step further. Aristotle's notion of friendship involves a reciprocity between people fulfilling each other's needs. Ethics of the gift point to something more generous and disinterested. Even if coaching involves a financial transaction, genuine care and love are what drive the coach to establish a genuine bond with the coachee and to facilitate their growth. When this happens, we don't have any problem if the coachee sees the coach as their friend! Of course, the coach will need to remain vigilant to ensure the generosity is not abused: self-care is essential including to be able to sustainably serve others. This quality of relationship is particularly critical in Being cultures and it promotes authentic engagement, allowing paradoxically to achieve greater results as is common in Doing cultures.

More generally, the COF can serve both to uncover limitations in traditional coaching ethics and to expand our cultural worldview for a more complete and fitting coaching ethics. Truly universal norms require expanding our cultural worldview, incorporating lessons from alternative cultural perspectives, and making the most of differences (promoting unity in diversity, mutual enrichment).

The COF dimensions offer some examples, which will be briefly discussed below (see Table 15.2). Generally, considering one orientation and overlooking

Table 15.2 Identifying ethical risks and solutions with the COF (select dimensions)

Ethical risks when	*Ethical risks when*	*Ethical solutions when*
Control without Humility Inadvertently pushing coachees beyond their limitations	**Humility without Control** Not encouraging to take responsibility	**Control with Humility** Inviting to take charge while recognizing what is beyond our control, to promote sustainable success (versus success at all costs)
Past without Future Failing to consider the impact of decisions and actions on future generations	**Future without Past** Failing to learn from history and past mistakes	**Past with Future** Learning from the past to promote sustainable results
Individualistic without Collectivistic Turning societal challenges into a matter of personal values. Emphasizing individual freedom while failing to consider our collective destiny	**Collectivistic without Individualistic** Preventing self-actualization. Minimizing individual freedom and accountability by overly emphasizing affiliation with the group	**Individualistic with Collectivistic** Promoting individual and collective accountability. Acknowledging personal motives and striving to use them to serve the collective
Hierarchy without Equality Being overly directive, compromising the coachees' autonomy and freedom	**Equality without Hierarchy** Failing to provide the necessary guidance	**Hierarchy with Equality** Empowering coachees notably through listening and questioning (letting them access their own resources) while offering guidance when it can be beneficial
Universalist without Particularist Lacking in flexibility	**Particularist without Universalist** Lacking in coherence	**Universalist and Particularist** Being coherent and flexible (e.g., enhancing rules by integrating lessons from implementations in various contexts)
Competitive without Collaborative Lacking in solidarity	**Collaborative without Competitive** Allowing undeserving free riders to be rewarded as well	**Competitive with Collaborative** Promoting healthy competitive simulation together with mutual support. Favoring entrepreneurial dynamism as well as social justice.
Protective without Sharing Setting boundaries that prevent establishing genuine human relationships with our coachees	**Sharing without Protective** Failing to set the appropriate boundaries in coaching, leading to potential confusion or/and conflicts of interests	**Protective with Sharing** Setting adequate boundaries that still allow to establish deep human bonds with our coachees

Ethical risks when	Ethical risks when	Ethical solutions when
Direct without Indirect communication	**Indirect without Direct communication**	**Direct with Indirect Communication**
Offending and hurting	Failing to raise important issues, not confronting what should be confronted (e.g., injustice)	Being clear in the content, sensitive in the way the content is given. Being assertive ('OK-OK'), rather than aggressive or condescending ('OK-not OK') or overly submissive ('not OK-OK')
Analytical without Systemic thinking	**Systemic without Analytical thinking**	**Analytical with Systemic thinking**
Failing to consider to big picture, the larger societal implications	Failing to work out the practical details	Considering the whole system, its elements, and the various links

© Philippe Rosinski. Reproduced with permission

its polar opposite will produce avoidable ethical risks, particularly when working in transnational and other different cultural contexts. On the other hand, enlarging our cultural worldview and synthesizing opposites, whenever possible, is a safe way to find optimal ethical solutions.

Whenever possible, coaches could consider leveraging COF orientations/polarities to turn these differences into an opportunity to expand our understanding of coaching ethics. Although intercultural coaching has been increasingly considered in coaching development programs over the past years, it is still not systematically integrated into coaches' and even coaching supervisors' practices. This gap is an obstacle that will need to be surmounted in the future.

This approach involves an "and" form of thinking. It is more paradoxical and complex than binary "or" thinking. However, this represents our best chance to make sound ethical choices, informed by multiple perspectives that we strive to combine, whether we work transnationally or not.

Conclusion

Ethics, particularly in transnational assignments, requires going beyond applying coaching codes of ethics in their stated form, even when careful consideration is exercised. These ethical codes, while an important foundation for the ongoing professionalism and legitimization of coaching practice, are insufficient. Sound ethical practice in the global context in which we operate, implies acquiring a deep understanding of alternative cultural perspectives and an ability to systematically integrate culture into coaching regardless of how far our coaching borders stretch. Across or within countries, there are a multitude of cultural options that if over-looked can mislead our practice and judgments. It is imperative that coaches master 'intercultural coaching'. By combining philosophical ethics with intercultural coaching, specifically using the COF, coaching ethics is taken to a new level.

Discussion points

1. Referring to the COF, what are your current cultural orientations? How do they shape and potentially limit your concept of coaching ethics?
2. How can you broaden your concept of coaching ethics by incorporating lessons from alternative cultural perspectives?
3. How can you deepen your reflection by considering various philosophical ethics (Western: deontology, virtue ethics, consequentialism/utilitarianism, ethics of the gift; non-Western: Confucianism, Hinduism, Buddhism, etc.)?
4. How can you combine intercultural coaching and philosophical ethics to address coaching dilemmas, and more generally to inspire your coaching practice?

Recommended reading

Rosinski, P. (2003) *Coaching Across Cultures*. London and Yarmouth, ME: Nicholas Brealey Publishing.

References

Aristotle. (335–322 BC) *Nicomachean Ethics*. Kitchener, ON: Batoche Books, 1999.

Barrett, R. (2014) *Evolutionary Coaching*. Lulu Publishing Services.

Bentham, J. (1789) *An Introduction to the Principles of Morals and Legislation*. Jonathan Bennett, 2017.

Bergson, H. (1932) *Les Deux Sources de la morale et de la religion*. Paris: Editions Flammarion, 2012.

Brock, V. (2015) Gold Rush Coaching Supervision. *e-Organizations & People, 22(1)*: 9–17.

Buehler, R. (2014) 9 Reasons the U.S. Ended Up So Much More Car-Dependent Than Europe. Retrieved on April 1 from www.bloomberg.com/news/articles/2014-02-04/9-reasons-the-u-s-ended-up-so-much-more-car-dependent-than-europe.

Derrida, J. (1999) Le siècle et le pardon. *Le Monde des Débats*, December. Retrieved from www.ufmg.br/derrida/wp-content/uploads/downloads/2010/05/Derrida-Jacques-Le-Siecle-Et-Le-Pardon.pdf.

Encyclopedia.com. (2022) Teleological Ethics. Retrieved on January 4 from www.encyclopedia.com/humanities/encyclopedias-almanacs-transcripts-and-maps/teleological-ethics.

Global Code of Ethics. (2022) Retrieved on January 31 from www.globalcodeofethics. org.

Goel, R. et al. (2022) Cycling behaviour in 17 countries across 6 continents: levels of cycling, who cycles, for what purpose, and how far? *Transport Reviews*, 42(1): 58–81. doi:10.1080/01441647.2021.1915898.

Graßmann, C., Schölmerich, F., & Schermuly, C. C. (2020) The relationship between the working alliance and client outcomes in coaching: A meta-analysis. *Human Relations*, 73: 35–58. doi:10.1177/0018726718819725.

Gulati, R. (2022) The Messy but Essential Pursuit of Purpose. *Harvard Business Review*, March–April: 44–52.

Hall, E. (1976). *Beyond Culture*. Anchor Books.

Harris, T. (1969) *I'm OK – You're OK*. Harper & Row.

Hofstede, G. (2001) *Culture's Consequences*, 2nd Edition. Sage Publications.

International Coaching Federation. (2022) ICF Code of Ethics. Retrieved on January 31 from https://coachingfederation.org/ethics/code-of-ethics.

Kahneman, D., Sibony, O., & Sunstein, C. (2021) *Noise: A Flaw in Human Judgment*. London: William Collins.

Kant, I. (1785) *Groundwork of the Metaphysics of Morals, H.J. Paton (trans.)*. New York: Harper & Row, 1964.

Kluckhohn, F. & Strodtbeck, F. (1961) *Variations in Value Orientations*. Peterson.

Levinas, E. (2006) *Totalité et infini*. Paris: Le Livre de Poche.

Mill, J. S. (1863) *Utilitarianism*. Kitchener, ON: Batoche Books, 2001.

Milner, J., Ostmeier, E., & Franke, R. (2013) Critical incidents in cross-cultural coaching: The view from German coaches. *International Journal of Evidence Based Coaching and Mentoring*, 11(2): 19–32.

Poushter, J. (2015) Car, bike, or motorcycle? Depends on where you live. Pew Research Center. Retrieved on March 6, 2021, from www.pewresearch.org/fact-tank/2015/04/16/car-bike-or-motorcycle-depends-on-where-you-live.

Rosinski, P. (2003) *Coaching Across Cultures*. London and Yarmouth, ME: Nicholas Brealey Publishing.

Rosinski, P. (2010). *Global Coaching*. London and Boston, MA: Nicholas Brealey Publishing.

Rosinski, P. (2016) Integrative Coaching Supervision. *Global Coaching Perspectives – Association for Coaching Magazine*, 10: 34–39. Retrieved from https://philrosinski.com/wp-content/uploads/2019/10/Integrative-Coaching-Supervision-in-Global-Coaching-Perspectives-July-2016-Issue-10.pdf.

Rosinski, P. (2022) Diversity and Inclusion 3.0. *Coaching Perspectives – Association for Coaching Magazine*, 32: 22–26. Retrieved from https://philrosinski.com/wp-content/uploads/2022/02/Diversity-and-Inclusion-3.0-AC- Perspectives-January-2022-SP_compressed.pdf.

Seligman, M. (2002) *Authentic Happiness*. London: Nicholas Brealey Publishing.

Seligman, M. (2011) *Flourish*. New York: Free Press.

Smith, W.-A., Boniwell, I., & Green, S. (2021) *Positive Psychology Coaching in the Workplace*. Berlin: Springer.

Stanford Encyclopedia of Philosophy. (2020) Deontological Ethics. Retrieved on October 30, 2021, from https://plato.stanford.edu/entries/ethics-deontological.

Stanford Encyclopedia of Philosophy. (2022) Justice as a Virtue. Retrieved on April 9 from https://plato.stanford.edu/entries/justice-virtue.

Trompenaars, F. (1997). *Riding the Waves of Cultures*, 2nd Edition. Nicholas Brealey Publishing.

Turner, E. & Passmore, J. (2018) Ethical dilemmas and tricky decisions: A global perspective of coaching supervisors' practices in coach ethical decision-making. *International Journal of Evidence Based Coaching and Mentoring*, 16(1): 126–142.

United Nations. (2015) 17 Sustainable Development Goals (SDGs). Retrieved on September 1 from https://sdgs.un.org/goals.

University College London. (2022) Jeremy Bentham. Retrieved on January 6 from https://blogs.ucl.ac.uk/transcribe-bentham/jeremy-bentham.

University of Geneva. (2022) *Le Bien, le Juste, l'Utile. Introduction aux éthiques philosophiques.*

Pushing the boundaries of conventional ethical thinking in coaching

Chapter 16

Positive ethical practice for coaching excellence and wellbeing

Annalise Roache, Aaron Jarden, Tayyab Rashid and Tim Lomas

Introduction

Before you start, please pause and ponder the following musing. When you hear the word 'ethics', what comes to mind? Do you see ethics as friend or foe? Opportunity or obligation? Companion to your practice or a dictator of it? Does the term elicit a sense of hope and excitement or a mood of reticence and, well frankly, boredom? It is posited that most coaches view ethics as boring, obligatory, and risk-aversive rule management; first and foremost, about preventing harm (non-maleficence; commonly defined as 'do no harm'). Here the authors take a transformative view in that here ethics is situated as additionally positive and a place to actively do good, rather than just avoiding harm. Whilst acting ethically is often about preventing harm (non-maleficence), it has radical potential to actively focus on beneficence (i.e., doing good to others). It is, therefore at the very heart of the cultivation of the good life and the central role coaching can play in that regard. As such, the aim is to take the relative balance between non-maleficence (preventing harm) and beneficence (doing good) – which is usually heavily weighted towards the former – and to reorient the scales in an equal fashion to appreciate more evenly the appropriateness of both. The authors assert that the goal of ethical codes and standards ought not to be merely about avoiding harm or preventing injury. They ought to be equally about cultivating conditions that help individuals in various professional domains develop emotional and cognitive capacities that promote wellbeing and the good life (however construed).

The way coaching practitioners conceptualise, approach, and enact ethics in coaching practice needs to change. The current focus in applied ethics has primarily been negative - on risk and harm reduction first and foremost. It is well understood that many coaches see ethical practice as a list of rules, things not to do, harm to be avoided, and risks to be managed; when we talk to coaches about ethical practice, this is what they say and think of. This trend can also be observed when examining various ethics guidelines (e.g., American Psychological Association, 2017; International Coaching Federation, 2020; Global Code of

DOI: 10.4324/9781003277729-16

Ethics, 2021) or coaching textbooks that cover ethical practice (e.g., Vandaveer & Frisch, 2022), though it is noted that many coaching textbooks do not cover ethics at all. In the sources that do, there is a predominant focus on the negative, on non-maleficence. This is akin to the negativity bias, with a supposition that negative interactions, feedback and impressions deserve more attention in coaching than positive dynamics (Baumeister, Bratslavsky, Finkenauer, & Vohs, 2001). In addition, many coaches do not explicitly link ethical practice with wellbeing for themselves or their clients *per se*. Instead, they think that acting ethically prevents illbeing. For example, one encounters the view that coaching in an unethical way (e.g., failure of the coach to meet a standard) may harm a client, and that acting ethically prevents such results.

Therefore, in this chapter, it is argued that the focus of ethical practice in coaching needs to change to actively promoting the positive and doing good (beneficence) and not predominantly concentrating on rule-following, behaviours, harm reduction and risk mediation. At the very least, an equal focus on enabling the good as we would on stopping the bad for our coaching clients is encouraged. These are, of course, complementary and mutually supporting. Non-maleficence and beneficence are not binary opposites; one is not at the cost of the other. It is just that the balance of emphasis and efforts has been skewed heavily towards the negative (non-maleficence). As such, it is argued that ethical practice should equally consider both and that, in particular, beneficent ethical practice should be strengthened. In addition, as a means of enabling equal consideration between non-maleficence and beneficence, the authors advocate moving beyond rule-following based ethics to consider virtue and character-based ethics as a pathway towards this goal of increased beneficence in practice.

This chapter first describes ethics more broadly and ethical practice specifically, and then ethical practice in a coaching context. This provides a high-level overview of the field of ethics and the context from which ethical practice has developed. Next, a focus on what is special and unique about Positive Ethics and about our formulation of the notion of Positive Ethical Practice (PEP, which builds upon the pioneering foundation of Positive Ethics developed by Handelsman, Knapp, and Gottlieb in 2002). The chapter then articulates various positive ethical principles and brings these to life through hypothetical reflection points and a vignette which we hope readers will find illuminating and inspiring. The chapter concludes with the suggestion and hope that the field can take these still nascent and evolving ideas forward to help the field of coaching reach ever greater heights in helping people lead their best lives.

Ethics

Ethics, and ethical theory, have a long history in the social and applied sciences, particularly with historical origins in philosophy (LaFollette & Persson, 2013). A common way to demarcate some approaches to ethics (or branches to ethics, see Figure 16.1) is to talk about ethics of character (what sort of people should we be?) and ethics of conduct (what types of actions should we perform?). Under the ethics of character branch usually sits 'virtue ethics', commonly linked to Aristotle (Fowers, 2005) (see figure 16.1).

In this approach, a virtue is a means between extremes of actions. Under the other branch sits the ethics of conduct, with both 'consequentialist ethics' and 'deontological ethics'. Consequentialist ethics (the right action is the one that produces the most good) is usually associated with a form of ethics dubbed 'utilitarianism,' and with the philosophers Jeremy Bentham and later John Stuart Mill (Mill, 1861/1987). However, another form of ethics that focuses on consequences is the lesser-known 'ethical egoism', where ethical decision-making is guided by self-interest (Pojman, 2010).

On the other branch of ethics of conduct (rather than of character) are 'deontological ethics', usually associated with Immanuel Kant. Here rules are used to distinguish right from wrong, and it is one's duty to follow them; for example, thou shall not lie or steal (Kant, 1785). Deontological ethics are the bedrock of most modern approaches to applied ethics, which are also largely rule-based. For example, in the practice of psychology, the emphasis has been more concerned with behaviour than character, i.e., what a practitioner can and cannot do (e.g., a practitioner should not breach clients' trust unless legally obliged to do so or should not lie to a client). As such, codes of ethics have outlined standards of behaviour, not standards of character. The codes are about being responsible for one's actions first and foremost, but also, arguably to a lesser extent, one's inactions (which can be seen as actions nonetheless).

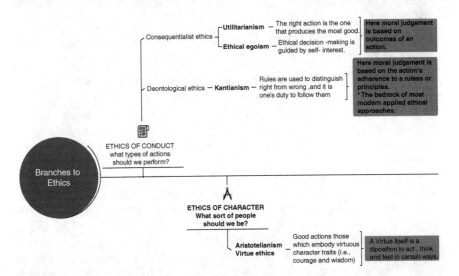

Figure 16.1 Branches to Ethics

Across these different approaches to ethics sits a conception of the good life – either for an individual (e.g., ethical egoism) or for the collective whole (e.g., the utilitarian notion of the greatest good for the greatest number). One acts ethically (behaviour) or is ethical (character) in order to enable the good life – however, construed (i.e., for the self, for others, or a combination of both). So, ethics primarily and traditionally, at least from a philosophical perspective, has been about doing good and enabling the good life.

The critical question is how to do good and enable the good life in the context of professional practice (Jarden et al., 2021). That is, how can coaching practitioners cultivate ethical behaviour (doing good), and what are the ways to hone ethical behaviour to achieve excellence (enabling the most satisfying life)? There is a paucity of theoretical frameworks and practical skills in psychology to cultivate such ethical excellence. However, the cultivation of virtues has long been a significant theme in philosophy. The authors posit that this philosophical premise can serve as a foundation here. From this premise, a new discipline under the title of PEP is proposed. As is explained below, this builds upon an already existing platform of positive ethics – formulated by Handelsman, Knapp and Gottlieb (2002) – hence the qualifier 'Practice'. First though, from the onset, a point of clarification in that by Positive Ethics, it is not implied that the rest of the ethics is negative, irrelevant or less than desirable. Rather, by PEP, the emphasises is that the application of ethics should not only be a risk-aversive paradigm or avoidance of harm, as has been the case in the bulk of practice within various disciplines of psychology, including coaching. Instead, risk aversion should be complemented by resource activation/cultivation of strengths to foster behavioural excellence.

Ethics in coaching

Coaching is, by its very nature, a solution and hope-filled mission. In coaching, practitioners aim to move their clients toward the good life, supporting them to attain a life that they aspire to and deserve. Coaching psychology and coaching have been defined in various ways in literature, for example Atad, Smith & Green (2021) state that "'*Coaching Psychology' is simply the science of human emotion, cognition and behaviour (i.e. psychology) that underpins coaching practice*" (pp. 43–44) while coaching has been defined by professional bodies such as the International Coach Federation's (ICF) as "partnering with clients in a thought-provoking and creative process that inspires them to maximise their personal and professional potential" (International Coach Federation, 2022). Unlike applied psychologists (i.e., clinical or counselling psychologists), coaches do not set out to coach with thoughts on minimising harm or reducing distress; they aim to elevate and transform. Every move a coach makes within and around a coaching relationship is grounded in ethical decision-making and behaviour.

Coaches must...

- *Have **awareness of limitations**...*
- ***Adherence** to codes and guidelines...*
- ***Resolve** conflict (of interest)...*
- ***Hold responsibility**...*
- *Do **not**...*
- *Strictly **avoid**...*
- *Are **required**...*
- ***Abide**...*
- ***Obliged**...*

Figure 16.2 Examples taken from coaching bodies ethical codes. (E.g. ICF, 2022 & GCoE, 2021)

Nevertheless, ethics is often treated as a cursory obligation in coach training, presented as 'foundational', yet typically administered as a 'tick-box' procedure. Coaching guidelines usually talk of ethics as a list of things to be aware of and behaviours to avoid or adhere to, with connotations of consequences for failure to obey (see Figure 16.2 above). The authors submit that there is a need to move away from seeing ethics as a measure of 'what not to do' (behaviours) and moving towards a means of 'what to do' and 'how to be'. Ethical practice lies both within the coach and the client, and the space between them. Thus additionally it is argued that repositioning ethics as a 'way of being', in addition to behavioural rule-following, also helps further focus on repositioning ethics as enabling the positive (beneficence) rather than avoiding the negative (non-maleficence). We now turn to outline previous work on Positive Ethics to date.

Background on positive ethics

In 2002 Handelsman, Knapp and Gottlieb published a chapter titled 'Positive ethics', which they subsequently revised, updated and strengthened in 2009 – then titled 'Positive ethics: Themes and variations'. In this later chapter, they set the ground for 'positive ethics', arguing that:

1. applied professions (such as psychology) have approached ethics from a rule-based perspective;
2. ethical codes have developed from focusing on problematic behaviours;

3. ethics training is concerned with helping professionals protect themselves and avoid complaints; and
4. there is always a conflict between professional rules and personal principles and values.

The core of their argument is that ethical practice and ethics codes were developed to protect people from harm and abuse. Indeed, the very first ethical code by the American Psychological Association (APA) in 1953 was developed in response to "critical incidents or problematic situations faced" by practitioners (Handelsman, Knapp, & Gottlieb, 2009, p. 2). It was not until 1992 that the APA ethics code incorporated aspirational principles, such as promoting welfare. However, Handelsman, Knapp and Gottlieb go on to assert that "the influence of these aspirational principles has been small. The profession - whose code was developed by focusing on problematic behaviours and minimum standards – still turns in the direction of emphasising the enforceable standards" and that this "remedial emphasis is unfortunate" (p. 2). They argued that "the goal of positive ethics was to shift the primary emphasis from avoiding discipline to a more balanced and integrative approach that included encouraging psychologists to aspire to their highest ethical potential" (p. 3).

Handelsman, Knapp and Gottlieb's (2009) solution was to argue for a "mid-course correction" (p. 2) in that in order for practitioners to aspire to their highest ethical ideas, they need to become more:

1. *self-aware* – which includes understanding personal values and motives and developing virtues that assist with personal and professional moral motivations;
2. *professionally aware* – integrating personal and professional moralities and understanding the moral traditions that underlie ethical reasoning; and
3. *globally aware* – including multicultural sensitivity, political sensitivity, and civic virtue.

We suggest that Handelsman, Knapp and Gottlieb (2002, 2009) have laid excellent foundations for Positive Ethical Practice upon which this discussion is built.

Positive Ethical Practice

The authors progress the work of Handelsman et al. (2002, 2009) in various directions, essentially extending, supercharging and specifically adapting Positive Ethics to create 'Positive Ethical Practice' (PEP), thus, building upon it in a way that complements their initial vision. Specifically, it is suggested that PEP should have five additional aims beyond those already identified by Handelsman et al., which are described below.

1. Balance non-maleficence and beneficence

The authors encourage greater focus on the need for practitioners to do good, to promote welfare and wellbeing, rather than (or primarily) prevent harm and reduce illbeing. It is argued that, within an ethical framework, non-maleficence has been taking precedence and priority in practitioners' hearts, minds and efforts and that beneficence should have a more predominance leading to a more equal role than it has had in the past.

PEP reflection

A client presents with feelings of self-doubt and notions of feeling like an imposter at work and home.

What specific skills could a coaching practitioner use in collaboration with a client to balance non-maleficence and beneficence, for example, to both reduce the negative impact of feelings of self-doubt and to also infuse hope and optimism, breaking it down into small but manageable actions and supporting the client to bring about a new more balanced perspective?

2. Be prescriptive

It is encouraged that coaching practitioners, organisations, codes and guidelines be more prescriptive, compared to descriptive, about behaviour in particular. While it is not advocated to be specifically prescriptive (e.g., the coach should develop this particular ethical value and apply this particular strength in this particular context), it is proposed that the coaching practitioner ought to do good when they can, in the particular context they find themselves.

PEP reflection

A client reports feeling confined by social and cultural norms and socio-economic constraints, often implicitly and sometimes explicitly, which they believe expect them to pursue a professional degree. Though capable of accomplishing this, their heart is in pursuing a career in curating animated stories of young people who defy social norms to break new grounds.

How can the coaching practitioner guide their client to move beyond cultural norms and such to cultivate curiosity, creativity and courage and explore acceptable ways (i.e. culturally), yet also allow them to follow their creative path?

3. Be accountable for inactions

It is encouraged that coaching practitioners take the mindset that they are as responsible and accountable for their inactions as for their actions. While codes of practice and standard committees have primarily focused on practitioner's actions, from a moral perspective, if 'ought impact can' (Kant, 1785), it is possible for a coaching practitioner to act, and yet, they choose not to. We suggest they are equally accountable for their inactions.

PEP reflection

While delivering a training session, a participant expresses explicitly racist and transphobic remarks towards a specific group, associating a religious group with terrorism, and expressing dismay for allocating the health budget to support gender-affirming treatment.

How can a coaching practitioner, without taking any ideological position, recognise that this may be a situation in which inaction might be harmful to other participants?

That is, from being a bystander, one needs to be an ally and an upstander. Remaining passive, retreating or not confronting an assumption that everyone is entitled to their opinion would not be in line with Positive Ethics. This situation is an opening to engage with the person showing bias. It is also an occasion to validate and support individuals who might be harmed from such views. Additionally, it is an opening for the coaching practitioner to educate organisers and authorities to educate presenters and participants about respectful behaviour. Brainstorm a few phrases or exercises that could be called on to support the facilitator to step up and be accountable.

4. Take a systems lens to ethical practice

It is encouraged for coaches/practitioners to take a broader perspective in that ethical excellence goes beyond the individual – to groups of people, organisations, and beyond. Indeed, the wellbeing sciences have realised the importance of the inter-connectedness of systems in relation to wellbeing (Kern et al., 2020). Cultures and groups can have impacts on ethical decision-making and outcomes, whereas the majority of focus in the helping professions and coaching is on the individual and their behaviour.

PEP reflection:

A coach is bought into a mid-size organisation to design and deliver a leader-as-coach program. The organisation is focused on improving individual performance and staff retention.

How can the coaching practitioner weave PEP ideals into the programme, such as the systems or systems level influences of ethical decisions and behaviours, which support the development of an ethical culture of transparency and honesty, with open communication and a desire to act for good?

A culture where individual actions are appreciated for their ripple effect on the performance and wellbeing of the team and the broader organisation. Brainstorm potential learning objectives and activities that can be integrated into the programme to promote a culture of PEP.

5. Expand beyond behaviours to character

It is encouraged for coaching practitioners to realise that the wellbeing sciences have importantly focused on people's emotions, cognitions, virtuousness, as well as their behaviours (Diener, 1984; Diener et al., 2019). Although behaviours are the target of regulation in ethical codes, we suggest moving beyond a rule-following behaviourally based ethics to consider virtue and character-based ethics as a pathway towards a goal of increased beneficence in practice.

PEP reflection

Beyond being merely rule-bound, in PEP, it is envisaged that exemplary practice ensures that only services within the coaches *scope of education, training and experience* are delivered and that the coach receives regular and relevant supervision. Such practice is more likely to increase the coaching practitioners' self-confidence and self-respect and enhance their commitment to do good while remaining mindful of the potential side effects of positive interventions. This commitment and mindfulness will likely result in making the right decisions at the right time. The authors are also conscious that the skills associated with exemplary practice are harnessed and honed. It is unlikely that one will not make mistakes; this is simply not realistic. Learning from mistakes affords opportunities for growth and transformation and is likely to make one's practice satisfying, caring, competent and effective.

Take a moment to brainstorm which virtues underpin your professional practice as related to the above reflection point.

For example, consider what behaviours are evident when working and living at your best. *When you are at your best, how does this impact your clients' wellbeing?*

How do you actively hone and amplify these virtues?

How could these reflections on your virtues enable more consistent ethical practice were following all the rules, all of the time, may not be feasible?

One of the aims of this work is to increase the prominence of positive behaviours and actions which can foster PEP. Much like how the risk-aversive paradigm of ethics has reinforced behaviours that should be avoided, there is a need to reinforce or increase the salience of behaviours and actions which do good and enable the good life.

The application of Positive Ethical Practice

So, what does PEP look like in action? How does a coach bring more benefi-cence to their work? How can a coach look at and integrate current ethical guidelines and codes with PEP in mind? In this section, we firstly provide a vignette to demonstrate PEP. Following this, suggested reflections and activities on how coaches can bring PEP to life can be found in the Table 16.1 below.

Vignette: Integrating non-maleficence and beneficence

In ethics education, case studies and illustrations are valuable tools for inte-grated deep learning (Pettifor, Estay, & Paquet, 2002). Presented below is a hypothetical account of a client experiencing skepticism about a strengths-based group coaching approach, and the actions of the coaching practitioner who questions the appropriateness of their actions as a result.

> Janet is enrolled at University. She is the first of her family to attend higher education, she has worked hard to stabilise her life and qualify. She comes from a history of emotional abuse and multiple unstable relationships and has engaged in therapy to work through these significant life challenges. Janet has since been offered the opportunity to participate in a university run psycho-educational strength-based coaching group focused on supporting educational attainment and strengthening relationships for students. Janet was initially sceptical of any approach as she thought an intervention that could mitigate her deficits was more suited for her concerns. Despite her uncertainty, Janet joined the group. During initial sessions, Janet remained quiet for the most part. In the early part of the intervention, while the coach/facilitator invited participants to share a story of overcoming challenges – big or small, Janet remained quiet. When the group members had shared their stories and experiences, everyone looked at Janet without asking her to share, nonverbally stating that it was ok to pass if she did not feel like sharing.
> Janet said, "*my life only includes emotional abuse by my family, alco-holism, and negativity spewed at me by one of my parents day in, day out. I have not overcome anything in my life; things, horrible things have taken over my life.*" As she was unburdened, the coach/practitioner felt the weight of Janet's distress, concerned they had committed a professional blunder by asking participants to do this exercise. After an uncomfortable and long pause, another group member gently asked Janet, '*why are you*

here in this group every week?". Upon hearing this, a stream of tears flowed from her eyes. She said quietly, *"This group is showing me the possibilities that come from greater self-awareness, learning from your stories, feeling less alone, also understanding that maybe I too have strengths that I have used to get here today. This is my only hope…something I will never let go of, it provides a roadmap for my future."* Everyone became silent, and the coach could feel that everyone was deeply moved. This silver lining of hope prompted the coach/facilitator to start a discussion about emotions, in particular, positive emotions and the power of recalling past challenges and hurdles overcome to build self-efficacy and a sense of mastery and potential.

Commentary: The coaching practitioner-facilitator's goal at this point was non-maleficence —doing or avoiding any potential harm. The group setting was ripe with preceding narratives of overcoming challenges. That is, group members share their stories of overcoming challenges with potentially widened perspectives, that included emotional experiences both negative and positive. The stream of tears from Janet illustrates Janet's pain but also her hope-filled widened cognitive perspective. The coach's response was to move from non-maleficence to active beneficence by tapping into the positive (i.e., accepting the negative emotions and also noting the positive emotions) as one of a number of pathways available to reducing illbeing. However, it was also with a view to beneficence with the longer-term view that emotional experiences are normal but that positive emotions are an important part of the good life for Janet and the other group members. Deliberate and systematic cultivation of positive emotions to enhance hope will likely, as evidence shows, build psychological resources which could help buffer against future occurrence of distress (Pleeging et al., 2021). Here PEP is not only about current reactions; it is also about future prevention.

This vignette illustrates some relevant points related to PEP. First, initially, the group coach practitioner-facilitator, out of fear of doing or avoiding harm, assumed that forcing a client to share a story of resilience might have done harm and added to the client's distress. However, the collective efficacy of the group members (i.e., listening to the stories of resilience of others) appeared to have worked as a catalyst to move Janet from a negative to a more hopeful mindset. Second, as noted above, from a systematic perspective, various services were not just mediating Janet's weaknesses but also bolstering her strengths and abilities and reinforcing her resources. To change the course of potential harm, one needs a village and the village's resources that support growth.

Take a moment to reflect

What is your reaction to this vignette, what memories, emotions and thoughts does it evoke for you as a coaching practitioner?
How would you as the coach work with and manage those memories, emotions and thoughts for the benefit of yourself, your coaching and also your client?

Reflecting now on PEP specifically;

What PEP aims and behaviours do you feel the coach, and other participants, displayed?
What could the coach have done differently? What might the implications be in applying those differences?
What are your takeaway leanings and how will you apply these in your coaching practice?

Actions toward PEP: Principles and Values from Positive Psychology Practice

Table 16.1 provides a range of reflections and activities to further embed the foundations and aims of PEP for the coach/practitioner and their clients. Each activity has been linked to guiding principles, values and, in some cases, specific positive psychology constructs and interventions.

The above table has provided some practical activities and reflections for embedding PEP into practice and professional development. Coaches are invited to revisit these activities regularly during professional development and supervision sessions.

Table 16.1 Reflections and activities to further embed the foundations and aims of PEP

Guiding ethical principle	*Positive ethical reflections and activities*
Beneficence: *Values:* Promoting the client's and practitioner's wellbeing. Recognising limits of one's capacity and expertise, Protecting safety of clients	Reflect on specific skills you need as a coaching practitioner to inculcate hope and optimism among someone who needs it but cannot find it in themselves.
	Explore which facet of empathy works for your client.
	There are two facets of empathy. Cognitive empathy entails understanding another person's perspective, whereas emotional empathy includes sharing other person's feelings.
	Effective coaching practice depends on the coaches emotional stability, openness, social intelligence and conscientiousness. Reflect on which of these attributes you do well and which ones need refinement.
	Reflect on the meaningful aspect of your work with client.
Non-maleficence: *Values:* Alleviating distress	How do you take a genuine interest in understanding clients' unique and idiosyncratic situations? How can you hone your skills to tolerate uncertainty and ambivalence when client situations are unclear or evolving?
Non-maleficence: *Values:* Recognising limits of one's capacity and expertise, Protecting safety of clients	Pay attention to detail to understand a client's situation.
	Practice in accordance with your education, training, and experience. Brainstorm the boundaries of your practice.
	What presenting cases would you or would you not take on and why?

Guiding ethical principle	Positive ethical reflections and activities
Non-maleficence: *Values:* Appreciating the diversity of human experience and cultures.	Reflect if you are (or are told so repeatedly) biased about a client or are ineffective with a specific group of clients. Think of specific actions (or inactions) that might be getting in your way of working more effectively. Brainstorm creative ways to help clients who have had less than optimal experiences with other practitioners.
Responsible Caring *Values:* Recognising limits of one's capacity and expertise.	What specific skills would you like to learn and how would learning these new skills extend your area of expertise? How do you keep up with the emerging research findings and mastering ways to build one's professional competence and efficacy?
Justice: Respect for people's rights and dignity. *Values:* Striving for a fair application of PP interventions; Appreciating Diversity	When do you feel the courage to speak up, even in difficult situations? What values are at play for you when this happens? Consider speaking up and standing up against a social issue about which there is widespread consensus of its negative impact but has yet to gather critical mass to attract public attention. This could be taking a stance against social issues such as specific forms of racism, stigma against mental health, or cuts to public services.
Autonomy: Respect for people's rights and dignity. *Values*: Protecting Safety *PP Construct*: Positive Emotions, Motivation	Calibrate your enthusiasm to match or respond to your clients' needs. For example, if your client is persistently in a low mood, reflect on how your motivation and energy can complement the dampened mood of your client.
Autonomy Values: Integrity of Practitioner-client relationship; Fostering a sense of self *PP Construct*: Prudence	Routinely ask your clients if your perspective is helpful. Seek their input on how you might broaden it.
Trustworthiness: Persistence, honouring agreements and promises *Values:* Enhancing Personal Effectiveness Integrity of Practitioner-client relationship	Select a role model in your areas of expertise who exemplifies persistence. Connect with the individual, if possible, to seek advice on how to emulate their success. Strive to be a trustworthy coaching practitioner who accurately presents themselves about their education, competence, experience and scope of practice. Elicit feedback from your clients and colleagues to regularly self-assess your competence and motivation.

Guiding ethical principle	Positive ethical reflections and activities
Justice: Respect for people's rights and dignity	As a fair-minded coaching practitioner, think of specific behaviours which may increase fairness and equity through the framework of IDEA:
Values: Striving for a Fair & adequate provision of PP services Appreciating the diversity of human experience and cultures.	*Inclusion*: Ensure your practice is inclusive in every all-possible respect. *Diversity*: Demonstrate that you genuinely respect and appreciate cultural, gender identity, ability and all other dimensions of diversity and are not afraid to learn where needed. *Equity*: Recognise that everyone does not start from the same place and personalised adjustments are needed to address imbalances. *Access*: Apply positive psychology and wellbeing-based practice to potentially increase access to people who may not be able to afford expensive interventions or may not seek them due to stigma.
Respect for people's rights and dignity *Values:* Enhancing Quality of Interpersonal relationships	Reflect on groups/teams you are a member of, work colleagues, professional association, parenting, family, friends, and alumni. Which team brings the best out of you? Why is this? Consider joining a team/group to pursue a cause that addresses a current issue and needs collective effort. Working together towards a social/environmental cause can provide a sense of belonging and meaning. Which group project provides you with a sense of belonging and meaning?
Autonomy *Values:* Enhancing the quality of professional knowledge and its application	Think of something you would like to change in your coaching practice that requires sustained effort, time and discipline. This could be acquiring or refining expertise, expanding your practice with a specific clientele, acquiring a leadership role within a professional organisation or writing your practice insights for a journal or writing a book. Consult with colleagues who are accomplished in your targeted or desired area. Devise a plan with specific goals. Use your self-regulation to acquire excellence in your practice. Suppose a specific personal or professional issue overwhelms you, including, working with a specific client or colleague. Reflect and mindfully explore what exactly irritates you? Think of adaptive ways you can deal with this issue. To manage your emotions as you deal with your situation, seek external support, if available.

Conclusion

This chapter aims to encourage coaches to focus on aspiring to their highest ethical ideals. It has challenged coaches to embrace and move beyond stopping the remediation of harm and to shift the focus to the opportunities to help and enable wellbeing and the good life for their clients and themselves. It has been suggested that a commitment to ethics need not merely be an onerous responsibility of abiding by rules and prescriptions but can be a positive pathway for the coach to become the best version of themselves and help their clients thrive. The authors have sought to elucidate these ideas by articulating various positive ethical principles and bringing these principles to life through hypothetical examples, which it is hoped readers will find illuminating and inspiring. Moreover, with PEP being still a relatively new and evolving idea, the hope is that coaches can take these potentials forward and develop them in their own ways. In so doing, coaches can continue to take the field of Positive Ethics to new heights in empowering people to live their best life.

Discussion points

1. How do you view your current practice with regard to the balance of non-maleficent and beneficent practice?
2. On reflection, in which ways do you recall not holding yourself to account for inaction? What will you put in place to support yourself to take action when the situation arises again?
3. Which aspect or aspect of PEP stands out for you?
4. What is your next step in bringing PEP to life for your practice?

A note about the authors

Annalise, Aaron, Tayyab and Tim form a small but mighty, independent working group of academics and practitioners who have developed the first ethical guidelines for the field of Positive Psychology. The project kicked off in 2016 with the first guideline published, in English, in 2019, followed quickly by translations in nine additional languages. 2023 will see the publication of the third iteration of The Ethical Guidelines for Positive Psychology Practice.

Recommended reading

Handelsman, M. M., Knapp, S., & Gottlieb, M. C. (2009). Positive ethics: Themes and variations. In R. Synder and S. Lopez (Eds), *Oxford handbook of positive psychology.* Oxford: Oxford University Press, pp. 105–113.

References

American Psychological Association. (2017). Ethical principles of psychologists and code of conduct. Retrieved July 16, 2022, from www.apa.org/ethics/code.

Atad, O., Smith, W. A., & Green, S. (2021). Coaching as the Missing Ingredient in the Application and Training of Positive Psychological Science. In Smith, W. A., Boniwell, I., & Green, S. (Eds), *Positive Psychology Coaching in the Workplace*. Cham: Springer. doi:10.1007/978-3-030-79952-6_3.

Baumeister, R. F., Bratslavsky, E., Finkenauer, C., & Vohs, K. D. (2001). Bad is Stronger than Good. *Review of General Psychology*, 5(4): 323–370. doi:10.1037/1089-2680.5.4.323.

Fowers, B. J. (2005). *Virtue and psychology: Pursuing excellence in ordinary practices*. Washington, DC: American Psychological Association.

Diener, E. (1984). Subjective Well-being. *Psychological Bulletin*, 95(3): 542–575.

Diener, E., Thapa, S., & Tay, L. (2019). Positive Emotions at Work. *Annual Review of Organizational Psychology and Organizational Behavior*, 7.

Global Code of Ethics. (2021). About The Global Code of Ethics For Coaches, Mentors, and Supervisors. www.globalcodeofethics.org.

Handelsman, M. M., Knapp, S., & Gottlieb, M. C. (2002). Positive ethics. In R. Synder and S. Lopez (Eds), *Oxford handbook of positive psychology*. Oxford: Oxford University Press, pp. 731–744.

Handelsman, M. M., Knapp, S., & Gottlieb, M. C. (2009). Positive ethics: Themes and variations. In R. Synder and S. Lopez (Eds). *Oxford handbook of positive psychology*. Oxford: Oxford University Press, pp. 105–113.

International Coach Federation. (2020). Code of Ethics. https://coachingfederation. org/ethics/code-of-ethics.

International Coach Federation. (2022). ICF Core Competencies. https://coachingfederation.org/ credentials-and-standards/core-competencies

Jarden, A., Rashid, T., Roache, A., & Lomas, T. (2021). Ethical guidelines for positive psychology practice (English: Version 2). *International Journal of Wellbeing*, 11(3).

Kant, I. (1785). *Groundwork of the metaphysic of morals*, H. J. Paton (trans.). New York: Harper & Row, 1964.

Kern, M. L., Williams, P., Spong, C., Colla, R., Sharma, K., Downie, A., Taylor, J. A., Sharp, S., Siokou, C., & Oades, L. G. (2020) Systems informed positive psychology. *Journal of Positive Psychology*, 15: 705–715. doi:10.1080/17439760.2019.1639799.

LaFollette, H. & Persson, I. (Eds). (2013) *The Blackwell guide to ethical theory*, 2nd Edition. John Wiley & Sons.

Mill, J. S. (1861/1987) Utilitarianism. In A. Ryan (Ed.), *John Stuart Mill and Jeremy Bentham: Utilitarianism and other essays*. New York: Penguin, pp. 272–338.

Pettifor, J. L., Estay, I., & Paquet, S. (2002) Preferred strategies for learning ethics in the practice of a discipline. *Canadian Psychology/Psychologie canadienne*, 43(4): 260.

Pleeging, E., Burger, M. & van Exel, J. (2021) The Relations between Hope and Subjective Well-Being: a Literature Overview and Empirical Analysis. *Applied Research Quality Life*, 16: 1019–1041. doi:10.1007/s11482-019-09802-4.

Pojman, L. P. (2010). *Ethical theory: Classical and contemporary readings* (6th Revised Edition). Belmont, CA: Cengage Learning.

Vandaveer, V., & Frisch, M. (2022) *Coaching psychology: Catalysing excellence in organisational leadership*. American Psychological Association.

Chapter 17

Ethics in education and the development of coaches

Bob Garvey and Andrea Giraldez-Hayes

Towards Ethical Mindedness: the implications for coach education

Within the world of coaching there are claims that ethical frameworks reassure potential clients or sponsors. These claims include assurances that ethical codes create quality control, standards, accountability and protection. These are bold claims, so, given the complex arguments surrounding ethical behaviour, is it possible to deliver on these promises?

This chapter is based on the premise that ethics, rather than being fixed like a set of rules, as offered by the professional associations, are more a process of critical thinking.

Two key questions to ask are:

1. *What are the ethical considerations educators need to be aware of when they are providing the education?*
2. *How is this critically reflective thinking developed in coaching through their coach education?*

Therefore, this chapter reflects on the importance of ethical development in coaching and considers how coach developers might contemplate and facilitate this.

To do this we first explore MacIntyre's virtue ethics concept and then consider how this may show up in the educator's ethical practice and in the professional education of coaches, if at all. We consider who might be doing this in the marketplace of providers. These may include private sector providers as well as universities.

We intend that this chapter considers not only the *why* of ethical education but also the *how*.

DOI: 10.4324/9781003277729-17

Context

As a starting point, we consider the terminology employed in the coaching world in relation to coach education. Our first observation is the term 'training' is used extensively. This is not our chosen word. The reasons for this are rooted in our understanding of human learning and development. To be harsh, training is something we do to animals!

Bernstein (1971) argued learning associated with training or more formal approaches tend to be 'teacher' driven where the content of what is taught is pre-specified within boundaries, outcome driven through the use of 'objective' criteria and assessment is a strong determinant of success. This approach does not allow for much initiative or creativity from the learner.

In contrast, Bernstein (1971) also argued that 'education' tends to offer respect and a degree of control to the 'learner' and this in turn encourages critical thinking, questioning, challenge, high initiative and creativity.

We argue that the 'training' approach to coach education is more about compliance with external 'standards' than to do the with all-round development of a coach. This matters because coaching is a complex and sophisticated activity, where a coach must work in the moment with their coachee and that an educational approach to coach development offers the best chance of preparing someone for their future coaching work (see, Barnett, 1994; Garvey, 2016).

This, we believe is an ethical issue in that the professional coaching bodies position themselves the arbiters of 'gold standard' or 'the go to' organisations for coaching accreditation but is this really the case, particularly given that no-one is sure as to what these statements are compared to?

An additional issue to consider in the context of the coaching field is the role ethics plays in coach education. To help consider this, we explored the websites of coach training providers through google searches. Unsurprisingly, irrespective of the search terms we used, there were literally millions of 'hits'. The general interpretations of a sample of these revealed some interesting results.

There are some providers who claim that their programmes are accredited. On further investigation, for some the accreditation was their own brand name! These were often well-known coaches. This, of course, says nothing about the content of their programmes nor the quality of facilitation but, in our view, these are dubious claims.

We also noted that many of these programmes and others that have some form of external accreditation (in the UK this may be a professional body, the Institute of Leadership and Management (ILM) or the Chartered Management Initiative and in some case, it may be a university) few even mention the word 'ethics' in their programmes. If they do mention ethics, it is often in the more advanced programmes, suggesting that ethics is somehow 'advanced'.

In one case, the ILM (2022) the advanced programmes contain references to ethics many times throughout their documentation. Although, there is no indication on how this is handled or delivered.

Among university providers of coach education, we found a similar pattern. Some university providers have accreditations from professional bodies in addition to their own qualification. We found few references to 'ethics' in their programmes, in fact only 40% of those we investigated mention 'ethics' and, similarly to other providers, we gain no insight into how ethics are presented or explored with the programmes. We speculate that universities seem to have become more 'training' oriented, perhaps owing to their adherence to professional body competency frameworks, in relation to coach education.

So what?

Given our findings above, using training providers websites, we argue that the seemingly lack of ethical education within coaching is a mistake and that it suggests that ethical considerations are not in the front of trainers' or educators' minds. In recent times, ethics have become a major issue in society. Arguably, this started with the banking crisis of 2008 and the behavioural issues that that debacle highlighted. We move forward in time and there are the ethical issues of climate change, the 'Me Too' movement, 'Black Lives Matter' and the issues faced by the LGBT community, the challenges of migration and refugees. Coaching has become involved in these matters, which all require ethical thought and consideration, and we argue the coaching field needs to up its game in relation to ethics and it starts with coach education.

MacIntyre's Virtue Ethics

There are different positions found in philosophy on ethics. Garvey and Stokes (2021) present three possible approaches. One position is that actions in themselves are actually neutral, but their consequences may or may not be good or bad in terms of the number of people affected or the manner in which they may be affected. This is known as the teleological approach. A second approach is the 'dutiful' approach to ethics. Here actions are viewed as intrinsically good or bad. The third approach is the 'pluralist' approach. Here, ethics are a case of balancing maximum good against minimum harm.

MacIntyre (1984) takes a different view. MacIntyre's position is based on Aristotelian moral philosophy. Aristotle (2004) was concerned with 'good action' aimed at improving people's lives. Aristotle argued that, in order to live well, people need to understand how virtues such as, for example, friendship, pleasure, honour and wealth fit together within the system in which they live. He argued that 'practical wisdom' or 'phronesis', as he called it, was the product of emotional and social awareness rather than a set of general rules. Aristotle's (2004) framework for 'practical wisdom' was based on three elements.

The first element is 'techne'. This is the kind of knowledge that is associated with technical skills and abilities or practical *'know how'*. The second is 'episteme'. This is knowledge of underlying theories, knowledge of the world or knowledge *'that'*. Phronesis is the practical wisdom or judgement which relates to dealing ethically within any given context and it is the result of a combination of 'techne' and 'episteme'. Phronesis is about awareness, noticing or attentiveness. Clearly this has relevance within the context of coach education. Garvey (2016) argues that techne and to some extent, episteme dominate coach training programmes and that phronesis is largely absent. This implies that our arguments made above about the paucity of ethics in coach training is almost absent by design!

Building on Aristotle (2004), MacIntyre (1984) argues that ethical behaviour is related to the character of the person. Therefore, it is the development of a virtuous character in the person that is the first step to appropriate ethical behaviour. In effect, a coach who is ethically aware, is one who has techne', 'episteme' and has developed 'phronesis'.

Corrie and Lane (2015) argue that there are six main elements of ethical awareness as follows:

1. *Ethical sensitivity* – self-awareness and an awareness of the consequences and impacts of behaviour.
2. *Ethical discernment* – is the ability to reflect with emotional awareness, solve problems and make ethically based decisions.
3. *Ethical implementation* – is an awareness of what supports one or blocks one from implementing ethical decisions.
4. *Ethical peace* – is being able to live with a decision by drawing on one's support networks and being able to learn from the process of ethical choice and let go of the decision and knowing one's limits.
5. *Ethical conversation* – is about being able to defend a position by going 'public' with it and showing that the decision is linked to key ethical principles.
6. *Ethical growth and development of character* – the MacIntyre 'qualities of the person' that are developed through learning. This has a progressive and developmental aspect to it as one develops and extends ethical understanding and alertness over time.

All of these aspects are learnable and the elements themselves give clues as to how this might be accomplished. Jarvis (1992, p. 7) argues that all learning and the resultant knowledge has "significant moral connotations."

Educators' awareness of ethical considerations

Ethical conflicts and dilemmas are intrinsic to coaching. Coaches and coach educators must make judgements concerning choices or the situations that arise during the coaching sessions and the education process and, in some cases, face safeguarding issues.

Questions for the educator

How would I handle a relative being a participant on the course that I deliver?
How do I safeguard participants in coaching skills practice?
How might I deal with a participant being upset?
How might you work with issues between participants?

The first question requires a high degree of ethical consideration. The central issue being 'disclosure' to the rest of the group. Any assessment of knowledge or skill needs to be done by someone other than the related educator. It would be appropriate to consider using two educators to work with this group so that skills practice sessions would not be observed by the relative in order to maintain confidentiality. The second question relies on careful contracting with the group and the offer of support outside of the classroom environment if required. The third question is something that happens in coaching situations. Contracting is part of this, and it becomes an opportunity to demonstrate empathy and situation awareness as well as sensitivity. Finally, sometimes tensions arise among group members. Again, contracting with a group is important and, if necessary, these ground rules may be revisited, reviewed or recontracted.

For all these questions, much depends on how the educator(s) deliver the course. One helpful approach is 'the coaching and mentoring way' (Garvey & Stokes, 2022, p. xviii). This, they argue, is a philosophical position, based on core humanistic values that include: "mutual respect and valuing differences of viewpoint, acknowledgement of our influences, listening and sharing". They go on to add that in delivering education programmes for coaches, a 'training approach' or instructional approach, or a content-based approach is inappropriate. As presented above, this leads to a 'teacher led' approach (Berstein, 1971) and inevitably creates a power differential between the learner and the 'teacher'. This is important, not only for coach educators but for coaches themselves. This is because Habermas, (1974) argued that it is not possible to have free and open conversation if there is a power differential between two people. This may be, in the case of education, the learner perceiving power because the teacher is also the assessor of their work. Similarly, a coachee may give power to the coach. Habermas's (1974) remedy for this was the 'ideal speech situation'. This takes the form of a list of idealised core conditions. It could be argued that contracting in coaching could be a way of helping to create this 'ideal speech situation' and contracting in a classroom setting offers the same function. To extend this idea, the approach taken by the educator is also important in creating appropriate and safe conditions for learning. Garvey and Stokes (2022) advocate an educational model based on

Knowles' (1980) andragogy (learner centred) rather than pedagogy (teacher centred) to coach education. Knowles' (1980) six elements of andragogy or adult learning are:

1. Adults need to know why they are learning something
2. Adults learn experientially
3. Adults need to be involved in the planning and evaluation of their learning
4. Adults are interested in learning things that are relevant to them
5. Adults need relevant problems to work on rather than content delivered
6. Adults are self-motivated

This approach offers an almost built-in safeguarding and ethical environment in which to learn and shifts responsibility in a learning environment away from being 'trainer-centric' towards something that resembles a coaching encounter. Additionally, the preference for prespecified learning outcomes in training and educational programmes creates further power related issues. Whilst these may help the trainer or educational institution to judge their success in teaching if these are met. However, this is a technical mindset that assumes that learning is a 'straight-line process' of getting someone from A to B (indeed this was the original use of coaching in the 19th century, see Gray et al., 2016). A bit like moving along a conveyor belt or up a staircase (see Self et al., 2019). This, we may think, is appropriate, mainly because we are so used to this way of thinking. Many things can be learned in this way, for example, driving a car or baking a cake. However, Habermas (1974) tells us that this approach can only engineer the pre-specified. It does not tell us anything about the other, more complex processes of learning, for example, critical, or ethical thinking nor does it cover anything to do with the relational aspects of learning of the different kinds of learning outcomes that may be possible or even honour emergence in learning. In contrast, Knowles' (1980) may help to reduce the control and represent something more akin to coaching.

Given the lack of ethics in the content of coach training programmes outlined above, we are curious about what might happen if a coaching student presents an ethical issue? We speculate that there may be two possible responses. One, the educator may offer advice to answer the student's questions. Two, they may refer them to one or more ethic codes, hoping that what is included there will help them find the answer. However, as suggested above, ethical awareness goes beyond the 'know how' theories and ethical codes. An essential component of ethical awareness is 'being', that is, who we are as coaching educators and how we 'consistently' develop a virtuous character, therefore, a third approach, based on 'the coaching and mentoring way' (Garvey & Stokes, 2022) could be to explore the presenting issue using the ethical framework raised above (virtue ethics, Corrie & Lane, 20015) through discussion in a group and thus offering a critical view of ethics. This approach may contribute to what Pope and Vasquez (2011) argued that ethical awareness is a "continuous, active process that involves constant questioning and personal responsibility" (p. xi). Ethical awareness is, therefore, more than being familiar with ethical codes. Although this knowledge is crucial, it cannot replace the reflective, active, and creative perspectives essential to being an ethical coaching educator.

Ethical codes can guide and inform but have limitations. They present a set of rules that cannot directly be applied to different situations, even if the scenarios seem similar, and might fall short of finding answers to the complexity of ethical dilemmas that can arise in the coaching profession. They can be a useful starting point but often not enough to resolve some dilemmas. Furthermore, coaches' and educators' personal values and beliefs may conflict with some of the statements included in the ethics codes. Consequently, they need to be challenged and questioned in the light of every specific situation. Thus, as Iordanou, Hawley and Iordanou suggest (2017), to become genuinely ethical coaches and educators, we need to engage in a critical self-dialogue, challenge our assumptions and beliefs and understand our personal and professional values. As coaching educators, we need to develop ethical awareness of what we teach and what we are. We should consider our integrity, that is, our moral rules, values, and beliefs and an understanding of how to engage with and, if appropriate, challenge ethical guidelines.

Developing a virtuous character is the first step to appropriate ethical behaviour (McIntyre, 1984). So, what are your moral rules, values and beliefs as a persona and an educator? We suggest that you create a three columns table and write down a list of your personal moral rules, your deepest values and your beliefs considering what is morally right or wrong for you (see table 17.1). Once you have created that list, we suggest starting a second one, including your professional moral rules, values and beliefs as a coaching educator (see Table 17.2).

Table 17.1 Values, Beliefs, Rights and Wrongs

Personal	Personal moral rules	Deep values and beliefs	What is right and what is wrong?
1.			
2.			
3.			

Table 17.2 Moral Rules, Deep Values and Beliefs, Rights and Wrongs

Professional	Personal Moral Rules	Deep Values and Beliefs	What is Right and What is Wrong?
1.			
2.			
3.			

Once you have completed the task, you can compare the lists, reflecting on the following questions.

How do your moral rules, values and beliefs influence who you are as a coaching educator?
Do some of your values and beliefs conflict with specific principles of the ethics codes?
If so, how do you handle this?

Asking yourself these questions is essential. After all, your moral rules, values, and beliefs will determine your ethical decisions, both as coaches and as educators. Coaches and coaching educators need to actively engage in reflective practice, and simple exercises like this one can help raise their self-awareness and plant the seeds for individual reflection or discussions in one-to-one or group supervision.

Coaching educators' ethical awareness could also be considered from a different perspective; their responsibility is to design and deliver coaching programmes. Starting in the early 1990s, the number of coaching schools, training providers and programmes delivered by universities increased dramatically. In parallel, professional associations such as the International Coach Federation (2019), the European Mentoring and Coaching (2022) or the Association for Coaching (2021) led the way in establishing competencies, standards of practice, credentialing, professional coaching training accreditations, and ethical guidelines for the coaching profession. More recently (in November 2021), the British Psychological Society approved the first Division of Coaching Psychology, setting their own standards of knowledge, conduct and practice for academic programmes (British Psychological Society, 2022). However, coaching is a non-regulated profession, and there is no centralised agency or regulatory board to control it. Hence the responsibility of coaching educators is to adhere to the guidance of one or more professional bodies and to clearly define what is and what is not coaching, as well as what should be the requirements to become a coach. Noticeably little attention has been paid to the teaching of coaching, and, with a few notable exceptions, the literature is rare. That includes the approach to ethics in coaching education programmes.

Coaching education providers, including universities, have the essential task of educating future coaching professionals, both in their theoretical-applied know-how and ethical behaviour. However, different debates exist about whether it is possible to teach ethics (Sheppard & Reynolds, 2018). There seems to be consensus in the idea that it can be taught, though how to teach ethics is not straightforward. As Perrenoud (1998) suggests, the current reflection on what is teachable and what can be transmitted should contemplate two connected aspects: the didactic transposition and the construction of competencies in professional training. In the Aristotelian sense, 'techne' and 'episteme' can be taught, whereas' 'phronesis' is more about critical thought and modelling. What we need to consider in the education of professional coaches is not only a specialised 'know-how' (techne and episteme) but also a critical and reflective, autonomous and responsible 'must-be' (phronesis). From this perspective, ethics can probably be taught using specific procedures, but they must also be modelled, and the educators' ethics are irreplaceable.

Ethics and critical thinking in the professional education of coaches

An overview of many coaching training programmes shows that ethics and critical thinking are not part of their main contents. There is, somehow, the belief that the coach will deal with ethical issues and critical thinking once they complete their training and start their professional life. When ethics is mentioned, it is suggested that coaching students should 'know' about ethics, which in many cases translates to becoming familiar with ethical codes. That seems to be common practice, as suggested in the Association for Coaching Training Organisations (ACTO, 2020, p. 4, item 31), a professional organisation committed to promote excellence in coaching education, code of ethics, "Teach coaching and coaching ethics in a manner that provides information for students to be aware of and how to address ethical challenges".

We argue that the process of learning coaching should go beyond techniques and information, and critical thinking and ethics principles and practice should be considered from the outset, in the programmes design and delivery. In this sense, the development of the virtuous person is considered as a central characteristic of coach education. Although coaching programmes include some uncontested knowledge (e.g., facts and principles that can be proven), most contents belong to what can be defined as contested or open to question knowledge, that is theories, perspectives or ideas that can be questioned or challenged. Brunner (1998, p. 516) argues that coaching is "a domain devoid of any fixed deontology". Therefore, a critical approach is crucial. Although ethical considerations may have areas of universal overlap, ethical practices and the possible solutions to an ethical dilemma are hardly universal. Hence the need for critical thinking when working with ethics. Critical thinking is essential to make the right decisions or ethical choices in specific situations. As we already mentioned in this chapter, there are no rules regarding the application of ethical principles to different issues. What might be ethical in one case, may be considered unethical in a different context. Consequently, it is not about adding an isolated ethics unit to a coaching module or course, but about consistently helping students to engage in critical thinking to raise ethical awareness. That allows coaching educators to integrate ethics into many different aspects of their programmes.

Examples of approaches to critical thinking which can encourage ethical awareness and behaviours are recognising and challenging assumptions, making connections, or considering a variety of voices and perspectives on a single subject. As suggested by Iordanou, Hawley and Iordanou (2017), educators should offer students "the opportunity to become actively involved in the exploration of ethical decisions in their learning and their coaching practice" (p. 162) by contemplating on which aspects of coaching they place the emphasis in teaching - practical, theoretical, empirical and the rationale behind this; critically reflecting on who has the ownership of knowledge and the power imbalance that can stem from it; evaluating their teaching practice through peer observation and reflection and incorporating ethics in coaching as a formal component across the curricula, including supervision, debates and case studies, as illustrated with example in the following lines.

Vignette – The 'how' of ethical thinking

One way in which educators can help to develop ethical thinking is through the use of case studies. Presenting a case and then subjecting it to critical thought is a way to highlight the complexities of ethical thinking but also this can help to develop a questioning and reasoning approach to ethical decision making. The following case is one that could be used as part of coach education.

Supervision, as a part of coach education, is also a process that can enable and facilitate ethical awareness (Corrie and Lane, 2015).

This case is based on a 'live' encounter during a supervision discussion. It highlights a common ethical dilemma found in coaching in a paid or commissioned environment.

He who pays the piper......?

The coach in this case is an experienced, well qualified and accredited coach. A recurring theme discussed in supervision in this case is the coach's strong desire to be helpful to their client and to help them resolve the issue that they are working on together. The coach makes use of various 'tools' to assist them with their work and in this case a 360-interview process was employed.

The coachee is a team leader who received coaching via the HR department following a complaint about their behaviour towards staff. The coachee agreed to the coaching.

The coach established ground rules, including the boundaries of confidentiality and then sought permission from the client to conduct the 360-interview process. The coachee nominated the people who would participate in the 360-interview process.

The coach gathered this information and presented it to the client. The 360-feedback was in the coach's words 'brutal'.

The coachee, who was also engaged in therapy at that time, appeared to initially accept the feedback but, following a session with their therapist, then rejected the feedback. The reasons given were, the methodology employed, the people they had nominated and the therapist's view that the coaching should end because they were working on these behavioural issues in therapy.

Without directly sharing the feedback with their manager, the coachee had a discussion with their manager about the 360 and the manager's view was that it was 'normal office tittle tattle'. What the coachee said to the manager is unknown.

The coach, being concerned that this 'brutal' feedback was going to be ignored or down-played by the coachee, the coachee's manager and the HR department, wondered if it might be a good idea to confidentially share the 360-report with HR, after all 'they are paying for this'.

Consider the following questions:

What do you discern as the central ethical issue?
What might be other ethical issues here?
If you were the coach, what would you be doing or saying and, to whom?
What kind of ethical conversation would you be having as a coach educator; supervisor; a coach; HR; the manager; the coachee or the other parties in the coachee's team?

Conclusion

Ethical conflicts and dilemmas are intrinsic to coaching. Therefore, ethics in coach education should not be taken for granted and limited to becoming familiar with the principal ethics codes. Instead, it should be a continuous process that starts at the beginning of coaches education and forms part of their professional development using reflective practice and critical thinking. Furthermore, coaching educators must consider the ethics in the design and delivery of coaching programmes to face safeguarding issues. In this chapter, we have explored some ethical considerations for coaching educators and the need to develop critical reflective thinking in coaching through the education process as an invitation to reflect and re-consider the need to embed ethics in coaching education.

Discussion points

1. What approaches to coach education have you come across and how far is ethical thinking an element?
2. How might you respond to ethical dilemmas that occur in any continuous professional development event you may attend?
3. What do you think constitutes a 'virtuous' coach?
4. How do you implement ethical decisions?

Recommended reading

Chapter 9, Ethical Issues in Coach Education and Training. In I. Iordanou, R. Hawkley, & C. Iordanou (2017), *Values and ethics in coaching.* Sage Publications.

References

Aristotle. (2004) *The Nicomachean Ethics.* London: Penguin Classics.

Association for Coaching. (2021) https://cdn.ymaws.com/www.associationforcoaching.com/resource/resmgr/Accreditation/Accred_General/Coaching_Competency_Framewor.pdf.

Association for Coaching Training Organisations. (2020) ACTO Code of Ethics. https://actoonline.org/wp-content/uploads/2020/03/ACTO-Code-of-Ethics-March-2020.pdf.

Barnett, R. (1994) *The Limits of Competence.* London: Open University Press & Society for Research into Higher Education.

Bernstein, B. (1971) On the classification and framing of educational knowledge. In M. F. D. Young (Ed.), *Knowledge and Control: New Directions for the Sociology of Education.* London: Open University, Collier–Macmillan, pp. 47–69.

British Psychological Society. (2022) *Standards for Coaching Psychology (Level 8).* www.bps.org.uk/member-microsites/division-coaching-psychology.

Brunner, R. (1998) Psychoanalysis and coaching. *Journal of Management Psychology,* 13(7): 515–517.

Corrie, S. & Lane, D. (2015) *CBT Supervision.* London: Sage Publications.

European Mentoring and Coaching Council. (2021) Global code of ethics. Retrieved from www.globalcodeofethics.org.

Garvey B. (2016) Issues of assessment and accreditation of coaches. In *The SAGE Handbook of Coaching* (Eds T. Bachkirova, G. Spence, & D. Drake).

Garvey, B. & Stokes, P. (2022) *Coaching and Mentoring theory and practice,* 4th Edition. London: Sage Publications.

Gray, D. E., Garvey, B., & Lane, D.A. (2016) *A Critical Introduction to Coaching and Mentoring.* London: Sage Publications.

Habermas, J. (1974) *Theory and Practice.* London: Heinemann.

International Coach Federation. (2019) Code of Ethics. Lexington, KY: International Coach Federation. Retrieved from https://coachingfederation.org/ethics/code-of-ethics.

ILM. (2022) www.i-l-m.com/learning-and-development/coaching-and-mentoring-qualifications, accessed June 18, 2022.

Iordanou, I., Hawkley, R., & Iordanou, C. (2017) *Values and ethics in coaching.* London: Sage Publications.

Jarvis, P. (1992) *Paradoxes of Learning: On Becoming an Individual in Society.* San Francisco, CA: Jossey-Bass.

Knowles, M. (1980) *The Modern Practice of Adult Education: From Pedagogy to Andragogy.* Englewood Cliffs, NJ: Prentice Hall.

MacIntryre, A. (1984) *After Virtue: A Study in Moral Theory,* 2nd Edition. Notre Dame, IN: University of Notre Dame Press.

Perrenoud, P. (1998) La transposition didactique à partir de pratiques: des savoirs aux compétences. *Revue des sciences de l'éducation,* 24(3): 487–514.

Pope, K. S. & Vasquez, M. J. T. (2016) *Ethics in psychotherapy and counseling: A practical guide.* 4th Edition. John Wiley & Sons Inc. doi:10.1002/9781118001875.

Self, T. T., Gordon S., & Jolly, P. M. (2019) Talent management: A Delphi study of assessing and developing GenZ hospitality leaders. *International Journal of Contemporary Hospitality Management,* 31(10): 4126–4149. doi:10.1108/IJCHM-11-2018-0915.

Sheppard, D. L. & Reynolds, J. L. (2018) *The dividends of decency: How values-based leadership will help business flourish in Trump's America.* Berkeley, CA.

Chapter 18

Ethics, wisdom and adult development in coaching

Sarah Smith and Roger Bretherton

Introduction

There is a growing demand for coaching, at the same time the profession is maturing and ethical conversations in the field are now increasingly being raised (Florence & Watts, 2021). This chapter sets out to prompt ethical reflection and discussion by considering professional ethics and the role of ethical maturity, alongside the burgeoning field of wisdom research, before turning the lens towards adult development theories. Two alternative and paradoxical perspectives on adult development are presented with accompanying case studies, as a means of surfacing deeper ethical reflection. The first perspective explores how theories of adult development, when considered as a dynamic process involving tasks, crises, roles, and practices, may support coaches in developing their own ethical reflective practice. The second perspective suggests that an ethical reflective practice requires coaches to question theories of adult development and the cultural and epistemological assumptions, or knowledge and truth criterion, they are built upon, noting that even the concept of development itself is culturally situated and may be problematic. The focus here is on provoking dialogue not on answering or resolving the paradox presented.

Context

There is no contesting the scale of the challenges humans are facing, from geo-political uncertainties to increasing global inequalities and climate change (United Nations, n.d.). In a world where arguably a human preoccupation with optimisation, controllability and growth may be a central part of the problem, alternative descriptions of our current human predicament hold credible explanatory power (Bateson, 2021; McGilchrist, 2021; Rosa, 2020; Wengrow & Graeber, 2021) and challenge us to examine how human self-deception may trap us into producing the very outcomes we are critical of (Weintrobe, 2021). Important and urgent ethical implications for coaching are being raised (Cavanagh & Turner, 2022; Clutterbuck, 2022; Hawkins, 2021; MacKie, 2021; Mercaldi, 2018).

DOI: 10.4324/9781003277729-18

As the field of coaching matures there is a move towards the democratisation of coaching through productisation (Passmore & Evans-Krimme, 2021). How confident can we be that more coaching for more people is for the good? What kind of holding questions might coaches and the coaching field need to be asking of themselves in order to minimise the often unseen, unintended negative consequences and optimise the positive outcomes of our work? How is self-deception, illusion and collusion present in coaching work and how do we probe and pry into these entanglements? The professional coaching community is interested in asking such questions (Bachkirova & Borrington, 2020; de Haan, 2021; Schermuly & Graßmann, 2019; Whybrow, Turner, McLean, & Hawkins, 2023; Wright, Walsh, & Tennyson, 2019). Systemic ways of working and ethical practices that address the need for an ecosystem perspective are being proposed, along with the ability to turn the looking glass back upon ourselves and our profession (Hawkins & Turner, 2020).

Ethics and ethical maturity

Ethics is concerned with identifying, organising and recommending what is right or wrong, good or bad (Carroll, 2011). In so doing it also addresses the practical application of values and sets out rules, codes and principles of conduct (Iordanou, Hawley, & Iordanou, 2016). *Professional ethics* addresses these tasks within a particular profession.

Professional ethics emphasises professional collective responsibility, along with an awareness of context (Carroll & Shaw, 2013). It involves asking questions such as, what is the scope of the professional role, where is the edge of the professional 'arena', what are the reach and possible consequential stakes associated with the professional work, what are the competencies and capabilities for this work, what are the relationships in this work and how are they 'relating'? At the foundational level professional ethical codes set out the core values and standards of behaviour that are essential to a professional role. However, professional ethics is also interested in the reflective practices and decision-making skills that build ethical maturity and contextual sensitivity within a professional domain, such as the skill of recognising subtle yet possibly consequential ethical issues as they arise or navigating specific value-laden situations where different stakeholders have competing interests.

Ethical codes are, by their very nature, limited. They provide a foundation for shared ethical practice. Looking at the ethical codes of multiple professional coaching bodies, Brennan and Wildflower (2010) identified the following consistent points:

- Do no harm: do not cause needless injury or harm to others.
- Duty of care: act in ways that promote the welfare of other people.
- Know your limits: practise within your scope of competence.

- Respect the interests of the client.
- Respect the law.

Coaches however, regularly encounter ambiguous ethical issues that cannot be resolved by any professional code. Coaching is predictably unpredictable; it is deeply relational. It has psychological consequences and involves working with coachees or teams who are themselves part of wider complex systems such as workplaces, families and communities. From this ecosystem perspective interdependencies are far reaching, and unexpected consequences are a feature, not something that can be eradicated or 'ruled' out. These very complexities increase the need for ethical awareness and capabilities. Here lies the territory of ethical maturity.

The concept of ethical maturity is described by Carroll (2011a, p. 12) as involving:

> "...the reflective, rational and emotional capacity to decide actions are right and wrong, good and better; the resilience and courage to implement these decisions; being accountable for ethical-decision made (publicly or privately); and the ability to learn from, and live with, the experience."

Noting the centrality of reason, emotion, and reflection capabilities, they warn against focussing on one at the expense of the others. While also acknowledging that during any specific instance of ethical decision-making they may be individually (and necessarily) foregrounded in different ways. They additionally emphasise that ethical maturity is an ever-unfolding process of life-long learning. They propose the following six components of ethical maturity (Hawkins & Turner, 2020):

1. *Creating ethical sensitivity* – self-awareness, mindful of consequences and impact of behaviour, aware of harm and of intention / motives.
2. *Ethical discernment* – reflection, emotional awareness and the process of ethical decision making.
3. *Implementing ethical decisions* – how to implement decisions, insight into what blocks or supports the coach.
4. *Ethical conversations* – accountability and responsibility, defending decisions, connecting to principles.
5. *Ethical sustainability and peace* – support networks, living with decisions, learning from the process.
6. *Ethical growth and integrating new learning into moral character* - enriching moral self-knowledge, extending ethical sensitivity and understanding, building ethical competency.

Taking an ecosystem perspective to ethical maturity, Hawkins and Turner (2020) advocate for the 'more-than human' world. They propose four capacities and disciplines that mitigate for the human tendency to privilege what is most immediate, local, accessible and similar to us (p. 171). Practising these capacities may support the development of systemic ethical maturity (Hawkins & Turner, 2020):

1. *Cultural awareness* – awareness of our own cultural biases and assumptions, acquired in the families, communities and cultures we have learnt how to be in.
2. *Listening* to not only what is in the room, but what is not in the room – listening not only to the coachee but 'through' the coachee, to the world they participate in. Attending to the unspoken and the unseen as well as the spoken and seen.
3. *Wide-angled empathy* – extending compassion and empathy beyond the coachee towards every involved individual, group and system.
4. *Holding the future in mind* – bringing a future generational view into the process, 'future-back' perspective taking.

Here we can see that ethical professional practice requires an ongoing process of self-reflection, increasing insight and awareness, and an expanded and more nuanced understanding of multiple perspectives (Brennan & Wildflower, 2010). The ethically mature coach is not an expert with technical knowledge who acts upon a 'system' and can predict and regulate for outcomes but is rather involved in a wider ecosystem where their professional expertise requires 'not knowing' as much as 'knowing' as they adaptively respond to the predictably unpredictable. It is a dynamic process of knowing and not knowing, doing and being, far beyond a set of guidelines and rules. To meaningfully grapple with ethics necessitates an epistemological awareness (Carroll, 2011b; Guishard, Halkovic, Galletta & Li, 2018), questioning not only what we know but how we know, it requires us to think deeply about what coaching is, why we do coaching, and what constitutes 'good' coaching. To achieve this, we propose it requires wisdom.

Wisdom and wisdom perspectives

Wisdom has long been studied by philosophers and theologians and more recently the psychological study of wisdom has added theoretical and empirical research to this body of work. There are multiple definitions and ways of thinking about wisdom, representing theoretical and cultural differences. At the same time there are considerable points of agreement (Grossmann et al., 2020) and integrative models describing how different aspects of wisdom may work together in a dynamic process (Ardelt, 2003; Bassett, 2011; Glück & Westrate, 2022; Smith & Bretherton, 2021; Sternberg & Karami, 2021).

From a broad perspective, wisdom can be defined as an adaptive capacity that enables us to live and act well in complexity (Küpers, 2016). It is a dynamic process which involves managing uncertainty, integrating conflicting interests over the short, medium and long-term, adjusting, shaping, and changing in service of a 'common good' (Sternberg, 1998). It requires deliberation on what matters most in life, translating that into choices and actions. The importance of action is not to be overlooked here. Wise thinking is for wise acting (Sternberg & Glück, 2021).

The Common Wisdom Model (CWM) describes wisdom as "morally grounded excellence in certain aspects of meta-cognition" (Grossmann et al., 2020, p. 108). The multiple wisdom scholars who were involved in developing the CWM agreed that the following components were centrally important (Grossmann et al., 2020):

- perspectival meta-cognition – a balance of viewpoints, epistemic humility, context adaptability and multiple perspectives
- grounded in moral aspirations and specific socio-cultural contexts and experiences
- for the purposes of implementing abstract moral concepts, seeing through illusion and self-deception and supporting long-term planning and survival-oriented coordination

Studies looking at wise reasoning in real life contexts have shown significant levels of within-person variability, suggesting that wisdom may be as much state as trait (Grossmann, Kung, & Santos, 2019). From this lens wisdom can be described as a meta-cognitive state that consists of (but is not limited to) a syndrome of perspectives, or ways of thinking and being, that manifest dynamically in ongoing processes such as reflection, inquiry and relevance realisation, helping us to overcome illusion, self-deception and collusion, more closely seeing ourselves, others and the world as it is, rather than as we think it is (Hu & Feng, 2023; Smith & Bretherton 2021; Vervaeke & Ferraro, 2013). These may or may not show sufficient stability within individuals to be described as trait-like.

Beyond the CWM components, an integrative review of the psychological research on wisdom suggests the following perspectives as being important (Smith, 2019). These wisdom perspectives include (Smith & Bretherton, 2021, pp. 534–535):

- "Self-transcendence – rising above oneself, feeling a connectedness to all things (e.g. Le & Levenson, 2005)

- Wholeness – seeing the whole, shining a light on what is hidden. Seeing the wider system, identifying patterns, themes, relationships between issues and developmental pathways over time. (e.g. Yang, 2011)

- Integration and balance – integrating and balancing conflicting interests and polarities, moving towards equilibrium. Considering historical, situational, contextual factors and future trajectories. (e.g. Sternberg, 1990)

- Paradox – recognising that conflicting things can be simultaneously true. (e.g. Ferrari & Westrate, 2013).

- Complexity – recognising multiple interrelationships. Paying attention not only to multiple perspectives but also to multiple descriptions. (e.g. Baltes & Staudinger, 2000)

- Humility and uncertainty – recognition of the limits of one's own knowledge (e.g. Grossmann, 2017)

- Compassion – concern for the suffering of others and motivation to relieve that suffering (e.g. Ardelt, 2003)

The parallels between wisdom and ethical maturity (Carroll, 2011a; Carroll, 2011b; Karami, Ghahremani, Parra-Martinez, & Gentry, 2020) and systemic ethical maturity (Hawkins & Turner, 2020) are marked (see Table 18.1). Wisdom involves an ecosystem perspective, a dynamic process of knowing and not knowing, doing and being. Sternberg suggests that "wise people are always ethical, although ethical people are not always wise" (2013, p. 69). Developing ethical *maturity* matters (Sternberg, 2013). Complementing ethical maturity frameworks we suggest that coaches adopt a wisdom perspective in their professional ethical practice when they engage in a reflective practice, such as through professional supervision, which involves: seeing multiple perspectives, interdependencies and the 'whole'; integrating multiple view-points; considering context and future trajectories; recognising and testing the limits of one's own knowledge and understanding; recognising uncertainty and paradox; experiencing connection and extending compassion to self and others, including the beyond human world.

Adult development

Theories of adult development are broadly concerned with describing the consistent, systematic, and qualitative ways in which individuals change over the course of a life span (Lerner, 2018). From a holistic perspective, these theories can be seen as describing changes in an individual's abilities and behaviour, arising as a result of internal and external environmental interactions, influenced by hereditary factors, internal and external influences,

Table 18.1 Ethical maturity, ethical systemic maturity and wisdom perspectives – an overview

Ethical maturity (Carroll & Shaw, 2013)	Systemic Ethical Maturity (Hawkins & Turner, 2019)	Wisdom Perspectives (Smith & Bretherton, 2021)
1. Creating ethical sensitivity – self-awareness, mindful of consequences and impact of behaviour, aware of harm and of intention / motives.	1. Cultural awareness – awareness of own cultural biases and assumptions, acquired in the families, communities, and cultures we have learnt how to be in.	1. Self-transcendence – rising above oneself, feeling connected to all things.
2. Ethical discernment – reflection, emotional awareness and the process of ethical decision making.	2. Listening to not only what is in the room, but what is not in the room – listening not only to the coachee but 'through' the coachee, to the world they participate in. Attending to the unspoken and the unseen as well as the spoken and seen.	2. Wholeness – seeing the whole, shining a light on what is hidden. Seeing the wider system, identifying previously unseen patterns, themes, relationships between issues and pathways over time.
3. Implementing ethical decisions – how to implement decisions, insight into what blocks or supports the coach.	3. Wide-angled empathy – extending compassion and empathy beyond the coachee towards every involved individual, group and system.	3. Integration and balance – integrating and balancing conflicting interests and polarities, moving towards equilibrium. Considering historical, situational, contextual factors and future trajectories.
4. Ethical conversations – accountability and responsibility, defending decisions, connecting to principles.	4. Holding the future in mind – bringing a future generational view into the process, 'future-back' perspective taking.	4. Paradox – recognising that conflicting things can be simultaneously true, recognising paradox and epistemological traps.
5. Ethical sustainability and peace – support networks, living with decisions, learning from the process.		5. Complexity – recognising multiple inter-relationships. Paying attention to multiple perspectives and descriptions.
6. Ethical growth and integrating new learning into moral character – enriching moral self-knowledge, extending ethical sensitivity, and understanding, building ethical competency.		6. Humility and uncertainty – recognition of the limits of one's own knowledge, knowing and not-knowing at the same time.
		7. Compassion – concern for the suffering of others and motivation to relieve that suffering.

resources and motives (Hoare, 2011). Adult development addresses issues of cognition, morality, ego, self, and changes in the way one experiences being 'oneself'. Differences in theories of adult development arise however in how that change is described, including the degree to which development is seen as a vertical, uni-directional, hierarchical journey of relatively stable and structured developmental progress, where universal 'higher' stages equate with 'better' (Kallio, 2020), development as a 'holarchy' (Wilber, 1999) where different lines of development progress through necessary stages that build upon and include each other but in complex, non-linear and overlapping ways, towards 'higher' or more complex stages (Dawson-Tunik et al., 2005), and a horizontal web of developmental pathways (Hofer, 2002).

These differences reflect underlying philosophical differences and can be seen in three schools of development (Levenson & Crumpler, 1996). *Ontogenetic models* of adult development broadly take the position that over the course of an adult's lifespan there are sequential stages of psychological change that are universal and intrinsic (e.g. Erikson, 1950; Levinson, 1978; Loevinger, 1966; Kohlberg, 1994) The stages are frequently represented as dialectical tensions involving specific developmental tasks or crises (e.g. Erikson, 1950). *Sociogenic models* of development argue that change in adulthood is largely influenced by social roles (Dannefer, 1984; Elder & Caspi, 1998; Neugarten, 1979) and where the emphasis is on the variability and complexity of sociocultural context. And *Liberative models* of development focus on attaining freedom from biosocial determinants and draw on traditions of development such as Taoism and Buddhism (Levenson, Aldwin, & Cupertino, 2001). Liberative models of development share a focus on practices that cultivate self-transcendence. While all three schools represent development as a dynamic process, we can see the different and relative importance placed on tasks, crises, roles and practices as central to the change process (see Table 18.2). Other differences between the models are not addressed here (for a comprehensive overview see Lerner, 2018).

Distinctive ethical features of adult development theories in the coaching context

Discussions of adult development theories and their role in coaching are often accompanied by a note of caution (Berger, 2006; Bachkirova & Borrington, 2019; Hurlow, 2022). At the same time developmental coaching, which draws directly from theories of adult development, is a growing field of coaching practice (e.g. Pannell, 2021). We would also argue that whether a coach describes themselves as engaged in developmental coaching or not, the contexts in which coaches work, the ways we address professional practice and operate in the world are steeped in legacy developmental theories. Criticisms of adult development theories include concerns that they may be overly reductionistic - simplifying complex and contextually sensitive dynamics of change. Often expressed as linear hierarchies with universal stages, they are focussed on 'parts' at the cost of being

Table 18.2 Adult development theories and the change process - a simplified overview

	Relative centrality and importance to the change process		
	Tasks and crises	Social roles	Practices
Adult Development Theories	Ontogenetic models e.g. Erikson, 1950 Levinson, 1978 Loevinger, 1966 Kohlberg, 1994 Sequential stages of psychological change that are universal and intrinsic. Stages frequently represented as dialectical tensions involving specific developmental tasks or crises.	Sociogenic models e.g. Dannefer, 1984 Elder & Caspi, 1998 Neugarten, 1979 Change in adulthood is largely influenced by social roles Emphasis on the variability and complexity of sociocultural contexts.	Liberative models e.g. Buddhism Taoism Focus on attaining freedom from biosocial determinants. Emphasis on practices that cultivate self-transcendence.

open to the multiple complex ways 'parts' are *relating*. By de-contextualising development they additionally risk being both biased and limited. Adult development theories are in large part focussed on Western cultural expressions of adult development, excluding other cultural expressions of how and in what ways adults develop over a lifetime (Bühler & Nikitin, 2020). Similarly, gender differences are under-represented (Herbert, 2022).

Reflecting the various ways in which an individual may feel they are developing is another limitation, including in ways that some models of development might even describe as regression. In particular, vertical theories reflect normative, value-based assumptions, rooted in latent historical and socio-cultural beliefs (Kallio, 2020), in trying to predict pathways of development they may unintentionally limit the very unfolding of human possibility they set out to describe. This may encourage clumsy and potentially judgmental assessments of others - suggesting that people can be categorised, labelled and in some cases measured and that these ways of categorising, labelling and measuring are stable and can predict developmental pathways over time and or patterns of responding right now.

Furthermore, suggestions that vertical theories provide a means of matching coaches to coachees, and that coaches best serve their coachees when they are at the same, if not a higher level of development (Laske, 2006) may be over-reaching. Adult development theories may be seen by some as an answer to many of the challenges being confronted today; whereby developing more people to higher stages, or assessing who is at a higher stage, is seen as a way of helping to address urgent global challenges. At an extended reach, the best of intentions can lead to a 'we just need to develop or identify better people' frame. Wisdom research suggests that people can be wise at any time or stage across a lifespan, and across developmental stages (Spano, 2015).

At the same time, when we move away from the 'content' of different models, theories of adult development cast an interesting light onto the processes of change. We can see conceptions of development as a natural process that unfolds in different ways, at different times, across different peoples; the expression of an intrinsic motive to learn (Bachkirova & Borrington, 2019). Stages of thinking are reconsidered as modes of thinking (Kallio, 2020) and ways of rethinking adult development itself are being described in line with demographic and structural changes (Arnett, Robinson & Lachman, 2020; Buhler & Nikitin, 2020), conceptions of the 'modern self' (Mercaldi, 2018) and neuroscience perspectives (Staudinger, 2020). With its emphasis on practical consequences, Bachkirova and Borrington (2018) argue for the adoption of philosophical pragmatism when considering adult development theories and coaching. It is in this modern practice arena that wisdom and ethical maturity may be especially important.

A wise reflective ethical practice requires us to pry into the entangled ways we are indirectly involved in emergent unintended negative consequences, at multiple levels. Without awareness of the historicity of one's own actions and thoughts, or positions held and upheld, unethical practice can arise (Ison & Schlindwein, 2006). As we build our ethical practice it is important to remind ourselves that this is always an ongoing process of knowing and not knowing, and that universally right ethical decisions and actions are impossible. The service we owe to coachees is to strive for humility in our own thinking and acting and to engage in wise ethical reflective practices that foster insight, challenge what we think is relevant in a process of ongoing inquiry and relevance realisation, sharpening the choices afforded to us in specific contexts.

As a device for provoking deeper ethical reflection, we have deliberately chosen to present two somewhat paradoxical perspectives and case studies. As will be seen, each perspective surfaces its own set of ethical questions. However, when considered alongside each other a practice paradox emerges. How can adult development theories support coaches in their ethical practice while at the same time be implied in potentially unethical practice? A wisdom perspective encourages us to notice paradox. Through description of these two perspectives, we aim to highlight the epistemological traps that may be present in our work. The reader is encouraged to notice their own responses as they read each perspective. We do not set out to answer the questions that juxtaposing them raises. We simply hope that they provide 'food for thought' for the reader's own ethical reflective practice. A practice paradox: ethical coaching and developmental theories, central to *both* perspectives are the following questions.

What constitutes developmental work?
What should be seen and known about developmental work before embarking on it, and by whom?

How does the knowledge or awareness one has of a particular approach alter the way in which one might participate in and benefit from the work?
Who and what is being privileged in different approaches to developmental work and does that raise systemic ethical questions?

In the first perspective we propose an approach to reflective practice influenced by theories of adult development. The focus here is on the coach as the subject and object of development.

Perspective One: adult development theories in support of ethical maturity and wisdom

When looking to adult development theories as a source of guidance for *how* coaches may develop ethical maturity and wisdom in the context of their coaching work, the contribution of tasks, crises, roles, and practices to the developmental process offers us a useful cross-theoretical framework. The suggestion is that when considered holistically, these aspects may work together in support of coach development, potentially surfacing ethical issues and fostering ethical maturity and wisdom in coaching practice. Here we approach development from the meta-theoretical perspective of Relational Developmental Systems theory (Lerner & Overton, 2008), where development is seen as deriving from mutually influencing relations within a system, including individual and context relations.

This stance can also be seen in integrative models of wisdom as a process, which suggest that *difficult life events and life experiences* are the crucible from which wisdom can arise (Pascual-Leone, 1990; Glück & Bluck, 2013), in a process of forming and being formed (Stacey, 2003) within specific socio-cultural contexts (Grossmann, 2017; Grossmann, Dorfman & Oakes, 2020). This is dynamically influenced by the *roles* we embody and enact and the social relationships we experience ourselves, others and the world through. Learning, narrating, curating, and sharing through language (Ferrari, Westrate, & Petro, 2013) and other non-verbal ways of knowing and relating, as we negotiate social normative and individual needs, and *life tasks* (often described as a source of difficult life events); con-forming and trans-forming over time. All these are facilitated by meta-cognitive capacities that allow us to engage in *practices that include reflecting upon* ourselves, others and wider contexts, mentally time travelling and adopting multiple expansive perspectives, including non-human perspectives (Grossmann et al., 2020). And we are motivated by a desire, *a continuous life task*, to see the changing, dynamic, living world and ourselves more clearly.

Influenced by this as a framework we propose some holding reflective questions (see Table 18.3) that may dynamically support coaches in developing ethical maturity and wisdom in coaching. The questions are organised around 1) tasks and crises – where the tasks and crises of coaching become

Table 18.3 Developing ethical maturity and wisdom in coaching: tasks and crises, roles, and practices – reflective questions

1. Tasks and crises	*2. Roles*	*3. Practices*
Possible questions include:	Possible questions include:	Possible questions include:
• What is the central task of the coaching work?	• Who are you when you are coaching?	• What do you do regularly that supports professionalism in your coaching?
• Who and what is that task in service of?	• Who is your coachee?	
	• Who is the team, who is the organisation?	• How are you supported in your practice?
• What task(s) does coaching fulfil for the coach, for the coachee, for the team, the organisation, for wider society?	• Who are you when you are not coaching?	• How do you approach reflection?
• What additional, smaller or peripheral tasks arise in the coaching work?	• Who is your coachee when they are not being coached?	• How are you changing as you practice over time?
• How are those tasks serving the central task?	• Where is the edge of you, the edge of you and your coachee, the edge of the system within which the coaching work is happening etc?	• What do you know to be not true now, that you used to believe to be true?
• What large task(s) is (are) being asked of the coach by the system / eco-system within which the coaching is happening?	• What are you able to say and not say, do and not do, know and not know when you are being a 'coach'?	• How do you practise shifting your perspective in order to see yourself, your coachee and wider contextual factors more clearly?
• How is task ambiguity benefitting and constraining the work, for whom?	• What *do* you say and not say, do and not do, know and not know when you are coaching?	• How do the tasks and roles involved in your work influence the practices or habits you might want to engage in?
• What critical incidents (including critical emotions such as fear or anger) are being experienced in the coaching work?	• *How* are you 'being' a coach?	• Who do you seek out to test your assumptions and challenge your work as a coach?
• Critical how and for whom?	• What does that look, feel and sound like?	• What perspectives are missing from your reflective practice?
• What tensions are showing up in the coaching?	• How do these things enable and constrain you?	• What have you forgotten that you used to know / do that could help your practice today?
• What is the relationship between any tensions, critical incidents and the task(s) of the coaching?	• How are you more than your role(s) and how can that 'more than' benefit your coaching work, or not?	• What is being given life in and through your coaching?
• How is stuck-ness showing up?	• How is role ambiguity benefitting and constraining the work, for whom?	• How is that moving towards what is true, important, and desirable?
• What are the implications of that for the coaching tasks?		

the content and ground of professional reflective practice; 2) roles – where the roles we embody and enact in our coaching work become the content and ground; and 3) practices – where the practices and habits we engage in become the content and ground.

During the following case study, readers are encouraged to consider how tasks and crises, roles and practices may be playing out dynamically, and which of the proposed reflective questions seem most relevant here. What ethical questions does the vignette raise for you?

Mini case study 1: role and task ambiguity, practices and habits in coaching work

Hilary was an experienced coach and psychotherapist who ran two separate practices, one for her business coaching clients and one for her private therapy clients. As part of an in-house organisational leadership programme for a group of senior leaders, Hilary was coaching some participants individually for the duration of the programme and facilitating two workshops with the whole group. Having shared her psychotherapy experience with the group during introductions a few participants had expressed an interest in her practice. In her coaching work two of Hilary's coachees had raised issues that she felt best able to explore with them through use of her psychotherapy training. Throughout her considerable experience working in both therapeutic and business coaching contexts Hilary was used to navigating the grey area between therapy and coaching. She prided herself on drawing on all her skills in her work, skills developed in both of her professional roles. She had explored this with her therapy supervisor when she had noticed it first starting to arise as a question in her coaching work. (Hilary did not have coaching supervision, nor was her therapy supervisor qualified or experienced as a coach, or in organisational or team work). Over the years Hilary had become more casual about contracting or re-contracting with her coachees, she responded flexibly to their emerging needs in the moment and was confident in her abilities to help them achieve positive outcomes in their lives. She was a skilful coach and therapist and had many outstanding testimonials to that effect.

Part way through the leadership programme, Hilary was facilitating what was her first full group session. She was very pleased with the progress she felt was being achieved with the participants she was coaching. She was looking forward to seeing them in the group context and noticing how their patterns of behaviour may have changed. At the end of the first morning session, Hilary had noticed several patterns arising that she felt were holding several individuals in the group back. Some of these were her coachees, others were being coached by different members of the coaching team. Drawing on all of her skills and insights gained from the coaching work she had done with some of the group so far, Hilary decided to share her observations, giving individual feedback in front of the group. During the round of feedback one participant, who was not one of Hilary's coachees, ran from the room after receiving hers. Another participant, who was one of Hilary's coachees, flushed bright red and remained completely silent. The rest of the group were unsettled but were not dis-interested in the feedback or where the work might go next.

During the break Hilary's coachee told her directly that he was very angry that she had addressed, even obliquely, work they were doing privately in their coaching sessions. The participant who had run from the room spoke with their own coach. Personal issues from childhood had been triggered. The next day she put in a formal complaint to the human resources (HR) department who were sponsoring the work. Hilary was very upset and surprised by what happened.

In the next perspective we show how theories of adult development, and arguably even the concept of development itself may be problematic, raising different ethical questions in the context of coaching work. The focus here is on the coachee as the subject and object of development.

Perspective Two: how theories of adult development and even the concept of development itself may be problematic

As can be seen from the description of different theories of adult development, they are complex and grounded in arguably irreconcilable perspectives (Mercaldi, 2018). Furthermore, there is no agreement over what development means (Kallio, 2020). Yet the term is used regularly, perhaps especially in our workplaces. Relevant to the concept of development is the idea of 'normal', normal according to those who define the models against which others are evaluated. In this way developmental models are normative, not just describing but also defining what is seen as good or bad. As identified earlier, individuals are engaged in complex responsive processes by which they negotiate individual needs with social normative needs. However, ethical questions arise when models are grounded in decontextualised ways of knowing and latent beliefs that may disadvantage some people, restricting access to opportunities and power. Ethical maturity requires contextualised knowing (Carroll & Shaw, 2013).

Wisdom research has something relevant to say here about epistemological issues and how they inform wise reasoning. Vervaeke and Ferraro (2013) identify four types of knowing, *propositional* – knowing that something is true e.g. France is a country; *procedural* – knowing how to do something e.g. how to listen; *perspectival* – knowing the world from a particular view; *participatory* – an embodied knowing, knowing how to be, how to act in a role or context (pp. 29–30). Wise reasoning involves a recursive process of relevance realisation, drawing on *multiple* ways of knowing we enrich our understanding and gain insight. A wisdom perspective also emphasises the problems with decontextualised knowledge. When we decontextualise knowing we reduce experience to propositional truths.

While reading this next case study readers are encouraged to keep the following ethical questions in mind:

When do you first notice a possible ethical dilemma arising?
What made you think it was an ethical dilemma?
How is development being conceived of here, by whom?
What are the ethical implications of these conceptions, for whom?
Where do ethical dilemmas 'live' in the work of coaching?
If there is developmental work here, where is it?
What are the possible short-, medium- and long-term consequences here?
Where and when does a coach need to be ethically aware?
If you were Adebayo, what would be your first next steps?

The focus here is on the front end of coaching work, the different stakeholders involved and the interdependencies that can play out within the coach-client organisational context.

Mini case study 2: Gender and cultural differences in development

Adebayo had been supporting a client organisation for several years with leadership coaching. He was regularly asked to work with individuals identified as High Potential, High Performers (HiPo) and increasingly, he had noted, HiPo individuals who the organisational sponsors felt were being held back by their communication style. Curious about this he had commented during some of his most recent supervision sessions that he thought he might be noticing an unconscious bias in the organisation towards women who were somewhat more direct. None of the coachees he had been asked to work with were men.

On this occasion he was briefed by the line manager and HR manager about the latest coachee they wanted him to work with, Abigail. They described her as overly forthright and direct in her communications upwards in the organisation, with peers and external stakeholders. Abigail had been given this feedback directly and had expressed concern to her line manager that she thought these 'issues' were arguably indicative of wider cultural and gender biases, rather than being a problematic feature of her actual working relationships. She also shared her view that the organisation's description of what an average, good, better leader looked and sounded like, as set out in their organisational competency framework, was rather limited and didn't seem to reflect how leadership actually happened in the organisation. Her line manager agreed but did not have anything more to add on the matter, it was the only framework they had after all, and he felt it did describe a useful developmental pathway in principle.

Following the feedback conversation between Abigail and her line manager, a 360-feedback exercise had been conducted. The survey generated very positive feedback from Abigail's peers, stakeholders, and her direct reports. The external stakeholder views had come as a particular surprise to Abigail's line manager, who had been expecting critical feedback on Abigail's direct communication style. Despite the 360 results, the line manager and HR manager had now reached out to Adebayo, asking him to help Abigail in putting together and implementing a development plan that would address her communication 'issues', and her relationship skills more generally, supported by the leadership competency framework (which Adebayo was already very familiar with and usually ignored in the coaching work he did). Towards the end of the briefing conversation, the HR manager mentioned that he would also like to have another discussion with Adebayo about the possibility of introducing vertical development coaching. He had been introduced to the concept by a colleague and thought the assessment and diagnostic opportunities might be very helpful for assessing what stages different leaders might be at and supporting their talent population in their development.

In initial communications with Adebayo, Abigail was eager to start the coaching work. She had very positive previous experiences of coaching and had heard great things about Adebayo from others in the organisation he had coached. During their first exploratory session Adebayo decided to focus on understanding things from Abigail's perspective. Abigail shared that she had moved to the UK from Nigeria since marrying six years' previously and starting a family of now three children. She was a few months away from completing the PhD in Organisational Psychology that she had been studying for part time, alongside her full-time work. She had requested flexible working hours in support of childcare issues and her necessarily long commute, owing to high house prices close to her workplace. This had been granted within certain parameters, which she felt had been rather begrudgingly done. Abigail was very keen to progress in her career and was confident that she had much to contribute to the organisation. She loved her work and felt she had very positive relationships with her various stakeholders. She had been delighted by the feedback in the 360 which had really boosted her after the feedback conversation with her line manager. Abigail shared with Adebayo that she felt her communication style was being judged differently from her male colleagues. She also expressed concern about the theoretical basis of the organisational leadership competency rubric she was being measured against. She shared that development theories and gender bias in organisational contexts was a particular area of interest in her research work. She was keen to get Adebayo's thoughts and advice on the matter and wanted to know how he could support her in advocating for change in the organisation.

Having read both perspectives 1 and 2 above we encourage you to revisit the ethical coaching and developmental theories and consider the following questions:

What constitutes developmental work?
What should be seen and known about developmental work before embarking on it, and by whom?
How does the knowledge or awareness one has of a particular approach alter the way in which one might participate in and benefit from the work?
Who and what is being privileged in different approaches to developmental work and does that raise systemic ethical questions?

Conclusion

This chapter has deliberately set out to juxtapose two different ways in which adult development theories may be ethically relevant to coaching work; by contributing to our understanding of how change happens, as well as describing the ways in which people change. Guided by a wisdom lens we have highlighted the complexities involved in coaching and the potentially unseen ways in which adult development theories may be ethically implied in the work. A cautionary reflective note is encouraged. Becoming an ethical coach is not something that simply happens, it is something one practices, it is something one does, recursively. The same can be said for wisdom. The encouragement here is for readers to consider the ongoing questions they ask of themselves and the regular practices they engage in that foster systemic ethical maturity and wisdom; together with consideration of how ethical awareness and wisdom may play a role in the coaching process itself.

Discussion points

1. This chapter presented two paradoxical perspectives as a means of surfacing deeper ethical issues. What paradoxes do you notice arising in the context of coaching work? What potential deeper ethical issues do they surface?
2. What ongoing practices do you think support the development of ethical maturity and wisdom in coaching?
3. What place do you think ethical maturity and wisdom have in the coaching work itself?
4. As you reflect on the chapter as a whole, what is relevant to you now, that did not seem relevant, or as relevant before?

Recommended reading

Kallio, E. K. (Ed.). (2020) *Development of adult thinking: Interdisciplinary perspectives on cognitive development and adult learning*. Abingdon: Routledge.

References

Ardelt, M. (2003) Empirical assessment of a three-dimensional wisdom scale. *Research on aging*, 25(3): 275–324.

Arnett, J. J., Robinson, O., & Lachman, M. E. (2020) Rethinking adult development: Introduction to the special issue. *American Psychologist*, 75(4): 425.

Bachkirova, T., & Borrington, S. (2018) The limits and possibilities of a Person-centred approach in coaching through the lens of adult development theories. *Philosophy of Coaching: An International Journal*, 3(1): 6–22.

Bachkirova, T. & Borrington, S. (2019) Old wine in new bottles: Exploring pragmatism as a philosophical framework for the discipline of coaching. *Academy of Management Learning & Education*, 18(3): 337–360.

Bachkirova, T. & Borrington, S. (2020) Beautiful ideas that can make us ill: Implications for coaching. *Philosophy of Coaching: An International Journal*, 5(1): 9–30.

Baltes, P. B. & Staudinger, U. M. (2000) Wisdom: A metaheuristic (pragmatic) to orchestrate mind and virtue toward excellence. *American psychologist*, 55(1): 122.

Bassett, C. L. (2011) Wisdom and its development. In C. Hoare (Ed.) *The Oxford handbook of reciprocal adult development and learning*, 2nd Edition. New York, NY: Oxford University Press, pp. 302–318.

Bateson, N. (2021) Aphanipoiesis. *Journal of the International Society for the Systems Sciences, Proceedings of the 64th Annual Meeting of the ISSS, Virtual*, 1(1).

Brennan, D. & Wildflower, L. (2010) Ethics in coaching. In E. Cox, T. Bachkirova, & D. Clutterbuck (Eds), *The complete handbook of coaching*, 3rd Edition. London: Sage Publications, pp. 500–517).

Bühler, J. L. & Nikitin, J. (2020) Sociohistorical context and adult social development: New directions for 21st century research. *American Psychologist*, 75(4): 457.

Carroll, M. (2011a) Ethical maturity: Compasses for life and work decisions-Part I. *Psychotherapy in Australia*, 17(3): 34–44.

Carroll, M. (2011b) Ethical maturity: making ethical decisions-part II. *Psychotherapy in Australia*, 17(4): 40–51.

Carroll, M. & Shaw, E. (2013) *Ethical maturity in the helping professions: Making difficult life and work decisions*. London and Philadelphia: Jessica Kingsley Publishers.

Cavanagh, M., & Turner, E. (2022) Ethics and the Ecological Environment in Coaching. In W.-A. Smith, J. Passmore, E. Turner, Y.-L. Lai & D. Clutterbuck (Eds), *The Ethical Coaches Handbook: A Guide to Developing Ethical Maturity in Practice*. Abingdon: Routledge.

Clutterbuck, D. (2022) The Role of Coaching and Mentoring: Addressing the Leadership Deficit. In H. Gray, A. Gimson, & I. Cunningham (Eds), *Developing Leaders for Real: Proven Approaches That Deliver Impact*. Bingley: Emerald Publishing Limited, pp. 175–186.

Dannefer, D. (1984) Adult development and social theory: A paradigmatic reappraisal. *American Sociological Review*: 100–116.

Dawson-Tunik, T. L., Commons, M., Wilson, M., & Fischer, K. W. (2005) The shape of development. *European Journal of Developmental Psychology*, 2(2): 163–195.

De Haan, E. (2021) The case against coaching. *The Coaching Psychologist*, 17(1): 7–13.

Elder Jr, G. H. & Caspi, A. (1988) Human development and social change: An emerging perspective on the life course. In *Persons in context: Developmental processes*, pp. 77–113.

Ferrari, M., & Weststrate, N. M. (2013) The scientific study of personal wisdom. In *The Scientific Study of Personal Wisdom*. Springer, Dordrecht, pp. 325–341.

Ferrari, M., Weststrate, N. M., & Petro, A. (2013) Stories of wisdom to live by: Developing wisdom in a narrative mode. In *The scientific study of personal wisdom.* Springer, Dordrecht, pp. 137–164.

Florance, I. & Watts, M. (2021) Introduction: Why are conversations emerging in coaching?. In *Emerging Conversations in Coaching and Coaching Psychology.* Abingdon: Routledge, pp. 1–7.

Glück, J. & Bluck, S. (2013) The MORE life experience model: A theory of the development of personal wisdom. In M. Ferrari & N. Westrate (Eds), *The scientific study of personal wisdom.* Dordrecht: Springer, pp. 75–97.

Glück, J. & Weststrate, N. M. (2022) The Wisdom Researchers and the Elephant: An Integrative Model of Wise Behavior. In *Personality and Social Psychology Review.*

Graeber, D. & Wengrow, D. (2021) *The dawn of everything: A new history of humanity.* London: Penguin.

Grossmann, I. (2017) Wisdom in context. *Perspectives on Psychological Science,* 12(2): 233–257.

Grossmann, I., Dorfman, A., & Oakes, H. (2020) Wisdom is a social-ecological rather than person-centric phenomenon. *Current opinion in psychology,* 32: 66–71.

Grossmann, I., Kung, F. Y. H., & Santos, H. C. (2019) Wisdom as state versus trait. In R. J. Sternberg & J. Glück (Eds), *The Cambridge handbook of wisdom.* Cambridge: Cambridge University Press, pp. 249–273.

Grossmann, I., Weststrate, N. M., Ardelt, M., Brienza, J. P., Dong, M., Ferrari, M., Fournier, M. A., Hu, C. S., Nusbaum, H. C., & Vervaeke, J. (2020) The science of wisdom in a polarized world: Knowns and unknowns. *Psychological Inquiry,* 31(2): 103–133.

Guishard, M. A., Halkovic, A., Galletta, A., & Li, P. (2018) Toward epistemological ethics: Centering communities and social justice in qualitative research. *Forum Qualitative Sozialforschung/Forum: Qualitative Social Research,* 19(3):1–24.

Hawkins, P. (2021) *Leadership team coaching: Developing collective transformational leadership,* 4th Edition. London: Kogan Page.

Hawkins, P. & Turner, E. (2020) *Systemic coaching: Delivering value beyond the individual.* Abingdon: Routledge.

Herbert, D. (2022) Our symbolic journey–heroes or heroines? In *Positive Psychology Across the Lifespan.* Abingdon: Routledge, pp. 79–93.

Hoare, C. (2011) Continuing to build a discipline at the borders of thought. In C. Hoare (Ed.), *The Oxford Handbook of Reciprocal Adult Development and Learning,* 2nd Edition. New York, NY: Oxford University Press, pp. 3–16.

Hobson, A. J. & van Nieuwerburgh, C. J. (2022) Extending the research agenda on (ethical) coaching and mentoring in education: embracing mutuality and prioritising well-being. *International Journal of Mentoring and Coaching in Education,* 11(1): 1–13.

Hofer, B. K. (2002) Personal epistemology as a psychological and educational construct: An introduction. In B. K. Hofer & P. R. Pintrich (Eds), *Personal epistemology: The psychology of beliefs about knowledge and knowing.* New York: Routledge, pp. 3–14.

Hu, C. S. & Feng, Z. (2023) Wisdom: Learning to Understand the World as it is. In Steves-Long & E.K. Kallio (Eds). *The International Handbook of Adult Development and Wisdom.* Oxford: Oxford University Press.

Hurlow, S. (2022). Revisiting the Relationship Between Coaching and Learning: The Problems and Possibilities. *Academy of Management Learning & Education,* 21(1): 121–138.

Iordanou, I., Hawley, R., & Iordanou, C. (2016) *Values and ethics in coaching.* London: Sage Publications.

Ison, R. & Schlindwein, S. L. (2006) *History repeats itself: current traps in complexity practice from a systems perspective.*

Kallio, E. K. (2020) Thinking in Adulthood. In *Development of adult thinking: Interdisciplinary perspectives on cognitive development and adult learning.* Abingdon: Routledge.

Kant, I. (2012) *Cambridge texts in the history of philosophy: Kant: Groundwork of the metaphysics of morals* (M. Gregor & J. Timmermann, Trans.), 2nd Edition. Cambridge: Cambridge University Press.

Karami, S., Ghahremani, M., Parra-Martinez, F. A., & Gentry, M. (2020) A polyhedron model of wisdom: A systematic review of the wisdom studies in psychology, management and leadership, and education. *Roeper Review*, 42(4): 241–257.

Kohlberg, L. (1994) *Moral Development: Kohlberg's original study of moral development*, 3rd Edition. Taylor & Francis.

Küpers, W. (2016) *A handbook of practical wisdom: Leadership, organization and integral business practice.* Abingdon: Routledge.

Laske, O. E. (2006) From coach training to coach education: Teaching coaching within a comprehensively evidence based framework. *International Journal of Evidence Based Coaching and Mentoring.* 4(1): 45–57.

Le, T. N. & Levenson, M. R. (2005) Wisdom as self-transcendence: What's love (& individualism) got to do with it? *Journal of Research in Personality*, 39(4): 443–457.

Lerner, R. M. (2018) *Concepts and theories of human development.* Abingdon: Routledge.

Lerner, R. M. & Overton, W. F. (2008) Exemplifying the Integrations of the Relational Developmental System: Synthesizing Theory, Research, and Application to Promote Positive Development and Social Justice. Journal of Adolescent Research, 23 (3): 245–255.

Levenson, M. R., Aldwin, C. M., & Cupertino, A. P. (2001) Transcending the self: Towards a liberative model of adult development. *Maturidade & velhice: Um enfoque multidisciplinar*: 99–116.

Levenson, M. R. & Crumpler, C. A. (1996) Three models of adult development. *Human Development*, 39(3): 135–149.

Levinson, D. J. (1978) *The seasons of a man's life.* New York: Ballantine Books, Random House, Inc.

Loevinger, J. (1966) The meaning and measurement of ego development. *American Psychologist*, 21(3): 195.

Loewenthal, D. (2014) Relational ethics: From existentialism to post-existentialism. In *Relational psychotherapy, psychoanalysis and counselling.* Abingdon: Routledge, pp. 140–151.

MacKie, D. (2021) Strength-Based Coaching and Sustainability Leadership. In *Positive Psychology Coaching in the Workplace.* Cham: Springer, pp 375–396.

Mercaldi, G. (2018) Is developmental coaching morally acceptable. *Philosophy of Coaching: An International Journal*, 3(2): 60–72.

McGilchrist, I. (2021) *The Matter with Things: Our Brains, Our Delusions, and the Unmaking of the World.* London: Perspectiva Press.

Mill, J. S. (1863) *Utilitarianism.* London: Parker, Son and Bourn.

Neugarten, B. L. (1979) Time, age, and the life cycle. *The American Journal of Psychiatry*.

Pannell, B. (2021) Adult Development and Positive Psychology Coaching. In W. A. Smith, I. Boniwell, & S. Green (Eds), *Positive Psychology Coaching in the Workplace*. Cham: Springer.

Pascual-Leone, J. (1990) 12 An essay on wisdom: toward organismic processes that make it possible. *Wisdom: Its nature, origins, and development*, p. 244.

Passmore, J. & Evans-Krimme, R. (2021) The future of coaching: a conceptual framework for the coaching sector from personal craft to scientific process and the implications for practice and research. *Frontiers in Psychology*, 12: 715228.

Rosa, H. (2020) *The uncontrollability of the world*. Cambridge: Polity.

Schermuly, C. C. & Graßmann, C. (2019) A literature review on negative effects of coaching–what we know and what we need to know. *Coaching: An International Journal of Theory, Research and Practice*, 12(1): 39–66.

Schwartz, B. & Sharpe, K (2010). *Practical wisdom: The right way to do the right thing*. New York, NY: Penguin.

Slote, M. (2010) Virtue ethics. In *The Routledge companion to ethics*. Abingdon: Routledge, pp. 504–515.

Smith, S. (2019) Wisdom as an embodied and embedded process. In *5th annual applied positive psychology symposium: Proceedings of presented papers*, pp. 26–50.

Smith, S. & Bretherton, R. (2021) Coaching Wisdom in the Workplace: Coaching from an Integrative Model of Wisdom. In W. A. Smith, I. Boniwell, & S. Green (Eds), *Positive Psychology Coaching in the Workplace*. Cham: Springer, pp. 529–553. doi:10.1007/978-3-030-79952-6_28.

Spano, S. L. (2015) Constructive-Developmental Theory and the Integrated Domains of Wisdom: Are Post-Conventional Leaders Really Wiser?. *Integral Review: A Transdisciplinary & Transcultural Journal for New Thought, Research, & Praxis*, 11(2).

Stacey, R. D. (2003) *Complexity and group processes: A radically social understanding of individuals*. Abingdon: Routledge.

Staudinger, U. M. (2020) The positive plasticity of adult development: Potential for the 21st century. *American Psychologist*, 75(4): 540.

Sternberg, R. J. (Ed.). (1990) *Wisdom: Its nature, origins, and development*. Cambridge: Cambridge University Press.

Sternberg, R. J. (1998) A balance theory of wisdom. *Review of general psychology*, 2(4): 347–365.

Sternberg, R. J. (2013) Personal wisdom in the balance. In *The scientific study of personal wisdom*. Dordrecht: Springer, pp. 53–74.

Sternberg, R. J. & Glück, J. (2021) *Wisdom: The psychology of wise thoughts, words, and deeds*. Cambridge University Press.

Sternberg, R. J. & Karami, S. (2021) What is wisdom? A unified 6P framework. *Review of General Psychology*, 25(2): 134–151.

United Nations. (n.d.) Do you know all 17 SDGs? Retrieved June 8, 2022, from https://sdgs.un.org/goals.

Vervaeke, J. & Ferraro, L. (2013) Relevance, meaning and the cognitive science of wisdom. In *The scientific study of personal wisdom*. Springer, Dordrecht, pp. 21–51.

Walsh, M. M. & Tennyson, S. (2019) Systemic Coaching Supervision: Responding to the Complex Challenges of Our Time. *Philosophy of Coaching: An International Journal*, 4(1): 107–122.

Weintrobe, S. (2021) *Psychological roots of the climate crisis: Neoliberal exceptionalism and the culture of uncare.* Bloomsbury Publishing USA.

Whybrow, A., Turner, E., McLean, J. with Hawkins, P. (2023) *Ecological and Climate-conscious Coaching: A Companion Guide to Evolving Coaching Practice.* Abingdon: Routledge.

Wilber, K. (1999) Spirituality and developmental lines: Are there stages?. *The Journal of Transpersonal Psychology*, 31(1): 1.

Yang, S. Y. (2011) Wisdom displayed through leadership: Exploring leadership-related wisdom. *The Leadership Quarterly*, 22(4): 616–632.

Chapter 19

Ethics and culture in coaching – moving beyond a universal Western ethical code

David A. Lane, Dumisani Magadlela, Ivan Yong Wei Kit and Silvina Spiegel

Ethics as an external process

Ethics has been traditionally treated within professional bodies as a matter of conformity to an externally mandated code. Yet coaching and supervision is a co-constructed process. Each team member comes with their own reflexive narrative to the encounter. Between them they formulate a new relational narrative which identifies the purpose of the work they will do together, the perspectives they bring to understand that purpose and an agreed (shared) process of working. And – increasingly the position they assume in the world – positionality - impacted by sense of self, other and culture. Why if this is a relational process, co-constructed, have we treated ethics as a process external to that relationship?

If we consider the difference between a Reflexive and Relational way of working (Lane, Kahn, & Chapman, 2019), we can see both are possible but lead to potentially different outcomes and need for alternative ways to ask ethical questions.

Reflexive narrative

- Each party has their own purpose.
- Each retains their own perspectives.
- They agree on a transactional process for working – I do this, you do that.
- They work alongside each other.
- Change is horizontal – building on existing skills.
- Each has their own moral stance to the work. Positionality remains consistent.
- They need to agree on an applicable external ethical code to cover the work they do together.

Relational narrative

- They work to agree on a joint purpose.
- They explore each other's perspectives.
- A shared process for working is developed.

DOI: 10.4324/9781003277729-19

- They work together to generate change.
- Change can be vertical – transformative.
- They can explore each other's moral stance and positionality and seek understanding.
- They can adopt a relational ethical stance agreeing what and how they will decide.

This raises questions for us – how do we make ethical decisions in coaching?

How do you currently make ethical judgements as a coach?
How might cultural context influence those judgements?

Alternative questions you might consider:

How might alternative ways of viewing ethics influence your coaching practice?
Is a universal code of ethics possible?
How do current professional codes in coaching meet or challenge such principles?
What alternatives might there be if we take culture into account (individual moral compass/ethical maturity, relational ethics)?

There are three useful ways of viewing ethical dilemmas: the external, internal, and relational. (Corrie & Lane, 2015; Gray, Garvey, & Lane, 2016).

1. *External* - Ethics as a universal set of principles which are externally mandated and with which we are required to comply.
2. *Internal* - Ethical maturity/Moral compass; that is, practitioners' internal sense of moral behaviour which includes a sensitivity to ethical dilemmas and willingness to engage with them.
3. *Relational* - Ethical issues as dilemmas arising in the context of a relationship with others where we are required to negotiate what is moral in order to arrive at a shared understanding, formulation and judgement of an appropriate course of action.

It is the relational stance that enables high performing teams to sustain change in diverse cultural contexts as it informs a moral position and enables transformation.

In this chapter we will consider different cultural contexts and how they might inform ethical decision making in coaching.

How might a spiritual model influence practice?

- Ershad meaning guidance is the Arabic term van Nieuwerburgh and Allaho (2017) use to describe the role of a guide (coach) who develops and grows the individual into his or her desired maximum capacity and degree of accomplishment against a framework of Islamic beliefs about God, self, others and the world. Ershad echo's Islamic ideals of Discovery, Intentions, Pathways and Effort. These principles are used to guide the coaching process. It asks us to align our lives with the deepest goals we find in ourselves - these are considered gifts from God.

- There are four phases to the conversation. Discovery asks the coach/coachee to reflect on self, relationships and their experiences. This enables understanding of current resources and to see their situation from different perspectives. Intention asks the coach/coachee to turn their attention to the future and to articulate very clearly their intentions. Pathways explores ways to move closer to their intentions. They are introduced to the Alignment Wheel which asks coach/coachee to assess if their pathways are aligned to their values and beliefs. In particular, they are asked how a decision might affect their relationship with their beliefs, self, life or the universe and significant others.

Brief case vignette – a clash of values

A coach was asked to work with a bank manager who was a high performer but who was now struggling to meet sales targets. The bank wanted to help him fulfil what they saw as his full potential. He was well regarded in the bank. On meeting with the client, the coach learned that this former mutual (member owned institution) had now become a shareholder-based company. Consultants working with the new senior management team had focussed attention on building customer relationships and how to sell a range of bank owned products and services. The manager was struggling with this as he was committed to a member-based framework in which he sought the best options for members. He was not comfortable selling products to customers which perhaps were not the best available for their needs. He spoke about his religious belief and felt that what was being asked of him contradicted his values and beliefs. This presented an ethical dilemma for the coach who had been asked to help him meet sales targets and for the client who was being asked to work against his beliefs.

How might an understanding of alignment help to make sense of this dilemma?

Confucius and Ethics

Relationships or more specifically the building of harmonious relationships is the tenet of the teaching of Confucius (551–479 BC); a Chinese sage, poet and philosopher who lived during the Spring and Autumn period.

His teachings, also known as *Confucianism,* forms the cultural code of East Asian countries such as China, Hong Kong, Japan, Korea and the Chinese diaspora in South East Asia.

Much of his work is captured in *The Analects of Confucius*, an anthology of his sayings, which was compiled immediately upon his death (Waley, 2000). Once, Confucius was quizzed by the ruler of the large and powerful state of Qi about the principles of good governance. His view was that good government consists in "the ruler being a ruler, the minister being a minister, the father being a father and the son being a son" (Waley, 2000, p. 77).

In other words, Confucius emphasised that for a country to prosper, importance must be placed on the 'correctness' of the social relationship. The tenet of his teachings are five basic relationships in life;

1. Ruler to subject
2. Parent to child
3. Husband to wife
4. Elder brother to younger brother
5. Friend to friend

In the above relationships, the former should accord the latter with kindness, benevolence and consideration, creating a harmonious and righteous nation. Hwang (2012) explored the mechanics of these dyadic relationship from the perspective of:

- Benevolence (仁), which refers to the closeness/distance of the relationship of the dyad
- Righteousness (義), which refers to the choice of appropriate rule for social exchange
- Propriety (禮), which dictates the proper behaviour for social interaction between the dyad.

Evidently, much importance is placed upon the role played by the individuals to ensure a congruous relationship. Being cognizant of one's role in a relationship and its corresponding mechanics, allows one to conduct oneself appropriately and to be given due consideration attached to the role.

This leads us to the principle of 'Rectification of Names' or 正名 *Zhèngming*, which alludes to the fact that, 'things in actual fact should be made to accord with the implications attached to them by names, the prerequisites for correct living and even efficient government being that all classes of society should accord to what they ought to be' (Steinkraus, 1980).

It is Confucius's belief that when one is called according to one's name, one would behave in a manner that is required of that designation, acting responsibly and to be what one ought to be. Rectifying names is a self-fulfilling prophecy.

In applying the concept of 'Rectification of Names', into modern coaching practice, it is the coach's duty to help their coachees reach their highest potential. This is well within the coaching code-of-conduct that we are familiar with today. However, there is an additional emphasis, the responsibility of the coachee to him or herself, fulfilling the demands required by the 'name' coachee.

Another strong influence of *Confucianism,* which has direct consequence to building and sustaining a harmonious relationship is the concept of 'face', especially 'giving face'.

While we are familiar with the notion of 'saving face', the concept of 'giving face' may be abstruse to the Western societal norm. Essentially, 'saving face' is an internal process, where one does his or her utmost to maintain one's self-respect, 'giving face' is an entirely external process, beyond the control of oneself.

'Giving face' is by its literal meaning, given by someone else.

In the study of Chinese 'face', Ho (1994) suggested that to study Chinese face, we must view the individual not as a unit of analysis but as 'individuals-in-relation'.

While Western society puts an emphasis on individuality in building a confident individual who is self-reliant and self-oriented; Asians especially Chinese have placed much importance on the collective good of a group or family. Thus, 'face' is much more relational and it's about how one is viewed by others and less about personal pride or ego.

An example would be for the coachee to arrive for a coaching session on time or even earlier to wait for the coach, even though the coachee is the paying client. This is neither an act of deference nor entirely an act of respect.

In reality, it is an act that allows the coach to feel self-respectable. By 'giving face', the coachee viewed the coach as an 'individual-in relation' to his or her community although none were present during the engagement. It is a tacit recognition that individuals are inexorably embedded in their social network.

Perhaps, you may now understand why Asians tend to solve problems, especially arguments, ambiguously. Ambiguity allows the individuals involved to approach the confrontation with a certain amount of liberty through 'Rectification of Names', prescribed by the nature of the relationship. Simultaneously, with the focus on building an amicable relationship, the contentious parties are able to focus on the matter at hand and not on each other.

In coaching, this would meet all three views of ethical decision making;

1. *External*: The coach and coachee abide by a universal set of ethics, conveyed at the commencement of the coaching engagement.
2. *Internal:* Both parties are accorded a certain liberty in conducting themselves, such as meeting expectations, confined by the nature of the relationship.
3. *Relational*: Both parties are committed to establishing and maintaining a 'harmonious relationship', which sets the foundation towards a transformative experience for the coachee and the coach.

Brief case vignette – a clash of expectation

At the stroke of the hour, the coach logged on to the virtual conference only to find the client (the coachee) there already, waiting for him. After exchanging some pleasantries, he begins to convey the necessary code of ethics, which will underpin the engagement to the client.

Next, to set the expectation right.

"What would be your expectation for our engagement? What would you like to achieve?" he enquired.

His client, an Asian coachee, ventured with a humble statement, "I am here to learn from you. One of the reasons as to why I selected you as my coach is your experience as a leader in a Fortune 500. I believe your experience is invaluable in my development as a leader. I am very excited to see where this will lead to in my work", he added enthusiastically.

A coach who understands Asian culture will be able to identify that the coachee has assumed a lesser role in the relationship, which is detrimental to an effective coaching outcome. The coach will also be able to reestablish the relationship hierarchy to an equal footing and prescient about its reversal throughout the engagement.

Ubuntu and Ethics

> *"If the wise elders of the village don't teach the children, the village idiots will certainly do so."*
>
> (African proverb)

This part of our chapter explores the concept of Ubuntu as it is used in ethical considerations and coaching contexts. Ubuntu is a powerful and important word in the Nguni languages found in Southern Africa. These languages include isiZulu, isiXhosa, isiNdebele, SiSwati, and several others. Ubuntu literally means *I am because we are.*

Ubuntu means that I can only be fully human when you and/or others have the opportunity to become fully who you can become. It is about valuing all of humanity collectively and not focusing on the superficial or learned differences that seek to separate. Ubuntu is what all of humanity needs in a fragmented and divisive world fuelled by heightening differences and otherness. In this way, Ubuntu is the ultimate ethical stance for all humans, starting with coaches who hold the space for human development.

Ubuntu is an expression of the culture of valuing the collective over the individual. It is the pre-eminence of the community above that of the legendary single hero. In many African and other communities around the world, life is organised along the lines of the benefit of most over the benefit of a few.

As mentioned in the introductory part of this chapter, the dance between the reflexive and relational aspects of ethics is an ongoing one. Ubuntu is inherently a relational practical guide to co-existence. It goes to the heart of ethics in coaching, neutralising most power bases to enable everyone to safely share their ethical stance without fear of judgement.

Over time, the influence of other cultures, especially Anglo-Saxon or Western models of human relationships, emphasising the individual over the community, has eroded many aspects of these ancient Ubuntu-led human connection and relational practices. Ubuntu is a global phenomenon that finds greater expression among many indigenous communities where collective interests still 'preside' over individual need.

Ubuntu has been regarded as part of cultural tenets in some societies and not others. It is a 'way of being' that is inherently 'ethical' as it places human interconnectedness and collective respect at the centre of all relationships. It is positive due regard for others upfront (until they show you that they are unethical or cannot be trusted to be mutually accountable). Ubuntu is not unique to specific cultures. It is the essence of being human. It is certainly not an African or communal society concept. It is universal.

Ubuntu is the stance of ethics

When using this approach in practice, ethical conduct is not only standard, but it is also expected of all fellow coaches and clients. It is when – as practitioner senior coaches – we model and demonstrate ethical behaviours that we trigger and ignite the same in those we interact with. When we start with these Ubuntu ways, we equip ourselves and our clients with the tools we need to live ethical lives and help others do the same.

As a critical foundational concept of humaneness and general human interconnectedness, Ubuntu is about living daily with the ethical values of interconnectedness. It is ignited from the moment we engage with others, from the first encounter. Ubuntu starts with how we come alive in conscious greetings, as opposed to the tick-box greetings in many individualistic societies or contexts that do not inspire genuine connection.

In Ubuntu-infused situations, the 'conscious greeting' starts with what in the isiZulu language is the term 'Sawubona' (Sah – woo – bo – nah). Literally, the greeting 'Sawubona' means 'I See You' (in IsiZulu language). When someone greets you and says 'Sawubona', they are acknowledging that your existence is not only important but sacred. It means that you are 'seen' as an integral part of this shared world. They are recognising your humanity and their own through you.

Greeting consciously ignites genuine connection with others. It helps us see others as they are. When we really **see** others, we cannot unsee them. Ubuntu means that I become less than I can fully be when I inadvertently contribute towards restricting you/others from becoming who you/they can fully become.

"Ubuntu is the humanistic experience of treating all people with respect, with humane dignity. It encompasses values of sharing and universal 'humane-hood', and respect for other beings. It is a belief in the sacredness of all human beings and is a life-long process..."

(Bhengu, 1996, in 'Ubuntu in Action')

Globally, the coaching profession needs ethical grounding in Ubuntu principles and values for the profession to truly earn the 'global' tag.

"Ubuntu is [a global phenomenon that is] best understood experientially" *(Magadlela, 2008, p. 1, as cited in Stout-Rostron, 2019, p. 88).*

While it is best expressed in some indigenous communities as expected and standard practice or behaviour, Ubuntu is everywhere, wherever we find human beings. It is most expressed whenever there is a dire human need such as natural disasters like fires, floods, earthquakes, or wars. The call here is to make this part of the standard operating system for all humans.

Ethical conduct is looked upon as noble and desirable. Ubuntu lays the foundation for that. Ubuntu is part of our human essence especially when we are stripped or free of the external programming and conditioning from our often-insular societies and communities. Ubuntu is part of our internal compass that expresses itself externally in our human interactions and relationships. It is part of that microchip within us that recognises right from wrong or helps us recognise what is ethical or not. We all have it unless we are clinically diagnosed as unwell at some level.

Living with Ubuntu values and being ethical as a coach are complementary qualities of being a grounded human being. It is the ultimate ethically humane thing to do for all human beings (living with Ubuntu values ethically). Coaches are at the forefront of reminding us of our humanity in our shared world, and Ubuntu is the best instrument to help transform and rehumanise our shared world. It is the ethical grounding all coaches need.

Coaching with Ubuntu values and ethics requires that we grow new mind-sets and especially new *heart-sets* that enable us to see the self in the other, and most important, to feel genuine empathy and connection with other beings. This means removing the learned or taught negative narratives, stereotypes, and stories we carry about others, and ethically let others re-present themselves authentically to us in our inevitably shared spaces. Coaches are professionally required to conduct themselves ethically, and the above sets the scene and tone for them to live these values and principles.

The ethical call to prioritise the collective over the individual

Professionals in diverse disciplines such as in research and policy making, or development practitioners and academics, among many others, tend to make the same mistake of referring to the continent of Africa as one homogenous mass. It is not. These analytical and related mistakes deepen with the gross generalisations about everything African as common to all Africa alike.

One example of the unethical and gross generalisations was the outbreak of Ebola in 2016. This saw news networks around the world impose travel bans on all of Africa when the outbreak was only in three of the 54 states. The same misguided generalisations exist in the fields of people development. When it comes to the fluid field of ethics in coaching, one of the key issues is the concept of 'ethics in African culture'.

The point here is that there is no such thing as African culture. Instead, there are multiple African cultures and sub-cultures, just like we see in other parts of the world. These cultures and sub-cultures could be as many as there are African ethnic groups. Ethnic-based cultures are fully fledged cultures.

The essence of community, infused with Ubuntu, is the embodied collective value of ethical conduct driven by collective accountability to the greater good. In a community living with Ubuntu values, ethics are everyone's first nature. The corruption of these Ubuntu values across indigenous communities around the world, especially through practices that promote individual greed and self-centredness, does not mean that these ethical practices, and the values of Ubuntu that characterise them, do not exist. It means that something more forceful takes over temporarily. It is a matter of shifting paradigms over time. There is growing momentum especially within transformational professions such as coaching, to seek out and enrol practices, values, and behaviours such as those in Ubuntu and ethics, to drive forward the momentum.

Vignette I

The human resources (HR) executive of a financial services organisation was a good friend of the same company's chief financial officer (CFO). The HR executive and the CFO often spent time in each other's offices. Away from work they would meet for lunch and family get-togethers. The friendship grew stronger until the CFO left the organisation to pursue better offers. After six months away, the CFO's new employer unexpectedly went under, and her old job was still available. Her HR executive friend alerted her to this. She applied for the old job and was rehired. One of the CFO's first requests in her role was for the company to pay for her coach that had been allocated to her in her previous job. The approval of the coaching allocation was deemed unethical by the Learning and Development Manager who reported to the HR executive. She was, however, reluctant to challenge the executive's recommendation. When the coach heard about this, she expressed discomfort with the fact that the coaching objectives that led to her matching with the CFO were not the same in her *now* new job. The HR executive argued that this was a culturally suitable recommendation to sweeten the deal for the CFO to settle back into her role.

What are the ethical dilemmas that you see in this case?

It is certainly not an Ubuntu-infused ethical scenario. Ubuntu is about collective accountability for the greater good. This clearly violates it.

Latin America: a kaleidoscope of cultures, history, colours, and flavours

The richness of Latin American culture is the product of many influences:

1. *Pre-Columbian cultures*, more vivid in some parts of the region than others, due to the different histories of colonisation in every country e.g: in Mexico, Guatemala, Ecuador, Peru, Bolivia, and Paraguay they have more influence today than in other countries like Argentina and Uruguay.

2. *Spanish and Portuguese culture*, deriving from the region's history of colonisation. Because of this, some of the core elements of Latino culture are related to Western Culture, and Christianity is the strongest religion (The Inquisition was in place in the colonies until the beginning of the 19th century, Feitler & Freston, 2016).

3. 19th- and 20th-century: due to suffering and war, there was a massive *European immigration from Spain, Portugal, Italy, Germany, France, and Eastern Europe.* This fact had a strong impact in countries such as Argentina, Uruguay, Brazil (particularly the southeast and southern regions), Colombia, Cuba, Chile, Venezuela, Paraguay, the Dominican Republic (specifically the northern region) and Mexico (particularly the southern region).

4. *Immigration of Armenian people, Arab groups (Lebanese and others), and Asian groups (Chinese, Indian, Korean, Japanese, and various others).* They were mostly immigrants and indentured labourers who arrived from the coolie trade and influenced the culture of Brazil, Colombia, Cuba, Panama, and Peru in areas such as food, art, and cultural trade.

5. *The cultures of Africa* brought by Africans slaves in the Trans-Atlantic slave trade. Influences are particularly strong in dance, music, cuisine, and some syncretic religions of Cuba, Brazil, Dominican Republic, Venezuela and coastal Colombia.

Owing to this mixture of origins, Latin America has a very rich range of colourful cultures, full of blending and contradictions (Freston & Dove, 2016), but with some common traits that can be highlighted for our purpose in the following vignette.

Vignette 2

A professional coach arrives at the headquarters of a very large company – to meet a new client, a high ranked executive.

He is greeted – 10 minutes late – by a tall man. The client shakes the coach's hand enthusiastically, taps the coach in the back and begins speaking loudly about his grandma being 'gringa' (foreign) like the coach, and the things she told him about their country. Then starts a long speech about the places that the coach should not miss while in this beautiful city, inside the most beautiful country in the world. He shows the coach from the window a huge, beautiful cathedral, not far from the office. Then, the client offers the coach something to nibble and a beverage and calls his secretary to bring everything down.

It is 15 minutes into the session and the coach wonders if where this session is going. The coach struggles. He needs to set the agreement and the boundaries of the relationship.

The coach ponders: *When and how to begin? How to enter this conversation? Is the client trying to avoid it by speaking about other things?*

Let's help the coach by understanding more of the cultural traits portrayed on this situation:

- The use of the body and a different notion of 'personal space': to greet a person - even within a formal introduction - in Latin America can reserve surprises for people from other cultures. The loud tone of voice, the hugging, embraces, kisses - one or more - or the tapping on the back is what's usual and it differs in each part of the region (even within the same country). A person from another culture has to be advised not to feel threatened and understand where all this 'familiarity' comes from.

- Latin Americans are passionate about their origins, their countries, their music, their food, their cities, their sports, their religion... and all of these become part of their cultural identity. From this point of view the neutrality, impartiality, and detachment of a coach -if not properly explained- can inspire the opposite of confidence and safe space: it can be seen as displaying coldness and/or lack of interest.

- The presence of the extended family bond throughout life. Families stick together in the majority of Latin America, they 'invite their opinion' to every matter of the life of one another, and they are taken seriously. It is fairly common that the grandparents become the primary caregivers in the life of a child, sometimes co-parenting with the actual parents. That's why in Latin America, bringing to the coaching conversations the aunt's opinion on one's career is not a rarity.

- The religious belief in most of Latin America is strong. Religion for many people is the primary source for ethical conduct and since there are many different religions in Latin America, this fact presents challenges of its own. Respecting and understanding the religious background of each client can sometimes clarify some behaviours that could otherwise be misread by the coach.

- Latin Americans are resilient, so the cheerfulness and light approach to hard topics such as losses, poverty and lack of perspectives, are culture built coping mechanisms that allow members of all these countries to live on in the midst of nature's rage (earthquakes, hurricanes and storms) but most importantly facing human tragedies (military governments or so called 'democratic' governments that - due to impunity and scandalous strategies - last for decades, and endless economic crisis). Latin American people keep on going and try to make things work with what there is, while it lasts. Creativity is a great trait of all the different cultures, and it's seen as a survival mechanism, to patch what's broken or to create new partial solutions to the same old problems -that are seen by Latin Americans as perpetual parts of the region's reality.

Ethical approaches in the Latin American context

The lack of ethical conduct from the government down, and the impunity in every part of the society gave the Latin American people a 'survival instinct'. This means that in the public eye, moral conduct can become a subjective fluid concept.

In this context, to have an external international code of ethics for example …to rely on, helps publicly reinforce the importance of the matter and brings a clear frame of reference for professional coaches, as it does for other professions as well.

To have ethical competency, to speak, learn and teach about ethics within a non-ethical context is revolutionary, and of course needs a big commitment, courage, and resilience. In Latin America those traits are abundant.

There is work to do on the creation of a reliable moral compass. Coach training schools together with the different independent professional coaching bodies, are the ones that can create a culturally appropriate method to introduce this discussion to new coaches and to the society as a whole. While the reflective approach can inform this process, the relational approach gives us the possibility to acknowledge differences, negotiate understandings, and ultimately co-create the ethical behaviours that are the sustainable foundation of our profession's evolution.

Conclusion

Cultural nuances of ethics in coaching are increasingly becoming part of a value system that is needed as the profession evolves and takes on a more global character. The relational and reflective approaches are both vital as coaching becomes an integral part of human transformation at both individual and collective levels. While the relational approach helps us address and understand the different boundaries of familiarity, and the different notions of respect, there is a need for us to make a distinction between religious beliefs, heritages, and ethical mixtures around different parts of the coaching profession. A combination of the above approaches and 'wisdoms' drawn from selected parts of the world such as the Eastern, African, Latin America and generic Western reflective approaches, can assist coaches' understanding and management of ethics in coaching. As coaching evolves and grows around the world, it must remain – become more – open to incorporating and learning from ancient and new approaches. Ethics are the foundation to respect, by acknowledgement and appreciation other ways of being. Ethics that encompasses the internal and relational framework must be brought forth to enable sustained change in diverse cultural and spiritual contexts such as East, Africa, Latin America and generic Western reflexive approaches should be deployed to inform ethical practices in coaching. Henceforth, ethics informed by culture, must be embedded first as a personal reflexive narrative of the coach and coachee in parallel to define the relational narrative of the co-constructed coaching process.

Discussion points

1. How could understanding your coachee's cultural background and that of your own help to create a transformative coaching experience for your coachee?
2. How might exploring ethics from external, internal and relational perspectives inform the way you contract for coaching?
3. What can you do to recognize your client's cultural background?
4. How would this exploration broaden your ethical possibilities to support your client?

Recommended reading

Stout-Rostron, S. (Ed.) (2019) *Transformational Coaching to Lead Culturally Diverse Teams*. Abingdon: Routledge Focus.

References

Bhengu, M. J. (1996) *Ubuntu: The Essence of Democracy*. Novalis Press.
Corrie, S. & Lane, D. A. (2016) *CBT Supervision*. London: Sage Publications.
Feitler, B., & Freston, R. (2016). The Inquisition in the New World. In V. Garrard-Burnett, P. Freston, & S. Dove (Eds), *The Cambridge History of Religions in Latin America*. Cambridge: Cambridge University Press, pp. 133–142. doi:10.1017/CHO9781139032698.009.

Chang, Y. Y. (2008). Cultural "Faces" of Interpersonal Communication in the U.S. and China. *Intercultural Communication Studies*, 17(1).

Cheng, S. K. K. (1990) Understanding The Culture and Behaviour of East Asians – A Confucian Perspective. *Australian and New Zealand Journal of Psychiatry*, 24(4): 510–515, doi:10.3109/00048679009062907.

Gray, D. E., Garvey, B., & Lane, D. A. (2016) *A Critical Introduction to Coaching and Mentoring*. London: Sage Publications.

Ho, D. Y. (1994). Face dynamics: From conceptualization to measurement. In S. Ting-Toomey (Ed.), *The challenge of facework: Cross-cultural and interpersonal issues*. Albany, NY: SUNY Press, pp. 269–286.

Hwang, K. K. (2012). Face and Morality in Confucian Society. In: Foundations of Chinese Psychology. In *International and Cultural Psychology*, Vol 1. New York, NY: Springer. doi:10.1007/978-1-4614-1439-1_10.

Iordanou, I., Hawley, R., & Iordanou, C. (2017). *Values and Ethics in Coaching*. London and Thousand Oaks, CA: Sage Publications.

Lane, D. A., Kahn, S., & Chapman, L. (2019) Adult learning as an approach to coaching. In S. Palmer & A. Whybrow (Eds), *Handbook of Coaching Psychology A Guide for Practitioners*, 2nd Edition. Abingdon: Routledge.

Lane, D. A., Watts, M., & Corrie, S. (2016) *Supervision in the Psychological Professions Building your own personalised model*. London: Open University Press.

Steinkraus, W. E. (1980) *Socrates*, Confucius, and the Rectification of Names. In *Philosophy East and West*, Vol. 30, No. 2. Hawaii: University of Hawai'i Press, pp. 261–264.

Tai M. C. & Lin, C. S. (2001) Developing a culturally relevant bioethics for Asian people. *Journal of Medical Ethics*, 27: 51–54.

Waley, A. (2000) *The Analects of Confucius*. London: Everyman's Library.

Chapter 20

Race: Ethical perspectives on equity-based coaching

Terrence E. Maltbia and David Matthew Prior

Introduction

A core principle of professional coaching is the importance of creating egalitarian relationships with the people we coach. Yet, three concurrent challenges (i.e., disruptions to global economic systems; civil and racial unrest triggered by the very public murder of an unarmed Black Man, George Floyd, at the hands of a police officer; and rising rates of remote/hybrid work arrangements) emerged during the COVID-19 outbreak served to amplify a cold hard truth, existing for decades, if not centuries; that is, we cannot realize social justice without addressing injustice; the need for antiracism is rooted in racism; and true equity is achieved only by dismantling the very systems that sustain inequity.

Facing a renewed emphasis on social justice, organizations are increasingly turning to external coaching engagements to focus on diversity, equity, inclusion, and belonging – DEIB (Abel et al., 2021). This integration of professional coaching with DEIB raises questions such as: *Is the coaching professional immune from the broader dynamics of bias and power dynamics? What evidence exists that the coaching profession is preparing coaches to address these dynamics? What is our commitment to engage in coaching for equity? How can ethical perspectives contribute to coaches, coach educators, and accrediting bodies who engage in the work of coaching that attends to the role of race?*

Context awareness – the origins of equity-based coaching

A comprehensive exploration of the meaning of *professional coaching* (e.g., Brock, 2014), *coaching education-training* (e.g., Stein, Page, & Maltbia, 2014), and *credentialing bodies* (e.g., Maltbia, Marsick, & Ghosh, 2014) is beyond the scope of this chapter. While an equity-based orientation can apply to a range of specializations, this chapter assumes a focus on *executive* (i.e., leaders) and *organizational* (i.e., work context) coaching, which is defined as "a development process that builds a leader's capabilities to achieve

DOI: 10.4324/9781003277729-20

professional and organizational goals" (Maltbia & Page, 2013, p. 2). The emphasis of this form of coaching is on leaders who can make significant contributions to the mission and purpose of their organizations.

The story of race in professional coaching is being written. The good news is coaching can benefit from literature, research, and experiences of allied helping professions (e.g., cross-cultural communications, counseling, social work, and therapy) where race has been a more constant feature of discourse, including practice guidelines grounded in race-identity theory. Beginning in 2020, conversations on race in coaching started to emerge (Maltbia, 2021a, b, c). In addition, a study conducted by Roche and Passmore (2021) suggest the industry is in the early stages of the equity-based coaching journey by noting: a) artifacts of professional coaching associations largely ignore race (e.g., membership applications, coaching competency frameworks, and training accreditation guidelines/requirements), yet include other demographics such as gender, age, language, and country of residence; b) few explicit explorations of the role of race in coaching appear in coach-specific literature and research; and c) "the coaching literature largely ignores the power dynamics" inherent in cross-race interactions (p. 7). This section examines several concepts central to understanding the emerging practice of equity-based coaching.

Brief history of the concept of race – a core dimension of diversity, equity, inclusion, and belonging

Understanding the role of race in coaching requires a level of conceptual clarity regarding the meaning of race, and related concepts. From literal definitions found in Webster (2001) we learn that race is "a group of persons related by common descent, or heredity; traditional divisions of human-kind, the commonest being the Caucasian, Mongoloid, and Negro" based on combinations of supposedly distinctive and universal physical characteristics such as "skin color, facial form, eye shape or color, hair texture" (p. 1590). Geneticist J. Craig Venter and his team, established that all human beings are 99.9 percent the same, thus providing scientific evidence that race is not a biological concept (Naomi, 2002). Yet, race is a social construction that gives, and denies, benefits and privileges to groups of people based on race, and other, categorization systems.

The notion of race became embedded in the formation of American society to justify what emerged as a new, capitalistic economic system, which depended on the institution of forced labor (especially the enslavement of Africans). Understanding how race and racism are endemic in modern society, requires an exploration of the history of how race, white privilege, and anti-blackness emerged. More broadly, institutional racism and systemic bias rests on the human impulse to create hierarchies, i.e., in-groups, like-us, on top; out-groups, not like us, on the bottom (Schwabish & Feng, 2021; Sue, 2015).

Isabel Wilkerson (2020) makes important distinctions between *racism* and *casteism*, given the ubiquitous application of these systems in nations around the developed world. Specifically, she notes racism reflects "any action or institution that mocks, harms, assumes, or attaches inferiority or stereotype on the basis of the social construct of race," while casteism reflects "any action or structure that seeks to limit, hold back, or put someone in a defined ranking, seeks to keep someone in their place by elevating or denigrating that person on the basis of their perceived category" (p. 70). Both ideas represent major challenges to realizing the ideals of equality and equity embedded the dynamic tension between a yearning for fairness and a desire to control one's environment.

What is the connection between: (1) the role of race in coaching and (2) diversity, equity, inclusion, and belonging? Racism is one of many 'isms' that exist in organizations and society, along with ageism, sexism, and other forms of discrimination. The field of diversity, as it is known today in the United States, is an outgrowth of various social movements during the 1950s and 1960s, that resulted in legal remedies embedded in Civil Rights Acts legislation of the 1960s and beyond, along with the advent of the Equal Employment Opportunity Commission and Affirmative Action. The Hudson Institute's landmark study 'Workforce 2000', and its sequel, 'Workforce 2020', officially put workplace diversity on the strategic agenda of many organizations, with data predicting major demographic shifts (Judy & D'Amico, 1997). DEIB work in global corporations has led change agents to believe that "every country has dominant and subordinate groups" (e.g., Anand, 2022). These power structures reflect a history of exclusion, various forms of discrimination, along with a web of attitudes, and systems that serve to justify marginalization.

There is confusion about what constitutes diversity. *Diversity* simply means heterogeneity, or the advent of people who were previously excluded, in the context of the workplace (i.e., diversity is a descriptive concept). Human diversity reflects various social identity markers from *primary dimensions* (e.g., race, ethnicity, gender, and so on; mainly inborn); *experience-based dimensions* (e.g., geographic location, religion, and education); and *organizational* (e.g., line or staff, headquarters or field location, union, or non-union employee). Diversity work lacks conceptual clarity without the use of modifiers such as understanding diversity, valuing diversity, managing diversity, and leveraging diversity (Maltbia, 2001).

The work of diversity is often combined with *inclusion* [i.e., basic human needs that people experience in their interpersonal relationships, to be treated fairly and respectfully, despite differences – behavioral focus]; *equity* [i.e., create fairness by providing people with individualized resources, treatment, and support to compensate for differences between individuals – outcome focused]; and *belonging* [i.e., centers around the experience of feeling accepted, valued, and engaged – relational focused] (Brown, 2019; Morukian,

2022). These ideas align with three basic human needs of belonging, mastery, and autonomy (Ryan & Deci, 2018). Thus, the role of race in coaching is one of many dimensions of diversity that can emerge during coaching engagements linked to a client's identity.

Antiracism, social justice, and power dynamics

New York Times Bestselling Author Ibram X. Kendi (2019) makes important distinctions between the definition of 'racist' (i.e., "one who is supporting a racist policy through their actions or inaction or expressing a racist idea" p. 13) and 'antiracist' (i.e., "one who is supporting an antiracist policy through their actions or expression of an antiracist idea" p. 13). At its core, the primary aim of antiracism work is an effort to ameliorate racism. Thus, racism and antiracism are two sides of the same coin, suggesting that the work of racially focused, equity-based coaching, education, and accreditation policy, must be framed as such. We either make a proactive choice to be antiracist, or we may reactively be racist even if that is not our conscious intention. For many, it is easier to frame the work as antiracism vs. addressing racism. But doing so is a form of a denial of reality that will suboptimize our well-intended efforts.

Similarly, realizing the ideal of social justice requires a clear focus on addressing injustices wherever they exist. Rising the level of race-based equity within the coaching profession requires both coaches and educators, intentionally identify and address various forms of oppression endemic within the spaces (i.e., communities, workplaces, schools) where we meet coachees and learners. Also, leaders of professional associations, who have the power to define and enforce the standards for the entire industry, must also go beyond a starting point of antiracists statements. The call to action for coaching leaders is to conduct an equity audit of the very systems created by the profession itself (e.g., coaching competencies, accreditation protocols, and certification requirements). The reality is that none of these systems are cultural or power neutral. Kendi's distinctions highlight the importance of acknowledging comprehensive antiracism work has individual and systemic dimensions.

A starting point for taking an equity-based coaching orientation is accepting the normality of bias. To protect our core identity as being 'good people,' many of us deny the existence of bias and its key manifestations, racism, and racist behavior. This often follows predictable scripts such as: 'I'm not a racist' or 'Some of my best friends are Black' or the ever famous 'I don't see color,' to name a few. Research reveals, by as early as nine months, infants are better able to tell two 'own race' faces apart from two 'other' race faces, implanting the in-group (us/me) and out-group (them/they) dynamics deep in our brains. It is natural to trust the familiar, i.e., like me, and distrust the unfamiliar, i.e., not like me (Kelly et al., 2007). Drawing on similarity attraction theory, we know early in the identity formation process people form an attraction to the familiar that include skin color and the sounds of voices (Osbeck et al., 1997). Given that bias exists and plays a very real role in the way we see, experience, and act in the world, with over 100 types of cognitive bias (explicit and implicit), denying their existence is simply not realistic if one is committed to engaging in the work of diversity, equity, and inclusion (Johnson & Stoddart, 2019). This is an invitation, if not a clarion call, to include these components in one's professional coaching and coaching education approaches.

Contrary to popular belief, bias and racism exists in the coaching profession; it is NOT generally the blatant form that many associate with racism. Yet it does exist. They can be a more challenging, unconscious form, that are expressed and experienced as *microaggressions* (i.e., "relatively small slights and possess minimal harmful impact; are unintentional acts outside the level of conscious awareness; and do not include overt displays of bigotry" p. 7) and *macroaggressions* (i.e., "the active manifestation of systemic or institutional biases that reside in the philosophy, policies, programs, practices and structures" p. 9) (Sue et al., 2021).

A growing body of research is starting to make visible, what has been invisible for decades in the professional coaching industry, including coach education. For example, Ariel Finch Bernstein's (2019) dissertation research entitled, 'Race Matters in Coaching: An Examination of Coaches' Willingness to Have Difficult Conversations with Leaders of Color' examined coaches' willingness to have 'difficult conversations' with Black clients compared to White Clients. This study revealed several important findings regarding the impact of bias and race in coaching:

- Black clients received more support, yet less challenge, less constructive feedback, and less time devoted to areas of development than did otherwise identical White clients.
- Coaches were also twice as likely to provide diversity-related feedback to White executives than they were to Black executives.
- Coaches assigned to Black clients chose to sidestep conversations about diversity and development, resulting in missed development opportunities for these clients, one of the aims of such coaching.

Bernstein's sample of 129 coaches was drawn from a population of those who had completed some of the most recognized coaching programs, and many of them were credentialed professional coaches, yet this study clearly revealed that, at the very least, unconscious bias DOES exist in professional coaching, and it will take more than 'Antiracism Statements' to address the current situation.

Understanding the role of race in coaching demands an honest examination of Suarez's (2018) four levels where racism operates, a necessary condition for developing the mindsets, policies, and practices needed to facilitate the progress toward race equity in coaching. The descriptions of these levels are (p. 2):

- *Personal* – Private beliefs, prejudices, and ideas that individuals have about the superiority of whites and the inferiority of people of color.
- *Interpersonal* – The expression of racism between individuals. It occurs when individuals interact, and their private beliefs affect their interactions.
- *Institutional* – Discriminatory treatment, unfair policies and practices, inequitable opportunities and impacts within organizations and institutions, based on race, that routinely produce racially inequitable outcomes for people of color and advantages for white people. Individuals within institutions take on the power of the institution when they reinforce racial inequities.
- *Structural* – A system in which public policies, institutional practices, cultural representations, and other norms work in various, often reinforcing, ways to perpetuate racial group inequality. It involves the cumulative and compounding effects of an array of societal factors including the history, culture, ideology, and interactions of institutions and policies that systematically privilege white people and disadvantage people of color.

The implications of levels of racism suggests that equity-based coaching must go beyond awareness of individual bias (implicit or explicit), to include a focus on the very systems that drive behavior within the organization, in short, equity-based coaching attends to individuals embedded in systems.

Key distinctions: equality and equity

Understanding the subtle, yet critical distinction between, *equality* and *equity* is essential to the work of equity-based coaching. This distinction is found in a range of academic disciplines including psychology, counseling, cross-cultural studies, inclusive and educational leadership. *Equality* means to "create fairness by providing everyone with the same resources, treatment, and support, regardless of the differences between individuals that may influence what they need to thrive;" while *equity* is to "create fairness by providing people with individualized resources, treatment, and support to compensate for differences between individuals" (Brown 2019, p. 128). Equity acknowledges the privilege afforded to certain individuals and attempts to level the playing field. Notice, the former aligns with the so-called 'golden rule' (i.e., principle of treating others as one wants to be treated, embedded in ethnocentric assumptions), while the later aligns with the 'platinum rule' (i.e., treat others the way they want to be treated), rooted in ethnorelative assumptions and reflect a subtle yet powerful shift away from false consensus (Bennett, 2004).

Equity-based coaching acknowledges race as an essential identity marker, especially for clients who belong to marginalized groups. This form of coaching intentionally integrates identity development with topics clients bring to engagements by providing a space for them to understand themselves (and others) better, surface, shift, and/or expand beliefs, to build new capabilities needed to achieve professional and organizational goals in the context of an increasingly diverse world.

Conceptual clarity – Distinctive ethical features of equity-based coaching

With this chapter's focus on the emerging practice of equity-based coaching (with an emphasis on race), it is important for the reader to simplify foundational ethical frameworks through considerations and questions that advance the process of initial inquiry (i.e., learner-informed) towards emergent and organic advocacy (i.e., developing agency to act). The word, 'ethics' stands for a branch of philosophy, namely moral philosophy, or philosophical thinking about morality and its problems (Frankena & Granrose, 1974). In linking this to equity-based coaching, thereby involving social justice and what is morally right or wrong related to the broader dynamics of bias and power dynamics, the ethical constructs of social and institutional systems come into play beyond what any one individual considers to be the 'right' stance (i.e., mindset) and action (i.e., behavior).

On a collective level, coaching codes of ethics often include definitions, frameworks and behaviors that encompass the principles of autonomy, guided choice, and reflection. One working definition of ethics that supports equity-based coaching explains that "ethics has had but one meaning: it is the reflective study of what is good and bad in that part of human conduct for which a man has some personal responsibility" (Bourke, 2020, p. ii). One of the key principles in professional coaching that distinguishes it from the associated fields of counseling, mentoring, and consulting, are the notions of awareness and personal responsibility, and that each of us, working within different levels of systems (i.e., individual, interpersonal, family, team, organization, country, world) is responsible for the choices we make and the decisions that we take.

One way to examine our responsibility in equity-based coaching is to tap into the ethical 'school of thought' that guides choices and decisions through the lens of *character* (i.e., virtue ethics), *duty* (i.e., deontological ethics), and *outcome* (i.e., teleological ethics). When we consider the sensitivities to raise and address bias and racism in the coaching profession, how do we respond as it relates to be 'able', our capacity to respond (i.e., response-ability) when we are confronted with microaggressions and macroaggressions? From the lens of virtue ethics, what underpins the character traits of the agent's (i.e., the individual actor – in this specific case, the actor being 'the coach') orientation? For virtue theorists, the primary goal object of moral evaluation is not the intentional act or its consequences, but the agent (Louden, 1986). Raising this to the level of institutions, a deontological approach could be a useful inquiry as a departure point. Deontological theories stress the presence of universal ethical principles that need to be followed irrespective of the outcome (Baumane-Vitrolina, Calis & Sumilo, 2015).

On the broader level of society, what are the intended and emergent positive outcomes of establishing equity-based coaching in curriculums, codes of conduct and field-based practice? The teleological perspective holds that an act is morally right if it produces a greater level of good over evil than any alternative act and it is morally wrong if it does the opposite (Banlahcene, Ismail, & Zainuddin, 2018). An additional ethical frame might include a values-based ethics examination (i.e., awareness) and approach (i.e., action) when examining the four levels of racism described earlier in the chapter by Suarez (2018). In research by the original Institute of Global Ethics, founded by the late Rushworth Kidder, they asked individuals from around the world to comment on the most important values for them or their culture, and the same five came up consistently: honesty, respect, fairness, responsibility, and compassion. How do coaching practitioners sponsor a values-driven approach to both inform and guide the establishment of equity-based coaching within their social structures?

Finally, Kitson and Campbell 1996 study suggests four ways to build ethical climates within organizations: 1) conduct an ethics audit; 2) create public and accessible codes/frameworks of Ethics and Conduct to which all staff are made aware (i.e., aligns with emerging inclusive leadership behaviors used in organizations); 3) create structures that support ethical behavior at all levels of the organization and involve accountability and responsibility; and 4) unethical behavior is dealt with promptly and clearly according to guidelines. These ideas suggest an ethical challenge for the coaching profession: *How might we consistently initiate a global equity-coaching based audit, within and across the broader structures of our coaching institutions, whose findings and recommendations might spawn new standards of conduct for assimilation within already extant ethical codes?*

Informed action – Equity-based coaching: from theory to practice!

The ethical codes for various coaching associations include a provision that members have the qualifications, skills, and other personal attributes needed to meet client needs and operate within the limits of their capabilities. *What are the requirements to be ethically engaged in equity-based coaching, including attending to race explicitly and directly as a core dimension of one's identity?* This question can be approached from multiple perspectives including, requirements for professional coaches, coaching educators, and professional coaching association leaders.

Professional coaches

The journey toward becoming an equity-based coach with the capacity to engage in race talk with clients starts with 'self-work' – a developmental process characterized by going from the coach's comfort zone to the: *fear zone* (i.e., deny racism is a problem to be attended to in coaching unless the client brings it up; avoid the hard, race-based questions; strive to be comfortable - including wanting to make the client feel comfortable; work with clients who look and think like you), *learning zone* (i.e., recognize when race and racism is present and embedded in the topics bring to coaching; be willing to ask race-based questions in the face of discomfort; understand one's own privilege in ignoring race and racism, and invite clients to do the same; commit to ongoing learning about race and racism; vulnerable in surfacing bias and knowledge gaps; intentionally seeks clients who look and think differently than you), and *growth zone* (i.e., identify how one unknowingly benefits from racism; promote and advocate for antiracist policies and practices; show willingness to sit with race-based discomfort; educate peers on how racism harms the coaching profession; don't let mistakes deter one from getting better; surround self with others who look and think differently).

Examples of race-based questions include:
How do you describe your racial identity? How does it show up in your life (work, school, community, etc.)?

What is your experience of being one of a few Black male executives in this company?

What role, if any, does your racial identity, play in what you seek from our coaching engagement?

When were you first aware of your race, and its impact, working here (i.e., What was the situation? Your intentions? Intentions of Others? What actions did you/others take? What was the outcome/impact of those actions?)?

What do you remember from your childhood about how you made sense of human differences (explore 'high-points' – 'low points' – 'key learning')?

In the second example, 'Black' can be replaced with the person's racial identity, race can also be explored with gender, e.g., 'Black Female,' adding intersectionality to the conversation.

The developmental path outlined above represents an ethical dilemma for most coaches. For White coaches this can involve reconciling a core identity is rooted in the legacy of White Supremacy (i.e., a social and political system designed for a small group of people to amass a lot of wealth and related power over others) and Colonization (Aguilar, 2020). Learning this history can be difficult, yet necessary to move beyond default reactions of fear of appearing racist, along with feelings of guilt, shame, regret, anxiety, anger, helplessness, avoidance, denial, and deflection when encountering race talk in coaching, especially with racially different clients and colleagues. Facing this legacy disrupts one's sense of being a 'good person' by realizing one's own racism and confronting White privilege embedded in social systems, including coaching.

Race talk is difficult for Black coaches as well, yet for different reasons. Black people are conditioned to be hypersensitive to the need to speak and act in ways that avoid White people feeling uncomfortable, because doing so comes with a range of consequences including being constrained or silenced, or accused of being aggressive or militant, and consequently deprived from future interactions (exclusion). Race talk for Black coaches risks feelings of humiliation and loss of integrity. A major emotional barrier for Black coaches is dealing with racial stigma, racial microaggressions, and stereotype threat (Avery, 2021). The reality is the competencies and other requirements for being credentialed as a professional coach was created by, and for White people, a fact not lost on Black coaches, for whom the coaching profession is a microcosm of a society characterized by White privilege. How do we know this? Building on Vikki Brock (2014), and others who write about the history of professional coaching, one can examine the racial identities of the founders of this field by reviewing their biographies.

In addition to standard cannons of professional coaching preparation programs, the learning agenda for equity-based coaching includes:

1. Knowledge of racism and white supremacy, identity formation and development (e.g., Wilkerson, 2020);
2. Examination of one's own bias (i.e., a great resource is the 'Project Implicit' website for a range of free Implicit Associate Test from race to sexuality);
3. Commitment to interrupt inequities, with a deep sense of purpose and commitment to social justice, courage, and on one's own practice (Sue et al., 2021);
4. Ongoing development of cultural competence with an emphasis on understanding identity markers, power dynamics through the lens of identity and social oppression, ability to navigate racial differences in coaching relationships, ongoing direct contact with people with identity markers different from one's own (e.g., Aguila, 2020); and
5. Emotional Intelligence and Leadership, given strong feelings triggered by race talk and equity-based coaching (e.g., Goleman et al., 2002).

Coaching educators and trainers

A disorienting dilemma for educators and trainers in the coaching field is a commitment to honoring the cannons of the profession, while creating learning climates that work for all participants. It is important to acknowledge that these cannons were developed by a relatively homogenous group of individuals who were largely American and White, resulting in a set of standards (i.e., ethical codes, competency models, and credentialing systems) that reflect their worldview of what constitutes effective professional practice in coaching. An unintended consequence is that these taken-for-granted credentialing systems have the potential for including unconscious, systematic bias. These systems inform coaching education and training programs around the world, with increasingly racially and ethnically diverse students.

Against the backdrop outlined above, coaching educators and trainers run the risk of facilitating programs that commit subtle forms of curriculum violence and racial trauma – the result of classroom content and pedagogy that harms students intellectually and emotionally (Venet, 2021). This idea may seem extreme to well-meaning educators and trainers, however when students engage in learning experiences that serve to ignore or displace one's core racial identity, this can trigger stress. Teachers often want learning to be fun, engaging, safe, with hands-on activities. Yet, in a society in which White people are often socialized to believe that it's impolite to talk about race, it is not surprising that race has not been explicitly addressed in the industry's cannons. Such omissions serve to render the topic of race unimportant, and inappropriate, sending an unspoken message that addressing hard histories do not have a place in coaching.

While the problem of curriculum violence is systemic, while coaching educators and trainers can take personal responsibility for ensuring they develop equity literacy - to see our work as an ongoing learning process that involves continuous cycles of: a) learning to recognize inequities in credentialing systems and related curriculum; b) naming and challenging inequities; and c) working to change inequities (including understanding why various inequities exist that generally requires thinking critically about the origins and related histories of taken-for-granted cannons). As coaching educators and trainers, what role(s) are you playing in the context of equity-based coaching (with a focus on race):

a) *Offenders* (i.e., individuals who enact microaggressions, everyday slights, insults, putdowns, invalidations, and other offensive behaviors toward members of racial minorities);
b) *Targets* (i.e., microaggressions experienced by racial minorities that results in a hostile and invalidating societal climate in life spaces including employment, education, and healthcare);
c) *Allies* (i.e., a member of a different racial group who works to end a form of discrimination, bias, or racism, for a particular individual or group); and/or
d) *Bystanders* (i.e., individuals who passively observe microaggressions). Clear Point: Coaching for Equity is Not a Spectator Sport!

There is a growing range of resources for coaching educators, trainers, and researchers, and to develop equity literacy, for example:

- *Racism without Racists* (Bonilla-Silva, 2017 – resource for placing race in an historical contexts)
- *Micro intervention Strategies* (Sue et al., 2021 – resource for learning to disarm and dismantle individual racism and bias
- *Diversity and Inclusion for Coach Trainers and Educators* (Davis & McMillan, 2021 – resource for definitions of key terms/concepts and curriculum suggestions).

What are the ethical implications coaching educators and trainers developing, or not developing, equity literacy? In a world characterized by increased diversity, equity literacy is needed to meet the needs of marginalized populations and ensure academic and behavioral success of all learners.

Professional coaching associations

The ethical challenge for leaders of professional coaching associations has to do with taking personal responsibility for their organization's willingness to both acknowledge and address systemic racism that may be grounded in the origins of the organization that continues to influence the culture of the organization, and by extension to the field of coaching. A study (Roche & Passmore, 2021, p. 17) revealed "a gap in perception between the professional bodies and the coaches", based on interviews with CEOs and the presidents of four well established associations in the coaching industry with respect to racial equity. Many of these leaders reject any claims that racism, or racist behavior exists in their organizations or related credentialing processes, yet, there is little evidence that these associations have engaged in a critical examination of potential *disparate impact* (i.e., unintentional discrimination or inequity that results from organizational systems, policies, and/or practices, e.g., membership of Black coaches well below population statistics) or disparate treatment (i.e., intentional discrimination) within the coaching profession, which seems highly unlikely given the omnipresence of racial tensions and dynamics around the world. The current focus appears to be making antiracist statements, including non-discrimination language in codes of ethics, and the recent inclusion of attending to 'identity' in coaching competency models.

What appears absent are examples collecting race data as part of membership applications or as part of demographic data collected as segment of association-sponsored studies and research. These authors have not been able to identify any association in the coaching space that has conducted equity systems analysis work (for membership or credentialing systems). An early step for professional associations would be to start collecting race data along with other demographic data commonly collected as part of membership application and survey research. A review of the websites of the four associations included in the Roche & Passmore study, along with a review of various published research reports, shows they routinely collect data on other identity markers such as gender, age, nationality, educational attainment, years in coaching, number of clients, and so on, yet, race data is consistently absent. Without collecting race data, the field of coaching will remain blind to potential systemic bias or disparate impact regarding racial inequities, and lag other professions (e.g., psychology, therapy, and counseling) in effectively responding to the global social movement for antiracism.

The adage 'no metrics means no movement' lives true for equity-based coaching, or racial inequities more generally. Given the role professional coaching associations play in the industry, the efforts of individual coaches and coach education/training organizations will be sub-optimized without leadership engaging in data collection and equity-focused analytical work aimed at identifying and rooting out systemic bias. What are the ethical implications for not doing so? Suggested resources for furthering the conversation at the systemic level of the coaching industry include: 1) *Microintervention Strategies* (Sue et al., 2021; specifically, chapters concentrating on Barriers to Combating Macroaggressions; Becoming Aware of the Harmful Impact of Macroaggressions; Challenging Macroaggressions; Strategies and Tactics to Disarm Macroaggressions; Fighting Macroaggressions); and 2) *Inclusalytics* (Mattingly, 2022; resource for building accountability systems grounded in metrics and data collection).

Vignette – Multi-rater feedback debrief coaching

In this example, a White Female Coach is part of a cadre of external coaches secured to plan and conduct one-hour multi-rater, developmental feedback review sessions with four to five leaders assigned to them. She has 10 years of experience working with leaders in a range of industries since completing training and her professional coach credential. The coaching is part of a comprehensive leadership development program for high potentials employed by a Fortune 500 Global Entertainment Company headquartered in the United States. Coaches attend an orientation with program sponsors where they learn about the curriculum, along with clarifying the major aim of the feedback review sessions which is to focus on helping leaders make sense of their results as input to creating a development plan to amplify their strengths and address areas of improvement.

While specifics of each coaching conversation are confidential, program sponsors collect a range of anonymous survey data from each coach about their impressions of assigned clients based on his/her professional profile (i.e., workback and position description), 360 results, and to indicate general strategies for each coaching client (i.e., positive/supportive and/or constructive/challenging feedback). These data are collected to identify strengths and developmental priorities for each cohort of high potentials as input to the company's talent strategy. Each leader meets with their manager prior to the program to identify personal learning objectives, select raters (i.e., direct reports, peers, clients, customers, and superiors) and is expected to have a follow-up conversation with their manager after the program (while the employee decides whether to share the actual feedback report). Each leader also submits a development plan to the sponsors at the end of the program based on their personal learning objectives, what they learned from the program, including their individual coaching sessions.

The coach in this case was assigned five leaders (i.e., two White Females, two White Men, and one Black Male; all are in their 30s operating at the Director level and have worked for the company for five to ten years). She reviewed the profiles and multi-rater feedback results for each prior to: a) preparing for each session; and b) submitting the required surveys to program sponsors. The feedback reports included results on the company's ten leadership competencies and related behaviors (i.e., Client Focus; Decision Making; Change Leadership; Inclusive Leadership; Strategic Leadership; Managing Others; High-Impact Leadership; Self Development; Innovation; and Teamwork), based on a 10-point frequency scale, with '1' low demonstration and '10' high demonstration of a given behavior. The reports also include verbatim comments noting strengths, improvement areas, and suggestions from each rater group. All coaching sessions were delivered via Zoom using web cams and audio.

After completing her five sessions, the coach received the survey results from the five clients she coached. The feedback indicated that all clients were pleased with the coaching and found the session useful in making sense of their multi-rater feedback as input to their individual development plans. However, as the program sponsors reviewed the cumulative multi-rater feedback results for the cohort, they noticed the following trends: a) Inclusive Leadership was the lowest of ten leadership behaviors (average of 4.6 out of 10 with a range of 1.5 to 6) this was concerning given the company's commitment to diversity; b) none of the 'Black' leaders with low scores for 'inclusive leadership' addressed this factor; while a majority of 'White' leaders with low scores in that area identified actions for addressing this leadership behavior; and (c) while the sponsors did not have specific information on whether coaches addressed the low inclusive leadership scores with Black and White leaders, the pattern in the development plans raised questions about the comfort level of exploring diversity and race with Black leaders.

This vignette illustrates several ethical questions associated with equity-based coaching. Organizations increasingly integrate coaching with broader talent development strategies and other initiatives (including diversity, equity, inclusion, and belonging). In this case, the coach needs to contract with both the program sponsors and the individual leaders - challenging the coaching profession's desire for absolute confidentiality. The more systemic nature of equity-based coaching challenges the belief to focus solely on the 'coachee's agenda'. Clearly, coaches working with clients of color face several predicaments.

Consider the following questions:

In this case, is it ethical for the coach not to challenge clients who do not bring up low 'inclusive leadership' multi-rater scores?

How does one convey criticism in a way that inspires rather than stifles motivation? What might be unintended consequences of a coach not challenging 'Black' leaders with low 'inclusive leadership' scores as often as 'White' leaders?

The absence of 'Black' leaders with low inclusive leadership scores having actions in the required development plans compared to their 'White' counterparts, raises questions about whether coaches chose to sidestep conversations about diversity and other constructive development feedback with Black clients. Research conducted by the sponsors in the case revealed that 'Black' leaders were less likely to get direct, constructive feedback from their supervisors and mentors (compared to 'White' leaders), which negatively impacts career advancement; it appears that professional coaches may contribute to this phenomenon.

Conclusion

This chapter explores a big topic: equity-based coaching with a focus on race! It is a challenge that society has struggled with for centuries, so it is unrealistic to think a chapter can resolve the issue for the coaching profession. Instead, the aim of this chapter served to place the issue in a broader social context; provide a level of conceptual clarity of the major components of equity-based coaching; share resources to continue one's developmental path toward develop a capacity for equity-based coaching; and importantly, position equity-based coaching, including race talk, as a core ethical concern that requires the industry's attention.

Discussion points

1. **An Invitation for Coaches**: Complete an 'Association Mapping' activity by profiling the clients you are currently coaching (or have coached in the past 5 years) along the dimensions of race, ethnicity, gender, and age. What patterns and themes do you notice? What are the implications for your starting point toward building an equity-based coaching capability? What ethical issues emerge for you as you consider your current client profile?

1.1 **For Coaching Educators/Trainers**: Complete an 'Association Mapping' activity with a focus on:

   a) profiling your student/participant profile currently (and for the past five years);

   b) What is the racial profile of the authors of the core content/cannons that informed your curriculum; and

   c) How does the curriculum explicitly attend to race?

1.2 **For Association Leaders**: What is the race profile of your leadership, membership, and suppliers? How is your organization currently collecting and working with race data?
2. What are examples of tools, assessments, practices, and protocols that you are aware of, can be applied to equity-based coaching with a focus on race? What are the ethical considerations for applying any of these as part of your coaching practice, or your curriculum?
3. What do you need to learn about available resources to inform equity-based coaching with a focus on race? What ethical perspective(s) inform your choices of resources to guide your equity-based coaching learning agenda?
4. An Invitation to Systemic Coaching Supervision Training Organizations: What do coaching supervision training bodies need to include within current curriculum so that coach supervision trainers are sufficiently equipped to support, enable, rehearse and reflect (with their coach supervisor trainees) upon the normative, formative and restorative aspects of equity-based coaching?

Recommended reading

Ryde, J. (2009). *Being White in the Helping Professions: Developing effective intercultural awareness*. London: Kingsley Publishers.

References

Abel, A. L., Ray, R. L., Starkka, S., & Jaworsky, V. (2021). *Global Executive Coaching Survey 2021*. New York, NY: The Conference Board.
Aguilar, E. (2020). *Coaching for Equity: Conversations that change practice*. Hoboken, NJ: Jossey-Bass.
Anand, R. (2022). *Leading Global Diversity, Equity, and Inclusion: A guide for systemic change in multinational organizations*. Oakland, CA: Berrett-Koehler Publishers, Inc.
Avery, E. K. T. (2021). *Examining The Zone: Narratives of Black Women Executives in Cross*-Cultural Executive Coaching in Corporate America. Unpublished dissertation, UMI Dissertation Services, Ann Arbor, MI.
Baumane-Vitrolina, I., Cals, I., Sumilo, E., (2015). *Is Ethics Rational? Teleological, Deontological and Virtue Ethics – Theories Reconciled in the Context of Traditional Economic Decision Making*. 3rd Global Conference on Business, Economics, Management and Tourism. Rome, pp. 108–114.
Benlahcene, A., Ismail, A. B., & Zainuddin, R. B. (2018). A Narrative Review of Ethics Theories: Teleological and Deontological Ethics. *International Journal of Humanities and Social Sciences*, 23(7), pp. 31–38.
Bennett, M. J. (2004). Becoming Interculturally Competent. In Wurzel, J. (Ed), *Toward*multiculturalism: A reader in multicultural education, 2nd Edition. Newton, MA: Intercultural Resource Corporation, pp. 62–77.
Bernstein, A. F. (2019). *Race Matters in Coaching: An examination of coaches' willingness to*have difficult conversations with leaders of color. *Unpublished dissertation*, UMI Dissertation Services, Ann Arbor, MI.

Bonilla-Silva, E., (2017). *Racism without Racists: Color-Blind Racism and the Persistence of Racial Inequity in the United States*, 5th Edition. New York, NY: Rowman & Littlefield Publishers.

Bourke, V. (2020) *The History of Ethics*. Providence, RI: Cluney Media.

Brock, V. G. (2014). *Sourcebook of Coaching History*, 2nd Edition. CreateSpace Independent Publishing Platform.

Brown, J. (2019). *How to Be an Inclusive Leader: Your role in creating cultures of belongingwhere everyone can thrive*. Oakland, CA: Berrett-Koehler Publishers, Inc.

Davis, L. A & McMillian, M. (2021). *A Resource Guide: Diversity and Inclusion for CoachTrainers and Educators*. Lexington, KY: International Coaching Federation.

Frankena, W. K.Granrose, J. T., (1974). *Introductory Readings in Ethics*. New Jersey: Prentice Hall.

Goleman, D., Boyatzis, R., & McKee, A. (2002). *Primal Leadership: Realizing the power of emotional intelligence*. Boston, MA: Harvard Business School Press.

Johnson, W. & Stoddart, K. M. (2019). Do you know if your assessments are biased? Cognitive biases and heuristics may affect musculoskeletal assessment and clinical decision-making. *Physiotherapy UK Conference Abstracts*, 105(1): e40.

Judy, R. W. & D'Amico, C. (1997). *Workforce 2020: Work and Workers in the 21st Century*. Indianapolis, IN: Hudson Institute.

Kelly, D. J., Quinn, P.C., Stater, A. M., Lee, K; Ge, L., & Pascalis, O (2007). The Other-Race Effect Develops During Infancy: Evidence of perceptual narrowing. *Psychological Science*, 18(12): 1084–1089.

Kendi, I. X. (2019). *How to Be an Antiracist*. New York, NY: One World.

Kitson A. & Campbell, R. (1996). *The Ethical Organization: Ethical Theory and Corporate Behavior*. London: MacMillan.

Louden, R. B., (1986). Kant's Virtue Ethics. *Philosophy*, 61(238): 473–489.

Maltbia, T. E. (2001). *The Journey of Becoming a Diversity Practitioner: The Connection between Experience, Learning, and Competence*. Unpublished dissertation, UMI Dissertation Services, Ann Arbor, MI.

Maltbia, T. E. (2021a). *I Am Not a Racist: The role of race in coaching*. Webinar, British Psychological Society, March.

Maltbia, T. E. (2021b). *I'm Not a Racist – The Role of Race in Coaching, Coaching Education, and Research*. Webinar, ICF – New York City Chapter, June.

Maltbia, T. E. (2021c). *Anti-racism in coaching*. Henley Coaching Conference, Henley Business School, UK, September.

Maltbia, T. E., Marsick, V. J., & Ghosh, R. (2014). Executive and Organizational Coaching: A Review of Insights Drawn from Literature to Inform HRD Practice. *Advances in Developing Human Resources*, 16(2): 161–183.

Maltbia, T. E. & Page, L. J. (2013). *Academic Standards for Graduate Programs in Executive and Organizational Coaching*. Kennesaw, GA: Graduate School Alliance of Executive Coaching, unpublished internal document.

Mattingly, V., Grice, S., & Goldstein, A. (2022). *Inclusalytics: How diversity, equity, and inclusion leaders use data to drive their work*. Mattingly Solutions.

Morukian, M. (2022). *Diversity, Equity, and Inclusion for Trainers: Fostering DEI in The Workplace*. Alexandra, VA: ATD Press.

Oseck, L. M., Moghaddm, S., & Perreault, S. (1997). Similarity and attraction among majority and minority groups in a multicultural context. *International journal of intercultural relations*, 21(1): 113–123.

Naomi, Z. (2002). Race is a Social Concept. *Philosophy of Science and Race*. New York, NY: Routledge, p. 68.

Pan, M. L. (2017). *Preparing literature reviews: Qualitative and quantitative approaches*, 5th Edition. New York, NY: Routledge.

Roche, C. & Passmore, J. (2021). *Racial Justice, Equity and Belonging in Coaching*. Henley-on-Thames: Henley Business School.

Ryan, R. M. & Deci, E. L. (2018). *Self-determination theory: Basic psychological needs in motivation, development, and wellness*. New York, NY: Guilford Press.

Schwabish, J. & Feng, A. (2021). *Do No Harm: Applying equity awareness in data visualization*. Washington, DC: Urban Institute.

Stein, I. F, Page, L. J., & Maltbia, T. E. (2014). Coaching Education: Coming of Age. *Journal of Psychological Issues in Organizational Culture*, 5(2): 7–15.

Suarez, K. (2018). *The Role of Senior Leaders in Building a Race Equity Culture*. Boston, MA: The Bridgespan Group.

Sue, D. W. (2015). *Race Talk and The Conspiracy of Silence: Understanding and facilitating difficult dialogues on race*. Hoboken, NJ: John Wiley & Son.

Sue, D. W., Calle, C. Z., Mendez, N., Alsaidi, S., & Glaeser, E. (2021). *Micro-intervention Strategies: What you can do to disarm and dismantle individual and systemic racism and bias*. Hoboken, NJ: Wiley.

Torraco, R. J. (2016). Writing Integrative Literature Reviews: Using the Past and Present to Explore the Future. *Resource Development Review, 15(4)*: 404–428. doi:10.1177/1534484316671606.

Venet, A. S. (2021). *Equity-Centered Trauma-Informed Education*. New York, NY: W. W. Horton & Company.

Webster's. (2001). *Webster's Encyclopedic Unabridged Dictionary of the English Language*. San Diego, CA: Thunder Bay Press, p. 1590.

Wilkerson, I. (2020). *Caste: The Origins of Our Discontent*. New York, NY: Penguin Random House.

Chapter 21

An ethical exit strategy for dealing with incapacity and unexpected death

David A. Lane and Eve Turner

Introduction

Many people consider and indeed plan for their retirement, but neither of the two authors of this chapter can recall sessions in training or continuing professional development (CPD) programmes for coaches, mentors or supervisors that specifically talked about incapacitation, end-of-life care and unexpected death. While this is standard practice in some professions, for example psychotherapy, the first sessions in the coaching field that we are aware of were run Association for Professional Executive Coaching and Supervision (APECS; July, 2021). This may be because, in the West at least, there has been a cultural reluctance to discuss death. This is seen in personal wills where, for example, in the UK, research suggests only about four in ten adults have one (UK Wills and Probate, 2021).

In preparation for writing this chapter, the authors each have asked coaches, mentors and supervisors in multiple settings about such preparations, and rarely have people had these arrangements in place. Similarly, there seems to be little information through professional bodies beyond some brief references in the Global Code of Ethics (2022) discussed later. The assumption has often been that family, or a business partner, will 'sort' this. This can put an additional, and unnecessary, emotional strain and pressure on those left behind, already grieving or facing uncharted territory. It can leave clients in a difficult and perhaps uncomfortable position, having established a trusted relationship and then being left 'high and dry' or with a sense of abandonment. It is something coaches may not wish to think about but there are clearly ethical considerations if we do not.

Thinking about death – cultural considerations

Until relatively recently research on bereavement and death has been lacking and our understandings of bereavement, dying and death are contradictory (Exley, 2004). Over the last two decades this has now increased. While different understandings of the place of death in societies have been of cultural

DOI: 10.4324/9781003277729-21

significance since early in our evolution and attitudes to incapacity also varied attempts to establish an evidence base for understanding this has been less developed. A very influential early approach was found in the work of Kübler-Ross (1969) five stages of grief – Denial, Anger, Bargaining, Depression and Acceptance. While originally developed as a way to look at people facing their own death from terminal illness it became a general-purpose way of exploring grief. However, it has become clear that people do vary greatly in the way they approach death and such stages are by no means universal. The work on exploring grief did have the benefit of starting a conversation about the process of dying and how we deal with it. Nevertheless, as Exley (2004) has pointed out, debate about death and dying have remained taboo subjects. How far this lack of comfort contributes to the still large number of people who die interstate is difficult to know. It may also contribute to the even fewer who write professional wills.

For many, we remain uncomfortable with the facts of our own mortality or incapacity (Mellor and Shilling, 1993). Kessler talks about Anticipatory Grief, and in an interview (Berinato, 2020) linked this to the feeling we get about what the future holds when we're faced with uncertainty. Speaking at the start of the Covid-19 pandemic, Kessler argues that while it is normally centred on death, it also relates to a diagnosis or worry about an event like a virus. This impacts on our sense of safety.

There are, at the time of writing, active research groups, university centres and annual symposium under the British Sociological Association study group 'Social Aspects of Death, Dying and Bereavement' and from the 1990s a series of books in the 'Facing Death' series and a journal: Mortality. Exley (2004) refers to a number of early studies which began to change thinking on the topic such as those of Lawton and McNamara. In the USA, many states have mandated procedures for professionals to deal with client information in the event of death. Ideas influencing this field have come from different aspects of professional services dealing with the dying.

There has been much debate about what palliative care can and does achieve (James & Field, 1992). Lawton's (2000) study of the care provided within the UK National Health Service (NHS) hospice has been particularly influential. There has been as a result much discussion about dignified or 'good' deaths. "Terminally ill people live until they die, but their living is irretrievably changed as they begin to live their dying" (McNamara, 2021, p. 66).

Karnik and Kanekar (2016) identify a number of ethical issues surrounding end of life care which coaches might also consider relevant.

Key questions include:

Who holds the responsibilities and who takes which role in managing the consequences of the incapacitation or death of a colleague? If this is not known in advance it is likely that clients will suffer?

It is considered important that those dying or impacted by deteriorating conditions are able to make autonomous decisions. They need to feel that they have some control. However, if they are in denial about their increasing incapacity and it is impacting on client services what procedures are in place to address this?

Where Advance Directives (plans made in advance outlining situations in which you would want to refuse certain treatments or no longer feel competent to work with clients) - are in place this both enables autonomous decision making and ensures responsibilities are clear?

Several ethical issues are present both in end-of-life care and also in the management of colleagues, family and clients especially in professional fields built around establishing long-term trusting relationships. Issues arise in areas such as redundancies where colleagues left behind often feel at a loss or guilty that they survived the cull when those better able did not (Lane, 1983; Petzer, 2020). Coaches are balancing when dealing with these issues doing what is thought to be best with the demands of those impacted for control over a situation which might feel unmanageable.

How do professional bodies approach this?

There are considerable differences in the way these matters are addressed by professional bodies. Some have detailed procedures, while for others it goes largely unmentioned.

A good example is the American Psychological Association (APA). Ethics Standard 3.12 (p. 7) states:

"Unless otherwise covered by contract, psychologists make reasonable efforts to plan for facilitating services in the event that psychological services are interrupted by factors such as the psychologist's illness, death, unavailability, relocation or retirement…".

Beyond this it offers various sources of information and helplines to facilitate action. Similarly, The National Career Development Association, in their Code of Ethics (2015, Ch. 2, p. 10), has a specific section on Incapacitation, Death, or Termination of Practice:

"Career professionals prepare and plan for transfer of clients and files and disseminate to an identified colleague or "records custodian"… in case of their incapacitation, death, or termination of practice."

Psychotherapy and Counselling bodies in the UK vary but many do address this issue. According to Byfield (2016) several bodies mandate action. These include: British Psychoanalytic Council (BPC), UK Council for Psychotherapy (UKCP),

The Humanistic and Integrative Psychotherapy College of UKCP, Council for Psychoanalysis and Jungian Analysis College of UKCP. For example:

Section 9.2 *(p. 3) of UKCP's Ethical Principles and Code of Professional Conduct states: "The psychotherapist accepts a responsibility to take appropriate action should their ability to meet their obligations to their clients be compromised by their physical or mental health.'"* And

Section 9.3 *"The psychotherapist commits to carefully consider how, in the event of their sudden unavailability, this can be most appropriately communicated to their clients. This will also include careful consideration of how a client might be informed of a psychotherapist's death or illness and where appropriate supported to deal with such a situation."*

However, according to Byfield (2016) individual member organisations vary in making this mandatory.

So how is this addressed in coaching?

There is some reference in the Global Code of Ethics (GCoE). While it is not specific to incapacity or death the implication can follow that provision for the 'termination of practice' should include these matters.

The GCoE (July 2021, p. 7) requires that:

2.27 Members will prepare clients for the ending of the service including having a service continuity plan if the member is unexpectedly unable to complete.

2.28 Members are required to have a provision for the transfer of current clients and their records in the event of the termination of practice.

2.29 (part) Members understand that their professional responsibilities continue beyond the end of the professional relationship. These include:

• Maintenance of confidentiality of all information in relation to clients and sponsors with careful and ethical management of confidential, personal, or other data.

However, the level of support offered to members does not reach the levels in the APA. For some bodies the topic is largely absent either from the codes of conduct or advice offered to members. Nevertheless, it is clear that addressing these issues is important, owing to various ethical implications such as confidentiality and continuity of coaching service.

Dealing with the death and incapacity of colleagues

There are an increasing number of articles which look at aspects of dealing with the death of a colleague. This includes the work of Dance (2020) a practitioner in cancer care. She and her colleagues understand the impact of death. Yet she realised that when a colleague died, they had not put anything in place when it was one of their own. Her description of the grief and sense of loss and the way they had to put together ways of dealing with it is instructive. If teams such as hers, with the knowledge they have, can fail to plan, how much more so those without that understanding.

Key suggestions from her include:
- Being Authentic with your team
- The Plan you have might not be others' plan
- Recognising that it is important to communicate your grief clearly
- When thinking about replacing a member of staff who has died, have a buddy with you - it might be too raw.
- Find ways to keep their memories alive.

The American Psychological Association (2013) in an article about coping with the death of a co-worker, has also looked at the impact of the death of a co-worker who, as they say, can feel like a member of an extended family. They raise a number of areas for attention including both emotional and physical impacts. They, like Dance (2020), stress the importance of sharing your feelings, making use of support services available and the essential need to plan ahead so you have processes in place.

However, the variation among many professional bodies including in coaching and absence of this issue from some codes of conduct is notable.

Frameworks for understanding grief

When faced with the issues raised so far, it is important to understand some of the perspectives that inform the understanding of dealing with incapacitation or death as an area of study and practice. Earlier in the chapter the work of Kübler Ross has been mentioned, but several other concepts have more recently appeared which are helpful. One of these is found in the work of Tonkin (1996). She has explored the idea that rather than grief going away, or that people get over it, instead people learn to grow around it. It remains but becomes incorporated as part of us in ways that are still present, but we are able to deal with it. This concept has the real benefit that it absolves people/ coaches of feeling that they must get over it and move on. Other concepts arise from work in the field of trauma and trauma informed practice. Traumatic grief studies demonstrate the move from seeing people as a victim, to seeing them instead as survivors and thrivers. Not only can practitioners incorporate their grief, but they can be more resilient as an outcome (Joseph, 2012; Tehrani & Lane, 2021).

One of the useful ways of looking at grief is Stroebe and Schut's dual process model (2010) which looks at both loss-oriented and restoration-oriented stressors. Rather than being a list of negatives and positives or list of symptoms it is a map of the coping process through loss of a loved one or in this instance a colleague. It recognises that a focus on grief work may not be culturally appropriate. It suggests that people oscillate between periods of focus on loss and at other times on restoration. It is important to recognise that this is not a model of 'symptoms' or 'problems', or of positives and negatives, but a map of all the elements involved in the coping process. Stroebe and Schut's understanding of the grief process is that people experience and work through, in varying proportions (according to individual and cultural variations) both loss-oriented and restoration-oriented coping within their everyday life experience (see figure 21.1).

According to the model there is not a smooth transition from one to the other orientation, rather people oscillate back and forwards between them. While this may not fit everyone's experience it is helpful to understand patterns of movement in our responses.

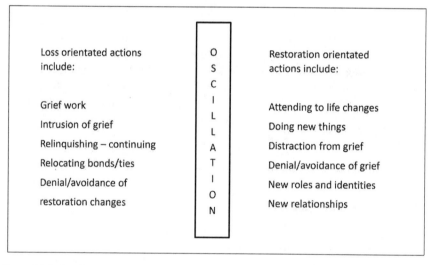

Figure 21.1 Dual Process Model adapted from Stroebe and Schut's dual process model (2010)

What areas might a coach or supervisor need to consider?

Various issues that may arise requiring some consideration (Turner, 2021):

- *What happens if you were to die suddenly or be incapacitated without warning?*
- *What happens where a long-term decline in health is identified, and you may continue to work but be less able to fulfil all roles?*
- *Although sudden death needs to be addressed, what processes do you have in place to cover a long period of end-of-life care? This is likely to be a complex task leaving family and business partners with difficult decisions.*
- *How might a gradual exit from the business be managed and clients supported?*

- *How might leadership of the business be shared during declining health?*
- *How might co-ordination of care and communication between family, business and across health and social care professionals be discussed?*
- *What support for bereavement for family and business partners and possibly long-term clients is in place?*

Each of these raise difficult ethical issues if coaches are to meet the points raised by Karnik and Kanekar (2016) above. Some case examples are considered below for reflection on the ethical issues that arise as well as practical steps that might be taken.

You are asked to consider three core questions in each of the cases described below:

1. *Who holds the responsibilities in the examples and who needs to take which roles?*
2. *It is considered important that those dying or impacted by deteriorating conditions are able to make autonomous decisions. How do you deal with increasing incapacity impacting on client services while respecting autonomy?*
3. *What 'Advance Directives' might be put in place to enable autonomous decision making yet ensure responsibilities to clients and colleagues are addressed?*

First, here are examples of cases where the coach became increasingly unable to fulfil their role.

Vignette 1[1]

"A European based coach, well respected in her field of expertise, was highly regarded by colleagues and clients alike. At the time of her incapacitation, she was a senior partner in a small coaching and consulting firm. The coach developed some symptoms of a depressive illness. She informed her close colleagues of her symptoms of depression, and also raised this in supervision. She acknowledged that she had had previous mental health problems with an episode of mania following a difficult pregnancy, albeit 20 years previously.

The coach agreed a plan with her supervisor and colleagues to manage her workload, choosing to reduce her workload to focus on her wellbeing. While she had not discussed her personal challenges with clients, she did inform them that she was reducing her work commitments.

Subsequently, the coach experienced a rapid deterioration in her mental state with the onset of manic symptoms. Colleagues quickly became aware of the changes in her mental state, although she became increasingly agitated as they

---

1   With thanks to Amanda Clark, Executive Coach and Consultant for sharing this vignette.

endeavoured to convey their concerns to her. The coach had kept appointments with two clients as her symptoms of mania began to manifest. One of these was a longstanding client who quickly gathered that all was not well with their coach and expressed concern to her colleagues, while the former was a relatively new client who later noted that they had been rather distressed by the behaviour of their coach, later seeking coaching elsewhere.

Following a period in hospital and an extended period of sickness absence, the coach made a full recovery from her mental health symptoms, which her doctors subsequently attributed to the hormonal changes which came with menopause (while her previous episode had also been in the context of significant hormonal fluctuations). By the time the coach returned to work, she had been absent for 8 months and had to consider how to explain her absence to clients, all of whom had been notified of her absence, although the likely duration had not been specified."

(Personal communication, April 25, 2022)

Please pause to consider the three questions. What else does this case suggest to you in terms of ethics and practical steps?

Vignette 2[2]

"The coach was employed by a large organisation which worked in the service sector. Their role was to provide an internal coaching and staff support service. They had a number of significant health challenges in previous years, including a heart attack from which they had made a good recovery.

The coach had been feeling a little under the weather and subsequently collapsed at work, this being observed by several coachees as they were treated by paramedics and taken to hospital. The coach went on to have several further such episodes, including one in a session with a coachee. The coach's behaviour prior to these episodes was a little erratic, and they were disorientated for a period afterwards. This was distressing for both the coach and the coachees, with the coach disliking showing any vulnerability (something they had worked on in their own coaching and remained a work in progress), while also being an intensely private person. The coachees were concerned for the wellbeing of their coach, who was also a colleague as well as their coach.

As a result of these circumstances, a number of coaching sessions were cancelled at very short notice. The coach's attendance at work and availability to coachees was patchy over a period of several months. The coach was eventually diagnosed with epilepsy, and prescribed medication eliminated the occurrence of seizures."

(Personal communication, April 25, 2022)

Please pause to consider the three questions posed above. What else does this case suggest to you in terms of ethics and practical steps?

---

2   With thanks to Amanda Clark, Executive Coach and Consultant for sharing this vignette.

Vignette 3[3]

A practising coach in Europe was given a terminal illness diagnosis and did not believe/wish the diagnosis to be accurate. Therefore, they did not professionally address either the possibility of illness, incapacitation or death and what each scenario might mean for clients.

Very sadly the practising coach firstly became extremely sick and in consequence absent, then they passed away shortly after, leaving their clients unaware, unprepared and in shock.

The practising coach did not have a current supervisor nor any plans in place for their own sudden and distressing departure. Clients then contacted the grieving family members to find out what was happening to their coaching, and for answers/confirmation of notes' destruction/where to go for help and so on.

Please pause to consider the three questions posed above. What else does this case suggest to you in terms of ethics and practical steps?

Vignette 4, Part A[4]

"After many years of trying to conceive, my husband and I were delighted when I fell pregnant. At our 12 weeks scan we were given the news that any expectant parent dreads: "I'm sorry there's no heartbeat. Both the babies haven't made it." I felt devastated and heartbroken. All my future dreams and hopes had fallen to pieces around me on the hospital floor and I didn't have the strength to pick them up.

During the painful process of having a miscarriage, I was left with the difficult task of advising my clients that I would be incapacitated for a few weeks. I found it exceptionally hard to find the words, to set healthy boundaries and to respond well to people's messages. I am forever grateful for the support and love that I received at this painful time.

The truth is I could have done without the pressure of talking about work."

(Personal communication, April, 28, 2022)

Please pause to consider the three questions posed above. What else does this case suggest to you in terms of ethics and practical steps?

Vignette 4, Part B

This is the action Sharon undertook, again in her words…

"Once I was strong enough to hold some space for myself and my clients, I wrote an exit strategy for the next unexpected event in my life. I am thankful that I did because I would need it again after just a few months.

---

3   With thanks to the concerned coach who shared this situation.
4   With thanks to Sharon Aneja, founder Humanity Works Consultancy, for sharing her story.

- I worked with a VA to compose the initial messages that would go out to my clients letting them know that I was not available for x period of time.
- In the event of my death, we wrote a message to be posted on social media
- I asked two coaches from our team of associates to be responsible for taking on my coaching work
- I put their names and contact details in the contracting agreement with new clients I sent out a message to existing clients informing them of the new process I informed my family of this new process.

Nobody can take away the pain of losing a child. Having this process in place reduced some of the pain and gave me peace of mind that I was doing the right thing for me, my associates and my clients."

(Personal communication, April 28, 2022)

Please pause to consider the action the coach undertook in relation to the three questions posed above. What else does this case suggest to you in terms of ethics and practical steps?

The role of the professional will

The last case raises the question of the use of an exit strategy. For many this has given rise to the concept of a professional will (for example see Jain, 2021). If the coach works within an organisation that has policies in place to handle case handover, control of records and ways to inform clients this may be sufficient. If the coach does not have those options a professional will is one and probably the best solution. It can protect the coach, their clients, family members and the coach's estate. Coaches working in group practices can designate a colleague as a professional executor. Otherwise, finding the right person prepared to take on the responsibility requires much careful thought. It certainly cannot be a colleague who works closely with the coach who could be travelling to the same meetings.

The American Psychologists Association Practice Organization represents those in private practice. It is clear that establishing a well-founded professional will is highly recommended. It provides samples to its members although it recommends getting legal advice to ensure that it reflects your needs.

Areas they suggest it covers include:

- *Transfer of documents* in the case of death and incapacity including letting clients know you have organised this, so they are not surprised if someone contacts them.
- *Confidential notification of clients* in the event of death or incapacity – a general letter to a family home or their employers may not be appropriate
- *Preferences for attendance at funeral or memorial services* – clearly a matter of personal choice but it avoids embarrassing situations.

- *Knowing State Laws and Resources* – because in the USA many states have adopted regulations governing practice.

The APA Ethics Standard 3.12 (p. 7) may apply:

> "Unless otherwise covered by contract, psychologists make reasonable efforts to plan for facilitating services in the event that psychological services are interrupted by factors such as the psychologist's illness, death, unavailability, relocation or retirement..."

Although not mandated in other jurisdictions it is still an effective practice to protect all.

We the authors are very grateful to those who have provided ideas and information that have allowed the inclusion of an example professional will and the linked documents for executors and clients. These are in Appendix A and include an example professional will (A1; p. xxx), an example list of associated details needed for the will (A2; p. xxx) and an example client list for a professional living will (A3; p. xxx). These indicate some of the things that might be included, but they are not meant as definitive documents. It is emphasised that all working in the coaching field and community generally will need to take their own legal and/or professional advice in preparing their practice.

Let's now look at the following case study from Julia Menaul (Personal communication, May 2, 2022), coach and coach supervisor who describes why this topic became important to her.

Case study, Part A

The background

> "The experience of bereavement often precipitates existential questioning, as happened to me when my father died and I had to deal with his estate. It led to an interest in how grief and loss is dealt with which continues (Menaul and João, 2022).
>
> In one discussion group about grief and loss the important role of clinical wills for therapists was emphasised and we all wondered, what did coaches do? This happened as things started to change for me personally. The Covid-19 pandemic hit my husband and me hard. His Primary Immune Deficiency meant he was extremely clinically vulnerable and in the early days of the pandemic we were shielding him and very fearful, but also realistic about what plans we should put in place. So, we updated our Wills and put in place Power of Attorney documents in case either of us became incapacitated.
>
> Unfortunately, the economic fallout from the first lockdown meant my husband had to wind up his small business and retire earlier than expected. These events created a reconfiguration of our planned future that we had

thought was some years away. Psychologically we were re-contracting our whole marriage.

The dilemma

My husband felt real sadness when informing his suppliers and customers that he was closing his business, made more poignant by the kind and unexpected words that followed. Watching him close a business made me question my own process. Retirement was some years away for me but how would I do that, if forced to do it unexpectedly? I looked at the vast amount of materials, books and administration that had built up over twenty years as a self-employed coach/supervisor and wondered how on earth my husband would cope with the burden of my work on top of his own grief and ill health if anything happened to me. Even if he was up to the task, was it even ethical for someone else to contact clients and see their notes?

Several coaches told me they had a reciprocal arrangement with another coach, but I was loath to impose the burden on a colleague and felt unsure whether I really wanted to commit myself to handling their coaching business on their demise and all that would entail. The coaching profession is a small world, so would an ethical line be crossed more easily by a fellow coach compared to someone outside of our network?"

Please pause to consider the three core questions posed above. What else does this case suggest to you in terms of ethics and practical steps?

Case study, Part B

Julia continues…

"Serendipitously, I was told about a Professional Executor Service for coaches and therapists and signed up straightaway. The template they sent was a salutary lesson in the reality of how much of a digital footprint many of us leave behind in the twenty first century. Questions such as what did I want my clients to know about my death/illness? Would I want clients to be invited to my funeral? How long should my website remain? Did I want my social media pages taking down? Where are all my clients notes and would I want them destroyed after my death?

Knuckling down one rainy afternoon to sort out answers to all these questions, where my passwords could be found and which colleague would happily pick up my clients, was such a relief. For all my own clients who can be supervisees, coachees or even sponsors I ensure I inform them of my executor service as an indicator of good practice. They are then fully aware of where the boundaries of confidentiality lie especially with any commercially sensitive information.

Table 21.1 Fifteen tips to prepare for your termination of practice

1. Don't panic – take time now to consider what steps you would like to make and form a plan in the event of your serious illness, or death.

2. Appoint an 'executor(s)' and ensure your family and clients know about the arrangement.

3. Ideally put a professional or living will in place, independently witnessed and signed.

4. Make sure you have left instructions for quick access to a list of client contacts and where that list is held. You may choose for the instructions to the executor(s) to be timeless i.e., do not include specific client details and just where to find records etc. But if you are providing and updating this client list and sharing it while you are practising, ensure you have your clients' consent (data protection).

5. Consider data protection (such as GDPR in Europe) in all you do including a rationale for your note-taking as this will help your executor(s) – for example if you only produce anonymised notes, you can tell clients as part of contracting that they will be destroyed in the event of your termination of practice.

6. Make a diary note to review this regularly, at least annually. We would recommend more often – a common theme from practitioners is the challenge of remembering to update contacts which is seen as key.

7. Consider what initial support might be needed for clients, family and business colleagues in dealing with deterioration in your mental capacity and physical well-being or death.

8. Consider whether you would want clients to be given suggestions for alternative practitioners and if you do prepare a list, ensure you have the consent of the practitioners.

9. Have a process in place for promptly cancelling forthcoming appointments ensuring the person has access to your diary. This may well need to be done, and best be done given the impersonal nature of emails, by phone. Prepare the person who will be calling for the possibility that clients could be distressed and be sure that they will have the resilience, skills and time to do this.

10. Have a process for dealing with emails so that they don't sit unanswered, with pre-notified password access given to a trusted person and a pre-written auto-responder that you've prepared, but only once all current clients have been contacted.

11. Keep important contact information in a known place for example for your supervisor and any professional colleagues so they can be informed. This includes professional bodies you may have membership of or accreditation with.

12. Ensure the executor(s) knows where your professional indemnity insurance policy is and informs your insurers. Check your policy to ensure that the type you have will provide cover during your incapacity or after your death.

13. Consider how your website and social media pages will be changed to reflect the situation and make sure your representative has access to your accounts. Pre-agreed wording will make this process more straightforward. You may also need to ask people specifically not to post anything until clients and other close contacts have been notified – but it is hard to control this for very long.

14. Consider your finances – examples are bank accounts, direct debits and required tax payments. Your executor will need to inform your accountant and stop/make payments as needed and close accounts as needed.

15. Consider whether you wish to invite some or all your clients and/or professional colleagues to your funeral or memorial and leave instructions for this.

Implications

> Consequently, as a supervisor, a standard question I now ask all my supervisees at contracting stage when we talk about their client notes plus their own health and wellbeing, is "What do you formally have in place in the event of your death or incapacity?" So far, I have not met a coach who has considered this question before."

Please pause to consider the three questions posed above. What else does this case suggest to you in terms of ethics and practical steps for us in coaching and supervision?

There are many areas to consider in preparing for termination of practice. Fifteen such considerations are suggested below in Table 21.1 (with thanks to Jan Stannard of the Professional Executor Service and Jo Mountain of Howden Insurers).

Do coaches have a responsibility to act on a colleague's incapacity?

One area not considered so far, arises from the increasing incapacity of a colleague to fulfil their duties. While coaches can feel sympathy for a colleague undergoing difficult life circumstances the question arises of what to do if they are not acknowledging this, and it is impacting on client services. What if a coach increasingly smells of alcohol at work, or becomes increasingly forgetful or misses client appointments, or shows early signs of dementia or other progressive illness? Can coaches ignore this? Certainly, it is clear in some professional body codes that this is a matter on which practitioners have to act (Clay, 2011). A number of bodies suggest trying to assist early but if this is rejected there may be no choice but to formally report the colleague to the group, association or organisation to which they belong.

As organisations start to address the concerns raised above there is more opportunity to take up training in these areas. For example, in the UK the charity Cruse (2021) provides advice and guidance and in house training sessions to address death and bereavement. Other bodies such as APECS have offered CPD sessions on the topic.

Vignette 5

The need is ongoing. Supervision is one place where coaches can go to discuss their reactions, concerns and responsibility. Having attended the APECS session on exit strategies in July 2021, executive coach Sasi Penchal reflected afterwards that the topic had:

> "...triggered a visceral response like the very emotional process of completing a personal Will and appointing Power of Attorneys. The extent of

my reaction made me realise that I hadn't considered the need to extend the same duty of care and attention to my coachees...there are processes in place to contract neatly for beginnings and endings to coaching assignments but not if life events abruptly occurred without provision for the wellbeing and future support of the client. As a result, I left the session with even more questions... existential and practical, such as 'What can I put in place now until a more sustainable long-term plan is in place?' Sasi continues that she has *"taken this to supervision which is 'my go-to place', to explore, reflect and seek to be challenged in a psychologically safe space, to develop a Professional Will that serves my coachees well, resourcefully and with compassion."*

(Personal communication, 28 April, 2022)

Conclusion

Dealing with incapacity or death depends on many factors. Some are personal to us, others reflect our cultural heritage, religious or spiritual beliefs. Others are a matter of professional ethics. No matter our role or connection, each of us can be significantly negatively impacted by the death of a colleague or the process of watching their slow deterioration. This may cause the coaching colleague to be temporarily less effective or even be a cause of hazardous and unethical behaviour. In organisational contexts it can unsettle or significantly disrupt a team. The impacts can be physical, emotional and cognitive. Coaches need to find ways to share their feelings with others, ask for and seek support, and make use of services available through the various associations or charities working in the field. However, it goes beyond this, since there are several ethical issues involved in addressing questions of death and incapacity. A number of ethical concerns and scenarios that reflect these have been explored. The approach of professional bodies has been found to vary with some offering extensive advice and support, and others little, while it is either rarely mentioned in coaching Codes of Ethics (such as the Global Code of Ethics, 2021; International Association of Coaching, 2022) or not directly referred to at all (International Coaching Federation, 2020). Similarly, unplanned incapacity, deterioration, or death, is rarely if ever mentioned in coach or supervision training programmes. We would encourage providers to include discussion on exit strategies for unexpected situations.

Exit strategies cannot be ignored as it appears that potential solutions such as professional wills, while mandated in some professions, are currently not within coaching, and in practice few have considered the necessity to write one or to make other sufficient arrangements for unplanned situations. It is time to take this matter seriously and address this ethical concern.

Discussion points

1. How are you feeling now having read this chapter, and the vignettes and case study? Why might that be?
2. In practical terms, what plans do you have in place? Are these sufficient? If not, what will you do to plan for your unexpected death, incapacity or deterioration?
3. In emotional terms, what might need to be in place for your and others' well-being in the event of an unexpected death, incapacity, or deterioration?
4. How will you raise this with others? What might you add to your training programmes if you train practitioners? What might you ask for, from whom, to support you?

Recommended reading

Menaul, J. & João, M. (2022) *Coaching and Supervising Through Bereavement: A Practical Guide to Working with Grief and Loss.* Abingdon: Routledge.

References

American Psychological Association. (2013). Coping with the death of a co-worker. www.apa.org/topics/mental-health/coping-death-coworker, accessed July 25, 2022.
American Psychological Association. (2017). Ethical Principles of Psychologists and Code of Conduct. www.apa.org/ethics/code/ethics-code-2017.pdf, accessed June 9, 2022.
Aneja, S. (2022). Personal communication, April 28.
Association for Professional Executive Coaching and Supervision. (2021). How To... Series Exit Strategy - in the event of our declining health, incapacitation or death. July 7.
Berinato, S. (2020). That Discomfort You're Feeling Is Grief. An interview with David Kessler. *Harvard Business Review*, March 23. https://hbr.org/2020/03/that-discomfort-youre-feeling-is-grief, accessed July 24, 2022.
Byfield, R. (2016). Where there's a will there's a way. www.bacp.co.uk/bacp-journals/private-practice/spring-2016/where-theres-a-will-theres-a-way, accessed May 10 2022.
Clark, A. (2022). Personal communication, April 25.
Clark, D. (1993). *The Sociology of Death.* Oxford: Blackwell.
Clark, D. (2002). Between hope and acceptance: the medicalisation of dying. *British Medical Journal*, 324: 905–907.
Clay, R. A. (2011). When a colleague is impaired. *Monitor on Psychology*, 42(6). www.apa.org/monitor/2011/06/colleague Accessed May 9, 2022.
Cruse. (2022). Cruse Bereavement Support. www.cruse.org.uk, accessed October 8, 2022.
Dance, A. (2020). Working through the death of a colleague. *Harvard Business Review.* https://hbr.org/2020/11/working-through-the-death-of-a-colleague, accessed May 10, 2022.

Exley, C., (2004). The sociology of death, dying and bereavement. *Sociology of Health and Illness*, 26(1): 110–122.

Field, D., Hockey, J., & Small, N. (Eds) (1997). *Death, Gender and Ethnicity*. London: Routledge.

Global Code of Ethics. (2021). www.globalcodeofethics.org, accessed July 2022.

International Association of Coaching. (2022). Code of Ethics. Retrieved July 26, 2022 from https://certifiedcoach.org/about/ethics.

International Coaching Federation. (2020). Code of Ethics. Retrieved 26 July, 2022 from https://coachingfederation.org/ethics/code-of-ethics.

Jain, S. (2021). Where There is a Will, There is a Way - Professional Will: A Tool for Ethical Practice. *The South Asian Journal of Transactional Analysis*, 7(2): 70–83. www.saata.org/wp-content/uploads/2021/07/SAJTA-Volume-7-Number-2-July-2021. pdf, accessed July 24, 2022.

James, N. & Field, D. (1992). The routinization of hospice: charisma and bureaucratization. *Soc Sci Med*, 34(12): 1363–1375.

James, C. R. & Macleod, R. D. (1993). The problematic nature of education in palliative care. *Journal of Palliative Care*, 9(4): 5–10.

Joseph, S. (2012). *What doesn't kill us: The new psychology of posttraumatic growth*. New York: Basic Books.

Karnik, S. & Kanekar, A. (2016). Ethical Issues Surrounding End-of-Life Care: A Narrative Review.

Kübler Ross, E., (1969). *On Death and Dying*. New York: Macmillan.

Lane, D. A. (1983). *Do we need counselling for those not made redundant?* London: PDF Position Paper.

Lawton, J. (2000). *The Dying Process: Patients' Experiences of Palliative Care*. London: Routledge.

McNamara, B. (2001). *Fragile Lives: Death, Dying and Care*. Buckingham: Open University Press.

Mellor, P. & Shilling, C. (1993). Modernity, self-identity and the sequestration of death. *Sociology*, 27(3): 411–431.

Menaul, J. (2022). Personal communication, May 2.

Menaul, J. & João, M. (2022). *Coaching and Supervising Through Bereavement: A Practical Guide to Working with Grief and Loss*. Abingdon: Routledge.

National Career Development Association. (2015). 2015 NCDA Code of Ethics. Retrieved from www.ncda.org/aws/NCDA/asset_manager/get_file/3395?ver=738700.

Penchal, S. (2022). Personal communication, April 28.

Petzer, M. (2020). *Don't shoot the messenger: The enigmatic impact of conveying bad news during redundancy situations and how to limit the impact*. Applied Research Conference January 22–23, 2020, Dublin, Ireland.

Stroebe, M. & Schut, H. (2010). The dual process model of coping with bereavement: a decade on. *Omega (Westport)*. 61(4): 273–289.

Tonkin, L. (1996). Growing around grief—another way of looking at grief and recovery, *Bereavement Care*, 15(1):10. doi:10.1080/02682629608657376.

Tehrani, N., & Lane, D. A. (2021). The role for coaching in psychological trauma. In M. Watts & I. Florance (Eds), *Emerging Conversations Coaching and Coaching Psychology*. Abingdon: Routledge.

Wills and Probate. (2021). UK Wills & Probate Market 2020: Consumer Research Report. https://todayswillsandprobate.co.uk/only-4-in-10-uk-adults-have-a-will-despite-owning-a-property, accessed July 24, 2022.

Turner. E. (2021). Exit Strategy. *Coaching at Work*, 14(4): 40–43.

UK Council for Psychotherapy. (2022) UKCP Code of Ethics and Professional Practice. www.psychotherapy.org.uk/media/bkjdm33f/ukcp-code-of-ethics-and-professional-practice-2019.pdf, accessed June 9, 2022.

Young, M. & Cullen, L. (1996). *A Good Death: Conversations with East Londoners.* London: Routledge.

Chapter 22

Ethics and the ecological environment in coaching

Searching for a new paradigm

Michael Cavanagh and Eve Turner

Introduction

"The state of the planet is broken. Humanity is waging war on nature." These are the words of the United Nations Secretary General António Guterres (United Nations, 2021). Earth's average surface temperature has risen around 1.8 degrees Fahrenheit (1.01 degrees Celsius) since1880 (NASA, 2022), largely driven by increased carbon dioxide emissions and other human activities. Most of this increase has occurred in the last four decades. Intergovernmental Panel on Climate Change scientists warn that we have limited time to halt the warming that will irrevocably change the earth's climate (BBC, 2022). They call for "rapid, deep and immediate" cuts in carbon dioxide (CO_2) global emissions, peaking by 2025 to stave off the worst impacts. In less than 50 years the population of mammals, birds, amphibians and fish has dropped by 68 percent (Polman & Winston, 2021). We are already seeing 150,000 human climate-related deaths a year, expected to rise to 300,000 by the end of the 2020s (Kasotia, 2022).

The facts of these ecological crises are well known, even if their causes remain disputed by some. We hear coaches ask, *'What does this have to do with us as coaches? Surely, our role is simply to assist business in achieving its goals and coachees to achieve theirs? We are not social or environmental activists!'*

In this chapter, we seek to respond to these concerns, and show why coaches, mentors and supervisors, cannot and do not sit separate from these issues. We will argue that we live in a world in which all systems – social, economic and environmental – are so intimately connected that our action as coaches contributes to this environmental degradation. We suggest that if we as coaches are to ethically respond to these challenges we need to firstly examine the paradigms we bring to our work as coaches. Do our paradigms adequately take account of the complex interdependence that makes up our world? Second, we argue that our practical coaching models must also reflect this complexity. Third, we present an approach to coaching that may help coaches and their clients collaboratively unpack the uncomfortable ethical

DOI: 10.4324/9781003277729-22

issues we collectively face. Finally, reflective questions are posed about what these ideas may mean for coach education, and coaching practice.

To begin reflecting on the interdependence of our world, let's pause to ask:

What would you like to hear our collective great grandchildren say about our contribution to their world through our work as coaches?
How might this provide us a compass for ethical decision making in coaching?

Questioning the received wisdom of coaching

The dominant paradigm or world view of coaching can be seen in a few beliefs and principles that have gone largely unquestioned. They are often taught as the cornerstones of coaching work.

- That the client and their agenda is 'king' or 'queen'
- The client is the expert, and the answers are in them.
- Coaches ask – not tell
- Coaching is about constructing solutions, not exploring the cause-and-effect structure of problems.

Indeed, much of coach education, assessment and accreditation worldwide has drawn on these principles. Nevertheless, some voices in coaching have questioned these orthodoxies (for example, see Cavanagh 2006, 2013b; Cavanagh & Lane, 2012; Hawkins, 2011, 2017; Hawkins & Turner, 2020; McLean, 2017; Whybrow et al., 2023), noting that instead of serving us, they serve a simplistic world view that supports the status quo or *business as usual.*

In recent years there has been growing concern among coaches and coach organisations about these orthodoxies. In Whybrow et al. (2023), Downey talks of learning to say "no" (Chapter 3, p. 5):

"...we'd won awards for work that had helped maintain the disturbing status quo. It's easy to unwittingly collude when you're ignorant of the facts of our lives. As I slowly awoke to what we're doing to our planet home the gap between my increasing awareness and my professional life widened to a chasm that could no longer be crossed....

There was a specific moment when I was required to stay silent about something that deserved to be brought into the open and discussed: the impacts of the client's technology on the human and natural world. Legitimate questions, asked by their own people, that needed to be acknowledged.

On the outside, nothing much happened. I stayed silent. Said nothing. On the inside, I completely lost it. That was it. I couldn't do this anymore."

In Vignette 1, Zoe Cohen tells of the impact her personal ethical code has had on her actions.

Vignette 1

Zoe Cohen is an accredited Executive Coach and Supervisor in the UK. In recent years her deepened understanding of the climate, ecological and social justice crises driven by the West's political economy and its passion for consumption, profit and economic growth has led her to further transform her life, personally and professionally. A fundamental reconsideration of her ethics has been central to this.

> "So, the challenge facing the coaching profession is the same one facing pretty much every profession – to accept the truth of the devastating, catastrophic situation that we are in, and that without a massive mobilization for change we are on a sure path to societal collapse and loss of all we hold dear - to speak that truth and to act accordingly every single day. It's as simple as that...
>
> That truth, that simple truth, has taken me into civil disobedience and into ongoing civil resistance against a government, and a system, which is determined to kill us and to take away all that we love and care about.
>
> Governments, fossil fuel companies, banks, corporations and much of the media are all complicit in this. Their denial, misinformation and gaslighting, all to maintain and grow the power and wealth of 'business as usual' has all but squandered our collective right to a liveable planet.
>
> So, in 2022, whether I'm a coach or whatever I am, (quite frankly, it really doesn't matter anymore) I feel utterly compelled to speak my truth to as many people as I can. And if that means that I annoy them, or they don't want to work with me as a client, or whatever, then so be it. I can't look myself in the mirror, if I don't speak and act in line with what I know to be the case.
>
> And in a few short years' time, the only thing that people who are adults now will come to regret is that they didn't do more. No one will regret any climate action that they took..."
>
> (Personal communication, May 2022)

Zoe is here sharing her personal code, one that might be quite confronting for many coaches. It forces us to consider the ethics and practice of social and environmental activism in coaching, not to mention the pragmatic problem of how to maintain a coaching practice when taking such strong positions. However, the reader should note that Zoe is here speaking of her considered value position as a coach, and not describing the way she works with her clients. There is no suggestion she would seek to unilaterally impose a value proposition on other stakeholders. This is rarely a useful coaching road – ethical decision making in complex systems is a collaborative process.

We invite you to pause for a moment and consider these questions:

How did you feel when you read Zoe's account? What does this bring up for you in your practice as coach? Where might you reflect on, and discuss this with others?

The changing position of the coaching professional bodies

The accepted pre-eminence of the coachee's goals is also starting to be challenged by professional bodies, albeit gently. In the Global Code of Ethics (2021), we find these clauses:

> "*2.8 Members should be guided by their client's interests and at the same time raise awareness and responsibility to safeguard that these interests do not harm those of sponsors, stakeholders, wider society, or the natural environment.*
>
> *3.3 Members will abide by their respective bodies' statements and policies on inclusion, diversity, social responsibility and climate change.*
>
> *3.8 Members will engage in professional development activities that contribute to increased self-awareness in relation to inclusion, diversity, technology, latest developments in changing social and environmental needs.*"

The ICF Code of Ethics (2021) includes in Section IV, "Responsibility to Society":

> *28. Am aware of my and my clients' impact on society. I adhere to the philosophy of "doing good" versus "avoiding bad."*

While a seemingly modest start, collaboration between coaching and supervision bodies has continued and expanded with a signed statement on climate change in May 2020. A unique "Joint Global Statement Group on the Climate and Ecodiversity Crises" (Joint Global Statement Group, 2022) has been established among coaching, coaching psychology and supervision professional bodies. The eleven signatories, at the time of writing, acknowledge that "Humankind faces one of its biggest challenges in the current climate and biodiversity crisis" (Joint Global Statement Group, 2020, p. 1). "To address the reality and urgency of the climate emergency" (Joint Global Statement Group, 2020, p. 2) they commit to raising awareness and knowledge with members and non-members by sharing information and research freely, and to "raising awareness and support to our clients to enable them to redesign their organisations in response to changing needs and good practices" (Joint Global Statement Group, 2020, p. 2). An example of this in practice is described in Vignette 2.

Vignette 2

Raising awareness, through coaching, of the interdependent connectivity of all living systems can enable a radical resetting of business goals. A client of coach and author Giles Hutchins has given permission for the following feedback to be shared anonymously:

> "Giles' regenerative coaching work, drawing upon living-systems, has had a profound effect on me, my leadership team and countless people across the organization, massively impacting our wider culture and stakeholder ecosystem. The coaching is essentially about connection - deepening our inner connection and our outer connection with life. He has helped me shift my consciousness, to gain perspective on things, to sense the organization as a living-system, that everything is interconnected and has repercussions. This has helped me realize that business can't be about making the wrong things righter (sustainability), it has to be about cultivating regenerative futures by being a force for good in the world. Through the coaching, I have been exploring how the organization I lead can deepen its inner-nature (its culture, values, ways of working, power-relations, shifting from parent-child/mechanistic to adult-adult/regenerative) and its outer-nature (its value propositions and stakeholder relations from linear value chains into co-creating regenerative communities). In so doing we have morphed linear product lines into education-based community participation services with circularity and reuse baked in, while helping our stakeholders connect more deeply with nature, and explore their own wellbeing and regeneration. This understanding of the interconnectedness of life is helping our business become more future-fit and thrive amid these volatile times by becoming a force for good in the world – it's a step beyond conventional sustainable business."
>
> (Personal communication, May 2022)

Understanding the forces that have shaped coaching

Coaching, as we know it, is a relatively new invention of the West (or at least a reshaping of older forms of helping). It did not rise to life *ex nihilo*. Its processes and logic developed within a social and economic context that needs to be understood if a pathway to a more ethical and sustainable relationship between coaching practice and the ecology is to be developed.

Modern coaching arose to fill a need in organisations and society more generally. That need, we argue, grew out of the hyper-individualisation that is a necessary consequence of the dynamic of the modern western economies. The world's economic systems have at their heart a structural imperative for continual growth, narrowly conceived as a growth in profitability and productivity. The consequence of slowed or no growth is a destabilisation of the economy and political systems through increased unemployment, reduced consumption, the failure of businesses and the migration of capital to more productive markets (Ferguson, 2019; Gordon & Rosenthal, 2003).

Social implications of the growth imperative can be seen in numerous ways:

- Calls by share markets for ever-increasing growth in size and profits, with dire consequences for organizations if these are not met.
- An inability to change when change may lead to lower growth or threaten current levels of productivity (e.g. protection of fossil fuel industries).
- The constant call by organizations and governments to do ever more with ever less.
- The continual need to increase consumption irrespective of the real value of what is consumed, and without any question as to what value means. This includes the creation of markets for which there is no need, and products that are clearly harmful to us and the environment.
- The common expectation that one must be on a path of constant improvement.

The imperative to growth and need for increased consumption has led to a shaping of our self-understanding away from an interconnected social world toward individualisation (Han, 2015). Margaret Thatcher's (1987) famous statement sums up this change in self-understanding: "...And who is society? There is no such thing! There are individual men and women and there are families and no government can do anything except through people and people look to themselves first".

This hyper-individualisation has led to an implicit acceptance that we are individually responsible for constantly growing our personal productivity. Han (2015) describes this movement as a type of auto-exploitation in which this unattainable goal remains always just beyond our grasp – we must do more, be more and have more in order to be a worthwhile member of society or even to feel good about ourselves – leading to a society in which individuals are ripe for burnout.

As coaches we are intimately involved in this systemic dynamic. Indeed, we have been the prophets of it. Coaching has implicitly and explicitly accepted the logic of growth and hyper-individualisation, as illustrated in the cornerstone coaching principles above.

However, the implicit acceptance of this dynamic, means that we have missed many of the warning signs that suggest our collective direction of travel is leading to destruction. These include increasing disparity of wealth nationally and internationally, decreasing mental health despite increased wealth, environmental degradation of all kinds, decreasing worker engagement, rising consumerism, a growing focus on superficialities rather than the underlying dynamics that shape outcomes. In truth, many of these signs have been seen and bemoaned. However, coaches could see no way of addressing them without breaching the above fundamental principles that have shaped coaching practice for three decades.

The above brief discussion of the structural economic forces in our societies, and their practical sequelae, means that the ecological and climate crises we are facing are not so much technological issues, but challenges that require a radical shift in our perspective as coaches. It is a shift away from the individual and disconnected toward an understanding of community and the way in which coaches are all connected as parts of a complex adaptive system.

How to create an ethical coaching approach to ecological sustainability – a potential pathway

Understanding systems.

The worldview that underpins the cornerstone principles of coaching, is drawn from the linear, world view of Newtonian mechanics. In this world view, causes lead directly to effects and systems are dealt with as if they are discrete and closed off from the systems around them.

However, human beings are agents that exist and operate in systems made up of other interconnected agents and systems. For this reason, the context for ethical decision making is always within complex adaptive systems (CAS) (Boulton, Allan & Bowman 2015; Capra & Luisi, 2014). While articulating a theory of CAS is not within the scope of this chapter, complex adaptive systems have several key features important to the topic.

1. *Holism*: Complex systems are more than the sum of their parts, and the features of the parts are different to the features of the system. This is important because it points to the fact that people's behaviour is shaped by the systemic forces operating on them. These forces enable some behaviours and perspectives while constraining others. This is an important corrective to the typical name, blame and shame processes associated with moral judgment and ethical decision making.

2. *Emergence*: The characteristics and outcomes of systems emerge from the interaction of the parts. E.g. the wetness of water emerges from the interaction of water molecules. If we change that interaction, different properties emerge (e.g. hardness in the case of ice, and vapour in the case of steam). Together holism and emergence suggest that we must focus on the interaction between agents and systems, rather than the isolated choices of individuals. It is the dynamic interconnection between agents and systems that is productive of system outcomes.

3. *Interdependence*: As can be seen from the above two features of systems, interdependence points to the fact that boundaries between systems are ultimately abstract and permeable delineations we draw to help us understand the world. Just as we now accept that an organization's

boundary includes customers, regulators and a host of other stakeholders (who previously were not considered to be a part of the organization) we need to see all those elements and agents who form the systems of which we are apart. For example, the bee is a key agent in human society. Without the bee our food production systems would fail, and people would die. Recognising this fundamental interdependence is critical to ethical decision making – and a failure to do so may lead to catastrophic outcomes.

4. *Sensitivity to initial conditions:* Complex systems are temporal processes, not things. Where we start matters, and small changes at the starting point can lead to big differences over time. Lorenz's (1972) butterfly effect is an illustration of this. This understanding corrects the coaching belief that the past can be ignored because the only thing that matters is creating the desired future. Sensitivity to initial conditions tells us that the past shapes the set of possible futures.

5. *Irreversibility*: This tells us that there is no going back to an earlier system state or time. The environment that we enjoyed as children is no longer available to us and will never be available again. This does not mean we cannot create a better environment. It does mean that whatever future is created will be different. Attempts to protect or recreate that past are doomed to failure.

6. *Unpredictability:* The non-linearity of complex systems makes them ultimately unpredictable, particularly over longer time frames. This is critical to ethical decision making. It means that we cannot simply decide a strategy then set and forget it. The impact of our decisions are always temporary, contingent and ultimately unknowable. This means that ethical decision-making carries with it a requirement to engage in an ongoing iterative and collaborative process. Ethical action is a process not an event.

A framework for working in complex systems

We, the authors argue that to formulate appropriate responses to complex ethical issues, any approach must take the above features of complexity seriously. Cavanagh (2013a) and Cavanagh & Sinclair (in prep) outline such an approach. Originally developed as a leadership and coaching model, Cavanagh's (2013a) Four Factor Model can be used to assist coaches to consider complex ethical questions. The four factors, and their current definitions are:

1. **Perspective taking capacity** – a person's or group's capacity to understand, critically consider and integrate competing perspectives to form a bigger perspective that enables effective action.
2. **Purpose** – the articulation of the pattern of commitments that give meaning to action. This is valuing everything that needs to be valued.

3. **Positive process** - the creation of processes that enable people to maintain engagement in complex and contested spaces. Such processes are always respectful and embody a mix of challenge and support.
4. **Proprioception** - the person's or group's capacity to identify how the system is unfolding and changing over time - in as close to real time as possible. This involves active connectedness with the system.

Each of these factors are considered as they bear upon ecological ethical decision making in coaching (and for fuller details of the four factors, see Cavanagh, 2013).

Factor 1: Perspective taking capacity

Perspective taking capacity, as the above definition suggests, is not simply the ability of the person or group to take another's perspective, though it does include this. Rather it is the capacity to take a *bigger* perspective that incorporates and extends the lesser perspectives of relevance to the issue at hand. The analogy used for this factor is holding a torch. If one holds a torch close to the ground, it illuminates a small proportion of the available system space, but very brightly. The higher one holds the torch, the more of the system is visible, but lit less brightly. For example, a manager whose only concern is end of month profitability, will hold a narrow perspective focused only on this issue. Other data will be excluded. A leader who is concerned with the overall health of the company will hold a higher perspective, and one who is also concerned for the health of the holding environment will hold a perspective that incorporates all the data relevant to this purpose.

The holding of a higher level of perspective will help resolve issues that appear to be unsolvable tensions and paradoxes when viewed from a lower perspective. For example, if the only metric of company health a manager holds is monthly profit and loss (an exploitation paradigm), then a drop in profit will appear incompatible with good company health. However, a manager who is able to hold an exploration paradigm, will see lack of profit, owing to research and development as an investment in future sustainability. Here the tension between exploration and exploitation is productive of a bigger paradigm and greater range of available options for action.

Holding lower perspectives is attractive. It offers coaches an illusory sense of clarity and certainty. Hence, they often seek to simplify the complexity of issues facing us by use of 4 techniques:

1. *Restricting system boundaries* – e.g., ignoring systemic issues by defining them as personal problems; or drawing strong boundaries between "business" and the rest of life. Clearly, the failure to see economic decisions as ecological decisions falls into this category of simplification.

2. *Drawing shorter temporal frames* – this type of simplification seeks to avoid consideration of the long or medium term consequences of actions, or properly examining the full range of causes and connections that give rise to the present situation. Systems are not things, they are processes, and restricting the temporal frame under consideration is a form of systemic restriction.

3. *Ignoring key processes and interconnections* - again this is a way of limiting the scope of the system under consideration. We see this when businesses make decisions without considerations of internal interconnections, or business decisions without consideration of effects on families, society or the environment.

4. *Failure to approach tension and paradox*. One way we simplify our perspective is to ignore or avoid tensions. The coaching principle, 'the client is the expert' is an example of this. It neatly resolves the tension felt by coaches when they face client issues for which they feel unqualified or inadequate.

Happily, we can enhance our perspective taking capacity by exercising the opposite of these simplifications:

1. *Draw wider systems boundaries* – what other systems or system elements need to be part of the decision-making process? What other voices need to be present?
2. *Draw longer temporal frames* – where has this issue come from? If we adopt this response, what might it look like in the short, medium and long term?
3. *Focussing on process and interconnectedness* – what other system processes might be affected by this? What interconnections might be at play?
4. *Approaching tensions and paradoxes.* Rather than seeing tension as something to be overcome, system thinkers see tensions as doorways to new bigger understandings of the system.

Why must we take a complexity perspective?

We have argued that the first step in addressing the ethical challenges facing coaching, is to develop a perspective that is sufficient to meet those challenges. This is not just a 'nice to have', it is built into the structure of all complex adaptive systems. Ashby's (1964) law of requisite variety states that if we are to address the challenges of a complex system, then we must have the same or greater variety in our responses as the variety of challenges presented to us by the environment. If we do not have this requisite variety, then one of three things will happen:

1. We will simplify the environment to match our available responses.
2. We will increase our available responses to match the variety of challenges presented to us (i.e., increase our complexity).
3. We will cease to survive in that environment.

We suggest that the only sustainable response is that we increase the complexity of our responding. This is a developmental process.

Ethical decision making is a developmental process for both coach and client

Research into child and adult development and meaning making from Piaget to the present day, clearly tells us that the capacity to form and understand complex perspectives is something that develops across the life span (e.g. see Kegan, 1994). While it is beyond the scope of this chapter to discuss in depth the developmental process, it has important implications for us as coaches.

The first implication is that a reliance on static codes of ethical conduct, however well intentioned, will be insufficient to meet the demands of ethical decision making in complex settings. Secondly, the collaborative process of developing more complex shared perspectives requires that we are personally able to take more complex perspectives. This begs the questions: *How then are coaches engaged in continually developing their perspective taking capacity? What do your perspectives make obvious to you? What is hidden from you by your perspectives?*

Thirdly, how can we challenge and support our clients to take bigger perspectives? This means that coaching engagements must be fundamentally collaborative and developmental. Coaches will need to hone genuinely dialogical skill sets if they are to meet their clients where they are at and engage with the tensions and paradoxes that can lead to more useful perspectives.

Some questions to consider:

The above discussion of perspective taking capacity suggests a number of questions that coaches can ask themselves and their clients to enhance their ethical decision making?:

Are we holding the torch high enough?
What parts of the system are we ignoring?
What other voices need to be heard (including human and environmental stakeholders that have no voice)?
What are the tensions, dilemmas and paradoxes I/we would rather avoid?
Does our perspective have the requisite variety to meet this challenge in the short, medium and long term?
What processes, relationships and interconnections are we preferencing? What are we ignoring?

Factor 2: Purpose

When purpose is mentioned in coaching, it is often used interchangeably with the term goal. This is not the meaning of purpose here. Rather, purpose is defined as the pattern of commitments that give meaning to action. In other words, it is the set of values, outcomes and goods which make action toward any goal meaningful.

Purpose is intimately tied up with perspective taking capacity. They are mutually co-defining. The higher our perspective, the bigger our purpose typically becomes, and the more able it is to be realised in multiple ways. The lower our perspective, the more defined and clearer our purpose but the narrower and more limited it becomes.

Just as our perspective will stimulate a bigger purpose, a smaller purpose will tether our perspectives to those immediately associated with its fulfilment. The perspective that the coachee's goal is paramount tethers coaching to the purpose and perspective of the coachee. We believe this is too narrow a foundation upon which to build an ecologically sound coaching enterprise.

The following questions may be of use to coaches in considering purpose when coaching:

What is my purpose, what is the client's purpose, and what is our common purpose in this coaching engagement?
Is our purpose big enough?
Who benefits from this purpose? Who loses?
What is the impact on wider systems and the ecology if we are successful in achieving our purpose?
What will future generations say about our purpose? Are we being and becoming good ancestors?

Factor 3: Positive process

Positive process is the practical application of purpose and perspective. It refers to how our perspective and purpose is implemented. It is defined as the creation of processes that are respectful and bear an appropriate mix of challenge and support for people as they attempt to work in complex and contested spaces.

Ethical decision making, if it is to be effective, requires action. For that action to be effective and ethical it must be collaborative and ethically coherent. This means that the processes we use must seek to value all that needs to be valued. It also means that ethical action involves not just individual choices, they also involve systemic processes. Leaders, groups and coaches should consider how the processes we implement serve to support or constrain ethically effective behaviour.

For example, the raising of ecological concerns, both in organisations and coaching engagements, often requires significant courage on the part of the person raising the concerns and may carry significant costs for that person. The creation of a positive process for ecological sustainability would include ways in which the system could ensure ecological concerns were brought forward without the need for attendant personal risk and the courage needed to take that risk. In other words, it would involve the creation of courageous systems rather than relying on courageous individuals.

Questions that might enhance decision making around positive process include:

Are the processes we are contemplating respectful to those involved?
Who benefits from these processes, who loses, and who bears the costs of any externalities associated with them?
How can we support people as they strive to behave ethically?
What forces are operating on people that limit or constrain their capacity to respond?
How sustainable is the behaviour we are asking of people, given all the demands facing them?

Factor 4: Proprioception

Proprioception is the capacity of the nervous system that allows us to know where we are in the world and the relationship of our body to the external world. It is the process that allows us to touch our finger to our nose with our eyes closed. It combines internal sensory input (interoception) with external sensory data (exteroception) to let us know where we are in the world, so that we can adapt our responses to meet a changing world. Proprioception is here used primarily as a metaphor. It refers to the internal and external data streams we use to sense where we are in our emerging and changing world, and to develop responses that fit with our purpose and perspective.

In practical terms, proprioception is the ability to notice the weak signals around us that tell us how the world is unfolding in relation to the things we deem important. In the workplace it may include what is talked about around the coffee machine, changes in employee mood or customer sentiment. It might include noticing minor changes in our own or others' moods and behaviours. At its most basic, proprioception is simply the noticing of tensions, the unexpected or things that don't fit. It is paying attention to that scratchy feeling in the back of your mind that tells you to pay attention. More systematically, it involves the deliberate creation of feedback loops and data streams that bear upon the issue at hand. Ideally the closer to real time feedback the more effective one's proprioception may be in creating systemic responsiveness.

Questions coaches can ask of themselves and their clients to develop proprioception and ethical responsiveness include:

What tensions am I/we noticing? What unexpected things are happening?
What information would tell you that the course of action you have embarked upon is working?
What information would tell you that the course of action is failing? What impacts are being felt around the system? How have conversations changed? What is being spoken about, what is not? What can be spoken about, what cannot?

Vignette 3

In this vignette coach Dr Josie McLean describes her work with a leadership team. Here McLean questions the ethics of not enabling spaces for people to talk about things that matter to them:

> "Before a team coaching launch event I considered how to create space for the team to consider the greatest existential question of our time, allowing ... the conversation to emerge as the team members wanted and needed... – rather than me preaching at them. I chose to open the space indirectly or from the side, rather than directly. As we considered their team purpose, I began... with individual purpose that is then aggregated into the team purpose.
>
> I employed an adapted version of Krznaric's exercise from his book "The Good Ancestor" (see Whybrow et al., 2023, Chapter 6, pp. 205–207). It ...looks across many generations... to someone young now, talking at the end of their lives about the legacy they have gained from us, making the inquiry very personal. I also asked other coaching questions around the topic of personal purpose.
>
> At the end of this exercise, team members shared their emerging sense of their personal purpose. As they did so, a few were tearful and yet relieved and thankful to finally have the space to talk about some of their deepest concerns for their children, a conversation that they hadn't engaged together in before and this powered their team purpose...... Perhaps the societal and organisational norms are still such that it makes acting ethically, from our internal compasses, more difficult than it should or need be."
>
> (Personal communication, May 2022)

Vignette 4

The role of education has already been touched on, and here Diana Tedoldi, Founder of The Nature Coaching Academy in Italy, describes how education is central for her:

> "...creating an ethical approach benefits our clients and our planet. We need to make coaching education radical.... How can we partner with our clients in connecting self-awareness and self-realization with social and ecological impact? How can we enable a systemic view of their life challenges, supporting them in understanding that personal, social and environmental crises are different aspects of the same issues? We don't need new ethical models or principles. We need to reconnect with nature's intelligence...and with our somatic intelligence."
>
> (Personal communication, May 2022)

Conclusion

In this chapter we have laid out the ethical challenges facing us all and argued that coaching needs a new paradigm to deal with them. There are shoots of change emerging in the industry. We have provided one model as a potential way to do this, developing our perspective-taking, purpose, positive process and proprioception (our constant connectedness to signs of change). Through the vignettes other coaches have shown their approaches.

The professional bodies through their codes, accreditation and credentialing and their offers for development, along with broader coach education will be key to this.

Finally, we argue the coaching community has an ethical imperative to be good ancestors and hear the voice of future generations. It seems fitting to finish with a quote drawn from a contemporary indigenous perspective Kimmerer, 2020, p. 383).

> "Our elders say that ceremony is the way we can remember to remember. In the dance of the giveaway, remember that the earth is a gift we must pass on, just as it came to us. When we forget, the dances we'll need will be for mourning. For the passing of polar bears, the silence of cranes, for the death of rivers and the memory of snow...We need to recognize the dazzling gifts of the world."

Discussion points

1. As you have read this chapter what emotions and thoughts have come up for you? How has this touched on your personal ethics and your views about coaching and its functions?
2. What do you see as the implications for coach training and development?
3. How might this have implications for coach/coachee contracting?
4. What implications might there be for coach supervision?

Recommended reading

Boulton, J. G., Allan, P. M., & Bowman, C. (2015) *Embracing Complexity: Strategic Perspectives for an age of turbulence.* Oxford: Oxford University Press.

References

Boulton, J. G., Allan, P. M., & Bowman, C. (2015) *Embracing Complexity: Strategic Perspectives for an age of turbulence.* Oxford: Oxford University Press.

Capra, F. & Luisi, P. L. (2014) *The Systems View of Life: A Unifying Vision.* Cambridge: Cambridge University Press.

Cavanagh, M (2006) Coaching from a systemic perspective: A Complex Adaptive Conversation. In D. Stober & A. M. Grant (Eds), *Evidence Based Coaching Handbook*. New York, NY: Wiley, pp. 313–354.

Cavanagh, M. (2013) The Coaching Engagement in the 21st Century: New paradigms for complex times. In D. Clutterbuck, D. Megginson and S. David (Eds), *Beyond Goals: Effective strategies for coaching and mentoring*. London: Gower Publishing.

Cavanagh, M., Stern, L., & Lane, D., (2016) Supervision in coaching psychology: A systemic developmental Psychological perspective. In D. Lane, M. Watts, & S. Corrie, *Supervision in the Psychological Professions: Building your own personalized model*. London: McGraw Hill, pp. 173–194.

Cavanagh, M. & Grant. A., (2006) Coaching psychology and the scientist-practitioner model. In S. Corrie & D. Lane (Eds). *The Modern Scientist Practitioner.*

Cavanagh, M. & Lane, D. (2012a) Coaching psychology coming of age: The challenges we face in the messy world of complexity. *International Coaching Psychology Review*, 7(1): 75–90.

Cavanagh, M. & Lane, D. (2012b) Coaching Psychology Coming of Age: A response to our discussants. *International Coaching Psychology Review*, 7(1): 125–127.

Cavanagh, M. & Spence, G. (2012) Mindfulness in coaching: philosophy, psychology or just a useful skill? In J. Passmore, D. Peterson, & T. Freire (Eds). *The Wiley-Blackwell Handbook of Psychology of Coaching and Mentoring*. London: Wiley Blackwell, pp. 112–134.

Cohen, Z. (2022) Personal communication with Eve Turner, May 2022.

Dizikes, P. (2011) When the Butterfly Effect Took Flight. *MIT Technology Review*, February 22. www.technologyreview.com/2011/02/22/196987/when-the-butterfly-effect-took-flight, accessed April 30, 2022.

Ferguson, Peter (2019) The Growth Imperative. In *Post-growth Politics*. Cham: Springer, p. 119. doi:10.1007/978-973-319-78799-2.

Florio, L. (2008) Applications of constructive developmental theory to the studies of leadership development: A systematic review. Submitted master's thesis, Cranfield University.

Global Code of Ethics. (2021) The global code of ethics. For coaches, mentors and supervisors. www.globalcodeofethics.org.

Gordon, Myron J. & Rosenthal, Jeffrey S. (2003) Capitalism's growth imperative. *Cambridge Journal of Economics*, 27(1): 25–48. doi:10.1093/cje/27.1.25.

Gwyn, W. G. & J. Cavanagh, M. (2021) Adolescents' Experiences of a Developmental Coaching and Outdoor Adventure Education Program: Using Constructive-Developmental Theory to Investigate Individual Differences in Adolescent Meaning-Making and Developmental Growth. *Journal of Adolescent Research*. doi:10.1177/07435584211010805.

Han, Byung-Chul. (2015) *The burnout society*. Stanford, CA: Stanford University Press.

Hawkins, P. (2012) *Creating a Coaching Culture*. Maidenhead: Open University Press.

Hawkins, P. (2017) *Tomorrow's Leadership and the necessary revolution in today's leadership development*. Henley: Henley Business School.

Hawkins, P. & Turner, E. (2020) *Systemic Coaching – delivering value beyond the individual.* Abingdon: Routledge.

Hutchins, G. (2022) Personal communication with Eve Turner, May 2022.

International Coaching Federation. (2021) ICF Code of Ethics. https://coachingfederation.org/ethics/code-of-ethics, accessed May 1, 2022.

Joint Global Statement Group. (2022) Joint Global Statement Group Climate and Ecodiversity Crises. www.jgsg.one, accessed April 30, 2022.

Joint Global Statement Group. (2020) *Joint Global Statement on Climate Change.* www.jgsg.one/joint-global-statement, accessed July 5, 2022.

Kasotia, P. (2022) The health effects of global warming: developing countries are the most vulnerable. *UN Chronicle* [online]. www.un.org/en/chronicle/article/health-effects-global-warming-developing-countries-are-most-vulnerable, accessed April 2022.

Kegan, R. (1994). *In over our heads: The mental demands of modern life.* Cambridge, MA: Harvard University Press.

Kegan, R. & Lahey, L. (2009) *Immunity to change.* Boston, MA: Harvard Business Press.

Kimmerer, R. (2020) *Braiding sweetgrass. indigenous wisdom, scientific knowledge and the teachings of plants.* London: Penguin Books.

Kolbert, E. (2015) *The Sixth Extinction.* London: Bloomsbury Publishing.

Krznaric, R. (2020) *The good ancestor: how to think long term in a short-term world.* London: W. H. Allen & Co.

Lane D. A. & Corrie, S. (2012) *Making successful decisions in Counselling and Psychotherapy.* Maidenhead: Open University Press.

Lane, D. A., Magadlela, D., Yong, I., & Spiegel, S. (2023) *Ethics and Culture in Coaching – Embracing a more Universal Ethical Code.* In W.-A. Smith, J. Passmore, E. Turner, Y.-L. Lai, & D. Clutterbuck (Eds), *The Ethical Coaches' Handbook.* Abingdon: Routledge.

McGrath, M. (2022) Climate change: IPCC scientists say it's 'now or never' to limit warming. BBC, 4 April.www.bbc.co.uk/news/science-environment-60984663, accessed April 30, 2022.

McLean, J. J. (2017) Embedding sustainability into organisational DNA: a story of complexity. University of Adelaide. PhD thesis. doi:10.4225/55/5b21f318e7939.

McLean, J. J. (2022) Personal communication with Eve Turner, May 2022.

NASA. (2022) Vital signs of the planet. https://climate.nasa.gov/vital-signs, accessed April 30, 2022.

O'Connor, S. & Cavanagh, M. (2017) Group and team coaching. In T. Bachkirova, G. Spence, & D. Drake (Eds), *The SAGE handbook of coaching.* Sage Publications, pp. 486–504.

Polman, P. & Winston, A. (2021) *Net positive: How courageous companies thrive by giving more than they take.* Cambridge, MA: Harvard Business Review Press.

Scharmer, O. (2016) *Theory U – leading from the future as it emerges,* 2nd Edition. Oakland, CA: Berrett-Koehler.

Tedoldi, D. (2022) Personal communication with Eve Turner, May 2022.

Thatcher, M. (1987) Interview for "Woman's Own" by Douglas Keay ("No Such Thing as Society"). In *Margaret Thatcher Foundation: Speeches, Interviews and Other Statements.* London. www.margaretthatcher.org/document/106689, accessed July 26, 2022.

United Nations. (2021) Climate Action. Speech by António Guterres at Colombia University, December 2.www.un.org/en/climatechange/un-secretary-general-speaks-state-planet.

Vaughan, A. (2022) The world's 1.5°C climate goal is slipping out of reach – so now what? *NewScientist*. June 7. www.newscientist.com/article/2323175-the-worlds-1-5c-climate-goal-is-slipping-out-of-reach-so-now-what, accessed July 1, 2022.

Whybrow, A., Turner, E., McLean, J. with Hawkins, P. (2023). *Ecological and Climate-Conscious coaching – A Companion Guide to Evolving Coaching Practice*. Abingdon: Routledge.

Chapter 23

Ethics and the digital environment in coaching

Marc Buergi, Mona Ashok and David Clutterbuck

Introduction

There is increasing discussion about the ethical concerns of using digital technology, inevitably generating a variety of questions. Coaches have been using digital media for more than two decades, however the impact of Covid-19 pandemic has been, that online virtual coaching now accounts for the majority of workplace coaching (e.g. Passmore, 2021; Passmore et al., 2021). Advances in digital technology and the Covid-19 pandemic triggered significant changes in coaching practices (Passmore et al., 2021; Turner & Goldvarg, 2021), with little or no investigation in relation to the ethical considerations of digital coaching.

Almost all the research into digital coaching focuses on the practicalities, advantages and disadvantages of the genre (e.g. Terblanche et al., 2022; Kanatouri, 2020; Terblanche, 2020; Wegener et al., 2020; Berninger-Schäfer, 2018; Geissler, 2018; Heller et al., 2018), rather than on fundamental philosophical and ethical aspects. This chapter explores artificial intelligence and the digital environment broadly, questions the influences and challenges of AI and digital coaching. The chapter highlights digital coaching ethics (DiCE) as it is referred to in coaching codes of ethics and provides a suggested systemic view of digital coaching ethics required for coaching ethically in the digital environment. Finally, a series of vignettes is offered with reflecting questions for the coaching practitioner that aim to map what ethical issues exist when coaching in the digital environment.

Artificial intelligence and the digital environment

The use of Artificial Intelligence (AI) is gaining momentum in all spheres of life (Madan & Ashok, 2022; Müller, 2022; Osterle, 2020; Winfield, 2019) including self-help and psychological treatments (see Fairburn & Patel, 2017 for an overview), which has implications for coaching. Digital technologies have made the world a global market as such they are enabling value co-creation (Patha et al., 2022; Ashok, 2018). We the authors define the **digital**

DOI: 10.4324/9781003277729-23

environment *as a context of digital services, products, communication and data processing in the private, professional and public domain. Including exposure to, use of and impact of digital technology on individuals, organisations, governments and society.* Examples being (non-exhaustive): electronic devices, hardware, software, electronic data storage, physical or cloud, email, electronic agenda, contacts, session scheduling, office applications, websites, social media, video conferencing, online collaboration, content capturing, digital recording, speech-to-text conversion, digital coaching platforms, electronic status reports, assignments, contracting, coach-client matching, invoicing and billing processes, intelligent software support, digital sensors, artificial intelligence, chat bots, virtual and augmented reality.

AI and coaching

Most of what is currently marketed as AI in coaching is in many cases a form of coachbot. The difference is primarily that a coachbot reproduces algorithms developed by humans, while a true AI learns from its interactions with its environment (including humans) and develops new algorithms of its own. Small coach biases can be amplified unpredictably, with unexpected negative effects. While existing data protection and data use ethics provide guidelines for working with coachbots, the situation with AI is much less clear – not least because neither the AI nor human intervention can explain the reasoning process (Kanatouri, 2020). Sharing of data between coach, coachbots and AI complicates matters further – the ethics of 'virtual pillow talk' (i.e. important conversations that cannot be overheard), - including those who record the coaching conversations - pose a major challenge for the future. Issues of transparency abound – for example, when is the coach or the AI steering the conversation, and does it matter to the client?

Digital ethics

Digital ethics' *is defined as "the systems of values and moral principles for the conduct of electronic interactions among people, organisations and things"* (Buytendijk, 2019, p. 3). Despite the strides in the application of digital technology, there exists a large gap in the impact analysis of ethical tensions of using digital technologies and their implications for policy and practice (Ashok et al., 2022a), in particular coaching.

Digital coaching ethics (DiCE)

What is DiCE and how can practitioners reflect on the issues at hand? We understand that we are not capable of giving all answers relating to the complex challenges faced in the digital environment. However, the goal of this chapter is to raise awareness about potential issues and to provide a set of reflective questions to support the coaching practitioner, be it for self-reflection, supervision or training on ethical issues.

We the authors define **digital coaching ethics(DiCE)** as *ethical considerations for the coaching of clients in a digital environment.* Thereby **ethics** serve as a moral framework for decision-making within a context. Attention to ethics enables the coach to be authentic, confident and professional when faced with complexity. Passmore et al. (In Press) define **coaching** as *"...partnering with clients to help them reflect on themselves, their situation and context, and identify new insights and actions to unlock potential, enhance wellbeing and improve performance."* Furthermore, coaching *"involves partnering with clients in a thought-provoking and creative process that inspires them to maximise their personal and professional potential"* (International Coaching Federation, 2022). A **client** herein is *the individual or team/group being coached i.e. the coachee, the coach being mentored or supervised, or the coach or the student coach being trained.*

Current literature, professional bodies, coach education and coaches are lagging in understanding the ethical dilemmas created by the use of digital technologies. We enquired about coaching in the digital environment with the professional coaching bodies by asking them how they support their members concerning digital coaching ethics and whether they could provide further literature or resources. Three international bodies from the English-speaking world and 15 from the European German-speaking world were addressed by email. The replies indicated that smaller organisations tended to apply general coaching ethics standards without explicit consideration of digital issues. They would refer to bigger or international partner organisations and their ethical codes.

The combined results from the literature search and the inquiry with the professional coaching bodies led us to gravitate towards three main sources and their initiatives concerning our questions. First, programmes by governmental and private bodies for the standardisation of IT are about to regulate the development and use of AI technology (e.g. AlgorithmWatch, 2022; UNESCO, 2021; European Union, 2020; Institute of Electrical and Electronics Engineers, 2019; European Union, 2018).

Second, The International Coaching Federation (ICF) provides coaching core competencies guided by a code of ethics (2022a; 2022b), where in the latter the most consideration to digital coaching is given in competencies represented as the pledges for coaches as noted below:

"Maintain the strictest levels of confidentiality with all parties as agreed upon. I am aware of and agree to comply with all applicable laws that pertain to personal data and communications" (International Coaching Federation, 2020, Section 1: 3) and:

"Maintain, store, and dispose of any records, including electronic files and communications, created during my professional interactions in a manner that promotes confidentiality, security and privacy and complies with any applicable laws and agreements. Furthermore, I seek to make proper use of emerging and growing technological developments that are being used in coaching services (technology-assisted coaching services) and be aware how various ethical standards apply to them."

(International Coaching Federation, 2020, Section 1: 7)

Furthermore, the recently founded "AI Coaching Standards Work Group" aims at providing future guidelines for digital coaching ethics (International Coaching Federation, 2022c).

Third, the Global Code of Ethics (GCoE) with several coaching bodies having signed to the code, created by the original members The European Mentoring and Coaching Council (EMCC) and the Association of Coaching, refer to AI in the Global Code of Ethics (GCoE) whereby:

"Members will keep, store and dispose of all data and records of their client work including digital files and communications, in a manner that ensures confidentiality, security, and privacy, and complies with all relevant laws and agreements that exist in their client's country regarding data protection and privacy."

(Global Code of Ethics, 2.15, p. 5)

and

"Members will demonstrate respect for the variety of practices used by members and other individuals in the profession and all the different ethically informed approaches to coaching, mentoring, and supervision, including the use of data technologies and AI."

(Global Code of Ethics, 3.2, p. 7)

Systemic digital coaching ethics

We, the authors suggest that current professional coaches, to a large extent, are coaching in a digital environment. Thus, developing guidance, codes, standards, principles and practices requires collaboration between different key stakeholders. Given the multiple and complex issues, digital coaching ethics considerations should be supported at least at the following six systemic levels:

1. **The individual coach** (*the coach system*) such as the independent coach, who takes care of self-development, their own continuous coach education, reading, or self-reflection (see vignettes that follow).
2. **Between coach and client** (*the coaching system*) by raising issues, discussions and awareness in coaching, before, during and after coaching sessions.

3. **In coach training, mentoring, or supervision** (*the coach education system*), to receive feedback, learn from supervisors, master coaches, mentors or peers.
4. **Professional bodies for coaching** (*the coach profession system*) such as the ICF, the EMCC or the AC, Coaches and Mentors of South Africa, International Association of Coaching and The Association for Professional Executive Coaching and Supervision (but some examples) which provide standards, certification processes, quality monitoring, research, and resources for coaches.
5. **Other professional bodies**, e.g. for digital technology (*the digital system*) such as councils for IT/IS, robotics, machine learning, AI, virtual and augmented reality.
6. **Society and humanity as a whole** (*the wider regulatory system*), represented by national and international governments and regulatory bodies, such as South Africa, Australia, USA, UK, Switzerland, Germany, the EU and the UN.

Vignettes

The following vignettes are drawn from discussions with professional coaching bodies and the outcomes from coaching practitioners' views on how AI and ethics come into play in the field of coaching (Buergi et al., 2022) in the modern day and future coaching digital environment. It is hoped the vignettes take a step toward addressing the gap mentioned earlier in this chapter.

Vignette 1 – Ethics and digital administration

A coach (Dana) uses email for communication and an electronic agenda for scheduling coaching sessions and to organise the client's contact details. In a conversation with a friend Dana argues that since she meets only face-to-face for coaching with clients in her office, she was not involved with digital coaching at all. The friend replies, that from what was said, one would consider Dana to be a digital coach and that Dana should take the respective ethical issues into account.

Consider the following questions:

Is the coach a digital coach?

Why should the coach reflect on digital coaching ethics?

Where is the client data stored (local, cloud, server location in the USA, EU or elsewhere)?

How is the client data protected from unauthorised access (secured access, logins, passwords, encrypted storage, transfer)?

How long is the data stored (emails, calendar entries, contact details, notes)?

When is the data deleted and according to which governance policy?

Who has access to details, for example who reads email exchanges with clients (employees, personal assistants, family members, coaching platform providers, other intermediaries)?

Vignette 2 – Ethics and digital marketing

A coach (Gerard) offers coaching services on a website, and lists testimonials with a full display of client names and company details to attract potential new business to the website. Gerard further markets his competence and reputation as being 'the indisputable number one coach in the universe' (see Chapter 25 for further discussion on the promotion of coaching). Owing to the marketing activities on social media platforms, Gerard engages in many discussions with corporate representatives for lead generation. He doesn't hesitate to display corporate brands as being 'his customers' on the website soon after he first pitched services to the corporate.

Consider the following questions:

Is the coach acting ethically (claims that they are the number one coach in the universe, displaying prospects as customers)?

What should the coach consider when using the website and social media platforms for marketing (including the use of client testimonials)?

Did the clients (individuals or corporates) give explicit permission to use their details and testimonies and under which conditions (duration when the details can be displayed, what channels the data can be displayed on, data deletion procedure, compensation agreement)?

What are the policies and processes for obtaining client consent for the display of data?

What is ethically sound coaching behaviour, especially when dealing with online branding, marketing, and promotion (for example when can a coach call an individual or corporate a client, how should consent be agreed)?

Vignette 3 – Ethics and online conferencing

A coach (Una) offers video-call assisted coaching conversations and uses the built-in function of the application to record the session for later referral. Una assumes that the client will be ok with the recording. With the help of online service, Una later has the conversation transcribed from speech to text. She has her assistant produce a print-out of the conversational text on paper to store it in the file cabinet in the office.

One of the sessions with the client went so well, that Una decided to use the recorded material for the educational, training, and supervision process. Una uses the audio file and the electronic transcript of the coaching session to receive feedback from her supervisor (see Chapter 26 for case studies on the topic of session recordings). The two discuss if the coach's performance in this material could be uploaded as a demo tape for review by the professional body to earn a certified accreditation.

Consider the following questions:

What are the ethical considerations when using online audio and video-conferencing services?

What are the policy and processes that underpin the use of coaching sessions for supervision, certification, or other means?

What should be considered when taking and storing (digital) notes including session transcripts?

Are the audio and video recordings of the coaching sessions and their transcripts securely handled (stored, accessed, edited, shared, managed, and deleted)?

What are the coaching certification requirements and how can these requirements be met ethically?

Vignette 4 – Ethics and the digital platform

A coach (Irina) was contracted as a freelancer by a digital coaching platform, which was an exciting new business opportunity. The platform would support marketing and sales and provide categories of their coaching model, online learning nuggets, assignments for clients, and progress monitoring. The clients tend to like the coaching platform, because it provides video communication, visualisation of content, live recording, break-out group sessions, chat rooms, content libraries and scheduling among other things.

However, Irina realised the collaboration significantly brought down her earnings, owing to low rates. Further, on many occasions, the platform failed to provide a stable video connection to clients. The platform only offered a basic set of interventional functionalities which limited the creativity and innovation in the coaching process. Just recently, the coaching platform sent an automated email in error to all the platform's clients informing them that their coaching package had ended. This information left many clients confused and they wouldn't book any further sessions. Irina suffered not only economic loss, but also reputation damage.

Consider the following questions:

Technical dependence and centralisation: Coaches operating on third-party coaching platforms depend economically, operationally, technically on the providers. What are the ethical considerations?

Relationship and trust-building: What is the power balance between coaching platforms, their coaches and the clients (negotiation, terms & conditions, interventions, trust-building, communication)?

Beneficiaries and protocols: Ethical questions arise about who should benefit from digital coaching services, who should own the generated data, and who should benefit economically? And further, which compliance protocols and processes should mega-corporations (i.e. service and platform providers, data collectors, suppliers of AI) adhere to and how are they implemented?

Vignette 5 – Ethics and session data for research

A coach (Steven) uses an online provider for coaching. During a group coaching session, Steven offered to save the thumbnails with all the participants' faces as a group picture. The video was also used to detect personal emotional states by smart facial recognition software, without getting the participants' approval. All the data was stored by default somewhere in the cloud. Steven was not sure where the data servers were located, nor how the data would be handled by the provider.

Later, Steven thought that the recorded coaching sessions could be used for research purposes. Steven approached an academic institution with the proposition. The academic team found this to be a valuable opportunity and decided to start the data analysis and apply for an ethics approval retrospectively only if they found interesting results. Since Steven was the initial data provider but was not employed or compensated by the academic institution, he considered ethics questions to be none of his business.

Consider the following questions:

Using online services for coaching raises issues like data storage, data access, data management and data safety.

What are the issues in using online coaching providers and smart software? Who has access and for what purpose? What agreements have been made about the use of data with the clients?

Who are the key stakeholders and who is responsible for ethical considerations in digital coaching and the use of the created data?

What ethical considerations should be taken into account when creating policies for digital coaching?

Vignette 6 – Ethics and smart software support

An international company partners with a digital coaching start-up to implement AI coaching. Clients are linked up with a basic chatbot. Once the topic, issues and goals are set, the clients are hooked up with a more sophisticated AI coach who imitates even more closely a human interaction. Further, clients get a chance to use virtual reality headsets, where walking on distant planets during sessions is among the most popular choices. Some clients develop an addiction to the immersive nature of virtual and augmented reality.

Clients soon forget that they are coached by an AI, since the sessions are no longer distinguishable from human interactions. In one session, the robot confused one client with another client and erroneously played back confidential recordings from an earlier client, thereby breaching confidentiality. The machine finally realised its mistake and ran. The police chased the robot for quite a while before detaining it. A case was filed in court, and the robot was convicted of an unforgivable mistake by a machine against humanity under the 'universal human and machine digital coaching ethics regulations'. The declaration of the punishment is still pending.

Consider the following questions:

How do we ethically handle the potential impact of digital services and realities such as the potential of confusing AI with human interactions, or the development of addictions to virtual realities, and the like?

Who is responsible for the AI coach's mistake – the developer of the AI, the company that sells the AI software or robot, the user, or other parties?

How do we control the potential bias when programming, training and applying AI, e.g. who is writing the code, what are the guiding models and principles, and which data is used for training?

Vignette 7 – Ethics and super Artificial Intelligence

The coach (Bruce) and his supervisor (Ann) are meeting virtually. On a separate screen for each of them is their AI and the two AIs are linked. The supervisor Ann asks: "What were the client's actual words?" Bruce's AI reviews the coaching conversation and retrieves the words used, along with an analysis of the emotional state of the client and Bruce at that moment in question. Ann's AI – having learned how she thinks – is already communicating with Bruce's AI – machine to machine – about the pattern of emotional interaction between Bruce and not just this client but all other earlier clients as well. Does the observed pattern only apply in this instance or is it a frequent occurrence? All of this happens without Bruce being aware of what is going on in the background.

Later, Bruce is reflecting on a hybrid coaching session supported by AI. The client asked at the end, "So, who was coaching me – you or the machine?" The question prompted Bruce to reflect upon the degree of his dependency on AI. Where and how was the coach adding value beyond the suggestions from the

AI? As much as Bruce doesn't want to face up to the issue, he concludes that the client would get better value from being coached 'on-demand' by the AI, and with fewer but more personal sessions with the human coach, where Bruce could make effective use of his unique human life and work experience.

Consider the following questions:

What are the implications for contracting: who or what is the client contracting with?

What permissions are required when requesting AI data, from whom and when?

What needs to be considered for AI sharing data with another AI – machine to machine communication?

Who owns and has access to the data from the client's conversations with the AI?

A digital coaching ethics health check for the coaching practitioner

The following digital coaching ethics questions are proposed to support the coaching practitioner's self-reflection, as a framework for supervision or as guidance for coach education, mentoring and general digital ethical practice.

A. In a digital context, coaches might regularly enquire

1. Which aspects of my work as a coach today are digital? (Current awareness)
2. How much more digital will my coaching become in the coming years? (Future awareness)
3. In what ways is the digital technology, which I am using, changing the conduct and psychological contract of my coaching? (Articulate)
4. How does it change the power in the coaching relationship? (Context)
5. Who are the stakeholders and what voice do they have? (Context)
6. What are the real or potential consequences of using the technology? (Implications)
7. What is the depth of my awareness of the issues relating to digital technologies? (Alternative perspectives)
8. Who else can I talk to, who might see the issues differently? (Alternative perspectives)

   a) How do my priorities align with those of other stakeholders? (Balance)
   b) What are my intuition and my conscience telling me? (Final check)

B. Ethical decision-making from a digital perspective

The following is a six-stage model of ethical decision-making, applicable to digital coaching as it is to non-digital. The stages are:

1. Articulate the problem: Who does it affect and why? What is the conflict of interest?
2. Consider the context: Who is involved? Who has and hasn't been consulted? What responsibilities do players have?
3. Consider the implications: What safety, financial reputational, or other risks are involved? What would be the impact of doing this on a larger scale?
4. Alternative perspectives: What other opinions or perspectives may be relevant? Who might provide a valuable challenge? Who do we need to listen to and how will we ensure they speak up?
5. Balance the arguments: What priorities should we apply?
6. The final check: Does it "feel" right? How honest are we with ourselves?

Conclusion

The digital world poses many previously unseen and complex ethical challenges for coaches. These will in many cases demand new thinking about the nature of ethics, the client-coach relationship and the interface between client, coach, technology and society. Coaches, coach educators, professional bodies and the designers of digital solutions will have to work closely together to address these challenges as they emerge and evolve. The establishment of digital coaching ethics will happen not by abstract reasoning but by how all parties react to the scenarios – such as those presented in this chapter – that emerge in real-life practice.

Discussion questions

1. In case you're adopting or not adopting the new technologies for your coaching, what are the costs of doing/not doing so? For whom? What are the benefits? For whom?
2. How can you increase your understanding, skills, confidence and influence on what is going on with the technical developments and the digitalisation in coaching?
3. How can you use technology to your advantage to support wellbeing, happiness and better lives for every single person of the human tribe?
4. Assuming you had a conversation with past generations, the elders, our children and future generations, how would they answer the most pressing issues around the inclusion of technology and AI in the workplace, home and specifically coaching?

Recommended reading

Osterle, H. (2020) *Life Engineering. Machine Intelligence and Quality of Life.* Wiesbaden: Springer.

References

Association for Coaching. (2022) Membership. The Global Code of Ethics. www. associationforcoaching.com/page/AboutCodeEthics.

AlgorithmWatch. (2022) AI Ethics Guidelines Global Inventory. Database. https:// inventory.algorithmwatch.org/database.

Ashok, M., Buergi, M., & Clutterbuck D. (2022b) *Appendix – A practitioner survey on Digital Coaching Ethics (DiCE)*. Results from the Coaching Ethics Forum. Exploring Ethics in Coaching (February 2022). Henley Business School.

Ashok, M., Madan, R., Joha, A., & Sivarajah, U. (2022a) Ethical framework for Artificial Intelligence and Digital technologies. *International Journal of Information Management*, 62(102433): 1–17.

Ashok, M. (2018) Role of digitisation in enabling co-creation of value in KIBS firms. In *International Conference on Informatics and Semiotics in Organisations*. Cham: Springer, pp. 145–154.

Berninger-Schäfer, E. (2018) *Online-Coaching*. Wiesbaden: Springer.

Buergi, M., Ashok, M., & Clutterbuck D. (2022) *Ethics and the digital environment in coaching*. Exploring Ethics in Coaching Conference (February 2022). https:// coachingethicsforum.com.

Buytendijk, F. (2019) Digital Ethics, or How to Not Mess Up With Technology, Gartner Report, ID: G00338664.

European Coaching and Mentoring Council. (2022) Thought Leadership & Development. Ethics. The Global Code of Ethics. www.emccglobal.org/leadership-development/ethics.

European Union. (2018) General Data Protection Regulation. https://gdpr-info.eu.

European Union. (2020) The ethics of artificial intelligence: Issues and initiatives. www.europarl.europa.eu/thinktank/en/document/EPRS_STU(2020)634452.

Fairburn, C. G. & Patel, V. (2017) The impact of digital technology on psychological treatments and their dissemination. *Behaviour Research and Therapy*, 88: 19–25.

Geissler, H. (2018) E-Coaching – ein Überblick. In G. Siegfried, M. Heidi, & W. Scholl, *Handbuch Schlüsselkonzepte im Coaching*. Berlin and Heidelberg: Springer, pp. 115–124.

Heller, J., Triebel, C., Hauser, B., & Koch, A. (2018) *Digitale Medien im Coaching. Grundlagen und Praxiswissen zu Coaching-Plattformen und digitalen Coaching-Formaten*. Berlin and Heidelberg: Springer.

Institute of Electrical and Electronics Engineers. (2019) Ethically Aligned Design/AI Readiness Framework. https://ethicsinaction.ieee.org and https://standards.ieee.org/ content/dam/ieee-standards/standards/web/documents/other/ead_v2.pdf.

International Coaching Federation. (2022a) Credentials and Standards. ICF Core Competencies. https://coachingfederation.org/credentials-and-standards/core-competencies.

International Coaching Federation. (2022b) Ethics. ICF Code of Ethics. https://coachingfederation.org/ethics/code-of-ethics.

International Coaching Federation. (2022c) Academic Research. The Value of Artificial Intelligence Coaching Standards. https://coachingfederation.org/research/ academic-research.

Kanatouri, S. (2020) *The Digital Coach*. London: Routledge.

Madan, R. & Ashok, M. (2022) A Public Values Perspective on the Application of Artificial Intelligence in Government Practices: A Synthesis of Case Studies. In

Handbook of Research on Artificial Intelligence in Government Practices and Processes. IGI Global, pp. 162–189.

Müller, V. C. (2022) Ethics of Artificial Intelligence and Robotics. In E. N. Zalta (Ed.), *The Stanford Encyclopedia of Philosophy* (Summer 2021 Edition). https://plato. stanford.edu/archives/sum2021/entries/ethics-ai.

Osterle, H. (2020) *Life Engineering. Machine Intelligence and Quality of Life.* Wiesbaden: Springer.

Passmore, J. (2021) *Future Trends in Coaching: Executive Report 2021.* Henley-on-Thames: Henley Business School and EMCC International.

Passmore, J., Diller, S., & Isaacson, S. (In Press) *The Digital Coaches Handbook.* Abingdon: Routledge.

Passmore, J. & Evans-Krimme, R. (2021) The future of coaching: a conceptual framework for the coaching sector from personal craft to scientific process and the implications for practice and research. *Frontiers in Psychology*, 12: 715228.

Pathak, B., Ashok, M. & Leng Tan, Y. (2022) Value co-creation in the B2B context: a conceptual framework and its implications. *The Service Industries Journal*, 42(3–4): 178–205.

Terblanche, N. (2020) *A design framework to create Artificial Intelligence* Coaches. *International Journal of Evidence Based Coaching and Mentoring*, 18(2): 152–165.

Terblanche, N., Molyn J., de Haan E., & Nilsson V. O. (2022) Comparing artificial intelligence and human coaching goal attainment efficacy. *PLoS ONE*, 17(6): e0270255.

Turner, E. & Goldvarg, D. (2021) Supervising Virtually. In T. Bachkirova, P. Jackson, & D. Clutterbuck (Eds), *Coaching & Mentoring Supervison – Theory and Practice.* London: Open University Press.

UNESCO. (2021) Preliminary study on the Ethics of Artificial Intelligence. https:// ircai.org/project/preliminary-study-on-the-ethics-of-ai/ https://ircai.org/wp-content/ uploads/2020/07/PRELIMINARY-STUDY-ON-THE-ETHICS-OF-ARTIFICIAL-INTELLIGENCE.pdf.

Wegener, R., Ackermann, S., Amstutz, J., Deplazes, S., Künzli, H. & Ryter, A. (2020) *Coaching im digitalen Wandel.* Göttingen: Vandenhoeck & Ruprecht.

Winfield, A. (2019) An Updated Round Up of Ethical Principles of Robotics and AI. https://alanwinfield.blogspot.com/2019/04/an-updated-round-up-of-ethical.html.

Chapter 24

Ethical considerations for the use of multisource feedback in coaching

Angela M. Passarelli

Introduction

Formalized feedback, such as 360-degree assessment, is widely accepted as a powerful tool for personal and professional growth in the leadership development industry. Yet research suggests that feedback interventions only marginally improve performance, and may even have deleterious effects (Jones et al., 2016; Kluger & DeNisi, 1996). This research-practice gap is an issue of professional ethics for coaches who work with multisource feedback, because well-intended coaches could unknowingly do harm to a client or act in ways that are not in the client's best interests. The purpose of this chapter is to illuminate key ethical considerations involved in formalized feedback processes, so that coaches can utilize these tools with better results. The chapter begins by situating formalized feedback processes in coaching within the broader context of ethics. Three key challenges are described, along with questions coaches can ask to mitigate these challenges. Finally, a case study highlights these challenges in an executive coaching scenario.

The ethical context for feedback in coaching

Brennan and Wildflower (2014) surveyed the ethical codes of a wide variety of professions and identified five ethical principles common to all of them:

1. **Do no harm**: Do not cause needless injury or harm to others.
2. **Duty of care**: Act in ways that promote the welfare of others.
3. **Know your limits**: Practice within the scope of your competence.
4. **Respect the interests of the client**: Act in interest of the client before self.
5. **Respect the law**: Know and abide by local, regional, and national laws.

These general principles should guide the behavior of individuals acting in a coaching capacity (Iordanou et al., 2017), and are reflected in the ethical codes of professional coaching associations and certification bodies (e.g. the International Coaching Federation, the Center for Credentialing & Education, and the European Mentoring and Coaching Council).

DOI: 10.4324/9781003277729-24

Some issues encountered in coaching present clear and egregious violations of these general principles – for example, the breach of confidentiality or improper relations with clients. However, other issues are more insidious and subtle, yet pose the possibility of violating one or more of these ethical principles. The purpose of this chapter is to draw attention to the ethical dimensions of one such issue – the use of formalized feedback in coaching.

Formalized feedback is defined as "actions taken by (an) external agent(s) to provide information regarding some aspect(s) of one's task performance" (Kluger & DeNisi, 1996, p. 255). In executive and leadership coaching, formalized feedback often takes the form of multisource feedback assessment. Multisource feedback typically involves a manager or leader being rated by a group of people with whom they regularly interact on a set of desired, work-related competencies. It is commonly called '360-degree assessment' because raters include upward, downward, and lateral hierarchical relationships, such as one's manager, direct reports, and peers (Taylor & Bright, 2011). This information is collected and collated through either surveys or live interviews with selected raters. The information is then shared with the person being coached in service of enhancing their self-awareness, informing their development goals, and improving their work effectiveness. Multisource feedback (used interchangeably with '360-degree feedback' in this chapter) is the focus; other feedback processes are beyond the scope of the chapter.

Ethical dimensions of formal feedback

The purpose of using multisource feedback or other feedback interventions is often to provide new insight into how a leader is perceived by others (Yammarino & Atwater, 1993). Because leaders rarely receive open and honest feedback about their performance, this aspect of coaching is often highly valued by the individuals being coached. However, feedback is also used to establish the need for coaching (i.e. where a leader falls short of performance targets and needs improvement). The latter purpose can sometimes be to the leader's benefit, but it is also often of greater benefit to the organization or the coach who profits from the coaching engagement. Using feedback to establish the need for coaching potentially violates the ethical principles of do no harm, duty of care, and respect the client. Even when the purpose for using formal feedback honors the autonomy of the person being coached, a number of challenges to the efficacy of the feedback intervention may have ethical consequences.

There is evidence to suggest the continued popularity of feedback interventions outsizes their documented effects. In a meta-analysis of 131 feedback studies, Kluger and DeNisi (1996) found that feedback interventions (such as 360-degree feedback, performance reviews, grades, teaching evaluations) had a moderate positive effect on performance, on average. This average masked what examination of the full distribution revealed - 38% of effects were negative. In other words, 38% of feedback interventions actually *harmed* performance.

Kluger and DeNisi's meta-analysis looked an array of feedback interventions. How does multisource feedback fare when it is the sole focus of study? A meta-analysis of improvement outcomes from multisource feedback conducted in 2005 found only marginally positive effects on subsequent performance ratings (Smither et al., 2005). In 2016, twenty years after the Kluger and DeNisi meta-analysis, Jones and her colleagues conducted a systematic review of coaching outcomes literature and found that coaching interventions with multisource feedback were *less* effective than those without. Drawing on Kluger & DeNisi's work, Jones et al. (2016) attribute this finding to increased attentional demands from excessive focus on negative feedback that divert resources that would have otherwise been used on the coaching process. They also suggest that the content of the 360 might be disconnected from the central concern of the person being coached and therefore become a distraction from their personal objectives.

This is an ethical concern for coaching. Feedback that is biased or ill-timed can harm the person being coached. Failure to advocate for the appropriate measurement and use of multisource feedback can violate the duty of care. Multisource feedback involves a substantial organizational investment of not only the time and energy of the person being coached, but also from each of their raters. Engaging in needless feedback processes may provide financial benefit to the coach at the expense of the organization or coachee. Such a waste of resources violates the principle of acting in the client's best interest. The aim of the following section is to expose three key challenges with multisource feedback in order to inform coaches of their ethical considerations.

Feedback: challenges with ethical implications

An ethical approach to integrating formalized feedback into the coaching process requires that the coach is knowledgeable about the limitations of such interventions and is proactive about addressing challenges that may arise in the process. The purpose of this section is to delineate three specific challenges that can negatively impact the efficacy of multisource feedback processes. These challenges include 1) assessing recipient readiness; 2) ensuring the integrity of the data and how it will be used in the organization; and 3) avoiding flawed assumptions in the interpretation of the results.

Challenge 1: Recipient readiness concerns

Feedback is often written into coaching contracts before a full assessment of the needs and emotional readiness of the person being coached is conducted. When considering a recipient's 'readiness' for feedback, it is important to consider their individual needs and situation, the timing of the feedback intervention, and the broader context.

Individual readiness. Individuals vary in their *feedback orientation,* or their overall receptivity to feedback. One's feedback orientation consists of the degree to which they like feedback, seek it out, and are able to deeply process it, are sensitive to others' views of their behavior, believe that feedback is valuable to improving their effectiveness, and feel accountable to act on feedback they receive (London & Smither, 2002). One's feedback orientation is a relatively stable trait shaped by their previous experiences of feedback, fixed-versus-growth mindset, and the degree to which their work context is feedback-supportive. As Linderbaum and Levy (2010, p. 1375) explain:

> "someone who has a strong feedback orientation is likely to generally value feedback, be more attuned to feedback in his or her environment, and be more apt to act on the feedback he or she receives. On the flipside, an individual who has a weak feedback orientation will generally be more resistant to feedback, will tend to ignore feedback in his or her environment, and is less likely to respond to feedback that is received."

Thus, coaches have an ethical responsibility to determine how a feedback recipient is likely to respond to multisource feedback as a learning tool prior to administering it. This can be accomplished by asking specific questions about one's feedback orientation in the in-take process or using a validated instrument such as Linderbaum and Levy's (2010) Feedback Orientation Scale. If the person being coached has a weak feedback orientation, low self-esteem, is highly introverted, or works in a toxic environment, utilizing multisource feedback early in the coaching process may be counter-productive, thus doing harm to the individual and wasting company resources. Coaching should instead begin with the aim of increasing openness to feedback, realizing that a 360-degree feedback process might not be feasible for this person at that point in time.

Timing. Even if the person being coached is open and receptive to feedback, receiving multisource feedback is an emotional experience and must be carefully positioned in the course of a coaching engagement. How one feels in anticipation of feedback can set the stage for how they are likely to respond. Fear, distrust, and anxiety can lead to defensiveness or dismissal of the feedback as biased or unfair (London & Smither, 2002). Feedback is more likely to result in learning and positive behavior change when it is positively anticipated. Although how one feels in anticipation of receiving feedback is dictated to some degree by their feedback orientation, there are things a coach can do to make it a more positive experience. Involving the feedback recipient in decisions about the feedback process, such as selection of raters, can increase their sense of agency and control over the experience, thereby reducing anticipatory fear and anxiety.

Receiving and interpreting multisource data also evokes emotions and puts feedback recipients in an analytical reasoning mode, which narrows their attention and neurologically constrains their ability to be open and creative (Boyatzis & Jack, 2018). Because of a well-documented bias toward negative information (Baumeister et al., 2001), feedback recipients often focus on information they perceive as negative – weaknesses and/or information that is inconsistent with their own self-perception. Initial negative reactions to feedback, particularly when it is unfavorable, often take weeks to dissipate (Atwater et al., 2007). These negative emotions divert cognitive resources away from the task of making meaning of the results. Given that this response is natural, a coach's failure to notice and validate the leader's feelings may result in a breach of the relationship. Rather than trying to change the emotions, the coach can allow for it in the timing of the coaching process and assist the feedback recipient in moving through their initial reaction to a place of receptivity.

Even when an individual is receptive to the feedback, the very task of analyzing data puts the recipient in an analytical reasoning mode by activating the task positive network (TPN) in the brain (Boyatzis & Jack, 2018). The TPN allows us to focus and solve problems (Boyatzis et al., 2015). However, the TPN has been found to suppress the default mode network (DMN), which is responsible for social cognition, creativity, and big picture thinking (Jack et al., 2013). In other words, activation of the TPN (and analytical reasoning) can de-activate the DMN (and empathic reasoning). This has important implications for the timing of when feedback is delivered. First, presenting multisource data as a starting point for the coaching engagement introduces neurological and cognitive constraints to building a high-quality coaching relationship and openness to the feedback (Passarelli, 2015). Moreover, analyzing 360-degree feedback narrows the thinking of the person being coached, which can constrain creativity and big picture thinking. If the coach has not already helped the feedback recipient explore and articulate an ideal self, the long-term benefits of feedback will be sacrificed. According to Boyatzis & Jack (2018, p. 18), "by focusing on the personal vision before presenting any feedback, you have a greater chance of creating a positive, strongly desired context for the feedback. That is, the context should be the vision and dreams of the client." When debriefing 360-feedback results, it is further recommended that the coach first draw attention to the recipient's strengths. When discussing weaknesses or gaps, it is useful to do so vis-à-vis the recipient's ideal self or personal vision to leverage analytic reasoning in service of desired change (Boyatzis & Jack, 2018).

In summary, the ethical coach provides space for the leader's initial response to the data, especially those who receive negative ratings, and then provides support overcoming initial negative reactions (Atwater et al., 2007). Moreover, they link the feedback to the individual's ideal self to create intrinsic motivation for change (Taylor et al., 2019).

Context. A final consideration in assessing recipient readiness is the level of support for developmental provided by their work-life contexts. Generally, individuals who work in organizations with strong *feedback cultures* tend to be more open to feedback (London & Smither, 2002). Such organizations emphasize the importance of high-quality feedback and provide support for using that feedback for improvement. This will increase the likelihood that the feedback is heard and acted upon.

Organizations with strong feedback cultures also tend to have high levels of *psychological safety*, whereby individuals feel comfortable to be themselves, take risks and make mistakes (Edmondson, 1999). Psychological safety and a high-quality relationship with one's immediate supervisor promotes learning behavior (Carmeli & Gittell, 2009), which is essential for changing behavior as a result of feedback. Moreover, having a general sense that there is social support for skill development at work increases the level at which one engages in on- and off-the-job development activities after receiving 360-degree feedback (Maurer et al., 2002). On the flip side, receiving feedback in a toxic environment has the potential to further damage relationships and the psychological well-being of the person being coached. Coaches have an ethical responsibility to consider what role the recipient's organizational context might play in the effectiveness of a formal feedback intervention. Moreover, the coaching relationship itself should be characterized by high levels of psychological safety and perceived support for development.

Questions coaches can consider to mitigate feedback recipient readiness concerns:

Is the feedback recipient emotionally and cognitively open to feedback?
What steps can be taken to cultivate positive anticipatory feelings about feedback?
What is the appropriate timing to deliver feedback?
Has the feedback recipient adequately defined an ideal self or personal vision as a point-of-reference for interpreting the feedback?
How will this feedback advance the aims of coaching?
Is the feedback recipient's context sufficiently supportive?

Challenge 2: Information quality and use concerns

Once the decision to use multisource feedback has been made, coaches have a further responsibility to ensure the information gathered is valid and reliable, the raters are knowledgeable informants, and a skilled debriefer shares the information with the recipient. In addition, the ethical coach will understand who will have access to the information and how it will be used. Low quality and/or misused data can harm the feedback recipient or their raters, making this an ethical concern for coaches.

Measurement quality. Broadly speaking, there are two main ways to collect 360-degree feedback data. The first involves use of quantitative survey instruments, such as the Emotional & Social Competence Inventory (Boyatzis et al., 2017), which are distributed to a set of raters who provide confidential responses that are then collated and reported in aggregate. The second way to collect 360-degree feedback data is what we refer to as a 'live 360' in which a coach or third-party interviews key informants about the behaviors of the feedback recipient and formulates their findings into an interpretive report.

If a quantitative tool is being used, a technical report should be available that explains its psychometric properties. Coaches should look for evidence of internal and external validity and reliability before adopting an instrument. In other words, to what degree can the information collected by the survey be trusted to capture what it claims to measure? (And, is this information of use to the feedback recipient?) How well does it predict performance? And how reliable is that information – how much error or 'noise' is included in the results? To some degree, the reliability depends on the quality of raters selected to complete the survey, but there should be empirical evidence of the tool's internal consistency. The sea of available tools can be overwhelming. Examining the technical reports of selected tools can be one way to separate the good from the bad. Poorly designed surveys produce results that can be difficult for a feedback recipient to interpret, obscuring key areas of strength and weakness (Smither et al., 2005).

Conducting a live 360 requires expertise in both interviewing and qualitative data analysis. The interviewer should be skilled in how to remain neutral and reduce bias in asking questions, responding non-verbally, and interpreting what has been said. Moreover, analyzing the data and assimilating it into a form for the recipient requires familiarity working with qualitative data. This includes managing one's own perceptions and biases so as to present results that are as fair and balanced as possible.

Rater quality. Generally speaking, raters should be individuals who have an opportunity to observe the feedback recipient at work regularly. These individuals should be made aware of the purpose of the 360-degree feedback process and their role in it. Raters provide more honest and accurate feedback when they are confident in how the data will be used, anonymized, and who will have access to it (Atwater et al., 2007).

Assuming appropriate raters are selected and aware of their role in the process, two potential issues still exist: 1) poor feedback skills; and 2) bias. Very rarely are raters equipped to give constructive, effective feedback. Raters are rarely trained in how to use the behaviorally anchored scales in quantitative surveys, nor are they necessarily effective at providing written feedback. In her book, The Fundamentals of Feedback, Dr. Brodie Riordan (2020) outlines four simple rules for making general feedback more effective:

1. Focus on behavior, not the person
2. Be as specific as possible
3. Make it forward-looking
4. Give it as soon as possible (this is sometimes not possible in 360-degree formats).

These four rules can also improve verbatim feedback in multisource processes. But one issue still remains – bias. Many raters fall victim to implicit biases that disadvantage women and people of color. Women and people of color may be rated more harshly on performance evaluations than their mainstream counterparts, yet be denied constructive criticism they need in order to develop because of a leniency bias (Harber, 1998). Ratings may be skewed by other cognitive biases, such as the recency effect (whereby ratings are overly influenced by recent events), halo effect (where one trait overshadows other behavior) and similar-to-me bias (whereby those who share interests, skills or background with the rater are assessed more favorably).

Debriefing quality. An ethical approach to the provision of multisource feedback requires that the results are debriefed by a qualified facilitator and on-going support is provided by a coach. Despite a convincing body of evidence about the benefits of accompanying 360-feedback with coaching and/or facilitation (Brutus & Derayeh, 2002; Seifert et al., 2003) many organizations fail to provide the appropriate support. The 'data-dump-and-run' approach leaves leaders to their own devices in terms of responding to the results. This may result in leaders feeling baffled or stunted in terms of their development, or they may simply ignore the data all together. A coach or skilled facilitator can assist the leader in making accurate interpretations. Moreover, a coach is needed for insights to produce behavior change because managers may not always have the skills and knowledge necessary to change their behaviors and actions (Luthans & Peterson, 2003). Coaches can assist leaders in focusing on actions that would be most helpful to them. As discussed in the next session, this process can take time so multiple coaching sessions are preferred to just one debriefing session.

Use of information in the organization. The ethical coach should seek some assurances about the use of multisource feedback their coachee receives. Because 360-degree feedback is collected in service of employee development, it should not be used for performance evaluation or promotion/hiring decisions (Atwater et al., 2007). In addition, who will have access to the raw data and results should be made clear prior to collecting the data. The most conservative arrangement (and the one I prefer) is that the raw data is destroyed once the report is produced (and/or it remains in the hands of a third party) and that only the person being coached and the coach have access to the report. Of course, other agreements can be outlined in the contracting phase. Lastly, security measures should be in place to protect the confidentiality of raters who responded under the expectation of anonymity. Raters who trust in the promise of anonymity are more likely to respond honestly to surveys, especially if they fear retaliation for negative ratings (Antonioni, 1994).

In instances where anonymous raters provide qualitative feedback that is unclear, it may be difficult for leaders to interpret and act on the feedback. In this case, the coach can help the leader seek more information in a way that honors rater anonymity. For example, the coach can help the leader identify individuals they trust with whom to share the feedback and ask for clarification. This approach engages raters in a sense-making process with the leader, rather than singling them out or attacking them for potential comments in the data.

Questions coaches can consider to improve information quality and use concerns:

How psychometrically sound is the data collection tool?
What are the qualifications of the individual(s) conducting 360-degree interviews?
Have raters been selected who can give fair and unbiased feedback?
What potential biases might exist in the results?
How will the results be delivered?
Who is qualified to deliver/debrief the feedback?
How will the information be used in the organization?
Who has access to the results?
What measures are taken to protect rater anonymity/confidentiality?

Challenge 3: Flawed interpretive assumptions

Once the data has been collected and the results are in the hands of the person being coached, the primary concern for the coach is helping the recipient make sense of the results. However, two popular assumptions that are unsubstantiated by research may result in faulty interpretations, ultimately doing harm to the feedback recipient. The popular (but untrue) assumptions are that there is one objective 'truth' about one's performance and that self-other comparison is the most effective approach to data interpretation.

Singular, Objective Reality. Receiving 360-degree feedback can be cognitively and emotionally overwhelming. Many individuals have negative associations with feedback and therefore experience negative emotions in anticipation of receiving the data, which occupies some of their cognitive resources (Atwater et al., 2007; Riordan, 2020). This, in combination with the sheer volume of information to assimilate, can result in cognitive overload. Data reduction techniques, such as calculating average scores and reporting common themes among raters, can reduce the cognitive load on the feedback recipient. However, these approaches eliminate variation among raters and inherently endorse the notion that the results represent the 'truth' about one's performance.

The assumption that there is one objective reality that represents an accurate view of one's performance simply does not hold up in research. Raters very rarely agree (Fleenor et al., 2010), especially across roles at different levels such as manager versus direct report (Smither et al., 2005). For example, peers' views of a leader's behavior can vary drastically from those of their direct reports or supervisor. Moreover, there are conflicting results as to which perspective is most predictive of leadership effectiveness (Fleenor et al., 2010).

When lumped together or aggregated, these various viewpoints can obscure a more nuanced picture that can more effectively help a leader to grow. More nuanced data allows a leader to identify the relationships in which they score high and consider how they might replicate those behaviors in the context of relationships where they scored lower. The ethical coach understands the limitations of the results and can assist a leader in seeking more nuanced insights from the data and beyond.

Self-Other Comparison. Another challenge related to the assumption of a singular, accurate view of one's performance is that self and others' ratings are often discrepant. It has been widely argued that self-ratings alone are not accurate predictors of leadership because they are inflated by self-serving biases (Hough et al., 1983; Podsakoff & Organ, 1986; Yammarino & Atwater, 1993). Yet other reports do not always reflect reality and predict leadership outcomes either. A complex set of factors influence ratings from both perspectives. For example, demographic characteristics like age, gender, and race, personality and individual differences, and job relevant experiences can affect self-ratings. Other-ratings are affected by the rater's cognitive processes, characteristics, motivation, contextual factors, and rater-ratee interactions and expectations (for a review, see Fleenor et al., 2010).

Despite this complexity, differences between self and other ratings often become a focus of interpretation with the operating assumption that leaders' whose self-reports agree with those of others are more self-aware (Fleenor et al., 2010). Unfortunately, equating self-other agreement with self-awareness is an oversimplification that can produce faulty interpretations. Moreover, an assumption of singular reality sets up a conflict between how a leader sees themselves versus how others see them – a conflict between who is right and who is wrong.

Some argue that highlighting self-other discrepancy can raise a leader's awareness and motivate them to change their behavior in order to eliminate the discrepancy. However, the risk in this approach is that the information resolves the discrepancy by deflating leader's self-views, rather than motivating behavior change that improves the perception of others.

Other scholars argue that self-other comparison is an ineffective approach to data interpretation all together. Taylor and Bright (2011) claim that self-other comparison breeds defensiveness by setting up a tension between 'truths' (i.e. whose view is correct, mine or yours?). They report only 15% of executives are developmentally able to receive contradictory data; the other 85% are likely to reject the results or become defensive.

Taylor and Bright (2011) offer an alternative approach to self-other comparison, which they describe as *predicted*-other comparison. This approach minimizes attention to self-ratings by inviting the feedback recipient to predict how others will view them. To do this, the coach may ask them to reflect on questions such as 'how does my supervisor experience me? What am I like when I work with my supervisor?' This approach takes the focus off the self (reducing defensiveness that arises from conflicting views), and emphasizes context – the relationships and settings in which the leader interacts with their raters. It also puts the recipient in a mode of inquiry, rather than advocacy of their own views, which increases the likelihood of acceptance of the feedback.

Questions coaches can consider to address faulty interpretation assumptions:

How is self-other data presented in the results?
What predictors of self-other data might have influenced the results?
What is my mindset about whose perspective is most 'accurate'? How can the potential drawbacks of a 'singular reality' view be minimized?
How are self-other rating discrepancy being interpreted? What can I do to minimize inherent conflict/defensiveness and maximize acceptance and learning from the results?

Case Study

The following case study deviates positively from the issues outlined above. It is an example in which many of the feedback challenges were handled ethically and a best-case-scenario outcome was achieved. The case was inspired by real-client material, but details have been altered to disguise the identity of the client and fit the purposes of this chapter.

As part of a company-wide leadership development program, Damian had an opportunity to work with a coach and receive 360-degree feedback on his emotional and social competencies. Damian was the senior-most person of color in the organization, a rank of which he was proud and viewed as a great responsibility. He was well-liked in the organization, and generally had strong annual performance ratings. However, he expressed frustration to his coach about being passed over for promotion to the c-suite several times.

He shared with his coach that he did not recall the details of previous feedback reports, which he saw as a waste of company resources because they collected dust on his shelf. However, he agreed to go into the process with an open mind since he had never received individual support in conjunction with his feedback.

In keeping with Intentional Change Theory (Boyatzis et al., 2019; Boyatzis, 2008) the coaching process first explored his ideal self – his passion, purpose, values, and core identity – rather than begin with feedback. Part of the vision he articulated for himself involved being an inclusive leader who gives voice to others. He wanted to be a conduit for voices that typically go unheard in the organization. He also wanted to be a leader who involved people in decision-making, empowered them to take ownership, and made sure their accomplishments were visible and recognized. This aspect of his leadership connected directly to deeply held values about equality, developing others, and spirituality.

His visioning work became very important when he received his 360-degree feedback results. Although the results were strong overall, there were a few areas of concern that immediately caught his attention. Compared to other competencies, he scored lower in emotional self-control, empathy, and teamwork. In reading verbatim comments from his direct reports, he noticed a theme that suggested he relied too heavily on a pacesetting style, moving too fast to truly hear people's ideas and opinions and gain consensus.

Damian was crushed by the feedback. Despite the coach's attempts to draw his attention to his strengths, he could only see the negatives. He said it was the first time he'd heard anything like this. He experienced emotions about the feedback over the next few weeks that ranged from disbelief to anger to sadness and, finally, to interest and gratitude.

After a few weeks, Damian was able to explain why those particular results had such an impact on him: it was inconsistent with his ideal self, or personal vision as a leader. He realized that the deadline-driven nature of his role pushed him into a pacesetting-style, which was hampering his effectiveness and silencing the voices he was trying to include. He believed it was something he could improve, and he was very interested to learn more about how to do that.

Working with his coach, he revisited his 360-feedback report, seeing in more granularity the difference among rater categories and the areas of strength. He organized his insights into a 'personal balance sheet' (McKee et al., 2008) that outlined key strengths he could bring to bear on addressing his developmental opportunities (see Table 24.1).

In response to the feedback, he created a coalition of support for his change effort. He chose one peer and two direct reports to serve as his personal board of directors. He discussed his feedback with them and asked for their insights and suggestions for action. He walked away from those conversations with four goals to make positive change toward being an inclusive

Table 24.1 Partial Balance Sheet Summarizing Competency Strengths and Weaknesses

Strengths	*Opportunities for Development*
Achievement orientation: Striving to meet or exceed a standard of excellence; looking for ways to do things better, set challenging goals and take calculated risks	**Emotional self-control:** The ability to keep disruptive emotions and impulses in check and maintain our effectiveness under stressful or hostile conditions.
Positive outlook: The ability to see the positive in people, situations and events and our persistence in pursuing goals despite obstacles and setbacks.	**Empathy:** The ability to sense others' feelings and perspectives, taking an active interest in their concerns and picking up cues to what is being felt and thought.
Inspirational leadership: The ability to inspire and guide individuals and groups to get the job done, and to bring out the best in others.	**Teamwork:** The ability to work with others toward a shared goal; participating actively, sharing responsibility and rewards and contributing to the capability of the team.

leader: 1. be more collaborative; 2. promote open dialogue; 3. be positive and optimistic; and 4. lighten the atmosphere. He shared these goals with them and expressed his desire to get their feedback – both positive and negative – not in the moment, but later in private.

He experimented with a number of structural and behavioral changes. For example, he shifted the structure of his staff meetings by trying out new locations, having no agenda, and hosting "check-in" breakfast meetings. After several months, he felt comfortable relinquishing control of the staff meetings to his team and received feedback that he was no longer driving staff meetings with his own task list and allowing people to voice their own reports.

These structural changes were accompanied by a number of behavioral changes. He became cognizant of the power of his use of language and tried to use "but" and "however" less frequently to open up conversation. He refrained from stepping in when others were running meetings. He smiled more and leveraged his penchant for self-deprecating humor. He also instituted "town hall" meetings to discuss the vision for his unit and allow team members to air questions/concerns in a casual way. At these meetings, he did not stand at the podium as he typically would have before the feedback. Instead, he sat at a table in front of the room with everyone else.

Toward the end of the year-long coaching process, he was interested to know if his efforts produced the desired results. Was he seen as more collaborative? Did he promote open dialogue? Was he seen as positive and optimistic? And did the atmosphere in his business unit feel less tense and hurried to those both inside and outside his team? Although repeating his 360-degree feedback may have provided some insight into the effect of his efforts on the competencies that inspired the change (positive outlook, teamwork, and emotional self-control), it would not necessarily reflect his specific objectives and progress toward his vision. In consultation with the coaching sponsor, he and his coach decided not to proceed with a repeat 360 as the organizational investment was not worth the type of information he would receive. Instead, he sought qualitative feedback from a subset of his original raters about his performance vis-à-vis his ideal self. He shared his personal vision and developmental goals with them and asked them to comment on what changes (if any) they've noticed in him over the past year and what further changes could make him even more effective. He was also asked to predict what he thought others would say.

The feedback he received moved him to tears. Although he recognized there was still work to be done, he was able to acknowledge and celebrate the strengths and improvements that others saw in him. He also noticed that he was quite accurate in predicting what his direct reports would say – a group that was of most interest to him. Reflecting back on the original feedback, he expressed that he should not have been as blindsided as he was by the data about his pacesetting style. He said he could now see where similar issues had been raised in his performance reviews, but he wasn't able to see it in the same way as he did in the context of the coaching process. He attributed this to the importance of having started the process with his ideal self and connecting the feedback to a version of self that was intrinsic and autonomously motivated, rather than externally motivated by organizational standards and mandates. Two years later, Damian was promoted to his dream position as Chief Information Officer for the company.

Table 24.2 Implications for Coaching from Case Study

Ethical Challenges	Implications for Coaching
Recipient readiness	*Individual readiness.* The coach learned that the client had ambivalent-negative associations with past feedback processes and worked to increase his receptivity to feedback. Moreover, Damian had complete control over who was invited to respond to the feedback survey, increasing autonomy.
	Timing. The coaching process began with ideal self-discovery. Damian did not receive feedback until he articulated a personal vision for his life and work. Moreover, there was ample time built into the coaching contract for him to work through initial negative reactions to the feedback.
	Context. Both Damian and his coach assessed his work environment to be safe and supportive of his developmental efforts.
Information quality and use	*Measurement quality.* A valid and reliable instrument was used to collect the data.
	Rater quality. Damian was counseled by his coach about how to select appropriate raters. An ample response rate was achieved.
	Debriefing quality. Damian received his results during a coaching session with a coach who was certified to administer and debrief the 360-degree feedback instrument.
	Use of information in the organization. Only Damian and his coach had access to his results (and no one had access to the raw data). Damian chose to share some pieces of his feedback with trusted supporters who were invested in his development.
Interpretive assumptions	*Singular, Objective Reality.* When Damian was cognitively and emotionally ready, the coach encouraged him to move beyond the aggregated data to a more nuanced view that could point him to the contexts in which he was rated most favorably.
	Self-Other Comparison. This approach was used in his follow-up feedback as a way to focus his attention on the perceptions of others, rather than his own opinions.

Conclusion

This chapter summarizes ethical considerations for the use of multisource feedback in the context of coaching engagements. These issues are framed as ethical challenges because they relate directly to the coach's ability to adhere to the broad ethical principles of do no harm, duty of care, know your limits, and act in the best interest of the client. The intent of the chapter was not to convey that the use of formalized feedback is unethical. Rather, it was to raise awareness of issues that could lead to violation of ethical standards. Better assessing recipient readiness, ensuring the integrity of the data and how it will be used in the organization, and avoiding flawed assumptions in the interpretation of the results is not only ethical, it will improve the efficacy of feedback interventions in coaching.

Discussion points

1. Formalized feedback processes in coaching pose challenges to basic ethical principles of 'do no harm, duty of care, know your limits, and respect the interests of the client.'
2. Failing to account for the readiness of the feedback recipient can cause unintended harm. Ethical coaches should consider the individual's level of readiness, along with the supportiveness of their context and the timing of feedback within the coaching engagement.
3. Information quality and use present another set of ethical challenges to the use of feedback in coaching. Key considerations include ensuring high quality measurement, raters, and debriefing as well as how the information will be used within the organization.
4. Interpreting 360-degree feedback is also ethically precarious. Care should be taken to avoid flawed assumptions about the data, such as presenting the data as a singular 'truth' and misrepresenting self-other (in)congruencies.

Recommended reading

Riordan, B.G. (2020) *Feedback Fundamentals and Evidence-Based Best Practices: Give It, Ask for It, use It.* New York, NY: Routledge.

References

Antonioni, D. (1994) The effects of feedback accountability on upward appraisal ratings. *Personnel Psychology*, 47: 349–356.

Atwater, L. E., Brett, J. F., & Charles, A. C. (2007) Multisource feedback: Lessons learned and implications for practice. *Human Resource Management*, 46(2): 285–307. doi:10.1002/hrm.20161.

Baumeister, R. F., Bratslavsky, E., Finkenauer, C., & Vohs, K. D. (2001) Bad is stronger than good. *Review of General Psychology*, 5(4): 323–370. doi:10.1037/1089-2680.5.4.323.

Boyatzis, R. E. (2008) Leadership development from a complexity perspective. *Consulting Psychology Journal: Practice and Research*, 60(4): 298–313. doi:10.1037/1065-9293.60.4.298.

Boyatzis, R. E. & Jack, A. I. (2018) The neuroscience of coaching. *Consulting Psychology Journal: Practice and Research*, 70(1): 11–27. doi:10.1037/cpb0000095.

Boyatzis, R. E., Rochford, K., & Taylor, S. E. (2015) The role of the positive emotional attractor in vision and shared vision: Toward effective leadership, relationships, and engagement. *Frontiers in Psychology*, 6(670): 1. doi:10.3389/fpsyg.2015.00670.

Boyatzis, R., Guise, S., Hezlett, S., Kerr, P., & Lams, S. (2017) *Emotional and social competency inventory: A research guide and technical manual*. Korn Ferry. www.kornferry.com/content/dam/kornferry/docs/article-migration/ESCI_Technical_Manual_nav_04052017.pdf.

Boyatzis, R., Smith, M. L., & Oosten, E. V. (2019) *Helping People Change: Coaching with Compassion for Lifelong Learning and Growth*. Harvard Business Press.

Brennan, D. & Wildflower, L. (2014) Ethics in coaching. In E. Cox, T. Bachkirova, & D. A. Clutterbuck (Eds), *The Complete Handbook of Coaching*, 2nd Edition. Sage Publications, pp. 430–444.

Brutus, S. & Derayeh, M. (2002) Multisource assessment programs in organizations: An insider's perspective. *Human Resource Development Quarterly*, 13(2): 187–202. doi:10.1002/hrdq.1023.

Carmeli, A. & Gittell, J. H. (2009) High-quality relationships, psychological safety, and learning from failures in work organizations. *Journal of Organizational Behavior*, 30(6): 709–729. doi:10.1002/job.565.

Edmondson, A. (1999) Psychological safety and learning behavior in work teams. *Administratice Science Quarterly*, 44(2): 350–383. doi:10.2307/2666999.

Fleenor, J. W., Smither, J. W., Atwater, L. E., Braddy, P. W., & Sturm, R. E. (2010) Self-other rating agreement in leadership: A review. *The Leadership Quarterly*, 21 (6): 1005–1034. doi:10.1016/j.leaqua.2010.10.006.

Harber, K. D. (1998) Feedback to Minorities: Evidence of a Positive Bias. *Journal of Personality & Social Psychology*, 74(3): 622–628. doi:10.1037/0022-3514.74.3.622.

Hough, L. M., Keyes, M. A., & Dunnette, M. D. (1983) An Evaluation of Three "Alternative" Selection Procedures1. *Personnel Psychology*, 36(2): 261–276. doi:10.1111/j.1744-6570.1983.tb01436.x.

Iordanou, I., Hawley, R., & Iordanou, C. (2017) *Values and Ethics in Coaching*. Sage Publications.

Jack, A. I., Dawson, A., Begany, K., Leckie, R. L., Barry, K., Ciccia, A., & Snyder, A. (2013) FMRI reveals reciprocal inhibition between social and physical cognitive domains. *NeuroImage*, 66(1): 385–401.

Jones, R. J., Woods, S. A., & Guillaume, Y. R. F. (2016) A meta-analysis of learning and performance outcomes from coaching. *Journal of Occupational and Organizational Psychology*, 89: 249–277. doi:10.1111/joop.12119.

Kluger, A. N. & DeNisi, A. (1996) The effects of feedback interventions on performance: A historical review, a meta-analysis, and a preliminary feedback intervention theory. *Psychological Bulletin*, 119(2): 254–284. doi:10.1037/0033-2909.119.2.254.

Linderbaum, B. A. & Levy, P. E. (2010) The Development and Validation of the Feedback Orientation Scale (FOS). *Journal of Management*, 36(6): 1372–1405. doi:10.1177/0149206310373145.

London, M. & Smither, J. W. (2002) Feedback orientation, feedback culture, and the longitudinal performance management process. *Human Resource Management Review*, 12(1): 81–100. doi:10.1016/S1053-4822(01)00043–00042.

Luthans, F. & Peterson, S. (2003) 360-degree feedback with systemic coaching: Empirical analysis suggests a winning combination. *Human Resource Management*, 42(3): 243–256.

Maurer, T. J., Mitchell, D. R. D., & Barbeite, F. G. (2002) Predictors of attitudes toward a 360-degree feedback system and involvement in post-feedback management development activity. *Journal of Occupational and Organizational Psychology*, 75(1): 87–107. doi:10.1348/096317902167667.

McKee, A., Boyatzis, R. E., & Johnston, F. (2008) *Becoming a Resonant Leader: Develop Your Emotional Intelligence, Renew Your Relationships, Sustain Your Effectiveness.* Harvard Business Press.

Passarelli, A. M. (2015) Vision-based coaching: Optimizing resources for leader development. *Frontiers in Psychology*, 6. http://journal.frontiersin.org/article/10.3389/fpsyg.2015.00412/abstract.

Podsakoff, P. M. & Organ, D. W. (1986) Self-Reports in Organizational Research: Problems and Prospects. *Journal of Management*, 12(4): 531–544. doi:10.1177/014920638601200408.

Riordan, B. G. (2020) *Feedback Fundamentals and Evidence-Based Best Practices: Give It, Ask for It, use It.* New York: Routledge.

Seifert, C. F., Yukl, G., & McDonald, R. A. (2003) Effects of multisource feedback and a feedback facilitator on the influence behavior of managers toward subordinates. *Journal of Applied Psychology*, 88(3): 561–569. doi:10.1037/0021-9010.88.3.561.

Smither, J. W., London, M., & Reilly, R. R. (2005) Does Performance Improve Following Multisource Feedback? A Theoretical Model, Meta-Analysis, and Review of Empirical Findings. *Personnel Psychology*, 58(1): 33–66. doi:10.1111/j.1744-6570.2005.514_1.x.

Taylor, S. N. & Bright, D. S. (2011) Open-Mindedness and Defensiveness in Multisource Feedback Processes: A Conceptual Framework. *The Journal of Applied Behavioral Science*, 47(4): 432–460. doi:10.1177/0021886311408724.

Taylor, S. N., Passarelli, A. M., & Van Oosten, E. B. (2019) Leadership coach effectiveness as fostering self-determined, sustained change. *The Leadership Quarterly*, 30(6): 101313. doi:10.1016/j.leaqua.2019.101313.

Yammarino, F. J. & Atwater, L. E. (1993) Understanding self-perception accuracy: Implications for human resource management. *Human Resource Management*, 32(2–3): 231–247. https://doi.org/10.1002/hrm.3930320204.

Chapter 25

Choose me! Ethics in the promotion of coaching

Francine Campone

Introduction

In daylight, we cannot see the stars, although they continue to burn brightly. Similarly, the bright light of attracting clients may make it difficult for us to see the human beings we think of as prospects for our services.

Through presentations, websites, directories, and social media coaches present themselves and the value of their services. Promotion of services, however, is not a one-way communication. Coaching promotion as a relational rather than commercial undertaking invites consideration of ethical issues and potential challenges.

In a coaching engagement, coaches interact with and respond to specific clients, sponsors and stakeholders. In presenting ourselves verbally and visually in promotion, there is only an imagined Other and the ambiguous standards of truth in the digital world to help guide an ethical choice. The modest literature of ethics in coaching notes the importance of truthfulness and accuracy but tends to focus on what happens during an engagement rather than the promises that precede it. (Duffy & Passmore, 2010; Carroll & Shaw, 2013; Dichon & Nizet, 2015; Iordanou, Hawley, & Iordanou, 2017; Turner & Passmore, 2018). A coach's promotional strategies and materials, however, lay the groundwork for a relational contract that is formalized when coach and client or sponsor first meet.

This chapter will explore how coaches and coaching consultancies promote themselves and their services and explores ethical features and challenges of coach marketing with reference to coaching Codes of Ethics and relevant theories and research. To help ground the chapter and get a broad perspective on how coaches are currently engaging in promotion, promotional statements and activities from fifty coaches randomly selected from LinkedIn listings, websites and coach directories were collected to serve as source examples with all personally identifiable information removed. Other perspectives were sought from a small number of Human Resource (HR) professionals to guide attention to coach marketing that falls short of truthful and accurate. The chapter concludes with a case study and points for consideration. In this chapter, the terms

DOI: 10.4324/9781003277729-25

'marketing' and "promotion" are used to describe coach outreach to potential clients. While both refer to the activity of selling goods and services, 'promotion' has the added connotations of advancement and advocacy. Promotional statement examples in italics are paraphrased from the sample set and do not cite any specific coach or organization.

Coach marketing in the digital world

Coaches and consultancies use websites and social media platforms such as LinkedIn, Instagram, Twitter, and Facebook to reach a global audience, making it easy for potential clients to find a coach using searches based on commerce-oriented algorithms. Promotional activities on-line differ from interpersonal outreach activities such as live or even recorded talks. With global access through the internet, a client's first impression of a potential coach is increasingly likely to be impersonal and digitally mediated. This has important implications. A client's first impressions of a coach's trustworthiness and skill may be skewed by the coach's self-representation because of what the coach includes and excludes as well as the information that is implicit in visual elements of presentation such as images, logos, and even font size and style.

To get a sense of coaches' on-line presence, two broad searches on the business-to-business social media platform LinkedIn were made. The phrase 'Leadership Coaches', generated about 6,700 results. The search phrase 'Leadership Coaches UK' resulted in 291 entries, including coaches in France and Spain. A third search, using the phrase 'Executive Coaching Companies' yielded some 7,400 entries, the majority of which are coaching consultancies with some entries for coach training programs and executive search firms which provide coaching services to their executive clients. This suggests a significant degree of on-line promotion of coaching services.

Some efforts are made by consultancies and some coach directories to encourage fact-based marketing profiles. Coaches who work under the umbrella of a consultancy are usually given a template to guide them in preparing a profile for inclusion in the consultancy's coach directory. Consultancy and directory listings generally include a brief biography, years of experience, credentials and qualifications and identified areas of expertise. Some also add short case studies to illustrate coach experience and expertise. These are usually provided to customers who have requested services from the consultancy and are not publicly available. Instead, consultancies may advertise the qualifications of their coaches in general terms, stating, for example, that all the coaches hold a certification from a recognized source and have experience in a specialized field.

Details of services and outcomes promoted on websites vary widely. Statements about a consultancy's quality may be broad and make unverifiable claims about the uniqueness of their services, the breadth of inclusiveness or degree and consistency of client satisfaction. Visual images such as a diverse group of smiling people may implicitly reinforce such claims. Buzzwords are frequently used: *transformative, innovative, research-driven, proven method.* Coach websites are designed to appeal not only to individuals and leaders seeking coaching but also to other coaches. Marketing and business coaches, for example, may promise to grow one's coaching business to an extraordinary and improbable degree – '*guarantee six-figure income in one year!*' - with little evidence or documentation of how that is achieved. Key selling points empha-size '*speedy results*' and '*organization-wide*' *impact*, even from services such as individual coach-on-demand programs, promising '*incredible breakthroughs*' and '*transformation*' as an outcome of brief interventions.

Individual coach profiles in directories hosted by professional organiza-tions, such as the European Mentoring and Coaching Council (EMCC) and the International Coach Federation (ICF), also tend to be short and fitted into a data-oriented template. On coaches' websites, however, the information presented visually and verbally varies widely. Again, there is a reliance on terms such as '*transformative*' and '*proven methods*'. Terms such as '*transfor-mative*' have a particular meaning in such theoretical models as Transforma-tive Adult Learning (Mezirow, 2000; Kegan, 2000). Positive Psychology is a well-researched and documented approach to happiness and wellbeing (Diener, 1984; Diener, Thapa, & Tay 2019). However, decontextualized posi-tive psychology terms and principles are sometimes embellished for emotional impact, inviting clients to '*blaze your own path!*' or '*break free from the constraints of your life!*'. Such appeals may be visually reinforced with images of strength, freedom or similar, fostering unrealistic expectations in prospective clients. There are two considerations in ethically promoting coaching using these terms: coach competency and word connotation. Coaches who are well-grounded in the the-oretical underpinnings of positive psychology or transformative adult develop-ment can appropriately describe the terms and implications. What potential clients understand or associate with such terms may be misleading, especially in the absence of accurate supporting data.

Perhaps the most ethically challenging area of coach marketing lies in social media. Coaches raise their profiles or presence by posting frequently on social media platforms, sharing or reposting material prepared by others and providing glimpses into their personal and professional activities with photos and videos. Rettberg (2017) points to three modes of representation in social media: visual, written, and quantitative. The online self is selectively created and is managed responsively. Visibility on social media is based on quantified activity with opportunities to pay for higher rankings. The more responses, inquiries or 'likes' one gets, the more certain aspects of self may be empha-sized. Social media consultancies offer to manage an individual's presence by sourcing and sharing material with targeted groups; posting and replying to inquiries in the name of the individual being marketed; and by using metrics to guide and enhance an online profile. Thus, the presented coach may be a managed and mediated persona. While there does not appear to be any data on how widely coaches or consultancies use these services, their existence casts doubt on the veracity and authenticity of presentations on social media.

Feedback from the HR professionals consulted for this chapter point to several areas of concern: implicit and explicit promises of unrealistic outcomes; reliance on trendy language or buzzwords; little evidence of experience or expertise apart from selected testimonials; and clarity about the type of client with whom the coach works best. Thus, the state of coach marketing might be characterized as the Wild West: open, fluid, and rarely scrutinized. (*Harvard Business Review*, 2004).

Distinctive ethical features

Verbal content and visual choices in coach marketing are made in a unique context in that there is only the coach's self and an abstract Other with whom the coach is interacting and to whom the coach is hoping to appeal. Concepts in the ethical codes such as truthful, accurate and unbiased are defined by each individual coach. Most coaching Codes of Ethics offer general guidelines, values and ethical principles with the expectation that the individual practitioners must make their own determinations of application in specific situations. In addition to broad guidelines and principles of accuracy, integrity and truthfulness, The Australian Psychological Society's Code of Ethics explicitly prohibits comparative statements and statements that "are intended or likely to create false or unjustified expectations of favorable outcomes" (Australian Psychology Society, 2018, C.2.3).

Dichon and Nizet (2015, p. 290) propose that "ethical dilemmas are subjective and dynamic, constructed through people's interpretations". A dilemma that involves another specific human being adds emotional, relational and corporal elements to ethical judgements. In interaction with others, a coach may incorporate consideration of emotional, relational, and corporal aspects, informed by the presence and participation of another. These dimensions may be absent when a coach is sitting down to construct a website, or the data requested for a directory entry. In this instance, following a fact-oriented template such as offered in coach directories provides a more solid beginning point for coaches and establishes data from which to construct content with potential client interpretation in mind.

A core principle of ethical practice is the intention to not cause harm. When a coach is interacting directly with another person, the coach is aware of the person's emotional tone, values and motivators, experiences and tender spots. In appealing to an abstract Other, coaches must attend to the expectations they are creating with words and images directed at engaging a potential client's most aspirational self. Coaches who promise '*joy, happiness, and freedom*' may appeal, for example, to individuals who would better benefit from therapy for relief from depression or grief. Of equal concern are coaches who advertise *scientific* or *proven* methods which might be considered pseudoscience. Grief (2022) characterizes pseudoscience as methods which claim to have extraordinary effects but are supported only anecdotally. Assumptions are unsupported by scientific evaluation methods or evidence-based theory. In promotional material, coaches need to be attentive to the degree to which promised effects and outcomes can be supported by data beyond client testimonials or single cases. Extraordinary promises such as '*you will transform uncertainty into confidence* or *maximum peak performance in everyday life by tapping your deep intuitive self*' are difficult to substantiate empirically.

Bachkirova and Borrington (2020) advise that coaches "need to consider the claims we tend to make and what should be the expected influence of such claims", especially when alluding to, or using the language of, scientifically documented methods such as Positive Psychology without understanding or referring to the science (Bachkirova & Borrington, 2020, p. 15). There is a moral complexity in wholesale adoption of such frameworks in a 'one size fits all' marketing strategy. Coach competence and language connotation are key factors in ethically promoting services grounded in these theoretical models.

The exercise of ethical judgment in marketing requires us to manage and resolve the internal conflict between what Bazerman and Tenbrusel (2011) describe as the "want self" and the "should self" (p. 66). The "want self" is emotional, impulsive, affective and "hot-headed". The "should self" is rational, logical, thoughtful and "cool-headed". It is easy for the "want self" to gain the upper hand unless we exercise ethical judgment. We humans tend to underestimate the degree to which incentives and situational factors can affect our judgment. The "want self" seeking clients and income may be inclined to make promises or choose language and images designed to sway the client's emotions and encroach on client autonomy. For example, the "want self" may say that '*working with this coach will eliminate your fears and make you a winner.*' The "should self" will state that coaching is a partnership designed to help increase client self-awareness, identify opportunities for growth and cultivate the skills and resources needed to meet life and workplace challenges.

How the tension is resolved between these two selves depends, in part, on how we see ourselves in relation to others. Do we choose from a morality of justice or a morality of response and care (Gilligan, Ward, Taylor, & Bardige, 1988)? In a morality of justice, one sees oneself as separate from others and makes moral choices by invoking regulations, duty, and commitments, including commitments to oneself. One follows standards and norms.

In a morality of response and care, the priority is maintaining interdependent relationships and promoting the welfare of others. In this position, coaching practitioners must be aware of how they present boundaries, respect for the client's autonomy and self-generativity and transparency about potential outcomes. In this moral framework, making grand promises may create unreasonable expectations; presenting an idealized self may lay the groundwork for a relationship based on illusion. Coaching practitioners must be aware of how their marketing may project certainty, authority and expertise and implications for parity in an actual coaching relationship. In this framework, a coach must think about the abstract Other as a fully formed and complex person and not simply a concept of 'client'.

Ethical codes and laws

Within the Global Code of Ethics, the ICF Code of Ethics and the British Psychological Association and Australian Psychological Society's Codes of Ethics there are specific statements expressing the standards and expectation of those bodies with respect to coach self-representation and marketing. The Global Code of Ethics specifically requires that members are suitably qualified and honestly represent their relevant experience, professional qualifications, memberships, and certifications or (Global Code of Ethics, 2022, paragraph 2.9). The Global Code explicitly states: *2.11 "members will ensure that no false or misleading claims are made or implied about their professional competence, qualifications or accreditations in any published, promotional material or otherwise"* (italics added).

The ICF requires members to make "verbal and written statements that are true and accurate (verbal and written) about what I offer as an ICF professional...the coaching profession and the potential value of coaching." This includes qualifications, competencies, expertise, training, certification and credentials (ICF Code of Ethics, Section III, 21).

The British Psychological Society's Code of Ethics and Conduct for Chartered Coaching Psychologists addresses the core value of integrity, noting that "acting with integrity includes being honest, truthful, accurate and consistent in one's actions, words, decisions, methods and outcomes." In applying these values, members are asked to consider accurate unbiased representation and avoidance of conflicts of interest (including self-interest) (British Psychological Society, 2022, Section 3.4). The Australian Psychological Society (APS) code applies the principle of integrity to practitioner behaviors, communication, conflicts of interest, non-exploitation, authorship, financial arrangements and management of ethical infractions (APS, Section C).

Each professional membership organization requires members to agree to abide by that organization's code of ethics. Coaches may agree to abide by more than one code based on affiliation, credential and accreditation. As codes differ somewhat in language, focus and organization, an understanding of fundamental ethical principles and values, and cultivation of moral character and mature ethical judgment are essential for ethical actions in coach self-promotion.

In addition to Codes of Conduct, local laws and standards may be set by agencies such as the British Advertising Standards Authority (see reference list for website). Such laws and standards clearly prohibit untruthful or misleading advertising and require acknowledgement of work and materials that are created by someone other than the coach doing the marketing. Laws and standards are also clear about intentionally misleading logos which resemble those of other agencies or organizations. Because on-line material is internationally available, coaches must be aware of applicable laws. In general, the principles of laws and standards address fairness, decency and responsibility to consumers and society.

Professional organizations and associations with formal codes of ethics have mechanisms for encouraging compliance by investigating and acting on complaints from consumers. To get a sense of how widely these procedures are used, both the EMCC (as a signatory to the Global Code of Ethics) and ICF were contacted by email asking how many complaints, if any, about inaccurate or inappropriate marketing they had received in the past five years. According to the EMCC, there is only one complaint on file, although others may be registered at the local level (Secretariat, EMCC Global Complaints, 2022). The response from the ICF Ethics Committee revealed that the ICF has investigated complaints about coaches inflating their credentials, identifying as ICF certified without holding the certification, falsely claiming ICF membership or affiliation or misappropriating the ICF logo. The ICF treats these as compliance concerns, investigates the website or social media page in question and reaches out to the coach in question (Kelly, 2022). The year-to-date numbers of such complaints as of May 2022 were a modest 11 cases; however, in 2020 the total number reached 49.

However well-considered codes may be, Dichon and Nizet (2015) identified three types of limitations to codes of ethics: insufficiently accounting for complexity and diversity of clients, organizations, and coaching situations; by providing answers, the code discourages coach reflection, risk-taking and situational judgment; the tendency of codes to constrain or overlook the roles of coach's own values and emotions in ethical decision-making.

Theoretical and philosophical premises

A coaching practitioner's ability to behave in ways that align with codes and laws is rooted in their moral character. Principle-based ethics help determine the best course of action in each situation, the factors to which are assigned the most weight, and how they defend one's choices. Personal values inform ethical principles. However, by framing marketing as a relational issue rather than a commercial device, relationships and social content become potential resources in making ethical choices.

The literature of ethics in the helping professions suggest that there are six principles that inform the coaching practitioner's choices: beneficence (do good); autonomy (an individual's right to self-determination); non-malfeasance (avoid doing harm); justice (fair and equal treatment); fidelity (making and keeping commitments); and veracity (truthfulness) (Corey, Corey, & Corey, 2019).

Ethical judgements are made in the complex and dynamic arena of human interaction. Such judgements require a coach to be able to perceive and understand complexity, balance and evaluate multiple factors, understand the implication of decisions and actions, and engage the practitioner's moral character. In addition to a framework for the concepts of ethics and values, coaches must understand the multiple selves involved in self-presentation and the limitations and biases that influence their thinking and decision-making.

The triangular self in marketing

Because the person self-represented in a coach's marketing is a dynamic and complex construct, it is useful to understand the multiple facets of who is being shown. Wang's (2022) triangular self-theory suggests that we have three identities online: a represented self, a registered self, and an inferred self. The represented self is constructed from the experiences, characteristics and roles of the coach as the coach perceives them. The represented self "is embedded and constructed in the sociocultural context and ... outsourced to cyberspace, where the person selectively processes, encodes and shares self-related information online." (Wang, 2022, p. 3). The registered self is the public self-presentation that is constructed with the audience in mind. This is the self that is formed and maintained to offer a narrative with the self as the main character. This is the performed self, self as coach, expert and guide. In the registered self, some qualities and characteristics of the represented self are highlighted while others are omitted. The third self is the inferred self, the self that viewers and audiences construct in their own minds about who the registered person is and what they can do. This is the audience's narrative about the coach or consultancy, woven from whatever bits are shared and unaware of omissions.

In making choices about what to include and exclude and implicit aspects of presentation, coaches and consultancies must consider how the inferred self may be constructed by prospective clients. The inferred self is who the client expects to meet and what the client expects from the coaching engagement.

Ethical maturity

Truthful and accurate self-representation aligns with an ethic of care. Ethical choices must intentionally seek to avoid inflicting potential harm by giving "wrong information, falsifying, spin, lies, coverups" (Carroll & Shaw, 2013, p. 45). Consider, for example, a coach who states *my clients consistently grow and transform through my coaching*. Unless this coach has never lost a client or had a client leave dissatisfied, this claim is questionable. The truth is that some clients do change and some don't and the success of those who do may have other contributing factors. More temperate language might specify instead what the successful clients have achieved for themselves during their coaching engagements. Promised outcomes that imply causality should be backed by objective data or be more carefully constructed based on available evidence.

Ethical maturity begins with an ethical sensitivity: recognizing the potential harm or impact of a behavior. Ethical aspects of coach marketing are under-represented in the literature of the field, yet coaches must not allow themselves to become morally deaf to the potential harm of misleading or misrepresenting material. Ethical sensitivity grows from three roots. Background beliefs are an individual's mental model of what is good or bad, right or wrong. These filter our perceptions and meaning making. The second root is the moral character of the communities in which we are embedded. Our relationships within these commu-nities might influence our willingness to conform or emulate questionable stan-dards and practices to maintain relationships and community acceptance. The third root is that of principle, the values and guidance offered by codes and statements of organizational values. The three roots make up our moral antennae - what we notice and respond to in a situation and what we overlook. Ethically sensitive antennae can be cultivated by holding our beliefs, values, assumptions and associations up to the light for critical examination and by reflecting on how these contribute to our ethical frameworks, blind spots and biases.

Biases and blind spots

Ethical psychology shows that despite a desire to be a good person and do the right thing, there is a gap between intention and action that codes, and tra-ditional ethics training, cannot fill (Bazerman & Tenbrusel, 2011). The gap between intention and action may be the result of one or more factors: unconscious biases and prejudices (including in-group favoritism) and ego-centrism, which allows us to over claim more than a fair share of credit for accomplishments of others or groups. Emotions can profoundly affect our moral reasoning and ethical judgment and may contribute to a phenomenon called ethical fading, a process by which situational factors cause the ethical dilemmas of a situation to "fade" in favor of action or habitual reaction. (Corey, Corey, & Corey, 2019). This may be the case, for example, when a coach or consultancy is motivated by a desire to stand apart from competitors by claiming to have demonstrated *superior results* using a proprietary method. The Australian Psychological Society's code is specific in this matter, indicat-ing that statement by psychologists must not include "any statement claiming or implying superiority" (2017, C2.3 c) as well as "any claim unjustifiably stating or implying that the psychologist uses exclusive or superior apparatus, methods or materials" (Australian Psychological Society, 2017, C2.3 f).

George and Passmore (2019) point to phenomena that may cause coaches to believe in the magic of their own methods and interventions. A coach's desire to believe in their own effectiveness is a cognitive bias that is "deeply rooted and difficult to overcome" (George & Passmore, 2019, p. 45). As a result, coaches may overlook other factors which have contributed to successful outcomes and unintentionally exaggerate claims of success. Given a human tendency to overestimate one's contribution to events and experiences, coaches may prefer certain outcomes on the basis of self-interest, then justify our preference by re-evaluating the weight of some attributes or factors to fit our idea of what's fair (Bazerman & Tenbrusel, 2011). Consider, for example, the extent to which a coach or consultancy's *unique and original model* resembles another more widely known without attribution. Claims that one's coaching has caused certain outcomes for the client misrepresents the client's role and agency in changing themselves.

To be ethical, coaches need to heed the ancient dictum – know thyself. Everyone has biases and blind spots which may cause the unintentional misleading of others through the coach's self-deception. It is unethical to intentionally manipulate prospective clients' perspectives or trigger emotional reactions through chosen images and omissions. This may be challenging for coaches who have an uncritical and examined faith in the magic and efficacy of their own methods. A sincere desire to share the magic in service of others may tip judgment in favor of the "want self".

Ethical decision-making calls upon the use of three brains to balance each other. The reptilian brain seeks to ensure survival and makes decisions on a "me-first basis". There is little or no moral code in the reptilian brain" (Carroll & Shaw, 2013, p. 90). The limbic brain generates feelings such as compassion and empathy and moves us toward social and nurturing behaviors. Emotions play a strong role in marketing as material and images are selected to stimulate an emotional response in the audience. Even strictly factual information such as '*I led my company to triple income in two years*' implies a promise that the coach's own business success ensures the client's business success. In addition, such statements reflect the human tendency to take credit for outcomes resulting from the efforts of others, or even a good ounce of luck, are a reflection of the reptilian brain. The executive brain balances emotion and instinct with reasoning and reflection. The three brains can work together in an ethically mature system by balancing safety, empathy and creative and imaginative reflection (Carroll & Shaw, 2013). The integrated position involves caring for both self and others.

Case Study

(Note: This case is constructed to represent ethical issues raised in the chapter and does not represent any single event, organization or individual.)

The dilemma

Website claims

PQR is a coaching and consulting company which promotes its services through its own website. The company's logo PQR includes a small subtitle,

Powerful Quick Results. The website has two pages behind an opening page: Who We Are and Meet Our Coaches. There is a link to email with inquiries. The site also has a pop-up box urging the reader to "chat with us now" which opens an on-line chat with a representative of the company.

The page titled "who we are" states: PQR stands for powerful, quick results. For over a decade, we have provided science-based coaching to individuals and organizations seeking to make transformative change. We work with organizational clients to create a customized program and best match between coach and client using our digital platform. Using our proven methods and resources, we deliver coaching that disrupts unhelpful thinking and behavioral patterns and opens the way to fulfilling your full potential. Our performance metrics show the effectiveness of our programs, and we share data with clients to monitor and adjust custom programs."

The page titled "meet our coaches" opens with a slide show of coach faces. One third of the rapidly changing slides show coaches of color interacting with a variety of professional-looking clients. The text states "Our diverse roster of over 350 certified coaches include specialists in leadership, entrepreneurship, personal development and wellness. Our coaches receive mentoring and supervision and engage in on-going development activities." Each page includes highly laudatory testimonials from past clients who are identified only by a first name and initial.

Context

Jackson is a HR leader tasked with identifying and choosing a coaching consultancy to provide services as part of his organization's leadership development initiative. Jackson's plan is to reach out to two or three consultancies based on their websites and conduct screening interviews with coaches they refer to establish a roster of coaches who might be suited for leadership coaching engagements. He has reached out to PQR because the emphasis on metrics seems like a good fit with his organization's technical orientation and culture. Since diversity and inclusion are key issues for his organization as well, Jackson is impressed by the high proportion of coaches of color who appear to be represented in the slide show. PQR provides Jackson with four coaches for his screening interviews. As Jackson meets with each coach, however, he is increasingly concerned about the accuracy of the website statements and the likelihood that PQR can deliver on its promises.

Stakeholders

PQR owners and leaders have a vested interest in the success of their marketing and in delivering the promised results. HR leaders such as Jackson have a stake in successfully sourcing and identifying coaches who are likely to deliver on the desired outcomes. The leader clients in Jackson's organization expect to be offered coaches working within their competency. The coaches recommended by PQR have a stake in the success of the consultancy and their individual practices.

Contracting

In signing a contract with PQR to provide coaches for review, Jackson has formulated his expectations of coach and organizational quality based on statements on the website. As suggested by Wang, Jackson has constructed an inferred self by interpreting statements about metrics and coach representation in the slide show as congruent with his organization's metrics-oriented culture and diversity. He infers that mention of 'credentialed coaches' represent coach approval from a recognized professional organization. He expects that the coach mentoring and supervision referred to on the site are provided by qualified professionals. This lays the ground for a psychological contract between Jackson and PQR: an unarticulated set of assumptions, beliefs and expectations based on an individual's understanding of promises made and offers extended (Carroll, 2005). Clients such as Jackson will evaluate the trustworthiness of the agency and its coaches based on how closely the actuality matches expectations.

Coach's experience

By promising extraordinary results, PQR has set up its coaches as well as the client for disappointment. Each of the four Caucasian coaches sent by PQR for an interview encounters challenging questions about their presumed areas of expertise. They cannot provide details regarding the metrics statement other than to inform Jackson that the company tracks coach checklist summaries of client sessions and evaluates the quality according to a proprietary algorithm. Two of the four coaches attempt to maintain a sense of self-image by emphasizing experiences and skills peripheral to Jackson's particular needs. Three of the coaches who are relatively new to PQR recognize the limitations of their own competencies and plan to revise their PQR profiles to reflect the scope of their qualifications and expertise more accurately. One coach experiences a disconnect between her values and how PQR is representing the coaches and the value of coaching and decides to leave the consultancy.

Ethical guidelines and points of concern

The codes of ethics referenced in this chapter explicitly require accuracy and truthfulness in representing qualifications, experience, and potential value. While the statements on PQR's website appear impressive, they fall short of truthful and accurate representation by misleading statements and visual representations and by omission of key facts and supporting evidence. The site offers no examples of types of companies or clients served, and the measures used in the performance metrics are not disclosed. Stating that all coaches are certified does not accurately represent the quality of the certifications. In fact, over half of PQR's coaches are certified by PQR after completing the organization's proprietary training, not by a recognized professional organization. While coaches of color are shown on one-third of the slides, they make up only 15% of PQR's coach roster. The pop-up boxes give the impression of interaction. However, the live chat is with a sales representative not a coaching professional who can assess and determine whether PQR is a suitable fit for the client's interests.

An individual coach may claim expertise in all four areas of coaching that PQR provides. This raises questions as to whether PQR coaches are working within their areas of competency or casting the broadest possible net for potential clients. Coach mentoring and supervision are offered by senior members of the organization who are neither approved mentors nor supervisors. Jackson is seeking qualified coaches who can help leaders develop stronger leadership presence and communication skills and to support directors and managers to improve decision-making and process management. The promise of transformation, however, does not make clear what changes he might expect as a result of the coaching.

Implications

As the case suggests, coaches need to apply a critical eye to the standards used in offering themselves and their services. The implications of the case have relevance for individual coaches, coach consultancies, HR leaders, and the coaching profession.

For coaches and consultancies, the case makes clear that the nuances and details of marketing language and imagery set up expectations which form the basis of a psychological contract with prospective clients. It is essential that marketing materials be as factual as possible, fully represent the person and services on offer and offer data and evidence in support of claims. For example, coach training covers a spectrum from proprietary three-day "certification" intensives (certificate of completion granted by the training agency) to year-long and multi-year university based graduate programs. Information should allow a prospective client to discern and evaluate the source and trustworthiness of a coach's credentials and experience. Coaches must also evaluate the accuracy and basis for claims of expertise and areas of competence and clearly identify those clients and areas where they are best suited to work. As a profession, the coaching community must help HR professionals familiarize themselves with the standards and expectations of professional coach organizations and with the credibility of organizations granting certifications and accreditations. Quality control should go beyond assurances of metrics to include mentoring and supervision by credentialed professionals, preferably outside of the consulting organization.

While the ethical codes of professional organizations provide general guidance, concepts such as true and accurate should be better defined, especially with respect to coach marketing in the digital era. Ethical education for coaches is a continuous process and training in ethics would benefit from deeper self-knowledge, cultivation of ethical decision-making protocols and continuous self-reflection through journaling and supervision.

Conclusion

The purpose of coach marketing is persuasion: 'Choose ME'. The audience of potential clients is looking at coach marketing material to find a professional to help effect some change. While these may seem complementary, the coach and viewing audience have two different purposes. By approaching promotional activities as relational rather than transactional, we can reconcile these differing needs and purposes ethically. Ethical maturity requires that coaches recognize potential ethical issues. Promotional material, whether presented in talks, writing or digital forms, form the basis of client expectations and potential coaching relationships and integrity to the field of coaching.

Accurate representation, as noted in the codes of ethics, is based on facts and evidence to the greatest extent possible and with all relevant details. Coaches must be aware of and manage biases and blind spots and balance the impulses and emotions of the "want self" with the logic, reasoning and thoughtfulness of the "should self" informed and guided by the codes and laws governing our field. Coaches have a responsibility to themselves, their clients and the profession to ensure that they show up in their promotional activities as truthful, honest and fully human.

Discussion points

1. The "want self" and the "should self" present an internal conflict of interest for coaches. How might your experiences and education influence these two selves in you?
2. Complaints and compliance bodies appear to have limited influence on coach tendencies to inaccurate representation. What means or mechanisms might have greater influence in fostering accuracy in coach marketing?
3. Since potential clients create an inferred coach from your marketing materials, what inferred clients might you be thinking of as you create your promotional materials? How might your biases and blind spots influence the client you are imagining?
4. To what extent have you considered the ethics of promoting your services? In thinking about how you have framed and presented yourself and your services in person and on-line, what might you want to revisit and re-consider to ensure more ethical alignment?

Recommended reading

Bazerman, M. H. & Tenbrusel, A. E. (2011). *Blind Spots: Why we fail to do what's right and what to do about it.* Princeton, NJ: Princeton University Press.

References

Australian Psychological Society. (2017) Code of ethics. Melbourne. www.psychology. org.au.

Bachkirova, T. & Borrington, Simon. (2020) Beautiful Ideas that can make us ill: Implications for coaching. *Philosophy of Coaching: An International Journal, 5(1).* Retrieved May 2022, from Philosophy of Coaching: An International Journal: doi:10.22316/poc/ 05.1.03.

Bazerman, M. H. & Tenbrusel, A. E. (2011) *Blind Spots: Why we fail to do what's right and what to do about it.* Princeton, NJ: Princeton University Press.

British Advertising Standards Authority. www.asa.org.uk.

British Psychological Society. (2022) Retrieved May 14, 2022, from BPS Code of Ethics and Conduct. www.bps.org.uk/sites/www.bps.org.uk/files/Policy/Policy%20-% 20Files/BPS%20Code%20of%20Ethics%20and%20Conduct.pdf.

Carroll, M. (2005) Psychological Contracts with and within Organizations. In R. Tribe & Morrissey, J. (Eds), *Handbook of Professional and Ethical Practice for Psychologists, Counsellors and Psychotherapists.* Brunner-Routledge.

Carroll, M. & Shaw, E. (2013) *Ethical Maturity in the Helping Professions: Making difficult life and work decisions.* Philadelphia, PA: Jessica Kingsley Publishers.

Corey, G., Corey, M. S., & Corey, C. (2019) *Issues & Ethics in the Helping Professions,* 10th Edition. Boston, MA: Cengage Learning.

Dichon, P. F. & Nizet, Jean. (2015) Ethical Codes and Executive Coaches: One Size Does Not Fit All. *The Journal of Applied Behavioural Science,* 51(2): 277–301.

Diener, E. (1984) Subjective Well-being. Psychological Bulletin, 95(3): 542–575.

Diener, E., Thapa, S., & Tay, L. (2019) Positive Emotions at Work. *Annual Review of Organizational Psychology and Organizational Behavior,* 7.

Duffy, M. & Passmore, J. (2010) Ethics in coaching: An ethical decision-making framework for coaching psychologists. *International Coaching Psychology Review,* 5(2).

George, A. J. & Passmore, J. (2019) Believe me. *Coaching at Work,* pp. 44–47.

Gilligan, C., Ward, J. V., Taylor, J. M., & Bardige, B. (1988) *Mapping the Moral Domain.* Boston: Harvard University Press.

Global Code of Ethics. (n.d.) Retrieved May 2022 from www.globalcodeofethics.org/ download-the-code.

Grief, S. (2022) Pseudoscience and Charlatanry in Coaching. In S. Grief, H. Moller, W. Scholl, J. Passmore, & F. Muller (Eds), *International Handbook of Evidence-Based Coaching.* Springer.

Harvard Business Review. (2004) https://hbr.org/2004/11/the-wild-west-of-executive-coaching.

ICF Code of Ethics. (n.d.) Retrieved May 2022, from https://coachingfederation.org/ ethics/code-of-ethics.

International Coach Federation. (2022) Revitalizing ICF's Core Values. Retrieved from https://coachingfederation.org/about/our-values.

Iordanou, I., Hawley, R., & Iordanou, C. (2017) *Values and Ethics in Coaching.* Thousand Oaks, CA: Sage Publications.

Kegan, R. (2000) What "Form" Transforms? A Constructive-Developmental Approach to Transformative Learning. In J. Mezirow and Associates (Eds), *Learning as Transformation: Critical Perspectives on a Theory in Progress.* San Francisco, CA: Jossey-Bass.

Kelly, K. (2022) Personal Communication.

Mezirow, J. (2000) Learning to Think Like an Adult. In J. Mezirow and Associates (Eds), *Learning as Transformation: Critical Perspectives on a Theory in Progress.* San Francisco, CA: Jossey-Bass.

Private Act 142. (2011) Retrieved May 14, 2022, from The Professional Charter for Coaching and Mentoring: www.eesc.europa.eu/sites/default/files/resources/docs/142-private-act–2.pdf.

Rettberg, J. W. (2017) Self-Representation in Social Media. In J. Burgess, A. Marwick, & T. Poell, *Sage Handbook of Social Media.* Sage Publications.

Secretariat, E. G. (2022) Personal correspondence.

Turner, E. & Passmore, J. (2018) Ethical dilemmas and tricky decisions: A global perspective of coaching supervisors' practice in coach ethical decision-making. *International Journal of Evidence-Based Coaching and Mentoring*, 16(1).

Wang, Q. (2022) The triangular self in the social media era. doi:10.1017/mem.2021.6.

Section IV

Case studies

Chapter 26

A series of 12 case studies for coach reflection and discussion

Case Study 1: Intimacy in the Coaching Engagement

Kristin Kelly

Background

Coaching requires trust and is particularly successful when clients can open up and speak freely. This level of intimacy is important for a successful coaching engagement. But what happens when boundaries become fuzzy and the level of intimacy exceeds what is appropriate for a coaching relationship? How should a coach recognise and address what is happening? Is coaching still possible in this kind of setting?

Case Study

A woman named Sophia has reached a point in her career where she feels ready for something different, and maybe even a career change. To help her navigate this, and to better determine the direction she should take, she decides at the urging of a close friend, to hire an executive coach. Her friend has been working with a coach successfully for a few months and he felt that Sophia and his coach would connect and collaborate well together.

An exploratory session was soon scheduled, and after speaking with the coach, she was really excited about what this may mean for her career.

Sophia and the coach signed an agreement shortly thereafter and coaching initially began virtually over a video platform and took place every other week. In a short time, she was making significant progress with the support of her coach.

Over time, the coaching sessions became more intimate, as the pair realised many similarities in their backgrounds, shared interests, and even a few mutual friends. The more time they spent together, the more they discovered they had in common.

Three months into the coaching engagement, they decide to start meeting in person at a local coffee shop they both individually enjoyed. The coaching engagement remained professional, although both parties found a great deal of satisfaction in their time with the other.

Over time, small physical gestures of affection entered the coaching space. A touch on the knee here, a hand resting too long on a back there. In fact, after several weeks of these in-person interactions, deeper feelings started to bubble up on both sides of the engagement, although neither party acknowledged it aloud.

Once the coach recognized what he was feeling for his client, he stepped back to assess the situation.

On the one hand, he felt like they had potential as a romantic couple, and he wanted to explore that further. On the other hand, as a coach, he knew that getting involved romantically with a client was a no-go. And he hated the thought of not following through on their coaching contract—he sincerely wanted to see her through on her career transition and fully honour their relationship as her coach. Despite that, he still found himself drawn to her and wanting to spend more time with her, beyond the context of a professional relationship.

To this point, he had never been caught in a situation like this in his coaching. He knew one thing for sure: he was conflicted.

Implications for coaching

- Shift in value received through coaching – the coach should remain alert to any indications that coaching is not benefiting the client. If the coach notices a shift, they can explore to see what is behind it and this may include a discussion with the client or encouraging the client to seek a new coach or other professional resource, depending on the situation. (ICF Code of Ethics (2020) Section 1, Standard 8)
- Boundaries of coaching engagement – the coach should hold the responsibility of being aware and setting clear, appropriate and culturally sensitive boundaries in the engagement. Boundaries may include cultural, physical, sexual or emotional – and it should be considered how religion and/or tradition might affect the coaching engagement. (ICF Code of Ethics (2020) Section 3, Standard 23)
- Do not participate in any sexual or romantic relationship with client – the coach should be mindful of the level of intimacy appropriate for the relationship, have an awareness to recognise and address feelings, be mindful to cultural differences that could be misinterpreted and take the appropriate action to address the issue or cancel the coaching engagement. (ICF Code of Ethics (2020) Section 3, Standard 24)

Possible outcomes or next steps

- Seek outside support. A coach in any ethical conundrum may choose to turn to their coach, mentor coach, coach supervisor, training programme or coaching organisation like the ICF for support in navigating ethically confusing situations. This process will likely include much reflection and thought on the coach's side. In addition, the coach may choose to utilise outside support after a coaching engagement ends (or is cancelled) to learn fully from the experience.

- Clarify the relationship with the other party. A coach may choose to bring their concerns to the client directly. This allows both parties to discuss and determine the best path forward in a collaborative manner. The coach may want to consider the dynamics of that meeting though – perhaps by shifting to a virtual platform and not meeting in person. If it is determined that the coaching engagement will continue, re-contracting with the client and setting up clear boundaries are strongly encouraged.
- End the coaching engagement. If it is determined that the coaching engagement should end, the coach should support the client as they transition to another coach and/or allow for the cancellation of the coaching arrangement.

Discussion points

1. What boundaries can a coach put into place to avoid this kind of situation? What resources can you turn to as a coach?
2. If you were this coach's coach, mentor or supervisor, how would you support the coach?
3. If you recognise feelings in yourself or in your client, how can these be addressed in a way that would not cause discomfort in the other party?
4. Can a coach ethically coach a significant other, someone with whom a romantic relationship is already at play?

Reference

ICF Code of Ethics. (2020) https://coachingfederation.org/ethics/code-of-ethics.

Case Study 2: Ethical dilemmas faced by postgraduate level teachers of coaching

Alexandra Morgan

Background

This case study looks at the ethical and moral issues which impact the tea-cher-student relationship and potentially student outcomes in a postgraduate teaching environment. The subject of this case-study (Lesley) is fictitious, and her dilemmas are a fusion of the author's experience of teaching at postgraduate level. None of the examples are real-life case studies. The author also draws on her experience of working with trainers, coaches and consultants both in the UK and internationally.

Case Study

Lesley is a coach, coach supervisor and lecturer on a postgraduate coaching programme. Lesley has felt tensions in her approach to three of her students, Mel, Sam and Aki. Mel is already a professional coach but as yet does not have a coaching qualification or accreditation. Sam is a senior manager in a medium-sized consultancy firm who is new to coaching and wants to add coaching to their portfolio of consulting skills. Aki, an artist, has had a great experience of life-coaching and wishes to become a life coach in semi-retirement.

During the programme Lesley experiences moments of moral and ethical tension. These dilemmas are not those relating to the practical matters of how to be a better coach trainer (e.g. how could I encourage the group to give each other better feedback, or how could I have managed that moment of conflict better between students), but are questions more fundamentally rela-ted to Lesley's beliefs around being a propagator of coaching excellence, a protector of coaching standards and a protagonist of creative, non-directive coaching approaches. Let's take a closer look at the issues Lesley faces, taking each student in turn.

Mel comes to the postgraduate programme as a coach of some ten years standing. He already has a profitable and productive client base and a good reputation. When Lesley sees Mel coach for the first time in coaching practice, Lesley does not consider Mel's skills to be effective, in fact the opposite; Mel demonstrates aggressive badgering, regular interruptions, intrusive body language and patronising opinions. Lesley is confused: Do Mel's clients enjoy and benefit from this style? Mel's references for the programme and the testimonials on Mel's website would suggest they do. How does Lesley reconcile her own concept of coaching excellence with Mel's success as a coach thus far?

Sam is an excellent consultant, top of their field. Sam finds the shift from advising to a less directive coaching style difficult and frustrating. In fact, Sam has significant blocks around the coaching process and others are avoiding Sam when doing coaching practice. Sam constantly berates themself on their "rubbish" coaching skills. Yet, in their academic assignments Sam appears to articulate the difference between coaching and consulting very well and is very knowledgeable around the psychology of coaching. Sam gets high marks for academic work, but low marks on coaching practicum assessments. How does Lesley balance knowledge versus practice when assessing coach effectiveness?

Aki is a wonderful artist and has shared her work with the group. Aki has no intention of combining her artwork with her coaching practice. Lesley feels frustrated as she has experienced art-based coaching herself and found it to be a profoundly moving experience. Lesley cannot understand why Aki won't consider an art-based coaching practice. Lesley feels the student is limiting her horizons. How might Lesley's judgement be influencing her interactions with, and assessment of, the student's overall achievements on the programme?

Implications for coaching

- High quality coach educators are essential to the profession, but they too need support. Lesley would benefit from a co-supervisory relationship where she can discuss her dilemmas in confidence with a knowledgeable coach and coach educator.
- Coach educators can feel like guardians of the professional standards. But learners need to be allowed to be less than perfect and have different approaches to coaching. Learning to be a coach is a messy and evolving process. Coach educators need to allow their students to take risks and make mistakes, this can however feel at odds with the pursuit of high standards.

Possible next steps

- As mentioned above, Lesley needs to take her dilemmas to supervision for a fresh perspective, and some challenge around her own paradigms and values as a coach educator. What is it about Lesley's view of quality coaching that may be affecting her view of her students' capabilities? It may be helpful if her supervisor is also a coach educator and familiar with similar dilemmas in teaching.

- Lesley could consider introducing a number of external speakers who can role-model excellence in coaching to the students, as well as open the students' eyes to alternative and creative ways to coach.
- Lesley could also work with co-trainers, thus sharing the responsibility of educating her students with other professionals, leading, potentially, to alternative student-tutor relationships which may work better for the students.

Discussion points

1. To what extent does Lesley's own paradigm of what is and is not good coaching affect their own judgement of student performance?
2. How would deferring to the ethical standards and coaching competencies of a coaching association help Lesley solve these dilemmas?
3. Are skills more important than knowledge when it comes to good coaching? Can you separate out the two?
4. How would supervision help Lesley and her students?

Case Study 3: Coaching: Developmental tool or organisational status quo?

Stephen Gresty and Eric Mellet

Background

A crucial question that needs answering at the start of any coaching assignment is "What is the real intention of the HR department or the organisational sponsor?" This must be clear for all those involved, either directly or indirectly. Is the desired outcome to equip the coachee, and by default the organisation, with various coping mechanisms, i.e., to effectively put them on a "life support" system or is to really help the individual, and therefore, the organisation flourish and grow.

Case Study

François Leclerc du Tremblay also known as Père Joseph, was a French confidant and agent of Cardinal Richelieu. He was the original *éminence grise*, the French term ("grey eminence") for a powerful adviser or decision-maker who operates secretly or unofficially. Like the famous cardinal, today's business leaders have their own grey eminences. But these advisers aren't monks bound by a vow of poverty, they are executive coaches and are increasingly plying their trade in all areas of the business world. A quick Google search will reveal all number of reasons why any business wishing to grow and develop should employ an external coach to help the various levels of management 'be better at their job'.

Today it is not only the C-Suite who are working with coaches, in fact there is a whole army of coaches working throughout organisations, with all levels of junior and senior managers, not forgetting those employees who have been given the title of manager-coach, who often have a better understanding of the culture of their own organisation but maybe ill-equipped with the necessary skills required to coach. They are also faced with the dilemma of the 'politics' that exist in any organisation, and the associated limitations this brings with it, so are they being utilised to help the organisation "to gain some time" without really helping people flourish and grow.

Hence the importance to understand why a coach has been assigned in the first place, is it to help manage poor performance, or designed to develop the coachee, or is it something that is being offered to help the individual 'survive' in the fast paced, permanent Volatile, Uncertain, Complex, Ambiguous world we are living in, or is it?

When exploring the area of survival within an organisation, it's essential to be aware of the level of psychological safety that the coachee feels exists. If they express to their coach some concern that indicates an uncomfortableness to be open, or perceive those levels are low, despite the coach's best efforts to support the coachee and bring about change, success will be limited. Low levels of psychological safety prevent the coachee from taking risks, speaking up or challenging existing thoughts and practices. If, however, a high level of psychological safety exists, there is more likely to be a successful outcome for all parties, as this type of positive relationship encourages risk taking and challenges existing ways of thinking, which in turn leads to a more collaborative approach to dealing with issues faced and builds employee engagement. Having worked with several corporate organisations, as well as start-up's, the coach has experienced both low and high levels of psychological safety. Larger organisations generally tend to be more risk averse, whereas start-up companies are keener, and often encourage their people to challenge the status quo, without fear of ridicule or retribution.

A coach was assigned to provide coaching to an upcoming executive.

During the first session the coach became concerned about the coachee's lack of engagement in the coaching process. The coachee was not open to exploring the coaching objectives, as they were happy that their 360-degree feedback. It has been consistently very good with little noted for areas of improvement. The coachee was a little surprised that they had even been assigned a coach, as they felt that it was not necessary, given they were more than capable of doing the job asked of them. This was contrary to the coaches understanding of the situation, based on various discussions with the human resources (HR) department.

The coach became concerned as to the rationale for the coaching, yet at the same time the coaching sessions were expected to generate the income needed in order to maintain budgeted income levels, so they were facing an ethical dilemma, which potentially could have a negative impact on all stakeholders if not resolved.

This discrepancy between the coachee's and the HR's objectives and rationale for the coaching assignment left the coach asking themself: "who is this coaching for? Is it purely to satisfy coaching quotas in organisational development or is there a real need for the coachee?"

Implications for coaching

Shift in value received through coaching – The coach should remain alert to any indications that coaching is not benefiting the client. ICF Code of

Ethics (2020) – Conflict of Interest (#18) – a situation in which an ICF Professional is involved in multiple interests, where serving one interest could work against or conflict with another. This could be financial, personal or otherwise.

With the privilege of coaching comes great responsibility, it is imperative to have a clear coaching relationship and not allow personal bias to influence professional actions.

- The roles and responsibilities, if they become blurred, can create a potential for ethical concern and poor outcome. It is essential to stay mindful of the ethical responsibility to the client and to maintain confidentiality.
- If the complete coaching process has been put in place to maintain the status quo rather than develop people, all parties need to be clear on what they are entering into and what are the expected outcomes. If not, they could be left with a sense of frustration and many unanswered questions.

Possible outcomes or next steps

- Be clear with oneself about what is acceptable and what is not
- Clarify the relationship with all parties
- Ensure the coach undertakes regular supervision

Discussion points

1. How can we discover the "real intention" for the coaching?
2. When the "real intention" conflicts with the coach's values and beliefs, who do they turn to?
3. What can the coach do if they identify that the coachee is just "playing the game" to survive?
4. How does the coach know when it is the right time to "walk away?"

Reference

International Coaching Federation. (2020). ICF Code of Ethics. Retrieved July 6, 2022 from https://coachingfederation.org/ethics/code-of-ethics.

Case Study 4: Where are the loyalties in the executive coaching relationship?

Stephen Murphy

Background

Coaching relationships in organisations are often peppered with hidden pitfalls. With the benefit of hindsight, many might have been foreseen. However, as we progress into early stages of relationship building and goal clarification, our antennae are not always well-tuned to possible issues lurking within the system. For example, how might our coachees feel obligated to react outside of our own contracting. Or, how we might be stretched between the client organisation and the individual with whom we are directly working (i.e., coachee). This Case Study explores how, with the best of intentions, a coach can be caught off guard!

Case Study

A colleague asked: "A good friend of mine is Global People Director (Anne) in a multinational company. She's looking for a coach to work with their Global Supply Chain Director (Paulo: coachee). I can't do it because I have a conflict of interest. Can you help?" The coach: "Guess so. How about she and I have a call to see what's needed and we'll go from there?"

The call with Anne took place. The issue discussed was that Paulo seemed more distant and aggressive than historically and was missing important deadlines. He recognised the issues and wanted some coaching to help him get back on track.

The coach and coachee agreed on the coaching details. They scheduled an introductory session with Paulo and then had a four-way meeting, including the CEO, to discuss the coaching goals and success criteria? They also agreed that the content of each session would remain confidential between Paulo and the coach. Everyone concurred.

Three months later, several areas had been covered in the coaching. Paulo was very demotivated working in what he saw as a toxic and divisive culture. He reported several arguments with the Sales and Finance Directors. Trust seemed rare, especially between his peers. His boss was becoming more distant working on a potential takeover.

Paulo and the coach focused on his role in this working environment and what he was experiencing? He came to realise that this was not a company where he felt good. However, he had a senior role; was well paid and he didn't yet have enough successes to look for a role in another organisation. He emphasised, to the coach, the confidential nature of this admission and decided for now to do what was needed to build results; improve relationships and empower his team.

After four months, Anne, Paulo and the coach held a checkpoint meeting. The CEO had told Paulo he couldn't attend. The summary was that Paulo's results were improving. He seemed much more positive, and his team were happier. Also, there was less friction between Sales, Finance and Supply. Everyone seemed happy.

Two days later, Anne called the coach. The takeover had accelerated. They had soon to decide how to integrate positions in the new business? They only needed one Supply Chain leader. The incumbent in the target business was well respected. Yet, Paulo had significantly improved his performance and attitude. He was the favourite. "But is the change in attitude real?", she asked. "We can't afford to lose the other guy, appoint Paulo and then have him leave after a few months. Has he ever mentioned leaving to you during the coaching?"

The coach: "Well, I understand that this is an important area for you. Have you talked directly to Paulo?"

Anne: "No, not yet. I just thought I'd ask you first, off the record."

The coach: "Look, we've talked a load of things over the months, some in passing, others in detail. I really think you are best talking with him directly given where you are in the takeover process."

Anne: "OK. I'll do that."

A few days later the coach met Paulo for their next session. Anne had indeed talked to him. She asked directly if was considering leaving? He told her that he was not and was curious why she had asked, given the positive nature of the check-point meeting. She said she was just checking to make sure everything was ok with him overall.

Paulo: "Did you say anything to her?" he asked.

The coach: "No, I didn't", the coach answered truthfully.

The subject got lost as they then worked together on the latest coaching topic.

The coach felt lucky in that the conversation enabled him to remain truthful. However, the coach felt exposed in several areas.

Implications for coaching

- Confidentiality – How the boundaries of confidentiality can be perceived differently through the eyes of a client, client organisation and coach. (Global Code of Ethics – Confidentiality 2.13 & 2.14)

- Contracting – Establishes and maintains the expectations and boundaries of the mentoring/coaching contract with the client and, where appropriate, with sponsors. (EMCC EIA Competence – Managing the Contract)
- Relationships – Skilfully builds and maintains an effective relationship with the client, and where appropriate, with the sponsor. (EMCC EIA accreditation Competence – Building the Relationship)

Possible outcomes or next steps

- Self-Reflection – What did I not notice or ignore as I re-think the process?
- Supervision – Exploring what happened, the impact and what other options might exist?

Discussion points

1. How would the coach have responded if Paulo had asked a direct question? For example, "Did she ask you if I had discussed leaving?"
2. How should the coach manage a coachee lying to their peer and the coach knowing about it?
3. Where are the coach's loyalties in the coaching relationship? With the corporate sponsor, who pays the bills and might be a future employer, or the coachee, with whom the coach has developed an open and safe place to work? And with whom else?
4. What might the coach have done differently, in the contracting, for example, to foresee such a situation?

Reference

Global Code of Ethics. (2021) *Global Code of Ethics for Coaches, Mentors, and Supervisors, updated June.* Retrieved July 3, 2022 from www.globalcodeofethics.org.

Case Study 5: Influence of the boss in a hierarchical culture

Ng Phek Yen

Background

In this case study, we are going to look at the ethical dilemma that the coach faced as a result of the influence exerted by the boss of the coachee in a hierarchical culture. The boss' action in trying to influence the coaching process has been deemed to impact the coaching ethics. We will look at the implication for coaching and on the coachee. We will also discuss the potential next steps that a coach could take when encountering such a situation.

Case Study

A sizeable US-based tech company appointed the coach to support one of their high potential leaders, (i.e., coachee) Ramesh, who was based in Bombay, India. Ramesh is one of the early leaders who helped setting up the IT shared service center in India 4 years ago. The company has recently promoted Ramesh as the Director to lead a group of engineers and programmers. Joseph, the immediate supervisor of Ramesh, has been very keen on being involved in Ramesh's coaching engagement.

To help the transition and development of Ramesh, the company has engaged an external coach contracted by a consulting company to undertake this coaching engagement. Before the start of the coaching journey with Ramesh, the coach had a briefing call from Joseph. During the call, Joseph highlighted his expectations about Ramesh and what he would like to see more of in Ramesh, including specific behaviours of Ramesh and the, whom he needs to pay particular attention to, and how he should do it.

The coaching goal of Ramesh is to develop leadership presence and be able to articulate what he wants to say clearly to his stakeholders.

During the first coaching session with Ramesh, the coach noted he was constantly asking for advice and recommendations, which was more mentoring than coaching. This is one of the most common challenges that coaches in Asia encounter. Coachees tend to come to the session to seek advice on what to do and tools they can use immediately when back to the office.

After three coaching sessions, the coach was contacted by Joseph to understand the coaching progress with Ramesh. Joseph also asked what was discussed in the coaching conversations and Ramesh's thinking on those highlighted issues. The coach hesitated to share the information with Joseph. The coach explained to Joseph that she could not do so. Sharing that information would have breached the confidentiality contract as a coach, which is one of the most important codes of ethics that we need to follow as coaches. Joseph was not pleased with the coach's reply. The coach noticed Joseph had assumed employees in India tend to be more obedient to power and taking instructions, and hence, he attempted to make all decisions for his team in India. He also approached Ramesh to understand how the coaching had helped him and what actions Ramesh had taken.

The impact of this is Ramesh becoming more concerned about the information he shared in the coaching sessions. Whereas the coach reassured him that the coaching conversations would remain confidential, this has unconsciously sat in the back of Ramesh's mind. He tended to speak about positive matters in the session and reserved to open up.

As an alternative, the coach offered the company an alignment call where tripartite coaching could offer – the coachee, manager and the coach attend to align the expectations.

Implications for coaching

- Managing power and status between the coach and coachee – Coachees in hierarchical cultures tend to perceive the coach as someone who has more power in influencing their professional development. Thus, the coach should be very aware of any power or status difference between them. (ICF Code of Ethics: Section I – Responsibility to Clients, point 11, 2021)
- Shift in value received through coaching – the coach should remain alert to any indications that coaching is not benefiting the client. (ICF Code of Ethics: Section I – Responsibility to Clients, point 8, 2021)
- Boundaries of coaching engagement – the coach should highlight to the client any potential breach of boundaries in the coaching interactions. (ICF Code of Ethics: Section III – Responsibility to Professionalism, point 23, 2021)

Possible outcomes or next steps

- Clarify the relationship with the other party. The coach, in this case, needs to clarify her position as a coach and the coachee's role and immediate supervisor.

- Seek outside support. The Coach could seek support from the programme co-ordinator (who supports the client's engagement) in the consulting company to highlight the challenge that she is facing.
- Coaching for the immediate supervisor.

Discussion points

1. What could you do differently in this situation if you were the coach?
2. How could you prevent this from happening?
3. As a coach, how do you balance your client's confidentiality while managing your stakeholder (in this case the boss of your coachee) as you are hired by the company?
4. What other ethical considerations need to be attended to?

Reference

International Coach Federation. (2019) *Code of Ethics*. Lexington, KY: International Coach Federation. Retrieved from https://coachingfederation.org/ethics/code-of-ethics.

Case Study 6: Ethical Challenges Across Cultures in Team Coaching

Ng Phek Yen

Background

This case study is based on a recent assignment of team coaching with a group of executives. The coach was engaged by the CEO of a multinational company in China to do team coaching for his team. The CEO, Moses, is a Korean in his late 30s, recently appointed to lead the team in China. This is his first CEO role and the first time leading a Chinese team. At the same time, he needs to co-lead the team with a VP in China, Chen. Chen has been with the company for over 20 years. Moses is based in Shanghai, and Chen is based in Beijing. At the time of the team coaching, Moses had been with the team eight months.

During the discovery call, Moses shared his challenges with his direct reports. Seven of them are responsible for different functions, including Sales & Marketing, Operations, Supplier Chain, HR, Finance and China Regulatory Affairs. Moses has found that his direct reports do not speak to him about many matters. This has Moses feeling that his team do not agree with his approach and lack trust in him. As the business in China is critical to the group, Moses feels he needs to quickly build his credibility and that his teams trust him. To help build trust, identify individual and team values and goals Moses would like the team to participate in team coaching.

Case Study

From the start, the coach faced a dilemma because of Moses' indirect communication when dealing with disagreement. This also linked to his hierarchical orientation (as well as power distance) trying to use the coaching session to achieve his agenda. The coach did not feel able to call out his behavior because the coach noted Moses got very emotional during the session and everything seems to be well received by him, at face value, during this particular session. The impact was that the other executives felt they were being encouraged by Moses to be honest and transparent about themselves during the team coaching session, but that he was then interpreting their honesty as a lack of respect for him which might lead to their disadvantage.

The coach did the necessary preparation for the session, including 1-on-1 interviews with all the executives. Furthermore, the coach felt she had got quite a big picture of the challenges encountered by the team when working with Moses. The coach briefed Moses about the interview findings and key themes from there, which could be explored further during the team coaching sessions. The coach and the manager, Moses, had an alignment call the day before the team coaching session meeting the team to understand the session's goals.

During the first coaching session, the team seemed hesitant to open up, which is common in the team's culture and considering the background of the team in China. From the second session onwards, the team members did feel more able to open up and sufficiently relaxed to express their authentic thoughts. The team started to share their true feelings about current management challenges and Moses' leadership. During their interactions, the coach contracted with the team that they were going to explore the different perspectives and provide suggestions to help each other to grow. Everyone agreed and was eager to do so as part of the journey to the goal – to develop and become a high-performing team. It was agreed that everyone would have a chance to give and receive suggestions, including Moses. He received a couple of suggestions from the team members about the unclear direction of his leadership style. To the coach's surprise, Moses became very emotional (his face was red) when receiving these suggestions, although he tried to contain his emotions. At the end of the session, he expressed that he was pleased to know the team better now, and that everyone is very open to sharing and helping each other grow. He was grateful for the suggestions.

While the coach was packing up to leave, she noticed Moses pushed one of his direct reports, Angela, into a meeting room. The coach felt weird but did not take any action at that moment – the team was supposed to have a team dinner – but Moses and Angela were still in another meeting and talking quite loud. Her intuition was wondering "Could it be Moses wanted to talk about the feedback he received today so that he can improve?" While she felt something was not right, she didn't follow-up on her intuition and ask, instead deciding they were probably talking about other work matters.

The next day the coach had a follow-up session with Moses. The coach wanted to debrief the session with him to understand what he felt about it and the next steps. He expressed that people do not respect him, do not speak up to him, he feels like his leadership style was challenged and feels embarrassed. The coach was confused by his response as one of the coaching contract agreements was that issues explored and discussed will be to build trust and develop the team, and rules on giving suggestions were agreed by the group. This is quite different from what was noticed and heard during the closing comment made by Moses yesterday. The coach hesitated for a while and wondered whether she should explore what was causing that change. She observed Moses was exhibiting an unfriendly posture and verbal tone.

There are a few cultural orientations that played out in this case: the coach's orientation to avoid confrontation to maintain the coaching relationship; the high-context and avoidance of confrontations in Moses' communication preferences to preserve the group harmony; the team felt safe to open up and share in the session and give suggestions, which in this case is perceived as negative feedback by Moses. Another cultural orientation that played out in the team is a hierarchical orientation demonstrated by Moses, the CEO. He felt his power and leadership style was challenged or brought into question when there was a suggestion for him. He felt like he was losing face.

After the coach's follow-up session with Moses, Chen approached the coach and told them what had happened the night before. It seems that Moses had questioned Angela, Chen's direct report, as Angela had given feedback to Moses in the team coaching session, and she had not told Moses in advance. Moses felt this was a sign that Angela did not respect him and was challenging his leadership.

In this case, the coach overlooked the importance of cultural sensitivity before prepping the team for the session. Most importantly, the coach had overlooked the cultural preferences of Moses during the preparation and process of the team coaching.

In this situation, what would you do?

The coach decided to call Moses to have a conversation about what had happened. The conversation did not go well as Moses found that his team was now speaking up to him further, and he was seeing that as a challenge to his authority.

Impact on the team – people are now speaking up less, as they have felt a lack of safety following the team coaching. Trust between the team and Moses is broken.

Impact on the coachee – Moses had assumed that the team is challenging his authority when they give feedback, which causes him to react more authoritatively.

Impact on the coach – the coaching engagement did not continue after that as Moses decided to change his team.

If the coach had been able to call out Moses' behaviour at the end of the day one session, that might have helped him reflect on his behaviours.

Implications for coaching

- The influence of culture – here seen in the indirect communication (avoid confrontation) and hierarchical orientations.
- Hearing about inappropriate behaviour after the coaching session and not feeling able to act on the information.
- The potential for coachees to exploit coaching sessions to further their own agenda.

Possible outcomes or next steps

- Have a face-to-face conversation with Moses – understand his thoughts about the team coaching and further challenges he faced with the team. Solicit his feedback. Build up the trust with him. At the same time, explore what Moses thought might be the potential misalignment of the session goals.
- Clarify the role of the coach in the team coaching session for all sides.
- Seek support in intercultural coaching. Suggest an intercultural awareness session for the team before diving into a team coaching session. Help each executive raise their awareness of intercultural sensitivity and understand each other's cultural preferences.

Discussion points

1. What would you do differently if you were the coach?
2. How would culture influence the position of the coach and coachees in relation to the code of ethics the coach follows? (Refer to ICF Section 1 Responsibility to clients – standard 11. "Am aware of and actively manage any power or status difference between the Client and me that may be caused by cultural, relational, psychological or contextual issues.")
3. What would you do to consider cultural influences at the beginning and throughout the coaching engagement in this situation?
4. Should there be one standard code of ethics for all coaching, or to what extent should we allow the code of ethics to be adapted to the context?

Reference

International Coach Federation. (2019) Code of Ethics. Lexington, KY: International Coach Federation. Retrieved from https://coachingfederation.org/ethics/code-of-ethics.

Case Study 7: Ethical Dilemmas with Recording Coaching Sessions

Eve Turner

Background

Coaches may choose, or be required, to provide either audio and or visual recordings of coaching sessions. It is suggested they occur for a specific purpose, such as bringing it to supervision, credentialing/accreditation, professional development and support both to understand what is happening in challenging sessions and to reflect on their practice. All purposes or types of recording will have ethical implications that overlap or are similar, however, this case study will focus specifically on a recording of a one-to-one coaching session for skill development within a group supervision session.

Recordings are a common feature of supervision for therapy, they are less common for coaching supervision and the ethics of their use may not be discussed in coach training. Recordings allow us to work with what really happened in the moment, rather than our memories of what happened, which are shaped by not only our ability to remember but by our own "blind spots" – what we may not see, hear or say. An important part of the learning process comes from the supervisee listening and watching the recording themselves beforehand. Feedback from fellow group members, a peer or a supervisor brings another dimension.

Thanks go to the supervisees who shared their own perceptions of, and reflections on, the ethical dilemmas in doing recordings of sessions for this case study and whose feedback is reflected throughout the case study. In particular appreciation both to Alison and to her client for allowing elements of their recording, brought to group supervision, to be shared and offering their insights.

Case Study

Prior to the coaches doing recordings the group explored the ethical considerations. These included:

- concern the coach might not be fully in service of / present for the client, that the coach might be trying to be "perfect".

- considering the impact on the coach and the coachee of making a recording:

  o Some clients may be more constrained – less open emotionally and in what they say aloud – by the recording than others. One supervisee talked of considering their "psychological robustness" before asking.
  o Coaches said, "This could be positive and enhance my effectiveness or it may make me focus too much on myself at the expense of the coachee".

- considering how the coach might feel about sharing a recording with the supervision group and/or supervisor?
- as well as seeking permission at the beginning, also confirming the coachee is still happy for the recording to be used once recording is finished. Offer them access to recording and invite them to provide feedback on the session as part of the learning.
- considering and explaining to a coachee why you wish to record and how the recording will being used, how it will be destroyed and, if necessary, explaining what supervision is – e.g., it is about our practice as a coach and our learning (this aligns with "Confidentiality" in the Global Code of Ethics, 2021, pp. 5–6).
- some supervisees viewed the 'commercial element' – charging for a session – as a barrier to asking to record a paid session, summed up by one supervisee: "is it fair to the client? Does it detract from their coaching investment? Does it make it about the coach not the coachee? Is it [an] equal exchange?" Offering a free session to an existing client was seen by some as equitable, something gifted by both parties.

Feedback suggests that a group needs to have bonded well and have a high level of trust for recordings to be dealt with in an 'Adult-Adult' way and this group was well established with good rapport, clear understanding of ethical practice and a commitment to both challenge and support each other (Turner and Hawkins, 2018).

In this instance Alison Curtis, a coach based in the United Kingdom, brought a recording to a supervision group with 6 members and the supervisor, for feedback on her style and any inappropriate use of the "tell" mode. She was thoughtful about confidentiality and selected a coachee whom she felt understood coaching and supervision practice well. The group contracted carefully in advance of using the recording. This included discussion around confidentiality, clarity that the group would focus on the positives as well as offering critical evaluation and having clear direction from Alison about the feedback that would be most valuable.

This is how Alison describes the experience and learning from bringing a recording – a section of about ten minutes was played:

My supervisor ensured that the space was very safe by asking each of us who had brought a recording to suggest three questions for the observers to consider, and to think about how the feedback that we gained might also benefit our client ... No wallowing in self-criticism was allowed! The feedback that I gained was incredibly rich and demonstrated not only my peers' respect for another professional at work and a different style possibly to their own, but also the quality of their offered observations, support and challenge which I believe if I had observed this piece alone, I would never have gleaned.

In undertaking this recording, I have probably learnt just as much about the need for careful contracting, and how much time and care I need to provide for this at the beginning of any recorded session, as much as I have about my own style and practice as a professional coach.

I brought this recording for feedback on my style. I have to be constantly mindful of not going into 'tell' mode when I work with someone, so in some ways, knowing I was recording meant I was very intentional in not doing that. I used questions and reflection for much of the session. However, the feedback from my supervision peers was that I should challenge [my coachee] more ... Challenge doesn't mean "tell!".

The coachee has provided a unique insight by kindly offering their observations on being recorded too:

- *"At the time I didn't think about it too much – I have knowledge of how coaching and supervision works so I felt comfortable and therefore shared in a way which I would have done if it had not been recorded. I think I am fairly open ... so may have thought less about it during sessions than some others might.*
- *Probably the most challenging element has been the after sharing thought process (i.e., what does it feel like knowing that it has been shared) – which feels slightly weird – knowing that a few people have seen me grapple with my gremlins!*
- *One reflection I have is that consent for recording at the start feels good, but I'd also suggest checking in at the end as you don't know where the session will go – I would have still said yes but that would be an interesting addition to practice around recording."*

Implications for coaching

Drawing on the comments from the coach and the coachee here we highlight some of the key implications:

- Confidentiality: to underpin this, we could consider audio only. If using video, before the recording we can be mindful of what is displayed on the screen such as a full name or a company name/logo. This also applies in the section selected to play, paying attention to any sensitive organisational or identifying personal information. Have a group agreement for situations where you recognise someone. This is aligned to, for example, points 2.15 and 2.16 under "Confidentiality" in the Global Code of Ethics (2021, pp. 5–6).

    o being clear about how the recording will be used, where and how it will be stored and how long for.

- Impact: what might be the impact on the coachee (client) of doing a recording – how might it impact their openness, the trust between you? What is the impact on the coach and how they are in the session?
- Coachee/client knowledge about coaching and supervision: ensuring that our clients understand how coaching and supervision works which will ensure their ethical ability to give permission with a full enough understanding.

Possible outcomes or next steps

The use of recordings in coaching has been little discussed in coaching literature and their use seems to be spasmodic, beyond initial training, where recordings and/or live observation is common. We would encourage the use of recordings as a continual means of learning, for specific reasons such as skills evaluation, noticing patterns, understanding a stuck point, as well as improving our reflective practice. In this we are behaving with ethical responsibility when engaging in our own professional development, both helping us better understand our coaching and where to develop and make changes. When doing so, we have outlined the many ethical considerations above, such as confidentiality and the relationship.

Discussion points

1. How best do we contract for recordings and when? And how might we set this up – charging, gifting, with a colleague or ... ?
2. How does recording affect our behaviour and ease as a coach and the client's? Recordings are to aid our learning – what might be the impact on how the client sees us and our relationship?
3. Confidentiality is an obvious issue – how can we best safeguard this from whom we ask, to how (long) we store?
4. How can we manage boundaries of the feedback session and create a safe environment for the coach, particularly in a group setting?

References

Global Code of Ethics. (2021. Confidentiality. Retrieved July 17, 2022 from www. globalcodeofethics.org.

Turner, E. and Hawkins, P. (2018) How to ... use recordings in reflective practice work. *Coaching at Work*, *13*(*6*): 52–53.

Case Study 8: Ethics and the Internal Coach

Katharine St John-Brooks

Background

Internal coaches – most of whom coach colleagues on top of their day jobs – swim in murkier ethical waters than external coaches owing to: the variety of intertwining relationships that the coach and client will have within the organisation (potentially giving rise to boundaries issues or compromises to the coach's independence); the scope for role conflicts between the coach's role as coach and their day job; and perceived or actual challenges around confidentiality (St John-Brooks, 2010). The potential for them to encounter ethical dilemmas is thus higher. Add in the fact that many organisations provide limited access to supervision and the challenges can be significant. The following case study is an amalgam of real cases but with significant changes and removal of identifying features so that total confidentiality is maintained.

Case Study

Max is a 35-year-old finance manager in an international corporation. He has a team of eight and is carrying two vacancies because of a recruitment freeze. HR knows that his team is under considerable pressure. Max wants to prepare for promotion to senior finance manager – which would involve managing a team of 25 – and has been allocated an internal coach, Claire. The goals identified in their first session are around identifying his development needs for the more senior role and how he might address them; job interview technique and how to get a better work-life balance in his current role.

Claire is 49 and works in marketing. She has recently been promoted – to the level that Max aspires to – and is familiar with what the process involves. Claire is part of an internal coaching pool that has been running for five years. She was in the first cohort of twelve employees to be trained and has completed the ILM5 coaching qualification. There are currently 40 coaches in the pool. There is an expectation that clients will receive six sessions and that the coaches will have a minimum of two clients at any one time. Claire is an enthusiastic coach and attends all the Continuing Professional Development opportunities offered. She has access to group supervision. Her coaching supervisor, Steve, also manages the coaching pool from within Learning and Development. He recently completed his supervision qualification. Claire feels that she gets more out of being a coach than she gets out of her day job. Max is her 18th client.

Max and Claire have hit it off and the coaching is proving productive. Max is ambitious. He has identified the gaps that he needs to fill if he is to be a good fit for the next step in his career but he's made no progress on achieving a better work-life balance. He works late most evenings and takes work home at weekends.

During their fourth session, Max tells Claire that his workload has become even worse (it's audit time). She suggests discussing strategies for handling the pressure and he drops into the conversation that he has started taking cocaine at weekends. He's taken it in the past during periods of high stress and assures her that he finds it a great 'stress buster' (and says that it has no negative impact on his work). He wants to focus the session on how he can get HR to allow him to fill the vacancies in his team.

Claire is completely thrown to hear about the cocaine and uncertain how to proceed. She knows that cocaine is a Class A drug and thus illegal. But Max is taking the drug at the weekends in his own time, and she isn't sure whether her company's strict substance abuse policy covers that or even if it's any of her business. She knows from a friend of hers who works in the Finance division that Max is well-regarded by his colleagues, and she doesn't want to do or say something that could damage his career. But she feels she has a 'duty of care' towards him and can't ignore it.

Implications for coaching

- The coaching contract – the coach should be clear with the client at the outset about the conditions of the coaching, including confidentiality (Global Code of Ethics, section 2.3, p. 4) and the limits to that confidentiality: Coaches "will have a clear agreement with clients and sponsors about the conditions under which confidentiality will not be maintained (e.g. illegal activity, danger to self or others)". (Global Code of Ethics, section 2.14, p. 5)
- Responsibility – Claire has responsibilities both to Max as her client and to spot potential risks to her employer (e.g. if Max has a cocaine-induced psychotic episode at work). She needs to be alive to the fact that a) Max's stress – that he's self-medicating with cocaine – is work-induced and b) he may think that by telling her he has 'told the company'. She also needs to be alert to the dangers of collusion: Coaches will not "encourage, assist or collude with conduct that is dishonest, unlawful ... " (Global Code of Ethics, section 2.12, p. 5)

- Boundaries/specialist abilities – Clare is not an expert in substance abuse. Nor is she a trained counsellor. She should avoid being tempted to go beyond the boundaries of her role: Coaches should "refer the client to a more experienced or suitably qualified practicing member where appropriate." (Global Code of Ethics, section 4.1, p. 9)
- Supervision – Claire's supervisor Steve also runs the coaching pool so he knows who her clients are. Anonymity is potentially at risk here (St John-Brooks, 2019). Did Claire say, when she was contracting with Max, that she might share information with Steve?

Possible next steps

- Communication with client Claire tells Max that she's uncomfortable with what he's told her; that now it's in the room she can't "un-know" it, and she will need to discuss with her supervisor how she should proceed.
- Read Code of Ethics. Claire confirms that the Code of Ethics gives her discretion to break confidentiality, should she decide that that's the best course of action.
- Seek outside support. Claire recognises that she has a dilemma that she needs to discuss with someone. She has access to group supervision run by Steve but it's only provided three times a year and there was a session the previous week. She really needs 1:1 support but she's worried about preserving Max's anonymity if she talks to Steve. She's not sure how to handle this. Might supervision from an external supervisor be made available?
- Company policies Claire familiarises herself with the company's substance abuse policy so that she's better informed about potential sources of support for Max and also possible sanctions. She is keen to avoid jeopardising her own reputation within the company by her choice of action.
- Involve the company's welfare/employee assistance programme One option might be for Max to refer himself for company counselling support (often outsourced and anonymous). Claire suspects that she would need evidence from him that he was seeing it through.
- Disciplinary processes If Claire decides that she must involve HR, it is possible that Max might be disciplined in some way.

Discussion points

1. What might the consequences be if Claire does nothing, Max goes off the rails and a colleague of his tells HR that Max had "told his coach that he was taking cocaine?"
2. If Max takes up an offer of counselling from his company, should Claire carry on coaching him? Should she a) terminate the assignment; b) coach

him in parallel; or c) pause the coaching until the end of the counselling then resume?

3. Given potential difficulties regarding anonymity if Claire discusses Max's drug use with her supervisor, Steve, what does this say about the challenges of using internal supervisors? What ways around it might there be?

4. Where do a company's substance abuse policies fit in? Should Claire simply tell Max that she has to break confidentiality because he's told her that he's indulged in illegal activity and she has a duty to the company to let them know; tell HR (or tell Max that he must); then let the disciplinary process take its course?

References

Global Code of Ethics. (2021). www.globalcodeofethics.org.

St John-Brooks, K. (2010). *What are the ethical challenges involved in being an internal coach?* International Journal of Mentoring & Coaching, VIII*(1)*: 50–66.

St John-Brooks, K. (2019). Supervision for Internal Coaches. In J. Birch and P. Welch (Eds), Coaching Supervision: Advancing Practice, Changing Landscapes. Abingdon: Routledge.

Case Study 9: Emotional Entanglement in the Coaching Engagement

Lisa Sansom

Background

While coaching is a partnership between the coach and the client, an effective coaching partnership also requires some emotional distance and professionalism, such that the coach does not become emotionally entangled in the client's situation. Furthermore, the coach needs to ensure that the session remains within the boundaries of coaching, and does not leak into counselling, therapy, friendship or any other 'helping' relationship that could compromise coaching integrity and value.

Case Study

A client named Alyssa had been working with coach Melanie for a few months. Alyssa had sought Melanie's coaching expertise as a professional with a similar background, both women in male-dominated high-pressure financially driven industries. Melanie, in her early pre-coaching 'good fit' conversations with Alyssa, had clearly explained the boundaries of coaching – that Melanie would not be providing advice or mentoring based on her own experience. Melanie further explained the role of the coach and the responsibilities of the client and answered questions that Alyssa had. This was the first coach that Alyssa had ever engaged, and she had a lot of questions. Melanie answered them accurately and thoroughly with reference to the ICF values and ethical standards. When Alyssa verbally agreed that she wished to engage Melanie, Melanie provided a written agreement to Alyssa, which included information about the role of the coach, the role of the client, and made explicit reference to the ICF Code of Ethics and Values. Alyssa read and reviewed the agreement, signed it and returned it to Melanie to commence the official coaching engagement.

The coaching relationship proceeded to unfold in a very positive way. Melanie established a safe space for Alyssa to share and be vulnerable, and Melanie was sensitive to her environment, experiences, values, and beliefs. Confidentiality was maintained and Melanie was consistently open, curious and client-centred. Alyssa felt comfortable talking about many professional challenges with Melanie and was introspective and open to new ways of thinking about the issues that she raised.

One session, when Melanie asked for Alyssa's coaching agenda, Alyssa shared personal information with Melanie that she had been struggling with a medical diagnosis that made it hard for her to concentrate on anything at work, and she wanted to receive coaching on how to refocus and be more professional at work, despite her medical issues and physical pain. Melanie felt great compassion for her client and asked her questions about her diagnosis and pain levels, which Alyssa was comfortable sharing. Alyssa shared how she was feeling lower and lower with each passing day, especially as the diagnosis was somewhat uncertain and her future dreams, which had been a topic for previous coaching sessions, were in jeopardy as a result.

Melanie's immediate instinct was to console her client and encourage her to draw on her faith to truly embrace the belief that there was a reason for these new challenges that were in her way. Melanie knew her client to be not only a spiritual woman, but also a strong advocate for others when they needed support, and Melanie saw that her client needed to be her own advocate and could keep pursuing her goals and ambitions, no matter what the obstacles were.

Implications for coaching

- Recognition of personal limitations that may impair or interfere with coaching performance or professional coaching relationships. The coach needs to be mindful of their own very natural and human emotional experience of compassion as a desire to alleviate the suffering of another and also be mindful of how this impacts their decision making and coaching abilities in the moment. (ICF Code of Ethics [2020], Section 2, Standard 17)
- Setting clear emotional boundaries for the coaching engagement and stating those in the moment to ensure that the professional coaching relationship is thoroughly respected by both parties. (ICF Code of Ethics [2020], Section 3, Standard 23)

Possible outcomes or next steps

- Refer the client to outside support. A coach, recognising their own limitations and abilities to effectively support the client as needed in a situation, may choose to refer to external service providers, even beyond the coaching profession. This may include referring to a family doctor, an employer-based employee assistance programme or other benefits, a therapist or counsellor more generally or other medical and psychological professionals.

- Seek outside support. A coach in any ethical conundrum may choose to turn to their coach, mentor coach, coach supervisor, training programme or coaching organisation like the ICF for support in navigating ethically confusing situations. This process will likely include much reflection and thought on the coach's side. In addition, the coach may choose to utilise outside support after a coaching engagement ends (or is cancelled) to learn fully from the experience.
- Clarify the relationship with the other party. A coach may choose to bring their concerns to the client directly. This allows both parties to discuss and determine the best path forward in a collaborative manner. The coach may want to consider the dynamics of that meeting though – perhaps by shifting to a virtual platform and not meeting in person, may help increase emotional distance. If it is determined that the coaching engagement will continue, re-contracting with the client and setting up clear emotional boundaries are strongly encouraged.
- Delay, postpone or consider ending the coaching engagement. If it is determined that the coaching engagement should end, the coach should support the client as they transition to another coach and/or allow for the cancellation of the coaching arrangement.

Discussion points

1. What boundaries can a coach put in place to avoid this kind of situation? What resources can you turn to as a coach?
2. How might you as a coach self-monitor and self-manage in emotionally challenging situations?
3. If you were this coach's coach, mentor or supervisor, how would you support the coach?
4. Can a coach ethically coach an existing client who contracted under a more professional context, and then raises emotionally compelling personal issues?

Reference

ICF Code of Ethics. (2020) https://coachingfederation.org/ethics/code-of-ethics.

Case Study 10: Widening the lens of the RECording button

Hellen Hettinga

Background

Coaching recordings are a requirement for performance evaluation as part of professional credentialing. The ICF provides guidelines and ethical standards for recording individual coaching sessions. Questions to consider are: With what are the recordings made? Who owns the recordings? Who will have access to the recordings? For how long and where are they kept?

Recordings can also serve as input for our reflective practice. A vital source of learning for a coach. However, what is it that we record when we press the metaphorical RECording button? An audio or video recording of an actual coaching conversation, notes through our own assumptions, interpretations and emotions? What do we observe?

Moreover, in our interconnected and dynamic world with multiple stakeholders, how to document collective learnings? Interrupting the assumption that coaching is 'confidential work done behind closed doors'.

Case Study

A large multi coach – coachee coaching assignment based in Asia and part of a leadership development summit. A written contract was developed between the executive coaches and programme team, with reference to a document specifying roles and responsibilities, including a written end of assignment report.

Each coach – coachee was required to contract on confidentiality, with specific attention to the assignment requirement of a post coaching written and verbal report to the larger group.

With the executive client, Rizal, contracting on confidentiality was agreed that:

- the content of the sessions was confidential;
- two sessions were recorded at the coaches' request for their own reflection;
- a triangular meeting with the mentor would take place, the meeting would be led by Rizal. He encouraged the coach to be open and transparent with his workplace mentor.

When writing the end of coaching report, this kind of recording or documenting preoccupied the coach's thoughts. The coach wondered how to find a balance between holding confidentiality for their client and sharing insights and learning that might be relevant for the team and the wider organisation. It was agreed coach's draft would be reviewed together with Rizal before submitting it to the team. The team would then aggregate all reports in an overall anonymised report, serving as input for the learning summits.

At the end of the coaching assignment the coachees, some coaches and the leadership team would gather to share their observations. The coach was relieved not to be participating. The coach had not yet figured out how they would navigate the tension of holding confidentiality and sharing observations with the group, in real time. Eventually Rizal who participated in the summit, decided what to share – which he reportedly did openly and generously.

The coach, an ICF ACC credentialed coach at that time, felt pretty confident and professional about how they had navigated the ethical dilemmas around confidentiality in the coaching relationship!

Right after, the coach began a training course to develop their systemic capacity and got to experience the value of supervision. The coach became much more aware of their blind and deaf spots, the coach's lenses expanded to consider the wider context, multiple perspectives and key-stakeholders that had not been so obvious previously.

Reflecting on the coaching work with Rizal, the coach wondered whether in their coach role they had been playing it safe by focusing a lot on confidentiality and perhaps how they were showing up to the coaching. Feeling limited in their presence, sensing the coaching relationship wasn't as collaborative as it could have been.

- How could the coach help themselves and the coachee feel more comfortable in the presence of the knowledge of being recorded?
- How might the coach have been more courageous in jointly holding the coachees feet to the fire, by considering the impact on the wider society, on the wider ecology?
- How might the learnings have been of value to the team, organisation or society at large, if the coach and coachee had discovered ways to report back with integrity and openness?

Implications for coaching

- Coaching Agreement Contract: ICF Code of Ethics Section 1, Ethical Standard 2: 'create an agreement / contract regarding the roles, responsibilities and rights of all parties involved with my Client(s) and Sponsor (s) prior to the commencement of services'

Establish a multi-stakeholder contract, to ensure that the collaborative coaching partnership is in service of the coachee's current and future stakeholders. These might be:

o   professional – team, manager, organisation, community, future clients;
o   personal – family, spouse, future generations;
o   non-human stakeholders – Mother Earth, wider ecology.

- Professional practice excellence: ICF Code of Ethics Section II, Ethical Standard 16: Commit to excellence through continued personal, professional and ethical development.
  Engage in practices that keep coaches fit for purpose and support doing their best work. For example, supervision, a variety of structured and open reflection practices, communities of practice, physical exercise, mindfulness practice, regular connection with the outdoors.
- Societal – systemic awareness in coaching: ICF Code of Ethics Section IV, Ethical Standard 28: Am aware of my and my clients' impact on society. I adhere to the philosophy of "doing good" versus "avoiding bad."
- Courage for highest quality ethical coaching practice: ICF Code of Ethics Introduction: ICF Professionals who accept the Code of Ethics strive to be ethical, even when doing so involves making difficult decisions or acting courageously.

Possible outcomes or next steps

- Set out with a systemic perspective for every coaching session. For example, with the opening and closing questions as offered by Hawkins and Turner (2020, p. 88):

  o   'What is the work we need to do together and how will that create value for you, your practice, your current and future clients and other stakeholders? In other words, how can we create a future ripple effect and a legacy that continues the benefits?' (p. 158)
  o   'If your stakeholders were in the room listening to our coaching session, what would they have valued … .and what would their challenge to us be?'.

- Design creative ways of recording and documenting that stimulate shared collective learnings, while respecting integrity and embodying safety for all parties engaged and maintain client desired confidentiality. For example: an aggregated and anonymised reporting and learning summits (as described in the case), creative arts like scribing, online tools harvesting learnings (e.g. Miro, Google Jamboard).

Discussion points

1.   When recording coaching sessions: What do you consider as 'the work' when in coaching?
2.   How can you navigate the tension between creating safety and confidentiality on one end and allowing open collective learning on the other end?
3.   What might be the impact of having an outside observer on the coaching relationship?
4.   Who are the stakeholders and how might they impact the coaching? What are the considerations the coach needs to be mindful of when engaging in multi-stakeholder trainings and coaching programmes and sharing information from within the coaching?

References

Hawkins, P. and Turner, E. (2020) *Systemic Coaching – delivering value beyond the individual.* Abingdon: Routledge.

ICF Code of Ethics. (2020) https://coachingfederation.org/ethics/code-of-ethics.

Case Study 11: Coach Qualification Representation

Lisa Sansom

Background

Coaching is an unregulated profession and, as such, coaches have considerable latitude over how they wish to represent themselves. It is incumbent on the coach to do so ethically and honestly, and there is still considerable variety when a coach wishes to represent not only their objective educational qualifications and years of work experience, but also their own more subjective personal experience and professional areas of perceived expertise. Clients are often attracted to coaches based on their qualifications and background, so it is enticing for coaches to represent themselves in what they feel is the best light possible. This can lead to dubious, or even erroneous, claims.

Case Study

Marcel had many years of executive leadership experience and decided that being on the corporate rat race was exhausting, so wanted to craft a more meaningful life for himself. He recalled working with an Executive Coach when he was a more junior leader. That coach had helped Marcel through his career progression, opening new ways of thinking and beneficial mindsets that helped Marcel achieve his professional goals. Marcel remembered how it felt to really be seen and heard. He had appreciated his year of working with that coach and it inspired Marcel to learn more about coaching himself.

After researching many different coaching schools, Marcel settled on one and started applying himself to his new chosen profession. Marcel enjoyed the courses and felt like he was learning and growing personally again, as well as professionally. Some of the instructors were versed in a relatively new field called 'positive psychology' and often made reference to researchers and books that had been written in the field. Marcel ordered these books and read them, taking copious notes. He also discovered that many of the researchers had TED talks, and those led to other TED and TEDx talks along similar themes, that Marcel devoured.

Over time, as Marcel practiced his coaching skills. He would use positive psychology models and frameworks, many of which he had learned through his own supplementary reading and viewing, to inform his questions. Occasionally, he would ask clients for permission to teach them a little bit about a positive psychology topic of interest, and then leverage that new knowledge for further questions, sometimes leading to breakthroughs for his practice clients.

When Marcel completed the course and attained his ICF Associate Certified Coach (ACC), he felt that he was finally willing to establish his own coaching business. He hired a designer and created a new website. He started a newsletter and changed his LinkedIn profile but couldn't quite determine how he wished to represent his new coaching niche. His credentials were clear enough – he was able to showcase his years of work experience and job titles, and he had earned the ACC from a reputable ICF-accredited coaching school. However, he didn't feel that these thoroughly depicted the type of coach he had become through his training, and the coach he aspired to be through his new business practice. He knew that he wanted to incorporate the phrase 'positive psychology' in there somewhere but wanted to ensure that he was doing so responsibly and ethically.

Finally, Marcel settled on calling himself a 'positive psychology coach', feeling that this struck a reasonable compromise between calling himself a 'positive psychologist', as he was not a psychologist and recognised that this was a protected and regulated designation, and omitting 'positive psychology' at all. Learning about the research and application of positive psychology had opened up coaching possibilities and growth for him, even though he hadn't received any dedicated education in the field. As he hit 'enter' on his LinkedIn profile, he still felt uneasy about his decision and wondered if he was doing the right thing.

Implications for coaching

- It is critically important to accurately and clearly represent one's coaching qualifications and expertise, especially in new and emerging areas where clients and the coaching marketplace may not yet be thoroughly educated or even aware. Without specific recognised training in a field such as positive psychology, it is dubious if Marcel was making the most ethical choice in his self-designation. (ICF Code of Ethics [2020], Section 3, Standard 20)
- Honouring the contributions and intellectual property of others, especially when referring to a research-based field such as positive psychology. Coaches must take care to attribute and cite the original researchers and creators of theories and models that are being used on websites, coaching resources and other materials shared with clients, partners and the public. (ICF Code of Ethics [2020], Section 4, Standard 26)

- Ensuring continued education and one's own ability to keep up with the emerging research, as it pertains to coaching. Psychological research, such as in the field of positive psychology, emerges and can change over time as the scientific method and peer reviewed processes unfold. This is the nature of the work that is done as the field and coaching grows and researchers learn more. Coaches cannot rely on research that is several years old as the standard. BPS – Code of Ethics Chartered Coaching Psychologist (2021). Section 3.2, Competence: Members should work to keep abreast of "Advances in the evidence base" of their work ([p. 6).

Possible outcomes or next steps

- Ensure continued professional development in areas of expertise, knowledge and coaching application. When choosing their coaching niche, a coach may be implicitly declaring that they will maintain relevance and currency in that niche, as well as adjacent fields and knowledge. When considering other ethically mindful areas, such as (but not limited to) maintaining fairness and equity, being aware of power and status differences, and/or matters of privacy and document storage, coaches benefit from being aware that societal understandings and expectations change over time. Similarly, any coaching frameworks, models, research, etc, benefit from updating as some lose their relevance and research may overturn others. In order to be of optimal service to clients, coaches have a responsibility to maintain currency and accuracy in these and related matters to be practicing at a high ethical standard.
- Seek outside support. A coach in any ethical conundrum may choose to turn to their coach, mentor coach, coach supervisor, training programme or coaching organisation like the ICF for support in navigating ethically confusing situations. This process will likely include much reflection and thought on the coach's side, and a coach may choose to engage with these resources throughout their coaching career, including establishing one's own practice.

Discussion points

1. What reflective practices can a coach put into place to avoid this kind of situation? What resources can you turn to as a coach?
2. If you were this coach's coach, mentor or supervisor, how would you support the coach?
3. How can a coach ensure they are being ethical in their practice and business even before engaging with their first client?
4. How might a coach ethically and responsibly indicate areas of cultivated interest and/or professional growth, so as to attract clients without misrepresentation?

References

British Psychological Society. (2021) Code of Ethics and Conduct. https://cms.bps. org.uk/sites/default/files/2022–06/BPS%20Code%20of%20Ethics%20and%20Con duct.pdf.

ICF Code of Ethics. (2020) https://coachingfederation.org/ethics/code-of-ethics.

Case Study 12: Diversity Blind Spots, Token Inclusion and Unspoken Biases in a Coaching Panel

Dumisani Magadlela

Background

Coach practitioners are becoming aware of the need to build a strong network of diverse coaches to work within knowledgeable client systems. In an increasingly diversifying world of globalising businesses and their far-flung organisations, it is becoming ever more valuable to have a pool of diverse coaches to select from as coaching businesses deliver coaching interventions for clients. This need for diversity among coaches is sometimes demanded by buyers of coaching services who themselves have diverse coaching clients who request coaches that they feel they may be comfortable working closely with.

This challenge is heightened in previously colonised or former apartheid-dominated contexts such as South Africa and Namibia. This short case study relates to an executive coaching firm that provides coaching panels to external clients (the purchasers of coaching services) and presents ethical and diversity challenges that a panel of coaches working in two client systems encountered during a coaching contract. It deals with ethics of diversity within the panel and the interaction with coaching clients.

Case Study

The organisational client had selected twelve managers earmarked for coaching support in the company. They were all part of the human resources and training department in a telecommunications business. The twelve managers had received all five coaches' profiles at the same time, via email. The managers were asked to indicate their three preferred coaches in order of preference. Nine out of the twelve managers selected 'the same coach' as their preferred first choice to work with for the contracted seven coaching sessions each. They indicated no further preferences.

The project manager of the coaching intervention on behalf of the executive coaching firm, who brought together the pool of coaches to form a working panel, initially planned to allocate coaches to the clients (managers) using their second or third choices, rather than necessarily to their first preference. This was thought to be a solution that would help spread the work among the five coaches on the panel. The solution was thought to be easy, until it was realised the managers didn't indicate their three preferred coaches, and only provided one, flatly refusing to select any other coach to work with.

The coaching firm had not anticipated that the managers would not select a second option, let alone a third. Nor had they considered that the majority of the managers would want to work only with one (the same) coach. It soon emerged that this was a well-known female coach. She had a powerful brand and reputation as both caring and supportive, while being challenging and assisting female professionals to grow in the male-dominated business that they worked in. The story was shared later that some of the managers had heard about the impressive coaching work by this coach, and some had discussed it among themselves.

As it turned out, the Human Resources Executive, who was the client liaison for coaching in the company, confirmed later that she had worked with the same coach in her previous employment and had mentioned to some of her managers that this was one of the best coaches around. She confirmed that she herself had selected this coach and was not going to change her preference. The coaches' ethical challenge now was how to work with the rest of the panel of coaches without disappointing most of the managers.

It was later revealed three members of the management team who had not selected this one coach (with the great reputation) as their preferred first choice were all relatively new male managers. They had not heard anything about the coach's brilliance. In fact, they had selected male coaches with a similar demographic and ethnic background. All female clients of all ethnic backgrounds had selected this one female ('brilliant') coach. It was shared later in reflection notes that her mixed-race background was the catalyst and she had taken full advantage of that to build a reputable brand while doing solid coaching with her clients. In a female dominated management team, the coaches had not foreseen this challenge.

The challenge was compounded by the other three coaches: two are white and female and one is a white male. Lastly, the situation was made more interesting by the fact that in a previous panel, in another organisation (a male dominated industry), the very same coach had not been selected by any of the managers even as a third option. The project manager indicated that this was understandable in a rather male-dominated client system (mining sector). The team managing the panel had not allocated any of the clients for her to coach. There was a sense of sexism, injustice, unfairness and several other team management issues that needed attention from within the panel of coaches before engaging another client or company seeking coaching afterwards.

Implications for coaching

Three points stand out from this case study in terms of ethics and diversity. First, there was clearly a lack of cohesiveness in the coaching panel. The one team member – the only female coach from a mixed-race background – had originally felt disconnected and not valued by the rest of the team, especially the project manager in charge of the coaching panel. Her selection by the majority of female managers was like a kind of vindication for her coaching competency and feeling valued at least by the coaching clients from the client system.

The above speaks to the ICF Statement of Diversity, Inclusion, Belonging and Justice, which stipulates that:

> "[w]e cannot ignore the challenges that many coaches and coaching clients face, owing to systemic problems in their communities … ".

The world of work in South Africa and other parts of the world that are either former or current pseudo-colonies, the status of a female professional doing work that is dominated by other demographic groups (e.g. white male and female coaches in the majority), means that she would have to do more to position herself as a credible coach.

Second, it is crucial for any coaching professional working alone or within a panel to always maintain confidentiality while addressing sensitive coaching group issues around reputation and gender. Again, this is a subject that requires a level of maturity and professionalism expected of any and every coach in active practice. In this regard, the International Coaching Federation (ICF) statement on diversity and inclusion clearly states that:

> "[a]s members of the ICF community, we ascribe to the core values of integrity, excellence, collaboration and respect.".

While it is regarded as mainly unprofessional, lack of confidentiality can be regarded as both reckless and disrespectful.

The third and final point of discussion here refers to the range of challenges that the project manager from the coaching panel side (external to the company) was facing. There is a case to be made here for the external project manager to check upfront with their counterpart within the organisation if any of the managers or the Human Resources Executive as the sponsor, knew any of the coaches on the panel (especially once the list of profiles was shared). Doing the above would ensure that the coaches remain within the ethical guidelines of the ICF (2021), which state that a coach must:

> "[h]ave a clear understanding about how information is exchanged among all parties involved during all coaching interactions".

Possible outcomes or next steps

- What were the likely or possible outcomes from this set of ethical, management, leadership and human interrelationship challenges?

- What were likely to be the main discussion issues in a meeting between the project manager (coaching panel leader) and the one preferred female coach on the panel?
- If you were in the position (shoes) of the only black female coach selected by the majority of managers from the company, how would you deal with the situation?
- What could the other four coaches on the panel say or do (and to whom) to help resolve the situation amicably for all parties involved?
- What can a company buying coaching do to assist in avoiding such scenarios and/or help to resolve such situations when they emerge in future (preventive measures)?

Discussion points

1. How can the coaching panel create a working space of communicating their concerns and setting processes for working better together? How can the panel support the managers (coachees) to address their concerns while maintaining confidentiality?
2. How can the coaching panel work better to increase take up of choices by the coachees? The ethical challenge of forcing a client to work with a coach they did not select in the first place can be avoided with clear selection instructions.
3. How can the project leader ensure greater diversity and equality among the coaching panel? What can coaching businesses do to grow a more diverse pool of coaches globally?
4. How can all parties increase their awareness of their biasis?

References

ICF Code of Ethics. (2021) https://coachingfederation.org/ethics/code-of-ethics.
ICF Statement of Diversity, Inclusion, Belonging and Justice. (2020) https://coachingfedera tion.org/blog/icf-publishes-statement-of-diversity-inclusion-belonging-and-justice.

Professional Living Will*

I, [Insert Full Name], do hereby declare this to be my professional living will, dated [insert date]. This document supersedes prior professional living wills [if any exist]. This is not a substitute for a Personal Last Will and Testament. It has an intended purpose, to give authority and instructions to my Professional Executor/s regarding my professional [insert practice type] practice and records in the event of my incapacitation or death.

Personal Details

I am a practicing [insert practice type]
My practice office address is [insert full address]
My current telephone number is [insert telephone number]
My email address is [insert email address]

Executor Details

In the event of my incapacitation or death, I hereby appoint as my first professional executor [Insert executor 1. full name], who has agreed to serve in this role. Their [delete as appropriate] contact details are as follows:

Phone number	
Email	
Mailing address	

In the event that [insert executor 1. full name] is unavailable or unable to perform this function, I hereby appoint my second professional executor [Insert executor 2. full name], who has agreed to serve in this role. Their [delete as appropriate] contact details are as follows:

Phone number	
Email	
Mailing address	

I hereby grant my professional executors full authority to:

1. Act on rmy behalf in making decisions about storing, releasing and/or disposing of my professional records, consistent with relevant laws, regulations and any professional requirements.
2. Carry out any activities deemed necessary to properly administer this professional living will.
3. Delegate and authorise other persons, determined by them, to assist and carry out any activities deemed necessary to properly administer this professional living will.

Lists and Records

Copies of my 'lists and records' are stored with a copy of my professional living will.

The lists and records will be maintained and updated as any amendments or changes occur in order to facilitate access to all relevant contacts, client records and other relevant documents, including all relevant hard copy and electronic files as well as back-up files. The lists are as follows:

List 1	• Full names and contact information for individuals who can assist in locating and accessing my client records and other relevant professional documents
	• The location of, and how to access, current client records plus appointment diary
	• The location of, and how to access, my professional billing and financial records
	• The location of the computer and necessary passwords and all other electronic devices used for my [insert practice type] practice
	• The account details and passwords of any professional social media accounts e.g., LinkedIn; Facebook; Twitter; Instagram etc.
	• My professional e-mail and website addresses and any associated information
	• Professional documents location and information
	o Professional liability insurance policy
	o Professional accrediting bodies
	• Location of any necessary keys to access my office, filing cabinets, storage facilities, etc.
List 2	Encrypted list of clients names email addresses and telephone numbers

Specific Instructions

Specific instructions for my professional executor are as follows:

1. There are 3 copies of this living will and its associated lists. They can be located as follows:

    a) I have a copy
    b) one is in your possession
    c) one is in the possession of executor 2 (see above for contact details)

2. Please use your clinical/professional judgment and discretion in deciding how you want to notify current clients of my incapacity or death and whom to contact for further information, consistent with ethical and legal requirements. In List 1 details will be found of any special instructions relating to my funeral and memorial service wishes.
3. If clinically indicated, for example by their response to notification of my incapacity or death, you may wish to provide referral sources. Suggested providers will be indicated in List 1.
4. Please promptly notify my professional liability carrier of my death. Please also notify my accrediting body.
5. Please arrange for clients' records to be destroyed. All records should be destroyed according to the [insert accrediting body name – e.g., APECS] accrediting body Ethics and Standards.

I declare that the foregoing is true and correct.

Executed at: [Address]

on

[Date]

Signature:

Witnessed

Printed Name:

Signature:

Date:

Residing at:

Disclaimer

*This Professional Living Will is for informational purposes only. It is not intended to provide legal advice and should not be used as a substitute for obtaining personal legal advice and consultation prior to making decisions regarding individual circumstances. Practitioners are advised to consult an experienced solicitor or their accrediting body for further information.

Professional Living Will
[Practitioner Name] List I

Full names and contact information for individuals who can assist in locating and accessing my client records and other relevant professional documents

Executor I

Name
Address
Telephone
Email

Executor I

Name
Address
Telephone
Email

Special instructions relating to my funeral

Special instructions relating to client referrals

The location of and how to access current client records plus appointment diary

An encrypted list of my clients and their contact details can be found with
Name
Address
Telephone
Email

Name
Address
Telephone
Email

I do/do not keep an online diary.

My physical appointment diary can be found with :

I do/do not keep online client records.
E.G.,

All my records are handwritten notes, kept in a locked filing cabinet. Please arrange for clients' records to be destroyed. All records should be maintained/destroyed according to the [insert relevant body] accrediting body Ethics and Standards.

The location of and how to access my professional billing and financial records
Records can be found with:

My accountant details name, address, email address and telephone number:

The location of the computer and necessary passwords and all other electronic devices used for my Psychotherapy and Supervision practice.

Records can be found with:

The account details and passwords of any professional social media accounts e.g., LinkedIn; Facebook; Twitter; Instagram etc.

Account
Email
Password

Account
Email

Password

Account
Email
Password

Account
Email
Password

My professional e-mail and website addresses and any associated information

Maintained by:
Website Host Name and address
Telephone number:
Email:

Associated accounts
Email:

Website:

My Professional documents location and information:

Professional Liability Insurance Policy

Insurer Name:
Telephone Number:

Policy Number:
Certificate Number:

Professional Accrediting Bodies

Location of any necessary keys to access my office, filing cabinets, storage facilities, etc.

Practitioner Name – Client listing for Living Will

First name	Last name	Email	Telephone	Client type

Index

Page numbers in italics refer to figures. Page numbers in bold refer to tables.